MW00720812

Windows® 98
Programming Secrets®

Windows® 98 Programming Secrets®

Clayton Walnum

IDG BOOKS WORLDWIDE

IDG Books Worldwide, Inc.
An International Data Group Company

Foster City, CA ♦ Chicago, IL ♦ Indianapolis, IN ♦ Southlake, TX

Windows® 98 Programming Secrets®

Published by
IDG Books Worldwide, Inc.
An International Data Group Company
919 E. Hillsdale Blvd., Suite 400
Foster City, CA 94404
www.idgbooks.com (IDG Books Worldwide Web site)

Copyright © 1998 IDG Books Worldwide, Inc. All rights reserved. No part of this book, including interior design, cover design, and icons, may be reproduced or transmitted in any form, by any means (electronic, photocopying, recording, or otherwise) without the prior written permission of the publisher.

Library of Congress Catalog Card No.: 97-078219

ISBN: 0-7645-3059-3

Printed in the United States of America

10 9 8 7 6 5 4 3 2

1E/SU/QT/ZY/FC

Distributed in the United States by IDG Books Worldwide, Inc.

Distributed by Macmillan Canada for Canada; by Transworld Publishers Limited in the United Kingdom; by IDG Norge Books for Norway; by IDG Sweden Books for Sweden; by Woodslane Pty. Ltd. for Australia; by Woodslane New Zealand Ltd. for New Zealand; by Addison Wesley Longman Singapore Pte Ltd. for Singapore, Malaysia, Thailand, and Indonesia; by Distribuidora Norma S.A.-Colombia for Colombia; by Intersoft for South Africa; by International Thompson Publishing for Germany, Austria, and Switzerland; by Toppan Company Ltd. for Japan; by Distribuidora Cuspide for Argentina; by Livraria Cultura for Brazil; by Ediciencia S.A. for Ecuador; by Addison-Wesley Publishing Company for Korea; by Ediciones ZETA S.C.R. Ltda. for Peru; by WS Computer Publishing Corporation, Inc., for the Philippines; by Unalis Corporation for Taiwan; by Contemporanea de Ediciones for Venezuela; by Computer Book & Magazine Store for Puerto Rico; by Express Computer Distributors for the Caribbean and West Indies. Authorized Sales Agent: Anthony Rudkin Associates for the Middle East and North Africa.

For general information on IDG Books Worldwide's books in the U.S., please call our Consumer Customer Service department at 800-762-2974. For reseller information, including discounts and premium sales, please call our Reseller Customer Service department at 800-434-3422.

For information on where to purchase IDG Books Worldwide's books outside the U.S., please contact our International Sales department at 650-655-3200 or fax 650-655-3297.

For information on foreign language translations, please contact our Foreign & Subsidiary Rights department at 650-655-3021 or fax 650-655-3281.

For sales inquiries and special prices for bulk quantities, please contact our Sales department at 650-655-3200 or write to the address above.

For information on using IDG Books Worldwide's books in the classroom or for ordering examination copies, please contact our Educational Sales department at 800-434-2086 or fax 817-421-5012.

For press review copies, author interviews, or other publicity information, please contact our Public Relations department at 650-655-3000 or fax 650-655-3299.

For authorization to photocopy items for corporate, personal, or educational use, please contact Copyright Clearance Center, 222 Rosewood Drive, Danvers, MA 01923, or fax 978-750-4470.

LIMIT OF LIABILITY/DISCLAIMER OF WARRANTY: AUTHOR AND PUBLISHER HAVE USED THEIR BEST EFFORTS IN PREPARING THIS BOOK. IDG BOOKS WORLDWIDE, INC., AND AUTHOR MAKE NO REPRESENTATIONS OR WARRANTIES WITH RESPECT TO THE ACCURACY OR COMPLETENESS OF THE CONTENTS OF THIS BOOK AND SPECIFICALLY DISCLAIM ANY IMPLIED WARRANTIES OF MERCHANTABILITY OR FITNESS FOR A PARTICULAR PURPOSE. THERE ARE NO WARRANTIES WHICH EXTEND BEYOND THE DESCRIPTIONS CONTAINED IN THIS PARAGRAPH. NO WARRANTY MAY BE CREATED OR EXTENDED BY SALES REPRESENTATIVES OR WRITTEN SALES MATERIALS. THE ACCURACY AND COMPLETENESS OF THE INFORMATION PROVIDED HEREIN AND THE OPINIONS STATED HEREIN ARE NOT GUARANTEED OR WARRANTED TO PRODUCE ANY PARTICULAR RESULTS, AND THE ADVICE AND STRATEGIES CONTAINED HEREIN MAY NOT BE SUITABLE FOR EVERY INDIVIDUAL. NEITHER IDG BOOKS WORLDWIDE, INC., NOR AUTHOR SHALL BE LIABLE FOR ANY LOSS OF PROFIT OR ANY OTHER COMMERCIAL DAMAGES, INCLUDING BUT NOT LIMITED TO SPECIAL, INCIDENTAL, CONSEQUENTIAL, OR OTHER DAMAGES.

Trademarks: All brand names and product names used in this book are trade names, service marks, trademarks, or registered trademarks of their respective owners. IDG Books Worldwide is not associated with any product or vendor mentioned in this book.

The IDG Books Worldwide logo is a trademark under exclusive license to IDG Books Worldwide, Inc., from International Data Group, Inc.

ABOUT IDG BOOKS WORLDWIDE

Welcome to the world of IDG Books Worldwide.

IDG Books Worldwide, Inc., is a subsidiary of International Data Group, the world's largest publisher of computer-related information and the leading global provider of information services on information technology. IDG was founded more than 25 years ago and now employs more than 8,500 people worldwide. IDG publishes more than 275 computer publications in over 75 countries (see listing below). More than 60 million people read one or more IDG publications each month.

Launched in 1990, IDG Books Worldwide is today the #1 publisher of best-selling computer books in the United States. We are proud to have received eight awards from the Computer Press Association in recognition of editorial excellence and three from *Computer Currents'* First Annual Readers' Choice Awards. Our best-selling ...*For Dummies*® series has more than 30 million copies in print with translations in 30 languages. IDG Books Worldwide, through a joint venture with IDG's Hi-Tech Beijing, became the first U.S. publisher to publish a computer book in the People's Republic of China. In record time, IDG Books Worldwide has become the first choice for millions of readers around the world who want to learn how to better manage their businesses.

Our mission is simple: Every one of our books is designed to bring extra value and skill-building instructions to the reader. Our books are written by experts who understand and care about our readers. The knowledge base of our editorial staff comes from years of experience in publishing, education, and journalism — experience we use to produce books for the '90s. In short, we care about books, so we attract the best people. We devote special attention to details such as audience, interior design, use of icons, and illustrations. And because we use an efficient process of authoring, editing, and desktop publishing our books electronically, we can spend more time ensuring superior content and spend less time on the technicalities of making books.

You can count on our commitment to deliver high-quality books at competitive prices on topics you want to read about. At IDG Books Worldwide, we continue in the IDG tradition of delivering quality for more than 25 years. You'll find no better book on a subject than one from IDG Books Worldwide.

John Kilcullen
CEO
IDG Books Worldwide, Inc.

Steven Berkowitz
President and Publisher
IDG Books Worldwide, Inc.

Eighth Annual Computer Press Awards ≥1992

Ninth Annual Computer Press Awards ≥1993

Tenth Annual Computer Press Awards ≥1994

Eleventh Annual Computer Press Awards ≥1995

IDG Books Worldwide, Inc., is a subsidiary of International Data Group, the world's largest publisher of computer-related information and the leading global provider of information services on information technology. International Data Group publishes over 275 computer publications in over 75 countries. Sixty million people read one or more International Data Group publications each month. International Data Group's publications include: **ARGENTINA:** Buyer's Guide, Computerworld Argentina, PC World Argentina; **AUSTRALIA:** Australian Macworld, Australian PC World, Australian Reseller News, Computerworld, IT Casebook, Network World, Publish, Webmaster; **AUSTRIA:** Computerwelt Osterreich, Networks Austria, PC Tip Austria; **BANGLADESH:** PC World Bangladesh; **BELARUS:** PC World Belarus; **BELGIUM:** Data News; **BRAZIL:** Annuário de Informática, Computerworld, Connections, Macworld, PC Player, PC World, Publish, Reseller News, Supergamepower; **BULGARIA:** Computerworld Bulgaria, Network World Bulgaria, PC & MacWorld Bulgaria; **CANADA:** CIO Canada, Client/Server World, ComputerWorld Canada, InfoWorld Canada, NetworkWorld Canada, WebWorld; **CHILE:** Computerworld Chile, PC World Chile; **COLOMBIA:** Computerworld Colombia, PC World Colombia; **COSTA RICA:** PC World Centro America; **THE CZECH AND SLOVAK REPUBLICS:** Computerworld Czechoslovakia, Macworld Czech Republic, PC World Czechoslovakia; **DENMARK:** Communications World Danmark, Computerworld Danmark, Macworld Danmark, PC World Danmark, Techworld Denmark; **DOMINICAN REPUBLIC:** PC World Republica Dominicana; **ECUADOR:** PC World Ecuador; **EGYPT:** Computerworld Middle East, PC World Middle East; **EL SALVADOR:** PC World Centro America; **FINLAND:** MikroPC, Tietoverkko, Tietoviikko; **FRANCE:** Distributique, Hebdo, Info PC, Le Monde Informatique, Macworld, Reseaux & Telecoms, WebMaster France; **GERMANY:** Computer Partner, Computerwoche, Computerwoche Extra, Computerwoche FOCUS, Global Online, Macwelt, PC Welt; **GREECE:** Amiga Computing, GamePro Greece, Multimedia World; **GUATEMALA:** PC World Centro America; **HONDURAS:** PC World Centro America; **HONG KONG:** Computerworld Hong Kong, PC World Hong Kong, Publish in Asia; **HUNGARY:** ABCD CD-ROM, Computerworld Szamitastechnika, Internetto online Magazine, PC World Hungary, PC-X Magazin Hungary; **ICELAND:** Tolvuheimur PC World Island; **INDIA:** Information Communications World, Information Systems Computerworld, PC World India, Publish in Asia; **INDONESIA:** InfoKomputer PC World, Komputek Computerworld, Publish in Asia; **IRELAND:** ComputerScope, PC Live!; **ISRAEL:** Macworld Israel, People & Computers/Computerworld; **ITALY:** Computerworld Italia, Macworld Italia, Networking Italia, PC World Italia; **JAPAN:** DTP World, Macworld Japan, Nikkei Personal Computing, OS/2 World Japan, SunWorld Japan, Windows NT World, Windows World Japan; **KENYA:** PC World East African; **KOREA:** Hi-Tech Information, Macworld Korea, PC World Korea; **MACEDONIA:** PC World Macedonia; **MALAYSIA:** Computerworld Malaysia, PC World Malaysia, Publish in Asia; **MALTA:** PC World Malta; **MEXICO:** Computerworld Mexico, PC World Mexico; **MYANMAR:** PC World Myanmar; **NETHERLANDS:** Computer! Totaal, LAN Internetworking Magazine, LAN World Buyers Guide, Macworld Netherlands, Net, WebWereld; **NEW ZEALAND:** Absolute Beginners Guide and Plain & Simple Series, Computer Buyer, Computer Industry Directory, Computerworld New Zealand, MTB, Network World, PC World New Zealand; **NICARAGUA:** PC World Centro America; **NORWAY:** Computerworld Norge, CW Rapport, Datamagasinet, Financial Rapport, Kursguide Norge, Macworld Norge, Multimediaworld Norge, PC World Ekspress Norge, PC World Nettverk, PC World Norge, PC World ProduktGuide Norge; **PAKISTAN:** Computerworld Pakistan; **PANAMA:** PC World Panama; **PEOPLE'S REPUBLIC OF CHINA:** China Computer Users, China Computerworld, China InfoWorld, China Telecom World Weekly, Computer & Communication, Electronic Design China, Electronics Today, Electronics Weekly, Game Software, PC World China, Popular Computer Week, Software Weekly, Software World, Telecom World; **PERU:** Computerworld Peru, PC World Profesional Peru, PC World SoHo Peru; **PHILIPPINES:** Click!, Computerworld Philippines, PC World Philippines, Publish in Asia; **POLAND:** Computerworld Poland, Computerworld Special Report Poland, Cyber, Macworld Poland, Networld Poland, PC World Komputer; **PORTUGAL:** Cerebro/PC World, Computerworld/Correio Informático, Dealer World Portugal, Mac*In/PC*In Portugal, Multimedia World; **PUERTO RICO:** PC World Puerto Rico; **ROMANIA:** Computerworld Romania, PC World Romania, Telecom Romania; **RUSSIA:** Computerworld Russia, Mir PK, Publish, Seti; **SINGAPORE:** Computerworld Singapore, PC World Singapore, Publish in Asia; **SLOVENIA:** Monitor; **SOUTH AFRICA:** Computing SA, Network World SA, Software World SA; **SPAIN:** Communicaciones World España, Computerworld España, Dealer World España, Macworld España, PC World España; **SRI LANKA:** Infolink PC World; **SWEDEN:** CAP&Design, Computer Sweden, Corporate Computing Sweden, Internetworld Sweden, it.branschen, Macworld Sweden, MaxiData Sweden, MikroDatorn, Nätverk & Kommunikation, PC World Sweden, PCAktiv, Windows World Sweden; **SWITZERLAND:** Computerworld Schweiz, Macworld Schweiz, PCtip; **TAIWAN:** Computerworld Taiwan, Macworld Taiwan, NEW ViSiON/Publish, PC World Taiwan, Windows World Taiwan; **THAILAND:** Publish in Asia, Thai Computerworld; **TURKEY:** Computerworld Turkiye, Macworld Turkiye, Network World Turkiye, PC World Turkiye; **UKRAINE:** Computerworld Kiev, Multimedia World Ukraine, PC World Ukraine; **UNITED KINGDOM:** Acorn User UK, Amiga Action UK, Amiga Computing UK, Apple Talk UK, Computing, Macworld, Parents and Computers UK, PC Advisor, PC Home, PSX Pro, The WEB; **UNITED STATES:** Cable in the Classroom, CIO Magazine, Computerworld, DOS World, Federal Computer Week, GamePro Magazine, InfoWorld, I-Way, Macworld, Network World, PC Games, PC World, Publish, Video Event, THE WEB Magazine, and WebMaster; online webzines: JavaWorld, NetscapeWorld, and SunWorld Online; **URUGUAY:** InfoWorld Uruguay; **VENEZUELA:** Computerworld Venezuela, PC World Venezuela; and **VIETNAM:** PC World Vietnam.   3/24/97

Credits

Acquisitions Editor
Greg Croy

Development Editor
Denise Santoro

Technical Editor
Greg Guntle

Copy Editors
Luann Rouff
Nicole Fountain
Carolyn Welch

Production Coordinator
Tom Debolski

**Graphics and
Production Specialists**
Maureen Moore
Jude Levinson
Elizabeth A. Pauw
Ed Penslien
Linda Marousek
Hector Mendoza

Quality Control Specialist
Mark Schumann

Proofreader
David Wise

Indexer
Ty Koontz

About the Author

Clayton Walnum started programming computers in 1982, when he traded in
an IBM Selectric typewriter to buy an Atari 400 computer (16K of RAM!). Mr.
Walnum soon learned to combine his interest in writing with his newly
acquired programming skills and started selling programs and articles to
computer magazines. In 1985, *ANALOG Computing*, a nationally distributed
computer magazine, hired him as a technical editor, and, before leaving the
magazine business in 1989 to become a freelance writer, Mr. Walnum had
worked his way up to Executive Editor. Mr. Walnum has since acquired a
degree in Computer Science, as well as written more than 30 books
(translated into many languages) covering everything from computer
gaming to 3D graphics programming. He's also written hundreds of
magazine articles and software reviews, as well as countless programs. His
recent books include *Special Edition Using MFC and ATL* (Que), *Java By
Example* (Que), and the award-winning *Building Windows 95 Applications
with Visual Basic* (Que). Mr. Walnum's biggest disappointment in life is that
he wasn't one of the Beatles. To compensate, he writes and records rock
music in his home studio. You can reach Mr. Walnum at his home page,
which is located at http://www.connix.com/~cwalnum.

Dedicated to the memory of Mary Wing, a good friend and a valiant soul

Preface

You may have heard that learning to program Windows 98 is a lot like studying to build a space ship, that there's so much to learn that only someone with an IQ of 180, and with 12 hours a day to study, could possibly master the techniques required. None of this is true, of course, although, as with all exaggerations, there's an element of truth. Yes, learning to program Windows 98 applications represents a big task. However, most people will be able to get the job done, and you don't have to dedicate your life to it either. A couple of hours a day will suffice.

Would-be Windows programmers today have a big advantage over those of a few years ago. Namely, the programming tools available to them are more sophisticated than ever. Not only can a basic Windows application be put together in minutes (as compared with hours the old-fashioned way), but extras such as toolbars, status bars, and dialog boxes are only a few button clicks away. In fact, with Visual C++ 5.0, you can create a Windows application by simply typing a program name and clicking the mouse five times. Pretty easy, eh?

Of course, creating a program like this isn't especially useful. Like a new house without electricity, plumbing, or furnishings, you still have to supply all the stuff that makes people want to visit. That's where this book comes in. In the pages that follow, you'll learn not only what makes a basic Windows 98 program work, but also how to add everything beyond the basic essentials to your programs. You'll learn about event-driven programming, responding to Windows messages, creating custom dialog boxes, drawing a window's display, printing documents, displaying bitmaps, creating threads, and much more.

Along the way, you'll also get an introduction to some advanced technologies, including ActiveX, DirectX, and Internet programming with WinInet. ActiveX is Microsoft's name for what you may know as OLE, a technology that enables applications to share not only data, but also program functionality. Using ActiveX, you can even create mini-applications, called ActiveX controls, that can be embedded into Web pages. DirectX, on the other hand, is a set of multimedia technologies used mostly for game programming, whereas WinInet is a set of classes that make creating Internet applications easier than you might believe possible.

Who Should Read This Book

This book is not a C++ tutorial. In order to understand the lessons here, you must already be fluent in C++ and understand object-oriented programming (OOP) concepts. If you're new to C++ and OOP, you should pick up a good general Visual C++ programming book such as *Visual C++ Bible 5* by Richard C. Leinecker and Paul Yao, published by IDG Books Worldwide. Once you've worked through that book (or some similar book), you can come back to this one.

Although this book assumes reasonable expertise with C++, it assumes no previous Windows programming knowledge. This book includes all the information you need to create most types of Windows applications. When you've completed this book, you'll have a solid grasp of Windows programming techniques and will be able to move on to more advanced books that concentrate on specific technologies, such as ActiveX or DirectX.

System Requirements

The system and software requirements for the programs and lessons in this book are the same as the requirements for Visual C++ 5.0 running under Windows 98:

- IBM-compatible with a 66MHz 486DX processor (Pentium processor recommended)
- Microsoft Windows 98
- 20MB RAM (24MB recommended)
- Hard disk
- CD-ROM drive
- VGA or better graphics (Super VGA recommended)
- Mouse
- Visual C++ 5.0

This Book's Overall Structure

This book covers a huge amount of Windows 98 programming territory and so is divided into seven sections, each of which is described below.

Part I: Introduction to Windows 98

Before you can get started with Windows 98 programming, you have to know what Windows 98 is and how to use the programming tools provided by Visual C++. This part of the book gets you started by providing a complete overview of the Windows 98 operating system. You'll learn about the basic graphical user interface (GUI) and about common types of windows and user controls. In addition, you'll learn about multitasking and event-driven operating systems.

This section moves on to provide an introduction to Visual C++ and its many programming tools, including AppWizard, ClassWizard, the compiler and debugger, and the resource editors. You'll then use Visual C++ in a hands-on project to create a complete Windows application using the tools to which you were introduced. Finally, you'll discover how Visual C++ MFC programs differ from conventional Windows applications. You'll also learn about the various types of Windows program modules, including Win32 applications, console applications, DLLs, and ActiveX controls.

Part II: User Interface

Every Windows application has a graphical user interface that enables the user to interact with the program, selecting commands, editing documents, and so on. Creating this interface for your applications is an important Windows 98 programming topic. This section introduces you to Windows' Graphics Device Interface (GDI), which enables applications to display data in their windows. You'll also study the various types of windows you can create, including frame windows, view windows, MDI windows, dialog boxes, property sheets, and wizards.

After presenting the basics, this section moves on to show how to manipulate text, create menu resources, and use standard and common controls. The standard controls include objects such as pushbuttons, edit boxes, checkboxes, radio buttons, list boxes, and combo boxes. The common controls include progress bars, status bars, sliders, spinners, list views, and tree views. After studying controls, you'll move on to printing documents under Windows 98, as well as managing and displaying device-dependent and device-independent bitmaps. You'll even get some advanced GDI training, as you learn about coordinate systems, mapping modes, rectangles, regions, paths, and metafiles.

Part III: OS Core

By this point in the book, you'll already have accumulated most of the basic skills you need to create Windows applications, so here you'll dig into some more advanced topics, including memory management, process control, input devices, and file handling. You'll learn how to allocate and manage memory, as well as how to create multithreaded applications. As you study these topics, you'll understand about movable, discardable, and virtual memory, as well as process and thread priorities, user-interface and worker threads, and thread synchronization.

In this part of the book, you also get the skinny on handling the mouse and keyboard, as well as how to use Visual C++'s MFC classes to manage files and create persistent classes. Finally, you'll get lessons in implementing Clipboard support in your programs, including using standard, registered, private, and multiple data formats. You'll learn how to open the Clipboard, place data on the Clipboard, and copy data from the Clipboard.

Part IV: ActiveX

The remainder of the book dedicates itself to the introduction of advanced technologies. In this part, you learn to create ActiveX applications with

Visual C++'s tools. These applications include container applications (which can hold data objects from other applications), server applications (which supply data objects, as well as editing services for those objects), automation applications (which can control or be controlled by other applications in the system), and ActiveX controls.

As you learn about the ActiveX technologies, you'll work through hands-on projects that create functional ActiveX programs. Sample programs include container and server applications for sharing and editing data objects, automation clients and servers, and an ActiveX control. When you finish this section, you'll have a basic understanding of ActiveX technology and how it's supported by Visual C++ and the MFC libraries.

Part V: Multimedia

This part of the book introduces you to Microsoft's DirectX multimedia technologies, which include DirectDraw, DirectSound, DirectInput, and Direct3D. (DirectPlay is not covered here.) You'll learn to create animated displays using DirectDraw and how to play wave files using DirectSound. In the DirectInput chapter, you'll see how this advanced library can give input devices interesting new capabilities, without a lot of programming on your part. You'll even display and rotate a 3D model using Direct3D.

Part VI: The Internet

The Internet is becoming more and more important to computer operators everywhere. No Windows programming book would be complete without a look into programming Internet applications. MFC's WinInet libraries make it easy to create HTTP, FTP, and Gopher applications. In this section, you'll not only get an overview of these handy Internet programming classes, you'll also build an FTP application that can browse the directories on an FTP server and even download files.

Later in this section, you'll learn to use Internet Explorer's programmable objects to create your own sophisticated Internet applications. By exposing Internet Explorer's impressive capabilities via ActiveX, Microsoft made it reasonably easy for you to add even Web browsing capabilities to any application, a good example of Microsoft's ActiveX vision coming of age.

Appendixes

In the book's appendixes, you'll read about Windows 98 logo certification. If you want to create commercial Windows 98 applications, you won't want to overlook this important topic.

Icons Used in This Book

As you read this book, you'll notice several types of icons designed to draw your attention to important notes and tips. The following list describes the icons used in this book:

On CD-ROM

This icon marks programs and files that you can find on this book's CD-ROM.

Note

This icon marks additional information about the current topic.

Tip

This icon marks tips that make programming tasks easier.

Moving On

As you can see, this book covers a lot of territory. Seems to me you have a lot of reading to do. And now just might be the perfect time to turn the page and get to work. I'll meet you there.

Acknowledgments

I would like to thank the many people whose hard work made this book as good as it could be. Special thanks go to Greg Croy for placing this important project in my care, to Denise Santoro for keeping things rolling and for providing valuable suggestions on a huge manuscript, to Carolyn Welch and Luann Rouff for polishing up the words, and to Greg Guntle for checking all the facts. As always, thanks goes to my family: Lynn, Christopher, Justin, Stephen, and Caitlynn.

Contents at a Glance

Contents

• •

Part I

Introduction to Windows 98

Chapter 1

A Windows 98 Overview

In This Chapter

▶ Introducing Windows 98

▶ Learning about Windows 98's user interface

▶ Exploring UI elements

▶ Familiarizing yourself with resource files

▶ Understanding event-driven applications

▶ Discovering multitasking and threads

Love it or hate it, Windows has become the operating system of choice for a majority of computer users. Besides making Bill Gates rich beyond comprehension, Windows has managed to establish the closest thing to an operating-system standard since the DOS command line popped up on computers the world over.

In 1990, with Windows 3.0, the Windows platform took over operating systems everywhere. Windows 3.0 transformed the fledgling Windows operating system (whose previous versions had very little luck in the marketplace) into a mature one for IBM-compatible computers. Since that time, Windows has gone through a lot of changes, as it moved from Windows 3.0 to Windows for Workgroups to Windows 95 (not to mention Windows NT).

With Windows 95, Microsoft rebuilt the operating system (OS) almost from the ground up, completely revamping the graphical user interface in an attempt to make Windows easier to use. (Whether Windows 95 was successful in making the operating system more accessible is a matter of hot debate.) Windows 98, the latest incarnation of the Windows operating system, promises to be just as popular as its predecessors. For this reason, the greatest programming opportunities are now available to programmers who can produce professional-quality Windows applications.

Introducing Windows 98

What exactly is Windows 98? Although it has a different name, Windows 98 is not all that different from Windows 95. The basic user interface is virtually identical, with only a few cosmetic changes thrown in. The biggest of these changes is the integration of the desktop with Microsoft's Web browser, Internet Explorer 4.0. If you choose to enable this integration (you can stick with the old-style user interface), the Internet becomes an integral part of your desktop, enabling you to access the Internet in almost the same way you access files on your own hard drive, a goal that Microsoft has been pursuing for some time.

The bottom line is, if you want to create software with the largest possible user base, Windows is your only choice. Learning to program Windows 98 is a task that brings with it not only the best chance of success, but also the security of knowing that the OS on which your software runs will be around for a long time to come. And I have to say that once you get the hang of it, Windows programming is downright fun!

In the rest of this chapter, you will examine the major elements of the Windows 98 operating system. If you're already a long-time Windows user, you may want to just skim this chapter and move on. However, if you're new to Windows, or need a review, this chapter provides a context for all the lessons to come.

The Windows 98 Desktop

Windows 98's main screen display is called the *desktop*. The user can configure the desktop in various ways, including integrating Internet Explorer to provide a Web view of all desktop elements. In the Web view, your desktop becomes much like a Web page, containing links to favorite Web sites, as well as hosting ActiveX controls and other forms of Web content. Figure 1-1 shows the desktop, set to its standard configuration (without Web integration). The main elements are labeled in the figure and described below:

Desktop icons	The user can place many types of objects on the desktop for easy access. These objects include files, shortcuts, applications, and more. To access an object represented by an icon, just double-click it.
Application windows	Each running application gets its own window, which can be displayed at various sizes or even hidden on the desktop's taskbar.
Taskbar	The taskbar displays buttons for currently loaded applications. The user can activate an application by clicking its button in the taskbar.

Band boxes	Much of the taskbar's contents is organized into band boxes. Band boxes look like sliding toolbars that can be horizontally resized as needed.
Start menu	The Start menu gives the user access to applications and documents stored on the system.
Tray	System utilities can display icons in the tray. These icons provide access to system settings such as the time and date, sound-card volume, and screen resolution.

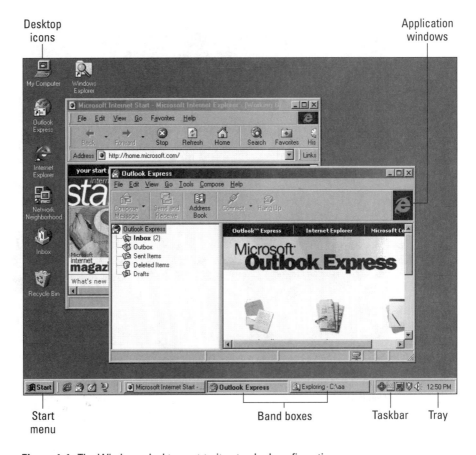

Figure 1-1: The Windows desktop set to its standard configuration

The desktop changes quite a bit when the user enables the Internet integration. The desktop's Web view, shown in Figure 1-2, includes icons that can be activated like Web links, with a single click; and a channel bar that provides quick access to favorite Web sites. The Web-like links are used throughout the system when the desktop is in Web view. For example, Figure 1-3 shows Windows Explorer in Web view. (Windows Explorer is Windows 98's main file-handling utility.) In Web view, all the entries in Explorer's panes are displayed like Web links. That is, the links are underlined like a link in a Web page, and the cursor changes into a hand when it's over the link.

Web link-like icons   Channel bar

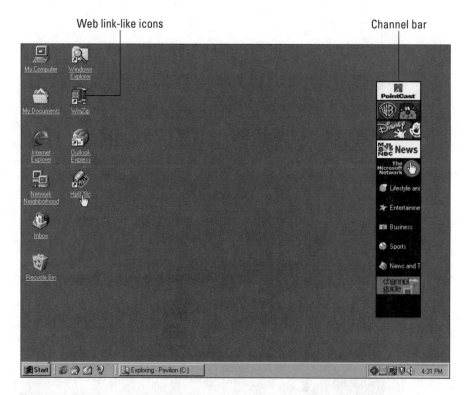

Figure 1-2: The Windows desktop in Web view showing icons that can be activated like Web links

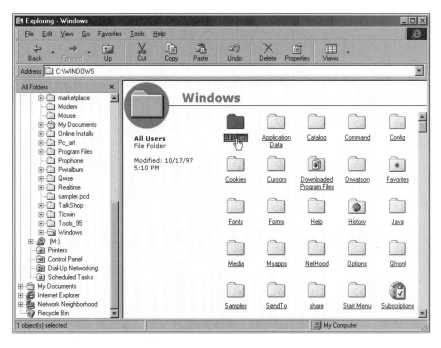

Figure 1-3: Windows Explorer set in Web view

Major Elements of the User Interface

The Windows 98 Graphical User Interface (GUI) features a number of major elements that are commonly used not only by the OS, but also by most Windows applications. The most obvious of these elements is the window, from which Windows gets its name. Although it may not be apparent at first glance, almost all graphical elements displayed by the user interface are windows of one sort or another. These elements include frame windows, dialog boxes, property sheets, and wizards, as well as various controls—like buttons, combo boxes, and edit boxes. The following sections introduce you to these various components.

Parts of a Window

Although most user interface elements are window objects, it is an application's main display area that most people think of as a window. This window is made up of features that work together to give the user complete control over the application. Figure 1-4 shows a generic window with its major parts labeled. The main parts of a window are described below:

Title bar   The title bar displays the application's name, along with the name of the open document. You can move the window by dragging the title bar with the mouse. The window may also be

	maximized or restored to its previous size by double-clicking the title bar.
Menu bar	The menu bar provides access to commands that control Windows applications. Most applications have at least File, Edit, and Help menus. Other standard menus—such as Tools, Format, and Window—may also be needed to comply with interface design guidelines for Windows applications.
Window border	The window's border frames the application and distinguishes it from other elements on your desktop. Dragging the border with the mouse allows you to resize the window, if the application allows window resizing.
Client area	The client area provides the surface where the application creates its display. Often, the client area contains a view window—a window containing no title bar, border, controls, or other graphical objects—that displays the application's native data. For example, a word processor may have in its client area a view window that displays the document being edited.
System menu	The system menu provides commands for moving, resizing, and closing windows. Applications may also have their own commands on the system menu, although this practice is not encouraged.
Minimize button	The Minimize button enables the user to hide the application on the taskbar.
Restore button	The Restore button restores the window to its previous size.
Maximize button	The Maximize button enables the user to enlarge the window to its maximum size, which is usually the full screen.

A Windows application can run as a single-document interface (SDI) application or a multiple-document interface (MDI) application. The generic window in Figure 1-4 employs the single-document interface, which allows only a single document to be open at a given point in time. An MDI application can display any number of child windows (additional windows owned by the application), each of which contains a different document or a different view of a document. Figure 1-5 shows an MDI application with several child windows open. Notice that in an MDI application, the main window acts as a type of mini-desktop in which minimized document windows appear as icons at the bottom of the window in much the same way that minimized applications appear as buttons in the desktop's taskbar.

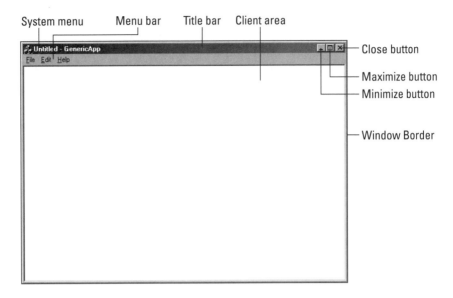

Figure 1-4: A generic Windows application with its major parts labeled

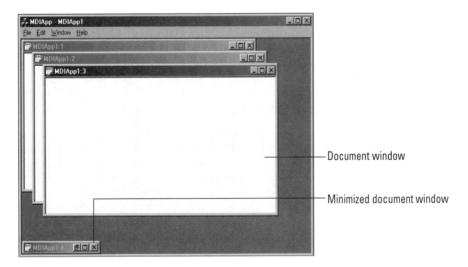

Figure 1-5: An MDI Windows application displaying several open child windows

Dialog boxes

Dialog boxes are a special type of window that facilitate communication between the user and the OS. They both obtain information from the user and provide information to the user. Dialog boxes often contain a number of controls—especially buttons and text boxes—that enable the user to make selections and enter data. Figure 1-6 shows a typical dialog box.

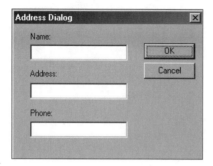

Figure 1-6: A typical dialog box

Dialog boxes are usually created with a *resource editor,* which enables the programmer to drag-and-drop controls onto the dialog box's display area. The resource editor then generates a resource file based on the dialog box the programmer created. When the programmer compiles the application, the resource file is merged into the application's executable file.

Message boxes

Message boxes are a special type of dialog box that don't require a dialog box resource file, which saves the programmer a bit of work. Instead of your having to create a resource script for the object, message boxes are built into the system and displayed programmatically. The function that creates a message box accepts a number of arguments that determine the contents of the message box, including the message text, the icon to display, and the buttons to include. Message boxes provide a quick and easy way for applications to interact with the user. Figure 1-7 shows a typical message box.

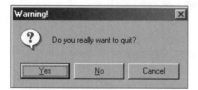

Figure 1-7: A message box set with standard arguments

Property sheets

Property sheets are often called *tabbed dialog boxes* because they contain tabs you can click. Their design allows programmers to organize many options into a single dialog box, by grouping the options into pages. Property sheets are used extensively in Windows 98, from setting system options to manipulating application attributes. Figure 1-8 shows a Windows 98 system property sheet.

Figure 1-8: A Windows 98 property sheet displaying system properties

Wizards

In order to make Windows 98 easy to use, Microsoft included lots of *wizards,* automated tasks that guide a user step-by-step through complex operations. Windows 98's wizards can help the user create an Internet connection, solve device conflicts, add and remove applications, and much more. Many modern applications (especially those from Microsoft) also include wizards to help the user complete tasks quickly and easily. Wizards are a bit like property sheets in that they have multiple pages; however, unlike property sheets, wizard pages have no tabs. Instead, the user moves from page to page by clicking buttons. Because the buttons allow access to only the previous or next pages in the wizard, the user must complete task steps in a sequential order. Figure 1-9 shows a Windows 98 wizard.

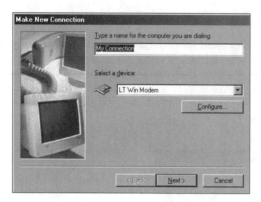

Figure 1-9: A Windows 98 wizard set to connect
your computer to your modem

Standard controls

Windows 98 uses dialog boxes and other windows to access information
from users. These controls include edit boxes for entering text, buttons for
making selections, list boxes for choosing items from a list, checkboxes for
selecting options, and more. These controls are a standard part of the
operating system, so you will get used to seeing and using them. Figure 1-10
shows a dialog box containing the standard controls. The controls and their
descriptions are listed below:

Static text	A string of text that cannot be edited. Static text controls are usually used to label other components in a dialog box.
Edit box	A box in which text can be entered. Text in the edit box can be edited and even copied and pasted via the Windows Clipboard.
Push button	A control that triggers a command when clicked. Push buttons usually contain a text label and are often animated so they appear pressed down when clicked.
Radio button	A button usually used in groups in which only one button can be selected at a time. When a radio button is selected, the previously selected button turns off.
Checkbox	A button used to turn options on and off. Unlike radio buttons, checkboxes are traditionally used to allow any or all of the selections in the group to be selected simultaneously.

List box

A list of items. You can use the mouse to select one or more items from the list. When there are more items in the list box than can fit, the list box will display a scroll bar that enables the user to view items not currently shown in the box.

Combo box

A list of items combined with an edit box. You can either click the combo box's arrow to display a list of choices, or type a selection into the associated edit box.

Group box

Used to group other controls. For example, a group box is often used to group a set of radio buttons. The box includes a caption that describes the contents of the box. In Figure 1-10, the term "Options" is used as a caption for the group box of radio buttons.

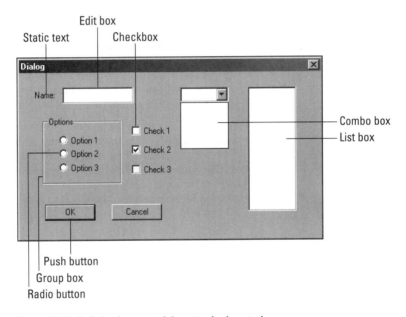

Figure 1-10: A dialog box containing standard controls

Common UI Elements

As Windows programmers became more and more proficient, they found better ways to interact with the user. Objects like toolbars and status bars started popping up in many Windows applications. The practice of including these interface elements in applications snowballed as other programmers saw how useful they were. When Microsoft designed Windows 95, they decided to incorporate these new types of controls into the system. Known as common controls, these graphical user interface objects (some of which are shown in Figure 1-11) are also part of Windows 98 and include the following:

Toolbar

A toolbar is a row of controls (usually buttons) that provide quick access to important commands. The buttons on a toolbar usually mirror the commands found in the application's menus. However, a toolbar also often features drop-down list boxes that enable you to select fonts, colors, and other document attributes.

Status bar

A status bar provides a place for an application to display command descriptions and status information, such as the state of the keyboard and the position of the text cursor. It usually sits at the bottom of an application's display.

Slider

A slider is a control for selecting a value from a range of values. The user drags the slider's thumb to select a value. When dragged, the thumb slides in the control's track, either horizontally or vertically, depending upon how the control was set up. Sliders can also be used to select a range of values.

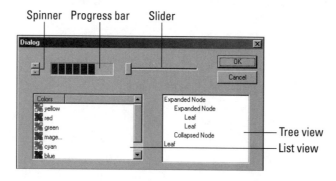

Figure 1-11: A dialog box containing common controls

Spinner	A spinner provides another way to select a value from a range of values. The spinner control is made up of two arrows, which enable the user to either raise or lower a displayed value.
Progress bar	A progress bar shows the status of an ongoing operation by filling the control's display area with a colored bar. The bar shows an operation's degree of completeness. For example, a progress bar might track the saving of a large file. When the file is half saved, the progress bar's display would be half filled.
List view	A list view control displays an organized group of items. How the items are displayed depends upon the list view's current setting. For instance, a list view control can display just a list of items or it can display the list in columns that include details about the items. A good example of a list view control is the display you see in the right-hand pane of Windows Explorer (see Figure 1-12).
Tree view	A tree view control displays items as a hierarchy. Parent items (such as folders on a disk) can contain child items (such as subfolders or files on a disk). You can open and close parent items by clicking them with a mouse. Closing a parent item hides its child items. A good example of a tree view control is the left-hand pane of Windows Explorer (see Figure 1-12), which shows the file hierarchy of the hard drive.
Image list	An image list is similar to an array of images. The image list control usually stores images for toolbar buttons, or stores the images used to display a tree in a tree view control. An image list can store images for any use. For example, you might use an image list to store a group of images that make up an animation sequence. The images are stored in memory and can't be seen on the screen until they're needed by the program.

Tree view   List view

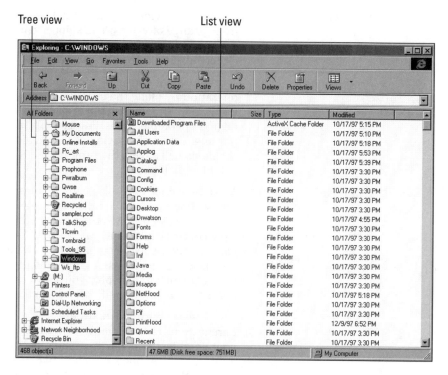

Figure 1-12: Windows Explorer uses tree view and list view controls.

Resource Files

Almost all Windows applications have resource files that define many of the
user interface elements that applications will display, as well as provide
storage for various types of data needed by the program. These elements
include dialog boxes, menus, and other important objects that Windows
users expect to find in an application. The following list describes each of
the types of data you can define and store in a resource file:

Dialog boxes   All of an application's dialog boxes must be
                               defined in a resource file. The dialog's resource
                               definition includes style flags (values that control
                               how the dialog box looks and acts), as well as the
                               size and position of the controls contained in the
                               dialog box. Figure 1-13 shows Visual C++'s dialog
                               box editor.

Menu bars   Your application's menu bar must also be defined
                               in a resource file. The file specifies menu
                               commands and IDs for the commands, as well as
                               the commands' positions in the menu. Figure 1-14
                               shows Visual C++'s menu bar editor.

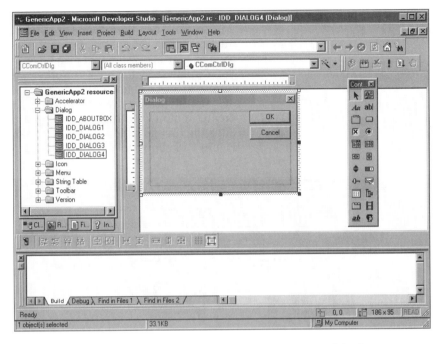

Figure 1-13: Visual C++'s dialog box editor enables you to create dialog box resources.

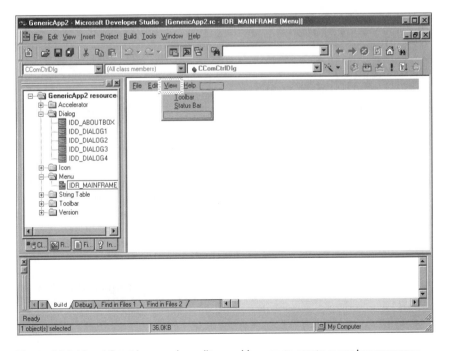

Figure 1-14: Visual C++'s menu bar editor enables you to create menu bar resources.

Bitmaps

Bitmaps are images that you use to create your application's user interface. For example, you might create a set of bitmaps for the images on toolbar buttons. You might also have bitmaps that you display in dialog boxes or other windows. Bitmaps can be defined byte-by-byte in a resource file. More typically, though, the programmer creates a bitmap with an image editor and then adds the bitmap's file name to the resource file. Figure 1-15 shows Visual C++'s bitmap editor.

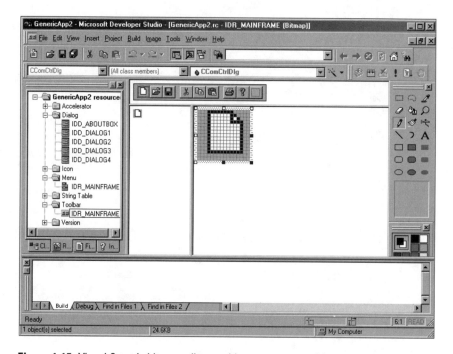

Figure 1-15: Visual C++'s bitmap editor enables you to create bitmap resources.

Icons

Icons are small images similar to bitmaps. However, whereas bitmaps can be any size, icons are much smaller, usually either 16x16 or 32x32 pixels. Icons can be used in many of the ways bitmaps are. However, they are commonly used for the image that represents the minimized application; for the images that represent the application's document type; and other similar system uses. Figure 1-16 shows Visual C++'s Icon editor.

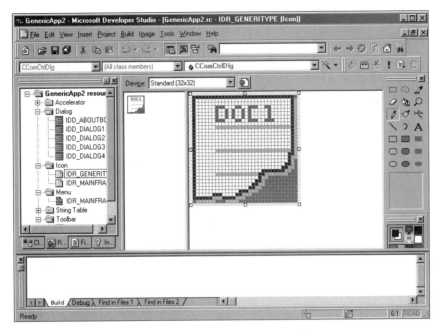

Figure 1-16: Visual C++'s icon editor enables you to create icon resources.

String tables

String tables are exactly what they sound like, a table of text strings. Often, text in a string table is used to display tool tips for menu commands or to display errors and other types of messages in dialog boxes or message boxes. However, you can use text strings in a string table any way you wish. To access a text string in the table, you reference the string's ID, which is associated with the string in the resource file that defines the table. Figure 1-17 shows Visual C++'s string table editor.

Cursors

A cursor is the image that represents the mouse's location on the screen. Although the Windows system defines a number of cursors you can assign to the mouse, you can also create your own. Such custom cursors can be defined in your application's resource file. Figure 1-18 shows Visual C++'s cursor editor.

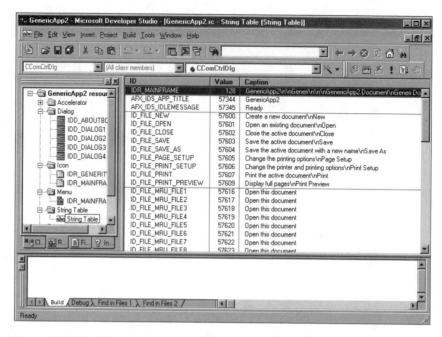

Figure 1-17: Visual C++'s string table editor enables you to create string table resources.

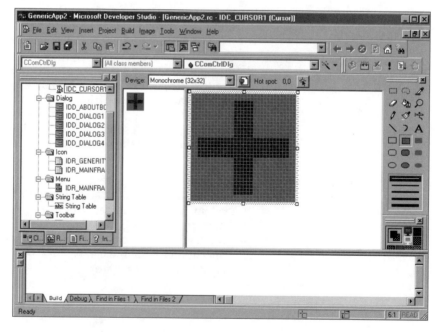

Figure 1-18: Visual C++'s cursor editor enables you to create cursor resources.

Accelerators

Accelerators are also known as hot keys. These are the key strokes the user presses to select a command instantly, without having to find the command in the application's menu. For example, most application's define Ctrl+V as the hot key for the Edit menu's Paste command. Accelerators are defined in a table that associates keystrokes with command resource IDs. Figure 1-19 shows Visual C++'s accelerator editor.

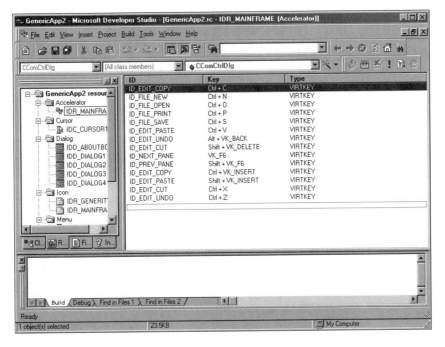

Figure 1-19: Visual C++'s accelerator editor enables you to create accelerator resources.

Custom resources

Custom resources are any other type of data that you want to store in your application's resource file. This can be text or binary data, and you can use the custom resource in the program any way you like. The resource file simply acts as a storage area. When you create a custom resource, you avoid having to load the data from disk files, because the data is loaded automatically with your resource file.

When folks first started programming Windows, they created resource files by hand, writing a resource script with the use of a text editor. The resource script was then compiled into a binary representation of the resource, which was then attached to the application's executable file. Resource files still come in both their script and binary forms, but nowadays programmers use visual editors (such as those shown in Figures 1-13 through 1-19) to create resource files. The editors generate the resource script from the objects the programmer creates with the editor. The resource compiler then handles the generated script in the same way it handled handwritten scripts. In the next chapter, you will see how Visual C++'s resource editors can speed resource development.

Maintaining a Consistent Look and Operation

From the user's point of view, one of the big advantages of an operating system like Windows 98 is that every application looks and works similarly. For example, Windows users know that, regardless of what application they're running, they can load and save files from an application's File menu. Similarly, commands to copy, paste, and delete data are always found in the application's Edit menu. In order to create professional Windows programs, you must be familiar with this design philosophy so that your applications meet users' expectations. If your program doesn't operate the way the user expects it to, the user is likely to put it aside for something more Windows-like.

Unfortunately, user interface design is a huge subject, one that could easily warrant a book of its own. If you need to brush up on the Windows interface design philosophy, you should read Microsoft's The Windows Interface Guidelines for Software Design, which is included on the Microsoft Developer Network library CD-ROM. For more information on this publication, check out Microsoft online at www.microsoft.com.

Understanding Windows' Event-Driven System

If you've never programmed applications for an operating system like Windows before, one of the hardest things to get used to is the event-driven architecture. The engine that drives a Windows application is its message loop. Whenever an event occurs that affects the application, such as the user typing on the keyboard or clicking with the mouse, Windows sends messages to the application.

The application's message loop processes and dispatches these messages to the functions that handle the events represented by the messages. For example, when the user clicks the mouse in an application's window, Windows sends the application a WM_LBUTTONDOWN message. If the application is designed to respond to the `WM_LBUTTONDOWN` message, the application's message loop routes the message to the function that handles the mouse click.

Windows defines hundreds of messages, way too many for the average person to ever remember. When you program Windows, you'll need to keep a good, general Windows reference at hand. A complete development environment also goes a long way toward helping you to make sense of the hundreds of messages and functions that make up the Windows API. The projects in this book were developed using Visual C++ 5.0, which includes the Microsoft Foundation Classes (MFC).

MFC is an extensive class library that speeds Windows application development by encapsulating the Windows API. One way MFC helps the developer is by shielding him or her from the details of message handling. In an MFC program, you need only define a message map that tells MFC where messages should be routed. The MFC framework takes care of the rest, including providing the message loop.

Visual C++ also provides a lot of help through its ClassWizard tool. When you use ClassWizard to manipulate the classes in a project, you don't have to remember the names of messages or figure out which class member functions can be overridden. ClassWizard takes out the drudgery by listing the available messages and functions for you. In most cases, you can associate a function with a Windows message with only a couple of mouse clicks. In the next two chapters, you will learn more about the Visual C++ Windows development environment and how to use it to create professional-quality Windows applications.

Multitasking

Another important feature of Windows 98 is *multitasking*, which allows many processes to run concurrently. Each process under Windows 98 is made up of one or more *threads,* each of which represents a flow of execution. Every process begins with its main thread. A process can create additional threads, with each thread running concurrently in the system. For example, a spreadsheet program might create a thread to recalculate the contents of the spreadsheet while the user continues to edit data.

You can think of a thread as a subprogram, a step down from a complete application. Whereas an application is a complete piece of software for performing a large-scale task like writing a report, a thread is a mini-program owned by the application that performs a specific, small-scale operation such as spooling data out to a printer. Although the thread is a part of the application, the two run concurrently.

Multitasking and threaded operations, however, can create problems when it comes to accessing shared resources. For example, an application may end up with invalid data if one thread reads from an array while another changes the same array. To avoid these types of conflicts, Windows 98 supports a number of thread synchronization objects, including events, critical sections, semaphores, and mutexes. You will learn about these important thread synchronization mechanisms in Chapter 15, "Process Control." For now, look over the following list to get a general idea of how thread synchronization works under Windows 98:

Events	Event objects are used to signal to a thread that a process can begin or has been completed. Until it receives this event signal, the thread remains suspended. When the event object enters its signaled state, the waiting thread can begin execution. An application might, for example, use an event object to notify a thread when data is ready to be processed.
Critical sections	Critical section objects control threads by providing an object that all threads must share. Only the thread that owns the object can access the protected resource. Before another thread can access the resource, the previous thread must release the critical-section object so that the new thread can claim it. An application might use a critical section to prevent two threads from accessing a loaded document at the same time.
Mutexes	Mutexes (the name comes from "mutually exclusive") work much like critical sections, except mutexes not only protect shared resources within a process, but also between processes in the system. A mutex might be used to prevent two applications from accessing a shared file simultaneously.
Semaphores	Semaphores are a bit unusual in that they don't limit access of a shared resource to a single thread. Instead, semaphores enable multiple threads—but only up to a preset limit—to access shared resources. For example, a semaphore could limit the number of processes that can access a file simultaneously.

Summary

Windows 98 is a complex operating system. To program professional Windows applications, you must spend a lot of time learning and practicing the required programming techniques. However, you don't have to go it alone. This book teaches you all the basic skills you need to create sophisticated Windows 98 applications. What you do with those skills is, of course, up to you!

Also discussed in this chapter:

▶ Windows 98 is a complex operating system that features a sophisticated graphical user interface.

▶ Windows' interface makes use of many standard types of windows and controls, such as dialog boxes, message boxes, menu bars, property sheets, edit boxes, buttons, checkboxes, and list boxes.

▶ Windows 98 also features a group of common controls—including toolbars, status bars, sliders, progress bars, and tree views—that make programming full-featured applications easier.

▶ Windows applications use resource files to store the application's dialog boxes, menus, icons, and other types of data.

▶ All Windows applications receive and process Windows messages. This event-driven type of programming is very different from traditional structured programming.

▶ Multitasking enables many applications to run concurrently under Windows 98. Applications can also start secondary threads to perform time-consuming operations concurrently with the main application.

Chapter 2

A Visual C++ Overview

Visual C++ is the most dynamic professional development environment available for Windows programmers. This shouldn't be all that surprising considering that it's published by Microsoft, the same company that brought you Windows 98. Using Visual C++, you can create not only conventional Windows applications, but also ActiveX servers and clients, database programs, ActiveX controls, programmable objects (using automation), and more. If you don't recognize some of these types of applications, don't worry. You'll know what they are by the end of this book. For now, though, take a few minutes in this chapter to explore the Visual C++ programming environment and the tools it features.

Introducing Visual C++ 5.0

The latest version, Visual C++ 5.0, includes many advanced features and tools, such as AppWizard and ClassWizard. Visual C++ is so extensive, in fact, it may take you a long time before you master all the ins and outs of programming with it. Luckily, getting started with Visual C++ 5.0 is easy, thanks to the many wizards—especially AppWizard—that guide you step-by-step through complex tasks.

In this chapter, you get a quick look at the major tools that make up the Visual C++ programming environment. Once you see what Visual C++ has to offer, you will be ready to get some hands-on experience with the package in the following chapter, "Programming with Visual C++."

Visual C++ Core Tools

Although Visual C++ 5.0 features many tools, you will use several again and
again as you develop your Windows applications. These tools, which include
AppWizard and ClassWizard, take a lot of the sweat out of Windows
programming by handling many of the tasks that must be performed every
time you start a new project or create new member functions and variables.
For example, using AppWizard, you can create a complete skeleton
application—including toolbar, status bar, and menu bar—with only a few
mouse clicks. This skeleton application contains all the source code needed
to compile and run the basic program. You then only need to add the code
that makes your application do what it's designed to do. In the following
sections, you examine each of these major tools.

AppWizard

Perhaps the most important Visual C++ tool (outside of the compiler) is
AppWizard, which enables you to create a skeleton application with only a
few mouse clicks. This skeleton application can support any number of
optional features, such as toolbars, menu bars, the multiple-document
interface, database connectivity, and even ActiveX controls.

When you start up AppWizard, you see the first page of the wizard, shown in
Figure 2-1. On this first page, select whether you want an SDI-, MDI-, or
dialog-based application. (A dialog-based application has a dialog box as its
main window.) You can also select a language for the application's resources.

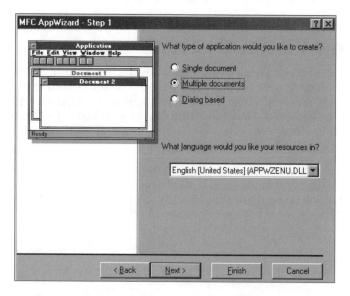

Figure 2-1: AppWizard's first page enables you to select whether
you want an SDI-, MDI-, or dialog-based application.

When you've selected the options you need, click the Next button to bring up AppWizard's second page (see Figure 2-2). Click the database support you would like to include in the application. The choices are as follows:

None	No database support
Header files only	AppWizard provides basic database support by including the database-class header files and libraries in the project. However, AppWizard creates no database classes for you. You must create the classes yourself.
Database view without file support	AppWizard provides full database support by including database-class header files and libraries in the project, as well as creating record view and record set classes. (Please refer to your Visual C++ online documentation for more information about the `CRecordView` and `CRecordset` classes.) However, this application will not support database serialization (transferring data to and from disk).
Database view with file support	AppWizard provides the same database support as in the previous support option, but with database serialization.

If you include a database view (a window that displays data from a database), you must also select a data source.

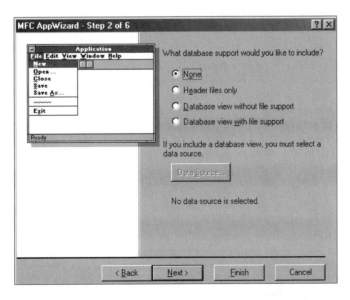

Figure 2-2: AppWizard's second page enables you to select the database support you would like to include in your application.

After making your database decisions, click the Next button to get to the
third AppWizard page. As you can see in Figure 2-3, this page enables you to
add various types of ActiveX (or OLE) support to the application. You can
decide to create a container and/or server, as well as whether to support
automation or ActiveX controls. (For more information on ActiveX, please
refer to Part 4 of this book.)

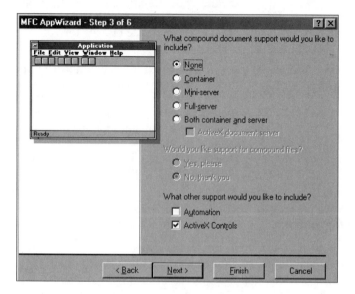

Figure 2-3: AppWizard's third page enables you to add various types
of ActiveX or OLE support to your application.

AppWizard's fourth page, shown in Figure 2-4, offers advanced features
(those not required by the application), such as a toolbar, status bar, and 3D
controls, for your application. You can even choose to include printing and
print preview support, which goes a long way toward giving your application
the kind of printer functionality Windows users expect. Other features you
can add to your application from this page include mail support, context-
sensitive help, and Windows sockets support (for creating Internet
applications).

The fifth AppWizard page, shown in Figure 2-5, provides options that affect
the way AppWizard generates the source code, as well as choices for how
the MFC libraries are linked to the application. Usually, you want to enable
AppWizard to generate comments in the source code. These comments can
be a great help when you're adding your own code to the generated files
because they provide basic usage instructions. You can also choose to link
to the static MFC library, which makes your executable file bigger, but
relieves you from installing the libraries on the user's computer. If you
choose to link to the MFC libraries as a shared DLL, you get a smaller
executable, but you must distribute the DLL with your application.

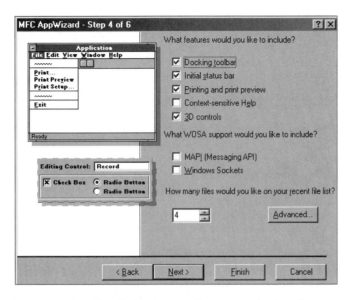

Figure 2-4: AppWizard's fourth page offers you a selection of advanced features to add to your application.

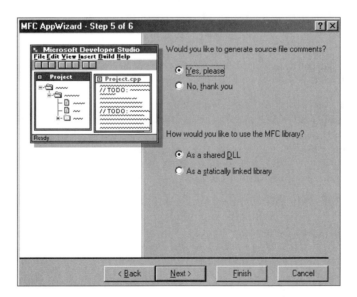

Figure 2-5: AppWizard's fifth page offers you options for generating source code and choices for how you would like to link MFC libraries to your application.

Finally, the sixth and last AppWizard page, shown in Figure 2-6, gives you a chance to change the suggested file names for your application's source code. In some cases, you can even change the MFC base classes from which your application's classes are derived.

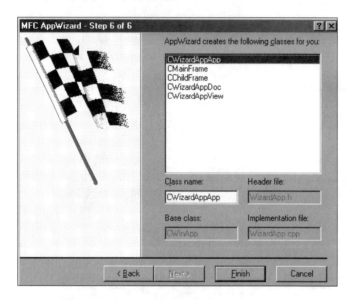

Figure 2-6: AppWizard's sixth page enables you to change the name of your application's source code files.

After you've completed each wizard step, click the Finish button to generate your source code. Actually, you can click the Finish button on any of the six AppWizard pages when you're sure that you don't want to change any remaining options. If you want the default application, just click Finish on the first page. If you choose all the default settings, AppWizard then generates the application shown in Figure 2-7. Pretty impressive, eh?

Right before generating your source code, AppWizard displays the New Project Information dialog box, which summarizes the choices you made with AppWizard. When you click the OK button on this dialog box, AppWizard generates your files. If you click Cancel, you go back to AppWizard, where you can make changes to the application's settings.

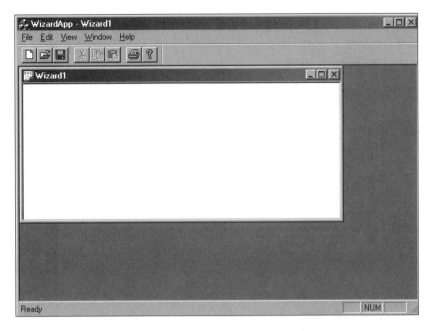

Figure 2-7: An application programmed with AppWizard's default settings

ClassWizard

One advantage of generating your application with AppWizard is that you get access to ClassWizard, which helps you, among other things, override class member functions and handle message-response functions. For an example of message-response functions, suppose you want the application to respond to the WM_LBUTTONDOWN Windows message. You bring up ClassWizard, find the WM_LBUTTONDOWN message in the message list, and create a message-response function with a couple of mouse clicks. Figure 2-8 shows ClassWizard after the programmer has created the OnLButtonDown() message-response function, which is the MFC function that handles the WM_LBUTTONDOWN Windows message.

ClassWizard has many other talents, too. It can create member variables that hold data in a dialog box, build ActiveX interfaces for objects, provide support for ActiveX controls, and even create new, custom classes. (Please refer to Chapter 23, "ActiveX Controls," for more information on ActiveX controls.) As you work your way through this book, you will call upon ClassWizard often.

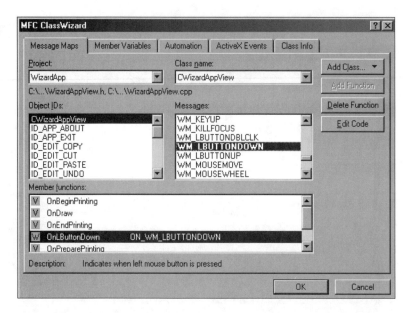

Figure 2-8: ClassWizard's appearance after a message-response function has been created

Resource editors

In the previous chapter, you learned about resource files, which define many of the graphical objects you use to build an application's user interface. Visual C++ features a complete set of resource editors (which you saw in Chapter 1) that make creating resource files a snap, whether you want to put together a dialog box loaded with controls, a menu bar, or just a bitmap for a button. Visual C++'s resource editors automatically generate the script that the resource compiler needs to create the resource binary file.

Figure 2-9, for example, shows the dialog box editor. You can build the dialog box by selecting controls from the toolbox and dropping them on the dialog box's window. Aligning controls is easy thanks to the adjustable grid and the many alignment commands in the editor's Layout menu. Setting dialog box and control styles is just a matter of selecting the object and pressing Enter to display the object's property sheet.

Visual C++'s other resource editors are equally as powerful. Figure 2-10 shows the bitmap editor, which is virtually a complete paint program, whereas the menu editor, shown in Figure 2-11, enables you to quickly and easily create your application's menu bar.

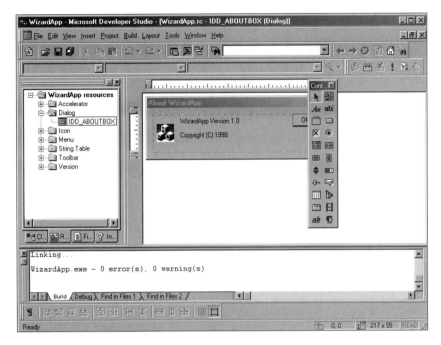

Figure 2-9: Here's the dialog box resource editor opened.

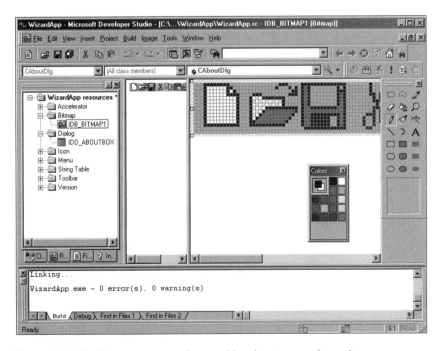

Figure 2-10: The bitmap resource editor provides almost a complete paint program.

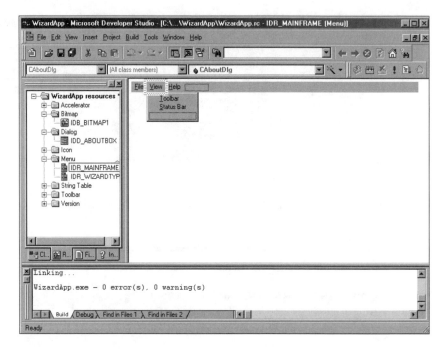

Figure 2-11: The menu resource editor provides an easy way to create menu bars.

Visual C++ supplies an editor for every other type of resource as well, including string tables, icons, and cursors. For a general review of resources and resource editors, please refer back to Chapter 1, "A Windows 98 Overview."

The compiler

The heart of Visual C++ is, of course, its compiler, which transforms your cleverly written source code into an executable file. The compiler doesn't have much of a visual presence, only displaying short messages as it works (see Figure 2-12), but you can set many options from Visual C++'s menu bar. Usually, the compiler runs just fine with its default options, leaving you to worry about more important things, like why your computer locked up when you tried to run the latest version of your application.

To run the compiler on your source code, simply select the Build button from the toolbar (see Figure 2-12). The compiler then sets to work, compiling any files that need to be updated. Files that haven't changed, or that don't rely on changed files, are left out of the compiler in order to speed things up. If you want to compile all files, regardless of whether they need it, Visual C++ offers the Rebuild All command. And, yes, you can even compile a single file if you like.

Compiler messages   Rebuild All command   Compile button   Build button

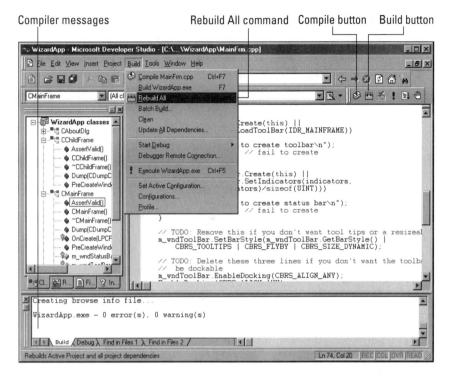

Figure 2-12: The compiler, which you control from the toolbar or menu bar, displays messages as it works.

As the compiler runs, it generates status messages (see Figure 2-12) that appear in the Build pane at the bottom of Visual C++'s window. These messages announce which files the compiler is processing and what errors the compiler finds. If you place the text cursor on an error message and press F1, Visual C++ displays a complete description of the error. Double-clicking the error message causes the appropriate source code file to appear in the editor, with the offending line visible and ready to edit.

For those of you who like to do things the hard way, Visual C++'s compiler also comes in a command-line version. However, throughout this book, you will stick with the visual tools. If you want to go back to the old-fashioned command line, you're on your own!

The debugger

If you manage to write a full-length program with no bugs, please let me know immediately because you clearly have some kind of magical touch. For the rest of us, Visual C++'s debugger provides an almost painless way to track down those digital critters that make your programs go awry. To use the debugger, you must first create a debug version of your program. This requires only setting the project configuration to Win32 Debug and rebuilding the program. Because the Win32 Debug configuration is the default for a new application, you don't even have to bother with the configuration unless you change it (though you should change the configuration to Win32 Release for the final compilation). The Set Active Configuration command on Visual C++'s Build menu takes care of this task.

Once you've compiled a debug version of your project, selecting the debugger's Go command gets things rolling. You can set breakpoints in your program, as well as trace program execution line by line. As variables come into scope, placing the mouse cursor over the variable's name in the source code window causes Visual C++ to display the variable's current value. For more detailed debugging, you can set up a watch window, listing all the variables whose values you want to keep an eye on.

The Visual C++ debugger also provides a register window, a memory window, and a call-stack window. The debugger can even disassemble your source code and display it in assembly-language form. You high-tech gurus will appreciate that.

The Project Workspace Window

Managing all the files, classes, and resources that make up a complete project would be a nightmare without the help of Visual C++'s Project Workspace window. This tabbed window normally docks on the left side of Visual C++'s main window, as shown in Figure 2-13. You can undock the window by dragging it with your mouse wherever you like.

In an AppWizard-generated project, the Project Workspace window holds four tabbed pages that provide access to all the elements that comprise a project. The tabs provide access to the ClassView, ResourceView, FileView, and InfoView pages. (In projects that you've created without AppWizard, the Project Workspace window may contain only the ClassView and FileView tabs.)

Docked Project Workspace window

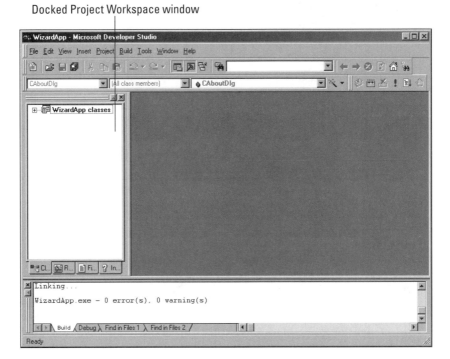

Figure 2-13: Visual C++'s Project Workspace window is docked on the left side of the main window.

The ClassView page

The ClassView page displays your program's classes, arranging them into a hierarchy (see Figure 2-14). At the top of the hierarchy is the application's name. The next step down in the hierarchy shows the classes that make up the project. Under the class names, the page lists all the member functions and variables defined in the class.

You can jump instantly to any function in the source code by double-clicking its name in the ClassView page. If you want to view a class's header file, which contains the class's declaration, double-click the class's name.

As you can see in Figure 2-14, Visual C++ marks each member function and variable with icons that indicate the member's type and accessibility. A purple box means that the item is a member function, whereas a blue box indicates a member variable. ClassView marks protected items with a key, and private items with a padlock. Public items have no additional icon.

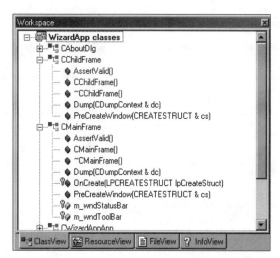

Figure 2-14: The ClassView page of the Project Workspace window, displaying the program's classes in a hierarchy

The ResourceView page

The ResourceView page, shown in Figure 2-15, lists all the resources you've defined in the project. As with the ClassView page, ResourceView organizes its entries into a hierarchy. At the top of the hierarchy is the application's name. The next step down in the hierarchy indicates the different types of resources. Finally, at the deepest level, are the IDs that represent actual resources. For example, in Figure 2-15, `IDD_ABOUTBOX` is the resource ID for the application's About dialog box. To display the dialog box in its resource editor, double-click the ID. You can display other resources in their respective editors the same way.

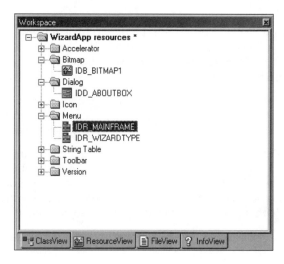

Figure 2-15: The ResourceView page of the Project Workspace window, listing the project's resources

The FileView page

If you want to see all the files in your project, click the FileView tab (see Figure 2-16). The FileView page organizes your files into the familiar hierarchical display, with the project name at the top of the hierarchy (you can have more than one project in a workspace), followed by the application's name, the file types, and finally the files themselves. The FileView page marks each file with an icon that indicates the file type. You can load any file by double-clicking it in the list.

Although the ClassView page is handier for loading source files (because you can jump right to a particular function), the FileView page enables you to access additional types of files—such as plain text files—that are part of the project, but not listed in the ClassView page.

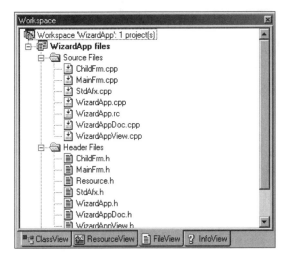

Figure 2-16: The FileView page of the Project Workspace window organizes your files into a hierarchy.

The InfoView page

InfoView is the last page in the Project Workspace window, and it's here that you can browse Visual C++'s significant online help (see Figure 2-17). What exactly appears in InfoView depends on the type of documentation you have installed on your computer. For example, although Visual C++ comes with its own online document set, you can also install the Microsoft Developer Network (MSDN) documentation CD. When you install MSDN, Visual C++ is smart enough to automatically include it in the InfoView page, putting a large amount of documentation right at your fingertips.

Figure 2-17: The InfoView page of the Project Workspace window enables you to browse Visual C++'s online help.

Utility Tools

Although the tools discussed in the previous sections are all you need to create an application, Visual C++ comes with other tools that can make your programming tasks easier. These tools include a class browser, a Windows message tracer, and an ActiveX control test container, to name a few. The following sections introduce you to these additional tools.

Source Browser

If you compile your project to include browser information, you can call upon Visual C++'s Source Browser tool to discover different types of information about a class. You start Source Browser from the Tools menu, after which Source Browser asks for a symbol to browse. Once you've entered a symbol name (usually a class, function, or variable name), you can browse the symbol in various ways, as listed below:

Definitions and References	Shows every place the symbol is defined and referenced in the project (see Figure 2-18).

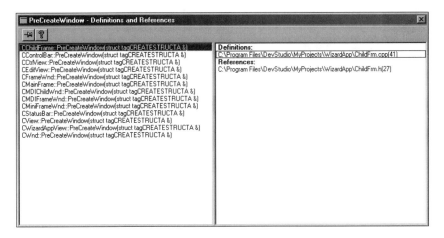

Figure 2-18: The Source Browser, showing definitions and references

File Outline   Displays all the symbols defined in a source code file (see Figure 2-19). Various filters enable you to specify exactly what type of information to view.

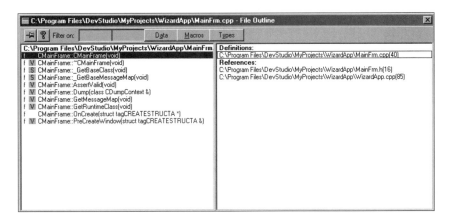

Figure 2-19: The Source Browser, showing a file outline

Base Classes and Members   Lists all base classes, including member functions, data members, definitions, and references. Using this view (see Figure 2-20), you can explore any class's inheritance tree in order to see where inherited member functions and variables are defined. Various filters enable you to display exactly the information you need.

Figure 2-20: The Source Browser, showing base classes and members

***Derived Classes
and Members***

Shows all classes derived from the selected class. Using this view (see Figure 2-21), you can explore a class's inheritance tree in reverse order, starting with the selected base class. Filters enable you to specify what types of functions and data members to display.

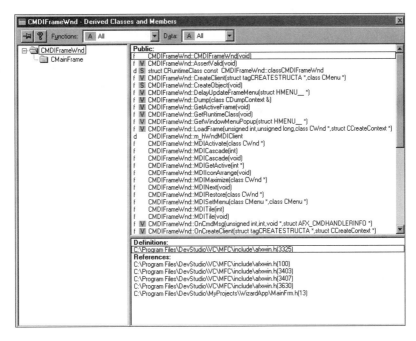

Figure 2-21: The Source Browser, showing derived classes and members

Call Graph   Lists all functions called by the selected function and shows where the listed functions are defined, as shown in Figure 2-22.

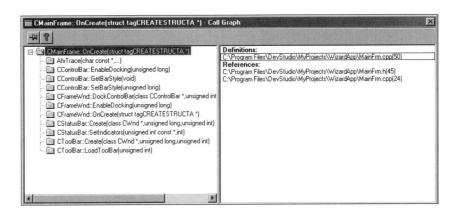

Figure 2-22: The Source Browser, showing a call graph

Callers Graph   Displays all functions that call the selected
                             function, as shown in Figure 2-23.

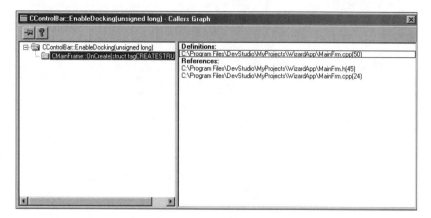

Figure 2-23: The Source Browser, showing a callers graph

Spy++

Programming with Windows presents unique debugging problems. For
example, while you can use Visual C++'s debugger to trace program flow,
how do you trace what's going on between Windows and the application? As
your application runs, there's a constant flow of information, with Windows
sending a stream of events to your application and your application handling
those events or passing them back to Windows.

Obviously, just as you can have program bugs internal to your program, so
too can you have bugs in the way the application responds to Windows
messages. When these occasions arise, you can load Spy++ and watch what's
going on under Windows' hood. Spy++ enables you to select a window and
then watch the flow of messages as they occur (see Figure 2-24). Not only is
this a great way to find program bugs, but it's also a great lesson on the
inner workings of Windows.

ActiveX Control Test Container

When you develop ActiveX controls (see Chapter 23, "ActiveX Controls"),
you'll need some way to test them. While you could go ahead and create a
test application, Visual C++ has already done that for you in the guise of the
ActiveX Control Test Container. Using this helpful utility, you can embed an
ActiveX control in the window and then set the control's properties, call the
control's methods, and even monitor events. Figure 2-25 shows the ActiveX
Control Test Container with a calendar control embedded in its window.

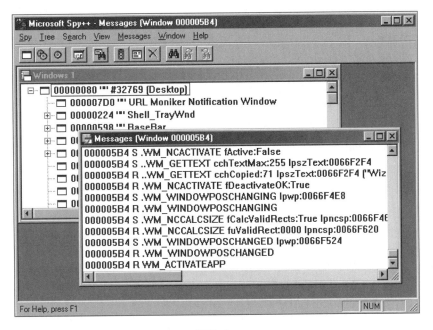

Figure 2-24: Spy++ displays a flow of Windows messages.

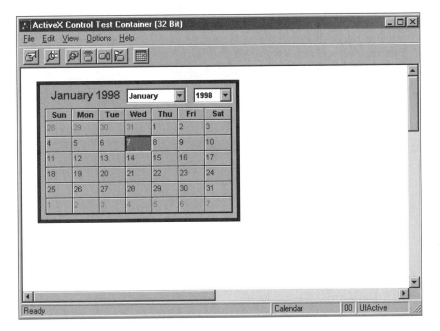

Figure 2-25: Here's the ActiveX Control Test Container window, displaying a calendar control.

Summary

As you become more familiar with the Visual C++ programming environment, take time to experiment with its more advanced features. The more familiar you are with the tools, the smoother your application development projects will go. Visual C++ provides everything you need to develop professional applications, but it's up to you to take advantage of all that's offered. In the next chapter, you get some hands-on experience creating a Visual C++ application and using its most important tools.

Also discussed in this chapter:

▶ AppWizard helps you create a skeleton application with only a few mouse clicks.

▶ Visual C++'s ClassWizard is a valuable tool for adding new member variables and functions to a class. ClassWizard can even create whole new classes.

▶ Resource editors provide a set of visual tools for creating dialog boxes, menus, and other graphical interface objects.

▶ Visual C++'s compiler can be as simple or as complex as you want it to be. Dozens of compiler options enable you to fine-tune your project's compilation to suit your needs.

▶ Visual C++'s debugger is a powerhouse for finding program bugs. You can step through program code, view variable values, examine the stack, disassemble your code, and much more.

▶ Visual C++'s Project Workspace window provides many ways to view the files that comprise your project. You can find almost any function in your source code with a click or two of your mouse.

▶ Additional tools such as Source Browser, Spy++, and ActiveX Control Test Container offer extra programming assistance.

Chapter 3

Programming with Visual C++

In This Chapter

▶ Introducing CircleApp

▶ Creating a skeleton application with AppWizard

▶ Completing your application's resources

▶ Exploring your application's classes

▶ Modifying your application's status bar

The projects in this book were developed using Visual C++ 5.0. For this reason, it's important that you have at least a nodding acquaintance with this popular development environment. In the previous chapter, you took a quick look at the main tools that make up Visual C++. In this chapter, you will put those tools to work as you create a complete Windows application.

Introducing the CircleApp Application

On CD-ROM

The application we will create in this chapter is called CircleApp. But before you start programming, you might like to see what the application looks like and what it does. (You can find the complete application on this book's CD-ROM, in the CircleApp folder.) To run the application, copy the CircleApp folder to your hard drive and double-click the CircleApp.exe executable file. When you do, the application's main window appears, as shown in Figure 3-1.

To get started, click the application's client area. The application is programmed to display a red circle wherever you click your mouse. To make your screen look more interesting, you can change the circle color and diameter by selecting the appropriate button from the toolbar or by selecting the command from the Circle menu. For example, to change the circle color, click the Change Color button on the toolbar, or select the Circle menu's Change Color command. The Color dialog box then appears, as shown in Figure 3-2. Select the color you want and click the OK button. CircleApp now draws new circles with the selected color.

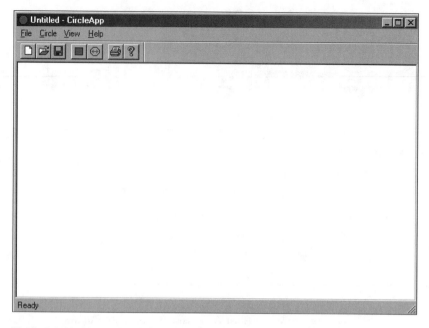

Figure 3-1: Here's the CircleApp application after it has been copied from your CD-ROM and opened from your hard drive.

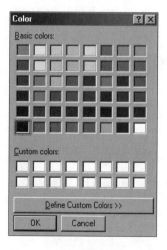

Figure 3-2: The Color dialog box enables you to change the color of your circles in CircleApp.

Changing the circle diameter is similar to changing the color. First, click the Change Diameter button on the toolbar, or select the Color menu's Change Diameter command. The Change Size dialog box appears, as shown in Figure 3-3. Type in a new diameter and click the OK button. CircleApp now draws new circles using the selected diameter. Figure 3-4 shows CircleApp after the user has drawn a number of circles.

Figure 3-3: The Change Size dialog box enables you to change the diameter of your circles in CircleApp.

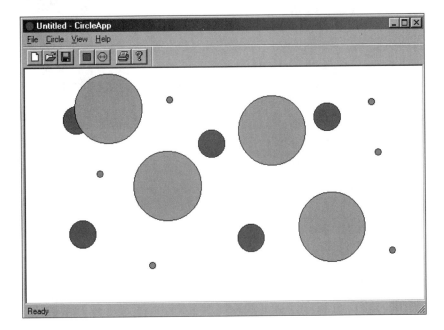

Figure 3-4: This is the CircleApp application, displaying a set of circles in various colors and sizes.

You can save your work by selecting the File menu's Save command. Conversely, you can load a saved file using the File menu's Open command. If you want to start a new circle masterpiece, select the File menu's New command. You can also select any of these commands from the toolbar by clicking the New, Open, or Save button.

Besides all its other skills, CircleApp fully supports printing and print preview. To see what the document will look like when printed, select the File menu's Print Preview command. A window displaying your circle document appears, as shown in Figure 3-5. Notice how small the printed image looks. This is because CircleApp does not employ printer-output scaling, so the number of pixels in the screen translate to exactly the same number of dots on the printer, which is usually too small for most applications. You learn more about printing in Chapter 11, "Printing."

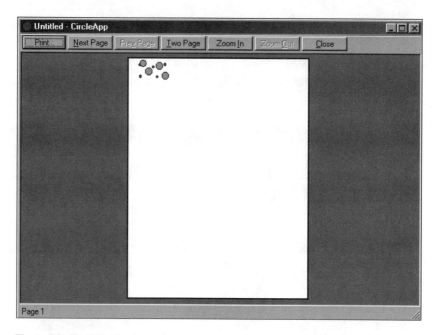

Figure 3-5: The Print Preview window displays your circle document without printer-output scaling.

You can print the document right from the Print Preview window, or you can print the document by selecting the File menu's Print command. You can even print the document by clicking the Print button on the toolbar. On the File menu, you can also find the Print Setup command, which enables you to change the attributes for your printer, such as page size and orientation. Finally, the File menu displays a list of the last four files opened, so that you can access a recently closed file with a single mouse click. Figure 3-6 shows the File menu. Notice that the mouse is over a recently opened document named test.cir.

The View menu contains two commands—Toolbar and Status Bar—that enable you to turn these two attributes on and off. The Help menu contains a single command for displaying the application's About CircleApp dialog box, as shown in Figure 3-7. The About CircleApp dialog box is an important part of every application, giving the user information about the application's author and copyright holder. You can also display the About CircleApp dialog box by clicking the About button on the toolbar. Because I created this application, my name appears here.

Although CircleApp is a trivial program (albeit kind of fun), it demonstrates most of the features users expect to find in a professional Windows application. Moreover, whenever you build an application yourself, you gain experience with most of Visual C++'s main tools, which prepares you for the programming lessons to come later in this book. Of course, if you're already a Visual C++ user, you may wish to skip the rest of this chapter. Still, it never hurts to review.

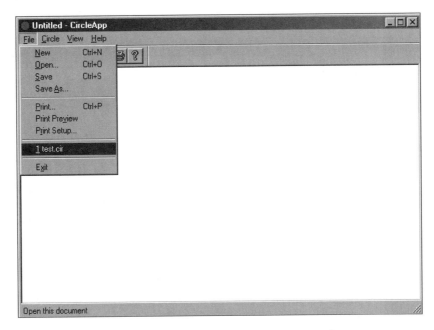

Figure 3-6: Here's the File menu list, displaying a recently opened file

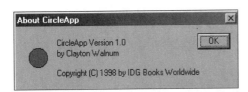

Figure 3-7: The About CircleApp dialog box displays the application's author name and copyright.

If you do choose to continue, you will build the CircleApp application from scratch. As you do, you will learn to use important tools such as AppWizard and ClassWizard. You will also learn to modify your application's resource file using Visual C++'s resource editors. By the time you complete CircleApp (it doesn't take too long), you will understand how to create message-response functions, add member functions and variables, create a dialog box class, edit a toolbar and status bar, draw an application's icon, and much more.

Creating CircleApp's skeleton application

The first step in building CircleApp is to have AppWizard create the skeleton application. AppWizard can generate about 90 percent of the source code needed to get the application up and running. All you need to do is add a few functions and modify existing functions and resources to complete the application. Perform the following steps to build the skeleton application.

1. Open Visual C++.

2. Select the New command from Visual C++'s File menu. The New property sheet appears, as shown in Figure 3-8.

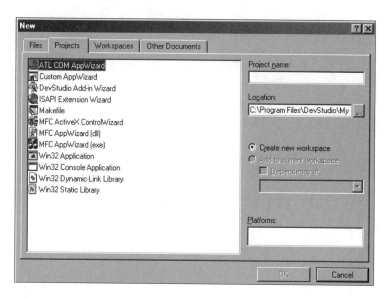

Figure 3-8: The New property sheet enables you to name your project and choose where you want to store your source code.

3. Select MFC AppWizard (exe) on the Projects page. The New property sheet enables you to name your project and choose where you want to store your source code. To do so, type **CircleApp** in the Project Name box and select a location folder for your source code in the Location box. Click OK. The MFC AppWizard Step 1 dialog box appears (see Figure 3-9).

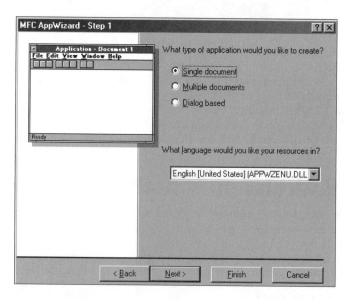

Figure 3-9: The AppWizard Step 1 dialog box enables you to choose the type of application you would like to create.

4. The MFC AppWizard Step 1 dialog box enables you to choose the type of application you want to create. For this application, select the Single Document option, as shown in Figure 3-9, which tells AppWizard that you want to create an SDI application. Click the Next button, and the Step 2 dialog box appears.

5. The MFC AppWizard Step 2 dialog box enables you to choose the type of database support you want to include in your application. For the CircleApp application, leave the Step 2 option set to None, as shown in Figure 3-10, as you don't want to include database support in this application. Click the Next button to display the Step 3 dialog box.

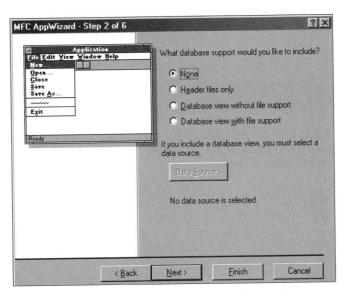

Figure 3-10: The AppWizard Step 2 dialog box enables you to choose the type of database support you would like to include in your application.

6. In the MFC AppWizard Step 3 dialog box, you may choose the type of compound document support you want in your application, along with either Automation or ActiveX Controls support. For the CircleApp application, leave compound document support set to None, as CircleApp does not need OLE or ActiveX support, and turn off the ActiveX Controls option, as shown in Figure 3-11. Click the Next button to display the Step 4 dialog box.

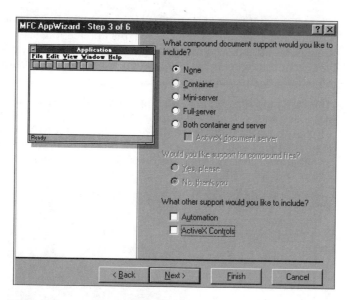

Figure 3-11: The MFC AppWizard Step 3 dialog box enables you to choose the type of compound document support you would like to include in your application.

7. In the AppWizard Step 4 dialog box, you may select extra features for your application, including a toolbar, a status bar, and 3D controls. For the CircleApp application, leave the Step 4 options set as they are, as shown in Figure 3-12. CircleApp features a toolbar, a status bar, printing and print preview, and 3D controls. You now need to set a few of AppWizard's advanced options. Click the Advanced button. The Advanced Options property sheet appears.

8. The Advanced Options property sheet enables you to program your applications' document template strings and window styles. For the CircleApp application, type **cir** in the File extension box of the Document Template Strings page, as shown in Figure 3-13. This is the default file extension for new CircleApp files. Click Close to exit the property sheet, and then click Next to display the Step 5 dialog box.

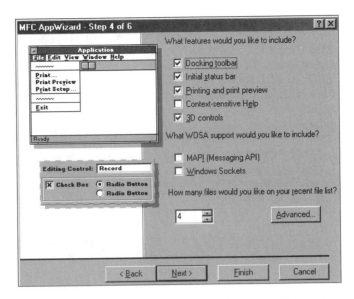

Figure 3-12: The MFC AppWizard Step 4 dialog box enables you to add extra features to your application.

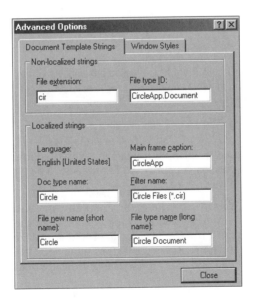

Figure 3-13: The Advanced Options property sheet enables you to program the document template strings and window styles for your application.

9. The MFC AppWizard Step 5 dialog box enables your application to generate source file comments and gives you two choices for using the MFC library. For the CircleApp application, select the "As a statically linked library" option, as shown in Figure 3-14, which enables the application to run on any system without having to install MFC DLL. Click Next, and the Step 6 dialog box appears.

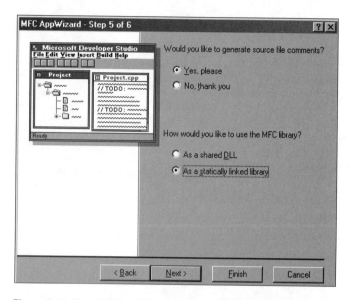

Figure 3-14: The MFC AppWizard Step 5 dialog box enables you to generate source file comments and choose how to use the MFC library.

10. The MFC AppWizard Step 6 dialog box creates classes for your application. For the CircleApp application, click the Finish button to accept the listed classes, as shown in Figure 3-15. The New Project Information dialog box appears.

11. The New Project Information dialog box lists the specifications for your new skeleton project. After taking a look at this, click the OK button and review the contents of the skeleton project that AppWizard is about to create, as shown in Figure 3-16. AppWizard generates the skeleton application's source code, and opens the project's workspace.

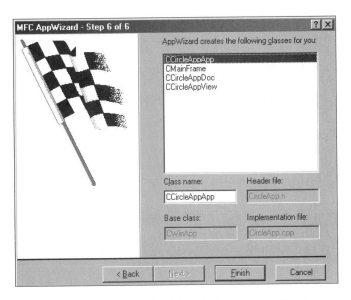

Figure 3-15: The MFC AppWizard Step 6 dialog box creates classes for you.

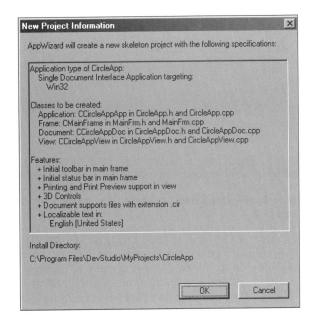

Figure 3-16: The New Project Information dialog box lists your project's specifications.

On CD-ROM

You've now completed the first part of the CircleApp application. (You can find the executable file and complete source code for this first version of CircleApp in the CircleApp1 folder of this book's CD-ROM.) To run your new version of CircleApp, select the Build menu's Execute CircleApp.exe command. Visual C++ asks whether you want to build the application's executable file. Click Yes, and Visual C++ compiles, links, and runs the application.

Figure 3-17 shows the application as it currently looks. Notice that the application's menu bar, toolbar, and status bar look nothing like the ones in the final application that you saw previously in this chapter. To change the appearance of these controls, you must edit the application's resources. But first, you need to examine the files generated by AppWizard.

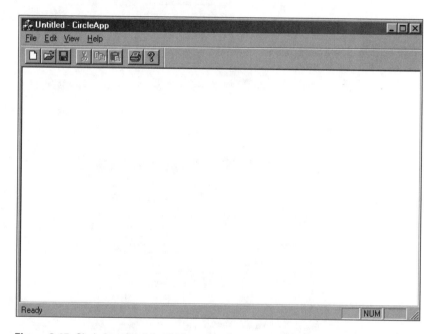

Figure 3-17: CircleApp displayed before you change the appearance of the menu bar, toolbar, and status bar

The files that AppWizard generates for your application are created from the options you selected in AppWizard. Several classes, however, appear in every AppWizard-generated application. When you generate the CircleApp application, you get the source code files shown in Table 3-1.

Table 3-1 CircleApp's source code files

Code	Description
CircleApp.h	This is the header file for the CCircleAppApp class, which represents the CircleApp's application object. The header file declares the class, but the class's .cpp file implements the class. The application's About dialog box class, CAboutDlg, is also declared in this header file.
CircleApp.cpp	This is the implementation file for the CCircleAppApp class. The class initializes the application and handles the File menu's New, Open, and Print Setup commands. The application's About dialog box class, CAboutDlg, is also defined in this file.
MainFrm.h	This is the header file for the CMainFrame class, which represents CircleApp's main window.
MainFrm.cpp	This is the implementation file for the CMainFrame class. This class initializes the frame window and creates the application's toolbar and status bar.
CircleAppDoc.h	This is the header file for the CCircleAppDoc class, which represents a CircleApp document.
CircleAppDoc.cpp	This is the implementation file for the CCircleAppDoc class. The document class holds the contents of the currently active document, as well as saves and loads the document.
CircleAppView.h	This is the header file for the CCircleAppView class, which represents the application's view window. The view window is an invisible (except for the document data it displays) window that MFC positions in the frame window's client area.
CircleAppView.cpp	This is the implementation file for the CCircleAppView class. The view class displays the currently active document, as well as enables the user to edit the document. By default, this class also handles the File menu's Print and Print Preview commands.
CircleApp.rc	This is CircleApp's resource file. Before you modify the resources (which you do later in this chapter), CircleApp.rc contains the program's default menu, toolbar, About dialog box, icon, accelerator table, and string table.

Completing CircleApp's resources

Your next task is to edit existing resources in the application's resource file, as well as add a couple of new resource objects. As you complete these tasks, you learn to create menus, dialog boxes, toolbar buttons, icons, and more. Perform the following steps to complete CircleApp's resources.

Editing the menu resource

1. Select the ResourceView tab at the bottom of the Project Workspace window, as shown in Figure 3-18. Click the plus sign next to the resource view's single entry to expand the resource list.

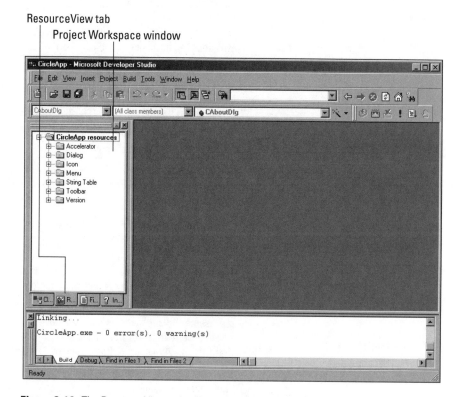

ResourceView tab

Project Workspace window

Figure 3-18: The ResourceView tab selected in the Project Workspace window

2. Double-click the Menu entry, and then double-click IDR_MAINFRAME to open the application's menu bar resource, as shown in Figure 3-19.

3. Click the resource's Edit menu and press the Delete key on your keyboard. Visual C++ asks whether you want to delete the menu. Click OK; the Edit menu vanishes from the resource.

Menu resource ID   Menu resource

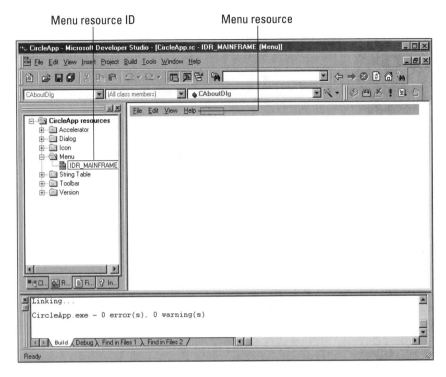

Figure 3-19: The application's menu resource, displayed with the menu resource ID

4. Click the empty menu item in the menu bar and press Enter. The Menu
   Item Properties property sheet appears. In the Caption box, type
   &Circle, as shown in Figure 3-20. Press Enter to finalize your changes.
   The selection rectangle on the menu bar moves to the first menu item
   below the new Circle menu.

   The ampersand in front of the "C" tells Windows which character to use
   as the menu's selection key. The "C" will be underlined in the menu bar,
   and then you can select the menu by pressing Alt+C.

Empty menu item   Menu Item Properties property sheet

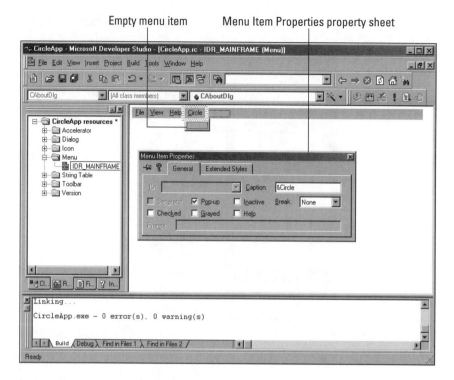

Figure 3-20: The Menu Item Properties property sheet displayed with the empty menu item

5. Press Enter. Visual C++ displays the Menu Item Properties property sheet for the blank menu item. In the ID box, type **ID_CIRCLE_ CHANGECOLOR**; in the Caption box, type **Change &Color**; and in the Prompt box, type **Change the circle color\nChange Color** (see Figure 3-21). Press Enter, and Visual C++ adds the Change Color command to the Circle menu.

   Visual C++ assigns the ID_CIRCLE_CHANGECOLOR resource ID to the command. The part of the prompt string before the \n defines the hint text that appears in the status bar when the mouse pointer is over the command, and the part after \n defines the tool tip that appears when the mouse is over the command's toolbar button.

6. Press Enter, and the Menu Item Properties property sheet appears for the next blank menu item. In the ID box, type **ID_CIRCLE_CHANGEDIAMETER**; in the Caption box, type **Change &Diameter**; and in the Prompt box, type **Change the circle diameter\nChange Diameter**. Press Enter, and Visual C++ adds the Change Diameter command to the Circle menu.

7. Click the Circle menu and, holding down the left mouse button, drag the menu into position just after the File menu, as shown in Figure 3-22.

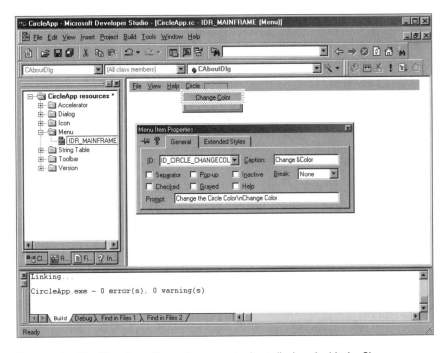

Figure 3-21: The Menu Item Properties property sheet displayed with the Change Color commands

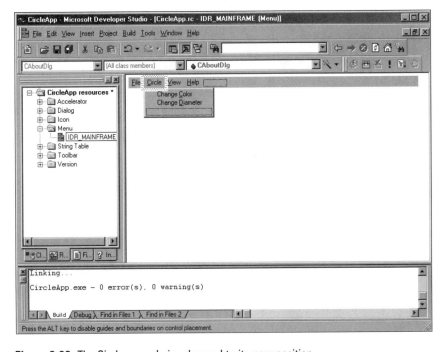

Figure 3-22: The Circle menu being dragged to its new position

You've now completed CircleApp's menu resource. The next step is to remove unneeded hot keys from the application's accelerator table.

Editing the accelerator table

Now that you've edited the application's menu commands, some menu hot keys are no longer valid. For example, because you deleted the Edit menu, you must delete the hot keys that were associated with the Edit menu's commands. You don't want the user accidentally selecting commands that don't exist.

To delete the unneeded hot keys, first double-click Accelerator in the Project Workspace window; then double-click the IDR_MAINFRAME resource ID. The application's accelerator table, which defines the application's hot keys, appears in the resource window. You can delete an accelerator by selecting the entry in the table with your mouse and pressing your keyboard's Delete key. Delete all entries in the table except ID_FILE_NEW, ID_FILE_OPEN, ID_FILE_PRINT, and ID_FILE_SAVE. The application's accelerators should then match the ones in Figure 3-23.

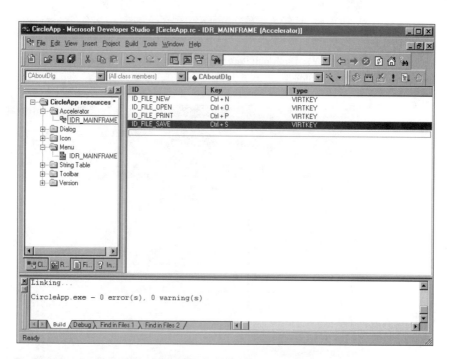

Figure 3-23: CircleApp's accelerator table after selected entries were deleted

Now that you've taken care of the accelerators, it's time to move on to the dialog boxes.

Editing the About CircleApp dialog box

The CircleApp application has three dialog boxes. The first is the About CircleApp dialog box, which AppWizard has already created for you; the second is the Color dialog box used to change circle color; and the third is the Change Diameter dialog box used to alter circle diameter. You will now modify the default About CircleApp dialog box and create the Color and Change Diameter dialog boxes.

To complete the About CircleApp dialog box:

1. Double-click Dialog in the Project Workspace window and then double-click the IDD_ABOUTBOX resource ID to display the About CircleApp dialog box in the resource window.

2. In the dialog box, click the "Copyright (C) 1988" text line, and press Enter. The Text Properties property sheet appears. Change the text in the Caption box to read **Copyright (C) 1998 by IDG Books Worldwide**, as shown in Figure 3-24. Press Enter to finalize the changes.

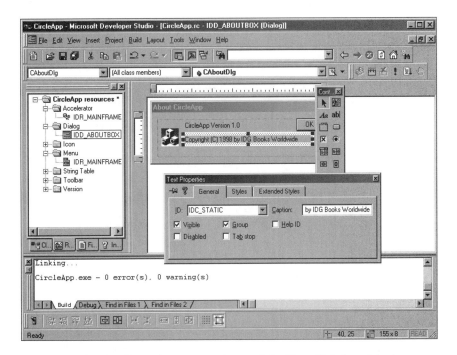

Figure 3-24: The Text Properties property sheet and the About CircleApp dialog box, displaying a revised caption

3. With the text line still selected, use your keyboard's down arrow key to move the line close to the bottom of the dialog box, as shown in Figure 3-25.

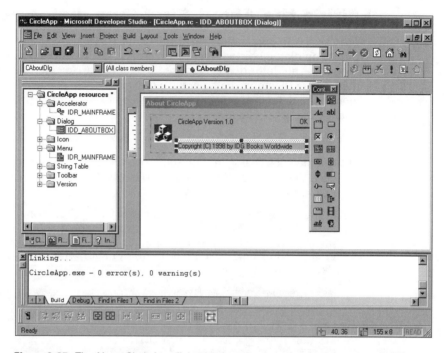

Figure 3-25: The About CircleApp dialog box's revised caption set in a new position

4. In the toolbox, click the Static Text tool (the one marked with *Aa*), and then click just below the "CircleApp Version 1.0" line in the dialog box. The new static text appears in the dialog box.

5. With the text still selected, press Enter to display the Text Properties property sheet. In the Caption box, type **by Clayton Walnum**, and press Enter. Use your keyboard's arrow keys to reposition the text just below the "CircleApp Version 1.0" text, as shown in Figure 3-26.

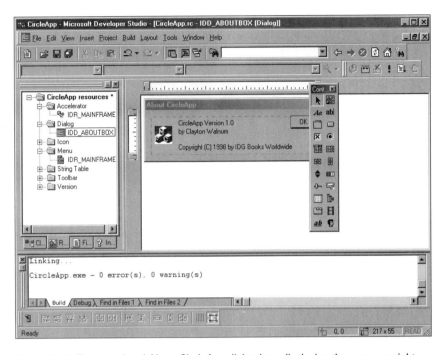

Figure 3-26: The completed About CircleApp dialog box, displaying the new copyright line and author's name

Creating the Change Diameter dialog box

As you've seen, modifying an existing dialog box is pretty easy. Now you'll discover that creating a whole new dialog box isn't much more difficult. Perform the following steps to create the application's Change Diameter dialog box:

1. Select the Resource command from Visual C++'s Insert menu. The Insert Resource dialog box appears, as shown in Figure 3-27. Select Dialog in the Resource type pane, and then click the New button. A new dialog box appears in the resource window.

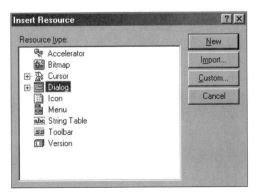

Figure 3-27: The Insert Resource dialog box set to create a new application dialog box

2. Place a new static text line on the dialog box and set its caption to **New Diameter:**. Position the text as shown in Figure 3-28.

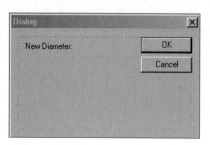

Figure 3-28: The Change Diameter dialog box displayed with the caption "New Diameter:"

3. Click the Edit Box control (the one marked **ab|**) in the toolbox, and add the control to the dialog box just below the "New Diameter:" text.

4. Press Enter and the edit control's Edit Properties property sheet appears. Change the ID to **IDC_DIAMETER**, as shown in Figure 3-29, and press Enter.

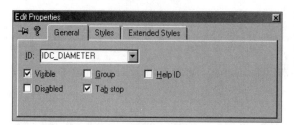

Figure 3-29: The Edit Properties property sheet displayed with a new ID name

5. Use your mouse to resize the control (by dragging the control's sizing handles), and then use your keyboard's arrow keys to reposition the control, as shown in Figure 3-30.

Figure 3-30: The dialog box displayed with a completed edit control

6. Resize the dialog box using its sizing handles. The dialog box should now look like the one in Figure 3-31.

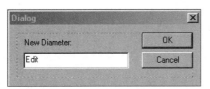

Figure 3-31: The resized dialog box surrounded by its sizing handles

7. With the dialog box selected, press Enter. The Dialog Properties property sheet appears. Change the ID to **IDD_DIAMETERDLG**, and change the caption to **Change Diameter**, as shown in Figure 3-32.

Figure 3-32: The Dialog Properties property sheet, displaying the dialog box's new ID and caption

8. Double-click the dialog box. The Adding a Class dialog box appears, as shown in Figure 3-33. Make sure the Create a new class option is selected, and click the OK button. The New Class dialog box appears.

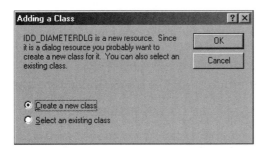

Figure 3-33: The Adding a Class dialog box displayed with the "Create a new class" option selected

9. In the Name box, type **CDiameterDlg** (see Figure 3-34), and then click the OK button. ClassWizard appears and creates the C++ class that represents the Change Diameter dialog box in your project.

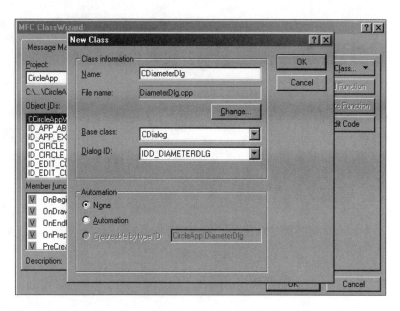

Figure 3-34: The New Class dialog box displayed with class information

10. In the MFC ClassWizard property sheet, select the Member Variables tab. Double-click `IDC_DIAMETER`, and the Add Member Variable dialog box appears.

11. In the Member Variable Name box, type **m_diameter;** and in the Variable Type box, select **int** (see Figure 3-35). Press Enter to finalize your choices. ClassWizard adds the member variable to the class.

    The `m_diameter` member variable stores the integer value that the user enters into the edit box. As you will see later in this chapter, `m_diameter` can also initialize the edit box to a default value.

12. At the bottom of the MFC ClassWizard property sheet, type **0** in the Minimum Value box and **100** in the Maximum Value box, as shown in Figure 3-36. Press Enter to finalize the new dialog box class.

    The dialog box class that ClassWizard generates will now automatically validate the user's input to ensure that the value entered into the edit box is within the range of 0 to 100.

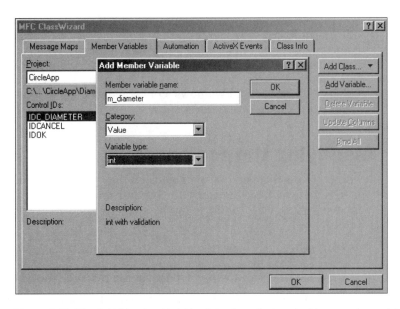

Figure 3-35: The Add Member Variable dialog box displayed with a member variable name, category, and variable type

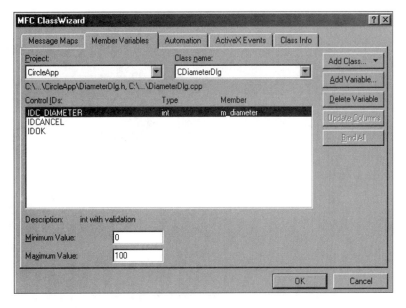

Figure 3-36: The MFC ClassWizard displayed with the variable's minimum and maximum values

You've now completed two of your application's three dialog boxes. You don't need to create resources for the Color dialog box because it's a common dialog box that's built into Windows. Instead, you create and manipulate the Color dialog box programmatically, as you will see later in this chapter in Step 17 of "Completing CircleApp's view class." For more detailed information on Windows' common dialog boxes, please refer to Chapter 6, "Windows and Dialogs."

Modifying the toolbar

Recently, you changed the commands on the application's menu bar. This means that you have to change the buttons on the toolbar to match the menu changes. Perform the following steps to complete the application's toolbar:

1. In the ResourceView page of the Project Workspace window, double-click the Toolbar entry, and then double-click the IDR_MAINFRAME resource ID. The application's toolbar appears in the resource window.

2. Click the Cut button (the one that looks like scissors). Holding down the left mouse button, drag the button off the toolbar. Do the same with the Copy and Paste buttons. Your toolbar resource should then look like the one in Figure 3-37.

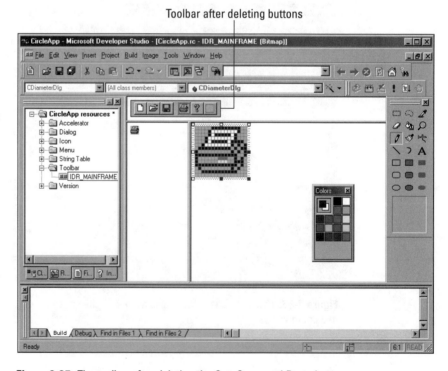

Toolbar after deleting buttons

Figure 3-37: The toolbar after deleting the Cut, Copy, and Paste buttons

3. Click the blank button in the toolbar. Using the drawing tools, draw a red rectangle on the button, as shown in Figure 3-38. This new button represents the Circle menu's Change Color command.

4. Double-click the new Change Color button in the toolbar. The Toolbar Button Properties property sheet appears. Change the ID to **ID_CIRCLE_CHANGECOLOR**, as shown in Figure 3-39. (Instead of typing the ID, you can also select it from the drop-down list.) The button's Prompt box automatically displays the correct string for the command. Press Enter to finalize your choices.

   Setting the button's ID to `ID_CIRCLE_CHANGECOLOR` associates the button with the Circle menu's Change Color command, which has the same ID. The prompt string that appears is the one you defined for the menu command.

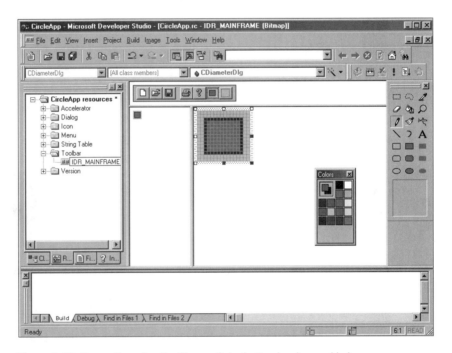

Figure 3-38: The toolbar after the Change Color button has been added

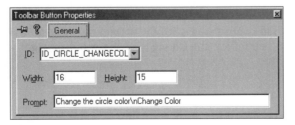

Figure 3-39: The Toolbar Button Properties property sheet set with a new ID for the Change Color button

5. Click the new blank button on the toolbar, and draw the icon shown in Figure 3-40 on the button. This new button represents the Circle menu's Change Diameter command.

6. Double-click the new Change Diameter button in the toolbar. The Toolbar Button Properties property sheet appears. Change the ID to **ID_CIRCLE_CHANGEDIAMETER**. (Instead of typing the ID, you can also select it from the drop-down list.) The button's Prompt box automatically displays the correct string for the command. Press Enter to finalize your choices.

Setting the button's ID to ID_CIRCLE_CHANGEDIAMETER associates the button with the Circle menu's Change Diameter command, which has the same ID. The prompt string that appears is the one you defined for the menu command.

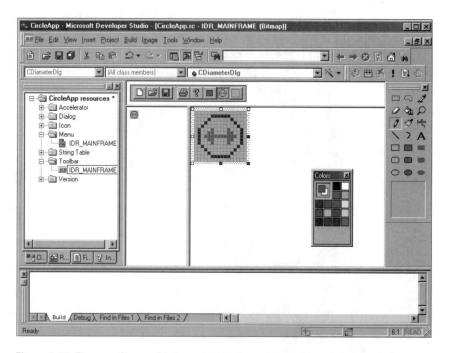

Figure 3-40: The new Change Diameter button drawn on the button's enlarged view

7. Click the Change Color button. Holding down the left mouse button, drag the button into position right before the Print button. Using the same technique, reposition the Change Diameter button right after the Change Color button.

8. Drag the Print button a little to the right in order to separate it from the Change Color and Change Diameter buttons, as shown in Figure 3-41.

Figure 3-41: The reordered toolbar with the print button set to the right of the Change Color and Change Diameter buttons

You've now completed the application's toolbar. The final step in creating the application's resources is to modify the default icon supplied by Visual C++. As you may have guessed, you do that in the next section. But first exit the resource editors and save your work by selecting the File menu's Save All command.

Modifying the application's icons

Each application has an icon that's displayed in the About CircleApp dialog box, in the application's title bar, and in any file lists that show the application's executable file (for example, in Windows Explorer's file list). The default application icon for an MFC application works just fine, but you should edit it so that it represents your specific application, rather than every other MFC application ever written (of which, no doubt, there are hundreds of thousands, maybe even millions).

Each application also has an icon that represents its document type. Much like the application icon, the document icon is used to represent the application's document files in a file list, such as that displayed by Windows Explorer. Users then know that they can double-click the document in order to automatically load it into the associated application. (AppWizard-generated applications also support *drag-and-drop*, meaning the user can drag a file from a file list and drop it onto the application's window, thus causing the application to display the document.) The following steps show you how to edit CircleApp's icons:

1. In the ResourceView page of the Project Workspace window, double-click the Icon entry. Then, double-click the IDR_MAINFRAME resource ID. The application's icon appears in the resource window.

2. Use the drawing tools to draw the image (a red circle) shown in Figure 3-42 on the enlarged view of the icon.

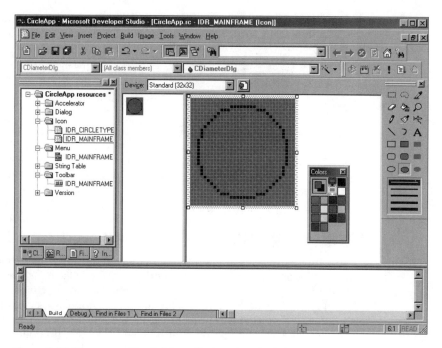

Figure 3-42: The new application icon displayed on the enlarged view

3. In the Device box above the icon editor, select the Small (16x16) icon. Draw the same image on the small icon that you drew on the large icon.

   Windows 98 applications actually have two versions of an icon. The large icon is used in Windows Explorer's Large Icon view, and the small icon is used in other Windows Explorer views, as well as in the application's title bar. In an AppWizard-generated application, the large icon is also displayed in the application's About CircleApp dialog box.

4. Back in the ResourceView page of the Project Workspace window, double-click the IDR_CIRCLETYPE icon resource ID. The application's document icon appears in the resource window.

5. Using the drawing tools, modify the icon so that it looks like the one in Figure 3-43.

6. In the Device box above the icon editor, select the Small (16x16) icon. Draw the same image on the small icon that you drew on the large icon.

You've now not only completed editing the application's icons, but you have also completed all of the application's resources. At this point, you can recompile the application and run it in order to see your changes. To do this, select the Execute Program button on the toolbar, or select the Build menu's Execute CircleApp.exe command, as shown in Figure 3-44. When Visual C++ asks whether you want to rebuild files, select Yes. Visual C++ then compiles any modified files and runs the application.

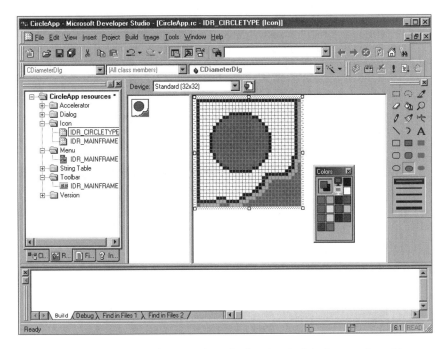

Figure 3-43: This is the new document icon displayed as both its large and small images.

Execute commands   Execute program button

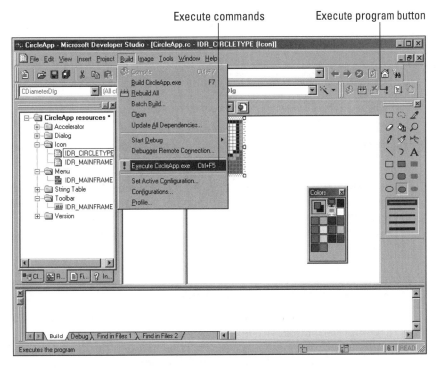

Figure 3-44: Select the execute command from either the toolbar or the Build menu.

Figure 3-45 shows the application at this point in its development. Notice that the Change Color and Change Diameter toolbar buttons are disabled. If you look at the Circle menu, you'll see that the Change Color and Change Diameter commands are also disabled. This is because you have not yet defined message-response functions for these commands. You do that later in this chapter, as you add source code to the CircleApp skeleton application.

On CD-ROM

(You can find the complete source code and executable file for this second version of CircleApp in the CircleApp2 folder of this book's CD-ROM.)

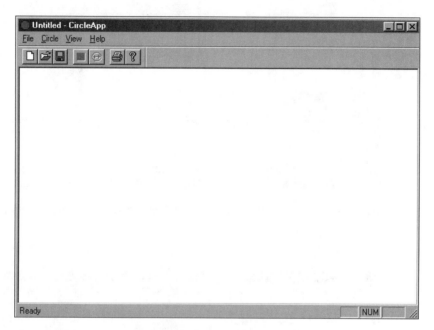

Figure 3-45: CircleApp displayed with its new resources

Modifying CircleApp's Classes

Now that you've got the application's resources completed, you can finish up the various classes that AppWizard created for your application. These classes represent the application object, as well as its frame window, document, and view objects. You'll learn more about these different classes in the sections that follow as you add the source code that makes CircleApp do what it's supposed to do.

The application class

You do not need to do anything substantive to the application class. It's complete and ready-to-go, just as AppWizard created it. However, because the application class's header file is included in the document and view classes, it's a good place to define data structures that you need in those other classes. In the case of CircleApp, you need to define the data structure that represents a circle object in the application's document. To do this, perform the following steps:

1. Click the ClassView tab in the Project Workspace window. The ClassView page appears.

2. Double-click "CircleApp classes." The application's classes appear in the window, as shown in Figure 3-46.

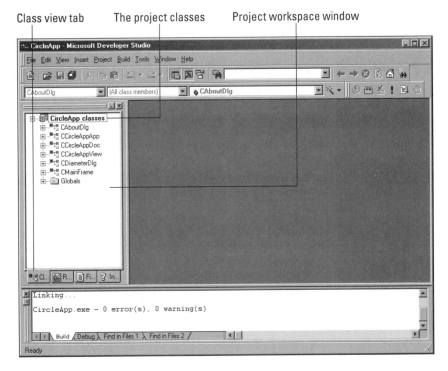

Figure 3-46: CircleApp's classes displayed in the Project Workspace window

3. Double-click the CCircleAppApp class. The application class's header file, CircleApp.h, appears in the edit window.

4. Add the following lines near the top of the file, right after the line `#include "resource.h"`:

```
struct CircleStruct
{
    CPoint point;
    COLORREF color;
    int diameter;
};
```

5. Close and save the CircleApp.h file.

The `CircleStruct` structure represents each circle in the application's document, holding the circle's position, color, and diameter. A `CPoint` object holds the circle's position. `CPoint` is an MFC class with member variables, x and y, that store the coordinates of a point. The circle's color is stored in a COLORREF object, which is a data type defined by Windows. COLORREF is actually a 32-bit value that holds a color's red, green, and blue (RGB) components. You will learn how to deal with CPoint and COLORREF objects as you write the rest of CircleApp's source code.

As you now know, CCircleAppApp represents CircleApp's application object. You will learn exactly what this means, for an MFC program, in the next chapter when you compare MFC programs with standard C Windows programs. For now, just keep in mind that the application object is what gets your application up and running. And, in the case of CircleApp, the CircleApp.h file contains the structure definition that represents circle objects. The structure definition is included in CircleApp.h because both the document and view classes #include this header file, which makes it easy to provide access to the structure in both classes.

The document class

An MFC application's document class is where the application's data is managed. This class contains member variables for holding the data and defining functions for saving and loading the document. In this section, you learn to modify CircleApp's default document class so that it can manage circle documents. Perform the following steps to complete this important task:

1. Right-click the CCircleAppDoc class in the ClassView page of the Project Workspace window. A context menu appears, as shown in Figure 3-47.

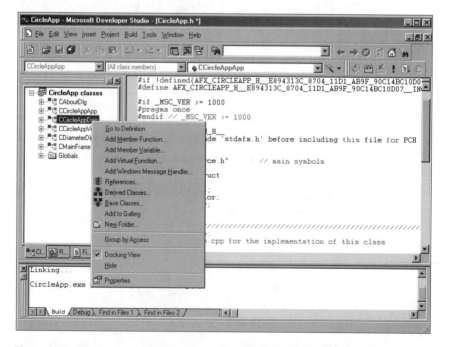

Figure 3-47: The document class's context menu is displayed after CCircleAppDoc is right-clicked.

2. Select the Add Member Variable command from the context menu. The Add Member Variable dialog box appears.

3. Type **CPtrArray** into the Variable Type box; type **m_circleArray** into the Variable Declaration box; and select Public in the Access box, as shown in Figure 3-48.

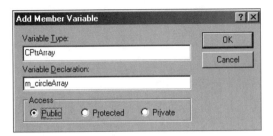

Figure 3-48: The Add Member Variable dialog box, displaying the application's Variable Type, Variable Declaration and Access attribute

This member variable declares the data structure that holds the document's data. CPtrArray is an MFC class that represents an array of pointers. In CircleApp's case, the CPtrArray object holds an array of pointers to CircleStruct objects, which, as you learned in the previous section, hold a circle's position, color, and diameter.

4. Click the plus sign next to CCircleAppDoc in the ClassView page of the Project Workspace window. The class's member functions and variables appear.

5. Double-click the Serialize() function. The document class's implementation file, called CircleAppDoc.cpp, appears in the edit window.

6. Add the lines shown in Listing 3-1 to the Serialize() function, right after the TODO: add storing code here comment:

Listing 3-1: Saving a CircleApp document

```
int size = m_circleArray.GetSize();
ar << size;

for (int x=0; x<size; ++x)
{
    CircleStruct* circle =
        (CircleStruct*)m_circleArray.GetAt(x);
    ar << circle->point;
    ar << circle->color;
    ar << circle->diameter;
}
```

These lines store the application's document when the user selects the Save or Save As commands. You learn more about this code later in the chapter.

7. Add the lines shown in Listing 3-2 to the `Serialize()` function, right after the `TODO: add loading code here` comment:

Listing 3-2: Loading a CircleApp document

```
int size;
ar > size;
m_circleArray.SetSize(size);

for (int x=0; x<size; ++x)
{
    CPoint point;
    COLORREF color;
    int diameter;
    ar >> point;
    ar >> color;
    ar >> diameter;
    CircleStruct* circle = new CircleStruct;
    circle->point = point;
    circle->color = color;
    circle->diameter = diameter;
    m_circleArray.SetAt(x, circle);
}

UpdateAllViews(NULL);
```

These lines load the application's document when the user selects the Open command. You learn more about this code later in the chapter.

8. Press Ctrl+W on your keyboard. Visual C++ displays the MFC ClassWizard.

9. Select the Message Maps tab and then select `CCircleAppDoc` in the Class Name box; double-click DeleteContents in the Messages box. ClassWizard overrides the `DeleteContents()` function in the application's document class, as shown in Figure 3-49.

10. Click the Edit Code button. MFC ClassWizard displays the document class's implementation file with the `DeleteContents()` function visible and ready to edit.

11. Add the following lines to the `DeleteContents()` function, right after the `TODO: Add your specialized code here and/or call the base class` comment:

```
int size = m_circleArray.GetSize();
for (int x=0; x<size; ++x)
{
    CircleStruct* circle =
        (CircleStruct*)m_circleArray.GetAt(x);
    delete circle;
}
m_circleArray.RemoveAll();
```

These lines ensure that a new document starts out empty, as you see when you examine `DeleteContents()` more closely later in the chapter.

12. Close and save the CircleAppDoc.cpp file.

The overridden function appears here
Double-click DeleteContents
Select CCircleAppDoc

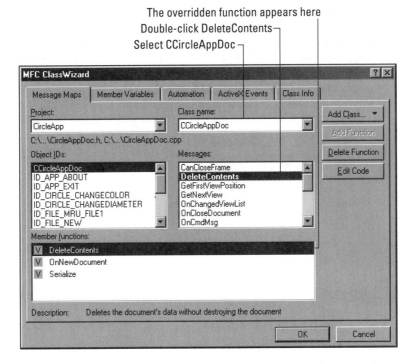

Figure 3-49: Overriding the `DeleteContents()` function in the document class

The `CCircleAppDoc` class represents a CircleApp document. The document object holds data for the currently active document, as well as saves and loads documents. Although you can compile the document class that AppWizard generates, and the default document class is capable of saving, loading, and managing the application's document, the document itself is empty. It's up to you to define exactly what a document contains and how that data should be managed.

The class's document data

The first step is to decide how you want to represent a document's data in the class. CircleApp represents its data as an array of pointers to `CircleStruct` objects. The class declares the data storage in its header file like this:

```
public:
    CPtrArray m_circleArray;
```

How the document object holds the document's contents is entirely up to you. In this case, `CPtrArray` is an MFC class that manages an array of pointers. For more information on this class, refer to your Visual C++ online documentation.

The `DeleteContents()` member function

When the document class is called upon to create a new document, which happens when the application is run and when the user selects the New command, MFC calls the `DeleteContents()` function to give the document a chance to release any data objects that might already exist. In order to gain control over this feature of MFC, you must override `DeleteContents()` in your document class, something you did in the previous section. In `CCircleAppDoc`, the `DeleteContents()` function looks like Listing 3-3.

Listing 3-3: The `DeleteContents()` function

```
void CCircleAppDoc::DeleteContents()
{
    // TODO: Add your specialized code here and/or call the base
class

    int size = m_circleArray.GetSize();
    for (int x=0; x<size; ++x)
    {
        CircleStruct* circle =
            (CircleStruct*)m_circleArray.GetAt(x);
        delete circle;
    }
    m_circleArray.RemoveAll();

    CDocument::DeleteContents();
}
```

`DeleteContents()` first gets the size of the array of `CircleStruct` objects. The `for` loop iterates through the array, getting a pointer to the currently indexed item in the array and deleting the object from memory. However, although the `for` loop deletes the `CircleStruct` objects from memory, the pointers still exist in the array. The call to the array class's `RemoveAll()` function removes all pointers from the array, leaving the array empty. Finally, `DeleteContents()` calls the base class's version of `DeleteContents()`.

It's important to remember that MFC calls `DeleteContents()` not only when the user explicitly starts a new document, but also when the application first runs. At this time, the document contains no data. For this reason, you must safeguard `DeleteContents()` from trying to delete data items that don't yet exist. In the case of `CCircleAppDoc`, if the call to `m_circleArray.GetSize()` returns 0, the `for` loop never executes.

The `OnNewDocument()` member function

After `DeleteContents()`, MFC calls the document class's `OnNewDocument()` function, which gives the class a chance to perform whatever document initialization is required. Listing 3-4 shows `CCircleAppDoc`'s `OnNewDocument()` function. As you can see, `CCircleAppDoc::OnNewDocument()` performs no initialization, because none is required for a CircleApp document. However, you could, in `OnNewDocument()`, do something like initialize an array of default circles for the document, if you needed to.

Listing 3-4: The OnNewDocument() **function**

```
BOOL CCircleAppDoc::OnNewDocument()
{
    if (!CDocument::OnNewDocument())
        return FALSE;

    // TODO: add reinitialization code here
    // (SDI documents will reuse this document)

    return TRUE;
}
```

Saving and loading document data

As I mentioned before, an application's document class is responsible for loading and saving documents. All this happens in the class's Serialize() function. CCircleAppDoc's Serialize() looks like Listing 3-5. The function receives a CArchive object as its single parameter. (You learn the details about CArchive in Chapter 17, "File Handling.") Serialize() can determine whether the document should be saved or loaded by calling the CArchive object's IsStoring() function. If IsStoring() returns TRUE, the document must be saved. CCircleAppDoc::Serialize() accomplishes this task by getting the size of the circle array, saving the size to the archive, and then extracting and saving to the archive each member—point, color, and diameter—of each circle object in the array.

If ar.IsStoring() returns FALSE, CCircleAppDoc::Serialize() first retrieves the array size from the archive and calls m_circleArray.SetSize() to set the size of the array. The function then retrieves each element of the array from the archive, creating new CircleStruct objects as it goes. The call to m_circleArray.SetAt() adds to the array a pointer to a new CircleStruct object.

Finally, after retrieving all document data from the archive, CCircleAppDoc::Serialize() calls the document class's UpdateAllViews(), which causes MFC to call the view class's OnUpdate(), which, in turn, initiates a call to the view class's OnDraw(), where the new data is displayed on the screen. A long and winding road (to quote some famous mop-tops)!

Listing 3-5: The Serialize() **function**

```
void CCircleAppDoc::Serialize(CArchive& ar)
{
    if (ar.IsStoring())
    {
        // TODO: add storing code here
        int size = m_circleArray.GetSize();
        ar << size;

        for (int x=0; x<size; ++x)
        {
            CircleStruct* circle =
                (CircleStruct*)m_circleArray.GetAt(x);
```

```
            ar << circle->point;
            ar << circle->color;
            ar << circle->diameter;
        }
    }
    else
    {
        // TODO: add loading code here
        int size;
        ar >> size;
        m_circleArray.SetSize(size);

        for (int x=0; x<size; ++x)
        {
            CPoint point;
            COLORREF color;
            int diameter;
            ar >> point;
            ar >> color;
            ar >> diameter;
            CircleStruct* circle = new CircleStruct;
            circle->point = point;
            circle->color = color;
            circle->diameter = diameter;
            m_circleArray.SetAt(x, circle);
        }

        UpdateAllViews(NULL);
    }
}
```

The view class

The application's document class may be where data gets stored, but it's the view class that presents that data to the user, as well as enables the user to edit the data. In CircleApp, the only way the user can edit a document is by adding new circles, but the principle is the same. In this section, you complete CircleApp's view class. Along the way, you learn to create message-response functions that handle Windows messages. Perform the steps below to modify CircleApp's view class:

1. In the ClassView page of the Project Workspace window, right-click the CCircleAppView class. The class's context menu appears.

2. Select the Add Member Variable command from the context menu. The Add Member Variable dialog box appears.

3. Type **COLORREF** into the Variable Type box; type **m_currentColor** into the Variable Declaration box; and select the Protected option, as shown in Figure 3-50. Press Enter to finalize your choices.

   The m_currentColor member variable stores the currently selected circle color.

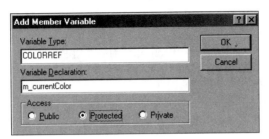

Figure 3-50: The Add Member Variable dialog box enables you to add a member variable to a class.

4. Create another member variable as described in Steps 1 through 3. The variable's type is **int**, the declaration is **m_currentDiameter**, and the access is Protected.

    The m_currentDiameter member variable stores the currently selected circle diameter.

5. In the ClassView page, click the plus sign next to the CCircleAppView class. The class's members appear. Double-click the class's constructor. The class's implementation file, called CircleAppView.cpp, appears in the edit window with the constructor visible and ready to edit.

6. Add the following lines to the constructor, right after the TODO: add construction code here comment:

    ```
    m_currentColor = RGB(255,0,0);
    m_currentDiameter = 40;
    ```

    These lines initialize the default circle color and diameter.

7. In the ClassView, double-click the OnDraw() function. Visual C++ displays OnDraw() in the edit window.

8. Add the lines shown in Listing 3-6 to OnDraw(), right after the TODO: add draw code for native data here comment:

Listing 3-6: The OnDraw() function

```
int size = pDoc->m_circleArray.GetSize();

for (int x=0; x<size; ++x)
{
    CircleStruct* circle =
        (CircleStruct*)pDoc->m_circleArray.GetAt(x);
    int radius = circle->diameter/2;
    int x1 = circle->point.x-radius;
    int y1 = circle->point.y-radius;
    int x2 = circle->point.x+radius;
    int y2 = circle->point.y+radius;
    COLORREF color = circle->color;
    CBrush brush(color);
    CBrush* oldBrush = pDC->SelectObject(&brush);
    pDC->Ellipse(x1, y1, x2, y2);
    pDC->SelectObject(oldBrush);
}
```

9. Press Ctrl+W on your keyboard. Visual C++ displays MFC's ClassWizard.

10. In the Class Name box, select `CCircleAppView`; in the Messages box, select `WM_LBUTTONDOWN`; and then click the Add Function button. ClassWizard adds the `OnLButtonDown()` message-response function to the class, as shown in Figure 3-51.

    Now, when the user clicks inside CircleApp's window, MFC calls the `OnLButtonDown()` function, responding to the `WM_LBUTTONDOWN` Windows message.

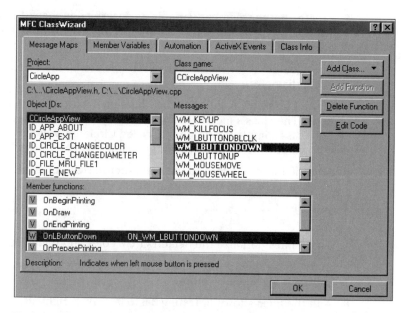

Figure 3-51: MFC's ClassWizard dialog box displays the parameters for creating the `OnLButtonDown()` message-response function.

11. Click the Edit Code button. The `OnLButtonDown()` function appears in the edit window. Add the lines shown in Listing 3-7, right after the `TODO: Add your message handler code here and/or call default` comment:

Listing 3-7: The `OnLButtonDown()` function

```
// Draw the new circle.
CClientDC clientDC(this);
CBrush brush(m_currentColor);
CBrush* oldBrush = clientDC.SelectObject(&brush);
int radius = m_currentDiameter / 2;
clientDC.Ellipse(point.x-radius, point.y-radius,
    point.x+radius, point.y+radius);
clientDC.SelectObject(oldBrush);
// Store the new circle in the document.
CCircleAppDoc* pDoc = GetDocument();
```

```
CircleStruct* circle = new CircleStruct;
circle->point = point;
circle->color = m_currentColor;
circle->diameter = m_currentDiameter;
pDoc->m_circleArray.Add(circle);
```

12. Press Ctrl+W on your keyboard. MFC's ClassWizard appears.

13. In the Class Name box, select CCircleAppView; in the Messages box, select OnUpdate; and then click the Add Function button. ClassWizard overrides the OnUpdate() message-response function in the class.

14. Click the Edit Code button and add the following line to OnUpdate(), right after the TODO: Add your specialized code here and/or call the base class comment:

    Invalidate();

15. Press Ctrl+W on your keyboard to display MFC's ClassWizard.

16. In the Class Name box, select CCircleAppView; in the Object IDs box, select ID_CIRCLE_CHANGECOLOR; in the Messages box, select COMMAND; and then click the Add Function button. When the Add Member Function dialog box appears, click OK to add the OnCircleChangecolor() message-response function to the class, as shown in Figure 3-52.

    Now, when the user clicks the Change Color toolbar button, or selects the Circle menu's Change Color command, MFC calls the OnCircleChangecolor() function, responding to the ID_CIRCLE_CHANGECOLOR message.

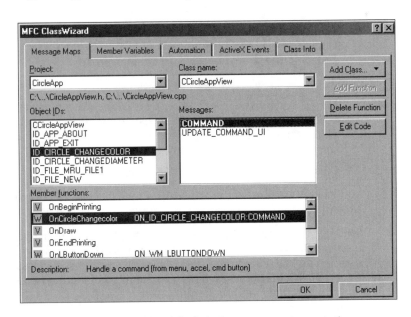

Figure 3-52: MFC's ClassWizard displays the parameters to create the OnCircleChangecolor() message-response function.

17. Click the Edit Code button and add the following lines to
    OnCircleChangecolor(), **right after the** TODO: Add your command handler
    code here **comment:**

    ```
    CColorDialog dialog;
    int result = dialog.DoModal();
    if (result == IDOK)
        m_currentColor = dialog.GetColor();
    ```

18. Press Ctrl+W on your keyboard to display MFC's ClassWizard.

19. In the Class Name box, select CCircleAppView; in the Object IDs box,
    select ID_CIRCLE_CHANGEDIAMETER; in the Messages box, select
    COMMAND; and then click the Add Function button. When the Add
    Member Function dialog box appears, click OK to add the
    OnCircleChangediameter() message-response function to the class.

    Now, when the user clicks the Change Diameter toolbar button, or
    selects the Circle menu's Change Diameter command, MFC calls the
    OnCircleChangediameter() function, responding to the
    ID_CIRCLE_CHANGEDIAMETER message.

20. Click the Edit Code button and add the following lines to
    OnCircleChangediameter(), **right after the** TODO: Add your command
    handler code here **comment:**

    ```
    CDiameterDlg dialog;
    dialog.m_diameter = m_currentDiameter;
    int result = dialog.DoModal();
    if (result == IDOK)
        m_currentDiameter = dialog.m_diameter;
    ```

21. Add the following line near the top of the view class's file (the
    CircleAppView.cpp file currently displayed in the editor), right after the
    line #include "CircleAppView.h" that's already there:

    ```
    #include "DiameterDlg.h"
    ```

    This line gives the view class access to the class that defines the Change
    Diameter dialog box. Without access to the dialog box class, the view
    class would be unable to display the dialog box when the user selected
    the Change Diameter command.

22. Close and save the CircleAppView.cpp file.

You've now completed the application's view class. You only need to tweak
the application's status bar and the application will be complete. Whew!

Whereas the document class's job is to hold, save, and load an application's
native data, the view class's task is to display the data, as well as enable the
user to edit the data. In the case of CircleApp, the view class also responds
to certain Windows messages and to menu command messages. In the rest
of this section, you'll discover how CCircleAppView, CircleApp's view class,
accomplishes these tasks.

The class's member variables

Because the view class must keep track of circle attributes as the user adds circles to the display, the class declares two member variables:

```
protected:
    int m_currentDiameter;
    COLORREF m_currentColor;
```

You already know that m_currentDiameter and m_currentColor hold the current circle diameter and color, respectively. These class members are initialized in CCircleAppView's constructor, as the following code segment shows:

```
CCircleAppView::CCircleAppView()
{
    // TODO: add construction code here

    m_currentColor = RGB(255,0,0);
    m_currentDiameter = 40;
}
```

The RGB macro makes it easy to create COLORREF values. The macro's three arguments are the red, green, and blue color components of the color. These values can be between 0 and 255; the higher the value, the brighter that color component. Arguments of 0,0,0 give you black, whereas 255,255,255 gives you white. In CCircleAppView's constructor, the call to RGB creates a COLORREF that represents the color red.

Responding to mouse clicks

When the user clicks the mouse in CircleApp's client area, MFC calls the view class's OnLButtonDown() message-response function, which you added to the class using ClassWizard. Listing 3-8 shows the complete OnLButtonDown() function. OnLButtonDown()'s first task is to draw the new circle in the application's display. It does this by getting a device context for the window's client area, creating a brush of the selected color, and drawing an ellipse of the selected diameter.

You learn about Windows graphics functions in Chapter 5, "Graphics Device Interface Basics," and in Chapter 13, "Advanced GDI." For now, you should know that a *device context* represents the attributes of a Windows application's drawing surface. You must obtain a device context before you can do any drawing. You customize the device context by creating pens, brushes, and other graphical objects that you need to create your display.

After drawing the new circle, CCircleAppView::OnLButtonDown() adds the new circle to the document's circle array. To do this, the function first gets a pointer to the document class. It then creates a new CircleStruct object, initializes the structure's members with the circle's attributes, and then adds the circle to the array. OnLButtonDown() can access the circle array through pDoc, a pointer to the document class.

Listing 3-8: The `OnLButtonDown()` **function**

```
void CCircleAppView::OnLButtonDown(UINT nFlags, CPoint point)
{
    // TODO: Add your message handler code here and/or call default

    // Draw the new circle.
    CClientDC clientDC(this);
    CBrush brush(m_currentColor);
    CBrush* oldBrush = clientDC.SelectObject(&brush);
    int radius = m_currentDiameter / 2;
    clientDC.Ellipse(point.x-radius, point.y-radius,
        point.x+radius, point.y+radius);
    clientDC.SelectObject(oldBrush);

    // Store the new circle in the document.
    CCircleAppDoc* pDoc = GetDocument();
    CircleStruct* circle = new CircleStruct;
    circle->point = point;
    circle->color = m_currentColor;
    circle->diameter = m_currentDiameter;
    pDoc->m_circleArray.Add(circle);

    CView::OnLButtonDown(nFlags, point);
}
```

Responding to menu commands

When the user clicks the toolbar's Change Color button, or selects the Circle menu's Change Color command, MFC calls the `OnCircleChangecolor()` message-response function, which you associated with the `ID_CIRCLE_CHANGECOLOR` command ID. Listing 3-9 shows the complete `OnCircleChangecolor()` function.

The `OnCircleChangecolor()` function first creates an instance of a `CColorDialog` object. The `CColorDialog` class represents Windows 98's common Color dialog box, which enables users to select colors from a palette. After creating an instance of the object, calling its `DoModal()` member function displays the dialog box to the user. When the user exits the dialog box, `OnCircleChangecolor()` checks whether the user exited via the OK button. If so, the function sets the current color to the color set by the user. (You learn more about common dialog boxes in Chapter 6, "Windows and Dialogs.")

Listing 3-9: The `OnCircleChangecolor()` **function**

```
void CCircleAppView::OnCircleChangecolor()
{
    // TODO: Add your command handler code here

    CColorDialog dialog;
    int result = dialog.DoModal();
    if (result == IDOK)
        m_currentColor = dialog.GetColor();
}
```

When the user clicks the toolbar's Change Diameter button, or selects the Circle menu's Change Diameter command, MFC calls the OnCircleChangediameter() message-response function, which you associated with the ID_CIRCLE_CHANGEDIAMETER command ID. Listing 3-10 shows the complete OnCircleChangediameter() function.

The OnCircleChangediameter() function first creates an instance of a CDiameterDlg object. The CDiameterDlg class, which you created previously with ClassWizard, represents the Change Diameter dialog box. (You may remember creating this dialog box resource earlier in this chapter.) After creating an instance of the object, calling its DoModal() member function displays the dialog box to the user. When the user exits the dialog box, OnCircleChangediameter() checks whether the user exited via the OK button. If so, the function sets the current diameter to the diameter set by the user. (You learn more about programming custom dialog boxes in Chapter 6, "Windows and Dialogs.")

Listing 3-10: The OnCircleChangediameter() **function**

```
void CCircleAppView::OnCircleChangediameter()
{
    // TODO: Add your command handler code here

    CDiameterDlg dialog;
    dialog.m_diameter = m_currentDiameter;
    int result = dialog.DoModal();
    if (result == IDOK)
        m_currentDiameter = dialog.m_diameter;
}
```

Drawing the application's display

In an MFC program, it's the view class's OnDraw() function that's charged with keeping the display up-to-date. Whenever the window's contents must be redrawn, MFC calls OnDraw(), the complete version of which you can see in Listing 3-11. After getting a pointer to the document object, OnDraw() gets the size of the circle array. It then uses the array size as a control value in a for loop. The for loop iterates through the array, extracting each circle's attributes and using the attributes to draw the circle in the display.

Listing 3-11: The OnDraw() **function**

```
void CCircleAppView::OnDraw(CDC* pDC)
{
    CCircleAppDoc* pDoc = GetDocument();
    ASSERT_VALID(pDoc);

    // TODO: add draw code for native data here
    int size = pDoc->m_circleArray.GetSize();

    for (int x=0; x<size; ++x)
    {
```

```
CircleStruct* circle =
    (CircleStruct*)pDoc->m_circleArray.GetAt(x);
int radius = circle->diameter/2;
int x1 = circle->point.x-radius;
int y1 = circle->point.y-radius;
int x2 = circle->point.x+radius;
int y2 = circle->point.y+radius;
COLORREF color = circle->color;
CBrush brush(color);
CBrush* oldBrush = pDC->SelectObject(&brush);
pDC->Ellipse(x1, y1, x2, y2);
pDC->SelectObject(oldBrush);
    }
}
```

The message map

You may now wonder how MFC knows which message-response functions to call for which messages. As it happens, the view class uses a message map to associate messages with the functions that handle those messages. Listing 3-12 shows `CCircleAppView`'s message map. You learn more about message maps in Chapter 4, "Application Fundamentals," but you can see in Listing 3-12 how each message is associated with its handler function.

Listing 3-12: The message map

```
BEGIN_MESSAGE_MAP(CCircleAppView, CView)
    //{{AFX_MSG_MAP(CCircleAppView)
    ON_WM_LBUTTONDOWN()
    ON_COMMAND(ID_CIRCLE_CHANGECOLOR, OnCircleChangecolor)
    ON_COMMAND(ID_CIRCLE_CHANGEDIAMETER, OnCircleChangediameter)
    //}}AFX_MSG_MAP
    // Standard printing commands
    ON_COMMAND(ID_FILE_PRINT, CView::OnFilePrint)
    ON_COMMAND(ID_FILE_PRINT_DIRECT, CView::OnFilePrint)
    ON_COMMAND(ID_FILE_PRINT_PREVIEW, CView::OnFilePrintPreview)
END_MESSAGE_MAP()
```

Modifying CircleApp's Status Bar

You're almost done now. Only one more thing to do. Currently, CircleApp's status bar contains a few panes that aren't appropriate for this particular application. Specifically, you need to remove the panes that display the status of the Caps Lock, Num Lock, and Scroll Lock keys, as these keys have no function in the CircleApp application. Perform the following steps to modify the status bar:

1. In the ClassView page of the Project Workspace window, click the plus sign next to the `CMainFrame` class. The members of the class appear.

2. Double-click the class's constructor. Visual C++ loads and displays the class's implementation file, called MainFrm.cpp.

3. Find the indicators[] array that's defined right before the class's constructor. This array specifies the types of panes that appear in the status bar.

4. Delete the ID_INDICATOR_CAPS, ID_INDICATOR_NUM, and ID_INDICATOR_SCRL panel IDs from the array, as shown in Figure 3-53. Removing these IDs removes the unwanted panels from the status bar.

The final indicators [ ] array

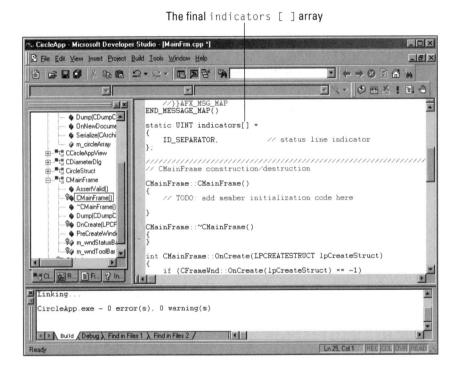

Figure 3-53: You modify the status bar from within the CMainFrame class.

And that finishes up the CircleApp application.

Summary

Over the course of creating this application, you've learned a lot about programming with Visual C++ and MFC. In fact, you've touched upon all the basic topics you need to know to create your own applications. Of course, there's a lot more to know about Windows 98 and Visual C++. In order to learn more about the way Visual C++ and MFC work, you might want to take some time now to explore Visual C++'s online tutorials. To learn more about C++ programming, you may also wish to take a look at Foundations™ of Visual C++® Programming for Windows 95 by Paul Yao and Joseph Yao, and Visual C++® 5 for Dummies® by Michael Hyman and Bob Arnson, both published by IDG Books Worldwide. The rest of this book also demonstrates many Visual C++ programming techniques for creating Windows 98 applications.

Also discussed in this chapter:

▶ One way to start a Visual C++ application is to generate skeleton source code with AppWizard. AppWizard creates the classes that represent your application, its document, and its windows.

▶ Although AppWizard creates a set of default resources, you must use the resource editors to modify the resources to suit your specific application.

▶ An MFC application's document class holds, saves, and loads document data.

▶ An MFC application's view class displays the document and enables the user to edit the document.

▶ ClassWizard makes it easy to create message-response functions for the Windows messages and menu messages to which your application must respond.

Chapter 4

Application Fundamentals

The Windows operating system has gone through many changes. During these changes many types of applications were created—both 16-bit and 32-bit—that run under the system. However, in this book, you won't be concerned with 16-bit applications, which are fast becoming extinct. Instead, you will focus on the types of applications that are designed for Windows 98. Specifically, you will examine Win32 applications.

Win32 Applications

There are many types of Win32 applications, from traditional programs to console applications and dynamic-link libraries (DLLs). You can even include ActiveX controls, which are programmable components that you can add to applications, Web pages, and even the Active Desktop. You will now examine several types of these Win32 applications.

Traditional Win32 applications

In the previous chapter, "Programming with Visual C++," you created a traditional Windows application. Such an application has all the features one would expect in a full-fledged application, including a frame window, menu bar, toolbar, and status bar. Most of the applications that you use every day, and most of the applications you'll create with Visual C++, fall into this category. Figure 4-1 shows Microsoft WordPad, a traditional Win32 application familiar to most Windows users.

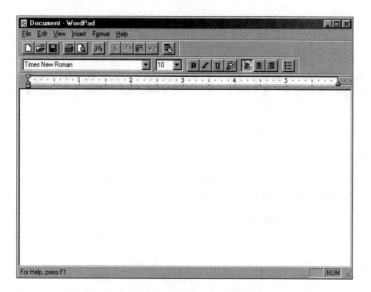

Figure 4-1: WordPad displayed on Windows 98

When you write a Win32 application, you must deal directly with the Windows operating system. This means creating an application that responds to Windows messages and follows the rules for creating a graphical user interface. These rules are so plentiful they are almost mind-boggling to the novice. Still, we Windows programmers manage to muddle through!

Win32 console applications

In your Windows explorations, you may have come across *console applications*. A console application is much like an old-fashioned DOS program in that, except for its frame window, it displays only text information. Console applications are often used for quickie utilities. Some programming environments also use console windows to display error messages and other information that, in the DOS days, would have appeared on the text screen.

Figure 4-2 shows a running console application. The code that created the application looks like this:

```
#include <stdio.h>

int main()
{
    printf("This is a console application.\n\n");
    return 0;
}
```

As you can see, you write a console application just as you used to write C applications in the good ol' days. This bit of simplicity—not having to deal with all the extra baggage Windows throws at you—makes console applications perfect for simple tasks in which you don't want to create windows classes, manage message maps, and draw to device contexts.

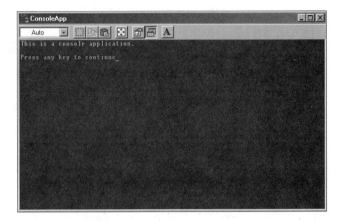

Figure 4-2: A Win32 console application displaying only text information

Dynamic-link libraries

A *Dynamic Link Library,* or *DLL,* as it's more commonly called, is not a complete program or even an executable file. Instead, a DLL is a library of functions that can be called from other modules in the system. Because a DLL is not an application, per se, it rarely has a visible presence and doesn't receive Windows messages. A DLL isn't even loaded into memory until some other module, such as an application, either explicitly loads the DLL or calls one of the DLL's functions. The "dynamic" in the name comes from the fact that the library is not linked to other modules at compile time, but rather is linked at run time.

As an example, a Windows programmer might write a DLL that contains image editing functions for a paint program. When the paint program runs, the user gets busy drawing an image. Because the program doesn't yet need the functions defined in the DLL, the DLL is not yet loaded into memory. After working for a while, though, the user decides to reduce the image by 50 percent. It just so happens that the functions the program must call to perform the reduction are located in the DLL. When the paint program calls these functions, Windows loads the DLL and dynamically (on the fly, so to speak) links the library with the paint program.

The big advantage of using a DLL is that many modules can share the same library without the modules having to be linked to the library at compile time. This saves the user disk space. In fact, DLLs can be shared between completely different applications, which can save not only disk space, but RAM. Windows itself is an excellent example of DLLs in action. Virtually all of Windows is implemented in DLLs that are loaded as needed. If you look in your Windows System folder, you'll see literally hundreds of files with the .DLL file extension, as shown in Figure 4-3. Most of these files came with Windows; others may have been placed there by applications you installed.

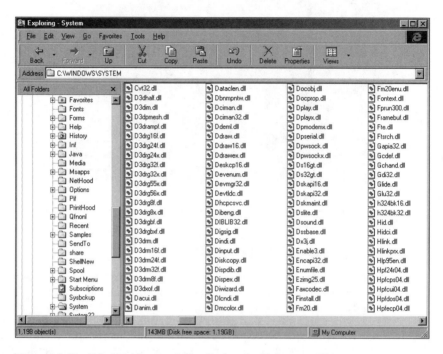

Figure 4-3: The Windows\System folder displayed with its many DLLs

ActiveX controls

ActiveX controls are kind of like mini-applications that can be embedded into some type of container object. The container is usually an application's frame window or an HTML document. In any case, an ActiveX control is not an executable file. That is, it cannot be run as a stand-alone application.

ActiveX controls enable programmers to add functionality to programs easily. For example, Figure 4-4 shows Microsoft's ActiveMovie ActiveX control loaded into Visual C++'s ActiveX Control Test Container application. If you were writing an application that needed to display video, you might opt to use the ActiveMovie ActiveX control rather than write your own code to play back video files. This way, you save a lot of time without having to compromise the final product.

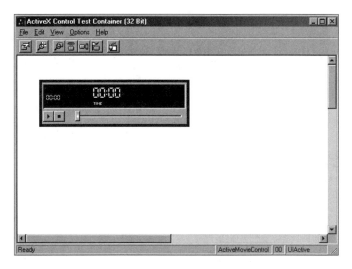

Figure 4-4: The ActiveMovie ActiveX control embedded in an application window

ActiveX controls have a programmable interface made up of properties and methods. The application or Web page containing the ActiveX control can determine how the control looks and acts by setting properties and calling methods. For example, an ActiveX control that implements a table might have properties that determine the number of rows and columns in the table. The control might have methods that enable the container to add elements to the table and sort the table entries in various ways.

You can download ActiveX controls from the Web, buy them from third-party vendors, or program your own using Visual C++. For more information on creating ActiveX controls, see Chapter 23, "ActiveX Controls."

Programming Windows the Hard Way

When Windows first become popular, sophisticated programming tools were as scarce as flies in a Raid factory. Programmers wrote Windows applications in straight C (no C++) and compiled them under DOS, strange as that sounds. There weren't any C compilers that ran under Windows, even though you could program Windows applications with the compilers. These days, complex libraries like MFC take a lot of the drudgery out of writing Windows applications, but such advantages come with a price. MFC itself has a steep learning curve. Moreover, if you don't understand how a conventional Windows program works, learning MFC is even harder. In this section, you learn to write basic Windows programs like the old timers did (and as many programmers still do). This experience will help you better appreciate MFC's capabilities.

On CD-ROM

Listing 4-1 is a simple Windows application called BasicApp that is written in C (you can find the executable file and complete source code for BasicApp in the BasicApp folder of this book's CD-ROM). Figure 4-5 shows BasicApp when you click in its window, which causes a message box to appear. It sure looks different from an MFC program, doesn't it? That's because an MFC program hides many of the details of programming Windows. However, MFC isn't magical. In order to get a Windows application up on the screen, an MFC application must perform exactly the same chores as a straight C program.

Figure 4-5: After you click in the Basic Application window, this message box appears.

Listing 4-1: A basic Win32 application

```
/***********************************************************
 * BASICAPP.C: A basic Windows application.
 ***********************************************************/

#include <windows.h>

LRESULT CALLBACK WndProc(HWND hWnd, UINT message,
    WPARAM wParam, LPARAM lParam);

int WINAPI WinMain(HINSTANCE hCurrentInst,
    HINSTANCE hPrevInstance, PSTR lpszCmdLine,
    int nCmdShow)
{
    WNDCLASS wndClass;
    HWND hWnd;
    MSG msg;
    UINT width;
    UINT height;

    wndClass.style = CS_HREDRAW | CS_VREDRAW;
    wndClass.lpfnWndProc = WndProc;
```

```
    wndClass.cbClsExtra = 0;
    wndClass.cbWndExtra = 0;
    wndClass.hInstance = hCurrentInst;
    wndClass.hIcon = LoadIcon(NULL, IDI_APPLICATION);
    wndClass.hCursor = LoadCursor(NULL, IDC_ARROW);
    wndClass.hbrBackground = GetStockObject(WHITE_BRUSH);
    wndClass.lpszMenuName = NULL;
    wndClass.lpszClassName = "BasicApp";

    RegisterClass(&wndClass);

    width = GetSystemMetrics(SM_CXSCREEN) / 2;
    height = GetSystemMetrics(SM_CYSCREEN) / 2;

    hWnd = CreateWindow(
        "BasicApp",              /* Window class's name.    */
        "Basic Application",     /* Title bar text.         */
        WS_OVERLAPPEDWINDOW,     /* The window's style.     */
        10,                      /* X position.             */
        10,                      /* Y position.             */
        width,                   /* Width.                  */
        height,                  /* Height.                 */
        NULL,                    /* Parent window's handle. */
        NULL,                    /* Menu handle.            */
        hCurrentInst,            /* Instance handle.        */
        NULL);                   /* No additional data.     */

    ShowWindow(hWnd, nCmdShow);
    UpdateWindow(hWnd);

    while (GetMessage(&msg, NULL, 0, 0))
    {
        TranslateMessage(&msg);
        DispatchMessage(&msg);
    }

    return msg.wParam;
}

LRESULT CALLBACK WndProc(HWND hWnd, UINT message,
    WPARAM wParam, LPARAM lParam)
{
    HDC hDC;
    PAINTSTRUCT paintStruct;

    switch(message)
    {
        case WM_PAINT:
            hDC = BeginPaint(hWnd, &paintStruct);
            TextOut(hDC, 10, 10, "This is a test.", 15);
            EndPaint(hWnd, &paintStruct);
            return 0;
```

```
        case WM_LBUTTONDOWN:
            MessageBox(hWnd, "Got mouse click!",
                "Basic Application",
                MB_ICONEXCLAMATION | MB_OK);
            return 0;

        case WM_DESTROY:
            PostQuitMessage(0);
            return 0;
    }

    return DefWindowProc(hWnd, message, wParam, lParam);
}
```

The first thing to notice in Listing 4-1 is the line

```
#include <windows.h>
```

near the top of the listing. The windows.h file contains many declarations that all Windows programs require. All Windows programs include this header file.

The next thing to notice is the WinMain() function, whose signature looks like this:

```
int WINAPI WinMain(HINSTANCE hCurrentInst,
    HINSTANCE hPrevInstance, PSTR lpszCmdLine,
    int nCmdShow)
```

WinMain() is the entry point for all Windows programs, in the same way main() is the entry point for DOS C programs. WinMain()'s four parameters are as follows:

hCurrentInst	The handle of this instance of the program
hPrevInstance	The handle of the previous instance
lpszCmdLine	A pointer to the command line used to run the program
nCmdShow	A set of flags that determine how the application's window should be displayed

Handles are one type of data you don't see very often in an MFC program, because MFC's classes manage handles internally. A handle is nothing more than a value that identifies a window or some other object. In a traditional C Windows program, you almost always refer to a window by its handle, and most Windows API functions that manipulate windows require a handle as their first argument.

An instance of an application is much the same thing as an instance of a class in object-oriented programming. For example, in most cases, the user can run the same Windows application multiple times, having several separate, but identical, windows on the screen. Each window represents an instance of the program. In 16-bit Windows programming, all application instances shared the same memory space. By checking the handle to the previous instance, programmers could prevent multiple instances. If hPrevInstance was NULL, there was no previous instance. If hPrevInstance was not NULL, the application had already been run, and the programmer could display the already existing window, rather than create a new instance of the application.

Under Windows 98, however, every application gets its own block of virtual memory. For this reason, the hPrevInstance handle in Windows 98 programs is always NULL. There are still ways to determine whether an application has already been run, but it's a more complicated process that requires searching running processes for a specific Window name.

Getting back to the program, the WinMain() function must create a class for its window, register the class with Windows, and then display the window. Windows defines a structure for holding the values that make up a window class. WinMain() declares an instance of this structure like this:

```
WNDCLASS wndClass;
```

WinMain() also initializes this structure to the values required for the window class, as shown in Listing 4-2:

Listing 4-2: Initializing the **WNDCLASS** structure

```
wndClass.style = CS_HREDRAW | CS_VREDRAW;
wndClass.lpfnWndProc = WndProc;
wndClass.cbClsExtra = 0;
wndClass.cbWndExtra = 0;
wndClass.hInstance = hCurrentInst;
wndClass.hIcon = LoadIcon(NULL, IDI_APPLICATION);
wndClass.hCursor = LoadCursor(NULL, IDC_ARROW);
wndClass.hbrBackground = GetStockObject(WHITE_BRUSH);
wndClass.lpszMenuName = NULL;
wndClass.lpszClassName = "BasicApp";
```

The WNDCLASS structure defines the window's style, as well as specifies the window's icons, cursor, background color, and menu. Because most programs in this book are written using MFC, fully describing the WNDCLASS structure (and all the values that are appropriate for the structure's members) is beyond the scope of this book. However, you can find plenty of details in your Visual C++ online documentation or in your favorite Windows programming manual, such as *Programming Windows 95* by Charles Petzold and Paul Yao. The important thing to know here is that every Windows application must create an instance of this structure and register it with Windows.

`WinMain()` registers the new window class with Windows by calling `RegisterClass()`, like this:

```
RegisterClass(&wndClass);
```

`RegisterClass()`'s single argument is the address of the initialized `WNDCLASS` structure.

Often in a Windows program, you need to know the size of the screen, fonts, and other objects. In the case of BasicApp, the application gets the size of the screen by calling `GetSystemMetrics()`. The program then divides the screen width and height by two in order to determine the initial size of the application's window:

```
width = GetSystemMetrics(SM_CXSCREEN) / 2;
height = GetSystemMetrics(SM_CYSCREEN) / 2;
```

Your online documentation describes the many other flags that can be used with `GetSystemMetrics()`. Using the appropriate flags as the function's single argument, you can determine the size of just about any part of the window or screen.

After determining the window's initial size, `WinMain()` creates an instance of the window class, as shown in Listing 4-3.

Listing 4-3: Creating the window object

```
hWnd = CreateWindow(
    "BasicApp",              /* Window class's name.    */
    "Basic Application",     /* Title bar text.         */
    WS_OVERLAPPEDWINDOW,     /* The window's style.     */
    10,                      /* X position.             */
    10,                      /* Y position.             */
    width,                   /* Width.                  */
    height,                  /* Height.                 */
    NULL,                    /* Parent window's handle. */
    NULL,                    /* Menu handle.            */
    hCurrentInst,            /* Instance handle.        */
    NULL);                   /* No additional data.     */
```

The comments in the listing describe `CreateWindow()`'s arguments.

At this point, the application has defined a window class and created an instance of that window class. But, so far, there is nothing on the screen. To display the new window, `WinMain()` calls the Windows API function `ShowWindow()`:

```
ShowWindow(hWnd, nCmdShow);
```

Finally, to ensure that the window updates its display, the program calls the Windows API function `UpdateWindow()`:

```
UpdateWindow(hWnd);
```

Notice how both of these functions, like most other window-manipulation functions, take a window handle as the first argument.

Now that the window is up on the screen, it can start to process the many messages that Windows will send it. The program does this by setting up a message loop, which looks like this:

```
while (GetMessage(&msg, NULL, 0, 0))
{
    TranslateMessage(&msg);
    DispatchMessage(&msg);
}
```

The `GetMessage()` Windows API function retrieves a message from the window's message queue. As long as `GetMessage()` returns a nonzero value, the message loop continues. In fact, you might say that a Windows program does nothing more than gather and respond to messages. The message loop continues until the user exits the application, at which point `GetMessage()` returns zero, and the message loop ends.

Inside the loop, the call to `TranslateMessage()` handles virtual-key messages (messages that represent keystrokes), translating them into character messages that go back into the message queue. The `DispatchMessage()` function sends the message off to the application's window procedure.

What's a window procedure? When you defined BasicApp's window class in the `WNDCLASS` structure, you specified the function to which Windows messages should be directed:

```
wndClass.lpfnWndProc = WndProc;
```

When the program registered the window class, Windows made note of the window procedure passed in the `lpfnWndProc` structure member. So, calls to `DispatchMessage()` result in Windows sending the message to `WndProc()`, where the messages are either handled by the application or sent back to Windows for default processing.

In BasicApp, `WndProc()`'s signature looks like this:

```
LRESULT CALLBACK WndProc(HWND hWnd, UINT message,
    WPARAM wParam, LPARAM lParam)
```

The function's four parameters are as follows:

hWnd	The handle of the window to which the message is directed
message	The message ID (for example, WM_CREATE)
wParam	A 32-bit message parameter
lParam	A 32-bit message parameterEnd list

The values of the two 32-bit parameters depend on the type of message. For example, when the user selects a menu item from an application's menu bar, the application gets a `WM_COMMAND` message, with the menu item's ID in the low word of the `wParam` parameter.

`WndProc()`'s job is to determine whether the application needs to handle the message or pass it back to Windows for default processing. (All messages must be dealt with in one of these ways.) In most Windows procedures, the programmer sets up a `switch` statement with `case` clauses for the messages the application should handle. BasicApp handles only three Windows messages. Its `switch` statement looks like the one in Listing 4-4.

Listing 4-4: Handling Windows messages

```
switch(message)
{
    case WM_PAINT:
        hDC = BeginPaint(hWnd, &paintStruct);
        TextOut(hDC, 10, 10, "This is a test.", 15);
        EndPaint(hWnd, &paintStruct);
        return 0;

    case WM_LBUTTONDOWN:
        MessageBox(hWnd, "Got mouse click!",
            "Basic Application",
            MB_ICONEXCLAMATION | MB_OK);
        return 0;

    case WM_DESTROY:
        PostQuitMessage(0);
        return 0;
}
```

`WndProc()` handles the following three Windows messages:

WM_PAINT	This message means that the window must redraw its display. Any Windows application with a visible display must handle WM_PAINT.
WM_LBUTTONDOWN	This message means that the user clicked the left mouse button inside the window's client area.
WM_DESTROY	This message means that the user wants to close the application. All Windows applications must handle WM_DESTROY.

Notice that, after handling a message, the function returns a value of zero. Messages that are not handled in the `switch` statement must be passed back to Windows. Failure to do this could result in the application being incapable of responding to the user. To pass a message back to Windows, the application calls `DefWindowProc()`:

```
return DefWindowProc(hWnd, message, wParam, lParam);
```

The function's arguments are the same as the parameters passed to the window procedure. Notice that `WndProc()` returns `DefWindowProc()`'s return value.

Now that you have a general idea of how a "handwritten" Windows application works, you can better appreciate what a class library like MFC does for you. In the next section, you see how MFC deals with the tasks you had to handle yourself in BasicApp.

MFC vs. C

As I said previously, there's nothing magical about MFC. An MFC program must perform all the same start-up procedures as any other Windows program. It must also receive and process Windows messages. In this section, you get an overview of how MFC performs these important tasks.

Initializing the application

When you create an MFC application with AppWizard, the generated source code—and the MFC classes on which that source code relies—takes care of many details, such as creating and registering the window class. MFC initializes a `WNDCLASS` structure for your application, registers the window class via the `RegisterClass()`, and displays the window. This doesn't mean, however, that you have no control over the window's styles. Various class member functions enable you to intercept MFC's default processing and change it to suit your needs. See the Problems & Solutions sections in this chapter for some MFC programming techniques that give you more control over your application's window.

Every MFC program has an application object, instantiated from a class that was derived from `CWinApp`. This application object contains the required `WinMain()` function, as well as the application's message loop. You don't have to do anything to get the message loop going; it's all automatic.

The application class also provides the `InitApplication()` and `InitInstance()` member functions so that you can perform your own custom application initialization. However, `InitApplication()` is only useful under 16-bit Windows, which allowed multiple instances of a single application. For 32-bit applications, you should ignore `InitApplication()` and use `InitInstance()` instead.

MFC message handling

When it comes to message handling in an MFC program, you must tell MFC what messages your application handles and where those message are handled. You do this by creating a message map in the class that accepts the messages. (Of course, if you're using AppWizard and ClassWizard, you don't have to create message maps by hand; AppWizard creates the basic message maps for you, and ClassWizard adds new entries to the message maps as needed.) To create a message map, perform the following steps:

1. Declare the message map in the class's header file.

2. Declare message-response functions in the class's header file.

3. Define the message map in the class's implementation file.

4. Define the message-response functions in the class's implementation file.

Declaring a message map is as easy as including the DECLARE_MESSAGE_MAP() macro in your class's header file. You declare message-response functions in much the same way as you declare any other class member function. However, MFC provides a special prefix, afx_msg, that marks a function as a message-response function. This prefix goes right before the function's return type, as shown here:

```
afx_msg void OnLButtonDown(UINT nFlags, CPoint point);
```

In the class's implementation file, you create the actual message map, which is made up of the BEGIN_MESSAGE_MAP() and END_MESSAGE_MAP() macros, between which are other macros that define each entry in the message map. For example, look at this message map:

```
BEGIN_MESSAGE_MAP(CCircleAppView, CView)
    ON_WM_LBUTTONDOWN()
    ON_COMMAND(ID_CIRCLE_CHANGECOLOR, OnCircleChangecolor)
    ON_COMMAND(ID_CIRCLE_CHANGEDIAMETER,
        OnCircleChangediameter)
END_MESSAGE_MAP()
```

The first line starts the message map. The BEGIN_MESSAGE_MAP() macro's two arguments are the name of the class in which the map is located and the name of the base class. The first argument tells MFC where to direct the messages. The second argument tells MFC where to direct the messages if the current class doesn't handle them. In this way, MFC can pass messages all the way up a class hierarchy until a class handles the message or MFC passes the message back to Windows for default processing.

After the BEGIN_MESSAGE_MAP() macro comes the message map entries, which tell MFC which function to associate with which message. MFC defines many macros for the different types of messages a class may handle in its message map. The most common are the macros that represent standard Windows messages. The names for these macros are derived from the message name.

For example, the message map macro for the WM_LBUTTONDOWN message is ON_WM_LBUTTONDOWN(). The macro name is formed by prefixing the message name with ON_ and adding parentheses to the end. The message-response functions for standard Windows messages are also named using a strict naming convention. To determine the name for a message, drop the WM_ from the message, lowercase all letters except for those that start a word, and add On to the front of the name. The message-response function for WM_LBUTTONDOWN is OnLButtonDown(), whereas the message-response function for WM_CREATE is OnCreate().

Another common message-map macro is ON_COMMAND, which usually associates menu commands with the functions that handle them. Unlike the standard Windows message macros, the ON_COMMAND macro requires two arguments: the message ID and the name of the function that handles the message.

When MFC receives a standard Windows message, it "cracks" the parameters into more easily usable data types. For example, the WM_LBUTTONDOWN message stores the mouse position in lParam, with the X coordinate in the low word and the Y coordinate in the high word. MFC extracts these values from lParam and stores them in a CPoint object, which it passes as an argument to the OnLButtonDown() message-response function. As an example, Listing 4-5 shows an OnLButtonDown() function from the CircleApp application that draws a circle where the user clicks. The function uses the CPoint object, which holds values that MFC extracted from the original Windows message, to determine where to draw the circle.

This message-cracking means that MFC message-response functions all have different signatures, depending on how MFC decides to crack the message parameters. When you use ClassWizard to add message handling to your application, you don't need to worry about the parameters, because ClassWizard creates the function for you. However, if you want to add message-response functions by hand, you need to look up the function signatures for the messages you want to handle.

Listing 4-5: The OnLButtonDown() **message-response function**

```
void CCircleAppView::OnLButtonDown(UINT nFlags,
    CPoint point)
{
    // TODO: Add your message handler code here
    //    and/or call default

    CClientDC clientDC(this);
    CBrush brush(RGB(255,0,0));
    CBrush* oldBrush = clientDC.SelectObject(&brush);
    clientDC.Ellipse(point.x-20, point.y-20,
        point.x+20, point.y+20);
    clientDC.SelectObject(oldBrush);

    CView::OnLButtonDown(nFlags, point);
}
```

PROBLEMS & SOLUTIONS

Finding Message-Response Function Signatures

PROBLEM: *When I'm not using ClassWizard, how can I easily define a message-response function for a Windows message? Each function's signature is different from the next. It's enough to drive me crazy!*

SOLUTION: Your Visual C++ online documentation can provide more than information. It also provides snippets of source code that you can paste right into your programs. For example, suppose you want to respond to the WM_CREATE Windows message in a window class. You already know from the Visual C++ naming conventions that the name of the message-response function is OnCreate(). Type OnCreate() into your code window, place the text cursor on the function name, and then press F1. The documentation for the function, including the function's signature, appears in the window, as shown in Figure 4-6. Use your mouse to highlight the function's signature, press Ctrl+C to copy the signature to the Clipboard, return to your source code, and press Ctrl+V to paste the signature into your code.

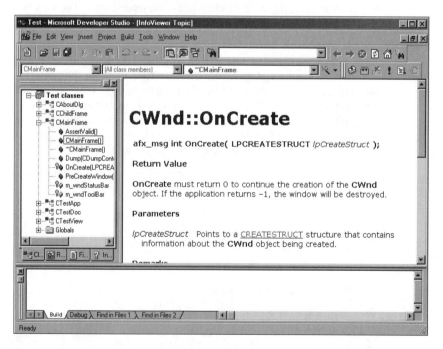

Figure 4-6: Obtaining a function signature from Visual C++'s online documentation

PROBLEMS & SOLUTIONS

Sizing MFC Windows

PROBLEM: *How can I specify the size and position of a frame window in an MFC program?*

SOLUTION: In your frame window class, usually called `CMainFrame`, find the `PreCreateWindow()` function. `CMainFrame`, and every other MFC window class, inherits `PreCreateWindow()` from `CWnd`. MFC calls this function just before it creates the window, so by placing your custom code in `PreCreateWindow()`, you can modify the way your window looks and acts.

`PreCreateWindow()` receives a reference to a `CREATESTRUCT` structure as a single parameter. The `CREATESTRUCT` structure contains four members that determine the window's size and position. These members are `cx`, `cy`, `x`, and `y`. To change the windows starting width and height, set `cx` and `cy`, respectively. To change the window's starting location, set `x` and `y`. Listing 4-6 shows the code required to set a window's starting size and position.

Note that the members of the `CREATESTRUCT` structure are the same values that you pass to the `CreateWindow()` function in a standard C Windows program.

Listing 4-6: Setting a window's starting size and position

```
BOOL CMainFrame::PreCreateWindow(CREATESTRUCT& cs)
{
    // TODO: Modify the Window class or styles
    //   here by modifying
    //   the CREATESTRUCT cs

    cs.cx = 400;
    cs.cy = 300;
    cs.x = 100;
    cs.y = 50;

    return CMDIFrameWnd::PreCreateWindow(cs);
```

PROBLEMS & SOLUTIONS

Modifying MFC Window Styles

PROBLEM: *How can I remove control buttons, such as the Maximize and Restore buttons, from a window's title bar?*

SOLUTION: Again, the answer lies in the `PreCreateWindow()` function. The `CREATESTRUCT` structure passed to the class contains a member, called `style`, that holds the window's style flags. By changing the style flags, you can change the way the window looks and acts. Listing 4-7, for example, creates a window that has only a Close button. Moreover, the window's border cannot be used to resize the window. This combination of styles creates a window that the user cannot resize. Figure 4-7 shows the resultant window. You can find all the window styles in your Visual C++ online documentation, by searching for "window styles."

Listing 4-7: Creating a window that cannot be resized

```
BOOL CMainFrame::PreCreateWindow(CREATESTRUCT& cs)
{
    // TODO: Modify the Window class or styles
    //   here by modifying
    //   the CREATESTRUCT cs

    cs.style = WS_OVERLAPPED | WS_SYSMENU | WS_BORDER;

    return CMDIFrameWnd::PreCreateWindow(cs);
}
```

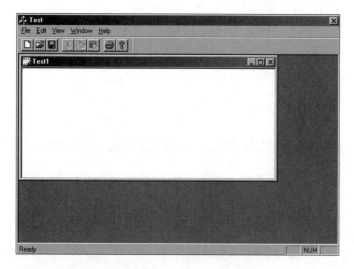

Figure 4-7: After changing this window's style flags, it cannot be resized.

Summary

Old-fashioned C Windows programs and modern MFC programs both have to perform the same tasks to get a window up on the screen. MFC, however, does a lot of the work that you would have to accomplish on your own, leaving you to concentrate on the implementation details of your specific application, rather than getting bogged down in the minutiae of Windows programming.

Also discussed in this chapter:

▶ Windows applications come in several forms, including traditional GUI applications, console applications, DLLs, and ActiveX controls.

▶ Before fancy tools like Visual C++ were available, Windows programs were written in C and compiled from the DOS command line.

▶ Every Windows application with a visible display must declare and register a window class. The application then creates its windows based on the registered classes.

▶ To provide custom initialization for an MFC application, you override the application object's `InitInstance()` function.

▶ Windows programs written in C contain a message loop that receives and dispatches a Windows message. MFC programs also have a message loop, but it's hidden from the programmer, along with the other overhead required to get a Windows application going.

▶ Whereas Windows programs written in C usually use a complex `switch` statement to route Windows messages to the appropriate functions, MFC uses a message map.

Part II

User Interface

Chapter 5

Graphics Device Interface Basics

Windows is a graphical operating system, which means that it displays everything on the screen as an image. The system even draws text as an image. For this reason, you shouldn't be surprised to discover that Windows has a library of functions that enables applications to handle graphics in various ways. Whether you want to print a line of text on the screen or draw a 3D background for a computer game, you're going to have to deal with Windows' Graphics Device Interface (GDI). In this chapter, you learn the basic skills required to create a Windows screen display. (In Chapter 13, "Advanced GDI," you learn more about the GDI.)

Introducing the GDI

The GDI is an extensive set of functions that you call whenever you draw or manage graphics from within a Windows application. Because everything seen on a Windows screen is graphical in nature, you must call a GDI function every time you display something in your application's window.

Besides the functions that perform display operations, the GDI also features a set of objects that programs use to render a display. These objects include the following:

Device context	A set of attributes that describes the surface on which images are displayed and the objects used to display those images.
Pen	A GDI object that draws lines.
Brush	A GDI object that fills onscreen shapes with color.

Font   A GDI object that determines the style of the characters used to draw text on the screen.

Bitmap   A GDI object that stores an image.

Palette   A set of colors that can be used when an application draws on the screen.

All these objects work together to create the displays you see in an application's window. In the following sections, you will examine device contexts, pens, and brushes in greater detail. For information on fonts, refer to Chapter 7, "Text," and for information on bitmaps and palettes, check out Chapter 12, "Bitmaps."

Device Contexts

As you learned in the previous section, a device context (DC) is a set of attributes that determines how graphics are displayed in an application's window. Before you can draw anything in a window, you must acquire a DC for the area of the window in which you will draw. You then route all graphics calls to the GDI, which carries out your commands as is appropriate for the DC.

You don't need to be concerned with many of these attributes because when you acquire a DC, Windows initializes a complete set of attributes and objects that you'll use to render a display. You can, however, change the attributes and objects in order to create your application's specific display.

For example, the default DC includes a black pen. Any lines you draw— including those that outline shapes like rectangles and circles—will be black. Obviously, there will be many times when you'll want to draw lines in another color. In this case, you must replace the default pen with a pen of the required color, which you create in your program and pass to the device context. In Windows programming jargon, the act of giving a new object to a DC is called selecting the object into the DC.

Note

A device context doesn't always represent a screen display. It can also represent the attributes of a printer or some other graphical device. That is, when you print a document from a Windows application, the application obtains a printer device context to which the program directs the data to be printed.

Keep in mind that a DC must always have a complete set of tools. This means that you cannot remove tools from the DC. Instead, you replace one tool with another. When your program is ready to destroy custom GDI objects you've selected into a DC, you must replace those objects with the old, default GDI objects.

A DC also represents the area in which you can draw. If you try to draw outside of this area, Windows *clips* the drawing to the edges of the valid area. This is one way Windows forces your display to stay within the confines of the application's window. More precisely, Windows usually restricts your drawing operations to the window's client area. Normally, you can't draw on the window's title bar or controls.

Visual C++'s MFC library encapsulates the GDI into a number of classes that simplify handling DCs and GDI objects such as pens, brushes, fonts, and palettes. The biggest of these classes is the CDC class, which represents a general DC from which the library derives specific types of DCs. Table 5-1 lists some of the more useful functions of the CDC class.

Table 5-1   Some useful functions of the CDC class

Message	*Description*
Arc()	Draws an elliptical arc
BitBlt()	Copies a bitmap from one DC to another
Draw3dRect()	Draws a three-dimensional rectangle
DrawDragRect()	Draws a rectangle that's being dragged by the mouse
DrawEdge()	Draws the edges of a rectangle
DrawIcon()	Draws an icon
Ellipse()	Draws an ellipse
FillRect()	Fills a rectangle with the color of the given brush
FillRgn()	Fills a region with the color of the given brush
FillSolidRect()	Fills a rectangle with the given color
FloodFill()	Fills an area with the color of the current brush
FrameRect()	Draws a rectangle border
FrameRgn()	Draws a region border
GetBkColor()	Gets the background color
GetCurrentBitmap()	Gets a pointer to the selected bitmap
GetCurrentBrush()	Gets a pointer to the selected brush
GetCurrentFont()	Gets a pointer to the selected font
GetCurrentPalette()	Gets a pointer to the selected palette
GetCurrentPen()	Gets a pointer to the selected pen
GetCurrentPosition()	Gets the pen's current position
GetDeviceCaps()	Gets information about the display device's capabilities
GetMapMode()	Gets the currently set mapping mode
GetPixel()	Gets an RGB color value for the given pixel
GetPolyFillMode()	Gets the polygon-filling mode
GetTextColor()	Gets the text color

(continued)

Table 5-1   *(Continued)*

Message	Description
GetTextExtent()	Gets the width and height of a text line
GetTextMetrics()	Gets information about the current font
GetWindow()	Gets a pointer to the DC's window
GrayString()	Draws grayed text
LineTo()	Draws a line
MoveTo()	Sets the current pen position
Pie()	Draws a pie slice
Polygon()	Draws a polygon
Polyline()	Draws a set of lines
RealizePalette()	Maps the logical palette to the system palette
Rectangle()	Draws a rectangle
RoundRect()	Draws a rectangle with rounded corners
SelectObject()	Selects a GDI drawing object
SelectPalette()	Selects the logical palette
SelectStockObject()	Selects a predefined stock drawing object
SetBkColor()	Sets the background color
SetMapMode()	Sets the mapping mode
SetPixel()	Sets a pixel to a given color
SetTextColor()	Sets the text color
StretchBlt()	Copies a bitmap from one DC to another, stretching or compressing the bitmap as needed
TextOut()	Draws a text string

The MFC library derives several specific device-context classes from the general CDC class. These classes are as follows:

CClientDC	A device context that provides drawing access to a window's client area. Use this type of DC when you want to draw in a window, except in response to a WM_PAINT Windows message.
CMetaFileDC	A device context that represents a Windows metafile, which is a file that holds a list of commands for reproducing an image. Use this type of DC when you want to create a device-independent file that you can play back to create an image.

(continued)

CPaintDC	A device context that MFC creates in response to a Windows WM_PAINT message. Your application uses this DC to update the window's display, usually in an MFC application's OnDraw() function.
CWindowDC	A device context that provides drawing access to an entire window, rather than just the client area.

In the following sections, you will examine the first three device-context classes in more detail. The CWindowDC class will not be discussed, as it is rarely used in applications.

Note

As you learn to use the device-context classes, remember that each of the classes inherits dozens of member functions from the CDC class. Only the CMetaFileDC class defines member functions specific to the class, in addition to those inherited from CDC.

The paint device context

As you learned in Chapter 4, "Application Fundamentals," when a window needs to redraw its display, Windows sends a WM_PAINT message. In a C Windows programs, you'd handle this message in the window's message loop something like this:

```
switch(message)
{
    case WM_PAINT:
        hDC = BeginPaint(hWnd, &paintStruct);

        // Draw window display here.

        EndPaint(hWnd, &paintStruct);
        return 0;

    // Handle other messages here.
}
```

To get the DC, you call the Windows BeginPaint() function, after which you call GDI functions to draw the window's display. After drawing the display, you call EndPaint(). You learned this process in Chapter 4, "Application Fundamentals."

In an MFC program, handling a paint DC is much easier because MFC handles the details of calling BeginPaint() and EndPaint() for you. MFC even creates the DC for you and passes it to the view class's OnDraw() function, which is the function in which you draw the window's display. A simple OnDraw() function might look like this:

```
void CPaintDCAppView::OnDraw(CDC* pDC)
{
    CPaintDCAppDoc* pDoc = GetDocument();
    ASSERT_VALID(pDoc);
```

```
        // TODO: add draw code for native data here

        pDC->Rectangle(20, 20, 300, 200);
}
```

As you can see, in an MFC program, you call GDI functions through an instance of a CDC-derived class. In the OnDraw() example, pDC is a pointer to an instance of the CPaintDC class, whose base class is CDC. The OnDraw() function draws a rectangle in the window's client area, as shown in Figure 5-1, by calling the CDC Rectangle() function through the pDC pointer.

Figure 5-1: An MFC application that draws a rectangle in response to a WM_PAINT message

MFC not only takes care of calling BeginPaint() and EndPaint(), it also deletes the DC object when the view class is through with it. You'll never have to create an instance of CPaintDC yourself; MFC handles this special type of DC object completely. All you need to do is call GDI functions through the supplied pointer in order to create the window's display.

The client-area device context

You don't have to wait for WM_PAINT messages in order to draw in a window. You can instead create a DC for the window's client area and then use this DC to call GDI functions. In a C Windows program, this involves calling the Windows API functions GetDC() and ReleaseDC(). GetDC() acquires a handle to a DC for the window's client area, whereas ReleaseDC() releases the DC, which you must be sure to do in order not to tie up this important system resource.

On CD-ROM

Listing 5-1 shows BasicDCApp, a Windows program written in C that creates a client-area device context in response to a left mouse-button click. When the user clicks in the window's client area, the word "Click" appears at the click location, as shown in Figure 5-2. You can find the executable file and

complete source code for BasicDCApp in the Chapter05\BasicDCApp folder
of this book's CD-ROM.

Listing 5-1: A basic Windows program that creates a client-area device context

```
#include <windows.h>

LRESULT CALLBACK WndProc(HWND hWnd, UINT message,
    WPARAM wParam, LPARAM lParam);

int WINAPI WinMain(HINSTANCE hCurrentInst,
    HINSTANCE hPrevInstance, PSTR lpszCmdLine,
    int nCmdShow)
{
    WNDCLASS wndClass;
    HWND hWnd;
    MSG msg;
    UINT width;
    UINT height;

    wndClass.style = CS_HREDRAW | CS_VREDRAW;
    wndClass.lpfnWndProc = WndProc;
    wndClass.cbClsExtra = 0;
    wndClass.cbWndExtra = 0;
    wndClass.hInstance = hCurrentInst;
    wndClass.hIcon = LoadIcon(NULL, IDI_APPLICATION);
    wndClass.hCursor = LoadCursor(NULL, IDC_ARROW);
    wndClass.hbrBackground = GetStockObject(WHITE_BRUSH);
    wndClass.lpszMenuName = NULL;
    wndClass.lpszClassName = "BasicDCApp";

    RegisterClass(&wndClass);

    width = GetSystemMetrics(SM_CXSCREEN) / 2;
    height = GetSystemMetrics(SM_CYSCREEN) / 2;

    hWnd = CreateWindow(
        "BasicDCApp",           /* Window class's name.    */
        "Basic DC Application", /* Title bar text.         */
        WS_OVERLAPPEDWINDOW,    /* The window's style.     */
        10,                     /* X position.             */
        10,                     /* Y position.             */
        width,                  /* Width.                  */
        height,                 /* Height.                 */
        NULL,                   /* Parent window's handle. */
        NULL,                   /* Menu handle.            */
        hCurrentInst,           /* Instance handle.        */
        NULL);                  /* No additional data.     */

    ShowWindow(hWnd, nCmdShow);
    UpdateWindow(hWnd);

    while (GetMessage(&msg, NULL, 0, 0))
    {
```

```
            TranslateMessage(&msg);
            DispatchMessage(&msg);
        }

    return msg.wParam;
}

LRESULT CALLBACK WndProc(HWND hWnd, UINT message,
    WPARAM wParam, LPARAM lParam)
{
    HDC hDC;
    int xPos, yPos;

    switch(message)
    {
        case WM_LBUTTONDOWN:
            hDC = GetDC(hWnd);
            xPos = LOWORD(lParam);
            yPos = HIWORD(lParam);
            TextOut(hDC, xPos, yPos, "Click", 5);
            ReleaseDC(hWnd, hDC);
            return 0;

        case WM_DESTROY:
            PostQuitMessage(0);
            return 0;
    }

    return DefWindowProc(hWnd, message, wParam, lParam);
}
```

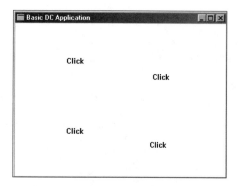

Figure 5-2: The BasicDCApp Windows application draws text in the window's client area.

If you like to do things the long way, you can create a client-area device context in an MFC program in almost exactly the same way that BasicDCApp does, by calling GetDC() and ReleaseDC(). For example, Listing 5-2 shows the MFC version of responding to the WM_LBUTTONDOWN message to draw the word "Click" in the window. This version of OnLButtonDown() creates a DC and draws to the screen with the same function calls that BasicDCApp did. The only difference is that OnLButtonDown() must call AfxGetMainWnd() to get a pointer to the MFC window object, which holds the window handle.

Listing 5-2: An `MFC` `OnLButtonDown()` **function that creates a client-area DC using standard Windows API calls**

```
void CClientDCAppView::OnLButtonDown(UINT nFlags,
    CPoint point)
{
    // TODO: Add your message handler code here
    //   and/or call default

    CWnd* pWnd = AfxGetMainWnd();
    HWND hWnd = pWnd->m_hWnd;
    HDC hDC = ::GetDC(hWnd);
    ::TextOut(hDC, point.x, point.y, "Click", 5);
    ::ReleaseDC(hWnd, hDC);

    CView::OnLButtonDown(nFlags, point);
}
```

MFC's `CClientDC` class makes handling client-area DCs much easier. You can create a local DC object without having to worry about calling `GetDC()` or `ReleaseDC()`. When you create the object, MFC calls `GetDC()` for you, and when the DC object goes out of scope, MFC automatically calls `ReleaseDC()` on behalf of the DC object. You just create the DC and use it. Listing 5-3 is a revised version of the `OnLButtonDown()` function that uses the MFC `CClientDC` class to create the client-area DC, rather than create the DC the standard Windows API way.

On CD-ROM

You can find the ClientDCApp application in the Chapter05\ClientDCApp folder of this book's CD-ROM. Figure 5-3 shows the running application. Just as with BasicDCApp, when the user clicks in the window, the word "Click" appears in the clicked location.

Listing 5-3: An MFC `OnLButtonDown()` **function that creates a** `CClientDC` **object**

```
void CClientDCAppView::OnLButtonDown(UINT nFlags,
    CPoint point)
{
    // TODO: Add your message handler code here
    //   and/or call default

    CClientDC clientDC(this);
    clientDC.TextOut(point.x, point.y, "Click");

    CView::OnLButtonDown(nFlags, point);
}
```

You create a `CClientDC` object by calling the class's constructor. You can create the DC object on the stack or on the heap (just as you can with most other MFC objects). Creating the DC object on the stack is easiest, because then you don't need to explicitly delete it; the system deletes the DC object when it goes out of scope. You create a `CClientDC` object on the stack like this:

```
CClientDC clientDC(this);
```

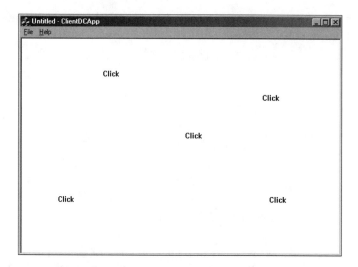

Figure 5-3: The MFC ClientDCApp application responds to clicks just as the BasicDCApp did.

The constructor's single argument is a pointer to the window with which the DC will be associated. The view class's `this` pointer fits the bill nicely.

You create the `CClientDC` object on the heap like this:

```
CClientDC* clientDC = new CClientDC(this);
```

You now have a pointer to the DC object. When you're finished with the object, you must delete it. This deletes the C++ object from memory, which forces the object's destructor to be called, which, in turn, causes `ReleaseDC()` to be called on behalf of the object. If you were to create a client-area DC in this way, the code in `OnLButtonDown()` might look like this:

```
CClientDC* clientDC = new CClientDC(this);
clientDC->TextOut(point.x, point.y, "Click");
delete clientDC;
```

The metafile device context

Although the third device context's name sounds fancy, a metafile is nothing more than a list of drawing commands. You use a metafile when you want to create a graphical object that can be redrawn again and again. For example, a drawing program might use metafiles to store the objects that make up the current drawing. By defining each object separately, the user can select the object to draw and place it anywhere on the screen. Most drawing programs even allow the user to select objects and move them around the screen.

You create a metafile DC in much the same way you create any other type of DC. The difference is that, when you call GDI functions to draw on the metafile DC, rather than appearing on the computer's screen, the DC stores the drawing commands in the metafile. You then later play the metafile back, which displays the drawing on the screen.

As you probably already suspect, Visual C++'s MFC library features a class that encapsulates the metafile DC object. This class, called CMetaFileDC, works a little differently than the other DC classes. To create and use the metafile DC, follow these steps:

1. Create an object of the CMetaFileDC class.

2. Call the CMetaFileDC object's Create() member function to create the device context.

3. Call the CMetaFileDC's drawing commands (inherited from CDC) to draw the image that will be stored in the metafile.

4. Call the CMetaFileDC's Close() member function, saving the metafile handle returned from the function.

5. Call the window's active DC's PlayMetaFile() function to draw the shape represented by it.

6. Call the Windows API function DeleteMetaFile() to delete the metafile when finished with the metafile.

On CD-ROM

In the Chapter05\MetafileDCApp folder of this book's CD-ROM, you can find the MetafileDCApp program, which demonstrates how to create and draw a metafile using MFC's CMetaFileDC class. When you run the program, you see a blank window. Click in the window, and the application draws the shape it created as a metafile, as shown in Figure 5-4.

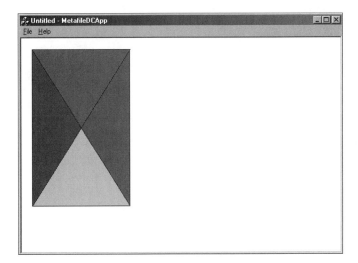

Figure 5-4: MetafileDCApp draws a shape that was stored in a metafile.

Now, take a look at the source code to see how the MetafileDCApp application works. The program creates its metafile in the OnCreate() member function of the view class. The OnCreate() function responds to the WM_CREATE message, which Windows sends to the application after the window has been created but before the window is displayed. In an MFC program, you can think of `OnCreate()` as a counterpart to the class's constructor. Whereas the constructor initializes data for the C++ class, `OnCreate()` is a good place to initialize data that requires the window element to have been created. Listing 5-4 shows the `OnCreate()` function.

Listing 5-4: The `OnCreate()` function

```
int CMetafileDCAppView::OnCreate
    (LPCREATESTRUCT lpCreateStruct)
{
    if (CView::OnCreate(lpCreateStruct) == -1)
        return -1;

    // TODO: Add your specialized creation code here

    CMetaFileDC metaFileDC;
    metaFileDC.Create(NULL);

    metaFileDC.Rectangle(20, 20, 200, 300);
    metaFileDC.MoveTo(20, 20);
    metaFileDC.LineTo(200, 300);
    metaFileDC.MoveTo(200, 20);
    metaFileDC.LineTo(20, 300);

    CBrush redBrush(RGB(255,0,0));
    CBrush* oldBrush =
        metaFileDC.SelectObject(&redBrush);
    metaFileDC.FloodFill(100, 50, RGB(0,0,0));

    CBrush greenBrush(RGB(0,255,0));
    metaFileDC.SelectObject(&greenBrush);
    metaFileDC.FloodFill(100, 250, RGB(0,0,0));

    CBrush blueBrush(RGB(0,0,255));
    metaFileDC.SelectObject(&blueBrush);
    metaFileDC.FloodFill(50, 150, RGB(0,0,0));

    CBrush purpleBrush(RGB(190,0,190));
    metaFileDC.SelectObject(&purpleBrush);
    metaFileDC.FloodFill(150, 150, RGB(0,0,0));

    metaFileDC.SelectObject(oldBrush);
    m_hMetaFile = metaFileDC.Close();

    return 0;
}
```

`OnCreate()` starts off by creating the metafile DC object:

```
CMetaFileDC metaFileDC;
metaFileDC.Create(NULL);
```

The `CMetaFileDC Create()` member function takes a single parameter, which is the file name where the metafile should be stored. If you provide `NULL` for this argument, MFC creates an in-memory metafile.

After creating the metafile DC, the program draws the shape on the DC. It starts by drawing a rectangle with lines connecting its corners:

```
metaFileDC.Rectangle(20, 20, 200, 300);
metaFileDC.MoveTo(20, 20);
metaFileDC.LineTo(200, 300);
metaFileDC.MoveTo(200, 20);
metaFileDC.LineTo(20, 300);
```

The `Rectangle()` method's arguments are the coordinates for the rectangle's upper-left corner and lower-right corner. The `MoveTo()` function positions the DC's pen at the given coordinates, and the `LineTo()` command draws a line from the pen's current position to the coordinates given as the function's arguments.

Note

`Rectangle()` and `LineTo()` are only two of the many DC functions you can use to draw shapes in a window's client area. You can also call `Draw3dRect()`, `Ellipse()`, `Arc()`, `Pie()`, `Polygon()`, `Polyline()`, `RoundRect()`, and other functions that the `CDC` class defines. Most of these functions are MFC versions of the Windows API functions of the same name.

The function then fills each triangle in the image with a color, starting with the top rectangle, which gets filled with red:

```
CBrush redBrush(RGB(255,0,0));
CBrush* oldBrush =
    metaFileDC.SelectObject(&redBrush);
metaFileDC.FloodFill(100, 50, RGB(0,0,0));
```

These lines create a new brush, select the brush into the DC, and then fill the rectangle section with the brush's color. You'll read about brushes a little later in this chapter. The FloodFill function takes three arguments: the coordinates at which to start filling and the color that acts as the fill's border. That is, the given color acts as a wall that contains the fill color. `OnCreate()` fills the other sections of the rectangle with color in the same way, but using brushes of a different color.

After the function completes the drawing, it restores the old brush to the DC and closes the metafile:

```
metaFileDC.SelectObject(oldBrush);
m_hMetaFile = metaFileDC.Close();
```

At this point, the program has a handle, stored in the m_hMetaFile data member, that it can use to access the metafile whenever it wants to draw the shape defined in the metafile. The program draws the shape in response to a user mouse click. This happens in the view class's `OnLButtonDown()` function, shown in Listing 5-5. `OnLButtonDown()` creates a client DC for the window and then call's the client DC's `PlayMetaFile()` function to draw the shape defined in the metafile. `PlayMetaFile()`'s single argument is the metafile's handle.

Listing 5-5: The `OnLButtonDown()` **function**

```
void CMetafileDCAppView::OnLButtonDown(UINT nFlags,
    CPoint point)
{
    // TODO: Add your message handler code here
    //    and/or call default

    CClientDC clientDC(this);
    clientDC.PlayMetaFile(m_hMetaFile);

    CView::OnLButtonDown(nFlags, point);
}
```

When the user quits the program, MFC calls the `OnDestroy()` function, which responds to the Windows message `WM_DESTROY`. Windows sends the `WM_DESTROY` message when the window has been removed from the screen and is about to be destroyed. `OnDestroy()` is the counterpart to `OnCreate()`. Just as `OnCreate()` acts as a constructor for a window element, `OnDestroy()` acts as the destructor. That is, whereas you do cleanup for the C++ object in the class's destructor, you do window cleanup in the `OnDestroy()` function. In the MetafileDCApp application, `OnDestroy()` looks like this:

```
void CMetafileDCAppView::OnDestroy()
{
    CView::OnDestroy();

    // TODO: Add your message handler code here

    ::DeleteMetaFile(m_hMetaFile);
}
```

Here, `OnDestroy()` calls the Windows API function `DeleteMetaFile()` to delete the metafile from memory. The function's single argument is the metafile's handle. If you specified a file name when you created the metafile, you may also want to delete the resultant file in `OnDestroy()`. You can do that by calling MFC's `Remove()` function, which is a static member of the `CFile` class:

```
CFile::Remove(pFileName);
```

`Remove()`'s single argument is the path and file name of the file to remove.

Device Capabilities

Now that you've taken a look at how a device context can represent any graphical device, you're ready to learn how to determine device capabilities. Most full-featured Windows programs wouldn't get too far if they weren't able to discover information about the devices on which they display data. For this reason, the Windows API includes a function called `GetDeviceCaps()` that can obtain most information you need to know about a device, whether it be a screen, a printer, or something else.

The `CDC` class, from which MFC derives all device context classes, defines its own version of `GetDeviceCaps()` as a member function of the class. Once you have a DC object, you can call `GetDeviceCaps()` to obtain whatever information you need about the display device. For example, if you want to get the resolution of the screen, you could do this:

```
CClientDC clientDC(this);
int horRes = clientDC.GetDeviceCaps(HORZRES);
int verRes = clientDC.GetDeviceCaps(VERTRES);
```

The `GetDeviceCaps()` function takes a single argument, which is the device capability that you want to obtain. Windows defines a set of constants that represent the available device capabilities. Table 5-2 lists these constants and their meaning. If you don't understand what some of the device capabilities mean, don't panic. You won't need to use most of them for a while. And by the time you need them, you'll know what they are!

Table 5-2   Some useful device capabilities

Constant	Description
ASPECTX	Relative width of a pixel
ASPECTXY	Diagonal width of a pixel
ASPECTY	Relative height of a pixel
BITSPIXEL	Number of color bits per pixel
CLIPCAPS	Device's clipping capabilities
COLORRES	Device's color resolution
HORZRES	Display width in pixels
HORZSIZE	Display width in millimeters
LOGPIXELSX	Number of horizontal pixels per inch
LOGPIXELSY	Number of vertical pixels per inch
NUMBRUSHES	Number of brushes
NUMCOLORS	Number of colors in the color table
NUMFONTS	Number of fonts
NUMPENS	Number of pens
NUMRESERVED	Number of reserved colors in the system palette
PLANES	Number of color planes
RASTERCAPS	Device's raster capabilities
SIZEPALETTE	Number of colors in the system palette
VERTRES	Display height in pixels
VERTSIZE	Display height in millimeters

On CD-ROM

In the DeviceCapsApp folder of this book's CD-ROM, you can find the DeviceCapsApp program, which displays some of the system's device capabilities by calling GetDeviceCaps(). When you run the program, you see seven capabilities listed in the window, as shown in Figure 5-5.

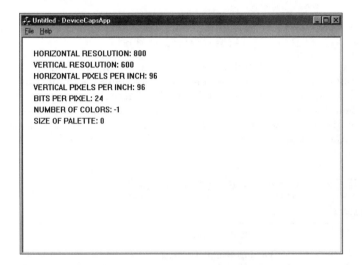

Figure 5-5: DeviceCapsApp displays capabilities for the current device.

In Figure 5-5, the application shows the device capabilities for a system that's set to 256 colors (8-bit color) and 800x600 resolution. The number of colors is shown as 20 because the Windows system reserves only 20 colors for its own use. In the shown configuration, an application that creates a palette should be able to display 256 colors. (When you run the program on a system set to True Color, you'll see -1 for the number of colors, because True Color displays don't use a color palette.) Listing 5-6 shows the code that creates DeviceCapsApp's display. The wsprintf() function is a Windows API function that works similarly to the C sprintf() function.

Listing 5-6: The DeviceCapsApp application's OnDraw() function

```
void CDeviceCapsAppView::OnDraw(CDC* pDC)
{
    CDeviceCapsAppDoc* pDoc = GetDocument();
    ASSERT_VALID(pDoc);

    // TODO: add draw code for native data here

    int horRes = pDC->GetDeviceCaps(HORZRES);
    int verRes = pDC->GetDeviceCaps(VERTRES);
    int logPixelsX = pDC->GetDeviceCaps(LOGPIXELSX);
    int logPixelsY = pDC->GetDeviceCaps(LOGPIXELSY);
    int bitsPixel = pDC->GetDeviceCaps(BITSPIXEL);
    int numColors = pDC->GetDeviceCaps(NUMCOLORS);
    int sizePalette = pDC->GetDeviceCaps(SIZEPALETTE);
```

```
            char s[81];
            wsprintf(s, "HORIZONTAL RESOLUTION: %d", horRes);
            pDC->TextOut(20, 20, s);
            wsprintf(s, "VERTICAL RESOLUTION: %d", verRes);
            pDC->TextOut(20, 40, s);
            wsprintf(s, "HORIZONTAL PIXELS PER INCH: %d",
                logPixelsX);
            pDC->TextOut(20, 60, s);
            wsprintf(s, "VERTICAL PIXELS PER INCH: %d",
                logPixelsY);
            pDC->TextOut(20, 80, s);
            wsprintf(s, "BITS PER PIXEL: %d", bitsPixel);
            pDC->TextOut(20, 100, s);
            wsprintf(s, "NUMBER OF COLORS: %d", numColors);
            pDC->TextOut(20, 120, s);
            wsprintf(s, "SIZE OF PALETTE: %d", sizePalette);
            pDC->TextOut(20, 140, s);
        }
```

The CPen Class

In order to enable your application to draw different types of lines, you create your own pens and select them into the DC. Pens are the most basic drawing tool that you use with a DC. They draw all lines in a display, including the lines that border shapes such as rectangles and circles. Once you've selected your pen into the DC, the DC automatically uses it for its line-drawing operations.

MFC's CPen class represents GDI pens. Creating a new pen is just a matter of calling the CPen class's constructor, whose signature looks like this:

```
CPen(int style, int width, COLORREF color);
```

The CPen constructor's arguments are as follows:

style   The pen's drawing style, which can be PS_SOLID, PS_DASH, PS_DOT, PS_DASHDOT, PS_DASHDOTDOT, PS_NULL, or PS_INSIDEFRAME. Most of these styles specify a pattern. The PS_NULL style is an invisible pen, and PS_INSIDEFRAME is a pen that draws shape borders within the shape, rather than outside of the shape.

width   The pen's width in pixels.

color   The pen's color as an RGB value.

On CD-ROM

In the PenApp folder of this book's CD-ROM, you can find the PenApp program, which demonstrates drawing with pens using MFC's CPen class. When you run the program, you see the window shown in Figure 5-6.

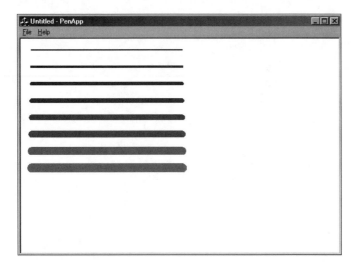

Figure 5-6: PenApp draws with pens of different sizes and colors.

All the drawing occurs in the view class's OnDraw() function. Listing 5-7 shows the OnDraw() function, which creates a different pen for each line displayed in the window. Within the for loop, the function creates a pen, selects the pen into the DC, draws a line, and then restores the old pen to the DC.

Restoring the old pen is important because, in each iteration of the loop, the newly created pen goes out of scope, causing the pen object to be deleted. You must never delete a pen that's selected into a DC. Selecting the old pen back into the DC before each loop iteration ends prevents the new pen from being deleted while it's still selected into the DC.

Listing 5-7: PenApp's OnDraw() function

```
void CPenAppView::OnDraw(CDC* pDC)
{
    CPenAppDoc* pDoc = GetDocument();
    ASSERT_VALID(pDoc);

    // TODO: add draw code for native data here

    int red = 0;
    int green = 0;
    int blue = 0;
    int width = 2;
    int row = 20;

    for (int x=0; x<8; ++x)
    {
```

```
        int color = RGB(red,green,blue);
        CPen newPen(PS_SOLID, width, color);
        CPen* oldPen = pDC->SelectObject(&newPen);
        pDC->MoveTo(20, row);
        pDC->LineTo(300, row);
        pDC->SelectObject(oldPen);

        red += 32;
        green += 16;
        blue += 8;
        width += 2;
        row += 30;
    }
}
```

On CD-ROM

If you'd like to see pen styles in action, check out the program in the Chapter05\PenApp2 folder of this book's CD-ROM. This program draws lines in the five different line styles shown in Figure 5-7. Listing 5-8, which is taken from PenApp2's source code, shows the view class's OnDraw() function, which works similarly to the previous version, except it changes pen drawing styles, rather than widths and color.

Listing 5-8: PenApp2's OnDraw() function

```
void CPenApp2View::OnDraw(CDC* pDC)
{
    CPenApp2Doc* pDoc = GetDocument();
    ASSERT_VALID(pDoc);

    // TODO: add draw code for native data here

    int styles[] =
        {PS_SOLID, PS_DASH, PS_DOT,
        PS_DASHDOT, PS_DASHDOTDOT};

    int row = 20;

    for (int x=0; x<5; ++x)
    {
        int color = RGB(0,0,0);
        CPen newPen(styles[x], 1, color);
        CPen* oldPen = pDC->SelectObject(&newPen);
        pDC->MoveTo(20, row);
        pDC->LineTo(300, row);
        pDC->SelectObject(oldPen);

        row += 30;
    }
}
```

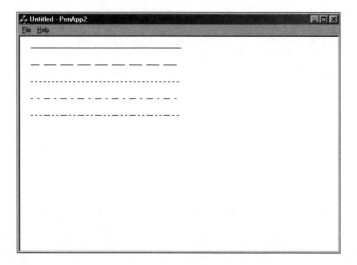

Figure 5-7: PenApp2 draws with different pen styles.

The CBrush Class

Whenever a program fills a shape with color, it uses the DC's current brush. A DC's default brush is white, which is why rectangles drawn in windows with white backgrounds don't look filled. If you were to draw two overlapping rectangles, as shown in Figure 5-8, however, you'd see that the rectangles aren't as empty as they appear; the fill color is indeed white.

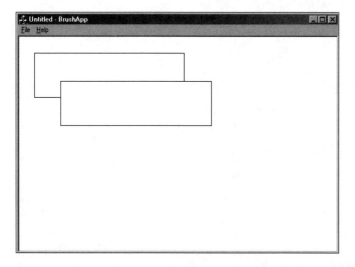

Figure 5-8: A DC's default brush is white, as shown by these overlapping rectangles.

Just as with pens, you can create your own brushes, and so control the way the DC draws and fills shapes. MFC features the `CBrush` class, which represents GDI brush objects. To create a new brush, you just call the class's constructor, whose signature looks like this:

```
CBrush(COLORREF color);
```

The constructor's single argument is the brush's color, specified as a `COLORREF` value. After creating the brush, you select it into the DC, after which all fill operations use the new brush. When you're finished with the brush, you reselect the old brush back into the DC.

On CD-ROM

In the BrushApp folder of this book's CD-ROM, you can find the BrushApp program, which demonstrates drawing with brushes using MFC's `CBrush` class. When you run the program, you see the window shown in Figure 5-9.

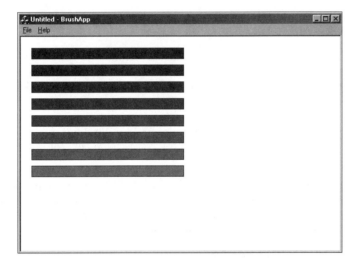

Figure 5-9: BrushApp draws with different brush colors.

Listing 5-9 shows BrushApp's `OnDraw()` function, which is where the application draws the filled rectangles in its display. Within the `for` loop, the function creates a brush, selects the brush into the DC, draws a rectangle, and then restores the old brush to the DC. As with the pens in PenApp and PenApp2, restoring the old brush is important because, in each iteration of the loop, the newly created brush goes out of scope, causing the brush object to be deleted.

Listing 5-9: BrushApp's `OnDraw()` function

```
void CBrushAppView::OnDraw(CDC* pDC)
{
    CBrushAppDoc* pDoc = GetDocument();
    ASSERT_VALID(pDoc);

    // TODO: add draw code for native data here
```

```
int red = 0;
int green = 0;
int blue = 0;
int row = 20;

for (int x=0; x<8; ++x)
{
    int color = RGB(red,green,blue);
    CBrush newBrush(color);
    CBrush* oldBrush = pDC->SelectObject(&newBrush);
    pDC->Rectangle(20, row, 300, row+20);
    pDC->SelectObject(oldBrush);

    red += 32;
    green += 16;
    blue += 8;
    row += 30;
}
}
```

Like many MFC classes, the CBrush class overloads its constructor, giving you several ways to create a brush. One constructor enables you to specify a fill pattern for your brush. That constructor's signature looks like this:

```
CBrush(int style, COLORREF color);
```

Here, style is one of the brush styles defined by Windows, which are HS_BDIAGONAL, HS_CROSS, HS_DIAGCROSS, HS_FDIAGONAL, HS_HORIZONTAL, and HS_VERTICAL.

On CD-ROM

In the PatternBrushApp folder of this book's CD-ROM, you can find the PatternBrushApp program, which demonstrates drawing with different brush styles. When you run the program, you see the window shown in Figure 5-10. Listing 5-10 is the revised OnDraw() function that creates the display.

Listing 5-10: PatternBrushApp's OnDraw() function

```
void CPatternBrushAppView::OnDraw(CDC* pDC)
{
    CPatternBrushAppDoc* pDoc = GetDocument();
    ASSERT_VALID(pDoc);

    // TODO: add draw code for native data here

    int styles[] = {HS_BDIAGONAL, HS_CROSS, HS_DIAGCROSS,
        HS_FDIAGONAL, HS_HORIZONTAL, HS_VERTICAL};
    int row = 20;

    for (int x=0; x<6; ++x)
    {
        CBrush newBrush(styles[x], RGB(255,0,0));
        CBrush* oldBrush = pDC->SelectObject(&newBrush);
        pDC->Rectangle(20, row, 300, row+30);
        pDC->SelectObject(oldBrush);
        row += 40;
    }
}
```

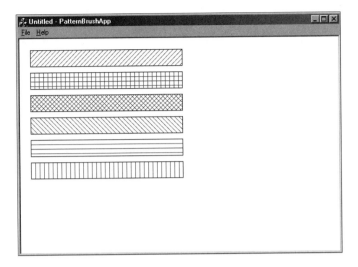

Figure 5-10: PatternBrushApp draws with different fill patterns.

 PROBLEMS & SOLUTIONS

Bitmapped Brushes

PROBLEM: *It's great that Windows enables me to choose from many types of pattern fills, but what if none of the standard fill patterns works for me? Can I create my own?*

SOLUTION: If you need to create a fill pattern for a brush, you can create a bitmap that holds the required pattern and use it as a brush. Although the process requires that you know a little something about bitmaps, you can easily modify the sample provided here for your own purposes. When you're ready to learn more about this subject, turn to Chapter 12, "Bitmaps."

First, you create a memory DC to hold the bitmap. A memory DC is like any other DC, except it remains hidden in memory and is never displayed on the screen. You can think of a memory DC as a buffer for holding off-screen graphics. To create a memory DC, you must already have a valid display DC. You then create the memory DC based on the settings in the display DC. The whole process looks like this:

```
CClientDC clientDC(this);
CDC memoryDC;
memoryDC.CreateCompatibleDC(&clientDC);
```

Here, an object of the CDC class represents the memory DC. The call to the object's CreateCompatibleDC() creates a device context with the same attributes as clientDC and attaches the DC to the memoryDC object.

Continued

Next, you create a bitmap object and select it into the memory DC:

```
CBitmap* pBitmap = new CBitmap();
pBitmap->CreateCompatibleBitmap(&memoryDC, 8, 8);
CBitmap* pOldBitmap =
    memoryDC.SelectObject(pBitmap);
```

The CBitmap object's CreateCompatibleBitmap() function creates a bitmap and attaches it to the CBitmap object. The function's three arguments are the DC with which the bitmap must be compatible, and the width and height of the bitmap. The smallest bitmap that can be used with a brush is 8x8 pixels, which is the size of the bitmap created here.

When you select the bitmap into the memory DC, the bitmap becomes the DC's drawing surface. All the drawing commands that you direct to the memory DC are rendered on the bitmap. Usually, the first thing you do is clear the bitmap to a single color:

```
CBrush whiteBrush(RGB(255,255,255));
memoryDC.FillRect(CRect(0,0,799,599),
    &whiteBrush);
```

Clearing the bitmap is important because, before you draw on it, the bitmap contains values that were in memory before the bitmap was created.

With the bitmap cleared, you can draw whatever pattern you like on its surface. When you've drawn the bitmap, use it to create a new brush and then select the brush into the display DC, like this:

```
CBrush brush(pBitmap);
CBrush* pOldBrush = clientDC.SelectObject(&brush);
```

Now, any shapes that use a brush will be filled with the pattern you created.

On CD-ROM

Check out the Chapter05\BitmapBrushApp folder of this book's CD-ROM. There, you can find the BitmapBrushApp application, which draws a rectangle filled with a custom brush pattern, as shown in Figure 5-11. Listing 5-11 shows the function that creates the display.

Listing 5-11: The BitmapBrushApp application's OnDraw() function

```
void CBitmapBrushAppView::OnDraw(CDC* pDC)
{
    CBitmapBrushAppDoc* pDoc = GetDocument();
    ASSERT_VALID(pDoc);

    // TODO: add draw code for native data here

    CDC memoryDC;
    memoryDC.CreateCompatibleDC(pDC);

    CBitmap* pBitmap = new CBitmap();
    pBitmap->CreateCompatibleBitmap(&memoryDC, 8, 8);
    CBitmap* pOldBitmap =
        memoryDC.SelectObject(pBitmap);

    CBrush whiteBrush(RGB(255,255,255));
    memoryDC.FillRect(CRect(0,0,799,599),
        &whiteBrush);
```

Continued

```
        memoryDC.Rectangle(2, 2, 6, 6);
        CBrush brush(pBitmap);
        CBrush* pOldBrush = pDC->SelectObject(&brush);
        pDC->Rectangle(20, 20, 200, 200);

        pDC->SelectObject(pOldBrush);
        memoryDC.SelectObject(pOldBitmap);
}
```

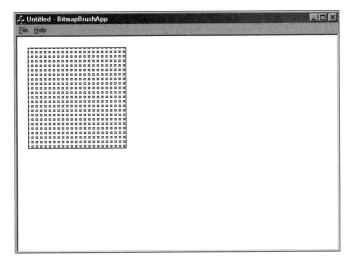

Figure 5-11: The BitmapBrushApp application displays a rectangle filled with a custom brush.

Summary

Device contexts are important to all Windows programmers because without them no application can display data in its window. By calling the many GDI functions, an application can draw anything from a simple line of text to commercial-quality images. Customizable GDI objects, such as pens and brushes, enable you to fine-tune the DC's attributes in order to create the exact graphics you need.

Also discussed in this chapter:

▶ The GDI is a huge library of graphics functions.

▶ A device context represents the attributes for a display device.

▶ Every DC is associated with a set of GDI objects, including a pen, a brush, and a font.

▶ A paint DC enables an application to update a window in response to a `WM_PAINT` message.

▶ A client DC enables an application to draw in a window's client area.

▶ A metafile DC enables an application to store drawing commands that the application can play back later.

▶ A GDI pen can have a pattern, a width, and a color.

▶ A GDI brush can fill shapes with a solid color or with patterns.

Chapter 6

Windows and Dialogs

In This Chapter

▶ Exploring the MFC window classes

▶ Using frame and view windows

▶ Creating a basic window without AppWizard

▶ Understanding window styles

▶ Understanding multiple-document interface application windows

▶ Creating custom and common dialog boxes

▶ Using property sheets

▶ Creating and adding wizards to a program

If there's one thing the Windows platform has it's plenty of windows. There are application windows, pop-up windows, wizard windows, dialog box windows, message box windows, SDI windows, MDI windows, property sheet windows and ... well ... you get the point. Let's just say that Windows definitely comes by its name well. The truth is that Windows is filled with objects—such as buttons, list boxes, and toolbars—that don't even look like windows but are, in fact, just other types of windows.

And just in case you feel you don't have enough windows to work with, Visual C++ and its MFC library break the window types down into even more categories, including frame, view, edit, MDI frame, MDI child, OLE, splitter, and database form windows, just to name a few. MFC also features classes for dialog boxes, property sheets, wizards, toolbars, status bars, and more, all of which are classes that represent—you guessed it—windows.

In its simplest form, a window is just a rectangular area on the screen that usually represents a running process. The window often displays, and enables the user to edit, whatever types of data are native to the application.

Of course, nothing is ever that simple. These days, windows also sport controls, menu bars, toolbars, status bars, and other adornments that users have come to expect and that programmers must supply. (For basic information on windows, please refer to Chapter 1, "A Windows 98 Overview.")

Windows are also the objects to which Windows 98 sends messages. An application can have a main window and several child windows, with specific messages being routed to each window. In fact, even controls in a window can and do receive messages; controls are, after all, windows themselves. Because Windows' messages enable the interactivity between a user and an application, it's clear that windows are the engines that drive all applications.

MFC applications, however, handle Windows messages much differently than straight C applications do. If you'd like to see the difference, refer back to Chapter 4, "Application Fundamentals," which demonstrates programming Windows 98 in C versus programming Windows 98 with MFC. In that chapter, you can see the difference between C and MFC message handling. However, although MFC programs seem to handle messages differently, way down in the innards of the MFC libraries, it's business as usual, with the application frameworks receiving and responding to messages at the same level C programs do.

In this chapter, because C Windows programming is falling out of fashion, you examine window objects from the MFC point of view. Along the way, you learn the relationship between frame and view windows, as well as get some experience with multiple-document-interface (MDI) windows. Dialog boxes, property sheets, and wizards are also introduced here.

The MFC Window Base Classes

As you've probably figured out by now, MFC represents a complicated hierarchy of classes. Most classes that you use in your Visual C++ programs have a long ancestry, and the window classes are no exception. A frame window, for example, traces its ancestry from `CFrameWnd` back through `CWnd` to `CCmdTarget` and finally to `CObject`. Each one of these base classes provides important functionality to the window, as you learn in the following sections.

The `CObject` class

The granddaddy of almost all MFC classes, `CObject` provides support for serialization (object persistence), debugging information, and run-time class information. The only MFC classes that can't trace their ancestry back to `CObject` are support classes like the value-type classes (`CPoint`, `CRect`, `CSize`, `CString`, `CTime`, and `CTimeSpan`) and Internet server classes (`CHtmlStream`, `CHttpFilter`, `CHttpFilterContext`, `CHttpServer`, and `CHttpServerContext`), as well as various other support classes and wrapper classes. The `CObject` member functions and their descriptions are listed below:

`AssertValid()`	Checks the validity of the object
`Dump()`	Prints the contents of the object
`IsKindOf()`	Compares the object to a given class
`IsSerializable( )`	Returns a nonzero value if the object can be serialized
`Serialize()`	Serializes (saves or loads) the object

Three of the `CObject` member functions—`AssertValid()`, `Dump()`, and `Serialize()`—must be overridden in your custom class in order to be useful.

The `CCmdTarget` class

`CCmdTarget` is the class that gives other MFC classes the ability to implement message maps in order to respond to Windows messages. Any MFC class that processes messages—including windows, dialog boxes, control bars, and controls—has `CCmdTarget` in its ancestry. Most of `CCmdTarget`'s functionality can be included in your MFC program with little additional effort on your part. In fact, the class has only a few member functions, the most useful of which are listed below:

`BeginWaitCursor( )`	Displays the hourglass cursor
`EnableAutomation( );`	Enables OLE automation for the object
`EndWaitCursor( )`	Changes the hourglass cursor back to the arrow
`RestoreWaitCursor( )`	Restores the hourglass cursor after another object, such as a dialog box, has changed the cursor to an arrow

The `CWnd` class

All window classes—including frame windows, control bars, dialog boxes, views, property sheets, and controls—have `CWnd` in their ancestry. This immense class is what makes a window a window, by providing member functions that enable a program to manipulate a window in various ways.

Your programs can create windows directly from the `CWnd` class, but more often they'll derive custom windows from one of the more specific window classes, such as `CFrameWnd` or `CMDIFrameWnd`. Table 6-1 lists some of the most useful `CWnd` member functions.

Table 6-1   Some useful `CWnd` member functions

Function	*Description*
`CenterWindow()`	Centers a window within its parent window
`Create()`	Creates a child window
`DestroyWindow()`	Destroys the window element
`EnableWindow()`	Enables or disables the window's mouse and keyboard input
`GetActiveWindow()`	Gets a pointer to the active window

(continued)

Table 6-1   *(Continued)*

Function	Description
GetCapture()	Retrieves a pointer to the window that has captured the mouse
GetClientRect()	Gets the dimensions of the window's client area
GetDlgItem()	Gets a pointer to a dialog box control
GetFocus()	Gets a pointer to the window that has the input focus
GetFont()	Gets a pointer to the window's font
GetIcon()	Gets the handle to the window's icon
GetMenu()	Gets a pointer to a menu
GetParent()	Gets a pointer to the window's parent window
GetParentFrame()	Gets a pointer to the window's parent frame window
GetParentOwner()	Gets a pointer to a child window's parent window
GetSafeHwnd()	Returns a window's handle
GetStyle()	Gets the window's style
GetSystemMenu()	Gets a pointer to the window's system menu
GetWindowRect()	Gets the window's screen coordinates
GetWindowText()	Gets the window's caption text
Invalidate()	Invalidates a window's entire client area
InvalidateRect()	Invalidates a rectangle within a window's client area
IsIconic()	Returns TRUE if the window is minimized
IsWindowEnabled()	Returns TRUE if the window can receive mouse and keyboard input
IsWindowVisible()	Returns TRUE if the window is visible
IsZoomed()	Returns TRUE if the window is maximized
KillTimer()	Kills a system timer
MessageBox()	Displays a message box
ModifyStyle()	Changes the window's style
MoveWindow()	Changes the window's position and dimensions
OpenClipboard()	Opens the Clipboard
PostMessage()	Sends a message to a window and returns immediately, without waiting for the message to be processed
PreCreateWindow()	Enables programs to change a window's style before the window is displayed
SendMessage()	Sends a message to a window, returning only after the window has processed the message

Function	Description
SetActiveWindow()	Activates a window
SetCapture()	Forces all mouse messages to be sent to the window
SetFocus()	Gives the window the input focus
SetFont()	Sets the window's font
SetIcon()	Sets the window's icon
SetMenu()	Sets the window's menu
SetTimer()	Starts a system timer
SetWindowText()	Sets the window's caption text
ShowWindow()	Shows or hides the window
UpdateData()	Transfers data to and from a dialog box

The functions listed in Table 6-1 are only a small sampling of what's available in the CWnd class and are intended to give you some idea of how much power the class gives you over window elements. When you become more familiar with Visual C++ and MFC, you'll probably want to examine the window classes more closely, which you can do by looking up the classes in your Visual C++ online documentation.

Tip

To quickly locate information about an MFC class, place the text cursor on the class name in the source code window and press F1.

Most conspicuously absent from Table 6-1 are the message-response functions that the CWnd class defines for standard Windows message. These functions are definitely useful, but are so numerous that they'd make the table too big. Just know that the CWnd class defines the functions that enable MFC windows to respond to Windows messages. These functions include OnLButtonDown() (which responds to WM_LBUTTONDOWN), OnCreate() (which responds to WM_CREATE), OnDestroy() (which responds to WM_DESTROY), OnChar() (which responds to WM_CHAR), and dozens of others.

Frame and View Windows

Now that you've explored MFC's base window classes, you're ready to learn about the many types of windows you can create in your programs. If you worked through Chapter 3, "Programming with Visual C++," you already have some experience with frame and view windows. A frame window, which is represented by MFC's CFrameWnd window class, is an application's main window, which is the window that contains the title bar, window controls, and menu bar. When programming a straight C Windows application, the main window also holds the area in which the application displays its document data. This document-display portion of the window is called the *client area*.

With MFC, however, the application framework separates a document from the way the user views the document. This document/view architecture relies upon three main objects: the document, frame window, and view window. (For more information on the document/view architecture, please refer to Chapter 17, "File Handling.") The frame window is much like the main window in a C Windows program. However, rather than drawing the document's data directly on the frame window's client area, the frame window's client area contains a view window.

The view window has no title bar, controls, or even a border. It's basically an invisible window that positions itself exactly over the frame window's client area. An MFC application then displays its document in the view window's client area, rather than in the frame window's client area.

This is a powerful programming technique because you can quickly change the way the user views and edits a document—just switch to a new view window. A document can be associated with any number of view windows.

Note

Not all MFC applications implement the document/view architecture. If you were to write an MFC program from scratch (that is, without using AppWizard to generate a skeleton application), you could create a frame window that displays data directly in its client area. However, if you use AppWizard to start a program, the resultant application always uses the document/view architecture.

The CFrameWnd class

As previously discussed, an MFC application's main window is represented by the CFrameWnd class, which the framework derives from CWnd. CFrameWnd has a rich ancestry, inheriting member variables and functions from CObject, CCmdTarget, and CWnd. In addition, CFrameWnd adds its own set of member functions, the most useful of which are listed in Table 6-2.

Table 6-2   The most useful CFrameWnd member functions

Function	Description
ActivateFrame()	Makes the window visible and available
Create()	Creates the Windows window associated with the CFrameWnd object
DockControlBar()	Docks a control bar
EnableDocking()	Enables control bar docking
FloatControlBar()	Floats a control bar
GetActiveDocument()	Gets a pointer to the document object
GetActiveFrame()	Gets a pointer to the active CFrameWnd object
GetActiveView()	Gets a pointer to the active view object

Function	Description
GetControlBar()	Gets a pointer to the toolbar
GetDockState()	Gets a frame window's dock state
GetMessageBar()	Gets a pointer to a frame window's status bar
LoadAccelTable()	Loads an accelerator table
LoadBarState()	Restores toolbar settings
SaveBarState()	Saves toolbar settings
SetActiveView()	Sets the active view object
SetMessageText()	Sets the status bar's text
ShowControlBar()	Shows the toolbar

The CView class

The CView class represents a document view in an MFC program. A document can have multiple views, but a view can be associated with only a single document. MFC programs implementing the document/viewing architecture always derive a custom view class from the CView base class, which then overrides member functions in the CView class, providing the functionality needed by the view object. Table 6-3 lists important CView member functions.

Table 6-3   The most useful CView member functions

Function	Description
DoPreparePrinting()	Displays the Print dialog box and creates a printer device context
GetDocument()	Gets a pointer to the document associated with the view
OnActivateFrame()	Called by MFC when the view's frame window becomes activated or deactivated
OnActivateView()	Called by MFC when a view is activated
OnBeginPrinting()	Called by MFC when printing begins
OnDraw()	Called by MFC to draw the document in the view window or on the printer
OnEndPrinting()	Called by MFC when printing ends
OnEndPrintPreview()	Called by MFC when preview mode is closed
OnInitialUpdate()	Called by MFC after a view is associated with its document
OnPrepareDC()	Called by MFC before OnDraw() renders the document or before OnPrint() starts printing or print preview

(continued)

Table 6-3   (Continued)

Function	Description
OnPreparePrinting()	Called by MFC to give a view window the chance to set up the Print dialog box
OnPrint()	Called by MFC in order to print one page of the document
OnUpdate()	Called by MFC when the associated document has been modified

All the entries in Table 6-3 whose descriptions begin with "Called by MFC" are functions that you can override in your own view class in order to implement some extra functionality in the class. For example, you almost always override OnDraw() in order to display the application's current document in the view window. The CView base class's OnDraw() does nothing on its own.

Some of the base class functions do, however, perform a useful service for your view class, even if you don't override the function in your class. OnUpdate(), for example, makes sure that the view window gets updated whenever the document changes. You can, however, override OnUpdate() to perform additional tasks before the view window gets updated.

Window Basics: Creating an Application Without AppWizard

One of the big problems with AppWizard is that it creates such sophisticated source code that it obscures much of what happens behind the scenes in an MFC program. To understand MFC window basics, you really need to see an MFC application that leaves out all the fancy stuff and performs the basic functions, which are creating a window and responding to Windows messages.

Creating the BasicApp application

On CD-ROM

Although most programmers don't bother, you can easily create a basic MFC application without cranking up AppWizard. The source code for such an application reveals much about the ways MFC windows perform. Listing 6-1 shows the source code for BasicApp, which is this type of MFC application. To create a project for this application, as well as to compile and link the application, complete the following steps:

1. From Visual C++'s File menu, select the New command (see Figure 6-1). The New dialog box appears.

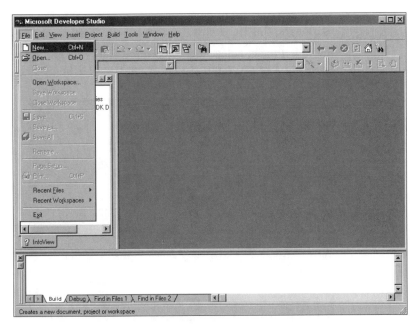

Figure 6-1: To start a new project, select New from the File menu.

2. In the left pane, select the Win32 Application project type, type
   BasicApp into the Project Name box, and select the destination
   directory in the Location box, as shown in Figure 6-2.

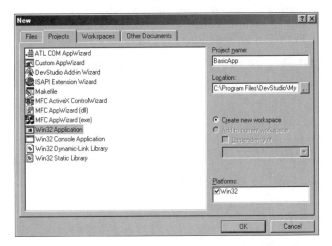

Figure 6-2: The New dialog box is displayed with the new
project's parameters.

3. Click OK in the New dialog box, and Visual C++ creates and opens the
   new project.

4. Select the File menu's New command a second time. The New dialog box reappears, this time with the Files tab selected.

5. In the left pane, select the C++ Source File type, and in the File Name box, type **BasicApp.cpp**, as shown in Figure 6-3.

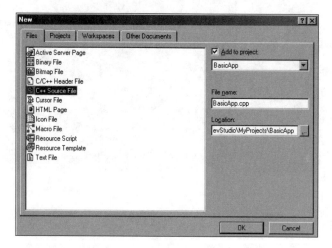

Figure 6-3: The New dialog box is displayed with parameters to add a source code file to the project.

6. Make sure the Add to Project checkbox is selected, and click OK. Visual C++ creates the new file and displays it in the text editor.

On CD-ROM

7. Type Listing 6-1 into the new source code window, or copy the source code into the window from this book's CD-ROM. (You can find the source code in the Chapter06\BasicApp directory.)

Listing 6-1: Source code for the BasicApp application

```
// Header file for all MFC classes.
#include <afxwin.h>

/////////////////////////////////////////
// Application class's declaration.
/////////////////////////////////////////

class CBasicApp : public CWinApp
{
public:
    CBasicApp();
    ~CBasicApp();
    BOOL InitInstance();
};

/////////////////////////////////////////
// Frame window class's declaration.
/////////////////////////////////////////
```

```cpp
class CSimpleFrame : public CFrameWnd
{
public:
    CSimpleFrame();
    ~CSimpleFrame();

    afx_msg void OnLButtonDown(UINT nFlags, CPoint point);

    DECLARE_MESSAGE_MAP()
};

/////////////////////////////////////////
// Application class's implementation.
/////////////////////////////////////////

// Global application object.
CBasicApp app;

CBasicApp::CBasicApp()
{
}

CBasicApp::~CBasicApp()
{
}

CBasicApp::InitInstance()
{
    m_pMainWnd = new CSimpleFrame();
    m_pMainWnd->ShowWindow(m_nCmdShow);

    return TRUE;
}

/////////////////////////////////////////
// Frame window class's implementation.
/////////////////////////////////////////

BEGIN_MESSAGE_MAP(CSimpleFrame, CFrameWnd)
    ON_WM_LBUTTONDOWN()
END_MESSAGE_MAP()

CSimpleFrame::CSimpleFrame()
{
    Create(NULL, "Basic MFC Application");
}

CSimpleFrame::~CSimpleFrame()
{
}

void CSimpleFrame::OnLButtonDown(UINT nFlags,
    CPoint point)
{
    CClientDC clientDC(this);
    clientDC.TextOut(20, 20, "Hello from BasicApp!");
}
```

8. Select the Project menu's Settings command (see Figure 6-4). The Project Settings property sheet appears.

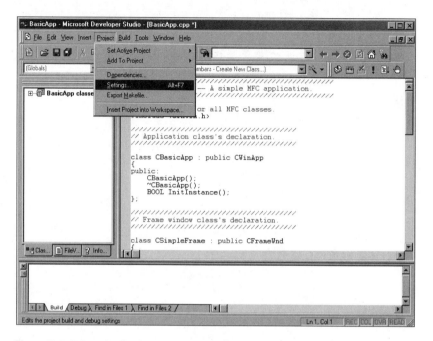

Figure 6-4: Select the Settings command from the Project menu to display the Project Settings property sheet.

9. In the Settings For box, select All Configurations, and in the Microsoft Foundation Classes box, select Using MFC in a Static Library, as shown in Figure 6-5. Click OK to finalize your choices.

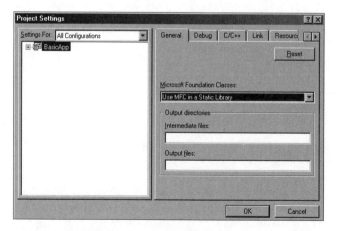

Figure 6-5: Here's the Project Settings property sheet, specifying that the project should use the static MFC library.

10. Click the Build button on the toolbar, or press F7, to compile and link your new application.

When you run BasicApp, you'll see a fairly plain frame window. This window has the basic window controls, but no extra adornments, such as a menu bar, toolbar, or status bar. Still, it's a fully functioning window that can respond to Windows messages. To prove this, click inside the window's client area. When you do, the message "Hello from BasicApp!" appears in the upper-left corner, as shown in Figure 6-6.

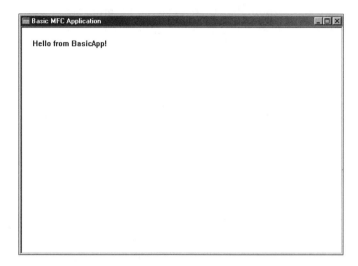

Figure 6-6: BasicApp responding to a mouse click

Understanding the BasicApp application

If you read Chapter 3, "Programming with Visual C++," you already know enough MFC to figure out Listing 6-1. In this section, you get a little review on how MFC works by looking at the application you just created, as well as touch on a few additional subjects.

The afxwin.h header file

First, BasicApp's source code includes the afxwin.h header file, like this:

```
#include <afxwin.h>
```

The afxwin.h file includes in your program all the header files for the many MFC classes. Any program that uses MFC must include this header file.

The application class

As you probably know by now, every MFC program must have an application object derived from CWinApp. In the BasicApp application, the application class is called CBasicApp and includes a constructor and a destructor. The class also overrides CWinApp's InitInstance(), which is where the application creates its main window. The class's declaration looks like this:

```
class CBasicApp : public CWinApp
{
public:
    CBasicApp();
    ~CBasicApp();
    BOOL InitInstance();
};
```

Because the application object must exist at program startup and because it must continue to exist while the application is running, every MFC program creates a global application object from its application class:

```
CBasicApp app;
```

As the MFC application starts up, MFC calls the application object's InitInstance() member function. In CBasicApp, you've overridden InitInstance() in order to create the application's frame window:

```
CBasicApp::InitInstance()
{
    m_pMainWnd = new CSimpleFrame();
    m_pMainWnd->ShowWindow(m_nCmdShow);

    return TRUE;
}
```

The application class has a data member called m_pMainWnd that holds a pointer to the application's frame window. In InitInstance(), CBasicApp creates a CSimpleFrame frame window object and assigns its pointer to m_pMainWnd. CSimpleFrame is the application's frame window class, which, as you soon see, is derived from MFC's CFrameWnd.

The application class also inherits the m_nCmdShow data member from CWinApp. This variable contains the flags that are normally passed to a Windows application's WinMain() function. This value determines how the window initially appears, and is usually set to SW_SHOW. (For more information, please refer to Chapter 4, "Application Fundamentals.") CBasicApp's InitInstance() passes this value to the frame window when it calls the frame window's ShowWindow() member function, which displays the window on the screen.

The frame window class

BasicApp's frame window class, CSimpleFrame, represents the application's main window and is derived from MFC's CFrameWnd. The class includes a constructor and a destructor, as well as the OnLButtonDown() message-response function. The class also declares a message map, as you can see in the class's declaration:

```
class CSimpleFrame : public CFrameWnd
{
public:
    CSimpleFrame();
```

```
    ~CSimpleFrame();

    afx_msg void OnLButtonDown(UINT nFlags,
        CPoint point);

    DECLARE_MESSAGE_MAP()
};
```

There's not much to say about CSimpleFrame's declaration that hasn't already been covered in this book. For information on message maps and message-response functions, please refer back to Chapter 4, "Application Fundamentals."

In the frame window's implementation, the class first defines its message map:

```
BEGIN_MESSAGE_MAP(CSimpleFrame, CFrameWnd)
    ON_WM_LBUTTONDOWN()
END_MESSAGE_MAP()
```

You can immediately tell from the message map that this window handles only the WM_LBUTTONDOWN Windows message.

In the constructor, the class calls Create() for the window:

```
CSimpleFrame::CSimpleFrame()
{
    Create(NULL, "Basic MFC Application");
}
```

The Create() member function creates the actual Windows window and attaches it to the MFC window class. If you don't call Create(), you will have no window to display. Although the call to Create() in the class's constructor has only two arguments, Create() actually takes eight arguments, all of which—except the first two—have default values. Create()'s signature looks like this:

```
BOOL Create(
    LPCTSTR lpszClassName,
    LPCTSTR lpszWindowName,
    DWORD dwStyle = WS_OVERLAPPEDWINDOW,
    const RECT& rect = rectDefault,
    CWnd* pParentWnd = NULL,
    LPCTSTR lpszMenuName = NULL,
    DWORD dwExStyle = 0,
    CCreateContext* pContext = NULL);
```

The function's arguments are listed in Table 6-4.

Table 6-4 `Create()` member function arguments	
Argument	**Description**
`lpszClassName`	The window class's name; or `NULL`, to accept `CFrameWnd`'s default class name
`lpszWindowName`	The text for the window's title bar
`dwStyle`	The window's style flags
`rect`	The size and position of the window
`pParentWnd`	The window's parent window, or `NULL` if there is no parent window
`lpszMenuName`	The name of the window's menu resource
`dwExStyle`	The window's extended styles
`pContext`	A pointer to a `CCreateContext` structure or `NULL`

The only other function of interest is `OnLButtonDown()`, which responds to the Windows message `WM_ONLBUTTONDOWN`:

```
void CSimpleFrame::OnLButtonDown(UINT nFlags,
    CPoint point)
{
    CClientDC clientDC(this);
    clientDC.TextOut(20, 20, "Hello from BasicApp!");
}
```

This function first creates a device context object for the window's client area and then displays the text "Hello from BasicApp!" in the window. Simply put, a device context is a set of attributes that the window needs in order to draw on the screen. If you would like more information on device contexts, check out Chapter 5, "Graphics Device Interface Basics."

Window Styles

You've now seen how to create an application that displays a basic window. What you haven't seen is how a window's style settings affect what you see on the screen. If every application window looked and acted exactly the same, what a boring world it would be (at least for those of us with IBM-compatible computers). Luckily, when Microsoft designed Windows, they knew that programmers would want to be able to control the way their windows look and act. To accommodate this desire, Windows defines a set of window styles that allow a window to be anything from an invisible rectangle to a full frame window.

These window styles are represented by a set of constants that you can combine in various ways to create the style of window you need for your application. Table 6-5 lists the window styles defined by Windows. As you can see, there are a lot of choices, making the creation of a window style as much an art as a science.

Table 6-5   Window style constants

Constant	Description
WS_BORDER	Creates a window with a border
WS_CAPTION	Creates a window with a title bar
WS_CHILD	Creates a child window
WS_CLIPCHILDREN	Prevents child windows from being drawn over when the application draws in the parent window's client area
WS_CLIPSIBLINGS	Prevents child windows from being drawn over when the application draws inside a child window that's overlapped by other child windows
WS_DISABLED	Creates a disabled window
WS_DLGFRAME	Creates a window with a double border and no title
WS_GROUP	Specifies the first control of a control group
WS_HSCROLL	Creates a window with a horizontal scroll bar
WS_MAXIMIZE	Creates a maximized window
WS_MAXIMIZEBOX	Creates a window with a Maximize button
WS_MINIMIZE	Creates a minimized window
WS_MINIMIZEBOX	Creates a window with a Minimize button
WS_OVERLAPPED	Creates a window with a caption and a border
WS_OVERLAPPEDWINDOW	Combines the WS_OVERLAPPED, WS_CAPTION, WS_SYSMENU, WS_THICKFRAME, WS_MINIMIZEBOX, and WS_MAXIMIZEBOX styles
WS_POPUP	Creates a pop-up window
WS_POPUPWINDOW	Combines the WS_BORDER, WS_POPUP, and WS_SYSMENU styles
WS_SYSMENU	Creates a window with a control menu
WS_TABSTOP	Specifies a control that can be selected with the Tab key
WS_THICKFRAME	Creates a window with a sizing frame
WS_VISIBLE	Creates a visible window
WS_VSCROLL	Creates a window with a vertical scroll bar

If you've read over Table 6-5, you can see that not all the styles apply to all types of windows. In fact, some of the window styles apply only to certain types of windows, including dialog boxes and controls. Moreover, while you can combine many styles, as WS_OVERLAPPEDWINDOW does, not all styles get along. For example, you can't have a system menu on a window that has no title bar. The title bar is, after all, where the system menu goes.

If you were programming Windows applications in straight C—that is, without the help of a sophisticated applications framework like MFC—you'd have a lot of flexibility in the type of windows your application creates. MFC, however, predetermines the basic look of a window, leaving you with only a few acceptable style modifications.

This makes sense when you think about it. The CFrameWnd class, for example, creates a frame window. In order to be a frame window, the window requires certain characteristics. MFC enables you to do things like remove the Minimize and Maximize buttons, but it won't let you remove the title bar.

Changing window styles

In an MFC program, you can change a window's style in the frame window class's PreCreateWindow() function, which MFC calls just before creating the window. To do this, override PreCreateWindow() in the class you derive from CFrameWnd. For example, in the BasicApp application that you created in the previous section, you could add a PreCreateWindow() function that changes the window's style, as well as sizes and positions the window. Listing 6-2 shows just such a PreCreateWindow() function. Figure 6-7 shows the resultant window.

Listing 6-2: The PreCreateWindow() function

```
BOOL CSimpleFrame::PreCreateWindow(CREATESTRUCT& cs)
{
    // Set window's size.
    cs.cx = 500;
    cs.cy = 400;

    // Set window's position.
    cs.x = 100;
    cs.y = 50;

    // Set window's style.
    cs.style = WS_OVERLAPPED | WS_SYSMENU;

    return CFrameWnd::PreCreateWindow(cs);
}
```

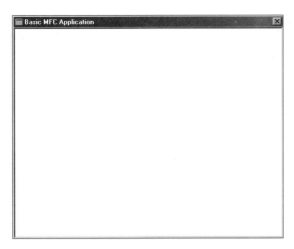

Figure 6-7: The BasicApp window displayed after a style change—notice that the window's Minimize and Maximize buttons have been removed.

The `PreCreateWindow()` has a single parameter, which is a reference to a `CREATESTRUCT` structure. This structure contains information that Windows needs in order to create the window. The structure is defined by Windows as shown in Listing 6-3:

Listing 6-3: The `CREATESTRUCT` structure

```
typedef struct tagCREATESTRUCT {
    LPVOID      lpCreateParams;
    HANDLE      hInstance;
    HMENU       hMenu;
    HWND        hwndParent;
    int         cy;
    int         cx;
    int         y;
    int         x;
    LONG        style;
    LPCSTR      lpszName;
    LPCSTR      lpszClass;
    DWORD       dwExStyle;
} CREATESTRUCT;
```

The window's style is in the structure's `style` member, but you can manipulate many of the `CREATESTRUCT` members in order to change the way the window looks. For example, the previous `PreCreateWindow()` example sets the window's size and position by changing the values in the `cy`, `cx`, `x`, and `y` members, respectively. The `PreCreateWindow()` example also sets the window's style to `WS_OVERLAPPED | WS_SYSMENU`.

Because the `WS_MINIMIZEBOX` and `WS_MAXIMIZEBOX` styles aren't included, the resultant window has no Minimize, Maximize, or Restore buttons. Similarly, because the `WS_THICKFRAME` style is missing, the window has no sizing border and so can't be resized by the user. Even the system menu reflects these changes, as shown in Figure 6-8. Notice how the Restore, Size, Minimize, and Maximize commands are all disabled in the system menu.

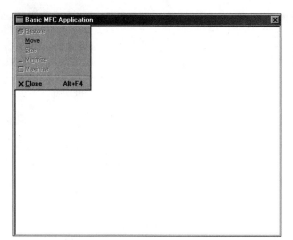

Figure 6-8: The application's system menu after its Restore, Size, Minimize, and Maximize commands have been disabled

Window styles in non-MFC programs

As I mentioned previously, MFC must insist that certain window styles be present in order to create windows associated with classes like CFrameWnd. Setting inappropriate window styles for these types of windows may lead to unpredictable behavior. However, if you really want to mess with windows styles, write a C windows program, leaving MFC out of the picture completely.

Listing 6-4, for example, shows the source code for BasicApp2, a C Windows application whose window has only the style WS_POPUP. You can find BasicApp2 in the Chapter06\BasicApp2 folder of the book's CD-ROM.

Listing 6-4: Source code for the BasicApp2 application

```
#include <windows.h>

LRESULT CALLBACK WndProc(HWND hWnd, UINT message,
    WPARAM wParam, LPARAM lParam);

int WINAPI WinMain(HINSTANCE hCurrentInst,
    HINSTANCE hPrevInstance, PSTR lpszCmdLine,
    int nCmdShow)
{
    WNDCLASS wndClass;
    HWND hWnd;
    MSG msg;
    UINT width;
    UINT height;

    wndClass.style = CS_HREDRAW | CS_VREDRAW;
    wndClass.lpfnWndProc = WndProc;
    wndClass.cbClsExtra = 0;
    wndClass.cbWndExtra = 0;
    wndClass.hInstance = hCurrentInst;
    wndClass.hIcon = LoadIcon(NULL, IDI_APPLICATION);
    wndClass.hCursor = LoadCursor(NULL, IDC_ARROW);
```

```
wndClass.hbrBackground = GetStockObject(WHITE_BRUSH);
wndClass.lpszMenuName = NULL;
wndClass.lpszClassName = "BasicApp2";

RegisterClass(&wndClass);

width = GetSystemMetrics(SM_CXSCREEN) / 2;
height = GetSystemMetrics(SM_CYSCREEN) / 2;

hWnd = CreateWindow(
    "BasicApp2",          /* Window class's name.     */
    "Basic Application", /* Title bar text.          */
    WS_POPUP,             /* The window's style.      */
    100,                  /* X position.              */
    100,                  /* Y position.              */
    width,                /* Width.                   */
    height,               /* Height.                  */
    NULL,                 /* Parent window's handle.  */
    NULL,                 /* Menu handle.             */
    hCurrentInst,         /* Instance handle.         */
    NULL);                /* No additional data.      */

ShowWindow(hWnd, nCmdShow);
UpdateWindow(hWnd);

while (GetMessage(&msg, NULL, 0, 0))
{
    TranslateMessage(&msg);
    DispatchMessage(&msg);
}

return msg.wParam;
}

LRESULT CALLBACK WndProc(HWND hWnd, UINT message,
    WPARAM wParam, LPARAM lParam)
{
    HDC hDC;
    PAINTSTRUCT paintStruct;

    switch(message)
    {
        case WM_PAINT:
            hDC = BeginPaint(hWnd, &paintStruct);
            TextOut(hDC, 20, 20,
                "This is a plain pop-up window.", 29);
            EndPaint(hWnd, &paintStruct);
            return 0;

        case WM_LBUTTONDOWN:
            PostMessage(hWnd, WM_DESTROY, 0, 0);
            return 0;

        case WM_DESTROY:
            PostQuitMessage(0);
            return 0;
```

```
        }

        return DefWindowProc(hWnd, message, wParam, lParam);
}
```

Providing only the WS_POPUP style causes the window to display only the white rectangle shown in Figure 6-9. Yep, that rectangle is a window. Although completely unadorned, the window can still function as a window. It can, for example, display data and even respond to Windows messages. To prove this, click in the window. The window receives a WM_LBUTTONDOWN message, to which the program responds in its WndProc() function. The program responds by sending its own window a WM_DESTROY message, which closes down the application.

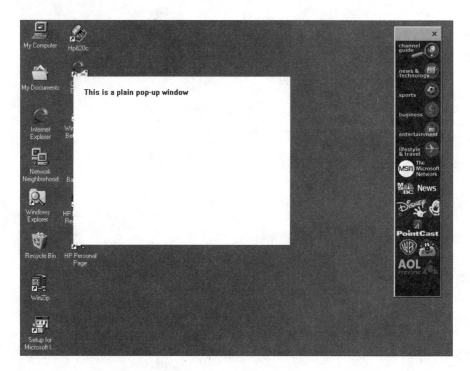

Figure 6-9: The BasicApp2 application window displayed with only the WS_POPUP style

You can get some really bizarre windows if you monkey with the styles and colors. For example, Figure 6-10 shows BasicApp2 when its background color is set to the NULL_BRUSH (no color) rather than the WHITE_BRUSH. Now all that appears on the screen is the text.

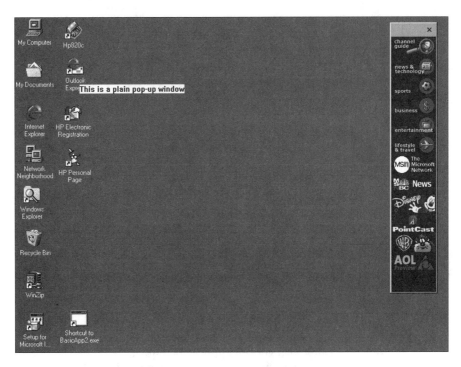

Figure 6-10: The BasicApp2 window displayed without a background color

Tip

When you use AppWizard to create a skeleton application, you can set window styles for the frame window from the Step 4 dialog box. To do this, click the Advanced button, select the Window Styles tab of the Advanced Options property sheet, and click the check boxes for the styles you want to add or remove.

MDI Windows

Up until now, all the applications you've seen in this book, such as the BasicApp2 application just created, have been SDI, or single-document interface applications. This type of application window can display only a single document at a time, which is sufficient for most applications. MDI, or multiple-document interface applications, can display more than one document at a time.

An MDI frame window is much like a mini-desktop on which the user can arrange several document windows (called MDI child windows). Document windows in an MDI application can even be reduced to icons inside the frame window, much like applications can be reduced to icons on Windows' taskbar.

AppWizard enables you to create MDI applications with little fuss. In fact, MDI applications are the default type in the AppWizard Step 1 dialog box. Figure 6-11 shows MFC AppWizard's Step 1 dialog box. Notice the options—

Single Document, Multiple Documents, and Dialog Based—you can select at the top of the dialog box. To create an MDI application, select the Multiple Documents option.

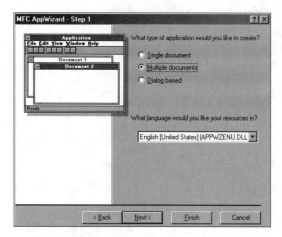

Figure 6-11: AppWizard's Step 1 dialog box, displayed with the parameters to create an MDI application

The other options in the remaining AppWizard dialog boxes are unaffected by the Multiple Documents selection. If you leave those options set to their default values, you get the application shown in Figure 6-12. As you can see, when the application runs, it displays two windows, the frame window and a child window. It's the child window that represents a document in the application. As such, the child window's client area contains the view window for the document.

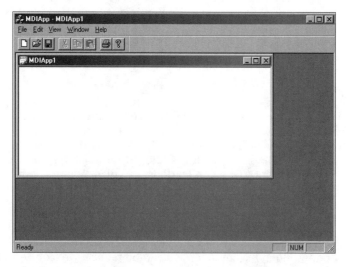

Figure 6-12: A basic MDI application displayed with its child and frame windows

An MFC MDI application derives some of its classes from different base classes than does an SDI application. Specifically, an MDI frame window is derived from the `CMDIFrameWnd` class, which is itself derived from `CFrameWnd`. This derivation should tell you that a `CMDIFrameWnd` window is just a frame window with some extra features. Those features include the ability to manage multiple documents.

The child window is represented by the `CChildFrame` class, which is derived from `CMDIChildWnd`. The child window is a frame window that appears inside an MDI frame window. Also, an MDI child frame window doesn't have a menu bar. Instead, it places menu commands in the MDI frame window's menu bar. MDI child windows can never leave the MDI frame window's client area.

Figure 6-13 shows an MDI application with several open document windows. Notice how the MDIApp3 child window is positioned so it doesn't fit entirely inside the MDI frame window. Rather than extend onto the window's desktop though, the portion of the child window that doesn't fit is not visible at all. This is similar to what happens on the Windows 98 desktop if you try to move an application window beyond the limits of the screen.

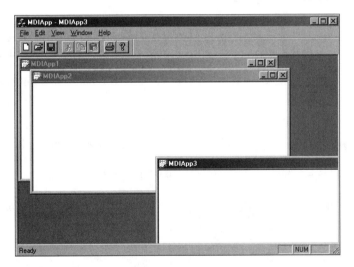

Figure 6-13: If you do not position a child window entirely within its frame window, the extended section is not visible.

AppWizard never creates a child window class for an SDI application, because SDI applications rarely display child windows—except for windows like dialog boxes and message boxes. Child document windows are, in fact, the main difference between SDI and MDI applications.

MDI applications are mostly out of vogue these days. Rather than trying to juggle multiple documents within a single frame window, Microsoft has suggested that it's easier and more practical to run multiple instances of an application in order to accommodate multiple-document manipulation. For this reason, this book doesn't cover the hairy details of programming MDI applications. You can find additional information on MDI applications in your Visual C++ online documentation.

Dialog Boxes

Dialog boxes are everywhere in Windows programs. Virtually every time a program must communicate with its user, a dialog box is involved. They don't call them dialog boxes for nothing! Your programs can incorporate two types of dialog boxes into the application. The first type is a custom dialog box that you create yourself, using the dialog box editor and creating a class to represent the dialog box in the program. The second type is the so-called common dialog box, which is part of the Windows operating system and for which MFC provides classes.

Custom dialog boxes

Probably more often than not, the dialog boxes you display in your application will be custom dialog boxes that you designed and created using Visual C++'s dialog box editor. You learned to create this type of dialog box back in Chapter 3, "Programming with Visual C++." If you'd like a hands-on dialog box tutorial, refer to that chapter. Here, you get a quick overview that serves as a refresher.

Creating a custom dialog box requires a number of steps:

1. Start a new dialog box resource by selecting the Insert menu's Resource command. When the Insert Resource dialog box appears, select Dialog in the Resource Type box (see Figure 6-14) and click New.

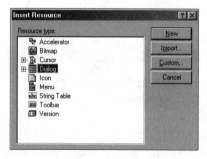

Figure 6-14: To create a new dialog box, choose Dialog as your resource type.

2. Use the dialog box editor to add the necessary controls and to set the controls' and dialog box's attributes (see Figure 6-15).

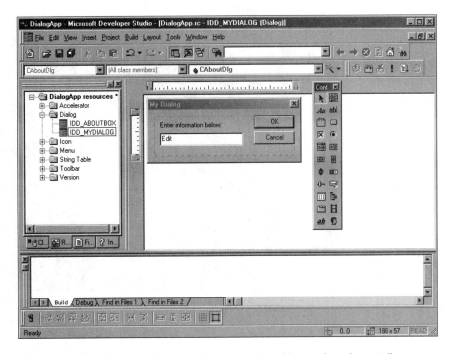

Figure 6-15: The editor provides the tools you need to add controls and set attributes.

3. Double-click the dialog box and create a class for the dialog by following the instructions in the dialog boxes that appear (see Figure 6-16).

4. From ClassWizard, add member variables to the class for the controls that you need to transfer data to and from, as shown in Figure 6-17.

5. In the source code file that uses the dialog box, include the dialog box class's header file, such as the following:

```
#include "MyDialog.h"
```

6. To display the dialog box, first create an object of the dialog class:

```
CMyDialog dialog;
```

7. Set the dialog box's member variables to the values that you want to appear in the dialog box's controls; for example:

```
dialog.m_info = "Default text";
```

8. Call the dialog box class's DoModal() function to display the dialog box and enable the user to manipulate the controls; for example:

```
int result = dialog.DoModal();
```

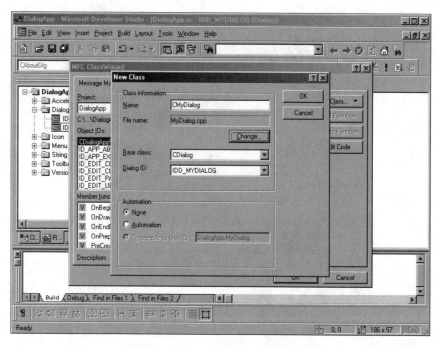

Figure 6-16: ClassWizard guides you through the process of creating a new class for the dialog box.

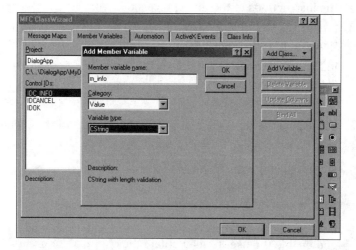

Figure 6-17: To add member variables to the dialog box class, choose a member variable name, category, and variable type.

9. If the return value from DoModal() is IDOK, extract data from the dialog box's controls; for example:

```
if (result == IDOK)
{
    m_info = dialog.m_info;
}
```

When it's all put together, a function that displays the custom dialog box and extracts information from its controls, might look like the one in Listing 6-5.

Listing 6-5: A function that initializes, displays, and handles a custom dialog box

```
void CDialogAppView::OnTestDialog()
{
    // TODO: Add your command handler code here

    CMyDialog dialog;
    dialog.m_info = "Default text";

    int result = dialog.DoModal();

    if (result == IDOK)
    {
        m_info = dialog.m_info;
    }
}
```

When the user exits a dialog box by clicking the Cancel button, DoModal()'s return value is IDCANCEL.

PROBLEMS & SOLUTIONS

Dialog Box OK and Cancel Buttons

PROBLEM: *In my application, I have to know when the user has clicked my dialog box's OK or Cancel button. How can I modify my dialog class to manage these buttons directly?*

SOLUTION: MFC defines message-response functions for both the OK and Cancel buttons. All you have to do is override the functions—called OnOK() and OnCancel()—in your dialog box's class. Here's an OnOK() function that displays a message box when the user clicks the OK button:

```
void CTestDialog::OnOK()
{
    MessageBox("You clicked OK.");

    CDialog::OnOK();
}
```

Continued

Of course, normally in `OnOK()`, you wouldn't display a message box; you'd do something more useful, such as validate the user's entries in the dialog box. Notice the call to the base class's version of `OnOK()`. If you don't call `CDialog::OnOK()`, the dialog box stays on the screen, which might be what you want if the user has entered some invalid data. Sooner or later, though, you have to call `CDialog::OnOK()` in order to close the dialog box when the user clicks OK.

The `OnCancel()` message-response function works similarly, as shown here:

```
void CTestDialog::OnCancel()
{
    MessageBox("You clicked Cancel.");

    CDialog::OnCancel();
}
```

As with `OnOK()`, a call to the base class's version of the function is required in order to retain the button's standard behavior.

PROBLEMS & SOLUTIONS

Creating Modeless Dialog Boxes

PROBLEM: *How can I create a dialog box that allows the application's user to switch back and forth between the dialog box and the application's window?*

SOLUTION: A dialog box that doesn't force the user to exit it before going back to the application's window is called a modeless dialog box. Other dialog boxes that you've worked with—the ones that must be dismissed before you can get back to the application window—are called modal dialog boxes.

Modeless dialog boxes are useful when the user needs to continually update values in the dialog box while working in the application's main window. The classic example of a modeless dialog box is the Find and Replace dialog. Creating and managing modeless dialog boxes, however, is a bit of a pain. You'll have to decide yourself whether it's worth the effort.

You create a modeless dialog box's resource the same way you would any other dialog box. The main difference between modal and modeless dialog boxes is the way you display them. You display a modeless dialog box by calling its `Create()` and `ShowWindow()` functions, rather than calling `DoModal()`.

The first step is to declare a pointer to the dialog box as a member variable of the class that will display the dialog box. Such a declaration might look like this:

```
CTestDialog* m_pDialog;
```

Continued

When you're ready to display the dialog box, first create the dialog box object with the `new` operator, and then initialize the dialog's controls. Finally, call the dialog's `Create()` function, and, if the dialog box doesn't have its Visible attribute set, also call `ShowWindow()`, like this:

```
m_pDialog = new CTestDialog(this);
m_pDialog->m_name = m_name;
m_pDialog->Create(IDD_DIALOG1);
m_pDialog->ShowWindow(SW_SHOW);
```

The `Create()` and `ShowWindow()` functions return immediately, rather than waiting for the user to click a button as `DoModal()` does. This means you've got the dialog box on the screen, but you need some way to communicate to the main program when the user clicks a button. You do this by overriding the dialog box class's `OnOK()` and `OnCancel()` functions and sending a Windows message to the application's window when the user clicks a button.

To implement this messaging system, you define custom Windows messages, where you can do something like this:

```
const WM_OKPRESSED = WM_USER + 100;
const WM_CANCELPRESSED = WM_USER + 101;
```

You can then use the `PostMessage()` function to send these messages to the application from the dialog box object. For example, your dialog's `OnOK()` function might look like this:

```
void CTestDialog::OnOK()
{
    UpdateData(TRUE);
    m_pViewWnd->PostMessage(WM_OKPRESSED, 0, 0);
}
```

First `OnOK()` calls `UpdateData()`, which causes MFC to transfer the contents of the dialog box controls to the appropriate member variables. Then the function calls the parent window's `PostMessage()` function to notify the program that the user clicked the OK button. In this version of `OnOK()`, *you do not call the base class's* `OnOK()` function. If you do, MFC will muddle everything up for you.

The dialog box's `OnCancel()` function looks similar, except it doesn't call `UpdateData()`, because the user wants to abandon any changes made to the dialog box's controls:

```
void CTestDialog::OnCancel()
{
    m_pViewWnd->PostMessage(WM_CANCELPRESSED, 0, 0);
}
```

In the parent window class, you use the `ON_MESSAGE` macro to define message-map entries for the custom messages:

```
BEGIN_MESSAGE_MAP(CDialogAppView, CView)
    ON_MESSAGE(WM_OKPRESSED, DialogOnOK)
    ON_MESSAGE(WM_CANCELPRESSED, DialogOnCancel)
END_MESSAGE_MAP()
```

Continued

With this message map in place, when the dialog box posts the `WM_OKPRESSED` message, MFC calls the window's `DialogOnOK()` function, which might look like this:

```
LONG CDialogAppView::DialogOnOK(UINT wParam, LONG lParam)
{
    m_name = m_pDialog->m_name;
    m_pDialog->DestroyWindow();
    delete m_pDialog;
    m_pDialog = NULL;

    return 0;
}
```

This function transfers the contents of the dialog's member variables to the window's member variables, destroys the dialog window, and deletes the dialog object.

The `DialogOnCancel()` function, which MFC calls when the dialog posts the `WM_CANCELPRESSED` message, might look like this:

```
LONG CDialogAppView::DialogOnCancel(UINT wParam,
    LONG lParam)
{
    m_pDialog->DestroyWindow();
    delete m_pDialog;
    m_pDialog = NULL;

    return 0;
}
```

On CD-ROM

If you want to experiment with a working modeless dialog box, look in the Chapter10\DialogApp folder of this book's CD-ROM. There you can find the DialogApp application, which enables you to display and manipulate a modeless dialog box. All of the source code shown in this section was taken from that application.

Common dialog boxes

Some tasks are common to so many applications that it's silly to expect programmers to have to write source code to accomplish them. Such tasks include getting file names, colors, and fonts. So common are these tasks that Microsoft decided to build dialog boxes into Windows 98 to handle them. Appropriately enough, these dialogs are referred to as the common dialog boxes. In this section, you learn how to program common dialog boxes into your applications. The common dialog boxes are as follows:

Color Dialog	Enables the user to select a color
File Dialog	Enables the user to select file names
Find-Replace Dialog	Enables the user to search and replace words in a document
Font Dialog	Enables the user to select a font and font attributes

Page Setup Dialog   Enables the user to select page options

Print Dialog   Enables the user to select printing options

The File dialog box

The vast majority of Windows applications (and most other applications, for that matter) require the user to load and save files. To help programmers with this ubiquitous task, Windows 98 features the File dialog box, which is represented in MFC by the `CFileDialog` class. In its simplest form, the File dialog box is criminally easy to display.

First, you must include the afxdlgs.h file in your source code (as you must do for any of the common dialog boxes):

```
#include "afxdlgs.h"
```

Then, create an object of the `CFileDialog` class:

```
CFileDialog fileDlg(TRUE);
```

A value of `TRUE` for the constructor's single argument specifies an Open dialog, and a value of `FALSE` specifies a Save As dialog box.

Then call the dialog object's `DoModal()` member function, just as you would for any dialog box:

```
int result = fileDlg.DoModal();
```

The File dialog box appears and the user locates and selects a file. If the user clicks the Open button to exit the dialog box, you can get the selected file name by calling the dialog box object's `GetFileName()` function, like this:

```
if (result == IDOK)
{
    m_openFileName = fileDlg.GetFileName();
}
```

Figure 6-18 shows the dialog box created by the previous example. Notice how the dialog box lacks some features that a professional application would offer. For example, there are no file types listed in the Files of Type box, nor does a default filter appear in the File Name box.

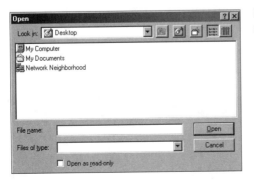

Figure 6-18: The Open dialog box is one of the common file dialog boxes.

In the previous example, the `CFileDialog` constructor received only a single argument, a `BOOL` value that specified whether the dialog box should be a Save As or Open box. The constructor actually has six arguments, all of which except the first have default values. The constructor's full signature looks like this:

```
CFileDialog(
    BOOL bOpenFileDialog,
    LPCTSTR lpszDefExt = NULL,
    LPCTSTR lpszFileName = NULL,
    DWORD dwFlags = OFN_HIDEREADONLY |
        OFN_OVERWRITEPROMPT,
    LPCTSTR lpszFilter = NULL,
    CWnd* pParentWnd = NULL);
```

The six arguments are used as follows:

bOpenFileDialog	A BOOL value specifying an Open (TRUE) or Save (FALSE) dialog box
lpszDefExt	The file extension that should be added to file names that have no extension
lpszFileName	The file name that should be initially selected
dwFlags	Customization flags
lpszFilter	The file filters for the Files of Type box
pParentWnd	A pointer to the dialog box's parent window

To create a full Open dialog box, you use the `lpszFileName` argument to specify a file filter for the File Name box. In addition, you use the `lpszFilter` argument to specify file filters for the Files of Type box. These file filters consist of two strings separated by an OR symbol (|). For example, one complete file filter looks like this:

```
Test Files (*.tst)|*.tst
```

The string on the left appears in the Files of Type box. The string on the right specifies the actual filter. You can string together as many of the filters as you need. You would, for example, always want to include the All Files filter, as well as the filters associated with your application's documents, like this:

```
char filters[] =
    "Test Files (*.tst)|*.tst|All Files (*.*)|*.*|";
```

The following lines create and display the dialog box shown in Figure 6-19:

```
char filters[] =
    "Test Files (*.tst)|*.tst|All Files (*.*)|*.*|";
CFileDialog fileDlg(TRUE, NULL, "*.tst",
    NULL, filters, NULL);
int result = fileDlg.DoModal();
```

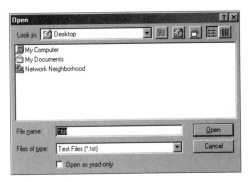

Figure 6-19: A complete Open dialog box created by the previous example lines

The Save As dialog box works much like the Open dialog box. The main difference is the arguments you pass to the `CFileDialog` constructor. Normally, you set the arguments as follows:

bOpenFileDialog	Set to FALSE to specify the Save dialog box
lpszDefExt	Set to the file extension associated with the application's documents
lpszFileName	Set to the currently loaded document's file name or, if the document has not yet been named, set to a default file name
dwFlags	Set to OFN_HIDEREADONLY | OFN_OVERWRITEPROMPT in order to hide read-only files and to prompt before overwriting existing files
lpszFilter	Set to the file filters for the Files of Type box
pParentWnd	Set to NULL

Considering these values, the lines that create and display a Save dialog box might look like those in Listing 6-6. Figure 6-20 shows the resultant dialog box.

Listing 6-6: Creating and displaying a Save dialog box

```
CString fileName;

char filters[] =
    "Test Files (*.tst)|*.tst|All Files (*.*)|*.*|";

if (m_saveFileName == "")
    fileName = "default.tst";
else
    fileName = m_saveFileName;

CFileDialog fileDlg(FALSE, "*.tst", fileName,
    OFN_HIDEREADONLY | OFN_OVERWRITEPROMPT,
    filters, NULL);

int result = fileDlg.DoModal();
```

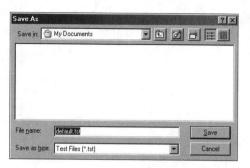

Figure 6-20: Here's the complete Save As dialog box created by the previous example's code lines.

If the user selects a file that already exists on the disk, the Save As dialog box displays the warning in Figure 6-21. As you can see, this warning box gives users a chance to change their minds before overwriting valuable data.

Figure 6-21: A Save As dialog box warning appears when you attempt to save with the name of an existing file.

As with the Open dialog box, you call the `GetFileName()` function to retrieve the file name the user selected. The `CFileDialog` class has many other member functions that you can call, the most useful of which are listed in Table 6-6.

Table 6-6   The most useful `CFileDialog` member functions

Function	Description
`DoModal()`	Displays the dialog box
`GetFileExt()`	Gets the selected file's extension
`GetFileName()`	Gets the selected file's name
`GetFileTitle()`	Gets the selected file's title
`GetPathName()`	Gets the selected file's path
`GetReadOnlyPref()`	Gets the selected file's read-only attribute
`OnFileNameOK()`	Called by MFC to validate the selected filename. Overridable in a derived class.
`OnShareViolation()`	Called by MFC in the event of a share violation. Overridable in a derived class.

The Font dialog box

While the File dialog boxes are common to most Windows 98 applications, the Font dialog box is used only with text-based applications. When using an application on Windows 98, the user usually expects to be able to select fonts and font sizes, as well as character attributes, such as bold and underlining. To accommodate these needs, Windows 98 features the Font dialog box, from which the user can select any font on the system and apply text attributes as needed.

The MFC `CFontDialog` class represents the Font dialog. Creating a Font dialog is even easier than creating a File dialog, because the `CFontDialog` class's constructor requires no arguments:

```
CFontDialog fontDialog;
```

After creating the dialog object, you display it by calling the `DoModal()` member function:

```
int result = fontDialog.DoModal();
```

These two lines result in the dialog box shown in Figure 6-22. Notice how the default Font dialog box enables the user to select not only a font, but also font styles, size, attributes, and color. That's a lot of power for only two lines of source code.

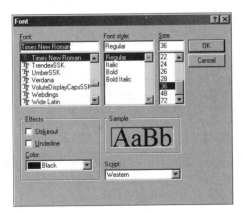

Figure 6-22: The default Font dialog box, which is created with only two lines of source code, enables users to select many font options.

If the user clicks OK to exit the Font dialog box, `DoModal()` returns `IDOK`. In this case, you can get the selected font by calling the `CFontDialog` member function `GetCurrentFont()`:

```
LOGFONT logFont;
fontDialog.GetCurrentFont(&logFont);
```

`GetCurrentFont()`'s single argument is the address of a `LOGFONT` structure, into which `GetCurrentFont()` stores the values that define the selected font.

After retrieving the LOGFONT structure, you create a CFont object and call that object's CreateFontIndirect() function to actually create the font:

```
CFont font;
font.CreateFontIndirect(&logFont);
```

You can then use the font by selecting it into the current device context. For more information on LOGFONT structures and the CFont class, please refer to Chapter 7, "Text." To learn more about device contexts, please refer back to Chapter 5, "Graphics Device Interface Basics."

Although the CFontDialog constructor requires no arguments, it defines four, all of which have default values. The constructor's full signature looks like this:

```
CFontDialog(
    LPLOGFONT lplfInitial = NULL,
    DWORD dwFlags = CF_EFFECTS | CF_SCREENFONTS,
    CDC* pdcPrinter = NULL,
    CWnd* pParentWnd = NULL);
```

The arguments are used as follows:

lplfInitial	A pointer to a LOGFONT structure
dwFlags	Font dialog box flags
pdcPrinter	A pointer to a printer device context
pParentWnd	A pointer to the dialog box's parent window

Because the default Font dialog box works fine in most cases, this chapter doesn't get into the details of modifying the dialog box's flags and attributes. If you'd like more control over the Font dialog box, look up the CFontDialog class in your Visual C++ online documentation. Table 6-7 lists the most useful CFontDialog member functions.

Tip

If you want the currently active font to be selected in the Font dialog box when it appears, pass a pointer to the font's LOGFONT structure as the CFontDialog constructor's first argument, like this:

```
CFontDialog fontDialog(logFont).
```

Table 6-7   The most useful CFontDialog member functions

Function	Description
DoModal()	Displays the dialog box
GetColor()	Gets the selected font's color
GetCurrentFont()	Gets the selected font's name
GetFaceName()	Gets the selected font's face name

Function	Description
GetSize()	Gets the selected font's point size
GetStyleName()	Gets the selected font's style name
GetWeight()	Gets the selected font's weight
IsBold()	Returns TRUE if the font is bold
IsItalic()	Returns TRUE if the font is italic
IsStrikeOut()	Returns TRUE if the font is struck through
IsUnderline()	Returns TRUE if the font is underlined

The Color dialog box

Although not as common a task as selecting files and fonts, the ability to select colors is often important in applications. As you've probably figured out, Windows 98 features a dialog box called the Color dialog box that makes selecting colors easy. Using the Color dialog box, the user can even create custom colors.

The MFC CColorDialog class represents the Color dialog. Because CColorDialog's constructor requires no arguments, you can create and display a Color dialog object easily:

```
CColorDialog colorDialog;
int result = colorDialog.DoModal();
```

These two lines result in the dialog box shown in Figure 6-23. Notice how the user can select from already defined colors or from a palette of custom colors. When the dialog box first appears, the custom color palette is empty. The user can fill the custom palette by clicking the Define Custom Colors button and selecting the color in the color window, as shown in Figure 6-24.

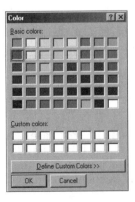

Figure 6-23: The default Color dialog box, which is created with only two lines of source code, enables users to choose from different color options.

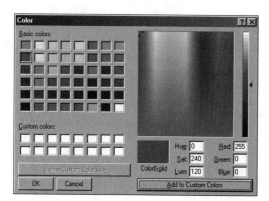

Figure 6-24: Defining custom colors is possible with the default Color dialog box.

If the user clicks OK to exit the Color dialog box, DoModal() returns IDOK. In this case, you can get the selected color by calling the CColorDialog member function GetColor():

```
COLORREF m_color = colorDialog.GetColor();
```

What you do with the selected color depends upon your application. You might, for example, use the color to create a custom pen or brush for the window's device context. For more information on device contexts, please refer to Chapter 5, "Graphics Device Interface Basics."

Although the CColorDialog constructor requires no arguments, it defines three, all of which have default values. The constructor's full signature looks like this:

```
CColorDialog(
    COLORREF clrInit = 0,
    DWORD dwFlags = 0,
    CWnd* pParentWnd = NULL);
```

The arguments are used as follows:

clrInit	The color that should be initially selected
dwFlags	Color dialog box flags
pParentWnd	A pointer to the dialog box's parent window

Because the default Color dialog box works fine in most cases, this chapter doesn't get into the details of modifying the dialog box's flags and attributes. If you'd like more control over the Color dialog box, look up the CColorDialog class in your Visual C++ online documentation. CColorDialog's member functions are listed as follows.

`DoModal()`	Displays a color dialog box
`GetColor()`	Returns a `COLORREF` representing the selected color
`GetSavedCustomColors()`	Gets the user's custom colors
`SetCurrentColor()`	Sets the current color selection
`OnColorOK()`	Called by MFC when the user selects the OK button. Overridable in a derived class.

The Common Dialog application

On CD-ROM

In the CommonDlgApp folder of this book's CD-ROM, you can find the Common Dialog application, which demonstrates programming common dialog boxes in the context of a full application. When you run the application, you see the application's main window. The Dialogs menu contains four commands—Open File Dialog, Save File Dialog, Font Dialog, and Color Dialog—that enable you to display and manipulate Open, Save, Font, and Color dialog boxes, respectively. The choices you make in the dialog boxes are reflected in the window's display, as shown in Figure 6-25.

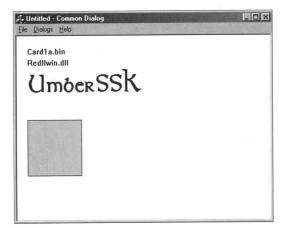

Figure 6-25: The Common Dialog application's window reflects the choices you make in your dialog boxes.

If you've read this chapter carefully, the source code for the Common Dialog application should be fairly easy to understand. The application was created using AppWizard and ClassWizard, so it is made up of source code files for application, main window, document, and view classes. However, all of the program's dialog boxes are managed in the view class. In this section, you quickly examine each of the view class's member functions that are relevant to common dialogs.

When you select the Open File Dialog command from the Dialogs menu, MFC calls the `OnDialogsOpenfiledialog()` message-response function. Listing 6-7 shows the function. Following the source code is a brief description of the function.

Listing 6-7: Handling the Open File dialog box

```
void CCommonDlgAppView::OnDialogsOpenfiledialog()
{
    // TODO: Add your command handler code here

    char filters[] =
        "Test Files (*.tst)|*.tst|All Files (*.*)|*.*|";
    CFileDialog fileDlg(TRUE, NULL, "*.tst",
        NULL, filters, NULL);

    int result = fileDlg.DoModal();

    if (result == IDOK)
    {
        m_openFileName = fileDlg.GetFileName();
        Invalidate();
    }
}
```

This function performs the following tasks:

- Creates an array of file filters
- Creates a `CFileDialog` object that represents an Open File dialog box
- Displays the dialog box to the user
- Extracts the selected file name
- Calls `Invalidate()` in order to force the window to repaint

When you select the Save File Dialog command from the Dialogs menu, MFC calls the `OnDialogsSavefiledialog()` message-response function. Listing 6-8 shows the function. Following the source code is a brief description of the function.

Listing 6-8: Handling the Save File dialog box

```
void CCommonDlgAppView::OnDialogsSavefiledialog()
{
    // TODO: Add your command handler code here

    CString fileName;

    char filters[] =
        "Test Files (*.tst)|*.tst|All Files (*.*)|*.*|";

    if (m_saveFileName == "NO FILE NAME SELECTED")
        fileName = "default.tst";
    else
        fileName = m_saveFileName;

    CFileDialog fileDlg(FALSE, "*.tst", fileName,
        OFN_HIDEREADONLY | OFN_OVERWRITEPROMPT,
        filters, NULL);

    int result = fileDlg.DoModal();
```

```
    if (result == IDOK)
    {
        m_saveFileName = fileDlg.GetFileName();
        Invalidate();
    }
}
```

This function performs the following tasks:

- Creates a string object (`fileName`) for storing the current file name
- Creates an array of file filter strings
- Determines whether to use the default or a selected file name
- Creates a `CFileDialog` object that represents a Save File dialog box
- Displays the dialog box to the user
- Deletes the old font and creates the selected font
- Calls `Invalidate()` in order to force the window to repaint

When you select the Font Dialog command from the Dialogs menu, MFC calls the `OnDialogsFontdialog()` message-response function. Listing 6-9 shows the function, and as you probably have guessed, following the source code is a brief description of the function.

Listing 6-9: Handling the Font dialog box

```
void CCommonDlgAppView::OnDialogsFontdialog()
{
    // TODO: Add your command handler code here

    CFontDialog fontDialog(&m_logFont);

    int result = fontDialog.DoModal();

    if (result == IDOK)
    {
        delete m_pFont;
        m_pFont = new CFont;
        m_pFont->CreateFontIndirect(&m_logFont);
        Invalidate();
    }
}
```

This function performs the following tasks:

- Creates a `CFontDialog` object that represents a Font dialog box
- Displays the dialog box to the user
- Extracts the selected file name
- Calls `Invalidate()` in order to force the window to repaint

Selecting the Color Dialog command from the Dialogs menu, causes MFC to call the `OnDialogsColordialog()` message-response function. This function's source code is shown in Listing 6-10, after which is a brief description of the function.

Listing 6-10: Handling the Color dialog box

```
void CCommonDlgAppView::OnDialogsColordialog()
{
    // TODO: Add your command handler code here

    CColorDialog colorDialog(m_color);

    int result = colorDialog.DoModal();

    if (result == IDOK)
    {
        m_color = colorDialog.GetColor();
        Invalidate();
    }
}
```

This function performs the following tasks:

- Creates a `CColorDialog` object that represents a Color dialog box
- Displays the dialog box to the user
- Extracts the selected color
- Calls `Invalidate()` in order to force the window to repaint

Each of the functions that display a common dialog box calls the `Invalidate()` function, which causes the program to repaint its window with the new values the user selected. The view class's `OnDraw()` function handles the repainting tasks, as shown in Listing 6-11. Once again, a brief description of the function follows the source code.

Listing 6-11: Rendering the new display

```
void CCommonDlgAppView::OnDraw(CDC* pDC)
{
    CCommonDlgAppDoc* pDoc = GetDocument();
    ASSERT_VALID(pDoc);

    // TODO: add draw code for native data here

    pDC->TextOut(20, 20, m_openFileName);
    pDC->TextOut(20, 40, m_saveFileName);

    CString fontName = m_logFont.lfFaceName;
    CFont* oldFont = (CFont*)pDC->SelectObject(m_pFont);
    pDC->TextOut(20, 60, fontName);
    pDC->SelectObject(oldFont);

    CBrush brush(m_color);
    CBrush* oldBrush =
        (CBrush*)pDC->SelectObject(&brush);
    pDC->Rectangle(20, 150, 120, 250);
    pDC->SelectObject(oldBrush);
}
```

This function performs the following tasks:

- Displays the selected file names
- Selects the selected font into the device context
- Displays a string in the selected font
- Restores the original font to the device context
- Creates a `CBrush` object from the selected color
- Selects the new brush into the device context
- Draws a rectangle in the selected color
- Restores the original brush to the device context

Property Sheets

Property sheets are a special type of dialog box suitable for organizing many options. A property sheet organizes options into a series of tabbed pages, each page (called a property page) of which holds a set of related settings. Figure 6-26, for example, shows the property sheet Windows 98 uses to enable the user to set the system's display properties. Each tab at the top of a property sheet is associated with a different page of properties. If you click the Appearance tab, for example, you see the property page shown in Figure 6-27.

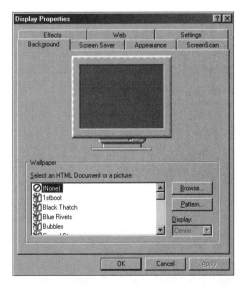

Figure 6-26: This Windows 98 property sheet enables users to set their system's background display.

You can create your own property sheets fairly easily using Visual C++'s dialog box editor. Each property page in the property sheet is actually a dialog box resource associated with MFC's `CPropertyPage` class. The property sheet itself, which contains the property pages, is an object of the `CPropertySheet` class.

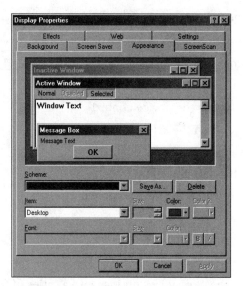

Figure 6-27: The Appearance property page enables you to change the way windows look. The message box is part of the graphic that shows what the current window settings look like.

Creating property pages and sheets

The following steps illustrate how to create a property page resource and how to derive your own classes from `CPropertyPage` and `CPropertySheet`. These steps assume that you've created a skeleton application with AppWizard.

1. Select the Resource command from Visual C++'s Insert menu and double-click Dialog in the Insert Resource dialog box, as shown in Figure 6-28.

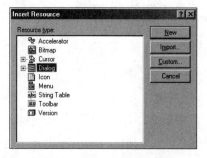

Figure 6-28: Selecting Dialog in the Insert Resource dialog box starts your creation of a property page resource.

2. When the new dialog box appears, press Enter to display its Dialog Properties property sheet. In the General page, change the ID and the Caption properties to appropriate values. You might, for example, set the ID to IDD_TEXTOPTIONS and set the caption to "Text Options," as shown in Figure 6-29. The caption appears in the property page's tab.

Figure 6-29: Set the dialog's properties in the General tab.

3. In the Dialog Properties property sheet, click the Styles tab in order to switch to the Styles page. Set the Style box to Child; set the Border box to Thin; and turn off the System Menu option, as shown in Figure 6-30. These are the window styles required by a property page.

Figure 6-30: Set the dialog's styles in the Styles tab.

4. Remove the OK and Cancel buttons from the dialog, and add the controls you need for the property page. Figure 6-31 shows an example of an assembled property page in Visual C++'s dialog box editor.

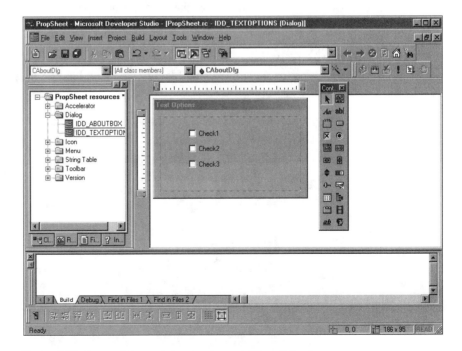

Figure 6-31: A complete property page is much like a dialog box.

5. With the property page selected, press Ctrl+W to display ClassWizard. The Adding a Class dialog box appears. Click OK to create a new class. The New Class dialog box appears.

6. Type the name of your property page class into the Name box, and select CPropertyPage in the Base Class box, as shown in Figure 6-32. Click OK to create the class.

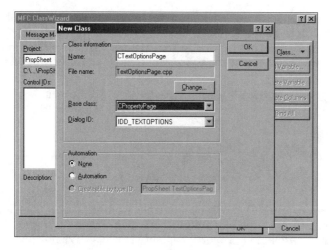

Figure 6-32: Defining a class for the property page occurs in the New Class dialog box.

7. In the ClassWizard's Add Member Variable page, create member variables for the controls with which your application must communicate (see Figure 6-33).

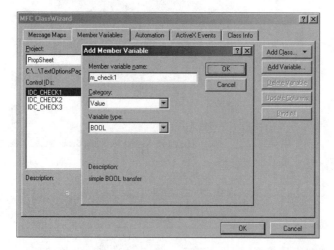

Figure 6-33: ClassWizard enables you to define member variables for the property page.

8. Repeat Steps 1 through 7 for each property page you want to display in your property sheet.

9. Click ClassWizard's Add Class button, and select New from the pop-up menu. The New Class dialog box appears.

10. Type a name for your property sheet class into the Name box, and select CPropertySheet in the Base Class box. Click OK to create the class, and then dismiss ClassWizard by clicking its OK button.

Programming the property sheet

Now that you have your property page resources defined and have derived your property page and property sheet classes from CPropertyPage and CPropertySheet, you're ready to write the source code that displays and manipulates the property sheet.

The first step is to include the property page header files in the property sheet class:

```
#include "TextOptionsPage.h"
#include "ColorOptionsPage.h"
```

Now that your property sheet class has access to your property page classes, you can create the property page objects as member variables of the property sheet class:

```
CColorOptionsPage m_colorPage;
CTextOptionsPage m_textPage;
```

I mentioned before that property pages are contained by the property sheet class. In order to enable you to add property pages, CPropertySheet offers the AddPage() member function. You should add your property pages to the property sheet in the property sheet's constructor:

```
CMyPropertySheet::CMyPropertySheet(
    LPCTSTR pszCaption, CWnd* pParentWnd,
    UINT iSelectPage):CPropertySheet(pszCaption,
    pParentWnd, iSelectPage)
{
    AddPage(&m_textPage);
    AddPage(&m_colorPage);
}
```

That's the minimum you need to do to finish up the property sheet class. Next, you must include the property sheet class in the source file that displays the property sheet. Often, in an AppWizard-generated application, this will be the view class. So, you might place a line like the following near the top of the view class's implementation file:

```
#include "MyPropertySheet.h"
```

Finally, displaying the property sheet is no different than displaying a dialog box. Just define a property sheet object and call its DoModal() member function:

```
CMyPropertySheet propertySheet("My Property Sheet");
int result = propertySheet.DoModal();
```

When creating the property sheet, the constructor requires one argument, which is the title that will appear in the property sheet's title bar.

Transferring values between your program and the property sheet works just as it does for dialog boxes. That is, to place data in a property sheet's controls before displaying the sheet, you initialize the property page classes' member variables. Conversely, you extract information from the property pages by copying the values of the property page's member variables into variables you've defined in the main program. Listing 6-12 shows a message-response function that initializes and displays a property sheet. If the user clicks OK to exit the property sheet, the program extracts the data entered by the user into the property pages.

Listing 6-12: Managing a property sheet

```
void CPropSheetView::OnTestPropertysheet()
{
    // TODO: Add your command handler code here

    CMyPropertySheet propertySheet("My Property Sheet");

    propertySheet.m_textPage.m_check1 = m_check1;
    propertySheet.m_textPage.m_check2 = m_check2;
    propertySheet.m_textPage.m_check3 = m_check3;

    propertySheet.m_colorPage.m_backgrnd = m_backgrnd;
    propertySheet.m_colorPage.m_red = m_red;
    propertySheet.m_colorPage.m_green = m_green;
    propertySheet.m_colorPage.m_blue = m_blue;

    int result = propertySheet.DoModal();

    if (result == IDOK)
    {
        m_check1 = propertySheet.m_textPage.m_check1;
        m_check2 = propertySheet.m_textPage.m_check2;
        m_check3 = propertySheet.m_textPage.m_check3;

        m_backgrnd =
            propertySheet.m_colorPage.m_backgrnd;
        m_red = propertySheet.m_colorPage.m_red;
        m_green = propertySheet.m_colorPage.m_green;
        m_blue = propertySheet.m_colorPage.m_blue;

        Invalidate();
    }
}
```

The PropSheet application

On CD-ROM

The function in Listing 6-12 was taken from a program called PropSheet that you can find in the Chapter06\PropSheet folder of this book's CD-ROM. This simple application gives you a chance to experiment with property sheets in the context of a running program. When you run the program, you see the window shown in Figure 6-34. Select the Test menu's Property Sheet command to display the property sheet.

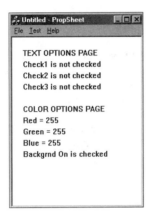

Figure 6-34: The PropSheet application window displayed

Figure 6-35 shows the property sheet's first page, and Figure 6-36 shows the second page. Change the values of the controls any way you like. When you click OK to exit the property sheet, the application's window displays the choices you made.

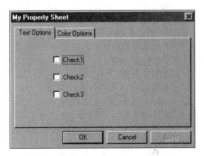

Figure 6-35: The property sheet's Text Options page displayed

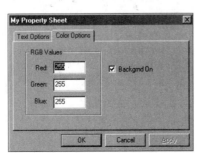

Figure 6-36: The property sheet's Color Options page displayed

Wizards

Wizards are special dialog boxes that guide a user step-by-step through complex tasks. You've already had a lot of experience with at least one wizard, Visual C++'s AppWizard. A wizard is a close cousin of the property sheet. The main differences are that a wizard uses buttons rather than tabs to move from page to page, and the user must view the pages consecutively, rather than being able to jump to any page as the user can with a property sheet.

Creating a wizard

So similar are wizards to property sheets that you construct your wizard pages exactly as you do property pages. You even associate the dialog resource for a page with the `CPropertyPage` class. The wizard itself is an object of the `CPropertySheet` class. What turns the property sheet into a wizard is a call to the property sheet object's `SetWizardMode()` member function. You can call `SetWizardMode()` right after you construct the object. So, you would create and display a wizard with code something like this:

```
CMyWizard wizard("My Wizard");
wizard.SetWizardMode();
int result = wizard.DoModal();
```

Setting a wizard's buttons

One thing you have to do differently with a wizard's pages is to override the `CPropertyPage` class's `OnSetActive()` member function. MFC calls `OnSetActive()` for a property (and wizard) page when the page is displayed. This gives the wizard a chance to perform whatever initialization is needed.

One bit of initialization that the wizard must perform is the enabling of buttons. A wizard has three important buttons: Back, Next, and Finish. The Back button brings the user back to the previous wizard page, the Next button brings the user to the next wizard page, and the Finish button closes the wizard.

Obviously, if the user is viewing the first wizard page, only the Next button should be enabled. Similarly, on the wizard's last page, only the Back and Finish buttons are usually enabled. You can have a Finish button on every page if you like, assuming that you provide default settings for any wizard options the user doesn't explicitly set.

To enable the correct wizard buttons, each wizard page calls the wizard's `SetWizardButtons()` function, which is a member function of the `CPropertySheet` class, as shown in Listing 6-13.

Listing 6-13: Setting the wizard buttons

```
BOOL CWizardPage1::OnSetActive()
{
    // TODO: Add your specialized code here
    //    and/or call the base class

    CPropertySheet* pParentSheet =
        (CPropertySheet*)GetParent();
    pParentSheet->SetWizardButtons(PSWIZB_NEXT);

    return CPropertyPage::OnSetActive();
}
```

Notice how the function first gets a pointer to the CPropertySheet object that is the wizard page's parent. Then, the program calls SetWizardButtons() through the pointer. Notice also SetWizardButtons()'s single argument. There are several constants you can use for this argument:

PSWIZB_NEXT	Enables the Next button
PSWIZB_BACK	Enables the Back button
PSWIZB_FINISH	Enables the Finish button
PSWIZB_DISABLEDFINISH	Disables the Finish button

You OR together the button constants in order to select which buttons to enable. For example, Listing 6-14 shows the OnSetActive() function for a second wizard page, which ORs together the PSWIZB_BACK and PSWIZB_NEXT constants.

Listing 6-14: Setting the wizard buttons for a second wizard page

```
BOOL CWizardPage2::OnSetActive()
{
    // TODO: Add your specialized code here
    //    and/or call the base class

    CPropertySheet* pParentSheet =
        (CPropertySheet*)GetParent();
    pParentSheet->
        SetWizardButtons(PSWIZB_BACK | PSWIZB_NEXT);

    return CPropertyPage::OnSetActive();
}
```

The last wizard page, which usually needs the Back and Finish buttons, might set its buttons like this:

```
CPropertySheet* pParentSheet =
    (CPropertySheet*)GetParent();
pParentSheet->
    SetWizardButtons(PSWIZB_BACK | PSWIZB_FINISH);
```

PROBLEMS & SOLUTIONS

Responding to Wizard Buttons

PROBLEM: *I need to know when the user has clicked a wizard button so that I can be sure that none of the options on a wizard page has been left blank. How can I do this?*

SOLUTION: Often, you need to know when the user has clicked the Back, Next, or Finish buttons. You might, for example want to validate the information the user has entered into the current wizard page. The CPropertyPage class provides several button-response functions that you can override in your own class:

OnWizardBack()	Called when the user clicks the Back button
OnWizardNext()	Called when the user clicks the Next button
OnWizardFinish()	Called when the user clicks the Finish button

Listing 6-15 shows overridden OnWizardBack() and OnWizardFinish() functions. Neither function does anything fancy—they just display a message box—but they demonstrate how these helpful button-response functions work.

Listing 6-15: Responding to wizard buttons

```
LRESULT CWizardPage3::OnWizardBack()
{
    // TODO: Add your specialized code here
    //    and/or call the base class

    MessageBox("You just clicked Back.",
        "Wizard Message");

    return CPropertyPage::OnWizardBack();
}

BOOL CWizardPage3::OnWizardFinish()
{
    // TODO: Add your specialized code here
    //    and/or call the base class

    MessageBox("Thanks for using MyWizard.",
        "Wizard Message");

    return CPropertyPage::OnWizardFinish();
}
```

The WizardApp application

On CD-ROM

In the WizardApp folder of this book's CD-ROM, you can find the WizardApp application, which demonstrates displaying and handling a wizard. When you run the program, select the Test menu's Wizard command. When you do, the application's sample wizard appears (see Figure 6-37). Experiment with the wizard's buttons to get a feel for how the wizard works.

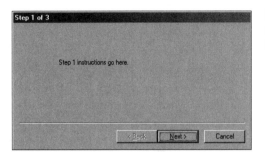

Figure 6-37: The WizardApp application's wizard, displaying its first of three steps.

Summary

Windows 98 features more kinds of windows than you can shake an icon at. These windows include not only application windows, but also dialog boxes, property sheets, and wizards. Even controls like buttons and text boxes are windows at heart.

Also discussed in this chapter:

- MFC window classes are part of a complex hierarchy of classes.
- A frame window acts as an application's main window.
- View windows display the data that makes up a document.
- Windows defines a set of styles that determine how a window looks and acts.
- MDI windows enable the user to open and edit more than one document at a time.
- Most dialog boxes are custom dialog boxes that you design using Visual C++'s dialog editor.
- Windows 98 features common dialog boxes for selecting files, fonts, and colors.
- Property sheets are dialog boxes with tabbed pages.
- Wizards are similar to property sheets, except they have buttons instead of tabs.

Chapter 7

Text

In This Chapter

▶ Displaying text

▶ Setting text color

▶ Setting character spacing

▶ Setting text alignment

▶ Getting text metrics

▶ Creating fonts

Windows can display many kinds of data, but even in a graphical OS like Windows, text remains the main way a program communicates with the user. Unfortunately, because text is displayed as an image in a window, creating text displays under Windows is a bit more complicated than it would be under a character-oriented OS like DOS. At the very least, you must deal with a device context (DC). You may also have to handle fonts, which under Windows can be complex critters.

Displaying Text

In previous programs in this book, you got an introduction to displaying text. Chapter 5, for example, discusses how in order to display text on the screen, you must have a device context. You then call the TextOut() function to display a line of text:

```
CClientDC clientDC(this);
clientDC.TextOut(20, 20, "This is a line of text.");
```

The MFC TextOut() function's three arguments are the X coordinate at which to print the text, the Y coordinate at which to print the text, and the text itself. This is an MFC version of a Windows API function of the same name. The Windows version's signature looks like this:

```
BOOL TextOut(
    HDC hdc,
    int X,
```

```
int Y,
LPCTSTR string,
int numChars);
```

The function's arguments are as follows:

hdc	A handle to the device context
X	The horizontal position at which to display the text
Y	The vertical position at which to display the text
string	The text to display
numChars	The number of character in the string to display

Setting Text Color

Normally, Windows draws black text, but you can change the text color by calling the SetTextColor() function. In an MFC program, this is a member function of the CDC class, and so is inherited by the other DC classes. A call to SetTextColor() might look like this:

```
CClientDC clientDC(this);
clientDC.SetTextColor(RGB(255,0,0));
```

SetTextColor()'s single argument is a COLORREF value that specifies the text color. In this example, SetTextColor() sets the text color to red.

You can retrieve the current text color by calling the GetTextColor() function:

```
COLORREF color = clientDC.GetTextColor();
```

You can also set the background color, which is the color that appears behind the text, by calling SetBkColor():

```
clientDC.SetBkColor(color);
```

This function's single argument is a COLORREF value specifying the new background color.

You can obtain the current background color by calling the GetBkColor() function:

```
COLORREF backColor = clientDC.GetBkColor();
```

Windows displays all text with a background color (the default is white) unless you change the background color mode. By changing the mode, you can tell Windows to ignore the background color and display only the text itself. To do this, you call the SetBkMode() function:

```
clientDC.SetBkMode(TRANSPARENT);
```

SetBkMode()'s single argument can be one of two values: TRANSPARENT or
OPAQUE. If you set the background mode to TRANSPARENT, Windows ignores the
background color.

You can obtain the current background mode by calling GetBkMode():

`int backMode = clientDC.GetBkMode();`

Note

When your program gets a DC, the DC's text attributes are always set to their
default values. This means the functions that obtain text attributes, such as
GetTextColor() and GetBkMode(), are really useful only if you've already
changed the DC's default attributes.

On CD-ROM

In the Chapter07\ColorTextApp folder of this book's CD-ROM, you can find
the ColorTextApp application that demonstrates setting text color,
background color, and background mode. When you run the application, you
will see a color version of the window shown in Figure 7-1. Notice how the
program displays the text in color with a black background.

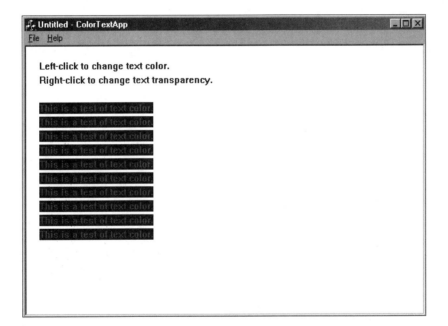

Figure 7-1: ColorTextApp displays text in color.

To change the text color, click in the window. You can also change the
text background mode by right-clicking the window. When you do, the
background mode toggles between OPAQUE (which is the Windows default)
and TRANSPARENT. Figure 7-2 shows the application with a transparent
background.

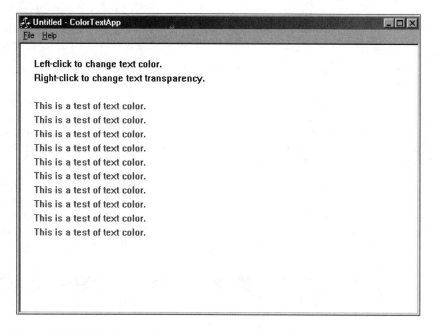

Figure 7-2: ColorTextApp can display transparent, as well as opaque, text backgrounds.

ColorTextApp's view class declares two data members for keeping track of the currently selected text color and background mode:

```
BOOL m_transparent;
COLORREF m_textColor;
```

The class's constructor sets these data members to their default values when the program starts:

```
CColorTextAppView::CColorTextAppView()
{
    // TODO: add construction code here

    m_textColor = RGB(255,0,0);
    m_transparent = FALSE;
}
```

The view class's `OnDraw()` function uses these values when it draws the application's display, as shown in Listing 7-1.

Listing 7-1: ColorTextApp's `OnDraw()` function

```
void CColorTextAppView::OnDraw(CDC* pDC)
{
    CColorTextAppDoc* pDoc = GetDocument();
    ASSERT_VALID(pDoc);
```

```
    // TODO: add draw code for native data here

    pDC->TextOut(20, 20,
        "Left-click to change text color.");
    pDC->TextOut(20, 40,
        "Right-click to change text transparency.");

    pDC->SetTextColor(m_textColor);
    pDC->SetBkColor(RGB(0,0,0));
    if (m_transparent)
        pDC->SetBkMode(TRANSPARENT);
    else
        pDC->SetBkMode(OPAQUE);

    for (int x=0; x<10; ++x)
        pDC->TextOut(20, 80+x*20,
            "This is a test of text color.");
}
```

The `OnDraw()` function performs the following tasks:

■ Displays instructions for using the program. This text output uses the DC's default settings.

■ Sets the text and background colors as selected by the user.

■ Sets the currently selected background mode.

■ Displays ten lines of text using the new attributes.

When the user clicks in the application's window, MFC calls the `OnLButtonDown()` function, which changes the currently selected text color. Listing 7-2 shows the source code for `OnLButtonDown()`.

Listing 7-2: ColorTextApp's `OnLButtonDown()` function

```
void CColorTextAppView::OnLButtonDown(UINT nFlags,
    CPoint point)
{
    // TODO: Add your message handler code here
    //    and/or call default

    COLORREF red = RGB(255,0,0);
    COLORREF green = RGB(0,255,0);
    COLORREF blue = RGB(0,0,255);

    if (m_textColor == red)
        m_textColor = green;
    else if (m_textColor == green)
        m_textColor = blue;
    else
        m_textColor = red;

    Invalidate();

    CView::OnLButtonDown(nFlags, point);
}
```

Finally, when the user right-clicks in the window, MFC calls the view class's `OnRButtonDown()` function, which toggles the background mode. Listing 7-3 shows the `OnRButtonDown()` function.

Listing 7-3: ColorTextApp's `OnRButtonDown()` function

```
void CColorTextAppView::OnRButtonDown(UINT nFlags,
    CPoint point)
{
    // TODO: Add your message handler code here
    //    and/or call default

    m_transparent = !m_transparent;
    Invalidate();

    CView::OnRButtonDown(nFlags, point);
}
```

Setting Character Spacing

Another attribute you can set is the spacing between the characters of text. You do this by calling `SetTextCharacterExtra()`:

```
clientDC.SetTextCharacterExtra(space);
```

Here, `space` is the number of pixels of extra space you want between text characters. You can obtain the current character spacing by calling the `GetTextCharacterExtra()` function:

```
int space = clientDC.GetTextCharacterExtra();
```

On CD-ROM

In the Chapter07\CharSpaceApp folder of this book's CD-ROM, you can find the CharSpaceApp application, which demonstrates character spacing. When you run the application, you see the window shown in Figure 7-3. Notice how each line of text has more space between the characters than the previous line. The first line is displayed with a spacing of 0, which is the Windows default.

There's not much to examine in CharSpaceApp. All the action happens in the `OnDraw()` method, shown in Listing 7-4. The function sets up a `for` loop that displays fifteen lines of text. Each time through the loop, the program sets the character spacing to the value of the loop variable `x`, which adds a pixel of space between characters for each text line. That is, the first line starts with a spacing of 0, which increases by one until the program displays the last line of text with a spacing of 14.

Listing 7-4: CharSpaceApp's `OnDraw()` function

```
void CCharSpaceAppView::OnDraw(CDC* pDC)
{
    CCharSpaceAppDoc* pDoc = GetDocument();
    ASSERT_VALID(pDoc);

    // TODO: add draw code for native data here
```

```
for (int x=0; x<15; ++x)
{
    pDC->SetTextCharacterExtra(x);
    pDC->TextOut(20, 20+x*20,
        "A test of character spacing.");
}
```

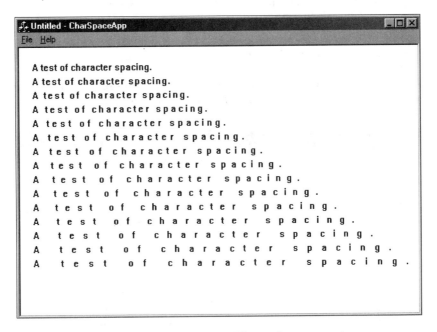

Figure 7-3: CharSpaceApp displays text with different character spacings.

Setting Text Alignment

There may be times when you need to align your application's text output in different ways. For example, you may want a paragraph of text centered in the window rather than displayed flush left. There may even be times when you want text to be flush right. The DC class provides functions for setting not only horizontal alignment, but also vertical alignment, which causes text to be displayed higher or lower than usual. In the following sections, you learn to manage text alignment in your programs.

Horizontal text alignment

Horizontal text alignment enables you to specify the horizontal position of text in a window. The type of horizontal alignment you choose determines how Windows interprets the coordinates you supply when displaying text. For example, when displaying a table of values, it might be handy to display text left- or center-aligned. Windows can handle this type of horizontal alignment for you. All you need to do is call SetTextaAlign():

```
clientDC.SetTextAlign(alignment);
```

Here, alignment is one of three values: TA_LEFT, TA_CENTER, or TA_RIGHT. The TA_LEFT constant represents Windows' default left text alignment. With this setting, Windows starts the left end of the text at the coordinate given as TextOut()'s first argument. With the TA_CENTER setting, Windows interprets the first TextOut() argument to be the point around which the string should be centered. And, finally, with the TA_RIGHT setting, Windows interprets TextOut()'s first argument as the coordinate for the right end of the text string.

On CD-ROM

In the Chapter07\HorizontalAlignApp folder of this book's CD-ROM, you can find the HorizontalAlignApp application, which demonstrates horizontal text alignment. When you run the application, you see the window shown in Figure 7-4, displaying the text with left alignment.

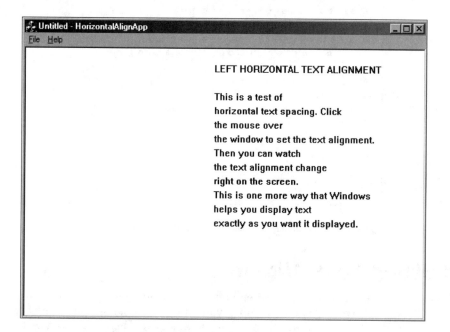

Figure 7-4: HorizontalAlignApp displaying left-aligned text.

Click the window, and the text alignment switches to center alignment, as shown in Figure 7-5.

Finally, click again, and you get right-aligned text, as shown in Figure 7-6. Continue clicking in order to cycle through the alignments as many times as you like.

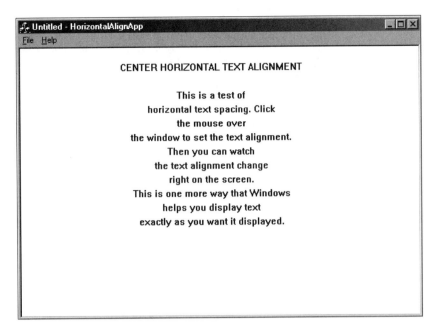

Figure 7-5: HorizontalAlignApp displaying center-aligned text.

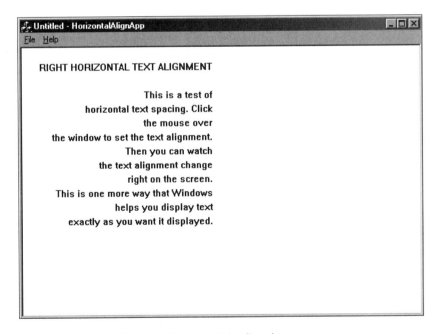

Figure 7-6: HorizontalAlignApp displaying right-aligned text.

On CD-ROM

HorizontalAlignApp creates its display in the view class's OnDraw() function, which is shown in Listing 7-5. Before drawing the text lines, OnDraw() calls SetTextAlign() to set the currently selected text alignment. Windows then automatically aligns the text as it's displayed.

Listing 7-5: HorizontalAlignApp's OnDraw() function

```
void CHorizontalAlignAppView::OnDraw(CDC* pDC)
{
    CHorizontalAlignAppDoc* pDoc = GetDocument();
    ASSERT_VALID(pDoc);

    // TODO: add draw code for native data here

    pDC->SetTextAlign(m_currentHAlign);

    CString string;
    if (m_currentHAlign == TA_LEFT)
        string = "LEFT HORIZONTAL TEXT ALIGNMENT";
    else if (m_currentHAlign == TA_CENTER)
        string = "CENTER HORIZONTAL TEXT ALIGNMENT";
    else
        string = "RIGHT HORIZONTAL TEXT ALIGNMENT";

    pDC->TextOut(280, 20, string);
    pDC->TextOut(280, 60, "This is a test of");
    pDC->TextOut(280, 80,
        "horizontal text spacing. Click");
    pDC->TextOut(280, 100, "the mouse over");
    pDC->TextOut(280, 120,
        "the window to set the text alignment.");
    pDC->TextOut(280, 140, "Then you can watch");
    pDC->TextOut(280, 160, "the text alignment change");
    pDC->TextOut(280, 180, "right on the screen.");
    pDC->TextOut(280, 200,
        "This is one more way that Windows");
    pDC->TextOut(280, 220, "helps you display text");
    pDC->TextOut(280, 240,
        "exactly as you want it displayed.");
}
```

When the user clicks the application's window, the text alignment changes. The view class's OnLButtonDown() function handles this task, as shown in Listing 7.6.

Listing 7-6: HorizontalAlignApp's OnLButtonDown() function

```
void CHorizontalAlignAppView::OnLButtonDown(UINT nFlags,
    CPoint point)
{
    // TODO: Add your message handler code here
    //    and/or call default

    if (m_currentHAlign == TA_LEFT)
        m_currentHAlign = TA_CENTER;
```

```
    else if (m_currentHAlign == TA_CENTER)
        m_currentHAlign = TA_RIGHT;
    else
        m_currentHAlign = TA_LEFT;

    Invalidate();

    CView::OnLButtonDown(nFlags, point);
}
```

Vertical text alignment

You can also set the text's vertical alignment, which controls how Windows interprets TextOut()'s second parameter, the vertical coordinate at which to place text. To set vertical alignment, you call SetTextAlign() with one of three values: TA_TOP, TA_BOTTOM, or TA_BASELINE. With TA_TOP, the default vertical alignment, Windows positions text with the top of the characters located at TextOut()'s second argument. TA_BOTTOM is just the opposite, with the text positioned above TextOut()'s vertical coordinate. Finally, TA_BASELINE specifies that a character's baseline (the bottom of a character, not including extenders) sits at TextOut()'s vertical coordinate.

On CD-ROM

In the Chapter07\VerticalAlignApp folder of this book's CD-ROM, you can find the VerticalAlignApp application, which demonstrates vertical text alignment. When you run the application, you see the window shown in Figure 7-7, displaying the text with the default TA_TOP alignment.

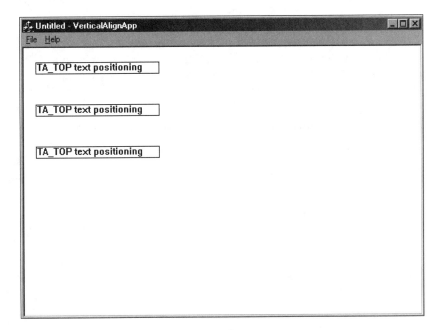

Figure 7-7: VerticalAlignApp displaying top-aligned text.

Click the window, and the text alignment in the second two lines of text switches to TA_BOTTOM and TA_BASELINE alignment, as shown in Figure 7-8. The rectangles drawn around the text lines show the position for the default TA_TOP alignment.

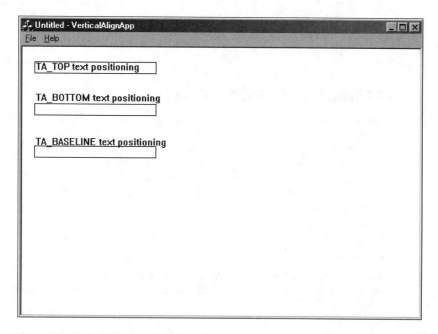

Figure 7-8: VerticalAlignApp displaying top-, bottom-, and baseline-aligned text

VerticalAlignApp, like HorizontalAlignApp, creates its display in the view class's OnDraw() function, which is shown in Listing 7-7. The m_showAllAlignments flag determines whether OnDraw() displays text lines with TA_TOP alignment or with all three alignments.

Listing 7-7: VerticalAlignApp's OnDraw() function

```
void CVerticalAlignAppView::OnDraw(CDC* pDC)
{
    CVerticalAlignAppDoc* pDoc = GetDocument();
    ASSERT_VALID(pDoc);

    // TODO: add draw code for native data here

    CBrush* oldBrush =
        (CBrush*)pDC->SelectStockObject(NULL_BRUSH);

    if (m_showAllAlignments)
    {
```

```
        pDC->SetTextAlign(TA_TOP);
        pDC->TextOut(20, 20, "TA_TOP text positioning");
        pDC->Rectangle(18, 21, 200, 38);

        pDC->SetTextAlign(TA_BOTTOM);
        pDC->TextOut(20, 80,
            "TA_BOTTOM text positioning");
        pDC->Rectangle(18, 81, 200, 98);

        pDC->SetTextAlign(TA_BASELINE);
        pDC->TextOut(20, 140,
            "TA_BASELINE text positioning");
        pDC->Rectangle(18, 141, 200, 158);
    }
    else
    {
        pDC->SetTextAlign(TA_TOP);
        pDC->TextOut(20, 20, "TA_TOP text positioning");
        pDC->Rectangle(18, 21, 200, 38);

        pDC->TextOut(20, 80, "TA_TOP text positioning");
        pDC->Rectangle(18, 81, 200, 98);

        pDC->TextOut(20, 140, "TA_TOP text positioning");
        pDC->Rectangle(18, 141, 200, 158);
    }

    pDC->SelectObject(oldBrush);
}
```

When the user clicks the application's window, the vertical text alignment of
the second and third text lines changes. The view class's OnLButtonDown()
function handles this task, as shown in Listing 7-8, by reversing the value of
the m_showAllAlignments flag. The call to Invalidate() then forces the
window to redraw its display.

Listing 7-8: VerticalAlignApp's OnLButtonDown() function

```
void CVerticalAlignAppView::OnLButtonDown(UINT nFlags,
    CPoint point)
{
    // TODO: Add your message handler code here
    //    and/or call default

    m_showAllAlignments = !m_showAllAlignments;

    Invalidate();

    CView::OnLButtonDown(nFlags, point);
}
```

PROBLEMS & SOLUTIONS

Displaying Tabbed Text

PROBLEM: *I have a table that I want to display in my application's window. How can I use tabs to position the table elements, rather than having to fool with a lot of special text alignments?*

SOLUTION: Sounds like a job for the `TabbedTextOut()` function, which is a member of the CDC class. `TabbedTextOut()` enables you to display text strings that contain tab characters. To use the function, perform these steps:

1. Create an array of integers that hold the tab positions you need.

2. Create the text strings you want to display, embedding tab characters (\t) as appropriate.

3. Call `TabbedTextOut()` to display each line of tabbed text.

`TabbedTextOut()` is a complicated function that requires several more arguments than the regular `TextOut()` function. Its signature looks like this:

```
TabbedTextOut(
    int x,
    int y,
    Const CString& str,
    int numTabs,
    LPINT tabs,
    int tabOrigin);
```

`TabbedTextOut()`'s arguments are as follows:

x	The horizontal position at which to display the string
y	The vertical position at which to display the string
str	The string to display, which can also be the address of a char array
numTabs	The number of tabs in the tab array
tabs	The address of the tab array
tabOrigin	The horizontal position at which tab measurement begins

On CD-ROM

To see TabbedTextOut() do its stuff, take a look at the Chapter07\TabTextApp folder of this book's CD-ROM for the TabTextApp application. This application displays a multicolumn table that uses tabs to space the columns. Figure 7-9 shows the application's display. Listing 7-9 shows the application's OnDraw() function, which creates the tabbed display.

Continued

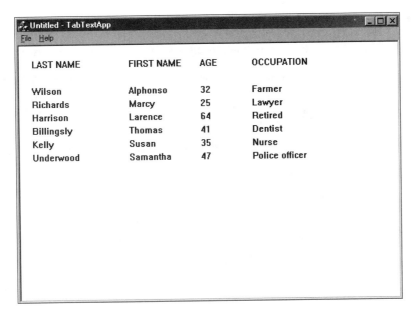

Figure 7-9: TabTextApp displays tabbed text.

Listing 7-9: TabTextApp's `OnDraw()` function

```
void CTabTextAppView::OnDraw(CDC* pDC)
{
    CTabTextAppDoc* pDoc = GetDocument();
    ASSERT_VALID(pDoc);

    // TODO: add draw code for native data here

    int tabs[] = {150, 260, 340};
    CString header =
        "LAST NAME\tFIRST NAME\tAGE\tOCCUPATION";
    CString row1 = "Wilson\tAlphonso\t32\tFarmer";
    CString row2 = "Richards\tMarcy\t25\tLawyer";
    CString row3 = "Harrison\tLarence\t64\tRetired";
    CString row4 = "Billingsly\tThomas\t41\tDentist";
    CString row5 = "Kelly\tSusan\t35\tNurse";
    CString row6 =
        "Underwood\tSamantha\t47\tPolice officer";

    pDC->TabbedTextOut(20, 20, header, 3, tabs, 20);
    pDC->TabbedTextOut(20, 60, row1, 3, tabs, 20);
    pDC->TabbedTextOut(20, 80, row2, 3, tabs, 20);
    pDC->TabbedTextOut(20, 100, row3, 3, tabs, 20);
    pDC->TabbedTextOut(20, 120, row4, 3, tabs, 20);
    pDC->TabbedTextOut(20, 140, row5, 3, tabs, 20);
    pDC->TabbedTextOut(20, 160, row6, 3, tabs, 20);
}
```

Getting Text Metrics

Up to this point in this book, programs have displayed text using hard-coded coordinates in the TextOut() function. This isn't the safest way to space text, because you can't always be sure of the current font's size. When you display multiple lines of text, it's a good idea to first determine the size of the font the application's using. Then, you can easily calculate the appropriate line spacing for the text the application will display.

To get information about the currently selected font, you call the GetTextMetrics() function:

```
TEXTMETRIC textMetric;
pDC->GetTextMetrics(&textMetric);
```

GetTextMetrics() single argument is the address of a TEXTMETRIC structure. Windows defines this structure as shown in Listing 7-10.

Listing 7-10: The TEXTMETRIC structure

```
typedef struct tagTEXTMETRIC {    /* tm */
    int   tmHeight;
    int   tmAscent;
    int   tmDescent;
    int   tmInternalLeadinga;
    int   tmExternalLeading;
    int   tmAveCharWidth;
    int   tmMaxCharWidth;
    int   tmWeight;
    BYTE  tmItalic;
    BYTE  tmUnderlined;
    BYTE  tmStruckOut;
    BYTE  tmFirstChar;
    BYTE  tmLastChar;
    BYTE  tmDefaultChar;
    BYTE  tmBreakChar;
    BYTE  tmPitchAndFamily;
    BYTE  tmCharSet;
    int   tmOverhang;
    int   tmDigitizedAspectX;
    int   tmDigitizedAspectY;
} TEXTMETRIC;
```

Table 7-1 describes each of the structure's members. Unless you know a bit about typography, some of the terms used in the table will be new to you. In most cases, however, you won't need to deal with the more esoteric members of the TEXTMETRIC structure.

Table 7-1 Members of the TEXTMETRIC structure

Member	Description
tmAscent	Character ascent, which is the height above the base-line
tmAveCharWidth	Average character width
tmBreakChar	Break character for text justification
tmCharSet	Font's character set
tmDefaultChar	Character that will be substituted for those not included in the font
tmDescent	Character descent, which is the height below the base-line
tmDigitizedAspectX	Horizontal element of the aspect ratio
tmDigitizedAspectY	Vertical element of the aspect ratio
tmExternalLeading	External leading, which is extra space between lines of text
tmFirstChar	Value of the font's first character
tmHeight	Character height
tmInternalLeading	Internal leading, which is space used for adding marks such as accents
tmItalic	Value indicating italic (0=no italic; nonzero=italic)
tmLastChar	Value of the font's last character
tmMaxCharWidth	Width of the widest character
tmOverhang	Extra width that may be added in order to add attributes, such as bold or italic, to characters
tmPitchAndFamily	Pitch, technology, and family of a physical font
tmStruckOut	Value indicating strikeout (0=no strikeout; nonzero=strikeout)
tmUnderlined	Value indicating an underline (0=no underline; nonzero=underlined)
tmWeight	Font weight (amount of "boldness")

On CD-ROM

In the Chapter07\TextMetricsApp folder of this book's CD-ROM, you can find the TextMetricsApp application, which demonstrates vertical text spacing. When you run the application, you see the window shown in Figure 7-10, which displays text using a character height obtained through the GetTextMetrics() function. Listing 7-11 shows the OnDraw() function, where the application determines the text height and displays several lines of text.

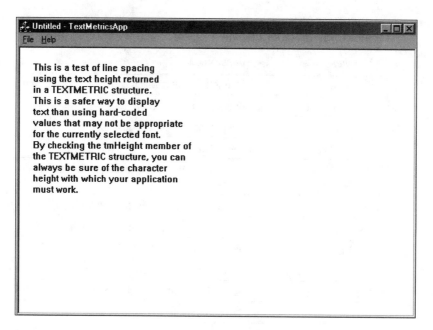

Figure 7-10: TextMetricsApp displaying lines of text

Listing 7-11: TextMetricsApp's `OnDraw( )` **function**

```
void CTextMetricsAppView::OnDraw(CDC* pDC)
{
    CTextMetricsAppDoc* pDoc = GetDocument();
    ASSERT_VALID(pDoc);

    // TODO: add draw code for native data here

    TEXTMETRIC textMetric;
    pDC->GetTextMetrics(&textMetric);
    int charHeight = textMetric.tmHeight;

    char* s[] = {
        "This is a test of line spacing",
        "using the text height returned",
        "in a TEXTMETRIC structure.",
        "This is a safer way to display",
        "text than using hard-coded",
        "values that may not be appropriate",
        "for the currently selected font.",
        "By checking the tmHeight member of",
        "the TEXTMETRIC structure, you can",
        "always be sure of the character",
        "height with which your application",
        "must work."};

    for (int x=0; x<12; ++x)
        pDC->TextOut(20, 20+x*charHeight, s[x]);
}
```

Creating Fonts

When you're writing simple applications, you don't have to deal much with fonts. The system font usually works fine for most purposes. However, if you need a specific font, you can create your own by creating an object of MFC's CFont class. To create a font, you first initialize an instance of the LOGFONT structure, which holds the information Windows needs to create the font. You then pass the structure to your CFont object in order to create the actual font. The process looks something like that in Listing 7-12.

Listing 7-12: Creating a font

```
LOGFONT logFont;
logFont.lfHeight = 24;
logFont.lfWidth = 0;
logFont.lfEscapement = 0;
logFont.lfOrientation = 0;
logFont.lfWeight = FW_NORMAL;
logFont.lfItalic = 0;
logFont.lfUnderline = 0;
logFont.lfStrikeOut = 0;
logFont.lfCharSet = ANSI_CHARSET;
logFont.lfOutPrecision = OUT_DEFAULT_PRECIS;
logFont.lfClipPrecision = CLIP_DEFAULT_PRECIS;
logFont.lfQuality = PROOF_QUALITY;
logFont.lfPitchAndFamily = VARIABLE_PITCH | FF_ROMAN;
strcpy(logFont.lfFaceName, "Times New Roman");

CFont font;
font.CreateFontIndirect(&logFont);
```

Obviously, before creating a font, you have to understand the LOGFONT structure, which Windows defines as shown in Listing 7-13.

Listing 7-13: The LOGFONT structure

```
typedef struct tagLOGFONT { // lf
    LONG lfHeight;
    LONG lfWidth;
    LONG lfEscapement;
    LONG lfOrientation;
    LONG lfWeight;
    BYTE lfItalic;
    BYTE lfUnderline;
    BYTE lfStrikeOut;
    BYTE lfCharSet;
    BYTE lfOutPrecision;
    BYTE lfClipPrecision;
    BYTE lfQuality;
    BYTE lfPitchAndFamily;
    TCHAR lfFaceName[LF_FACESIZE];
} LOGFONT;
```

Table 7-2 describes each of the LOGFONT members. Unfortunately, a complete discussion of fonts could take up an entire book of its own. So, if some of the descriptions in Table 7-2 make your head spin, know that you're in good company. As luck would have it, most of the LOGFONT members have default values (see the FontApp application's source code later in this chapter) that you can plug in, leaving you to concentrate on more useful aspects of the font, such as height, width, and attributes like bold and underline. For more information on the LOGFONT structure, check your Visual C++ online documentation.

Table 7-2 Members of the LOGFONT structure

Member	Description
lfCharSet	Font's character set. Can be ANSI_CHARSET, DEFAULT_CHARSET, SYMBOL_CHARSET, SHIFTJIS_CHARSET, GB2312_CHARSET, HANGEUL_CHARSET, CHINESEBIG5_CHARSET, OEM_CHARSET, JOHAB_CHARSET, HEBREW_CHARSET, ARABIC_CHARSET, GREEK_ CHARSET, TURKISH_CHARSET, THAI_CHARSET, EASTEUROPE_ CHARSET, RUSSIAN_CHARSET, MAC_CHARSET, or BALTIC_CHARSET.
lfClipPrecision	Font's clipping precision, which specifies how to clip characters that fall partially outside the clipping region. Can be CLIP_DEFAULT_ PRECIS, CLIP_CHARACTER_PRECIS, CLIP_STROKE_PRECIS, CLIP_MASK, CLIP_EMBEDDED, CLIP_LH_ANGLES, or CLIP_TT_ ALWAYS.
lfEscapement	Font angle
lfFaceName	Font's typeface name
lfHeight	Font height
lfItalic	Font's italic attribute. A nonzero value turns on the attribute.
lfOrientation	Font angle
lfOutPrecision	Font's output precision, which determines how closely Windows must match the font with existing fonts. Can be OUT_CHARACTER_ PRECIS, OUT_DEFAULT_PRECIS, OUT_DEVICE_PRECIS, OUT_RASTER_PRECIS, OUT_STRING_PRECIS, OUT_STROKE_PRECIS, OUT_TT_ONLY_PRECIS, or OUT_TT_PRECIS.
lfPitchAnd Family	Font's pitch and family. Can be DEFAULT_PITCH, FIXED_PITCH, or VARIABLE_PITCH using the OR operator with one of the following: FF_DECORATIVE, FF_DONTCARE, FF_MODERN, FF_ROMAN, FF_SCRIPT, or FF_SWISS.
lfQuality	Font's output quality, which is how well the GDI matches the logical-font attributes to those of a physical font. Can be DEFAULT_QUALITY, DRAFT_QUALITY, PROOF_QUALITY.

Member	Description
lfStrikeOut	Font's strikeout attribute. A nonzero value turns on the attribute.
lfUnderline	Font's underline attribute. A nonzero value turns on the attribute.
lfWeight	Font weight (degree of boldness). Can be FW_DONTCARE, FW_THIN, FW_EXTRALIGHT, FW_ULTRALIGHT, FW_LIGHT, FW_NORMAL, FW_REGULAR, FW_MEDIUM, FW_SEMIBOLD, FW_DEMIBOLD, FW_BOLD, FW_EXTRABOLD, FW_ULTRABOLD, FW_HEAVY, FW_BLACK, or any value between 0 and 1000.
lfWidth	Font width

On CD-ROM

In the Chapter07\FontApp folder of this book's CD-ROM, you can find the FontApp application, which demonstrates creating fonts. When you run the application, you see the window shown in Figure 7-11.

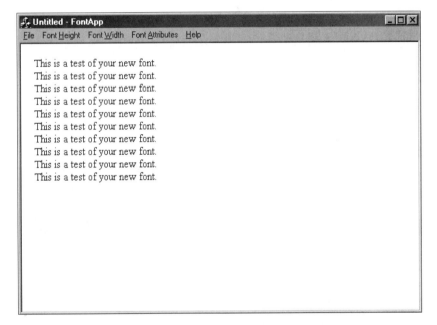

Figure 7-11: FontApp displays ten lines of text using its own font.

You can change the size and look of the displayed font from the application's menus. Figure 7-12 shows the application after the user has increased the font height to 36.

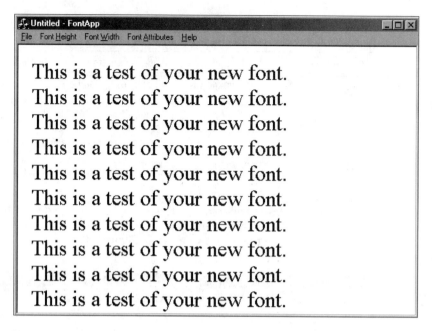

Figure 7-12: Here's FontApp after the user has enlarged the font.

Figure 7-13 shows the font with a larger width and its italics attribute selected.

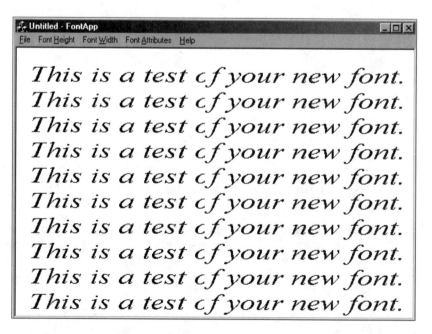

Figure 7-13: Here's FontApp after the user has selected the wide and italics attributes.

FontApp seems to do quite a bit of work, but all the application does is change the values of a few variables and create a new font based on the newly selected values. These values are members of the application's view class and are initialized in the class's constructor, as shown in Listing 7-14.

Listing 7-14: The view class's constructor

```
CFontAppView::CFontAppView()
{
    // TODO: add construction code here

    m_height = 12;
    m_width = 0;
    m_italic = 0;
    m_underline = 0;
    m_strikeout = 0;
    m_weight = FW_NORMAL;
}
```

When FontApp must update its window, MFC calls the view class's OnDraw() function. In OnDraw(), shown in Listing 7-15, the program creates a new font based on the user's selections; selects the font into the DC; and displays text with the new font. OnDraw() spaces the text in the window by using the font's height (as stored in the LOGFONT structure) to calculate the vertical position for each line.

Listing 7-15: FontApp's OnDraw() function

```
void CFontAppView::OnDraw(CDC* pDC)
{
    CFontAppDoc* pDoc = GetDocument();
    ASSERT_VALID(pDoc);

    // TODO: add draw code for native data here

    LOGFONT logFont;
    logFont.lfHeight = m_height;
    logFont.lfWidth = m_width;
    logFont.lfEscapement = 0;
    logFont.lfOrientation = 0;
    logFont.lfWeight = m_weight;
    logFont.lfItalic = m_italic;
    logFont.lfUnderline = m_underline;
    logFont.lfStrikeOut = m_strikeout;
    logFont.lfCharSet = ANSI_CHARSET;
    logFont.lfOutPrecision = OUT_DEFAULT_PRECIS;
    logFont.lfClipPrecision = CLIP_DEFAULT_PRECIS;
    logFont.lfQuality = PROOF_QUALITY;
    logFont.lfPitchAndFamily = VARIABLE_PITCH | FF_ROMAN;
    strcpy(logFont.lfFaceName, "Times New Roman");

    CFont font;
    font.CreateFontIndirect(&logFont);

    CFont* pOldFont = pDC->SelectObject(&font);
```

```
    for (int x=0; x<10; ++x)
        pDC->TextOut(20, 20+x*logFont.lfHeight,
            "This is a test of your new font.");

    pDC->SelectObject(pOldFont);
}
```

PROBLEMS & SOLUTIONS

The Size of a Text Line

PROBLEM: *Most Windows fonts use proportionate character spacing, making it difficult to determine the actual size of a line of text. This problem is multiplied by the fact that in the application I'm writing, the user can select a different font, which changes the size of the text string. How can my application accurately determine the size of a text string on the screen?*

SOLUTION: Proportionate fonts sure make life interesting. They look great on the screen, but because every character is a different width, you can't find the length of a string as easily as you can with a proportionate font.

Or can you? Windows has just the function to solve this dilemma. With the impressive name GetTextExtentPoint32(), this function returns the height and width of a text string based on the currently active font. This Windows API function's signature looks like this:

```
::GetTextExtentPoint32(
    HDC hDC,
    LPCTSTR pText,
    int numChars,
    LPSIZE pSize);
```

GetTextExtentPoint32()'s arguments are as follows:

hDC	A handle to the current device context
pText	The address of the text for which you want the size
numChars	The number of characters in the text string
pSize	The address of a SIZE structure

Continued

GetTextExtentPoint32() stores the size of the string in a SIZE structure, a pointer to which you supply as the function's fourth argument. Windows defines the SIZE structure like this:

```
typedef struct tagSIZE {
    LONG cx;
    LONG cy;
} SIZE;
```

The width of the string ends up in the cx member and the height in the cy member. You can use these values to determine other coordinates based on the size of the string.

On CD-ROM

For example, in the Chapter07\FontApp2 folder of this book's CD-ROM, you can find a new version of the FontApp application. This version works much like the previous version, enabling you to select font sizes and attributes for the text on the screen. However, this new version draws a rectangle around each string, calculating the rectangle's width from the string size returned by a call to GetTextExtentPoint32(). Figure 7-14 shows the program running, and Listing 7-16 shows the program's OnDraw() function.

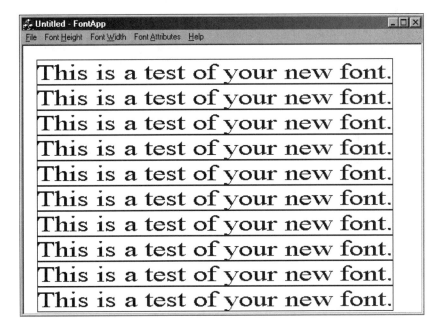

Figure 7-14: This version of FontApp calculates the size of each string in the display, regardless of the string's attributes.

Continued

Listing 7-16: FontApp's new `OnDraw( )` function

```
void CFontAppView::OnDraw(CDC* pDC)
{
    CFontAppDoc* pDoc = GetDocument();
    ASSERT_VALID(pDoc);

    // TODO: add draw code for native data here

    LOGFONT logFont;
    logFont.lfHeight = m_height;
    logFont.lfWidth = m_width;
    logFont.lfEscapement = 0;
    logFont.lfOrientation = 0;
    logFont.lfWeight = m_weight;
    logFont.lfItalic = m_italic;
    logFont.lfUnderline = m_underline;
    logFont.lfStrikeOut = m_strikeout;
    logFont.lfCharSet = ANSI_CHARSET;
    logFont.lfOutPrecision = OUT_DEFAULT_PRECIS;
    logFont.lfClipPrecision = CLIP_DEFAULT_PRECIS;
    logFont.lfQuality = PROOF_QUALITY;
    logFont.lfPitchAndFamily = VARIABLE_PITCH | FF_ROMAN;
    strcpy(logFont.lfFaceName, "Times New Roman");

    CFont font;
    font.CreateFontIndirect(&logFont);

    CFont* pOldFont = pDC->SelectObject(&font);
    CBrush* pOldBrush =
        (CBrush*)pDC->SelectStockObject(NULL_BRUSH);

    SIZE size;
    ::GetTextExtentPoint32(pDC->m_hDC,
        "This is a test of your new font.", 32, &size);

    for (int x=0; x<10; ++x)
    {
        pDC->TextOut(20, 20+x*logFont.lfHeight,
            "This is a test of your new font.");

        int top = 20+x*logFont.lfHeight;
        int right = 20+size.cx;
        int bottom = 20+x*logFont.lfHeight +
            logFont.lfHeight;
        pDC->Rectangle(20, top, right, bottom);
    }

    pDC->SelectObject(pOldFont);
    pDC->SelectObject(pOldBrush);
}
```

Summary

Most applications display text in one form or another. Unfortunately, due to Windows' graphical nature, creating the perfect text display can be a chore. Proportional fonts of different sizes with different attributes complicate matters by making it tricky to determine the right line spacing. Although there's a lot to know about displaying text and handling fonts, Windows provides all the tools you need to generate your application's display. In this chapter, you got an overview of the most useful techniques for displaying text.

Also discussed in this chapter:

▶ The `TextOut()` function displays text easily, if you're not too fussy about the outcome.

▶ An application can set the text color, as well as the background color.

▶ An application can change the character spacing in a line of text.

▶ An application can use left, center, or right horizontal alignment with text.

▶ An application can display text with top, bottom, or baseline vertical alignment.

▶ The `TabbedTextOut()` function displays text containing embedded tabs.

▶ The `GetTextMetrics()` acquires information about a font.

▶ An application can create its own fonts using MFC's `CFont` class.

Chapter 8

Menus

Windows 98 applications that do not contain menu bars are few and far between. It is, after all, the menu bar that gives the user access to the commands that control the application. Luckily, creating menus for your application is a simple task when programming with MFC. Although some menu programming techniques require that you roll up your sleeves and write a few lines of code from scratch, ClassWizard can help with most conventional menu-coding tasks. In this chapter, you get the inside scoop on programming professional-looking menus.

Creating Menu Resources

The first thing you must do to add menus to your Visual C++ application is create your menus' resources with the menu editor, as shown in Figure 8-1. Using the menu editor not only enables you to create new menus and add menu items, but also enables you to set the attributes for the menus. These attributes include whether each menu item should be initially checked or enabled. You saw how to use the menu editor to create menu resources in Chapter 3, "Programming with Visual C++." Please refer to that chapter or to your Visual C++ online documentation for more information on using the resource editors. Following is a quick review of the steps required to define a new menu.

1. Double-click the menu ID in the ResourceView pane of the Project Workspace window, as shown in Figure 8-1. The menu appears in the menu editor.

Menu ID   Resource view pane   Menu editor

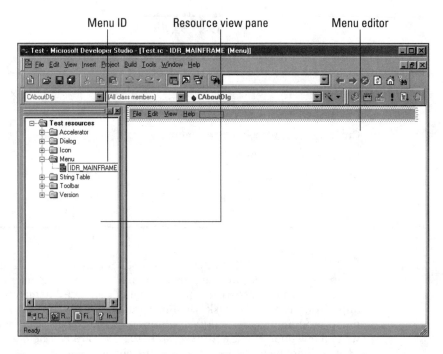

Figure 8-1: When you double-click a menu ID, the menu appears in the editor.

2. Select the blank menu in the menu bar, and press Enter. The Menu Item Properties property sheet appears, as shown in Figure 8-2.

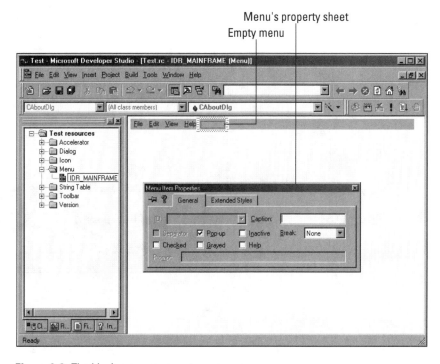

Figure 8-2: The blank menu represents a new pop-up menu.

3. Type the menu's name into the Caption box, using an ampersand (&) to indicate the menu's hot key, as shown in Figure 8-3.

Menu's name

The new menu

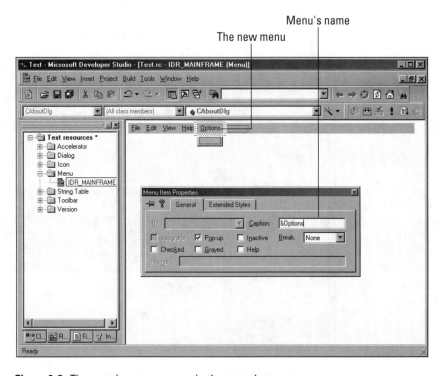

Figure 8-3: The menu's name appears in the menu bar.

4. Double-click the first empty menu item in the new menu. The Menu Item Properties sheet reappears, as shown in Figure 8-4.

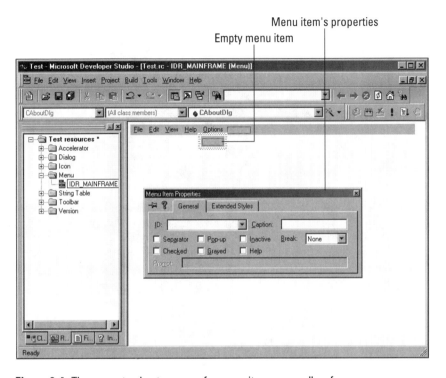

Figure 8-4: The property sheet appears for menu items, as well as for pop-up menus.

5. Type the menu item's command ID into the ID box, and type an ampersand followed by the command's caption into the Caption box, as shown in Figure 8-5.

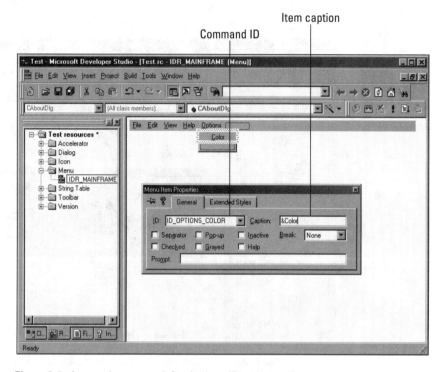

Command ID

Item caption

Figure 8-5: A menu item must define both an ID and a caption.

6. Repeat Steps 4 and 5 for each menu item in the menu.

Creating Message Response Functions

Once you have created the menu resource, you must associate each menu item with a message response function. This enables MFC to call the associated function when the user selects a menu item. The program can then process the user's request with the associated function. Creating message response functions is a snap with ClassWizard, as shown in Figure 8-6. You simply follow the proceeding steps:

1. Select the class that will define the function.

2. Select the menu ID that will be associated with the function.

3. Add the function to the program.

ClassWizard enables you to perform these tasks with a few mouse clicks, as you learned in Chapter 3, "Programming with Visual C++."

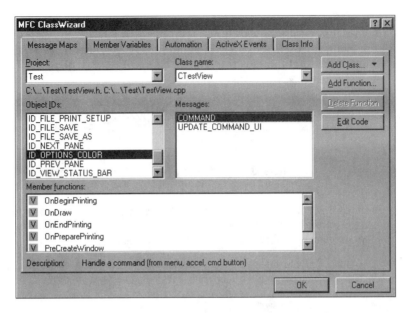

Figure 8-6: ClassWizard makes it easy to add message response functions to your application.

When ClassWizard adds a message response function to a class, it first declares the new function in the class's header file:

```
afx_msg void OnOptionsTime();
```

The `afx_msg` prefix simply marks the line as a message response function. The prefix isn't required, but should be supplied to differentiate message response functions from other class member functions.

After declaring the function in the class's header file, ClassWizard adds the function to the class's message map:

```
BEGIN_MESSAGE_MAP(CMenuAppView, CView)
    //{{AFX_MSG_MAP(CMenuAppView)
    ON_COMMAND(ID_OPTIONS_TIME, OnOptionsTime)
    //}}AFX_MSG_MAP
END_MESSAGE_MAP()
```

You may remember from Chapter 3 that the message map associates a message ID with a message response function. That is, the above message map tells MFC that when the application receives a command with the `ID_OPTIONS_TIME` ID, it should call the `OnOptionsTime()` message response function.

Finally, after adding the function to the message map, MFC defines the function's skeleton in the class's implementation file:

```
void CTestView::OnOptionsTime()
{
    // TODO: Add your command handler code here

}
```

MFC defines an empty message response function. (MFC, after all, doesn't have a clue what you want to do with the menu item that the function represents.) You must write the function's body yourself, providing the source code that handles the request represented by the menu item.

 PROBLEMS & SOLUTIONS

Handling a Range of Menu Items

PROBLEM: *My application's menus have several related commands that I'd like to manage in one message response function. Is this possible, or do I have to have a separate message response function for every menu item?*

SOLUTION: You can manage several, related menu items in a single message response function. The problem with this technique is that you have to write the code by hand, without ClassWizard's help. Still, it's a simple enough process.

The trick is to use the ON_COMMAND_RANGE macro in your message map, rather than the usual ON_COMMAND macro:

```
BEGIN_MESSAGE_MAP(CTestView, CView)
    ON_COMMAND_RANGE(ID_COLORS_RED,
        ID_COLORS_BLUE, OnColors)
END_MESSAGE_MAP()
```

The ON_COMMAND_RANGE macro's three arguments are the first ID in the range, the last ID in the range, and the name of the message response function that will handle the range. In order for this macro to work, all the command IDs in the range must be consecutive. For example, the above example sets up a range of command IDs that includes ID_COLORS_RED, ID_COLORS_GREEN, and ID_COLORS_BLUE, in that order. The IDs are defined like this:

```
#define ID_COLORS_RED 32771
#define ID_COLORS_GREEN 32772
#define ID_COLORS_BLUE 32773
```

As you can see, the IDs are numbered consecutively, a requirement for the ON_COMMAND_RANGE macro.

Next, you must declare the message response function in the class's header file. The declaration looks something like this:

```
afx_msg void OnColors(UINT commandID);
```

A message response function that's associated with an ON_COMMAND_RANGE macro must accept a single UINT argument, which is the ID of the command on whose behalf MFC called the function. You use commandID to determine which command the user selected and how you should respond to it.

Continued

Finally, you must define the message response function that will handle the command range. Such a function might look like this:

```
void CTestView::OnColors(UINT commandID)
{
    if (commandID == ID_COLORS_RED)
        m_color = RED;
    else if (commandID == ID_COLORS_GREEN)
        m_color = GREEN;
    else
        m_color = BLUE;
}
```

The function checks to see which command resulted in a call to the function, and acts accordingly. The above function replaces the three functions shown in Listing 8-1. The disadvantage is that although ClassWizard can generate the three functions in Listing 8-1 for you (except for the body of the function), but you have to write your own code from scratch when using command ranges.

Listing 8-1: Responding to the Colors menu items without using ID ranges

```
void CTestView::OnColorsRed()
{
    // TODO: Add your command handler code here

    m_color = RED;
}

void CTestView::OnColorsGreen()
{
    // TODO: Add your command handler code here

    m_color = GREEN;
}

void CTestView::OnColorsBlue()
{
    // TODO: Add your command handler code here

    m_color = BLUE;
}
```

Understanding Menu UI Functions

Your application must maintain the appearance of menu items. For example, the application may have menu items that must be checked or disabled depending upon the current settings of the program's options. MFC provides a mechanism for keeping menu items properly updated. Each time a menu item is about to be displayed, MFC checks whether the program has defined an update command UI function for the menu item. If so, MFC runs the update command UI function immediately before it displays the menu item, giving the application a chance to add checkmarks, disable options, change a menu item's text, and so on.

Creating Update Command UI Functions

You add update command UI functions to a program in exactly the same way that you add message response functions. Call up ClassWizard and select a menu command ID in the Object IDs box. When you do, you see COMMAND and UPDATE_COMMAND_UI function types in the Messages pane. Double-click UPDATE_COMMAND_UI, and ClassWizard displays the Add Member Function dialog box containing a suggested name for the new update command UI function, as shown in Figure 8-7. Accept the name by clicking OK, and MFC adds the function to the application.

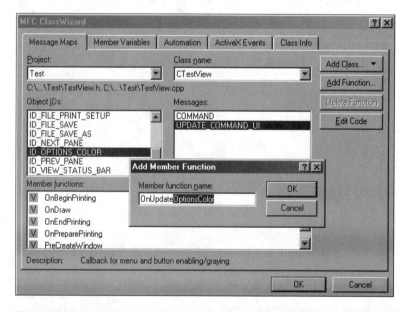

Figure 8-7: ClassWizard can add update command UI functions to your application.

Just adding the function to the application, however, is not enough. Once you have the update command UI function, it's your task to complete the function. Exactly how you do this depends upon what you want to do with the menu item before MFC displays it. In any case, you set the menu item's attributes by calling member functions of the CCmdUI class, an object that is passed to the update command UI function as its single parameter. In the following sections, you'll discover how to manipulate the CCmdUI object.

Marking menu items with checks

One way you can manipulate a `CCmdUI` object is to set checks on menu items. When you create menu items that represent option toggles—commands that turn an option on and off—you usually use checkmarks to notify the user that a particular option is on. For example, you may have an option that turns the application's toolbar on and off. When the attribute is on, the application places a checkmark next to the menu item, as shown in Figure 8-8.

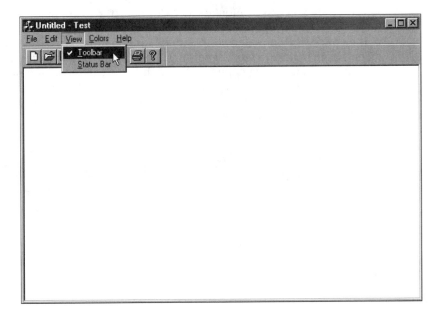

Figure 8-8: Checkmarks indicate whether an application option is selected.

An update command UI function that handles the checkmark might look like this:

```
void CTestView::OnUpdateViewToolbar(CCmdUI* pCmdUI)
{
    // TODO: Add your command update UI handler code here

    pCmdUI->SetCheck(m_toolbar);
}
```

As you can see, the update command UI function receives a pointer to a `CCmdUI` object as its single parameter. To set a checkmark on the menu item, the program calls the `CCmdUI` object's `SetCheck()` member function. The function's single argument is a `boolean` value: a value of `TRUE` turns the checkmark on; a value of `FALSE` turns the checkmark off. In the toolbar example, the `m_toolbar` member variable holds the current state of the option. That is, `m_toolbar` is either `TRUE` or `FALSE` depending on whether the user has the toolbar turned on or off.

When the user opens the View menu, MFC calls `OnUpdateViewToolbar()` in order to set the Toolbar command's checkmark. This occurs right before MFC displays the menu, so the user never sees the checkmark being turned on or off. When the menu appears, all the menu items' update command UI functions have already been called and the menu items' attributes set.

Bulleting menu items

Another way you can manipulate a `CCmdUI` object is to set bullets on menu items. Some menu option settings are mutually exclusive. That is, only one of the options can be selected at a time. These mutually exclusive items display bullets next to current settings. An example of this might be a set of commands for selecting colors. Because the user can draw with only one color in a given moment, only one color at a time can be selected. In this case, the application's menu would use a bullet to indicate the currently selected color, as shown in Figure 8-9.

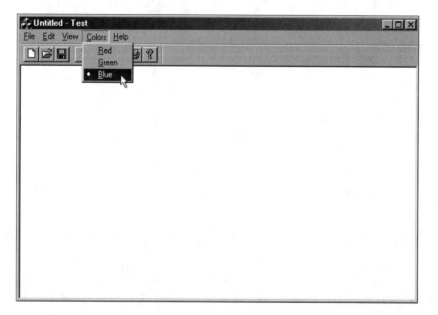

Figure 8-9: A bullet indicates the current selection in a set of mutually exclusive options.

The update command UI function for a color menu item might look like this:

```
void CTestView::OnUpdateColorsRed(CCmdUI* pCmdUI)
{
    // TODO: Add your command update UI handler code here

    pCmdUI->SetRadio(m_color == RED);
}
```

The `CCmdUI` member function `SetRadio()` adds or removes bullets from menu items. The function's single argument is a `boolean` value that indicates whether the bullet should or should not be visible. In this case, the boolean expression `m_color == RED` evaluates to either `TRUE` or `FALSE`. The `m_color` member variable holds the current color setting.

Note

You may wonder why `SetRadio()` isn't called `SetBullet()`. The function gets its name from radio buttons, which are Windows buttons that represent mutually exclusive selections. This concept comes from the buttons you have on your car radio, which also represent mutually exclusive settings. You sure wouldn't want to listen to more than one radio station at a time!

Enabling and Disabling Menu Items

`CCmdUI` objects can also enable or disable menu items. The state of an application and the currently selected options often dictates which menu items are selectable. For example, before you load a document into a word processor, the word processor disables all editing commands in its Edit menu, as shown in Figure 8-10. You can't, after all, edit text that doesn't yet exist in the application's window.

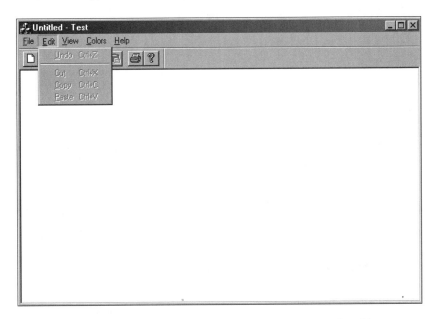

Figure 8-10: An application disables menu items that are not currently valid.

In an MFC program, you enable and disable a menu item in the item's update command UI function by calling the `CCmdUI` object's `Enable()` member function, as shown here:

```
void CTestView::OnUpdateEditCut(CCmdUI* pCmdUI)
{
```

```
    // TODO: Add your command update UI handler code here

    pCmdUI->Enable(m_cut);
}
```

The `Enable()` member function requires a single argument, a `boolean` value indicating whether the item should be enabled (`TRUE`) or disabled (`FALSE`).

Changing Menu Item Text

When you create a menu item, you define the item's caption, which is the text that appears in the menu. Although the text of most menu items remains unchanged throughout the application's run, some do change, based on the program's state or the currently selected options. As an example, reconsider the option toggle commands that you learned about in the section on menu checkmarks. Another way to handle such options is to change the menu text to reflect the current setting, rather than checkmark the option. For example, a command that toggles the toolbar could change its text from Show Toolbar to Hide Toolbar, depending on whether the toolbar were currently visible.

You handle this text change in the menu item's update command UI function:

```
void CTestView::OnUpdateViewToolbar(CCmdUI* pCmdUI)
{
    // TODO: Add your command update UI handler code here

    if (m_toolbar)
        pCmdUI->SetText("&Hide Toolbar");
    else
        pCmdUI->SetText("&Show Toolbar");
}
```

To change the menu item's text, you call the `CCmdUI` object's `SetText()` member function, which takes the new text as its single argument.

PROBLEMS & SOLUTIONS

Update Command UI Functions and Menu Item Ranges

PROBLEM: *Now that I know that I can use the* `ON_COMMAND_RANGE` *macro to handle a range of related commands in a single message response function, what about the update command UI functions for that same ID range?*

SOLUTION: As you may have guessed, MFC also provides a mechanism for creating a single update command UI function for a group of related menu items. In fact, the programming works much like what you learned for creating a command-range message response function.

Continued

The trick this time is to use the ON_UPDATE_COMMAND_UI_RANGE macro in your message map, rather than the usual ON_UPDATE_COMMAND_UI macro:

```
BEGIN_MESSAGE_MAP(CTestView, CView)
    ON_COMMAND_RANGE(ID_COLORS_RED,
        ID_COLORS_BLUE, OnColors)
    ON_UPDATE_COMMAND_UI_RANGE(ID_COLORS_RED,
        ID_COLORS_BLUE, OnUpdateColors)
END_MESSAGE_MAP()
```

The ON_UPDATE_COMMAND_UI_RANGE macro's three arguments are the first ID in the range, the last ID in the range, and the name of the update command UI function that will handle the range. As with ON_COMMAND_RANGE, in order for this macro to work, all the command IDs in the range must be consecutive:

```
#define ID_COLORS_RED 32771
#define ID_COLORS_GREEN 32772
#define ID_COLORS_BLUE 32773
```

Next, you declare the update command UI function in the class's header file. The declaration looks something like this:

```
afx_msg void OnUpdateColors(CCmdUI* pCmdUI);
```

Notice that this declaration looks like any other update command UI function declaration, receiving a pointer to a CCmdUI object as its single parameter.

Finally, you must define the update command UI function that will handle the command range. Such a function might look like Listing 8-2.

Listing 8-2: The update command UI function for the Colors menu

```
void CTestView::OnUpdateColors(CCmdUI* pCmdUI)
{
    // TODO: Add your command update UI handler code here

    if (pCmdUI->m_nID == ID_COLORS_RED)
        pCmdUI->SetRadio(m_color == RED);
    else if (pCmdUI->m_nID == ID_COLORS_GREEN)
        pCmdUI->SetRadio(m_color == GREEN);
    else
        pCmdUI->SetRadio(m_color == BLUE);
}
```

The function determines the command that resulted in the function call by examining the CCmdUI object's m_nID member variable. With the ID in hand, the function can determine what action to take. The above function replaces the three functions shown in Listing 8-3. The disadvantage is that, as with message response functions for ranges, although ClassWizard can generate the three functions in Listing 8-3 for you (except for the body of the function), you have to write your own code from scratch when using command ranges.

Continued

Listing 8-3: Responding to the Colors menu items without using ID ranges

```
void CTestView::OnUpdateColorsBlue(CCmdUI* pCmdUI)
{
    // TODO: Add your command update UI handler code here

    pCmdUI->SetRadio(m_color == BLUE);
}

void CTestView::OnUpdateColorsGreen(CCmdUI* pCmdUI)
{
    // TODO: Add your command update UI handler code here

    pCmdUI->SetRadio(m_color == GREEN);
}

void CTestView::OnUpdateColorsRed(CCmdUI* pCmdUI)
{
    // TODO: Add your command update UI handler code here

    pCmdUI->SetRadio(m_color == RED);
}
```

The MenuApp Sample Application

On CD-ROM

In the Chapter08\MenuApp folder of this book's CD-ROM, you'll find the MenuApp application, which demonstrates all the techniques discussed in this chapter. When you run the application, you see the window shown in Figure 8-11. Besides the usual File and Help menus, MenuApp has On/Off, Options 1, and Options 2 menus, each of which demonstrate various types of menu items.

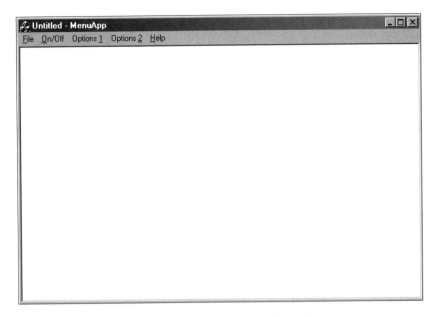

Figure 8-11: The MenuApp application displays a set of sample menus.

Using the MenuApp Sample Application

You will now use some of the information discussed in this chapter. First, select the On command in the On/Off menu. When you do, the On command changes to Off, and the other items in the menu become enabled, as shown in Figure 8-12. This menu demonstrates changing a menu item's text, as well as enabling and disabling menu items.

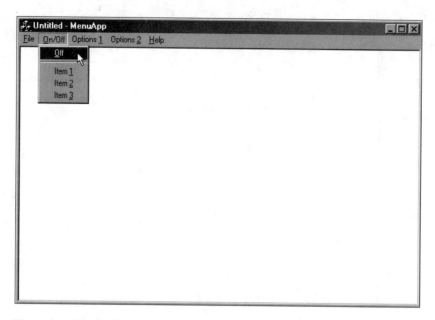

Figure 8-12: The On/Off menu demonstrates enabling and disabling menu items.

Next, check out the Options 1 menu. When you select an item on this menu, it becomes check marked, as shown in Figure 8-13. You can checkmark any or all of the menu items.

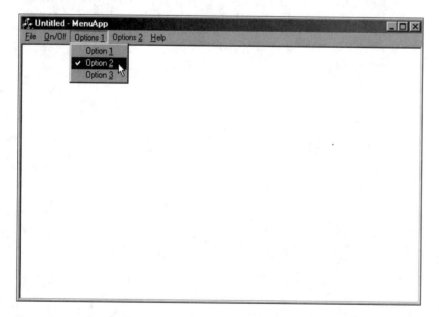

Figure 8-13: The Options 1 menu demonstrates checkmarking menu items.

Finally, the Options 2 menu shows how bullets work. In this menu, you can select any option, but only one option at a time, as shown in Figure 8-14. These options work like radio button controls, allowing the user to select from among mutually exclusive options.

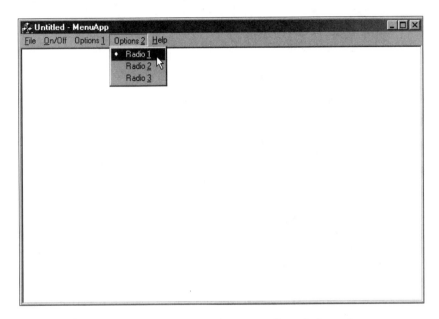

Figure 8-14: The Options 2 menu demonstrates mutually exclusive options.

Understanding the MenuApp Sample Application

The MenuApp application's view class defines both message response and update command UI functions. ClassWizard created the skeleton functions, and I added the source code lines that make the functions do what they're designed to do. Listing 8-4 shows how the functions are declared in the view class's header file. (The member variables that hold the status of the program's options are also declared in the listing.)

Listing 8-4: Declarations of the message response and update command UI functions

```
// Generated message map functions
protected:
    int m_radio;
    boolean m_option3;
    boolean m_option2;
    boolean m_option1;
    boolean m_onOff;
    //{{AFX_MSG(CMenuAppView)
    afx_msg void OnOnoffOn();
```

```
afx_msg void OnUpdateOnoffOn(CCmdUI* pCmdUI);
afx_msg void OnOnoffItem1();
afx_msg void OnUpdateOnoffItem1(CCmdUI* pCmdUI);
afx_msg void OnOnoffItem2();
afx_msg void OnUpdateOnoffItem2(CCmdUI* pCmdUI);
afx_msg void OnOnoffItem3();
afx_msg void OnUpdateOnoffItem3(CCmdUI* pCmdUI);
afx_msg void OnOptions1Option1();
afx_msg void OnUpdateOptions1Option1(CCmdUI* pCmdUI);
afx_msg void OnOptions1Option2();
afx_msg void OnUpdateOptions1Option2(CCmdUI* pCmdUI);
afx_msg void OnOptions1Option3();
afx_msg void OnUpdateOptions1Option3(CCmdUI* pCmdUI);
afx_msg void OnOptions2Radio1();
afx_msg void OnUpdateOptions2Radio1(CCmdUI* pCmdUI);
afx_msg void OnOptions2Radio2();
afx_msg void OnUpdateOptions2Radio2(CCmdUI* pCmdUI);
afx_msg void OnOptions2Radio3();
afx_msg void OnUpdateOptions2Radio3(CCmdUI* pCmdUI);
//}}AFX_MSG
```

Notice how each of the function declarations starts with the `afx_msg` prefix. Also notice the naming convention that ClassWizard uses to name the functions. The message response functions all start with the word "On" followed by the name of the menu and the menu item, whereas all the update command UI functions start with the words "OnUpdate."

Listing 8-5 shows the message map that ClassWizard created for the functions. The message map function entries use the `ON_COMMAND` macro to associate the command ID with the function, whereas the update command UI functions use the `ON_UPDATE_COMMAND_UI` macro for the same purpose.

Listing 8-5: The application's message map

```
BEGIN_MESSAGE_MAP(CMenuAppView, CView)
    //{{AFX_MSG_MAP(CMenuAppView)
    ON_COMMAND(ID_ONOFF_ON, OnOnoffOn)
    ON_UPDATE_COMMAND_UI(ID_ONOFF_ON, OnUpdateOnoffOn)
    ON_COMMAND(ID_ONOFF_ITEM1, OnOnoffItem1)
    ON_UPDATE_COMMAND_UI(ID_ONOFF_ITEM1,
      OnUpdateOnoffItem1)
    ON_COMMAND(ID_ONOFF_ITEM2, OnOnoffItem2)
    ON_UPDATE_COMMAND_UI(ID_ONOFF_ITEM2,
      OnUpdateOnoffItem2)
    ON_COMMAND(ID_ONOFF_ITEM3, OnOnoffItem3)
    ON_UPDATE_COMMAND_UI(ID_ONOFF_ITEM3,
      OnUpdateOnoffItem3)
    ON_COMMAND(ID_OPTIONS1_OPTION1, OnOptions1Option1)
    ON_UPDATE_COMMAND_UI(ID_OPTIONS1_OPTION1,
      OnUpdateOptions1Option1)
    ON_COMMAND(ID_OPTIONS1_OPTION2, OnOptions1Option2)
    ON_UPDATE_COMMAND_UI(ID_OPTIONS1_OPTION2,
      OnUpdateOptions1Option2)
    ON_COMMAND(ID_OPTIONS1_OPTION3, OnOptions1Option3)
    ON_UPDATE_COMMAND_UI(ID_OPTIONS1_OPTION3,
      OnUpdateOptions1Option3)
```

```
    ON_COMMAND(ID_OPTIONS2_RADIO1, OnOptions2Radio1)
    ON_UPDATE_COMMAND_UI(ID_OPTIONS2_RADIO1,
        OnUpdateOptions2Radio1)
    ON_COMMAND(ID_OPTIONS2_RADIO2, OnOptions2Radio2)
    ON_UPDATE_COMMAND_UI(ID_OPTIONS2_RADIO2,
        OnUpdateOptions2Radio2)
    ON_COMMAND(ID_OPTIONS2_RADIO3, OnOptions2Radio3)
    ON_UPDATE_COMMAND_UI(ID_OPTIONS2_RADIO3,
        OnUpdateOptions2Radio3)
    //}}AFX_MSG_MAP
END_MESSAGE_MAP()
```

The message response functions respond to the user's command by
performing some action in the application. In MenuApp, that action is
changing the value of an option. The options start off with the settings they
get in the view class's constructor, shown in Listing 8-6. When the user
selects a menu item, the program assigns a new value to the appropriate
member variable.

For example, if the user selects the Option 1 command from the Options 1
menu, the program toggles the `boolean` value assigned to the `m_option1`
member variable. The menu item's update command UI function uses this
value to determine whether or not to display a checkmark next to the menu
item. Listing 8-7 shows the message response functions defined in the
application's view class.

Listing 8-6: The view class's constructor

```
CMenuAppView::CMenuAppView()
{
    // TODO: add construction code here

    m_onOff = false;
    m_option1 = false;
    m_option2 = false;
    m_option3 = false;
    m_radio = 1;
}
```

Listing 8-7: The MenuApp application's message response functions

```
void CMenuAppView::OnOnoffOn()
{
    // TODO: Add your command handler code here

    m_onOff = !m_onOff;
}


void CMenuAppView::OnOnoffItem1()
{
    // TODO: Add your command handler code here

    MessageBox("Item 1");
}
```

```
void CMenuAppView::OnOnoffItem2()
{
    // TODO: Add your command handler code here

    MessageBox("Item 2");
}

void CMenuAppView::OnOnoffItem3()
{
    // TODO: Add your command handler code here

    MessageBox("Item 3");
}

void CMenuAppView::OnOptions1Option1()
{
    // TODO: Add your command handler code here

    m_option1 = !m_option1;
}

void CMenuAppView::OnOptions1Option2()
{
    // TODO: Add your command handler code here

    m_option2 = !m_option2;
}

void CMenuAppView::OnOptions1Option3()
{
    // TODO: Add your command handler code here

    m_option3 = !m_option3;
}

void CMenuAppView::OnOptions2Radio1()
{
    // TODO: Add your command handler code here

    m_radio = 1;
}

void CMenuAppView::OnOptions2Radio2()
{
    // TODO: Add your command handler code here

    m_radio = 2;
}

void CMenuAppView::OnOptions2Radio3()
{
    // TODO: Add your command handler code here

    m_radio = 3;
}
```

MFC calls the update command UI functions just before displaying menu items so that the menu items are properly displayed when the menu appears. As you now know, the application can display menu items in several ways, including disabled, checkmarked, and bulleted. Listing 8-8 shows MenuApp's update command UI functions.

Listing 8-8: The MenuApp application's update command UI functions

```
void CMenuAppView::OnUpdateOnoffOn(CCmdUI* pCmdUI)
{
    // TODO: Add your command update UI handler code here

    if (m_onOff)
        pCmdUI->SetText("&Off");
    else
        pCmdUI->SetText("&On");
}

void CMenuAppView::OnUpdateOnoffItem1(CCmdUI* pCmdUI)
{
    // TODO: Add your command update UI handler code here

    pCmdUI->Enable(m_onOff);
}

void CMenuAppView::OnUpdateOnoffItem2(CCmdUI* pCmdUI)
{
    // TODO: Add your command update UI handler code here

    pCmdUI->Enable(m_onOff);
}

void CMenuAppView::OnUpdateOnoffItem3(CCmdUI* pCmdUI)
{
    // TODO: Add your command update UI handler code here

    pCmdUI->Enable(m_onOff);
}

void CMenuAppView::OnUpdateOptions1Option1
    (CCmdUI* pCmdUI)
{
    // TODO: Add your command update UI handler code here

    pCmdUI->SetCheck(m_option1);
}

void CMenuAppView::OnUpdateOptions1Option2
    (CCmdUI* pCmdUI)
{
    // TODO: Add your command update UI handler code here

    pCmdUI->SetCheck(m_option2);
}

void CMenuAppView::OnUpdateOptions1Option3
```

```
    (CCmdUI* pCmdUI)
{
    // TODO: Add your command update UI handler code here

    pCmdUI->SetCheck(m_option3);
}

void CMenuAppView::OnUpdateOptions2Radio1(CCmdUI* pCmdUI)
{
    // TODO: Add your command update UI handler code here

    pCmdUI->SetRadio(m_radio == 1);
}

void CMenuAppView::OnUpdateOptions2Radio2(CCmdUI* pCmdUI)
{
    // TODO: Add your command update UI handler code here

    pCmdUI->SetRadio(m_radio == 2);
}

void CMenuAppView::OnUpdateOptions2Radio3(CCmdUI* pCmdUI)
{
    // TODO: Add your command update UI handler code here

    pCmdUI->SetRadio(m_radio == 3);
}
```

Summary

Menus are an important part of most Windows 98 applications. In fact, almost every application has a menu bar, which contains the commands the user needs to manipulate the program. Visual C++ features powerful and easy-to-use tools for creating and programming your application's menus.

Also discussed in this chapter:

▶ An application defines its menus in the application's resources.

▶ MFC programs contain message response functions that handle menu commands.

▶ MFC programs also frequently contain update command UI functions, which add attributes such as checkmarks and bullets to menu items.

▶ Applications usually checkmark menu items that represent selected options.

▶ Mutually exclusive options display a bullet next to the current setting.

▶ Besides checkmarking and bulleting menu items, an application can also change a menu item's text.

Chapter 9

Standard Controls

In This Chapter

▶ Introducing the standard controls

▶ Placing controls in nondialog windows

▶ Creating and programming standard controls

▶ Changing a control's color

▶ Manipulating controls in dialog boxes

If you took away its controls, Windows would be a crippled operating system. The system's interactivity is almost completely based upon Windows controls, whether the user is clicking a button to issue a command, typing in an edit box to give data to a program, or selecting a file from a dialog box. Without these objects that Windows users take so much for granted, applications would be about as useful as a car without pedals and a steering wheel. The bottom line is that if you want to be a Windows programmer, you have to know about controls. In this chapter, you learn the basic programming techniques required to add the standard controls to your applications. In the following chapter, you learn about Windows 98's common controls.

Introducing the Standard Controls

If you've used Windows for a while, you're well familiar with the operating system's standard controls. You may also remember that they were briefly discussed in Chapter 1. Standard controls are interactive objects, which appear mostly in dialog boxes, but can also appear in main windows and even in toolbars. The standard controls enable a Windows application to receive information from, and pass information to, the user. Following are the most common controls and their descriptions:

Static text	A string of text that cannot be edited. Static text controls are usually used to label other components in a dialog box.
Edit box	A box in which text can be entered. Text in the edit box can be edited and even copied and pasted via the Windows Clipboard.

Pushbutton   A control that triggers a command when clicked. Pushbuttons usually contain a text label and are often animated so they appear pressed down when clicked.

Radio button A button usually used in groups in which only one button can be selected at a time. When a radio button is selected, the previously selected button turns off.

Checkbox   A button used to turn options on and off. Unlike radio buttons, check buttons are traditionally used to allow any or all of the selections in the group to be selected simultaneously.

List box   A list of items. You can use the mouse to select one or more items from the list. When there are more items in the list box than can fit, the list box will display a scroll bar that enables the user to view items not currently shown in the box.

Combo box   A list of items combined with an edit box. You can either click the combo box's arrow to display a list of choices or type a selection into the associated edit box.

Group box   Used to group other controls. For example, a group box is often used to group a set of radio buttons. The box includes a caption that describes the contents of the box.

Some controls are more complex than others. Combo boxes, for example, require that the application fill the control with a list of items from which the user can select. A pushbutton, on the other hand, is ready to go as soon as the application creates it. In the sections that follow, you learn to add the standard controls to your applications, as well as how to manage the controls and respond to the messages they generate. The controls are presented in the order of their complexity.

Placing Controls in Nondialog Windows

Most often, you find standard controls like edit boxes and pushbuttons in dialog boxes. However, there's no reason you can't place these controls in any type of window. For example, an application can display and manipulate standard controls in its main window. This flexibility enables developers to create a variety of user interfaces.

To place, and respond to, controls in a nondialog window, you must perform the following several steps:

1. Create an object of the appropriate MFC class. For example, if you want to display a list box in the window, create an object of the `CListBox` class.

2. Call the control object's `Create()` member function to create the control element and associate it with the class. For example, after creating an object of the `CListBox` class called `listBox`, call `listBox.Create()`.

3. Add the appropriate messages to the application's message map. For a list box, you might add the `ON_LBN_DBLCLK()` macro so that the application can respond to selections in the list box.

4. Implement the message-response functions associated with the message-map macros you added in Step 3.

You can create objects of MFC's various control classes on the stack by creating them as member variables of a window class; you can also create them on the heap, by using the `new` operator. Once you've created the objects, you must call their `Create()` member functions. You can't, however, call `Create()` in a window class's constructor because the window element is not yet created at that point. Instead, you override the window class's `OnCreate()` function, which MFC calls in response to the Windows `WM_CREATE` message just before the window is about to be displayed.

In the following sections, you'll examine a sample program that illustrates how to create and manage standard controls in a nondialog window.

Running the ControlApp2 Sample Application

On CD-ROM

In the Chapter09\ControlApp2 folder of this book's CD-ROM, you'll find the ControlApp2 application, which demonstrates using standard controls in a nondialog window. (Many of the techniques used to program controls in a nondialog window are the same for dialogs.) Run the program and perform the following steps to experiment with the various controls:

1. Type text into the first edit control. The second edit control mirrors your typing, as shown in Figure 9-1. Every time you type a character, Windows sends a message to the application, which copies the text from the first control to the second.

First edit box

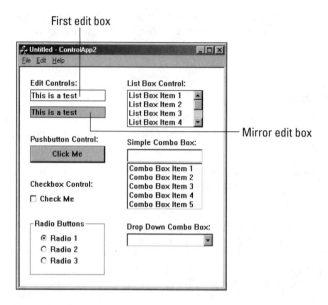

Mirror edit box

Figure 9-1: The second edit box mirrors the contents of the first edit box.

2. Click the Click Me button. When you do, a message box appears in response to the message Windows sends to the application, as shown in Figure 9-2.

Push Button

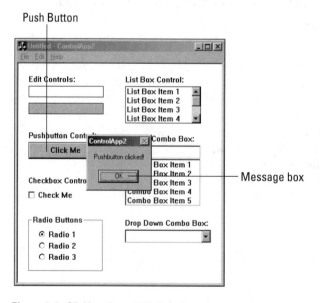

Message box

Figure 9-2: Clicking the pushbutton causes a message box to appear.

3. Click the Check Me checkbox. A check appears in the box, and a message box appears, telling you whether the box is checked or unchecked. The message box, shown in Figure 9-3, appears in response to the message Windows sends the application when the checkbox gets clicked. If you click the checkbox again, the checkmark turns off.

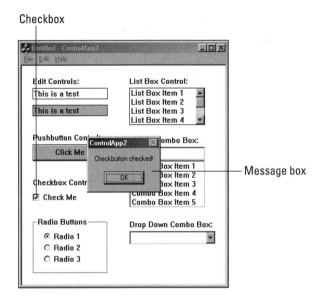

Figure 9-3: Clicking the checkbox turns its checkmark on and off.

4. Click a radio button in the Radio Buttons group. The new button becomes selected, while the old button becomes deselected. At the same time, Windows sends a message to the application, prompting a message box with the radio button's name to appear, as seen in Figure 9-4.

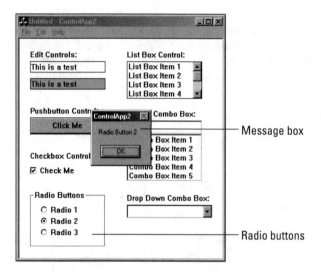

Figure 9-4: Clicking a radio button deselects the previous radio button.

5. Double-click a selection in the List Box Control box. When you do, Windows sends a message to the application, which copies the selected item from the list box and displays the item in a message box, as shown in Figure 9-5.

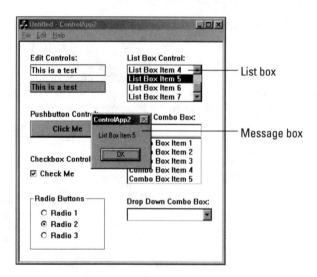

Figure 9-5: A message box displays the selected list-box item's name.

6. Double-click a selection in the Simple Combo Box. Windows sends a message to the application, which copies the selected item from the combo box and displays the item's name in a message box, as shown in Figure 9-6.

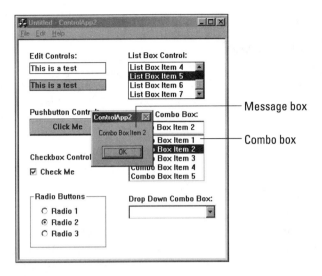

Figure 9-6: A message box displays the simple combo box's selected item name.

7. Click the arrow on the Drop Down Combo Box. The box's drop-down list appears. Select an item from the list, and a message box containing the selected item's name appears in response to the Windows message. Figure 9-7 shows the combo box with its drop-down list displayed.

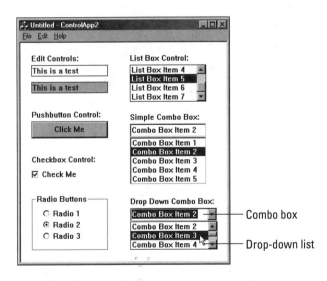

Figure 9-7: The Drop Down combo box stores its items in a drop-down list.

Creating and Programming Standard Controls

The basic techniques used to create and manipulate the various standard controls are similar. That is, in every case, you first create an object of the appropriate control class, and then call the object's `Create()` function. However, each control has its own set of style flags and member functions. In this section, you'll explore each type of standard control and see what makes them tick.

Static controls

One type of control that you didn't do much with in the preceding section is the static text control. Figure 9-8 shows static controls being used in a typical dialog box. Most often, static controls are used to display text, but they can also display icons, bitmaps, and other types of images.

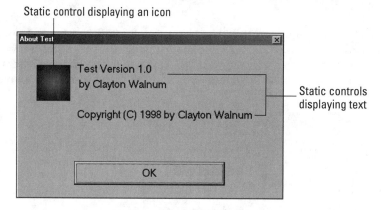

Figure 9-8: A dialog box displaying static controls

All of the text labels in ControlApp2's window are static text controls, which can display not only text, but also images. ControlApp2 declares the static text controls, which are objects of the MFC `CStatic` class, in the view class's header files, as follows:

```
CStatic m_editStatic;
CStatic m_buttonStatic;
CStatic m_checkStatic;
CStatic m_listStatic;
CStatic m_comboStatic;
CStatic m_comboStatic2;
```

Each of these static controls represents the descriptive label on one of the other controls. For example, `m_editStatic` is the edit box's descriptive label, whereas `m_buttonStatic` is the pushbutton control's descriptive label.

As you learned previously, all controls that you want to appear in a window must be created in the window class's `OnCreate()` function. This is true of the static text control as well. Listing 9-1 shows the `OnCreate()` function from ControlApp2's view class. As you can see, `OnCreate()` calls several member functions, each of which creates a specific type of control.

Listing 9-1: The view class's `OnCreate()` function

```
int CControlApp2View::OnCreate
   (LPCREATESTRUCT lpCreateStruct)
{
    if (CView::OnCreate(lpCreateStruct) == -1)
        return -1;

    // TODO: Add your specialized creation code here

    CreateStaticText();
    CreateEditBoxes();
    CreatePushbutton();
    CreateCheckbox();
    CreateRadioButtons();
    CreateListBox();
    CreateComboBoxes();

    m_whiteBrush.CreateSolidBrush(RGB(255,255,255));

    return 0;
}
```

In Listing 9-1, `OnCreate()` calls `CreateStaticText()` to create the window's static text controls. As you can see in Listing 9-2, `CreateStaticText()` calls each static text object's `Create()` function to create the control element and associate it with the `CStatic` object.

Listing 9-2: The view class's `CreateStaticText()` function

```
void CControlApp2View::CreateStaticText()
{
    m_editStatic.Create("Edit Controls:",
        WS_CHILD | WS_VISIBLE,
        CRect(20, 20, 220, 40), this, 0);

    m_buttonStatic.Create("Pushbutton Control:",
        WS_CHILD | WS_VISIBLE,
        CRect(20, 120, 220, 140), this, 0);

    m_checkStatic.Create("Checkbox Control:",
        WS_CHILD | WS_VISIBLE,
        CRect(20, 200, 220, 220), this, 0);

    m_listStatic.Create("List Box Control:",
        WS_CHILD | WS_VISIBLE,
        CRect(200, 20, 320, 40), this, 0);

    m_comboStatic.Create("Simple Combo Box:",
        WS_CHILD | WS_VISIBLE,
```

```
                    CRect(200, 125, 350, 145), this, 0);

         m_comboStatic2.Create("Drop Down Combo Box:",
             WS_CHILD | WS_VISIBLE,
             CRect(200, 275, 390, 295), this, 0);

}
```

The `CStatic` class's `Create()` function has the following signature (the
arguments' descriptions are listed after the signature):

```
BOOL Create(
    LPCTSTR lpszText,
    DWORD dwStyle,
    const RECT& rect,
    CWnd* pParentWnd,
    UINT nID = 0xffff);
```

lpszText	The address of the text to display in the control
dwStyle	The control's style flags
rect	A RECT or CRect object that specifies the control's size and position
pParentWnd	A pointer to the control's parent window
nID	The control's ID

Because the ControlApp2 application doesn't need to access the static
controls, the program gives all the static controls an ID of 0. You can also
leave the ID argument off, and so accept the `Create()` function's default ID of
`0xffff`.

Most of the function's arguments are fully described in the previous list. The
control's `dwStyle` argument, however, specifies the window and control flags
that determine the way the control looks and acts. You combine these flags,
using the OR operator, into a single `DWORD` value. You should at least specify
the `WS_VISIBLE` and `WS_CHILD` window styles. You may also want to use one
or more of the flags defined specifically for a static control. Table 9-1 lists
these style flags and their descriptions.

Table 9-1 Static control styles

Style Constant	*Description*
SS_BLACKFRAME	Draws the control's frame with the same color as the window frame, usually black
SS_BLACKRECT	Fills the control's rectangle with the same color as the window frame, usually black
SS_CENTER	Centers text in the control

Style Constant	Description
SS_GRAYFRAME	Draw's the control's frame with the same color as the desktop background, usually gray
SS_GRAYRECT	Draws the control's rectangle with the same color as the desktop background, usually gray
SS_ICON	Specifies that the control holds an icon
SS_LEFT	Left-aligns text in the control
SS_LEFTNOWORDWRAP	Disables word wrapping
SS_NOPREFIX	Prevents Windows from interpreting an ampersand in the control's text as a hot key indicator
SS_RIGHT	Right-aligns text in the control
SS_SIMPLE	Specifies a simple, single-line control
SS_USERITEM	Specifies a user-defined control
SS_WHITEFRAME	Draws the control's frame with the same color used to draw the window's background, usually white
SS_WHITERECT	Draws the control's rectangle with the same color used for the window's background, usually white

Tip

Most controls require unique IDs that you can use to access the control. Visual C++ offers a quick and easy way to define these IDs. Select the View menu's Resource Symbols command. When the Resource Symbols dialog box appears, click the New button. Enter the new ID's name and click OK. (Visual C++ suggests a unique value for the ID, so you don't even need to keep track of all the used ID numbers.) Visual C++ places all the defined IDs in the resource.h file.

In most cases, you won't need to manipulate a CStatic control once it's been created. However, the CStatic class does define a number of member functions in addition to those it inherits from its base classes. Table 9-2 lists those functions and their descriptions.

Table 9-2 CStatic **member functions**

Function	Description
Create()	Creates the control element and associates it with the CStatic object
GetBitmap()	Gets a handle to the control's bitmap
GetCursor()	Gets a handle to the control's cursor
GetEnhMetaFile()	Gets a handle to the control's metafile
GetIcon()	Gets a handle to the control's icon
SetBitmap()	Specifies the bitmap the control should display

(continued)

Table 9-2 *(Continued)*

Function	Description
SetCursor()	Specifies the cursor the control should display
SetEnhMetaFile()	Specifies the metafile the control should display
SetIcon()	Specifies the icon the control should display

Edit controls

Edit controls, represented in MFC by the CEdit class, are the main object used to obtain text responses from an application's user. These handy controls not only enable the user to type text, but also to edit the text in various ways. The user can even cut and paste text between the control and Windows' Clipboard. The edit control is so powerful in fact, it can be used to create a mini word processing application, similar to Windows' Notepad. Figure 9-9 shows a dialog box containing several edit controls, including a multiline edit control.

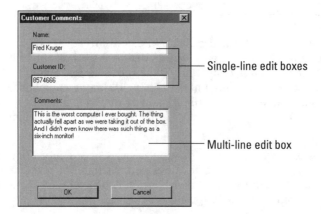

Figure 9-9: A dialog box displayed with both single-line and multiline edit boxes

In most cases, you find edit controls in their single-line incarnation, which, although they retain many editing features, can display only a single line of text at a time. This is the type of edit control displayed in ControlApp2's window. ControlApp2's edit control objects are declared in the view classes' header file:

```
CEdit m_edit;
CEdit m_edit2;
```

As with the static controls, the program creates the edit controls in the view class's OnCreate() function, which calls the local CreateEditBoxes() function to accomplish the task. CreateEditBoxes() looks like this:

```
void CControlApp2View::CreateEditBoxes()
{
    m_edit.Create(ES_AUTOHSCROLL | WS_CHILD | WS_VISIBLE
        | WS_BORDER, CRect(20, 40, 160, 60),
        this, IDC_EDIT);

    m_edit2.Create(ES_READONLY | WS_CHILD | WS_VISIBLE
        | WS_BORDER, CRect(20, 70, 160, 90), this, 0);
}
```

This function creates two edit controls: the control in which the user can type and the control that mirrors the user's typing. This second control is read-only, meaning that the user cannot change the text it displays.

The CEdit class's Create() function has the following signature (the arguments' descriptions are listed after the signature):

```
BOOL Create(
    DWORD dwStyle,
    const RECT& rect,
    CWnd* pParentWnd,
    UINT nID);
```

dwStyle	The control's style flags
rect	A RECT or CRect object that specifies the control's size and position
pParentWnd	A pointer to the control's parent window
nID	The control's ID

As with the CStatic control, the edit control's dwStyle argument specifies the window and control flags that determine the way the control looks and acts. You combine these flags, using the OR operator, into a single DWORD value. You should at least specify the WS_VISIBLE and WS_CHILD window styles. You may also want to use one or more of the flags defined specifically for an edit control. Table 9-3 lists these style flags and their descriptions.

Table 9-3 Edit control styles

Style Constant	Description
ES_AUTOHSCROLL	Selects automatic horizontal scrolling
ES_AUTOVSCROLL	Selects automatic vertical scrolling
ES_CENTER	Selects center text alignment in a multiline control

(continued)

Table 9-3 *(Continued)*

Style Constant	Description
ES_LEFT	Selects left text alignment
ES_LOWERCASE	Forces all text to lowercase
ES_MULTI-LINE	Specifies that the control should allow multiple text lines
ES_NOHIDESEL	Forces selected text to remain highlighted even when the control no longer has the input focus
ES_OEMCONVERT	Converts ANSI text entered in the edit control to OEM text and back to ANSI
ES_PASSWORD	Replaces all typed text with the current password character, usually an asterisk (*)
ES_RIGHT	Selects right text alignment in a multiline control
ES_UPPERCASE	Forces all text to uppercase
ES_READONLY	Locks the control from user editing
ES_WANTRETURN	Specifies that the control should insert a return character when the user presses Enter

When the user manipulates the text in the edit control, Windows sends a series of notification messages to the parent window. The types of messages Windows sends depends on the type of edit control you've created, which itself depends on the flags you specified in the call to Create(). For example, a single-line control receives a more limited set of messages than a multiline control does.

In order to respond to the user's action, the application must respond to the edit messages it receives. You set this mechanism up by adding entries to the window class's message map, which associates message-response functions with the notification messages. MFC defines a number of macros for the various edit messages. ControlApp2, for example, responds to the EN_CHANGE notification message, which Windows sends whenever the user changes the text in the control. To add this notification to the message map, you use the ON_EN_CHANGE macro:

ON_EN_CHANGE(IDC_EDIT, OnEditChange)

The macro's two arguments are the control's ID and the name of the function to be associated with the notification. ControlApp2's OnEditChange() function appears as follows:

```
void CControlApp2View::OnEditChange()
{
    char str[81];
    m_edit.GetWindowText(str, 80);
    m_edit2.SetWindowText(str);
}
```

Thanks to the new message-map entry, when the user changes the text in the control, MFC calls OnEditChange(). In that function, the program calls the control's GetWindowText() member function to obtain the text in the control. The function then calls the second edit control's SetWindowText() member function, setting the second control's text to that of the first.

The EN_CHANGE notification is one of many messages an edit control generates. Table 9-4 lists the entire set of edit control notifications along with their descriptions.

Table 9-4 Edit control notifications

Message Constant	Description
EN_CHANGE	Signals that the control's text has been changed (This notification comes after ON_EN_UPDATE)
EN_ERRSPACE	Signals a lack of memory
EN_HSCROLL	Signals that the user changed the horizontal scroll bar
EN_KILLFOCUS	Signals that the control has lost the input focus
EN_MAXTEXT	Signals that the user attempted to enter more text than the control can hold
EN_SETFOCUS	Signals that the control has received the input focus
EN_UPDATE	Signals that the control is about to display changed text. (This notification comes before ON_EN_CHANGE.)
EN_VSCROLL	Signals that the user has changed the vertical scroll bar

Tip

To get the name of a macro for a control notification, add ON_ to the front of the notification name. For example, the message-map macro for the EN_HSCROLL notification is ON_EN_HSCROLL.

In ControlApp2's OnEditChange() function, you saw how to use two of the CEdit class's many member functions. Table 9-5 lists all the member functions, along with their descriptions. As you can see from the list, there's a lot you can do with an edit control, even build a simple word processing application.

Table 9-5 CEdit member functions

Function	Description
CanUndo()	Returns TRUE if an edit operation can be undone
CharFromPos()	Gets the character and line indexes for the given position
Clear()	Clears the current selection

(continued)

Table 9-5 *(Continued)*

Function	Description
Copy()	Copies the current selection to the Clipboard
Create()	Creates the edit control element and associates it with the CEdit object
Cut()	Cuts the current selection to the Clipboard
EmptyUndoBuffer()	Clears the control's undo flag
FmtLines()	Toggles soft line-break characters in a multiple-line control
GetFirstVisibleLine()	Gets the index of the visible line at the top of the control
GetHandle()	Gets a handle to the control's contents
GetLimitText()	Gets the control's maximum capacity
GetLine()	Gets a text line from the control
GetLineCount()	Gets the number of text lines in the control
GetMargins()	Gets the control's left and right margins
GetModify()	Returns TRUE if the control's contents have been modified
GetPasswordChar()	Gets the control's password character
GetRect()	Gets the control's formatting rectangle
GetSel()	Gets the current selection's starting and ending indexes
GetWindowText()	Gets the contents of a single-line control
LimitText()	Limits the length of the text that the user may enter into an edit control
LineFromChar()	Gets the index of the line containing the given character index
LineIndex()	Gets the character index of the beginning of a text line
LineLength()	Gets the control's line length
LineScroll()	Scrolls a multiline control's text
Paste()	Pastes text from the Clipboard into the control
PosFromChar()	Gets the coordinates of a character, given its index
ReplaceSel()	Replaces a selection with the given text
SetHandle()	Sets the handle to the control's contents
SetLimitText()	Sets the control's maximum capacity

(continued)

Function	Description
SetMargins()	Sets the control's left and right margins
SetModify()	Toggles the control's modification flag
SetPasswordChar()	Sets the control's password character
SetReadOnly()	Sets the control's read-only state
SetRect()	Sets a multiline control's formatting rectangle
SetRectNP()	Sets a multiline control's formatting rectangle without redrawing the control
SetSel()	Selects a range of characters in the control
SetTabStops()	Sets a multiline control's tab stops
Undo()	Undoes the most recent edit

PROBLEMS & SOLUTIONS

Using the Tab Key in Non-Dialog Windows

PROBLEM: When I place controls in a dialog box, I can use the tab key to move from one control to another. But when I place controls in a nondialog window, the tab key doesn't seem to work. How can I fix this?

SOLUTION: A nondialog window processes keystrokes differently than a dialog box does. However, you can get that tab key back by overriding the window's PreTranslateaMessage() function and adding a couple of lines of code.

The steps to this process are as follows:

1. Call up ClassWizard.

2. Select your window's class (the class that acts as parent to the controls) in the Class Name box.

3. Select the PreTranslateMessage in the Messages box.

4. Click the Add Function button.

ClassWizard then adds the function to the class. Figure 9-10 shows ClassWizard after the programmer has overridden the PreTranslateMessage() function.

Continued

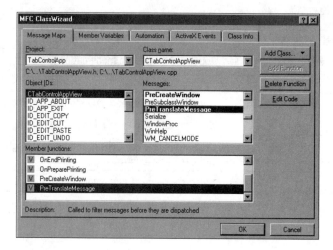

Figure 9-10: Use ClassWizard to override the window's
`PreTranslateMessage()` function.

After overriding `PreTranslateMessage()`, add the following lines to the function:

```
BOOL dlgMsg = IsDialogMessage(pMsg);

if(dlgMsg)
    return TRUE;
else
    return CView::PreTranslateMessage(pMsg);
```

The call to `IsDialogMessage()` determines whether the message is for a dialog box. If so, the function handles the message and returns `TRUE`. In this case, you should return `TRUE` from `PreTranslateMessage()`, which tells MFC not to continue processing the message. If the message is not intended for a dialog box, `IsDialogMessage()` returns `FALSE`. In this case, you should call the base class's `PreTranslateMessage()` and return its return value.

Finally, in order for a control to respond to the tab key, it must have been created with the `WS_TABSTOP` style flag. For example, the following lines create a combo box to which the user can tab:

```
m_comboBox.Create(CBS_SIMPLE | CBS_SORT |
    WS_TABSTOP | WS_CHILD | WS_VISIBLE | WS_GROUP,
    CRect(200, 145, 340, 255), this, IDC_COMBOBOX);
```

Don't add the `WS_TABSTOP` style to static controls or to group boxes, because the user can never select those controls and so can never tab to them.

Pushbuttons

Clicking a button is one of the simplest ways a user can issue a command to a Windows application. For this reason, pushbutton objects are everywhere in Windows, most conspicuously in dialog boxes and toolbars. MFC's `CButton` class represents pushbuttons and several other types of buttons, including checkboxes and radio buttons. In the window shown in Figure 9-11, both the toolbar and the dialog box contain pushbutton controls.

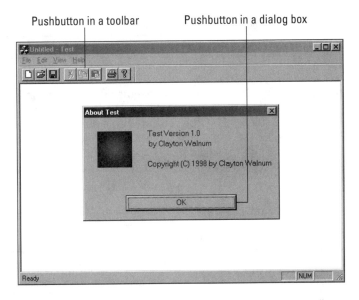

Figure 9-11: Windows applications often use pushbuttons in toolbars and dialog boxes.

In ControlApp2, the program declares its single pushbutton in the view class's header file, as follows:

```
CButton m_button;
```

The application creates the button element in the `OnCreate()` function, by calling the `CreatePushbutton()` member function, which looks like this:

```
void CControlApp2View::CreatePushbutton()
{
    m_buttaon.Create("Click Me", BS_PUSHBUTTON |
        WS_BORDER | WS_CHILD | WS_VISIBLE,
        CRect(20, 140, 160, 170), this, IDC_PUSHBUTTON);
}
```

The `CButton` class's `Create()` function has the following signature (the arguments' descriptions are listed after the signature):

```
BOOL Create(
    LPCTSTR lpszCaption,
    DWORD dwStyle,
    const RECT& rect,
```

```
CWnd* pParentWnd,
UINT nID);
```

lpszCaption	The button's caption
dwStyle	The button's style flags
rect	A RECT or CRect object that specifies the button's size and position
pParentWnd	A pointer to the button's parent window
nID	The button's ID

The button control's dwStyle argument specifies the window and control flags that determine the way the control looks and acts. As always, you combine these flags, using the OR operator, into a single DWORD value. You should at least specify the WS_VISIBLE and WS_CHILD window styles. You will also use one or more of the flags defined specifically for a button control. Table 9-6 lists these style flags and their descriptions.

Table 9-6 Button control styles

Style Constant	*Description*
BS_3STATE	Creates a three-state checkbox
BS_AUTO3STATE	Selects an automatic three-state checkbox
BS_AUTOCHECKBOX	Selects automatic checkmarks in a checkbox
BS_AUTORADIOBUTTON	Selects automatic radio buttons
BS_CHECKBOX	Creates a checkbox style button
BS_DEFPUSHBUTTON	Specifies that the button should have a thick border
BS_GROUPBOX	Creates a group box object
BS_LEFTTEXT	Selects left-hand text for a checkbox or radio button
BS_OWNERDRAW	Creates an owner-drawn style button
BS_PUSHBUTTON	Creates a pushbutton style button
BS_RADIOBUTTON	Creates a radio button style button

When the user clicks the button, Windows sends a notification message to the parent window. This message is BN_CLICKED for a single click and BN_DOUBLECLICKED for a double click. In order to respond to the user's action, the application must respond to the button messages it receives. MFC defines the ON_BN_CLICKED and ON_BN_DOUBLECLICKED macros for adding button messages to your application's message map. ControlApp2 responds to the BN_CLICKED notification, and so defines the following message-map entry:

```
ON_BN_CLICKED(IDC_PUSHBUTTON, OnPushbuttonClicked)
```

The macro's two arguments are the control's ID and the name of the function to be associated with the notification. ControlApp2's `OnPushbuttonClicked()` function, which only displays a message box in response to the `BN_CLICKED` notification, looks as follows:

```
void CControlApp2View::OnPushbuttonClicked()
{
    MessageBox("Pushbutton clicked!");
}
```

Although pushbuttons tend to work without your program having to call `CButton` member functions, `CButton` does define a set of member functions that are mostly useful for manipulating the other types of buttons. Later in this chapter, you'll see how to manage these other types of buttons. For now, Table 9-7 lists the `CButton` class's member functions.

Table 9-7 `CButton` **member functions**

Function	Description
Create()	Creates a button element and associates it with the CButton object
DrawItem()	Draws an owner-drawn CButton object
GetBitmap()	Gets a handle to the button's bitmap
GetButtonStyle()	Gets the button's style info
GetCheck()	Gets the control's checked state
GetCursor()	Gets a handle to the button's cursor
GetIcon()	Gets a handle to the button's icon
GetState()	Gets state information from the control
SetBitmap()	Sets the button's bitmap
SetButtonStyle()	Sets the button's style
SetCheck()	Sets the button's checked state
SetCursor()	Sets the button's cursor
SetIcon()	Sets the button's icon
SetState()	Sets the button's highlight state

Checkboxes

In the previous section, you got a close look at the `CButton` class, as well as discovered the types of notification messages your program receives from button objects. A checkbox is another type of button that you can create from the `CButton` class. Checkboxes usually enable the user to turn options on and off. If the checkbox is checked, the associated option is on; otherwise, the option is off. Figure 9-12 shows a dialog box that contains several checkboxes.

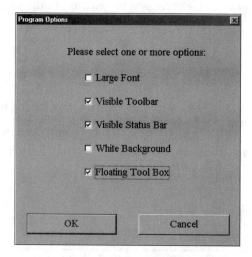

Figure 9-12: Checkboxes usually represent program options.

ControlApp2 displays a single checkbox that you can checkmark by clicking with your mouse. Although this button doesn't represent a program option, it does demonstrate all the programming techniques you need to know to use checkboxes. The program declares the checkbox button object in the view class's header file:

```
CButton m_checkButton;
```

The view class's OnCreate() function calls CreateCheckbox(), which creates the checkbox object. CreateCheckbox() looks as follows:

```
void CControlApp2View::CreateCheckbox()
{
    m_checkButton.Create("Check Me",
        BS_AUTOCHECKBOX | WS_CHILD | WS_VISIBLE,
        CRect(20, 215, 140, 255), this, IDC_CHECKBUTTON);
}
```

Notice that this call to CButton's Create() function uses the BS_AUTOCHECKBOX style, which tells MFC to create a checkbox that doesn't need to be checked or unchecked by the program. Instead, the button automatically toggles its checkmark when the user clicks it.

The program handles the checkbox in much the same way it handles the pushbutton, by responding to the BN_CLICKED notification. The message-map entry that associates the notification with a message-response function looks like this:

```
ON_BN_CLICKED(IDC_CHECKBUTTON, OnCheckboxClicked)
```

Now, whenever the user clicks the checkbox, MFC calls the
OnCheckboxClicked() function, which displays a message box. The function
uses a CButton member function, GetCheck(), to determine whether the
checkbox is currently checked, and then displays the result in the message
box. The BST_CHECKED and BST_UNCHECKED constants are defined by Windows
and represent the button's checked or unchecked state, respectively. The
OnCheckboxClicked() function looks like this:

```
void CControlApp2View::OnCheckboxClicked()
{
    int checked = m_checkButton.GetCheck();

    if (checked == BST_CHECKED)
        MessageBox("Checkbutton checked!");
    else if (checked == BST_UNCHECKED)
        MessageBox("Checkbutton unchecked!");
}
```

Radio buttons

Another object you can create with the CButton class is a radio button,
which represents a selection from a mutually exclusive set of options. That
is, radio buttons usually come in sets of two or more, with only one button
at a time being selectable. ControlApp2 displays three radio buttons in a
group box. Strangely, the group box, too, is another object of the CButton
class. Figure 9-13 shows a dialog box containing a set of radio buttons
organized by a group box.

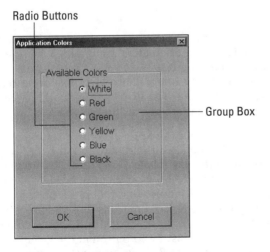

Figure 9-13: Radio buttons represent
mutually exclusive selections.

ControlApp2 declares these button objects in the view class's header file:

```
CButton m_radioGroup;
CButton m_radioButton1;
```

```
CButton m_radioButton2;
CButton m_radioButton3;
```

The view class's `OnCreate()` function calls `CreateRadioButtons()`, which creates the group box and radio button objects. Listing 9-3 shows the `CreateRadioButtons()` function.

Listing 9-3: The view class's `CreateRadioButtons()` function

```
void CControlApp2View::CreateRadioButtons()
{
    m_radioGroup.Create("Radio Buttons",
        BS_GROUPBOX | WS_CHILD | WS_VISIBLE,
        CRect(20, 270, 160, 370), this, 0);

    m_radioButton1.Create("Radio 1",
        BS_AUTORADIOBUTTON | WS_CHILD | WS_VISIBLE |
        WS_GROUP, CRect(40, 295, 110, 315),
        this, IDC_RADIOBUTTON1);

    m_radioButton1.SetCheck(BST_CHECKED);

    m_radioButton2.Create("Radio 2",
        BS_AUTORADIOBUTTON | WS_CHILD | WS_VISIBLE,
        CRect(40, 315, 110, 335), this,
        IDC_RADIOBUTTON2);

    m_radioButton3.Create("Radio 3",
        BS_AUTORADIOBUTTON | WS_CHILD | WS_VISIBLE,
        CRect(40, 335, 110, 355), this,
        IDC_RADIOBUTTON3);
}
```

Notice that the first call to `CButton`'s `Create()` function specifies the `BS_GROUPBOX` style, which tells MFC to create a group box, which really isn't much of a button at all. Instead, a group box is just a rectangular frame with a caption, and is used to organize a set of controls. Unlike other buttons, a group box is a noninteractive object. The user cannot manipulate the control, nor does the control generate notification messages.

The second call to `Create()` specifies the `BS_AUTORADIOBUTTON` and `WS_GROUP` styles. The former tells MFC to create a radio button that handles its own selection tasks (that is, when the user clicks the button, it automatically turns on its check and turns off the check on the previously selected control), whereas the latter tells Windows that this radio button is the first of the group. Because the remaining radio buttons don't specify the `WS_GROUP` style, Windows adds them to the group started with the first radio button. The next control created after the last radio button in the group should also specify the `WS_GROUP` style. That way Windows knows that the radio button group has ended and a new group has started.

Note

Why must you tell Windows which radio buttons belong together in a group? Remember that only a single radio button in a group can be selected at a time. With automatic radio buttons, Windows handles the checking and unchecking of the buttons. Obviously, Windows can't ensure that only a single button is selected at a time if it doesn't know which buttons belong to the group.

The program handles radio buttons in much the same way it handles the pushbutton, by responding to the BN_CLICKED notification. The message-map entries that associate the notifications with message-response functions for each button look like this:

```
ON_BN_CLICKED(IDC_RADIOBUTTON1, OnRadio1Clicked)
ON_BN_CLICKED(IDC_RADIOBUTTON2, OnRadio2Clicked)
ON_BN_CLICKED(IDC_RADIOBUTTON3, OnRadio3Clicked)
```

Now, whenever the user clicks a radio button, MFC calls the appropriate message-response function, which displays a message box telling you which button was clicked. Listing 9-4 shows the OnRadio1Clicked(), OnRadio2Clicked(), and OnRadio3Clicked() functions.

Listing 9-4: The radio button message-response functions

```
void CControlApp2View::OnRadio1Clicked()
{
    MessageBox("Radio Button 1");
}

void CControlApp2View::OnRadio2Clicked()
{
    MessageBox("Radio Button 2");
}

void CControlApp2View::OnRadio3Clicked()
{
    MessageBox("Radio Button 3");
}
```

List boxes

Often, programs need to present the user with a list of items from which the user can select. Windows provides two types of controls to handle this task: list boxes and combo boxes. List boxes, represented in MFC by the CListBox class, are the simplest of these two controls, amounting to little more than a rectangular border containing a list of items. Figure 9-14 shows a list box displayed in an application's window.

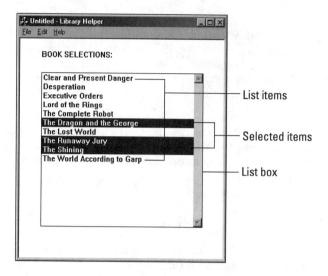

Figure 9-14: List boxes enable the user to select
one or more items from a list.

ControlApp2 displays a list box that contains seven data items. The program
declares its list box in the view class's header file:

```
CListBox m_listBox;
```

The view class's `OnCreate()` function calls `CreateListBox()`, which creates
the list box object. Listing 9-5 shows the `CreateListBox()` function.

Listing 9-5: The `CreateListBox()` function

```
void CControlApp2View::CreateListBox()
{
    m_listBox.Create(LBS_STANDARD | WS_CHILD |
        WS_VISIBLE | WS_GROUP,
        CRect(200, 40, 340, 120), this, IDC_LIST);

    m_listBox.AddString("List Box Item 1");
    m_listBox.AddString("List Box Item 2");
    m_listBox.AddString("List Box Item 3");
    m_listBox.AddString("List Box Item 4");
    m_listBox.AddString("List Box Item 5");
    m_listBox.AddString("List Box Item 6");
    m_listBox.AddString("List Box Item 7");
}
```

The `CListBox` class's `Create()` function has the following signature (the
arguments' descriptions are listed after the signature):

```
BOOL Create(
    DWORD dwStyle,
    const RECT& rect,
    CWnd* pParentWnd,
    UINT nID);
```

dwStyle	The list box's style flags
rect	A RECT or CRect object that specifies the list box's size and position
pParentWnd	A pointer to the list box's parent window
nID	The list box's ID

The list box control's dwStyle argument specifies the window and control flags that determine the way the list box looks and acts. As always, you combine these flags, using the OR operator, into a single DWORD value. You should at least specify the WS_VISIBLE and WS_CHILD window styles. You will also use one or more of the flags defined specifically for a list box control. Table 9-8 lists these style flags and their descriptions.

Table 9-8 List box control styles

Style Constant	Description
LBS_DISABLENOSCROLL	Specifies that the scroll bar should remain visible even when it's not needed
LBS_EXTENDEDSEL	Specifies that the user can extend the selection of multiple items by using the Shift key and the mouse
LBS_HASSTRINGS	Specifies that the control is an owner-drawn list box containing string items
LBS_MULTICOLUMN	Specifies a multicolumn list box that can be horizontally scrolled
LBS_MULTIPLESEL	Specifies that the user can select multiple items by clicking each item with the mouse
LBS_NOINTEGRALHEIGHT	Specifies that the list box should be exactly the size given, rather than automatically adjusted to an even line-height
LBS_NOREDRAW	Specifies that the list-box display should not be updated when changes are made
LBS_NOTIFY	Specifies that the parent window should receive notifications when the user clicks an item
LBS_OWNERDRAWFIXED	Specifies that the list box's owner will draw the list box's contents, each item of which is the same height
LBS_OWNERDRAWVARIABLE	Specifies that the list box's owner will draw the list box's contents, each item of which can be a different height

(continued)

Table 9-8 *(Continued)*

Style Constant	Description
LBS_SORT	Specifies that the list box's contents should be alphabetically sorted
LBS_STANDARD	Combines the WS_BORDER, WS_VSCROLL, LBS_NOTIFY, and LBS_SORT styles
LBS_USETABSTOPS	Specifies that the list box should expand tab characters in its item strings
LBS_WANTKEYBOARDINPUT	Specifies that the list box's owner should receive WM_VKEYTOITEM or WM_CHARTOITEM messages when the user types in the list box

When the user clicks an item in the list box, Windows sends a notification message to the parent window. This message can be LBN_SELCHANGE for a single click and LBN_DBLCLK for a double click. In order to respond to the user's action, the application must respond to the list box messages it receives. MFC defines macros you can use to add notifications to the window's message map. ControlApp2 responds to the LBN_DBLCLK notification, and so defines the following message-map entry:

```
ON_LBN_DBLCLK(IDC_LIST, OnListItemDblClk)
```

The OnListItemDblClk() message-response function gets the current selection and displays it in a message box. The source code looks like this:

```
void CControlApp2View::OnListItemDblClk()
{
    int selection = m_listBox.GetCurSel();
    char str[81];
    m_listBox.GetText(selection, str);
    MessageBox(str);
}
```

Here, the program first calls the list box's GetCurSel() member function, which returns the zero-based index of the currently selected item. Then, the program calls the list box's GetText() member function to get the text of the selected item, finally displaying the text in a message box.

The LBN_DBLCLK notification is one of several messages a list box generates. Table 9-9 lists the entire set of list box control notifications, along with their descriptions.

Table 9-9 List box notifications

Message Constant	Description
LBN_DBLCLK	Signals that the user has double-clicked an item in the list box
LBN_ERRSPACE	Signals that the list box couldn't allocate memory
LBN_KILLFOCUS	Signals that the list box has lost the input focus
LBN_SELCANCEL	Signals that the current selection was canceled
LBN_SELCHANGE	Signals that the list box selection has changed
LBN_SETFOCUS	Signals that the list box has received the input focus

Besides the member functions CListBox inherits from its base classes, CListBox defines many of its own functions. Table 9-10 lists those functions, along with their descriptions.

Table 9-10 CListBox **member functions**

Function	Description
AddString()	Adds a string to the list box
CharToItem()	Handles WM_CHAR messages for owner-draw list boxes without strings
CompareItem()	Called by MFC to get an item's position in a sorted owner-draw list box
Create()	Creates a list box element and associates it with the CListBox object
DeleteItem()	Called by MFC when the user deletes an item from an owner-draw list box
DeleteString()	Deletes a string from the list box
Dir()	Adds file names to the list box
DrawItem()	Called by MFC when an element of an owner-draw list box must be redrawn
FindString()	Finds a string in the list box
FindStringExact()	Finds the first matching string
GetAnchorIndex()	Gets the current anchor's index
GetCaretIndex()	Gets the index of the item with the focus rectangle
GetCount()	Gets the number of strings in the list box
GetCurSel()	Gets the selected item's index
GetHorizontalExtent()	Gets the list box's horizontally scrollable width

(continued)

Table 9-10   *(Continued)*

Function	Description
GetItemData()	Gets the 32-bit value associated with the given item in the list box
GetItemDataPtr()	Gets a pointer to a given item in the list box
GetItemHeight()	Gets the list box's item height
GetItemRect()	Gets an item's bounding rectangle
GetLocale()	Gets the list box's locale identifier
GetSel()	Gets an item's selection state
GetSelCount()	Gets the number of selected strings
GetSelItems()	Gets the indexes of the selected strings
GetText()	Gets a list-box item
GetTextLen()	Gets an item's length in bytes
GetTopIndex()	Gets the index of the list box's first visible string
InitStorage()	Allocates memory for list-box items
InsertString()	Inserts a string into the list box
ItemFromPoint()	Gets the index of the item nearest the given point
MeasureItem()	Called by MFC to determine list box dimensions
ResetContent()	Removes all items from the list box
SelectString()	Selects a string in the list box
SelItemRange()	Toggles the selected range of strings
SetAnchorIndex()	Sets the extended selection anchor
SetCaretIndex()	Sets the index of the item with the focus rectangle
SetColumnWidth()	Sets the list box's column width
SetCurSel()	Selects a string in a list box
SetHorizontalExtent()	Sets the list box's horizontally scrollable width
SetItemData()	Sets the 32-bit value associated with a given item in the list box
SetItemDataPtr()	Sets a pointer to the given item in the list box
SetItemHeight()	Sets the list box's item height
SetLocale()	Sets the list box's locale identifier
SetSel()	Toggles an item's selection state
SetTabStops()	Sets the list box's tab positions

(continued)

Function	Description
SetTopIndex()	Sets the index of the list box's first visible string
VKeyToItem()	Handles WM_KEYDOWN messages for list boxes with the LBS_WANTKEYBOARDINPUT style

Combo boxes

Combo boxes are a lot like list boxes, the main difference being that a combo box has both a list and an edit box, which holds the current selection from the list. Moreover, the user can type a selection into the edit box, rather than select it from the list. Combo boxes are great for places where you don't want to take up a lot of space with a long list, because you can create the combo box with a drop-down list. This way, the list doesn't appear until the user requests it by clicking an arrow next to the edit box. Figure 9-15 shows a combo box in an application's main window.

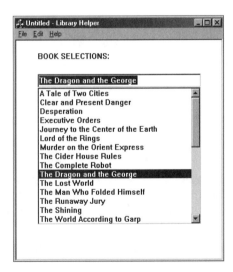

Figure 9-15: Combo boxes combine a list box and an edit control.

ControlApp2 displays two combo boxes: one simple box that always shows its list and one with a drop-down list. The program declares its combo boxes in the view class's header file:

```
CComboBox m_comboBox;
CComboBox m_comboBox2;
```

As you can see, the MFC CComboBox class represents Windows combo box controls.

The view class's OnCreate() function calls CreateComboBoxes(), which creates the combo box objects. Listing 9-6 shows the CreateComboBoxes() function.

Listing 9-6: The CreateComboBoxes() **function**

```
void CControlApp2View::CreateComboBoxes()
{
    m_comboBox.Create(CBS_SIMPLE | CBS_SORT |
        WS_CHILD | WS_VISIBLE | WS_GROUP,
        CRect(200, 145, 340, 255), this, IDC_COMBOBOX);

    m_comboBox.AddString("Combo Box Item 1");
    m_comboBox.AddString("Combo Box Item 2");
    m_comboBox.AddString("Combo Box Item 3");
    m_comboBox.AddString("Combo Box Item 4");
    m_comboBox.AddString("Combo Box Item 5");
    m_comboBox.AddString("Combo Box Item 6");
    m_comboBox.AddString("Combo Box Item 7");

    m_comboBox2.Create(CBS_DROPDOWN | CBS_SORT |
        WS_CHILD | WS_VISIBLE | WS_VSCROLL,
        CRect(200, 295, 360, 375), this, IDC_COMBOBOX2);

    m_comboBox2.AddString("Combo Box Item 1");
    m_comboBox2.AddString("Combo Box Item 2");
    m_comboBox2.AddString("Combo Box Item 3");
    m_comboBox2.AddString("Combo Box Item 4");
    m_comboBox2.AddString("Combo Box Item 5");
    m_comboBox2.AddString("Combo Box Item 6");
    m_comboBox2.AddString("Combo Box Item 7");
}
```

In CreateComboBoxes(), the program creates two combo boxes, populating the boxes with items by calling their AddString() member functions. Each call to AddString() adds one item to the combo box. When the combo boxes appear on the screen, these items will be in their lists.

The CComboBox class's Create() function has the following signature. The arguments' descriptions are listed after the signature.

```
BOOL Create(
    DWORD dwStyle,
    const RECT& rect,
    CWnd* pParentWnd,
    UINT nID);
```

dwStyle	The combo box's style flags
rect	A RECT or CRect object that specifies the combo box's size and position
pParentWnd	A pointer to the combo box's parent window
nID	The combo box's ID

The combo box control's `dwStyle` argument specifies the window and control flags that determine the way the combo box looks and acts. You should at least specify the `WS_VISIBLE` and `WS_CHILD` window styles. You will also use one or more of the flags defined specifically for a combo box control. Table 9-11 lists these style flags and their descriptions.

Table 9-11 Combo box control styles

Style Constant	Description
`CBS_AUTOHSCROLL`	Specifies automatic horizontal scrolling in the combo box's edit control
`CBS_DROPDOWN`	Specifies a drop-down list
`CBS_DROPDOWNLIST`	Specifies a combo box with a drop-down list and a static text control in place of the edit box
`CBS_HASSTRINGS`	Specifies an owner-draw combo box containing string items
`CBS_OEMCONVERT`	Specifies that text entered in the combo-box edit control should be converted from ANSI characters to OEM characters and back to ANSI
`CBS_OWNERDRAWFIXED`	Specifies that the combo box's owner will draw the combo box's contents, each item of which is the same height
`CBS_OWNERDRAWVARIABLE`	Specifies that the combo box's owner will draw the combo box's contents, each item of which can be a different height
`CBS_SIMPLE`	Specifies that the combo box's list should always be visible
`CBS_SORT`	Specifies that the combo box's contents should be alphabetically sorted
`CBS_DISABLENOSCROLL`	Specifies that the scroll bar should be visible even when it's not needed
`CBS_NOINTEGRALHEIGHT`	Specifies that the combo box should be exactly the size given, rather than automatically adjusted to an even line-height

When the user manipulates the combo box, Windows sends a notification message to the parent window. Because a combo box contains not only a list, but also an edit box, it can receive more types of notifications than a list box. Clicking an item in the list, however, results in similar notifications: `CBN_SELCHANGE` (or `CBN_SELENDOK`) for a single click and `CBN_DBLCLK` for a double click. A combo box also receives notifications when the user changes the text in the text box, or when the combo box displays or closes its drop-down list.

In order to respond to the user's action, the application must respond to the combo box messages it receives. MFC defines macros you can use to add notifications to the window's message map. ControlApp2 responds to the `CBN_DBLCLK` notification for the first combo box (the one without the drop-down list) and responds to `CBN_SELENDOK` for the second combo box (the one with the drop-down list). In order to respond to these notifications, the program defines the following message-map entries:

```
ON_CBN_DBLCLK(IDC_COMBOBOX, OnComboItemDblClk)
ON_CBN_SELENDOK(IDC_COMBOBOX2, OnComboSelEndOk)
```

In either case, the message-response functions `OnComboItemDblClk()` and `OnComboSelEndOk()` call the `GetCurSel()` member function to get the index of the selected item, and then call the `GetLBText()` member function to get the actual item, displaying the text in a message box. Listing 9-7 shows the `OnComboItemDblClk()` and `OnComboSelEndOk()` functions.

Listing 9-7: The combo box message-response functions

```
void CControlApp2View::OnComboItemDblClk()
{
    int selection = m_comboBox.GetCurSel();
    char str[81];
    m_comboBox.GetLBText(selection, str);
    MessageBox(str);
}

void CControlApp2View::OnComboSelEndOk()
{
    int selection = m_comboBox2.GetCurSel();
    char str[81];
    m_comboBox2.GetLBText(selection, str);
    MessageBox(str);
}
```

Table 9-12 lists the many types of notification messages that combo boxes can generate. These notifications represent not only selections by the user, but also other events that occur in the edit box and list components.

Table 9-12 Combo box notifications

Message	Description
CBN_CLOSEUP	Signals that the combo box's list has closed
CBN_DBLCLK	Signals that the user has double-clicked an item in the combo box
CBN_DROPDOWN	Signals that the combo box's list is dropping down
CBN_EDITCHANGE	Signals that the user has changed the text in the combo box's edit control (sent after CBN_EDITUPDATE)

(continued)

Message	Description
CBN_EDITUPDATE	Signals that the user has changed the text in the combo box's edit control, but before the change has appeared on the screen (sent before CBN_EDITCHANGE)
CBN_ERRSPACE	Signals that the combo box could not allocate memory
CBN_KILLFOCUS	Signals that the combo box has lost the input focus
CBN_SELCHANGE	Signals that the combo box's current selection is changing
CBN_SELENDCANCEL	Signals that the combo box's current selection should be canceled
CBN_SELENDOK	Signals that the combo box's current selection is valid, rather than canceled
CBN_SETFOCUS	Signals that the combo box has received the input focus

Changing a Control's Color

If you were to just throw a bunch of controls into a window, you might be surprised at what you get, as shown in Figure 9-16. Notice that the controls' background colors don't match the window's white background. If you were to place these controls in a dialog box, which normally has a gray background, they'd fit right in. But when you place the controls in a nondialog window, you have to deal with color.

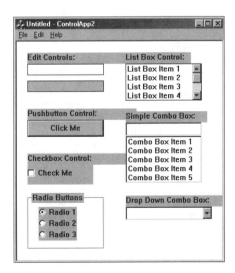

Figure 9-16: The controls' background colors don't match the window background color.

Unfortunately, setting a control's background color isn't as easy as you might think. You won't find anything like a SetBackgroundColor() member function in the control classes. Instead, you must respond to the `WM_CTLCOLOR` message, which Windows sends just before it draws a control. To add this message to your window's message map, use the `ON_WM_CTLCOLOR` macro:

```
ON_WM_CTLCOLOR()
```

As you can see, this macro requires no arguments. If you include the macro in your message map, you must also implement the `OnCtlColor()` function, which MFC calls when it receives the `WM_CTLCOLOR` message. That function's signature and a description of its arguments follow:

```
HBRUSH CControlApp2View::OnCtlColor(
    CDC* pDC,
    CWnd* pWnd,
    UINT nCtrlColor);
```

pDC	A pointer to the device context that will be used to draw the control
pWnd	A pointer to the control
nID	The type of `WM_CTLCOLOR` message

The third argument requires a little extra explanation. There are actually several types of `WM_CTLCOLOR` messages, each with its own ID. The message types represent the type of control that generated the `WM_CTLCOLOR` message. Table 9-13 lists these IDs, along with their descriptions.

Table 9-13 Types of `WM_CTLCOLOR` **messages**

Message ID	Description
CTLCOLOR_BTN	Message generated by a button control
CTLCOLOR_DLG	Message generated by a dialog box
CTLCOLOR_EDIT	Message generated by an edit control
CTLCOLOR_LISTBOX	Message generated by a list box
CTLCOLOR_MSGBOX	Message generated by a message box
CTLCOLOR_SCROLLBAR	Message generated by a scroll bar
CTLCOLOR_STATIC	Message generated by a static control, as well as by checkboxes, radio buttons, group boxes, and disabled edit boxes

In ControlApp2, the `OnCtlColor()` function looks like this:

```
HBRUSH CControlApp2View::OnCtlColor
    (CDC* pDC, CWnd* pWnd, UINT nCtrlColor)
{
    if ((nCtrlColor == CTLCOLOR_STATIC) &&
            (pWnd->m_hWnd != m_edit2.m_hWnd))
        return (HBRUSH)m_whiteBrush;

    return CView::OnCtlColor(pDC, pWnd, nCtrlColor);
}
```

Here, the `OnCtlColor()` first checks whether it has received a `CTLCOLOR_STATIC` type of `WM_CTLCOLOR` message. The function also checks that the control that generated the message isn't the read-only edit control, because the program needs to retain that edit control's gray background color. If the message is one the function is waiting for, it returns a white brush from the function. Windows will then use the brush to paint the control's background, rather than using the default gray brush.

If you want to change the text color in `OnCtlColor()`, you can call the device context's `SetTextColor()` function. If you want to change the text background color, you can call the DC's `SetBkColor()` function. Those function calls might look like this:

```
pDC->SetTextColor(RGB(255,255,255));
pDC->SetBkColor(RGB(0,0,255));
```

These lines set the text color to white and the text background color to blue.

 PROBLEMS & SOLUTIONS

Dialogs As Main Windows

PROBLEM: I want my application's main window to contain a number of controls, but I don't want to go through all the hassle of creating and positioning the controls in the window class. Isn't there an easier way?

SOLUTION: One technique you might want to try is creating your application using a dialog box as its main window. This handy trick can be accomplished easily through MFC and AppWizard. The big bonus is, because the main window holds a dialog box, you can define the controls using Visual C++'s dialog box editor.

First, create a new AppWizard application. When the Step 1 dialog box appears, select the Dialog Based option, as shown in Figure 9-17.

Continued

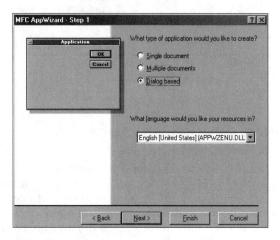

Figure 9-17: In AppWizard's Step 1 dialog box, you can select a dialog box as a main window.

This selection will change the remaining AppWizard steps. For example, Figure 9-18 shows the Step 2 dialog box, which now displays options that are applicable only to dialog-based windows, rather than options for a regular frame window, as you're used to seeing.

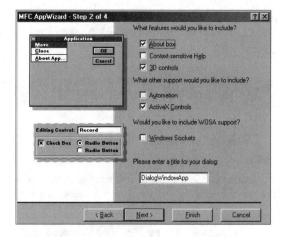

Figure 9-18: AppWizard provides different options for dialog-based windows.

When you finish selecting your application's options, AppWizard creates the skeleton application. Now, however, the program consists of as few as two classes: the application class and the dialog box class that represents the window's display. (You may also have a `CAboutDlg` class if you opted to include an About dialog box in the program.)

Continued

To create your window's user interface, first switch to the ResourceView page of the project workspace window. There, you'll find a dialog box with an ID created from your application's name. For example, if you called the project MyApp, the dialog box ID would be ID_MYAPP_DIALOG. This is the dialog box resource that represents your application's user interface. Double-click the ID to open the dialog box into the editor, as shown in Figure 9-19.

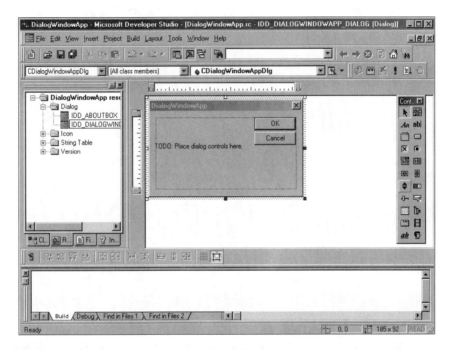

Figure 9-19: You create your application's user interface in the dialog box editor.

All the controls you place in the dialog box will appear in your application's main window. Moreover, the main window will be the same size as the dialog box resource. As an example, suppose that you leave the dialog box in its default state, as shown in Figure 9-19. When you compile and run the application, you'll see the window shown in Figure 9-20.

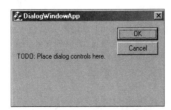

Figure 9-20: Here's the application as it appears with the default dialog box resource.

Continued

You can respond to the dialog box's controls within the dialog box class by handling notification messages. In fact, in every way, the dialog box class that represents the application's user interface works just like a normal dialog box. Everything you know about dialog boxes can be applied to the construction of your application's dialog-based window.

The application creates and displays the dialog box in the application class's InitInstance() function. Listing 9-8 shows the code that accomplishes this task. Notice the comments that indicate where you process dialog box data when the user dismisses the dialog box with the OK or Cancel buttons.

Listing 9-8: The CControlDlg **class's header file**

```
CMyAppDlg dlg;
m_pMainWnd = &dlg;
int nResponse = dlg.DoModal();
if (nResponse == IDOK)
{
    // TODO: Place code here to handle
    //   when the dialog is
    //   dismissed with OK
}
else if (nResponse == IDCANCEL)
{
    // TODO: Place code here to handle
    //   when the dialog is
    //   dismissed with Cancel
}
```

Manipulating Controls in Dialog Boxes

Most often, you'll see the standard controls used in dialog boxes. In Chapter 2, "Programming with Visual C++," and in Chapter 6, "Windows and Dialogs," you learned to create and manage dialog boxes. In both cases, you added controls to a dialog box using Visual C++'s dialog box editor. This is the standard way of creating dialog boxes. The controls you place in the dialog box handle themselves, although you may have to initialize some controls, such as list boxes and combo boxes.

If you haven't worked much with MFC dialog boxes, managing controls other than edit boxes and buttons in a dialog box can be a little tricky. In this section, you'll see how to create a new dialog box and add source code to the classes.

Creating the application skeleton

To better understand how to manipulate controls in dialog boxes, you will create the DialogControlsApp application. This application is also in the Chapter09\ControlApp2 folder of this book's CD-ROM. To create the first part of DialogControlsApp, you'll need to perform the following steps:

1. Start a new AppWizard project called DialogControlsApp, as shown in
   Figure 9-21.

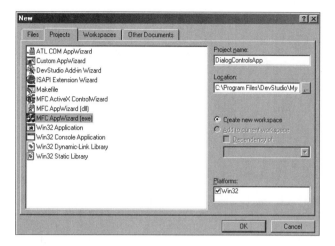

Figure 9-21: MFC's New dialog box is displayed when you create
the DialogControlsApp project.

2. In the Step 1 dialog box, select the Single Document option, as shown in
   Figure 9-22.

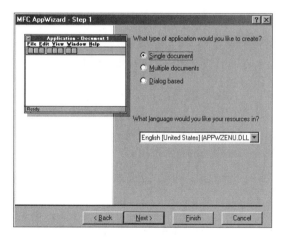

Figure 9-22: DialogControlsApp uses a single-document window.

3. In the Step 2 dialog box, keep the database support setting to None, its
   default option, as shown in Figure 9-23.

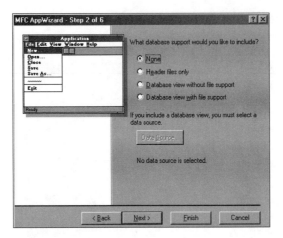

Figure 9-23: DialogControlsApp needs no database support.

4. In the Step 3 dialog box, turn off the ActiveX Controls option, as shown in Figure 9-24.

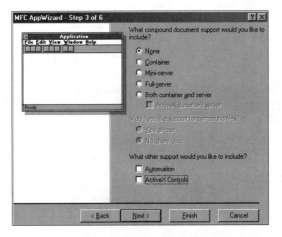

Figure 9-24: DialogControlsApp needs no ActiveX support.

5. In the Step 4 dialog box, turn off all options except 3D Controls, as shown in Figure 9-25.

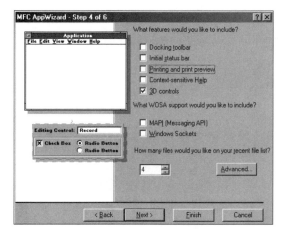

Figure 9-25: DialogControlsApp doesn't have a toolbar, a status bar, printing, or context-sensitive help support.

6. In the Step 5 dialog box, select the option to include MFC as a statically linked library, as shown in Figure 9-26.

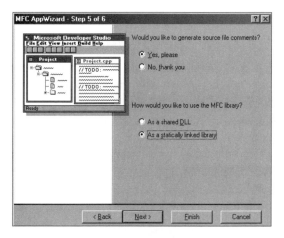

Figure 9-26: This project will link to MFC's static library.

7. In the Step 6 dialog box (see Figure 9-27), click Finish to accept the suggested classes. When the New Project Information dialog box appears, click OK to create the skeleton application.

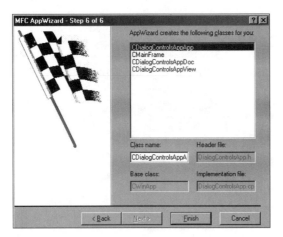

Figure 9-27: AppWizard suggests the final classes for the application.

At this point, you've created the basic application. You can compile and run the program if you like. You should at least save your work before moving on to the next section, where you'll create the dialog box resource.

Creating the new dialog box

Now that you have the basic application created, it's time to put together the dialog box resource and its associated class. Perform the following steps to complete this task:

1. Select the Resource command from Visual C++'s Insert menu. The Insert Resource dialog box appears, as shown in Figure 9-28.

Figure 9-28: You can add resource objects from the Insert resource dialog box.

2. Double-click Dialog in the Resource Type box. A new dialog box appears in Visual C++'s dialog box editor (see Figure 9-29).

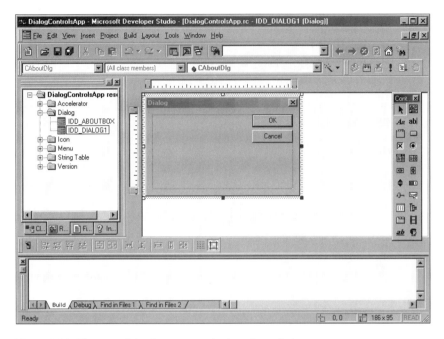

Figure 9-29: The new dialog box appears in the editor window.

3. Enlarge the box and add the list box shown in Figure 9-30.

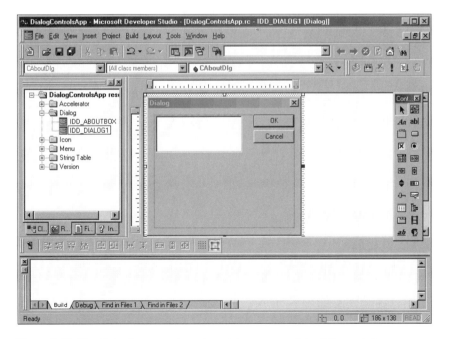

Figure 9-30: The dialog box must be enlarged to accommodate all its controls.

4. Add a pushbutton control to the dialog box, setting its label to "Click Me" (see Figure 9-31).

Figure 9-31: The dialog box gets a new button.

5. Add two edit controls to the dialog box, as shown in Figure 9-32.

Figure 9-32: Here's the dialog box displayed with its two new edit controls.

6. Change the second edit box's style to read-only, as shown in Figure 9-33.

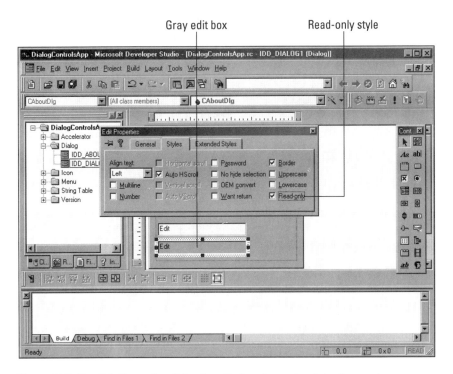

Figure 9-33: The Edit Properties dialog box displayed over the dialog box you're creating—notice that the read-only style grays out the edit box's background.

7. Double-click the dialog box. The Adding a Class dialog box appears, as shown in Figure 9-34.

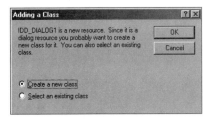

Figure 9-34: You need to create a class for the new dialog box.

8. Make sure the Create a New Class option is selected and click OK. The New Class dialog box appears.

9. Type `CControlDlg` into the Name box (see Figure 9-35). This will be the new dialog box class's name.

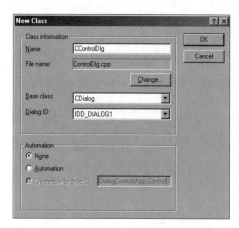

Figure 9-35: The dialog box class gets a name.

10. Click OK to dismiss the New Class dialog box, revealing the ClassWizard property sheet. Select the Member Variables page, as shown in Figure 9-36.

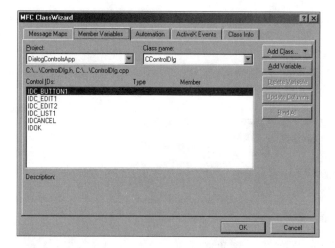

Figure 9-36: On the Member Variables page, you can add variables to the new class.

11. Double-click `IDC_LIST1` in the Control IDs box. The Add Member Variable dialog box appears. Name the new variable `m_listStr`, as shown in Figure 9-37.

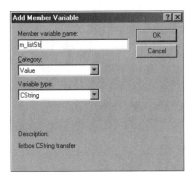

Figure 9-37: The `m_listStr` variable will hold the list box's selection.

12. Click OK to dismiss the Add Member Variable dialog box, and then click OK to dismiss ClassWizard.

You've now created the dialog box and the class that will represent the dialog box in the application. The final step is to add the source code needed to complete the application, which you'll do in the next section.

Adding source code to the view class

At this point, the application doesn't do much. For example, although you've created a new dialog box, you have no way to display it on the screen. Moreover, the program doesn't even add items to the list box in the dialog box. An empty list box isn't too useful. In this section, you add the program lines that enable the application to display the dialog box. Perform the following steps to add this functionality:

1. Load the DialogControlsAppView.cpp file, and add the following line near the top of the file, after the line `#include DialogControlsAppView.h` that's already there:

   ```
   #include "ControlDlg.h"
   ```

2. Press Ctrl+W to bring up ClassWizard. Add a message-response function for the `WM_LBUTTONDOWN` message, as shown in Figure 9-38. (Make sure you have `CDialogControlsAppView` selected in the Class Name box.)

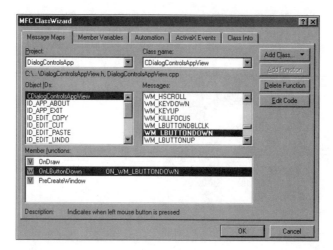

Figure 9-38: ClassWizard adding the OnLButtonDown() message-response function

3. Click the Edit Code button to bring the new function up in the editor (see Figure 9-39).

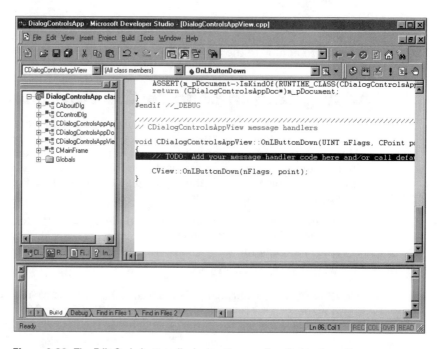

Figure 9-39: The Edit Code button displaying the new function in the editor

4. Add the following lines to the `OnLButtonDown()` function, right after the `// TODO: Add your message handler code here and/or call default` comment:

```
CControlDlg dlg(this);

int result = dlg.DoModal();

if (result == IDOK)
{
    CString str = dlg.m_listStr;
    if (str != "")
        MessageBox(str);
}
```

You've now completed the application's view class. Press Ctrl+F5 to compile and run the program. When you do, the application's main window appears. Click in the window, and your new dialog box appears, as shown in Figure 9-40. You can manipulate the dialog box's controls, but the program won't yet respond to your changes. You will take care of that in the next section, where you complete the application.

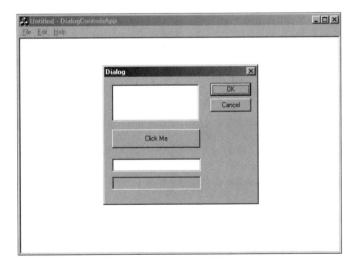

Figure 9-40: The application can now display the dialog box.

Adding source code to the dialog class

Now that you've created a new dialog box and finished the application's view class, you're ready to complete the dialog box class, `CControlDlg`. Along the way, you'll discover how to initialize controls in a dialog box and respond to the controls' notifications. Perform the following steps to complete the DialogControlsApp application:

1. In the ClassView page of the Project Window, right-click the `CControlDlg` class. The class's context menu appears (see Figure 9-41).

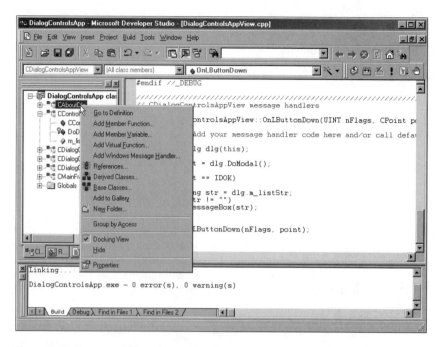

Figure 9-41: You can add functions and variables from the context menu.

2. Select the context menu's Add Member Function command. The Add Member Function dialog box appears.

3. Type `BOOL` into the Function Type box, type `OnInitDialog()` into the Function Declaration box, and select the Protected Access option, as shown in Figure 9-42.

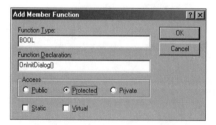

Figure 9-42: Use the Add Member Function
dialog box to define the new function.

4. Add the lines shown in Listing 9-9 to the new `OnInitDialog()` function:

Listing 9-9: Program lines for the new `OnInitDialog()` **function**

```
CDialog::OnInitDialog();

CListBox* listBox = (CListBox*)GetDlgItem(IDC_LIST1);
listBox->AddString("List Box Item 1");
listBox->AddString("List Box Item 2");
listBox->AddString("List Box Item 3");
listBox->AddString("List Box Item 4");
listBox->AddString("List Box Item 5");
listBox->AddString("List Box Item 6");

return TRUE;
```

5. Press Ctrl+W to display ClassWizard. Make the following selections: `CControlDlg` from the drop-down list in the Class Name box, `IDC_LIST1` in the Object IDs box, and `LBN_SELCHANGE` in the Messages box (see Figure 9-43).

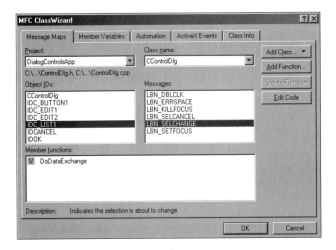

Figure 9-43: You can add notification response functions to a dialog box with ClassWizard.

6. Click the Add Function button. When the Add Member Function dialog box appears, click OK to accept the suggested function name. ClassWizard adds the function to the class.

7. Click the Edit Code button. The new `OnSelchangeList1()` function appears in the edit window. Add the following lines to the function:

```
CListBox* listBox = (CListBox*)GetDlgItem(IDC_LIST1);
int selection = listBox->GetCurSel();
listBox->GetText(selection, m_listStr);
```

8. Use ClassWizard to add the `OnButton1()` function to the dialog box class, as shown in Figure 9-44.

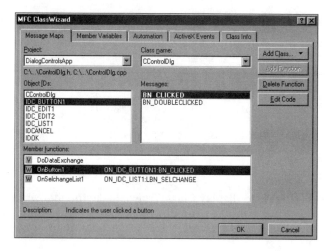

Figure 9-44: The OnButton1() function responds to button clicks.

9. Click the Edit code button. The new OnButton1() function appears in the edit window. Add the following lines to the function:

```
CButton* button = (CButton*)GetDlgItem(IDC_BUTTON1);
CString str;
button->GetWindowText(str);
if (str == "Click Me")
    button->SetWindowText("I've Been Clicked!");
else
    button->SetWindowText("Click Me");
```

10. Use ClassWizard to add the OnChangeEdit1() function to the dialog box class, as shown in Figure 9-45.

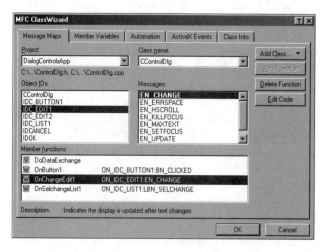

Figure 9-45: The OnChangeEdit1() function responds to changes in the first edit control.

11. Click the Edit code button. The new `OnChangeEdit1()` function appears in the edit window. Add the following lines to the function:

```
CEdit* edit1 = (CEdit*)GetDlgItem(IDC_EDIT1);
CEdit* edit2 = (CEdit*)GetDlgItem(IDC_EDIT2);
CString str;
edit1->GetWindowText(str);
edit2->SetWindowText(str);
```

You've now completed the DialogControlsApp application. You can compile and run the program by pressing Ctrl+F5 on your keyboard. Listings 9-10 and 9-11 show the completed `ControlDlg` class (the header and implementation files, respectively) and are included here so that you can see the source code you added, in the context of the entire class. The executable file and source code for DialogControlsApp is available in the Chapter09\DialogControlsApp file on this book's CD-ROM.

Listing 9-10: The `CControlDlg` class's header file

```
/////////////////////////////////////////////////////////////
// CControlDlg dialog

class CControlDlg : public CDialog
{
// Construction
public:
    CControlDlg(CWnd* pParent = NULL);

// Dialog Data
    //{{AFX_DATA(CControlDlg)
    enum { IDD = IDD_DIALOG1 };
    CString    m_listStr;
    //}}AFX_DATA


// Overrides
    // ClassWizard generated virtual function overrides
    //{{AFX_VIRTUAL(CControlDlg)
    protected:
    // DDX/DDV support
    virtual void DoDataExchange(CDataExchange* pDX);
    //}}AFX_VIRTUAL

// Implementation
protected:
    BOOL OnInitDialog();

    // Generated message map functions
    //{{AFX_MSG(CControlDlg)
    afx_msg void OnSelchangeList1();
    afx_msg void OnButton1();
    afx_msg void OnChangeEdit1();
    //}}AFX_MSG
    DECLARE_MESSAGE_MAP()
};
```

Listing 9-11: The `CControlDlg` **class's header file**

```cpp
// ControlDlg.cpp : implementation file
//

#include "stdafx.h"
#include "DialogControlsApp.h"
#include "ControlDlg.h"

#ifdef _DEBUG
#define new DEBUG_NEW
#undef THIS_FILE
static char THIS_FILE[] = __FILE__;
#endif

/////////////////////////////////////////////////////////
// CControlDlg dialog


CControlDlg::CControlDlg(CWnd* pParent /*=NULL*/)
    : CDialog(CControlDlg::IDD, pParent)
{
    //{{AFX_DATA_INIT(CControlDlg)
    m_listStr = _T("");
    //}}AFX_DATA_INIT
}


void CControlDlg::DoDataExchange(CDataExchange* pDX)
{
    CDialog::DoDataExchange(pDX);
    //{{AFX_DATA_MAP(CControlDlg)
    DDX_LBString(pDX, IDC_LIST1, m_listStr);
    //}}AFX_DATA_MAP
}


BEGIN_MESSAGE_MAP(CControlDlg, CDialog)
    //{{AFX_MSG_MAP(CControlDlg)
    ON_LBN_SELCHANGE(IDC_LIST1, OnSelchangeList1)
    ON_BN_CLICKED(IDC_BUTTON1, OnButton1)
    ON_EN_CHANGE(IDC_EDIT1, OnChangeEdit1)
    //}}AFX_MSG_MAP
END_MESSAGE_MAP()

/////////////////////////////////////////////////////////
// CControlDlg message handlers

BOOL CControlDlg::OnInitDialog()
{
    CDialog::OnInitDialog();

    CListBox* listBox = (CListBox*)GetDlgItem(IDC_LIST1);
    listBox->AddString("List Box Item 1");
    listBox->AddString("List Box Item 2");
```

```
        listBox->AddString("List Box Item 3");
        listBox->AddString("List Box Item 4");
        listBox->AddString("List Box Item 5");
        listBox->AddString("List Box Item 6");

    return TRUE;
}

void CControlDlg::OnSelchangeList1()
{
    // TODO: Add your control notification
    //   handler code here

    CListBox* listBox = (CListBox*)GetDlgItem(IDC_LIST1);
    int selection = listBox->GetCurSel();
    listBox->GetText(selection, m_listStr);
}

void CControlDlg::OnButton1()
{
    // TODO: Add your control notification
    //   handler code here

    CButton* button = (CButton*)GetDlgItem(IDC_BUTTON1);
    CString str;
    button->GetWindowText(str);
    if (str == "Click Me")
        button->SetWindowText("I've Been Clicked!");
    else
        button->SetWindowText("Click Me");
}

void CControlDlg::OnChangeEdit1()
{
    // TODO: If this is a RICHEDIT control,
    //   the control will not
    //   send this notification unless you
    //   override the CDialog::OnInitDialog()
    //   function to send the EM_SETEVENTMASK
    //   message to the control
    //   with the ENM_CHANGE flag ORed into
    //   the lParam mask.

    // TODO: Add your control notification
    //   handler code here

    CEdit* edit1 = (CEdit*)GetDlgItem(IDC_EDIT1);
    CEdit* edit2 = (CEdit*)GetDlgItem(IDC_EDIT2);
    CString str;
    edit1->GetWindowText(str);
    edit2->SetWindowText(str);
}
```

Running DialogControlsApp

When you run DialogControlsApp, you see the application's main window. Note that the program's menu bar contains commands that you didn't implement in the previous steps. The only valid menu commands are the File menu's Exit command and the Help menu's About DialogControlsApp command. (The other commands are defaults added by AppWizard. Normally, you'd either implement the commands or remove them from the menus. Although the Open and Save commands display dialog boxes, they don't actually open or save anything.)

To display the program's dialog box, click in the window. When the dialog appears (see Figure 9-46), you can experiment with the controls. Click the button and its caption changes. Type something into the edit control, and the read-only control displays the same text. Finally, select an item in the list box and click OK to dismiss the dialog box. When you do, a message box appears, displaying the item you picked.

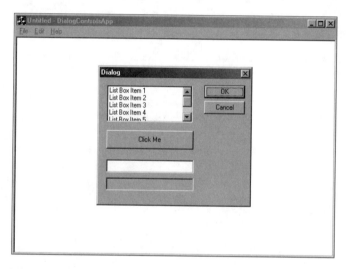

Figure 9-46: DialogControlsApp's dialog box illustrates how to manage standard controls.

Understanding DialogControlsApp

DialogControlsApp demonstrates some important techniques for manipulating controls in a dialog box. First, just as you could initialize window controls in a class's `OnCreate()` function, so you can initialize dialog box controls in the dialog class's `OnInitDialog()` function, which responds to the `WM_INITDIALOG` window's message. MFC calls `OnInitDialog()` just before the dialog box is displayed, so it's a great place to do any last-minute processing for the dialog box. In the `CControlDlg` class's `OnInitDialog()` function, the program adds items to the list box.

The other controls in the dialog box don't require initializing in `OnInitDialog()`, but they all generate notification messages that the dialog box handles. When you click the pushbutton, for example, the control generates a `BN_CLICKED` notification, which the dialog class handles in its `OnButton1()` member function. In that function, the program first gets a pointer to the pushbutton control:

```
CButton* button = (CButton*)GetDlgItem(IDC_BUTTON1);
```

`GetDlgItem()` takes one argument, the ID of the control for which you want a pointer. The function returns a `CWnd` pointer, so the returned value must be cast to a pointer of the correct type, which in this case is `CButton*`.

After getting a pointer to the button, the program retrieves the button's current text label:

```
CString str;
button->GetWindowText(str);
```

The program then compares the button's label to the original value and sets the label to the appropriate new value:

```
if (str == "Click Me")
    button->SetWindowText("I've Been Clicked!");
else
    button->SetWindowText("Click Me");
```

When you type in the edit control box, the control generates `EN_CHANGE` notifications, handled by the `OnChangeEdit1()` message-response function. In that function, the program first gets pointers to the two edit controls:

```
CEdit* edit1 = (CEdit*)GetDlgItem(IDC_EDIT1);
CEdit* edit2 = (CEdit*)GetDlgItem(IDC_EDIT2);
```

The program then copies the text from the first control to the second, read-only control:

```
CString str;
edit1->GetWindowText(str);
edit2->SetWindowText(str);
```

The last control is the list box. When you make a selection in the list box, the control generates an `LBN_SELCHANGE` notification, which the dialog class handles in its `OnSelchangeList1()` function. That function first gets a pointer to the list box control:

```
CListBox* listBox = (CListBox*)GetDlgItem(IDC_LIST1);
```

The function then gets the currently selected item's index:

```
int selection = listBox->GetCurSel();
```

Finally, the function copies the selected item's text into the dialog class's member variable m_listStr, which holds the list box string so the view class can access it:

```
listBox->GetText(selection, m_listStr);
```

The view class creates and displays the dialog box in its OnLButtonDown() function. When the user dismisses the dialog box, OnLButtonDown() gets the selected string from the dialog box and displays it in a message box:

```
if (result == IDOK)
{
    CString str = dlg.m_listStr;
    if (str != "")
        MessageBox(str);
}
```

Summary

As you've learned, you can add controls to both dialog boxes and nondialog windows. When adding controls to a dialog box, you use Visual C++'s dialog box editor to create the user interface. However, when adding controls to a nondialog window, you must create instances of the control classes and call the objects' Create() functions. The arguments you supply to Create() determine not only the control's position, but also the way the control looks and acts.

Also discussed in this chapter:

▶ Standard controls include static text, edit boxes, pushbuttons, checkboxes, radio buttons, list boxes, group boxes, and combo box controls.

▶ When placing controls in nondialog windows, you must explicitly specify the control's location and style flags when you call the control's Create() function.

▶ You respond to controls by creating message-response functions for the control's notifications.

▶ You can change a control's colors by implementing the MFC OnCtlColor() function.

▶ In a dialog box class, you override the OnInitDialog() function to initialize the dialog box's controls.

▶ When you place controls in a dialog box, you can respond to the controls' notifications to manage the user's interaction with the controls.

Chapter 10

Common Controls

In the previous chapter, you learned to incorporate Windows' standard controls into your applications. While these basic controls are the building blocks of most user interfaces, they aren't anywhere near as sophisticated as the newer common controls. Windows 98's common controls, which include list views and tree views, add sizzle to mundane applications, while providing the user with a fully modern user interface. In this chapter, you'll discover how to create and manage these important elements of a modern Windows application.

Introducing the Common Controls

Windows 98's common controls include some handy devices that you've seen often, not only in applications but also in Windows itself. In fact, many of Windows' utilities, such as Windows Explorer, rely on these advanced controls in order to present an elegant user interface. These extended controls, which were first introduced with Windows 95, include the following:

Progress bar	A progress bar shows the status of an ongoing operation by filling the control's display area with a colored bar. The bar shows an operation's degree of completion. For example, a progress bar might track the saving of a large file. When the file is half saved, the progress bar's display would be half filled.
Slider	A slider is a control for selecting a value from a range of values. The user drags the slider's thumb to select a value. When dragged, the thumb slides in the control's track, either horizontally or vertically, depending upon how the control was set up. Sliders also can be used to select a range of values.

Spinner	A spinner provides another way to select a value from a range of values. The spinner control is made up of two arrows, which enable the user to raise or lower a displayed value.
Image list	An image list control usually stores images for toolbar buttons or stores the images used to display a tree in a tree view control. An image list, however, can store images for any use. For example, you might use an image list to store a group of images that make up an animation sequence. The images are stored in memory and can't be seen on the screen until they're needed by the program.
List view	A list view control displays an organized group of items. How the items are displayed depends upon the list view's current setting. For instance, a list view control can display just a list of items or it can display the list in columns that include details about the items.
Tree view	A tree view control displays items as a hierarchy. Parent items (like folders on a disk) can contain child items (like subfolders or files on a disk). You can open and close parent items by clicking them with a mouse. Closing a parent item hides its child items.
Toolbar	A toolbar is a row of controls (usually buttons) that provide quick access to important commands. The buttons on a toolbar often mirror the commands found in the application's menus. However, a toolbar often also features drop-down list boxes that enable you to select fonts, colors, and other document attributes.
Status bar	A status bar provides a place for an application to display command descriptions and status information, such as the state of the keyboard and the position of the text cursor. It usually sits at the bottom of an application's display.

Because the toolbar and status bar controls are so fully integrated into AppWizard applications, you won't spend any time here exploring their classes. However, there's a lot to learn about the other controls. In the remainder of this chapter, you not only learn to program the common controls (starting with the simplest and moving to the most complex), but you also get hands-on experience with applications that demonstrate the controls.

Basic Common Controls

Some common controls are easier to program than others. Specifically, you can add progress bar, slider, and spinner controls to your applications with little fuss. Tree view and list view controls, on the other hand, require a lot of initialization and handling. In this section, you'll examine the more basic progress bar, slider, and spinner controls, learning how to add them to your applications, as well as learning how to manage them once they're created.

The CommonControlsApp Sample Application

On CD-ROM

Before you look at how to create and program the progress bar, slider, and spinner controls, you should take some time out to see them in action. In the Chapter10\CommonControlsApp folder of this book's CD-ROM, you'll find the CommonControlsApp application, which lists and demonstrates the basic common controls. When you run the program, you'll see the window shown in Figure 10-1.

Note

The image list control is not part of CommonControlsApp as it is a nonvisual control that cannot be manipulated by the user.

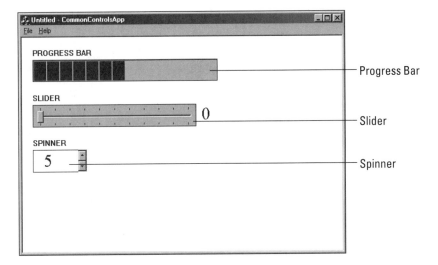

Figure 10-1: The CommonControlsApp application displays a progress bar, slider, and spinner in action.

To get the progress bar going, click in the window. When you do, the progress bar starts to fill with colored blocks. Of course, in this case, the progress bar doesn't represent any ongoing process (except arriving timer events), but you can get an idea of how the control looks. To stop the progress bar, click again in the window.

To try out the slider, use your mouse to move the slider's thumb. When you do, the number to the right of the control displays the slider's new current setting. The spinner control works similarly, except you change the value by clicking the arrows.

Understanding the OnCreate() function

As creating each control in the view class is almost identical, you'll take a look at how the CommonControlsApp completes this task at once. The parts of the program that implement the controls are fairly simple. First the program creates the controls in the view class's `OnCreate()` function (see Listing 10-1), which responds to the Windows `WM_CREATE` message.

Listing 10-1: CommonControlsApp's `OnCreate()` function

```
int CCommonControlsAppView::OnCreate
    (LPCREATESTRUCT lpCreateStruct)
{
    if (CView::OnCreate(lpCreateStruct) == -1)
        return -1;

    // TODO: Add your specialized creation code here

    InitStaticText();
    InitProgressBar();
    InitSlider();
    InitSpinner();

    m_whiteBrush.CreateSolidBrush(RGB(255,255,255));

    return 0;
}
```

As you can see in Listing 10-1, `OnCreate()` doesn't create the program's controls directly. Instead, it calls four member functions—`InitStaticText()`, `InitProgressBar()`, `InitSlider()`, and `InitSpinner()`—to handle the task. `OnCreate()` also creates a white brush that the program uses to draw the controls' backgrounds so that they match the window background. The program changes the background color in response to the `WM_CTLCOLOR` windows message, which is handled by the `OnCtlColor()` function, shown below:

```
HBRUSH CCommonControlsAppView::OnCtlColor
    (CDC* pDC, CWnd* pWnd, UINT nCtrlColor)
{
    if ((nCtrlColor == CTLCOLOR_STATIC) &&
        (pWnd->m_hWnd != m_slider.m_hWnd))
        return (HBRUSH)m_whiteBrush;

    return CView::OnCtlColor(pDC, pWnd, nCtrlColor);
}
```

You learned to modify control colors in Chapter 9, "Standard Controls." Please refer to that chapter if you don't understand how the `OnCtlColor()` message-response function works.

Note

To take a closer look at how static controls are used in this application, please take a look at the code in the CommonControlsApp folder in Chapter 10 of this book's CD-ROM. You might also be interested in looking at how the code is written to display text in a larger font.

The Progress Bar Control

As mentioned above, the progress bar control graphically displays the status of an ongoing operation. It does this by filling the bar with colored blocks as the operation progresses. Represented in MFC by the CProgressCtrl class, the progress bar is the easiest of the common controls to use. You just display the control and increment its display at appropriate times during the operation the bar represents. Figure 10-2 shows a progress bar control that indicates an operation about half completed.

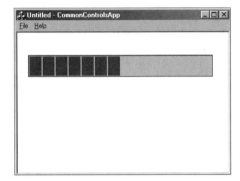

Figure 10-2: A progress bar fills with colored blocks as an operation progresses.

Creating and programming a progress bar control

To create a progress bar, you first define an object of the CProgressCtrl class:

```
CProgressCtrl m_progBar;
```

You then call the object's Create() member function, which creates the actual progress bar control and associates it with the CProgressCtrl object. The CProgressCtrl class's Create() function has the following signature. The arguments' descriptions are listed after the signature.

```
BOOL Create(
    DWORD dwStyle,
    const RECT& rect,
    CWnd* pParentWnd,
    UINT nID);
```

dwStyle	The progress bar's style flags
rect	A RECT or CRect object that specifies the progress bar's size and position
pParentWnd	A pointer to the progress bar's parent window
nID	The progress bar's ID

A call to `Create()` might look something like this:

```
m_progBar.Create(WS_CHILD | WS_BORDER | WS_VISIBLE,
    CRect(20, 40, 360, 80), this, IDC_PROGBAR);
```

Notice that the progress bar's style flags are all standard window styles. (Windows doesn't define any special styles for a progress bar.) You'll at least want to specify the `WS_CHILD` and `WS_VISIBLE` styles. Other window styles may also be useful in specific circumstances. For example, the above progress bar specifies the `WS_BORDER` style so that the edges of the control stand out against the window's white background.

Once you have the progress bar created, you can set its attributes, including the control's range, step size, and initial position. The range is the scope of values represented by the bar. For example, if you were using the bar to represent a percentage, you'd probably give the control a range of 0 to 100. The step size is the portion of the bar that fills when the application increments the control. In the case of a percentage progress bar, you might set the step size to 10, which means the control must be incremented ten times before its bar is filled. The initial position is the portion of the bar that's already filled when the application displays the control. Typically, you'd set this value to 0.

To set the control's range, step, and position, you call the `CProgressCtrl` class's `SetRange()`, `SetStep()`, and `SetPos()` member functions:

```
m_progBar.SetRange(1, 100);
m_progBar.SetStep(10);
m_progBar.SetPos(0);
```

The only thing left to do is increment the control as the task it represents progresses. You do this by calling the `StepIt()` member function:

```
m_progBar.StepIt();
```

The `StepIt()` function increments the control by its step value. In the case of a control with a range of 0 to 100 and a step value of 10, an application would have to call `StepIt()` ten times to fill the control's bar. Table 10-1 lists all of the `CProgressCtrl` class's member functions, along with their descriptions.

Table 10-1 `CProgressCtrl` **member functions**

Function	Description
Create()	Creates the progress bar element and associates it with the CProgressCtrl object
OffsetPos()	Advances the progress bar's position by a given amount
SetPos()	Sets the progress bar's current position
SetRange()	Sets the progress bar's minimum and maximum range
SetStep()	Sets the progress bar's step increment
StepIt()	Advances the progress bar's position by the step increment

Understanding CommonControlsApp's progress bar

The application creates its progress bar in the `InitProgressBar()` function, just as described in the previous section. The `InitProgressBar()` function looks like this:

```
void CCommonControlsAppView::InitProgressBar()
{
    m_progBar.Create(WS_CHILD | WS_BORDER | WS_VISIBLE,
        CRect(20, 40, 360, 80), this, IDC_PROGBAR);
    m_progBar.SetRange(1, 100);
    m_progBar.SetStep(10);
    m_progBar.SetPos(50);
}
```

This progress bar has a range of 1 to 100, a step value of 10, and starts off at a position of 50, which means the progress bar is half filled when it first appears. When the user clicks in the application's window, Windows sends a `WM_LBUTTONDOWN` message, which the program handles in the `OnLButtonDown()` function, as shown in Listing 10-2.

Listing 10-2: The application's `OnLButtonDown()` function

```
void CCommonControlsAppView::OnLButtonDown
    (UINT nFlags, CPoint point)
{
    // TODO: Add your message handler code here
    //    and/or call default

    if (m_timerSet)
    {
        KillTimer(1);
        m_timerSet = FALSE;
    }
    else
    {
        SetTimer(1, 250, NULL);
        m_timerSet = TRUE;
    }

    CView::OnLButtonDown(nFlags, point);
}
```

The `m_timerSet` variable is a member of the view class that acts as a timer flag. When `m_timerSet` equals `TRUE`, the timer is running; otherwise, the timer is off. `OnLButtonDown()` first checks the value of `m_timerSet`. If `m_timerSet` is `FALSE`, the program calls `SetTimer()` to start a Windows timer.

`SetTimer()`'s three arguments are the timer number, the number of milliseconds between timer events, and the address of a callback function. If the third argument is `FALSE` (that is, there's no callback function), Windows places the timer messages on the Windows message queue. You'll soon see what happens to those messages.

If `m_timerSet` is `FALSE`, `OnLButtonDown()` stops the timer by calling the `KillTimer()` function. This function takes the timer number as its single argument. After the program calls `KillTimer()`, Windows stops sending timer messages.

When the timer starts running, Windows sends a `WM_TIMER` message to the window. By now, you should be MFC-savvy enough to realize that you can respond to these messages by adding the `ON_WM_TIMER()` macro to your window class's message map and implementing the `OnTimer()` message-response function, as shown below:

```
void CCommonControlsAppView::OnTimer(UINT nIDEvent)
{
    // TODO: Add your message handler code here
    //    and/or call default

    m_progBar.StepIt();

    CView::OnTimer(nIDEvent);
}
```

Every time the application receives a `WM_TIMER` message, MFC calls `OnTimer()`, which calls the progress bar's `StepIt()` function. As long as the timer runs, the progress bar continues to cycle through its display.

The Slider Control

The slider control is a snazzy way of getting input from the user when you want the input value constrained to a given range. For example, if you create a slider with a range of 0 to 100, the user can select only values (or ranges of values) from 0 to 100. Figure 10-3 shows a slider control displayed in a window. To select a value, the user moves the sliding thumb with his mouse (the user can also use arrow keys on the keyboard). The further to the right the user drags the thumb, the higher the value being selected, up to the set maximum.

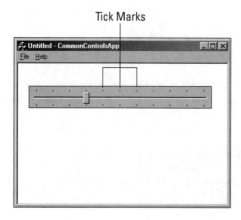

Tick Marks

Figure 10-3: A slider represents a range of values from which a user can choose.

Creating and programming a slider control

To create a slider control, you first define an object of the `CSliderCtrl` class:

```
CSliderCtrl m_slider;
```

You then call the object's `Create()` member function, which creates the actual control and associates it with the `CSliderCtrl` object. The `CSliderCtrl` class's `Create()` function has the following signature. The arguments' descriptions are listed after the signature.

```
BOOL Create(
    DWORD dwStyle,
    const RECT& rect,
    CWnd* pParentWnd,
    UINT nID);
```

dwStyle	The slider's style flags
rect	A `RECT` or `CRect` object that specifies the slider's size and position
pParentWnd	A pointer to the slider's parent window
nID	The slider's ID

A call to `Create()` might look something like this:

```
m_slider.Create(WS_CHILD | WS_VISIBLE | WS_BORDER |
    TBS_BOTH | TBS_AUTOTICKS | TBS_HORZ,
    CRect(20, 120, 320, 160), this, IDC_SLIDER);
```

Notice that, unlike the progress bar, the slider does have styles of its own, besides the standard window styles. For the window styles, you'll at least want to specify the WS_CHILD and WS_VISIBLE styles. Other window styles may also be useful in specific circumstances. For instance, like the previous progress bar example, the above slider specifies the WS_BORDER style so that the edges of the control stand out against the window's white background. The remaining styles are specific to slider controls. Table 10-2 lists all these styles, along with their descriptions.

Table 10-2   Slider control styles

Style	Description
TBS_AUTOTICKS	Gives the slider the capability to draw tick marks
TBS_BOTH	Displays tick marks on both sides of the slider
TBS_BOTTOM	Displays tick marks on the bottom of a horizontal slider
TBS_ENABLESELRANGE	Enables the slider to show selection ranges
TBS_HORZ	Creates a horizontal slider
TBS_LEFT	Places tick marks on the left side of a vertical slider

(continued)

Table 10-2   *(Continued)*

Style	*Description*
TBS_NOTICKS	Creates a slider with no tick marks
TBS_RIGHT	Places tick marks on the right side of a vertical slider
TBS_TOP	Places tick marks on the top of a horizontal slider
TBS_VERT	Creates a vertical slider

Once you have a slider up on the screen, you need some way to know what the user is doing with it. When the user moves the control's thumb, the control generates WM_HSCROLL messages, which you can respond to in the application. To do this, use ClassWizard to add the OnHScroll() message-response function to your application, as shown in Figure 10-4.

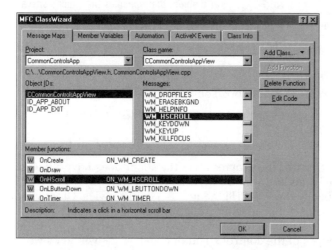

Figure 10-4: Sliders generate WM_HSCROLL messages to which your application can respond.

Listing 10-3 shows what the OnHScroll() function might look like in an application. The function receives three parameters: the scroll-bar code, the new scroll position, and a pointer to the scroller. (In this case, the scroller is the slider control.) For the most part, you don't need to be concerned with the scroll-bar code. If you want to know more about the code's possible values, look up the OnHScroll() function in your Visual C++ online documentation.

Listing 10-3: The OnHScroll() **function**

```
void CCommonControlsAppView::OnHScroll
    (UINT nSBCode, UINT nPos, CScrollBar* pScrollBar)
{
    // TODO: Add your message handler code here
```

```
//   and/or call default

CSliderCtrl* s = (CSliderCtrl*)pScrollBar;
int pos = s->GetPos();

// Do something with the new position here.

CView::OnHScroll(nSBCode, nPos, pScrollBar);
}
```

In Listing 10-3, the program first casts the scroller pointer to a `CSliderCtrl` pointer, which gives the function access to the slider object. The program then gets the slider's current position by calling the slider's `GetPos()` member function. The `CSliderCtrl` class defines many other member functions that you might find useful. Table 10-3 lists these functions, along with their descriptions.

Table 10-3   `CSliderCtrl` **member functions**

Function	Description
ClearSel()	Clears the slider's current selection
ClearTics()	Erases the slider's tick marks
Create()	Creates the slider element and associates it with the `CSliderCtrl` object
GetChannelRect()	Gets the slider's channel size
GetLineSize()	Gets the slider's line size
GetNumTics()	Gets the slider's tick-mark count
GetPageSize()	Gets the slider's page size
GetPos()	Gets the slider's current position
GetRange()	Gets the slider's minimum and maximum positions
GetRangeMax()	Gets the slider's maximum position
GetRangeMin()	Gets the slider's minimum position
GetSelection()	Gets the current selection's range
GetThumbRect()	Gets the slider's thumb size
GetTic()	Gets a single tick-mark position
GetTicArray()	Gets the slider's tick-mark positions
GetTicPos()	Gets a single tick-mark position in client coordinates
SetLineSize()	Sets the slider's line size
SetPageSize()	Sets the slider's page size
SetPos()	Sets the slider's current position
SetRange()	Sets the slider's minimum and maximum positions

(continued)

Table 10-3 *(Continued)*

Function	Description
SetRangeMax()	Sets the slider's maximum position
SetRangeMin()	Sets the slider's minimum position
SetSelection()	Sets the current selection's range
SetTic()	Sets a tick mark's position
SetTicFreq()	Sets the tick-mark frequency
VerifyPos()	Verifies that a slider is between the minimum and maximum position

Understanding CommonControlsApp's slider

The InitSlider() function gets the honor of creating and initializing the CommonControlsApps application's slider control. That function, shown in Listing 10-4, creates a horizontal slider with tick marks both above and below the slider track. The function then calls SetRange() to set the control's range to 0 through 100. The call to SetTicFreq() determines how many tick marks appear on the control.

Finally, the SetLineSize() and SetPageSize() function calls determine how far the slider moves when the user presses a key or clicks the mouse. The line size determines the increment value when the user uses the keyboard's up and down arrow keys. The page size determines the increment value when the user clicks the slider track with the mouse or presses the keyboard's PageUp and PageDown keys.

Listing 10-4: The application's InitSlider() function

```
void CCommonControlsAppView::InitSlider()
{
    m_slider.Create(WS_CHILD | WS_VISIBLE | WS_BORDER |
        TBS_BOTH | TBS_AUTOTICKS | TBS_HORZ,
        CRect(20, 120, 320, 160), this, IDC_SLIDER);
    m_slider.SetRange(0, 100, TRUE);
    m_slider.SetTicFreq(10);
    m_slider.SetLineSize(1);
    m_slider.SetPageSize(10);
}
```

When the slider moves, it generates WM_HSCROLL messages, to which the program responds in its OnHScroll() function, shown in Listing 10-5. OnHScroll() gets the current value of the slider, converts the value to a string, and then displays the string in the m_sliderStatic2 static text control, which displays text in a large font.

Listing 10-5: The application's `OnHScroll()` **function**

```
void CCommonControlsAppView::OnHScroll
    (UINT nSBCode, UINT nPos, CScrollBar* pScrollBar)
{
    // TODO: Add your message handler code here
    //    and/or call default

    CSliderCtrl* s = (CSliderCtrl*)pScrollBar;
    int pos = s->GetPos();
    char str[10];
    wsprintf(str, "%d    ", pos);
    m_sliderStatic2.SetWindowText(str);

    CView::OnHScroll(nSBCode, nPos, pScrollBar);
}
```

 PROBLEMS & SOLUTIONS

Enabling Slider Range Selection

PROBLEM: From what I've seen and read, I should be able to set up a slider control so that the user can select not only a single value, but also a range of values. How can I get this feature to work?

SOLUTION: It's easy to set a slider to display a range of values. Just include the `TBS_ENABLESELRANGE` style when you create the slider, and call the slider's `SetSelection()` member function to set the desired range. A problem rears its ugly head, however, if you want the user to make the range selection. You could create a dialog box into which the user enters the minimum and maximum values of the range, and then apply the range to the slider, but that's not particularly elegant. What you really want is to give the slider control its own range-selection capability.

Customizing the slider control is easier than you might think. The first step is to create your own slider class based on the `CSliderCtrl` class. If you're writing an MFC program using AppWizard and ClassWizard, you can use ClassWizard to create the new class and add it to your project. To do this, follow these steps:

1. Press Ctrl+W to display ClassWizard. Click the Add Class button and select New from the drop-down selections, as shown in Figure 10-5.

2. In the New Class dialog box, type your new class's name (for example, `CMySlider`) into the Name box, and select the `CSliderCtrl` class in the Base Class box (see Figure 10-6).

3. Click the OK button to finalize your entries. ClassWizard creates the new class and adds it to your project.

Continued

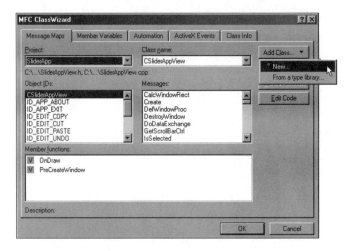

Figure 10-5: You can create new classes with ClassWizard.

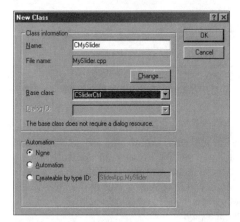

Figure 10-6: The New Class dialog box enables you to
name your new class, as well as select a base class.

Now that you have your new class created, you can start fiddling with the way a slider works.
A common way of enabling the user to select a range of values is to use the Shift key
combined with the mouse. With this method, the user drags the slider to the starting position.
Then she holds down the Shift key, places the mouse pointer over the slider's thumb, clicks
and holds the left mouse button, and drags the slider to the ending position. When the user
releases the mouse button (while still holding down Shift), the range selection is complete.

Continued

To add this functionality to your new slider class, add the `OnLButtonDown()` and `OnLButtonUp()` message-response functions to the slider class, as shown in Figures 10-7 and 10-8. You will use these functions to track mouse movement when the Shift key is pressed. When the user clicks the slider's thumb, MFC calls `OnLButtonDown()`, and when the user releases the mouse, MFC calls `OnLButtonUp()`.

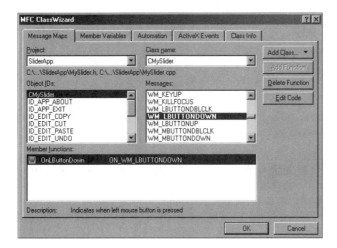

Figure 10-7: Here's ClassWizard adding the `OnLButtonDown()` function.

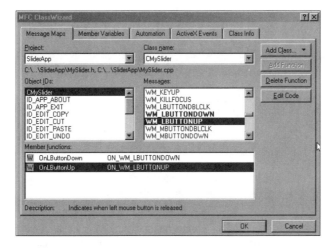

Figure 10-8: Here's ClassWizard adding the `OnLButtonUp()` function.

In the `OnLButtonDown()` function, the slider has to initialize the range-selection operation. This means initializing some member variables. You'll need to add four member variables to the class's header file, as shown here:

```
BOOL m_rangeSelected;
int m_rangeStart;
int m_rangeEnd;
int m_rangeValue;
```

In OnLButtonDown(), you want to check for the Shift key. If it's pressed, you set the range's starting position to the slider's current position and set the range value (the difference between the start and end of the range) to zero. Here are the lines to add to OnLButtonDown():

```
m_rangeSelected = FALSE;

if (nFlags & MK_SHIFT)
{
    m_rangeStart = GetPos();
    m_rangeValue = 0;
}
```

In OnLButtonUp(), you need to check whether the Shift key is still held down. If it's not, you don't want to do anything further. If it is, you want to set the range's end to the slider's current position. Then you can calculate the range value by subtracting the start from the end. You also need to plan for the user dragging the control to the left rather than to the right. To do this, you need to swap the starting and ending values. After all the calculations, you call the slider's SetSelection() member function to display the selected range in the control. Listing 10-6 shows the code for the OnLButtonUp() function:

Listing 10-6: The OnLButtonUp() function

```
if (nFlags & MK_SHIFT)
{
    m_rangeSelected = TRUE;

    int pos = GetPos();
    if (pos < m_rangeStart)
    {
        m_rangeEnd = m_rangeStart;
        m_rangeStart = pos;
    }
    else
        m_rangeEnd = pos;

    SetSelection(m_rangeStart, m_rangeEnd);
    m_rangeValue = m_rangeEnd - m_rangeStart;
}
```

To complete the class, you should create member functions called GetRangeStart(), GetRangeEnd(), GetRangeValue(), and IsRangeSelected() so that the slider's parent object can obtain information about the slider. The first three functions should have public access and do nothing more than return the values of the m_rangeStart, m_rangeEnd, and m_rangeValue member variables. The IsRangeSelected() function should return the value of m_rangeSelected, which indicates whether a new range is ready to be read. IsRangeSelected() should also turn off the m_rangeSelected flag. Listing 10-7 shows the new class's header file, whereas Listing 10-8 shows the class's implementation file.

Continued

Listing 10-7: The MySlider **class's header file**

```
// MySlider.h : header file
//

/////////////////////////////////////////////////////////
// CMySlider window

class CMySlider : public CSliderCtrl
{
// Construction
public:
    CMySlider();

// Attributes
public:

// Operations
public:

// Overrides
    // ClassWizard generated virtual function overrides
    //{{AFX_VIRTUAL(CMySlider)
    //}}AFX_VIRTUAL

// Implementation
public:
    BOOL IsRangeSelected();
    int GetRangeValue();
    int GetRangeEnd();
    int GetRangeStart();
    virtual ~CMySlider();

    // Generated message map functions
protected:
    BOOL m_rangeSelected;
    int m_rangeValue;
    int m_rangeEnd;
    int m_rangeStart;
    //{{AFX_MSG(CMySlider)
    afx_msg void OnLButtonDown(UINT nFlags,
        CPoint point);
    afx_msg void OnLButtonUp(UINT nFlags, CPoint point);
    //}}AFX_MSG

    DECLARE_MESSAGE_MAP()
};
```

Listing 10-8: The MySlider **class's implementation file**

```
// MySlider.cpp : implementation file
//

#include "stdafx.h"
```

Continued

```cpp
#include "SliderApp.h"
#include "MySlider.h"

#ifdef _DEBUG
#define new DEBUG_NEW
#undef THIS_FILE
static char THIS_FILE[] = __FILE__;
#endif

/////////////////////////////////////////////////////////
// CMySlider

CMySlider::CMySlider()
{
}

CMySlider::~CMySlider()
{
}


BEGIN_MESSAGE_MAP(CMySlider, CSliderCtrl)
    //{{AFX_MSG_MAP(CMySlider)
    ON_WM_LBUTTONDOWN()
    ON_WM_LBUTTONUP()
    //}}AFX_MSG_MAP
END_MESSAGE_MAP()

/////////////////////////////////////////////////////////
// CMySlider message handlers

void CMySlider::OnLButtonDown(UINT nFlags, CPoint point)
{
    // TODO: Add your message handler code here
    //    and/or call default

    m_rangeSelected = FALSE;

    if (nFlags & MK_SHIFT)
    {
        m_rangeStart = GetPos();
        m_rangeValue = 0;
    }

    CSliderCtrl::OnLButtonDown(nFlags, point);
}

void CMySlider::OnLButtonUp(UINT nFlags, CPoint point)
{
    // TODO: Add your message handler code here
    //    and/or call default

    if (nFlags & MK_SHIFT)
    {
```

Continued

```
                     m_rangeSelected = TRUE;

                     int pos = GetPos();
                     if (pos < m_rangeStart)
                     {
                         m_rangeEnd = m_rangeStart;
                         m_rangeStart = pos;
                     }
                     else
                         m_rangeEnd = pos;

                     SetSelection(m_rangeStart, m_rangeEnd);
                     m_rangeValue = m_rangeEnd - m_rangeStart;
                 }

             CSliderCtrl::OnLButtonUp(nFlags, point);
         }

         int CMySlider::GetRangeStart()
         {
             return m_rangeStart;
         }

         int CMySlider::GetRangeEnd()
         {
             return m_rangeEnd;
         }

         int CMySlider::GetRangeValue()
         {
             return m_rangeValue;
         }

         BOOL CMySlider::IsRangeSelected()
         {
             BOOL selected = m_rangeSelected;
             m_rangeSelected = FALSE;

             return selected;
         }
```

On CD-ROM

In the Chapter10\SliderApp folder of this book's CD-ROM, you'll find the Slider application, which demonstrates the custom slider control. When you run the program, select a range with the slider by dragging the slider's thumb while holding down the Shift key. Figure 10-9 shows the application after the user has selected a range of values.

Continued

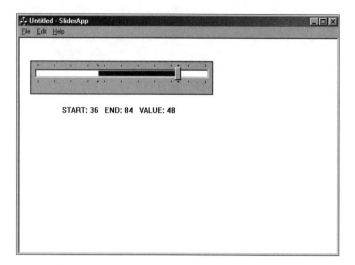

Figure 10-9: This custom slider enables a user to select a range of values.

The Spinner Control

The spinner control provides another way of getting input from the user when you want the input value constrained to a given range. But rather than moving a slider in a track, the user clicks onscreen arrows to change the control's value. Figure 10-10 shows a spinner control displayed in a window. To raise the control's value, the user clicks the up arrow. To lower the control's value, the user clicks the down arrow.

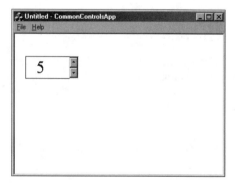

Figure 10-10: A spinner is another control that represents a range of values.

Creating and programming the spinner control

To create a spinner control, you first define an object of the `CSpinButtonCtrl` class:

```
CSpinButtonCtrl m_spin;
```

You then call the object's `Create()` member function, which creates the actual control and associates it with the `CSpinButtonCtrl` object. The `CSpinButtonCtrl` **class's** `Create()` function has the following signature. The arguments' descriptions are listed after the signature.

```
BOOL Create(
    DWORD dwStyle,
    const RECT& rect,
    CWnd* pParentWnd,
    UINT nID);
```

dwStyle	The spinner's style flags
rect	A `RECT` or `CRect` object that specifies the spinner's size and position
pParentWnd	A pointer to the spinner's parent window
nID	The spinner's ID

A call to `Create()` might look something like this:

```
m_spinEdit.Create(WS_CHILD | WS_VISIBLE | WS_BORDER |
    UDS_ALIGNLEFT | UDS_WRAP,
    CRect(20, 200, 120, 240), this, IDC_SPINNER);
```

Besides the standard window styles, a spinner control defines styles of its own. Table 10-4 lists all these styles, along with their descriptions. For the window styles, you'll at least want to specify the WS_CHILD and WS_VISIBLE styles. Other window styles may also be useful in specific circumstances.

Table 10-4   Spinner control styles

Style	*Description*
UDS_ALIGNLEFT	Places the spin button on the left of the buddy control
UDS_ALIGNRIGHT	Places the spin button on the right of the buddy control
UDS_ARROWKEYS	Enables the control to respond to the keyboard's up and down arrow keys
UDS_AUTOBUDDY	Automatically specifies the previous control as the buddy control
UDS_HORZ	Points the control's arrows left and right instead of up and down
UDS_NOTHOUSANDS	Stops the control from displaying thousands of separators (usually commas)

(continued)

Table 10-4	*(Continued)*
Style	*Description*
UDS_SETBUDDYINT	Sets the text of the buddy control when the user changes the spinner's position
UDS_WRAP	Creates a spinner that wraps around from its highest value to its lowest, and vice versa

A spinner control is little more than a pair of arrows. If you want the control's value to be visible on the screen, you must associate the spinner with a *buddy control*. Then, when the spinner's value changes, MFC automatically updates the buddy control. In most cases, the buddy control is a CEdit object. After creating the spinner control, you'll want to create the buddy control and give it to the spinner by calling the spinner's SetBuddy() function:

```
m_edit.Create(WS_CHILD | WS_VISIBLE | WS_BORDER,
    CRect(20, 200, 120, 240), this, IDC_SPINNER);
m_spin.SetBuddy(&m_edit);
```

As you did with the slider control, you also need to set the spinner's range and position:

```
m_spin.SetRange(1, 10);
m_spin.SetPos(5);
```

SetRange() and SetPos() are only two of the CSpinButtonCtrl class's member functions. Table 10-5 lists all the member functions and their descriptions.

Table 10-5	CSpinButtonCtrl **member functions**
Function	*Description*
Create()	Creates a spin button element and associates it with the CSpinButtonCtrl object
GetAccel()	Gets the spinner's acceleration information
GetBase()	Gets the spinner's current base
GetBuddy()	Gets a pointer to the spinner's buddy control
GetPos()	Gets the spinner's current position
GetRange()	Gets the spinner's upper and lower limits
SetAccel()	Sets the spinner's acceleration
SetBase()	Sets the spinner's base
SetBuddy()	Sets the spinner's buddy control
SetPos()	Sets the spinner's current position
SetRange()	Sets the spinner's upper and lower limits

Understanding CommonControlsApp's spinner

The last common control demonstrated in CommonControlsApp is the spinner. The program creates this handy control in its `InitSpinner()` function. In `InitSpinner()`, the program first creates the spinner's buddy control:

```
m_spinEdit.Create(WS_CHILD | WS_VISIBLE | WS_BORDER,
    CRect(20, 200, 120, 240), this, IDC_SPINNER);
```

The program then creates a large font for displaying text in the buddy edit box. Listing 10-9 shows how the program creates the font and gives it to the edit buddy control.

Listing 10-9: Creating a font for the buddy edit control

```
LOGFONT logFont;
logFont.lfHeight = 36;
logFont.lfWidth = 0;
logFont.lfEscapement = 0;
logFont.lfOrientation = 0;
logFont.lfWeight = FW_NORMAL;
logFont.lfItalic = 0;
logFont.lfUnderline = 0;
logFont.lfStrikeOut = 0;
logFont.lfCharSet = ANSI_CHARSET;
logFont.lfOutPrecision = OUT_DEFAULT_PRECIS;
logFont.lfClipPrecision = CLIP_DEFAULT_PRECIS;
logFont.lfQuality = PROOF_QUALITY;
logFont.lfPitchAndFamily = VARIABLE_PITCH | FF_ROMAN;
strcpy(logFont.lfFaceName, "Times New Roman");
m_spinEditFont.CreateFontIndirect(&logFont);
m_spinEdit.SetFont(&m_spinEditFont);
```

After getting the buddy control ready to go, the program creates the spinner control:

```
m_spin.Create(WS_CHILD | WS_VISIBLE | WS_BORDER |
    UDS_SETBUDDYINT | UDS_ALIGNRIGHT | UDS_ARROWKEYS,
    CRect(0, 0, 0, 0), this, 104);
```

The flags passed to the spinner's `Create()` function result in a spinner that automatically updates its buddy control, aligns the arrows to the right of the buddy control, and enables the user to manipulate the spinner with the keyboard's up and down arrow keys. The control's position and size are all set to zero because these values are determined by the size and position of the buddy control.

After creating the spinner, the program gives it the buddy control, as well as sets it range and initial position:

```
m_spin.SetBuddy(&m_spinEdit);
m_spin.SetRange(1, 10);
m_spin.SetPos(5);
```

The Image List Control

Image list controls are very different from the other types of controls you've learned about so far. They don't appear on the screen and they can't be manipulated by the user. It is for these reasons that image list controls do not appear in any of this chapter's sample applications. However, while they don't appear on the screen as part of your application's user interface, they do, nevertheless, contribute to the construction of that interface. Using image controls, you can manage images for other types of controls, including list view and tree view controls, which you learn about in the following section.

To create an image list control, you first define an object of the `CImageList` class:

```
CImageList m_imageList;
```

You then call the object's `Create()` member function, which creates the actual control and associates it with the `CImageList` object. The `CImageList` class's `Create()` function has the following signature. The arguments' descriptions are listed after the signature.

```
BOOL Create(
    int cx,
    int cy,
    UINT nFlags,
    int nInitial,
    int nGrow);
```

cx	The width of each image in the list
cy	The height of each image in the list
nFlags	The list's color flags
nInitial	The initial number of images in the list
nGrow	The amount that the list should grow to accommodate additional images

A call to `Create()` might look something like this:

```
m_imageList.Create(16, 16, ILC_COLOR4, 6, 4);
```

This call to `Create()` results in an image list that holds 16x16-pixel images. The `ILC_COLOR4` flag specifies that the images are 4-bit (16-color) bitmaps, and the last two arguments specify that the image list will start with six images and should grow to accommodate four additional images whenever it needs to.

After creating the image list, you add your images by calling the object's `Add()` member function:

```
m_treeImages.Add(hIcon);
```

Here, the program is adding an icon to the image list. In this case, the `Add()` function's single argument is the icon's handle. There are several versions of

Add(), however, so that you can add icons or bitmaps to the image list. The CImageList class defines many other member functions as well, all of which are listed in Table 10-6. Although CImageList is a powerful class, in most cases you'll just create your image list and hand it off to another control, such as a tree view or list view control.

Table 10-6 CImageList **member functions**

Function	Description
Add()	Adds images to an image list
Attach()	Associates an image list with a CImageList object
BeginDrag()	Starts image dragging
Create()	Creates an image list element and associates it with the CImageList object
DeleteImageList()	Deletes an image list
Detach()	Disassociates an image list element from a CImageList object
DragEnter()	Shows the drag image at the given position
DragLeave()	Erases the drag image
DragMove()	Moves the drag image
DragShowNolock()	Shows or erases the drag image without locking the window
Draw()	Draws the dragged image during a drag-and-drop operation
EndDrag()	Ends a drag operation
ExtractIcon()	Creates an icon from an image and mask
GetBkColor()	Gets the image list's background color
GetDragImage()	Gets the image list used for dragging
GetImageCount()	Gets the image list's image count
GetImageInfo()	Fills an IMAGEINFO structure with image list information
GetSafeHandle()	Gets the image list's handle
Read()	Reads an image list from an archive
Remove()	Removes an image from the image list
Replace()	Replaces an image in an image list
SetBkColor()	Sets the image list's background color
SetDragCursorImage()	Creates a new drag image
SetOverlayImage()	Sets an image as an overlay mask
Write()	Writes an image list to an archive

PROBLEMS & SOLUTIONS

Creating Composite Icons

PROBLEM: *I've noticed that many Windows 98 objects require two types of icons, a small 16x16-pixel icon and a full-size 32x32-pixel icon. Isn't there some sort of object that simplifies managing this pair of icons?*

SOLUTION: It's true that many Windows 98 objects require a standard pair of large and small icons. For example, document and application icons that appear in Windows Explorer require large and small icons so that Explorer can display them properly regardless of the current view. In order to manage such icon pairs, Windows came up with composite icons.

Composite icons are two icons—the standard 16x16 and 32x32 icons—stored in a single file. Although many icon editors don't support composite icons, Visual C++'s icon editor does. Once you've created a composite icon, you have a single icon resource—with a single ID—that contains both icons.

To create a composite icon, first select the Resource command from Visual C++'s Insert command. The Insert Resource dialog box appears, as shown in Figure 10-11.

Figure 10-11: The Insert Resource dialog box enables you to add a new resource object to a project.

Double-click the icon resource and Visual C++ opens the icon editor with a standard 32x32 icon displayed (see Figure 10-12). This will be the large image of your composite icon. Use the drawing tools to create the icon. Figure 10-13 shows the large icon after being drawn.

Now that you've drawn the 32x32 image, it's time to add the 16x16 image to the composite icon. To do this, click the New Device Image button (the small button to the right of the Device box). The New Icon Image dialog box appears, as seen in Figure 10-14.

Double-click the Small (16x16) entry in the dialog box. A 16x16 icon appears in the icon editor. Draw the 16x16 image (see Figure 10-15), and your composite icon is complete.

Continued

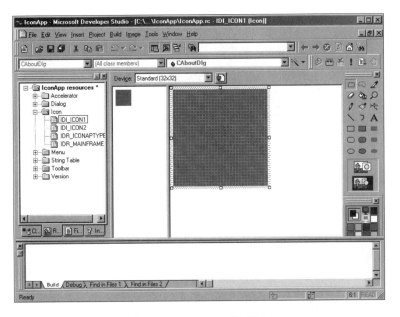

Figure 10-12: The icon editor opens to a new 32x32 icon.

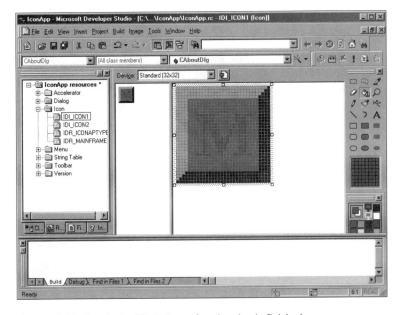

Figure 10-13: Here's the 32x32 icon after drawing is finished.

Continued

New Device Image Button

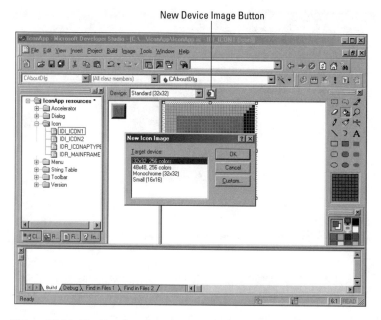

Figure 10-14: The New Icon Image dialog box enables you to add a second image to your composite icon.

Device Box

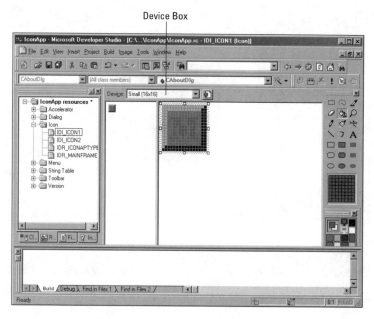

Figure 10-15: Here's the 16x16 image fully drawn.

Continued

When editing a composite icon, you can select the image on which to work from the Device box, which lists both the 32x32 and 16x16 images. When you refer to the composite image in a program, you use the icon's single ID for either image. Windows automatically accesses the specific icon it needs.

Advanced Common Controls

Now things get really interesting. The list view and tree view controls are among the most complex controls available in Windows 98. Although these controls aren't difficult to program, you do have to perform a number of often meticulous steps to get them up and running. These steps include setting styles, creating image lists, and defining columns and subitems, among other things. In the following sections, you'll see how to handle the list view and tree view controls.

The CommonControlsApp2 Sample Application

On CD-ROM

Before examining how to create and program the more complex common controls, you should take some time out to see what they look like. In the Chapter10\CommonControlsApp2 folder of this book's CD-ROM, you'll find the CommonControlsApp2 application, which demonstrates the list view and tree view controls in action. When you run the program, you see the window shown in Figure 10-16.

Start by clicking a main item in the list view control. When you do, a message box appears showing the data associated with the chosen item (see Figure 10-17). Notice that the message box appears only when you click a main item. If you click a subitem, nothing happens.

The columns have a special ability of which you may not yet be aware. Place your mouse cursor over the line between the first and second columns. The cursor changes into a cross with a horizontal arrow. Hold down the left button and drag to enlarge the first column, as shown in Figure 10-18.

List view control   Tree view control

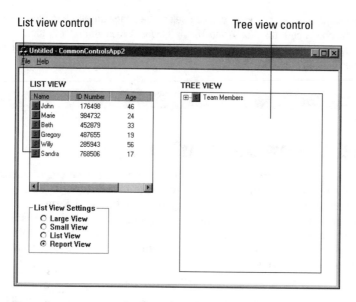

Figure 10-16: Here's the CommonControlsApp2 application with its list view and tree view controls

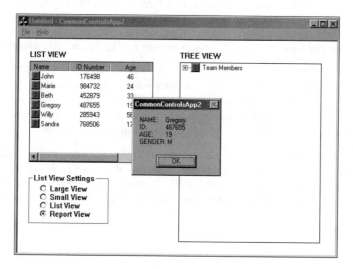

Figure 10-17: The message box displays data for a selected item.

Expanded column

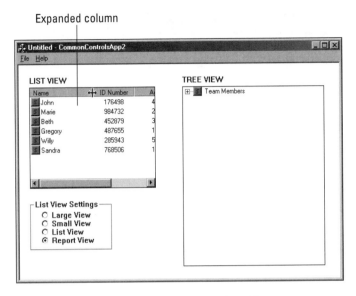

Figure 10-18: The list view's columns are adjustable.

Below the list view controls you'll see a group of radio buttons. These buttons control the type of view displayed in the list view control. Currently, the list view control is in its report view. Click the radio buttons to see the other views. Figures 10-19, 10-20, and 10-21 show the large icon, small icon, and list views, respectively.

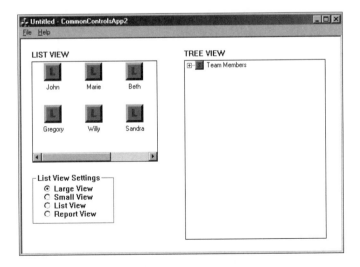

Figure 10-19: Here's the list view control in large-icon view.

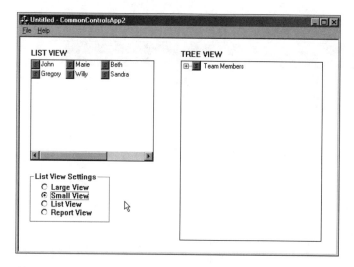

Figure 10-20: The list view control in small-icon view

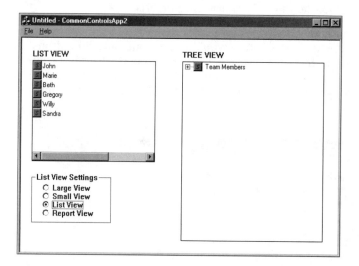

Figure 10-21: The list view control in list view

Finally, the tree view control contains the same data as the list view control, but organized into a tree hierarchy. Click the plus sign next to an item to expand the item. Click the minus sign to collapse an item. Double-click on any item to display a message box containing the item's text. Figure 10-22 shows the tree view control fully expanded. Notice that the items no longer fit in the control, so a scroll bar has appeared.

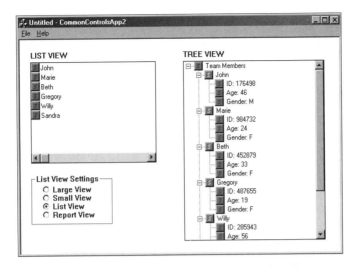

Figure 10-22: The tree view control with its items expanded

Understanding the `OnCreate()` function

As you now know, the best place in an MFC program to create controls is in the window class's `OnCreate()` function, which responds to Windows' `WM_CREATE` message. Listing 10-10 shows CommonControlsApp2's `OnCreate()` function, from which the program calls the `InitStaticText()`, `InitListView()`, `InitRadioButtons()`, and `InitTreeView()` functions. `OnCreate()` also creates the white brush that the program will use for the static controls' backgrounds, which are normally colored gray.

Listing 10-10: CommonControlsApp2's `OnCreate()` function

```
int CCommonControlsApp2View::OnCreate
    (LPCREATESTRUCT lpCreateStruct)
{
    if (CView::OnCreate(lpCreateStruct) == -1)
        return -1;

    // TODO: Add your specialized creation code here

    InitStaticText();
    InitListView();
    InitRadioButtons();
    InitTreeView();

    m_whiteBrush.CreateSolidBrush(RGB(255,255,255));

    return 0;
}
```

The program changes the background color in response to the `WM_CTLCOLOR` windows message, which is handled by the `OnCtlColor()` function:

```
HBRUSH CCommonControlsApp2View::OnCtlColor
    (CDC * pDC, CWnd * pWnd, UINT nCtrlColor)
{
    if (nCtrlColor == CTLCOLOR_STATIC)
        return (HBRUSH)m_whiteBrush;

    return CView::OnCtlColor(pDC, pWnd, nCtrlColor);
}
```

The List View Control

In this section, you'll learn to incorporate list view controls into your programs. There are four types of list views, as indexed below. Figures 10-23 through 10-26 show an example of each.

■ Report view

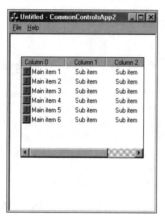

Figure 10-23: The list view control in its report view

■ Small icon view

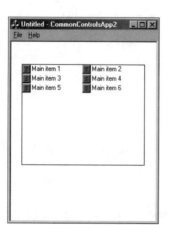

Figure 10-24: The list view control in its small icon view

■ Large icon view

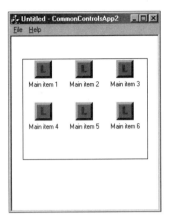

Figure 10-25: The list view control in its large icon view

■ List view

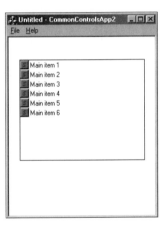

Figure 10-26: The list view control in its list view

Creating the list view control object

To create a list view control, you first define an object of the CListCtrl class:

```
CListCtrl m_listView;
```

You then call the object's Create() member function, which creates the actual control and associates it with the CListCtrl object. The CListCtrl class's Create() function has the following signature. The arguments' descriptions are listed after the signature.

```
BOOL Create(
    DWORD dwStyle,
    const RECT& rect,
    CWnd* pParentWnd,
    UINT nID);
```

`dwStyle`	The list view's style flags
`rect`	A `RECT` or `CRect` object that specifies the list view's size and position
`pParentWnd`	A pointer to the list view's parent window
`nID`	The list view's ID

A call to `Create()` might look something like this:

```
m_listView.Create(WS_VISIBLE | WS_CHILD |
    WS_BORDER | LVS_REPORT | LVS_NOSORTHEADER,
    CRect(20, 40, 250, 220), this, IDC_LISTVIEW);
```

For the standard window styles, you'll at least want to specify `WS_CHILD` and `WS_VISIBLE`. Other window styles may also be useful in specific circumstances. For example, the above list view control specifies the `WS_BORDER` style so that the edges of the control stand out against the window's white background.

The `CListCtrl` class defines a set of styles specific to the list view control. Table 10-7 lists these styles and their descriptions. You use these styles to specify how the list view control should look and act. Probably the most important styles are `LVS_ICON`, `LVS_SMALLICON`, `LVS_LIST`, and `LVS_REPORT`, which determine the type of view the list view control will display.

Table 10-7   List view control styles

Style	Description
`LVS_ALIGNLEFT`	Left-aligns items in large and small icon view
`LVS_ALIGNTOP`	Top-aligns items in large and small icon view
`LVS_AUTOARRANGE`	Automatically arranges icons in large and small icon view
`LVS_EDITLABELS`	Enables text editing of items
`LVS_ICON`	Creates the list in large icon view
`LVS_LIST`	Creates the list in list view
`LVS_NOCOLUMNHEADER`	Hides column headers in report view
`LVS_NOLABELWRAP`	Disables text wrapping for item text
`LVS_NOSCROLL`	Disables list scrolling
`LVS_NOSORTHEADER`	Disables column header buttons
`LVS_OWNERDRAWFIXED`	Creates an owner-draw list view control
`LVS_REPORT`	Creates the list in report view
`LVS_SHAREIMAGELISTS`	Enables multiple components to share the list view control's image list

(continued)

Style	Description
LVS_SHOWSELALWAYS	Shows the current selection whether or not the list has the input focus
LVS_SINGLESEL	Allows the user to select only one item at a time
LVS_SMALLICON	Creates the list in small icon view
LVS_SORTASCENDING	Sorts items in ascending order
LVS_SORTDESCENDING	Sorts items in descending order

Setting the control's image lists

After creating the list view control, you set the control's image lists. You'll at least want to specify small and large icons. You can also specify an icon for how an item looks when selected. You might, for example, want a folder icon to look closed when not selected and open when selected. You store the icons for your list view in image list controls. Here's how to specify the large and small icons:

```
m_listView.SetImageList(&smlImageList, LVSIL_SMALL);
m_listView.SetImageList(&lrgImageList, LVSIL_NORMAL);
```

The `CListCtrl` class's `SetImageList()` member function takes two arguments: a pointer to the image list and a flag indicating how the control should use the images in the list. You can specify `LVSIL_SMALL` (small icons), `LVSIL_NORMAL` (large icons), and `LVSIL_STATE` (state icons) for the second argument. (State icons enable the list item to change appearance when it's selected.)

Creating the control's columns

After setting the list view's icons, you can define the columns that the list displays in report view. To accomplish this task, you initialize an `LV_COLUMN` structure with the values that define a column and then call the `CListCtrl`'s `InsertColumn()` member function to add the column to the control.

Windows defines the `LV_COLUMN` structure as follows. Descriptions of each of the structure's members appears after the structure declaration.

```
typedef struct _LV_COLUMN {
    UINT mask;
    int fmt;
    int cx;
    LPTSTR pszText;
    int cchTextMax;
    int iSubItem;
} LV_COLUMN;
```

mask	A flag that specifies which of the structure's members contain information. The flag can be a combination of any or all of the following: LVCF_FMT, LVCF_SUBITEM, LVCF_TEXT, and LVCF_WIDTH.

(continued)

Continued	
fmt	A flag that indicates the column's text alignment. Can be LVCFMT_CENTER, LVCFMT_LEFT, or LVCFMT_RIGHT.
cx	The column's width
pszText	A pointer to the string that will be used for the column's heading
cchTextMax	The size of the pszText buffer. (Not used when setting columns.)
iSubItem	The index of the item within the column

You define the column's header using code something like this:

```
LV_COLUMN lvColumn;
lvColumn.mask = LVCF_WIDTH | LVCF_TEXT |
    LVCF_FMT | LVCF_SUBITEM;
lvColumn.fmt = LVCFMT_LEFT;
lvColumn.cx = 75;
lvColumn.iSubItem = 0;
lvColumn.pszText = "Column 0";
m_listView.InsertColumn(0, &lvColumn);
```

The InsertColumn() function requires two arguments: the column's index (the first column is 0, the second is 1, and so on) and a pointer to the LV_COLUMN structure containing the column information.

After defining the first column, you can define additional columns using the same LV_COLUMN structure, just changing the appropriate values. For example, after creating the first column, as shown previously, you could create a second column with code something like this:

```
lvColumn.iSubItem = 1;
lvColumn.pszText = "Column 1";
m_listView.InsertColumn(1, &lvColumn);
```

Note

The first column of a list view control always uses left alignment. If you specify another type of alignment for the first column, the control will ignore your request and still use left alignment.

Adding main items to the control

Now that you have the columns created, you need to put items into the columns. List view controls hold two types of items. The first type is the main item that appears in the first column. In a directory list, for example, this item might be the name of a file. The second type of item is a subitem, which you can think of as a child to the main item. In the directory list, the subitems might be the file's size and date of creation.

To create a main item, you initialize an LV_ITEM structure with the values that define an item and then call CListCtrl's InsertItem() member function to add the item to the control. Windows defines the LV_ITEM structure as follows. A description of each of the structure's members appears after the structure declaration.

```
typedef struct _LV_ITEM {
    UINT    mask;
```

```
int     iItem;
int     iSubItem;
UINT    state;
UINT    stateMask;
LPTSTR  pszText;
int     cchTextMax;
int     iImage;
LPARAM  lParam;
} LV_ITEM;
```

mask	A flag that specifies which of the structure's members contain information. The flag can be a combination of any or all of the following: LVIF_TEXT, LVIF_IMAGE, LVIF_PARAM, and LVIF_STATE.
iItem	The main item's index
iSubItem	The subitem's index
state	The item's state, which can be one or more of LVIS_CUT (marked for cut-and-paste), LVIS_DROPHILITED (highlighted as a drag-and-drop target), LVIS_FOCUSED (has the focus), and LVIS_SELECTED (selected)
stateMask	A flag that specifies which of the state member's bits contain information
pszText	A pointer to the item's text
cchTextMax	The size of the pszText buffer. (Not used when adding items.)
iImage	The index of the item's image in the image lists for the small and large icons
lParam	An application-specific 32-bit value

You define a main item using code something like this:

```
LV_ITEM lvItem;
lvItem.mask = LVIF_TEXT | LVIF_IMAGE | LVIF_STATE;
lvItem.state = 0;
lvItem.stateMask = 0;
lvItem.iImage = 0;
lvItem.iItem = 0;
lvItem.iSubItem = 0;
lvItem.pszText = "John";
m_listView.InsertItem(&lvItem);
```

Adding subitems to the control

Once you have a main item defined, you can add subitems. After all the
details you needed to know about columns and main items, you'll be pleased
to learn that adding a subitem requires only a single call to the list view's
SetItemText() function. You can add as many subitems as you need:

```
m_listView.SetItemText(0, 1, "Subitem 1");
m_listView.SetItemText(0, 2, "Subitem 2");
```

```
m_listView.SetItemText(0, 3, "Subitem 3");
```

The `SetItemText()` function takes three arguments: the main item's index, the subitem's index (starting with 1), and the subitem's text.

Responding to user selections

Often, you'll use a list view control to do more than just display data to the user. You may also want the user to be able to select items in the control. When the user double-clicks an item in the list view control, the control generates an `NM_DBLCLK` notification to which your application can respond. To accomplish this task, you must first add the notification to your window's message map:

```
ON_NOTIFY(NM_DBLCLK, IDC_LISTVIEW, OnListViewDblClk)
```

The `ON_NOTIFY` macro requires three arguments: the notification's ID, the control's ID, and the name of the message-response function.

In the message-response function, you can get the index of the selected item by calling the list view object's `GetNextItem()` member function:

```
int index = m_listView.GetNextItem(-1, LVNI_SELECTED);
```

The function's two arguments are the item index at which to start searching and the relationship of the requested item to the given item. To find the first item that matches the flag, use -1 for the first argument. The second argument can be one of the following flags: `LVNI_ABOVE`, `LVNI_ALL`, `LVNI_BELOW`, `LVNI_TOLEFT`, `LVNI_TORIGHT`, `LVNI_DROPHILITED`, `LVNI_FOCUSED`, or `LVNI_SELECTED`. If you need more information about these flags, look up `GetNextItem()` in your Visual C++ online documentation.

If the value returned from `GetNextItem()` is -1, there is no selected item. If `GetNextItem()` returns a valid index, you can call `GetItemText()` to get the selected item's text:

```
CString str = m_listView.GetItemText(index, 0);
```

This function's two arguments are the index of the main item and the index of a subitem. If the subitem index is 0, `GetItemText()` returns the main item text; otherwise, it returns the subitem text. So, to get the text for the subitems, you might make these calls to `GetItemText()`:

```
CString subItem1 = m_listView.GetItemText(index, 1);
CString subItem2 = m_listView.GetItemText(index, 2);
CString subItem3 = m_listView.GetItemText(index, 3);
```

The MFC list view shortcuts

You just learned the standard methods for constructing and initializing a list view control. Now that you know how the control works, you might be interested in a few MFC shortcuts that make it easier to create a list view control.

The `CListCtrl` class overloads its `InsertColumn()` and `InsertItem()` member functions with versions that don't require that you initialize `LV_COLUMN` and `LV_ITEM` structures in your program. You simply pass a few arguments to `InsertColumn()` and `InsertItem()`, and MFC fills in the structures for you.

Following is the overloaded version of `InsertColumn()`. Descriptions of each of its arguments follows.

```
int InsertColumn(
    int nCol,
    LPCTSTR lpszColumnHeading,
    int nFormat = LVCFMT_LEFT,
    int nWidth = -1,
    int nSubItem = -1);
```

nCol	The zero-based column number
lpszColumnHeading	The text for the column heading
nFormat	The column's alignment
nWidth	The column's width
nSubItem	The subitem index

The shortcut version of `InsertItem()` looks like the following; the arguments' descriptions are listed after the signature.

```
int InsertItem(
    int nItem,
    LPCTSTR lpszItem,
    int nImage);
```

nItem	The main item index
lpszItem	The main item's text
nImage	The index of the image-list image associated with the item

Using these alternative versions of `InsertColumn()` and `InsertItem()` simplify the code needed to create and initialize a list view control. Listing 10-11 shows the code required to create the list view control in Figure 10-27. The `m_lrgImageList`, `m_smlImageList`, and `m_listView` objects are all members of the window's class and are declared in the window class's header file.

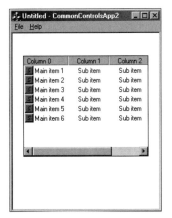

Figure 10-27: This is the list view control created by Listing 10-7.

Listing 10-11: Creating a list view control using MFC's shortcuts

```
// Create the image list controls.
m_lrgImageList.Create(32, 32, ILC_COLOR4, 1, 0);
m_smlImageList.Create(16, 16, ILC_COLOR4, 1, 0);

// Add images to the image lists.
HICON hIcon = ::LoadIcon (AfxGetResourceHandle(),
    MAKEINTRESOURCE(IDI_ICON1));
m_lrgImageList.Add(hIcon);
hIcon = ::LoadIcon (AfxGetResourceHandle(),
    MAKEINTRESOURCE(IDI_ICON1));
m_smlImageList.Add(hIcon);

// Create the list view control.
m_listView.Create(WS_VISIBLE | WS_CHILD | WS_BORDER |
    LVS_REPORT | LVS_NOSORTHEADER,
    CRect(20, 40, 250, 220), this, IDC_LISTVIEW);
m_listView.SetImageList(&m_smlImageList,
    LVSIL_SMALL);
m_listView.SetImageList(&m_lrgImageList,
    LVSIL_NORMAL);

// Add the columns.
m_listView.InsertColumn(0, "Column 0",
    LVCFMT_LEFT, 75);
m_listView.InsertColumn(1, "Column 1",
    LVCFMT_CENTER, 75);
m_listView.InsertColumn(2, "Column 2",
    LVCFMT_LEFT, 75);

// Add the main items.
m_listView.InsertItem(0, "Main Item 1", 0);
m_listView.InsertItem(1, "Main Item 2", 0);
m_listView.InsertItem(2, "Main Item 3", 0);
m_listView.InsertItem(3, "Main Item 4", 0);
m_listView.InsertItem(4, "Main Item 5", 0);
m_listView.InsertItem(5, "Main Item 6", 0);

// Add the subitems to each main item.
m_listView.SetItemText(0, 1, "Subitem");
m_listView.SetItemText(0, 2, "Subitem");

m_listView.SetItemText(1, 1, "Subitem");
m_listView.SetItemText(1, 2, "Subitem");

m_listView.SetItemText(2, 1, "Subitem");
m_listView.SetItemText(2, 2, "Subitem");

m_listView.SetItemText(3, 1, "Subitem");
m_listView.SetItemText(3, 2, "Subitem");

m_listView.SetItemText(4, 1, "Subitem");
m_listView.SetItemText(4, 2, "Subitem");
```

```
m_listView.SetItemText(5, 1, "Subitem");
m_listView.SetItemText(5, 2, "Subitem");
```

The list view control's member functions

The CListCtrl class defines many more member functions than the few you've learned about so far. Table 10-8 lists some of these functions and their descriptions. As there are a multitude of member functions, supplying a complete description of them all is beyond the scope of this book. However, you should have little difficulty figuring out and using most of the functions in the table.

Table 10-8   CListCtrl **member functions**

Function	Description
Arrange()	Arranges items on a grid
Create()	Creates a list control element and associates it with the CListCtrl object
CreateDragImage()	Creates an item's drag image list
DeleteAllItems()	Deletes all items
DeleteColumn()	Deletes a column
DeleteItem()	Deletes individual items
DrawItem()	Called by MFC when an owner-draw control must be redrawn
EditLabel()	Begins item text editing
EnsureVisible()	Ensures that a specified item is visible
FindItem()	Searches for a list view item
GetBkColor()	Gets the list view's background color
GetCallbackMask()	Gets the list view's callback mask
GetColumn()	Gets a column's attributes
GetColumnWidth()	Gets a column's report- or list-view width
GetCountPerPage()	Determines how many items fit vertically in the list view
GetEditControl()	Gets the handle of an item's edit control
GetImageList()	Gets a handle to the list view's image list
GetItem()	Gets a list view item's attributes
GetItemCount()	Gets the list view's item count
GetItemData()	Gets an item's application-specific value
GetItemPosition()	Gets a list view item's position
GetItemRect()	Gets an item's bounding rectangle

(continued)

Table 10-8 *(Continued)*

Function	Description
GetItemState()	Gets an item's state
GetItemText()	Gets an item's text
GetNextItem()	Finds a list view item
GetOrigin()	Gets the list view's view origin
GetSelectedCount()	Gets the list view's selected item count
GetStringWidth()	Gets the column width required to display a given string
GetTextBkColor()	Retrieves the list view's text background color
GetTextColor()	Gets the list view's text color
GetTopIndex()	Gets the index of the visible item at the top of the list view
GetViewRect()	Gets the bounding rectangle of all items
HitTest()	Returns the index of the item at a given position
InsertColumn()	Inserts a new column
InsertItem()	Inserts a new item
RedrawItems()	Repaints a range of items
Scroll()	Scrolls the list view's contents
SetBkColor()	Sets the list view's background color
SetCallbackMask()	Sets the list view's callback mask
SetColumn()	Sets a list view column's attributes
SetColumnWidth()	Changes the report- or list-view column width
SetImageList()	Sets the list view's image list
SetItem()	Sets item attributes
SetItemCount()	Allocates resources to accommodate adding multiple items
SetItemData()	Sets the item's application-specific value
SetItemPosition()	Sets an item's position
SetItemState()	Sets an item's state
SetItemText()	Sets an item's text
SetTextBkColor()	Sets the list view's background color
SetTextColor()	Sets the list view's text color
SortItems()	Sorts list view items
Update()	Repaints a specified item

PROBLEMS & SOLUTIONS

Enabling List View Item Editing

PROBLEM: *When I click on an item in some list view controls (such as that in Windows Explorer), the item text turns into an edit box. I can then edit the item text, changing it to anything I want. But when I create my own list view, the editing doesn't work. What's up?*

SOLUTION: A snazzy feature of list view controls is the ability to edit item text. A good example of this is when you click a file in Windows Explorer and press F2. The file's name then becomes an edit box into which you can type a new file name. However, handy as this feature can be for some list views, it doesn't come for free. There are several things you must do to make it work.

First, when you create your list view control, you must include the LVS_EDITLABELS style:

```
m_listView.Create(WS_VISIBLE | WS_CHILD | WS_BORDER |
    LVS_REPORT | LVS_NOSORTHEADER | LVS_EDITLABELS,
    CRect(20, 40, 250, 220), this, IDC_LISTVIEW);
```

Now, when the user clicks a selected main item in the list view, the item's label changes to an edit control. The user can edit the item, but when he presses enter to end the editing, the label returns to its old text. This occurs because your application must accept the user's changes before they become permanent.

To manage user edits, you respond to two list view notifications, LVN_BEGINLABELEDIT and LVN_ENDLABELEDIT. To do this, first use ClassWizard to override the OnNotify() member function in the window class, as shown in Figure 10-28. The OnNotify() message responds to WM_NOTIFY messages into which Windows packages the LVN_BEGINLABELEDIT and LVN_ENDLABELEDIT notifications.

Here is OnNotify()'s signature, followed by descriptions of each of its arguments:

```
virtual BOOL CWnd::OnNotify(
    WPARAM wParam,
    LPARAM lParam,
    LRESULT* pResult);
```

wParam	The WM_NOTIFY message's WPARAM value
lParam	The WM_NOTIFY message's LPARAM value
pResult	A pointer to a result code

Continued

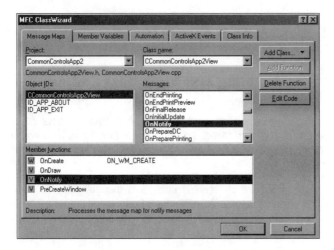

Figure 10-28: The `OnNotify()` function responds to Windows notifications.

How you interpret the three parameters received by `OnNotify()` depends on the type of message you're processing. In the case of a list view control, `wParam` holds the control's ID. The value of `lParam` depends also on the type of notification. In the case of `LVN_BEGINLABELEDIT` and `LVN_ENDLABELEDIT`, `lParam` holds a pointer to an `LV_DISPINFO` structure, which contains the information you need to process the user's editing request.

In `OnNotify()`, the first step is to cast `lParam` to an `LV_DISPINFO` pointer:

```
LV_DISPINFO* pDispInfo = (LV_DISPINFO*)lParam;
```

With a pointer to the structure in hand, the program can get the notification code, which is tucked away in the structure's `hdr.code` member:

```
UINT notificationID = pDispInfo->hdr.code;
```

If the notification ID is `LVN_BEGINLABELEDIT`, the program can do whatever it needs to do to process the request:

```
if (notificationID == LVN_BEGINLABELEDIT)
{
    // Perform pre-edit processing here.
}
```

If the notification ID is `LVN_ENDLABELEDIT`, you need to copy the new label from the edit control into the list view item. The `item.iItem` member of the `LV_DISPINFO` structure holds the item's ID:

```
UINT itemIndex = pDispInfo->item.iItem;
```

You can get the new text from the structure's `item.pszText` member:

```
CString newText = pDispInfo->item.pszText;
```

Continued

You must be sure to test for an empty string (or NULL, if you use a character array), because that's what the text will be if the user decides to exit the edit box by pressing Esc to cancel the editing operation.

If the new text is valid, you call the list view's SetItemText() function to complete the operation:

```
if (newText != "")
    m_listView.SetItemText(itemIndex, 0, newText);
```

On CD-ROM

In the Chapter10\EditControls folder of this book's CD-ROM, you'll find an application that demonstrates label editing in a list view control.

Understanding CommonControlApp2's list view control

CommonControlsApp2 creates its list view control in the view-window class's InitListView() member function. Listing 10-12 shows InitListView(), which begins by creating the list view's image lists. The function then creates the list view objects and assigns the image lists to the objects. Finally, the function calls the CreateListColumns() and AddListItems() member functions to complete the list view control.

Listing 10-12: CommonControlsApp2's InitListView() function

```
void CCommonControlsApp2View::InitListView()
{
    // Create the Image List controls.
    m_lrgImageList.Create(32, 32, ILC_COLOR4, 1, 0);
    m_smlImageList.Create(16, 16, ILC_COLOR4, 1, 0);

    HICON hIcon = ::LoadIcon (AfxGetResourceHandle(),
        MAKEINTRESOURCE(IDI_ICON1));
    m_lrgImageList.Add(hIcon);
    hIcon = ::LoadIcon (AfxGetResourceHandle(),
        MAKEINTRESOURCE(IDI_ICON1));
    m_smlImageList.Add(hIcon);

    // Create the List-view control.
    m_listView.Create(WS_VISIBLE | WS_CHILD | WS_BORDER |
        LVS_REPORT | LVS_NOSORTHEADER,
        CRect(20, 40, 250, 220), this, IDC_LISTVIEW);
    m_listView.SetImageList(&m_smlImageList,
        LVSIL_SMALL);
    m_listView.SetImageList(&m_lrgImageList,
        LVSIL_NORMAL);

    CreateListColumns();
    AddListItems();
}
```

The `CreateListColumns()` function, shown in Listing 10-13, creates and adds columns to the list view control. The function first creates and initializes an `LV_COLUMN` structure. The program then uses the structure in several calls to the list view object's `InsertColumn()` member function to create the four columns.

Listing 10-13: CommonControlsApp2's `CreateListColumns()` function

```
void CCommonControlsApp2View::CreateListColumns()
{
    LV_COLUMN lvColumn;
    lvColumn.mask = LVCF_WIDTH | LVCF_TEXT |
        LVCF_FMT | LVCF_SUBITEM;
    lvColumn.fmt = LVCFMT_CENTER;
    lvColumn.cx = 75;
    lvColumn.iSubItem = 0;
    lvColumn.pszText = "Name";
    m_listView.InsertColumn(0, &lvColumn);

    lvColumn.iSubItem = 1;
    lvColumn.pszText = "ID Number";
    m_listView.InsertColumn(1, &lvColumn);

    lvColumn.iSubItem = 2;
    lvColumn.pszText = "Age";
    m_listView.InsertColumn(2, &lvColumn);

    lvColumn.iSubItem = 3;
    lvColumn.pszText = "Gender";
    m_listView.InsertColumn(3, &lvColumn);
}
```

The `AddListItems()` function, shown in Listing 10-14, adds the main items and subitems to the list view control. The function creates the main items by setting up an `LV_ITEM` structure and using it in calls to the list view object's `InsertItem()` member function. The program adds the subitems by calling the `SetItemText()` member function.

Listing 10-14: CommonControlsApp2's `AddListItems()` function

```
void CCommonControlsApp2View::AddListItems()
{
    LV_ITEM lvItem;
    lvItem.mask = LVIF_TEXT | LVIF_IMAGE | LVIF_STATE;
    lvItem.state = 0;
    lvItem.stateMask = 0;
    lvItem.iImage = 0;

    lvItem.iItem = 0;
    lvItem.iSubItem = 0;
    lvItem.pszText = "John";
    m_listView.InsertItem(&lvItem);
    m_listView.SetItemText(0, 1, "176498");
    m_listView.SetItemText(0, 2, "46");
    m_listView.SetItemText(0, 3, "M");
```

```
        lvItem.iItem = 1;
        lvItem.iSubItem = 0;
        lvItem.pszText = "Marie";
        m_listView.InsertItem(&lvItem);
        m_listView.SetItemText(1, 1, "984732");
        m_listView.SetItemText(1, 2, "24");
        m_listView.SetItemText(1, 3, "F");

        lvItem.iItem = 2;
        lvItem.iSubItem = 0;
        lvItem.pszText = "Beth";
        m_listView.InsertItem(&lvItem);
        m_listView.SetItemText(2, 1, "452879");
        m_listView.SetItemText(2, 2, "33");
        m_listView.SetItemText(2, 3, "F");

        lvItem.iItem = 3;
        lvItem.iSubItem = 0;
        lvItem.pszText = "Gregory";
        m_listView.InsertItem(&lvItem);
        m_listView.SetItemText(3, 1, "487655");
        m_listView.SetItemText(3, 2, "19");
        m_listView.SetItemText(3, 3, "M");

        lvItem.iItem = 4;
        lvItem.iSubItem = 0;
        lvItem.pszText = "Willy";
        m_listView.InsertItem(&lvItem);
        m_listView.SetItemText(4, 1, "285943");
        m_listView.SetItemText(4, 2, "56");
        m_listView.SetItemText(4, 3, "M");

        lvItem.iItem = 5;
        lvItem.iSubItem = 0;
        lvItem.pszText = "Sandra";
        m_listView.InsertItem(&lvItem);
        m_listView.SetItemText(5, 1, "768506");
        m_listView.SetItemText(5, 2, "17");
        m_listView.SetItemText(5, 3, "F");
}
```

A set of radio buttons controls the list view control's current view setting. The program creates the radio button group in the InitRadioButtons() function, shown in Listing 10-15. You should already understand the way this function works. If you need a refresher on radio buttons, please refer back to Chapter 9, "Standard Controls."

Listing 10-15: CommonControlsApp2's InitRadioButtons() function

```
void CCommonControlsApp2View::InitRadioButtons()
{
    m_radioGroup.Create("List View Settings",
        BS_GROUPBOX | WS_CHILD | WS_VISIBLE,
        CRect(20, 240, 170, 330), this, 0);

    m_radioLarge.Create("Large View",
```

```
        BS_AUTORADIOBUTTON | WS_CHILD | WS_VISIBLE |
        WS_GROUP, CRect(40, 260, 130, 275),
        this, IDC_RADIOLARGE);

    m_radioSmall.Create("Small View",
        BS_AUTORADIOBUTTON | WS_CHILD | WS_VISIBLE,
        CRect(40, 275, 130, 290),
        this, IDC_RADIOSMALL);

    m_radioList.Create("List View",
        BS_AUTORADIOBUTTON | WS_CHILD | WS_VISIBLE,
        CRect(40, 290, 130, 305), this,
        IDC_RADIOLIST);

    m_radioReport.Create("Report View",
        BS_AUTORADIOBUTTON | WS_CHILD | WS_VISIBLE,
        CRect(40, 305, 150, 320), this,
        IDC_RADIOREPORT);

    m_radioReport.SetCheck(BST_CHECKED);
}
```

When the user clicks one of the radio button controls, the control generates
a BN_CLICKED notification, to which the program responds in the
OnRadioLargeClicked(), OnRadioSmallClicked(), OnRadioListClicked(), or
OnRadioReportClicked() function. These functions, which are shown in
Listing 10-16, change the view type by modifying the list view control's style
flags. They do this by calling the view window's SetWindowLong() function.

SetWindowLong() takes three arguments: the handle of the window whose
style is to be changed, the index of the value to change, and the new value.
The second argument can be one of the following values: GWL_EXSTYLE
(changes the extended window style), GWL_STYLE (changes the window style),
GWL_WNDPROC (changes the window procedure's address), GWL_HINSTANCE
(changes the application instance handle), GWL_ID (changes the window
identifier), or GWL_USERDATA (changes the window's application-specific 32-bit
value).

Listing 10-16: CommonControlsApp2's radio button handlers

```
void CCommonControlsApp2View::OnRadioLargeClicked()
{
    SetWindowLong(m_listView.m_hWnd, GWL_STYLE,
        WS_VISIBLE | WS_CHILD | WS_BORDER |
        LVS_ICON);
}

void CCommonControlsApp2View::OnRadioSmallClicked()
{
    SetWindowLong(m_listView.m_hWnd, GWL_STYLE,
        WS_CHILD | WS_VISIBLE | WS_BORDER |
        LVS_SMALLICON);
}

void CCommonControlsApp2View::OnRadioListClicked()
```

```
{
    SetWindowLong(m_listView.m_hWnd, GWL_STYLE,
        WS_CHILD | WS_VISIBLE | WS_BORDER |
        LVS_LIST);
}

void CCommonControlsApp2View::OnRadioReportClicked()
{
    SetWindowLong(m_listView.m_hWnd, GWL_STYLE,
        WS_CHILD | WS_VISIBLE | WS_BORDER |
        LVS_REPORT);
}
```

Last but not least, when the user double-clicks an item in the list view control, the control generates an NM_DBLCLK notification, which is managed by the view window's OnListViewDblClk() function. Listing 10-17 shows OnListViewDblClk(). The function first gets the index of the clicked item. It then gets the text for all the subitems, using the text to build a string that the program displays in a message box.

Listing 10-17: CommonControlsApp2's OnListViewDblClk() function

```
void CCommonControlsApp2View::OnListViewDblClk
    (NMHDR* pNMHDR, LRESULT* pResult)
{
    int index =
        m_listView.GetNextItem(-1, LVNI_SELECTED);

    if (index != -1)
    {
        CString str = "NAME:\t" +
            m_listView.GetItemText(index, 0);
        str += "\nID:\t" +
            m_listView.GetItemText(index, 1);
        str += "\nAGE:\t"
            + m_listView.GetItemText(index, 2);
        str += "\nGENDER: "
            + m_listView.GetItemText(index, 3);

        MessageBox(str);
    }
}
```

The Tree View Control

The tree view control is every bit as complex as the list view control. You have to perform similar steps to get the tree view up and running. In this section, you'll learn to incorporate tree view controls into your programs. Figure 10-29 shows a simple tree view control displayed in a window. The program is displaying the control with only its root item visible. Because the root item is in its collapsed state, you can't see any of the child items in the control.

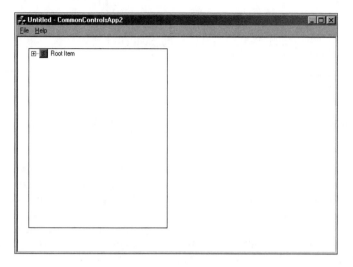

Figure 10-29: The tree view control with the root item in its collapsed state

To see the child items, you must click the plus sign next to the root item (or you can double-click the root item). When you do, the tree expands to show its next level, as shown in Figure 10-30. As you can see in the figure, the child items are also marked with plus signs, which means each can be expanded to reveal another level of the tree. Figure 10-31 shows the tree completely expanded.

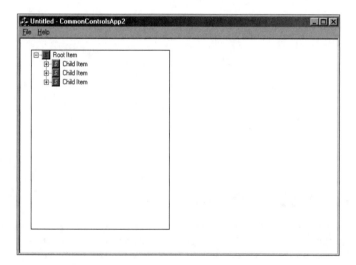

Figure 10-30: The tree view control with the first level of child items revealed

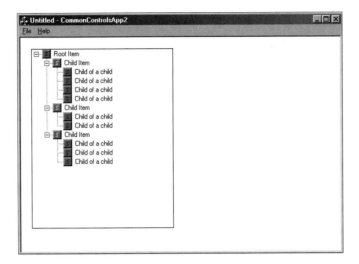

Figure 10-31: The tree view control with all child items revealed

Creating the tree view control object

To create a tree view control, you first define an object of the CTreeCtrl class:

```
CTreeCtrl m_treeView;
```

You then call the object's Create() member function, which creates the actual control and associates it with the CTreeCtrl object. The CTreeCtrl class's Create() function has the following signature. The arguments' descriptions are listed after the signature.

```
BOOL Create(
    DWORD dwStyle,
    const RECT& rect,
    CWnd* pParentWnd,
    UINT nID);
```

dwStyle	The tree view's style flags
rect	A RECT or CRect object that specifies the tree view's size and position
pParentWnd	A pointer to the tree view's parent window
nID	The tree view's ID

A call to Create() might look something like this:

```
m_treeView.Create(WS_VISIBLE | WS_CHILD | WS_BORDER |
    TVS_HASLINES | TVS_LINESATROOT | TVS_HASBUTTONS,
    CRect(300, 40, 560, 360), this, IDC_TREEVIEW);
```

For the standard window styles, you'll at least want to specify WS_CHILD and WS_VISIBLE. Other window styles may also be useful in specific circumstances. For example, the above tree view control specifies the WS_BORDER style so that the edges of the control stand out against the window's white background.

The CTreeCtrl class defines a set of styles specific to the tree view control. The following list describes these styles, which you use to specify how the tree view control should look and act.

TVS_DISABLEDRAGDROP	Prevents TVN_BEGINDRAG notifications
TVS_EDITLABELS	Enables the user to edit item labels
TVS_HASBUTTONS	Adds a button to the left of each parent item
TVS_HASLINES	Draws lines linking child and parent items
TVS_LINESATROOT	Draws lines linking child items to the root item
TVS_SHOWSELALWAYS	Forces a selected item to stay highlighted whether or not the tree view has the input focus

Adding items to the tree view control

An empty tree view control isn't going to do your application much good. So, after creating the control, you need to add the tree items. You do this by calling the tree view's InsertItem() member function. The first step in adding an item is to create and initialize a TV_ITEM structure. Windows defines the TV_ITEM structure as follows. A description of each of the structure's members appears after the structure declaration.

```
typedef struct _TV_ITEM {
    UINT mask;
    HTREEITEM hItem;
    UINT state;
    UINT stateMask;
    LPSTR pszText;
    int cchTextMax;
    int iImage;
    int iSelectedImage;
    int cChildren;
    LPARAM lParam;
} TV_ITEM, FAR *LPTV_ITEM;
```

mask	A flag that specifies which of the structure's members contain information. The flag can be a combination of any or all of the following: TVIF_CHILDREN, TVIF_HANDLE, TVIF_IMAGE, TVIF_PARAM, TVIF_SELECTEDIMAGE, TVIF_STATE, and TVIF_TEXT.
hItem	The item's handle
state	The item's state
stateMask	Flags that indicate the valid bits in the state member

Continued	
pszText	A pointer to the item text
cchTextMax	The size of the buffer pointed to by pszText
iImage	The image-list index of the item's image
iSelectedImage	The image-list index of the item's selected image
cChildren	A flag that specifies whether the item has child items
lParam	An application-specific 32-bit value for the item

To create a new root item, you might start with the following code, which sets up the TV_ITEM structure:

```
TV_ITEM tvItem;
tvItem.mask =
    TVIF_TEXT | TVIF_IMAGE | TVIF_SELECTEDIMAGE;
tvItem.pszText = "Root Item";
tvItem.cchTextMax = 10;
tvItem.iImage = 0;
tvItem.iSelectedImage = 0;
```

Next, you need to set up a TV_INSERTSTRUCT structure. Windows defines the TV_INSERTSTRUCT structure as follows. A description of each of the structure's members appears after the structure declaration.

```
typedef struct _TV_INSERTSTRUCT {
    HTREEITEM hParent;
    HTREEITEM hInsertAfter;
    TV_ITEM   item;
} TV_INSERTSTRUCT, FAR *LPTV_INSERTSTRUCT;
```

hParent	The parent item's handle or TVI_ROOT
hInsertAfter	The handle of the item after which to place the new item or one of the following flags: TVI_FIRST (place at the start of the list), TVI_LAST (place at the end of the list), or TVI_SORT (place in alphabetical order)
item	The TV_ITEM structure that defines the new item

For the root item, you might write the following code to create and initialize the TV_INSERTSTRUCT structure:

```
TV_INSERTSTRUCT tvInsert;
tvInsert.hParent = TVI_ROOT;
tvInsert.hInsertAfter = TVI_FIRST;
tvInsert.item = tvItem;
```

Finally, you can add the item by calling InsertItem():

```
HTREEITEM hRoot = m_treeView.InsertItem(&tvInsert);
```

The InsertItem() function takes the address of a TV_INSERTSTRUCT structure as its single argument and returns the handle of the newly inserted item. You should save the handle because you'll need it to add child items to the tree's root.

To add child items to the root, you follow similar steps, using slightly different flags, a different image, and the handle to the parent item. For example, the following lines add a child item to the previously created root item:

```
tvItem.pszText = "Child Item 1";
tvItem.cchTextMax = 13;
tvItem.iImage = 1;
tvItem.iSelectedImage = 1;
tvInsert.hParent = hRoot;
tvInsert.hInsertAfter = TVI_FIRST;
tvInsert.item = tvItem;
HTREEITEM hChild1 = m_treeView.InsertItem(&tvInsert);
```

To add a second child item on the same level (called a sibling), you change the hInsertAfter flag to TVI_LAST, which tells Windows to add the item at the end of the list:

```
tvItem.pszText = "Child Item 2";
tvItem.cchTextMax = 13;
tvItem.iImage = 1;
tvItem.iSelectedImage = 1;
tvInsert.hParent = hRoot;
tvInsert.hInsertAfter = TVI_LAST;
tvInsert.item = tvItem;
HTREEITEM hChild2 = m_treeView.InsertItem(&tvInsert);
```

To add a child item to another child item (that is, to create a third level to the tree), you use the first child's handle as the parent:

```
tvItem.pszText = "Child of a child";
tvItem.cchTextMax = 17;
tvItem.iImage = 2;
tvItem.iSelectedImage = 2;
tvInsert.hParent = hChild1;
tvInsert.hInsertAfter = TVI_FIRST;
tvInsert.item = tvItem;
HTREEITEM hChildChild1 =
    m_treeView.InsertItem(&tvInsert);
```

Responding to user selections

Just as with a list view control, often you'll use a tree view control to do more than just display data to the user. You may also want the user to be able to select items in the control. When the user double-clicks an item in the tree view control, the control generates an NM_DBLCLK notification to which your application can respond. To accomplish this task, you must first add the notification to your window's message map:

```
ON_NOTIFY(NM_DBLCLK, IDC_TREEVIEW, OnTreeViewDblClk)
```

In the message-response function, you can get the handle of the selected item by calling the tree view object's GetSelectedItem() member function:

```
HTREEITEM hItem = m_treeView.GetSelectedItem();
```

If the value returned from `GetSelectedItem()` is `NULL`, there is no selected item. If `GetNextItem()` returns a valid handle, you can call `GetItemText()` to get the selected item's text:

```
CString str = m_treeView.GetItemText(hItem);
```

This function's single argument is the handle of the item for which you want the text.

PROBLEMS & SOLUTIONS

Enabling Tree View Item Editing

PROBLEM: *Now that I have item editing working on my list view control, what about tree view controls?*

SOLUTION: Enabling editing in a tree view control is very similar to enabling editing in a list view control. First, when you create your tree view control, you must include the `TVS_EDITLABELS` style:

```
m_treeView.Create(WS_VISIBLE | WS_CHILD | WS_BORDER |
    TVS_HASLINES | TVS_LINESATROOT | TVS_HASBUTTONS |
    TVS_EDITLABELS, CRect(300, 40, 560, 360),
    this, IDC_TREEVIEW);
```

Now, when the user clicks a selected item in the tree view, the item's label changes to an edit control. The user can edit the item, but when he presses enter to end the editing, the label returns to its old text. As you know from the list view control, this action occurs because your application must accept the user's changes before they become permanent.

To manage user edits, the application responds to two tree view notifications, `TVN_BEGINLABELEDIT` and `TVN_ENDLABELEDIT`. To do this, first use ClassWizard to override the `OnNotify()` member function in the window class. The `OnNotify()` message responds to `WM_NOTIFY` messages into which Windows packages the `TVN_BEGINLABELEDIT` and `TVN_ENDLABELEDIT` notifications.

Here is `OnNotify()`'s signature, followed by descriptions of each its arguments:

```
virtual BOOL CWnd::OnNotify(
    WPARAM wParam,
    LPARAM lParam,
    LRESULT* pResult);
```

wParam	The WM_NOTIFY message's WPARAM value
lParam	The WM_NOTIFY message's LPARAM value
pResult	A pointer to a result code

Continued

How you interpret the three parameters received by `OnNotify()` depends on the type of message you're processing. In the case of a tree view control, `wParam` holds the control's ID. The value of `lParam` depends also on the type of notification. In the case of `TVN_BEGINLABELEDIT` and `TVN_ENDLABELEDIT`, `lParam` holds a pointer to a `TV_DISPINFO` structure, which contains the information you need to process the user's editing request.

In `OnNotify()`, the first step is to cast `lParam` to an `TV_DISPINFO` pointer, like this:

```
TV_DISPINFO* pDispInfo = (TV_DISPINFO*)lParam;
```

With a pointer to the structure in hand, the program can get the notification code, which is tucked away in the structure's `hdr.code` member:

```
UINT notificationID = pDispInfo->hdr.code;
```

If the notification ID is `TVN_BEGINLABELEDIT`, the program can do whatever it needs to do before the editing actually begins:

```
if (notificationID == TVN_BEGINLABELEDIT)
{
    // Perform pre-edit processing here.
}
```

If the notification ID is `TVN_ENDLABELEDIT`, you need to copy the new label from the edit control into the tree view item. The `item.hItem` member of the `TV_DISPINFO` structure holds the item's handle:

```
HTREEITEM hItem = pDispInfo->item.hItem;
```

You can get the new text from the structure's `item.pszText` member:

```
CString newText = pDispInfo->item.pszText;
```

You must be sure to test for an empty string (or `NULL`, if you use a character array), because that's what the text will be if the user decides to exit the edit box by pressing Esc to cancel the editing operation. If the new text is valid, you call the tree view's `SetItemText()` function to complete the operation:

```
if (newText != "")
    m_treeView.SetItemText(hItem, newText);
```

On CD-ROM

In the Chapter10\EditControls folder of this book's CD-ROM, you'll find an application, EditControls, that demonstrates label editing in a tree view control.

The MFC tree view shortcuts

You just learned the standard methods for constructing and initializing a tree view control. Now that you know how the control works, you probably suspect that, as you discovered with the list view control, MFC features shortcuts that make it easier to create a tree view control.

The `CTreeCtrl` class overloads its `InsertItem()` member function with versions that don't require you to initialize `TV_ITEM` and `TV_INSERTSTRUCT` structures in your program. You simply pass a few arguments to `InsertItem()`, and MFC fills in the structures for you. Following is the signature of the handiest overloaded version of `InsertItem()`, followed by its arguments:

```
HTREEITEM InsertItem(
    LPCTSTR lpszItem,
    int nImage,
    int nSelectedImage,
    HTREEITEM hParent = TVI_ROOT,
    HTREEITEM hInsertAfter = TVI_LAST);
```

`lpszItem`	The item's text
`nImage`	The image-list index of the item's image
`nSelectedImage`	The image-list index of the item's selected image
`hParent`	The parent item's handle or `TVI_ROOT`
`hInsertAfter`	The handle of the item after which to place the new item or one of the following flags: `TVI_FIRST`, `TVI_LAST`, or `TVI_SORT`

Using the alternate version of `InsertItem()` simplifies the code needed to create and initialize a tree view control. Listing 10-18 shows the code required to create the tree view control shown in Figure 10-32. The `m_treeImages` and `m_treeView` objects are members of the window's class and are declared in the window class's header file.

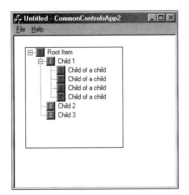

Figure 10-32: This is the tree view control created by Listing 10-18.

Listing 10-18: Creating a tree view control using MFC's shortcuts

```
// Create the tree view's image list
m_treeImages.Create(16, 16, ILC_COLOR4, 3, 0);
HICON hIcon = ::LoadIcon(AfxGetResourceHandle(),
    MAKEINTRESOURCE(IDI_ICON1));
m_treeImages.Add(hIcon);
hIcon = ::LoadIcon(AfxGetResourceHandle(),
    MAKEINTRESOURCE(IDI_ICON2));
```

```
m_treeImages.Add(hIcon);
hIcon = ::LoadIcon(AfxGetResourceHandle(),
    MAKEINTRESOURCE(IDI_ICON3));
m_treeImages.Add(hIcon);

// Create the Tree View control.
m_treeView.Create(WS_VISIBLE | WS_CHILD | WS_BORDER |
    TVS_HASLINES | TVS_LINESATROOT | TVS_HASBUTTONS,
    CRect(300, 40, 560, 360), this, 110);
m_treeView.SetImageList(&m_treeImages, TVSIL_NORMAL);

// Create the root item.
HTREEITEM hRoot = m_treeView.InsertItem("Root Item",
    0, 0, TVI_ROOT, TVI_FIRST);

// Create the first-level child items.
HTREEITEM hChild1 = m_treeView.InsertItem("Child 1",
        1, 1, hRoot, TVI_FIRST);
HTREEITEM hChild2 = m_treeView.InsertItem("Child 2",
    1, 1, hRoot, TVI_LAST);
HTREEITEM hChild3 = m_treeView.InsertItem("Child 3",
    1, 1, hRoot, TVI_LAST);

// Create the second-level child items.
m_treeView.InsertItem("Child of a child",
    2, 2, hChild1, TVI_FIRST);
m_treeView.InsertItem("Child of a child",
    2, 2, hChild1, TVI_LAST);
m_treeView.InsertItem("Child of a child",
    2, 2, hChild1, TVI_LAST);
m_treeView.InsertItem("Child of a child",
    2, 2, hChild1, TVI_LAST);
```

The tree view control's member functions

The CTreeCtrl class defines many more member functions than the few you've learned about so far. Table 10-9 lists some these functions and their descriptions. A complete description of so many member functions is beyond the scope of this book. However, you should have little difficulty figuring out and using most of the functions in the table.

Table 10-9 CTreeCtrl member functions

Function	Description
Create()	Creates a tree view element and associates it with the CTreeCtrl object
CreateDragImage()	Creates an item's dragging bitmap
DeleteAllItems()	Deletes all items
DeleteItem()	Deletes a new item
EditLabel()	Edits an item

Function	*Description*
EnsureVisible()	Ensures that an item is visible
Expand()	Expands or collapses child items
GetChildItem()	Gets an item's child
GetCount()	Gets the tree view's item count
GetDropHilightItem()	Gets the drag-and-drop target
GetEditControl()	Gets a handle to an item's edit control
GetFirstVisibleItem()	Gets the first visible item
GetImageList()	Gets a handle to the tree view's image list
GetIndent()	Gets the number of pixels an item is indented from its parent
GetItem()	Gets an item's attributes
GetItemData()	Gets an item's 32-bit application-specific value
GetItemImage()	Gets an item's images
GetItemRect()	Gets an item's bounding rectangle
GetItemState()	Gets an item's state
GetItemText()	Gets an item's text
GetNextItem()	Gets the next tree view item
GetNextSiblingItem()	Gets an item's next sibling
GetNextVisibleItem()	Gets the next visible item
GetParentItem()	Gets an item's parent
GetPrevSiblingItem()	Gets an item's previous sibling
GetPrevVisibleItem()	Gets the previous visible item
GetRootItem()	Gets the root item
GetSelectedItem()	Gets the currently selected item
GetVisibleCount()	Gets tree view's visible-item count
HitTest()	Returns the index of the item at a given position
InsertItem()	Inserts an item
ItemHasChildren()	Determines whether an item has child items
Select()	Performs a selection, highlight, or scrolling action for an item
SelectDropTarget()	Redraws an item as a drag-and-drop target
SelectItem()	Selects an item
SelectSetFirstVisible()	Specifies the first visible item
SetImageList()	Sets the tree view's image list

(continued)

Table 10-9	(Continued)
Function	*Description*
SetIndent()	Sets an item's indent
SetItem()	Sets an item's attributes
SetItemData()	Sets an item's 32-bit application-specific value
SetItemImage()	Sets an item's images
SetItemState()	Sets an item's state
SetItemText()	Sets an item's text
SortChildren()	Sorts the children of a parent item
SortChildrenCB()	Sorts the children of a parent item using a custom sort function

Understanding CommonControlApp2's tree view control

CommonControlsApp2 creates its tree view control in the view-window class's InitTreeView() member function. Listing 10-19 shows InitTreeView(), which begins by creating the tree view's image lists. The function then creates the tree view object and assigns the image lists to the object. Finally, the function calls the AddTreeItem() member function for each item in the control.

Listing 10-19: CommonControlsApp2's InitTreeView() function

```
void CCommonControlsApp2View::InitTreeView()
{
    // Create the Image List.
    m_treeImages.Create(16, 16, ILC_COLOR4, 3, 0);
    HICON hIcon = ::LoadIcon(AfxGetResourceHandle(),
        MAKEINTRESOURCE(IDI_ICON1));
    m_treeImages.Add(hIcon);
    hIcon = ::LoadIcon(AfxGetResourceHandle(),
        MAKEINTRESOURCE(IDI_ICON2));
    m_treeImages.Add(hIcon);
    hIcon = ::LoadIcon(AfxGetResourceHandle(),
        MAKEINTRESOURCE(IDI_ICON3));
    m_treeImages.Add(hIcon);

    // Create the Tree View control.
    m_treeView.Create(WS_VISIBLE | WS_CHILD | WS_BORDER |
        TVS_HASLINES | TVS_LINESATROOT | TVS_HASBUTTONS,
        CRect(300, 40, 560, 360), this, IDC_TREEVIEW);
    m_treeView.SetImageList(&m_treeImages, TVSIL_NORMAL);

    // Create the root item.
    HTREEITEM hRoot = AddTreeItem("Team Members",
        15, 0, 0, TVI_ROOT, TVI_FIRST);
```

```
HTREEITEM hChildItem = AddTreeItem("John",
    12, 1, 1, hRoot, TVI_FIRST);
AddTreeItem("ID: 176498", 12, 2, 2,
    hChildItem, TVI_FIRST);
AddTreeItem("Age: 46", 12, 2, 2,
    hChildItem, TVI_LAST);
AddTreeItem("Gender: M", 12, 2, 2,
    hChildItem, TVI_LAST);

HTREEITEM hChildItem2 = AddTreeItem("Marie",
    12, 1, 1, hRoot, TVI_LAST);
AddTreeItem("ID: 984732", 12, 2, 2,
    hChildItem2, TVI_FIRST);
AddTreeItem("Age: 24", 12, 2, 2,
    hChildItem2, TVI_LAST);
AddTreeItem("Gender: F", 12, 2, 2,
    hChildItem2, TVI_LAST);

HTREEITEM hChildItem3 = AddTreeItem("Beth",
    12, 1, 1, hRoot, TVI_LAST);
AddTreeItem("ID: 452879", 12, 2, 2,
    hChildItem3, TVI_FIRST);
AddTreeItem("Age: 33", 12, 2, 2,
    hChildItem3, TVI_LAST);
AddTreeItem("Gender: F", 12, 2, 2,
    hChildItem3, TVI_LAST);

HTREEITEM hChildItem4 = AddTreeItem("Gregory",
    12, 1, 1, hRoot, TVI_LAST);
AddTreeItem("ID: 487655", 12, 2, 2,
    hChildItem4, TVI_FIRST);
AddTreeItem("Age: 19", 12, 2, 2,
    hChildItem4, TVI_LAST);
AddTreeItem("Gender: F", 12, 2, 2,
    hChildItem4, TVI_LAST);

HTREEITEM hChildItem5 = AddTreeItem("Willy",
    12, 1, 1, hRoot, TVI_LAST);
AddTreeItem("ID: 285943", 12, 2, 2,
    hChildItem5, TVI_FIRST);
AddTreeItem("Age: 56", 12, 2, 2,
    hChildItem5, TVI_LAST);
AddTreeItem("Gender: M", 12, 2, 2,
    hChildItem5, TVI_LAST);

HTREEITEM hChildItem6 = AddTreeItem("Sandra",
    12, 1, 1, hRoot, TVI_LAST);
AddTreeItem("ID: 768506", 12, 2, 2,
    hChildItem6, TVI_FIRST);
AddTreeItem("Age: 17", 12, 2, 2,
    hChildItem6, TVI_LAST);
AddTreeItem("Gender: F", 12, 2, 2,
    hChildItem6, TVI_LAST);
}
```

`AddTreeItem()` is a member function of the view window's class. Its task is to take some of the hassle out of managing the `TV_ITEM` and `TV_INSERTSTRUCT` structures. The calling function supplies the data needed to create an item, and `AddTreeItem()` initializes the structures with the data and creates the item, returning the item's handle. Listing 10-20 shows the `AddTreeItem()` function.

Listing 10-20: **CommonControlsApp2's** `AddTreeItem()` **function**

```
HTREEITEM CCommonControlsApp2View::AddTreeItem
    (LPSTR pText, UINT max, UINT image, UINT selImage,
    HTREEITEM hParent, HTREEITEM hInsert)
{
    TV_ITEM tvItem;
    tvItem.mask =
        TVIF_TEXT | TVIF_IMAGE | TVIF_SELECTEDIMAGE;
    tvItem.pszText = pText;
    tvItem.cchTextMax = max;
    tvItem.iImage = image;
    tvItem.iSelectedImage = selImage;

    TV_INSERTSTRUCT tvInsert;
    tvInsert.hParent = hParent;
    tvInsert.hInsertAfter = hInsert;
    tvInsert.item = tvItem;
    HTREEITEM hItem =
        m_treeView.InsertItem(&tvInsert);

    return hItem;
}
```

Finally, when the user clicks an item in the tree view control, the control generates an `NM_DBLCLK` notification, which is managed by the view window's `OnTreeViewDblClk()` function. Listing 10-21 shows `OnTreeViewDblClk()`. The function first gets the handle of the clicked item. It then gets the text for the item and displays it in a message box.

Listing 10-21: **CommonControlsApp2's** `OnTreeViewDblClk` **function**

```
void CCommonControlsApp2View::OnTreeViewDblClk
    (NMHDR* pNMHDR, LRESULT* pResult)
{
    HTREEITEM hItem =
        m_treeView.GetSelectedItem();

    if (hItem != NULL)
    {
        CString str = m_treeView.GetItemText(hItem);
        MessageBox(str);
    }
}
```

Summary

Windows 98's common controls are great tools for putting together sophisticated user interfaces. Whether you need to retrieve a single value from the user or must display a large data set in an organized way, the common controls can fit the bill. Unfortunately, there wasn't enough room in this chapter to cover all the myriad ways in which the common controls can be used. You should therefore take the time to explore the common control classes on your own in order to discover details not presented here.

Also discussed in this chapter:

▶ The progress bar control displays the status of an ongoing operation.

▶ The slider control enables the user to select a value from a given range.

▶ The spinner control also provides a method for obtaining values within a given range.

▶ Image list controls hold images that other controls need to complete their displays.

▶ A list view control enables applications to organize large amounts of data in a table-like format.

▶ A tree view control also organizes data, but it uses a hierarchical display, rather than a table.

Chapter 11

Printing

In This Chapter

▶ Printing from a traditional Windows application

▶ Printing text in an MFC application

▶ Printing graphics in an MFC application

Handling printers under Windows was once a task that made even experienced programmers shudder. Nowadays, printing documents from a Windows application is easier, but it still requires that you handle many details. This complexity is due to the fact that you can never be sure exactly what printer is connected to the user's computer. This complication forces you to write code that adapts itself to the current printer's attributes. You do this by using variables in place of hard-coded values wherever the printer's attributes can affect the output. In this chapter, you discover the techniques you need to know to successfully print text and graphics from a Windows application.

An Overview of Printing in Windows

Most of this chapter covers printing documents from MFC programs. However, in order to understand what's going on behind the scenes in MFC, it helps to know how you print data from a traditional C Windows program. You'll tackle that topic in this section, where you'll not only learn the traditional Windows printing process, but also study a small sample application that demonstrates the concepts.

The six steps to printing a document

Under Windows, the basic printing process involves six steps:

1. Call the `CreateDC()` function to acquire a printer DC.

2. Call the `StartDoc()` function to begin the document.

3. Call the `StartPage()` function to begin a page.

4. Render the document onto the printer DC.

5. Call the `EndPage()` function to end a page. (Repeat Steps 3 through 5 for each page in the document.)

6. Call the `EndDoc()` function to end the print job.

You call `CreateDC()` to create a printer device context first because, just as you need a device context to draw data in an application's window, so too you need a DC to send data to a printer. To determine the type of printer connected to the system, the application must search the user's WIN.INI file or call the Windows API `EnumPrinters()` function. Calling `EnumPrinters()` is the easiest method. The `EnumPrinters()` function's signature looks like this:

```
BOOL EnumPrinters(
    DWORD Flags,
    LPTSTR Name,
    DWORD Level,
    LPBYTE pPrinterEnum,
    DWORD cbBuf,
    LPDWORD pcbNeeded,
    LPDWORD pcReturned,
);
```

The function's arguments are described as follows:

`Flags`	A flag indicating the type of printer needed
`Name`	The name of the printer object
`Level`	The type of printer info structure
`pPrinterEnum`	A pointer to the printer info structures
`cbBuf`	The size of the printer info array
`pcbNeeded`	A pointer to the variable that'll hold the number of bytes copied to the printer info array
`pcReturned`	A pointer to the variable that'll hold the number of print info structures that was copied to the array

Some of `EnumPrinters()`'s arguments have many different possible values, depending upon how you want Windows to describe the printers available on the system. For the most part, however, you'll be concerned only with getting the default printer. (If you're interested in all the other hairy details, look up `EnumPrinters()` in your Visual C++ online documentation.) To program your application to ask Windows for the default printer, use the following code:

```
PRINTER_INFO_5 printerInfo5[3];
DWORD needed, returned;

EnumPrinters(PRINTER_ENUM_DEFAULT, NULL, 5,
    (LPBYTE)printerInfo5, sizeof(printerInfo5),
    &needed, &returned);
```

If the previous lines execute successfully, you'll have the name of the default printer in the first printer info structure's `pPrinterName` member, which you can access like this:

```
printerInfo5[0].pPrinterName
```

The printer name is exactly what you need in order to create a DC for the printer. To get the DC, call `CreateDC()`:

```
HDC printDC;

printDC = CreateDC(NULL,
    printerInfo5[0].pPrinterName, NULL, NULL);
```

Here, you provide the printer's system name as the second argument. The remaining arguments should be `NULL`.

Once you have a DC for the user's printer, you can start printing the document. To do this, you first call the Windows API function `StartDoc()`, which sets up Windows to begin spooling your document to the system print spooler. This process is similar to how you call `BeginPaint()` in a C Windows program (see Chapter 4, "Application Fundamentals") to start displaying data in an application's window. If `StartDoc()` succeeds, it returns an ID for the print job; otherwise, it returns a value less than or equal to zero.

One of `StartDoc()`'s arguments is a pointer to a `DOCINFO` structure. You must initialize the members of the structure before calling `StartDoc()`. In most cases, you just place the size of the structure in the `cbSize` member and a pointer to the document's name in the `lpszDocName` member. The remaining members can be `NULL` or zero. The entire process looks something like Listing 11-1.

Listing 11-1: Calling the `StartDoc()` function

```
char docName[] = "RectangleDoc";
DOCINFO docInfo;
docInfo.cbSize = sizeof(docInfo);
docInfo.lpszDocName = docName;
docInfo.lpszOutput = NULL;
docInfo.lpszDatatype = NULL;
docInfo.fwType = 0;

result = StartDoc(printDC, &docInfo);

if (result <= 0)
{
    MessageBox(0, "StartDoc() failed",
        "Basic Print App", MB_OK | MB_ICONERROR );
    return;
}
```

If the call to `StartDoc()` succeeds, you can start your first page by calling `StartPage()`. The `StartPage()` function takes only a single argument, which is the printer DC. The function returns a value greater than zero if it succeeds; otherwise, it returns a value less than or equal to zero. The code to start a page will be similar to the following snippet:

```
result = StartPage(printDC);
if (result <= 0)
{
    MessageBox(0, "StartPage() failed",
        "Basic Print App", MB_OK | MB_ICONERROR );
    return;
}
```

Once you have the page started, sending data to the printer is just like sending data to an application's window. You just direct the output to the printer DC, rather than to a window DC. Of course, a printer isn't as versatile as a video display. For example, your printer probably can't display a bitmap the same way a window does. Also, the dots on the screen are a different size than the dots on most printers, so you often need to scale data destined for the printer.

After printing a page, you call the EndPage() function to end the current page. EndPage(), like StartPage(), requires the printer DC as its single argument. Also like StartPage(), EndPage() returns a value greater than zero if it succeeds, and zero or less if it doesn't succeed. The code to end a page will be similar to the following snippet:

```
result = EndPage(printDC);
if (result <= 0)
{
    MessageBox(0, "EndPage() failed",
        "Basic Print App", MB_OK | MB_ICONERROR );
    return;
}
```

At this point, the application can call StartPage() again to begin another page, or, if there are no other pages to print, the application should call EndDoc() to end the print job:

```
EndDoc(printDC);
```

The BasicPrintApp sample program

Now that you've explored the basic process for printing a document under Windows, you can put all that knowledge to the test. Listing 11-2 shows BasicPrintApp, a short Windows program that prints a rectangle and a line of text on the default printer. When you run the application, you see the window shown in Figure 11-1. Just click in the window to send the rectangle data to your printer. If the printing process fails anywhere along the way, a message box appears, indicating where the problem occurred (see Figure 11-2).

On CD-ROM

BasicPrintApp handles all its printing chores in the PrintRectangle() function, using the same techniques you just learned. In that function, you can see how all the function calls work together to produce a complete, albeit simple, document. Each step of the six printing steps is marked with a comment, making it easier for you to decipher the code. You can find this application and it's source code in the Chapter11\BasicPrintApp directory of this book's CD-ROM.

Listing 11-2: Source code for the BasicPrintApp application

```
#include <windows.h>

LRESULT CALLBACK WndProc(HWND hWnd, UINT message,
    WPARAM wParam, LPARAM lParam);
void PrintRectangle();

int WINAPI WinMain(HINSTANCE hCurrentInst,
    HINSTANCE hPrevInstance, PSTR lpszCmdLine,
    int nCmdShow)
{

    WNDCLASS wndClass;
    HWND hWnd;
    MSG msg;
    UINT width;
    UINT height;

    wndClass.style = CS_HREDRAW | CS_VREDRAW;
    wndClass.lpfnWndProc = WndProc;
    wndClass.cbClsExtra = 0;
    wndClass.cbWndExtra = 0;
    wndClass.hInstance = hCurrentInst;
    wndClass.hIcon = LoadIcon(NULL, IDI_APPLICATION);
    wndClass.hCursor = LoadCursor(NULL, IDC_ARROW);
    wndClass.hbrBackground = GetStockObject(WHITE_BRUSH);
    wndClass.lpszMenuName = NULL;
    wndClass.lpszClassName = "BasicPrintApp";

    RegisterClass(&wndClass);

    width = GetSystemMetrics(SM_CXSCREEN) / 2;
    height = GetSystemMetrics(SM_CYSCREEN) / 2;

    hWnd = CreateWindow(
        "BasicPrintApp",    /* Window class's name.    */
        "Basic Print App",  /* Title bar text.         */
        WS_OVERLAPPEDWINDOW,/* The window's style.     */
        10,                 /* X position.             */
        10,                 /* Y position.             */
        width,              /* Width.                  */
        height,             /* Height.                 */
        NULL,               /* Parent window's handle. */
        NULL,               /* Menu handle.            */
        hCurrentInst,       /* Instance handle.        */
        NULL);              /* No additional data.     */

    ShowWindow(hWnd, nCmdShow);
    UpdateWindow(hWnd);

    while (GetMessage(&msg, NULL, 0, 0))
    {
        TranslateMessage(&msg);
        DispatchMessage(&msg);
    }
```

```
            return msg.wParam;
    }

    LRESULT CALLBACK WndProc(HWND hWnd, UINT message,
        WPARAM wParam, LPARAM lParam)
    {
        HDC hDC;
        PAINTSTRUCT paintStruct;

        switch(message)
        {
            case WM_PAINT:
                hDC = BeginPaint(hWnd, &paintStruct);
                TextOut(hDC, 10, 10,
                    "Click in the window to print.", 29);
                EndPaint(hWnd, &paintStruct);
                return 0;

            case WM_LBUTTONDOWN:
                PrintRectangle();
                return 0;

            case WM_DESTROY:
                PostQuitMessage(0);
                return 0;
        }

        return DefWindowProc(hWnd, message, wParam, lParam);
    }

    void PrintRectangle()
    {
        PRINTER_INFO_5 printerInfo5[3];
        DWORD needed, returned;
        HDC printDC;
        DOCINFO docInfo;
        char docName[] = "RectangleDoc";
        int result;

        // Step 1: Get a printer DC.
        EnumPrinters(PRINTER_ENUM_DEFAULT, NULL, 5,
            (LPBYTE)printerInfo5, sizeof(printerInfo5),
            &needed, &returned);
        printDC = CreateDC(NULL,
            printerInfo5[0].pPrinterName, NULL, NULL);

        // Step 2: Call StartDoc().
        docInfo.cbSize = sizeof(docInfo);
        docInfo.lpszDocName = docName;
        docInfo.lpszOutput = NULL;
        docInfo.lpszDatatype = NULL;
        docInfo.fwType = 0;
        result = StartDoc(printDC, &docInfo);
        if (result <= 0)
        {
```

```
        MessageBox(0, "StartDoc() failed",
            "Basic Print App", MB_OK | MB_ICONERROR );
        return;
    }

    // Step 3: Call StartPage().
    result = StartPage(printDC);
    if (result <= 0)
    {
        MessageBox(0, "StartPage() failed",
            "Basic Print App", MB_OK | MB_ICONERROR );
        return;
    }

    // Step 4: Print data.
    Rectangle(printDC, 20, 20, 1000, 200);
    TextOut(printDC, 100, 90,
        "Windows printing in action!", 27);

    // Step 5: Call EndPage().
    result = EndPage(printDC);
    if (result <= 0)
    {
        MessageBox(0, "EndPage() failed",
            "Basic Print App", MB_OK | MB_ICONERROR );
        return;
    }

    // Step 6: Call EndDoc().
    EndDoc(printDC);
    MessageBox(0, "Document printed", "Basic Print App",
        MB_OK | MB_ICONINFORMATION);
}
```

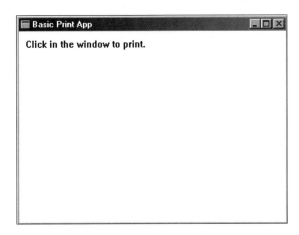

Figure 11-1: The BasicPrintApp application puts Windows printing to the test.

Figure 11-2: The application notifies you when the print job has failed.

Printing Text in an MFC Application

If you use MFC AppWizard to put together your application, you can get basic printing and print preview functions very easily. To get this functionality, just be sure that you select the Printing and Print Preview option in AppWizard's Step 4 of 6 dialog box, as shown in Figure 11-3. Such an AppWizard application handles all the details of getting the printer's name and acquiring the printer DC. You only need to refine the generated source code to produce the kind of printout that's appropriate for the application.

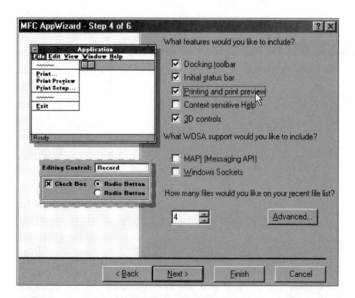

Figure 11-3: The AppWizard Printing and Print Preview option generates printing functions in your application.

In Chapter 3, you created an application called CircleApp that features basic printing and print preview functions. You may remember that a CircleApp document consists of a number of circles of various sizes and colors (see Figure 11-4). After creating a document with the application, you can select the File menu's Print Preview command. You then see a window something like that shown in Figure 11-5. Notice that the document in the print preview window seems small compared with the original document. This size difference is due to the fact that the window's pixels are larger than the printer's dots.

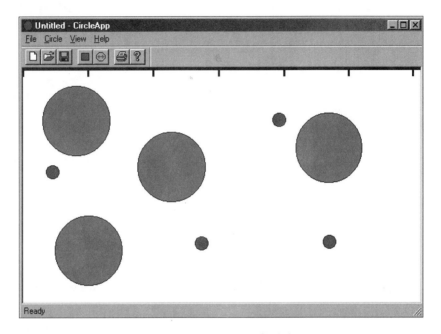

Figure 11-4: You can create circle documents with CircleApp.

When you use MFC's default printing functions, the application's document is both displayed on the screen and sent to the printer in the OnDraw() function. The difference is that, in the case of screen display, the DC object sent to OnDraw() is for the client window, whereas in the case of printing, the DC is for the current printer. This clever bit of DC switching enables one function to render output for both the screen and the printer, making it easier to produce WYSIWYG (What You See Is What You Get) output. The complication sets in when the coordinates used for screen display don't match those needed for printing. This is where scaling printer output comes in.

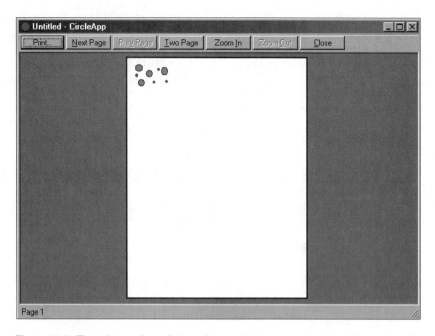

Figure 11-5: The print preview window shows what seems to be a smaller version of the document.

Scaling the printer output so that it appears to be the correct size is just one of the printing details with which you must contend, depending on the type of document you're printing. You may also need to deal with pagination, generating headers and footers, creating fonts, and other tasks that Windows applications must complete to print professional-looking documents. Luckily, MFC takes much of the busywork out of printing documents, by not only creating the printer context, but also by providing member functions in the CView class that enable view windows to access the printing process at various stages. In the next section, you get a look at those functions and how they work. Along the way, you'll learn printing skills such as pagination and scaling.

The PrintApp sample application

On CD-ROM

Before examining how to print in an MFC application, you should take some time out to see what such an application can do. In the Chapter11\PrintApp directory of this book's CD-ROM, you can find the PrintApp application from which the previous code examples were drawn. When you run the application, you'll see its main window. Although the window contains no scroll bars for displaying the full document, the application can hold any number of text lines. To increase the number of lines in the document, click in the window (see Figure 11-6). To reduce the number of lines in the document, right-click in the window. Use the File menu's Print Preview and Print commands to test the application's printing features, or select the Print command to print the document.

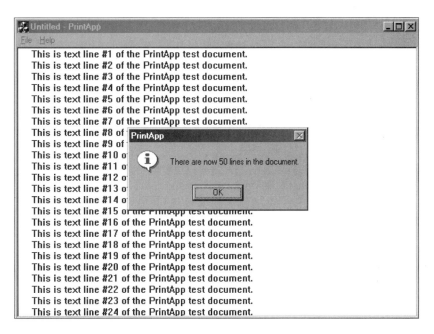

Figure 11-6: You add or remove lines to the display by clicking in the window.

MFC member functions for printing

When you write an MFC program with printing features, you don't have to worry about getting the name of the current printer and creating the printer DC. You also don't have to worry about displaying the Print dialog box. In many cases, you don't even have to worry about sending the application's document to the printer. MFC handles all these details for you. Often, though, you need to refine the default MFC printing features for a specific application. The CView class, from which you derive your application's view window, defines five functions that enable you to take control of different phases of the printing process:

- OnPreparePrinting()

- OnBeginPrinting()

- OnPrepareDC()

- OnPrint()

- OnEndPrinting()

In the following sections, you'll examine these five functions in detail to see how you can use them to customize MFC's printing capabilities.

The OnPreparePrinting() **function**

OnPreparePrinting() is the first of the five special functions that MFC calls for a print or print preview job. You must override this function in the view window's class and call the DoPreparePrinting() function, which displays the Print dialog box and creates the printer DC. You can also, in OnPreparePrinting(), change some of the values displayed in the Print dialog box to set the minimum and maximum page count—if you can calculate the page count without the printer DC. When MFC calls OnPreparePrinting(), the printer DC has not yet been created.

When you create your application with MFC AppWizard and select the Printing and Print Preview option for the application, AppWizard automatically overrides the OnPreparePrinting() function for you, as shown here:

```
BOOL CPrintAppView::OnPreparePrinting(CPrintInfo* pInfo)
{
    // default preparation
    return DoPreparePrinting(pInfo);
}
```

As you can see, the OnPreparePrinting() override calls DoPreparePrinting(), which is where the Print dialog box gets displayed (see Figure 11-7). You can control the options displayed in the dialog box by initializing members of the CPrintInfo object that's passed to the function as its single parameter. For example, if you know that the document will be three pages, you can add calls to the CPrintInfo object's SetMinPage() and SetMaxPage() member functions, as follows:

```
BOOL CPrintAppView::OnPreparePrinting(CPrintInfo* pInfo)
{
    // default preparation

    pInfo->SetMinPage(1);
    pInfo->SetMaxPage(3);

    return DoPreparePrinting(pInfo);
}
```

The SetMinPage() and SetMaxPage() functions not only tell MFC how many pages are to be printed, but also determine the values shown in the Print dialog box's From and To boxes. If you don't call SetMinPage() and SetMaxPage(), the From box defaults to 1 and the To box remains empty (although MFC will assume only one page is to be printed).

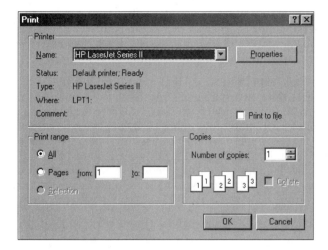

Figure 11-7: The `DoPreparePrinting()` function automatically displays the Print dialog box.

If your document is a fixed size, as in the preceding example, you'll know in advance how many pages will be printed. This will enable you to set the minimum and maximum pages in `OnPreparePrinting()`. The problem with `OnPreparePrinting()` is that the application does not yet have access to the printer DC, which limits how much information you can determine about the current document and printer. In many cases, you need the printer DC in order to determine how much of the document will fit on a page. If this is the case, you can modify the `OnBeginPrinting()` function.

The `OnBeginPrinting()` function

MFC calls the `OnBeginPrinting()` function after calling `OnPreparePrinting()`. The `CView` version does nothing, but if you override `OnBeginPrinting()` in your application's view window class, you can create GDI resources needed by the print job. Such resources include pens, brushes, and fonts. Also, because `OnBeginPrinting()` is the first place the view window has access to both the printer DC and the `CPrintInfo` structure, you can set page counts and other values here when those values may depend upon the settings of the printer DC.

When you create your application with MFC AppWizard and select the Printing and Print Preview option for the application, AppWizard automatically overrides the `OnBeginPrinting()` function for you, as shown here:

```
void CPrintAppView::OnBeginPrinting(CDC* /*pDC*/,
    CPrintInfo* /*pInfo*/)
{
    // TODO: add extra initialization before printing
}
```

Presumably to avoid compilation warnings about unreferenced variables, the AppWizard version of `OnBeginPrinting()` comments out the names of the printer DC and `CPrintInfo` objects. Obviously, if you're going to access these parameters, you must remove the comments.

Many applications, especially those that must properly space lines of text, need to calculate different character sizes for the screen and printer. This is because screen and printer fonts are rarely the same size from a DPI point of view. For example, a 10-point font might be 20 pixels high on the screen, but 50 dots high on the printer. If you try to use the same character height for the screen and the printer, the printer output will almost certainly overlap. Figure 11-8 shows an application displaying text, whereas Figure 11-9 shows the print preview window using the same character height for the same text.

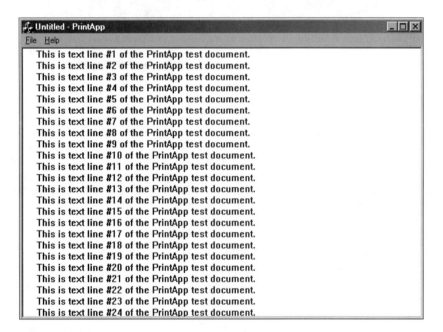

Figure 11-8: Text displayed on the screen uses screen font sizes.

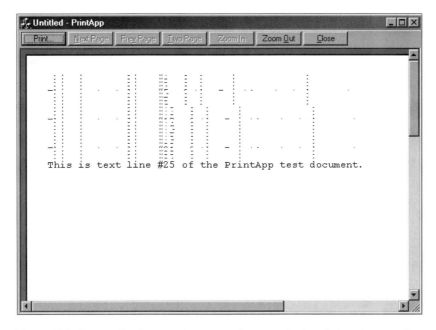

Figure 11-9: If an application uses the screen character size for printing, the text will probably overlap.

When you need to scale text output or calculate page sizes based on printer attributes, you override OnBeginPrinting(), which is the first place you have access to the printer DC. By calling printer DC member functions such as GetTextMetrics(), you can determine the correct character height for the printer, as well as calculate the number of lines per page and the number of pages needed to display the entire document. Listing 11-3 shows an example of the OnBeginPrinting() function calculating character sizes and page counts.

Listing 11-3: The OnBeginPrinting() **function**

```
void CPrintAppView::OnBeginPrinting(CDC* pDC,
    CPrintInfo* pInfo)
{
    // TODO: add extra initialization before printing

    TEXTMETRIC textMetric;
    pDC->GetTextMetrics(&textMetric);
    m_printerCharHeight = textMetric.tmHeight +
        textMetric.tmExternalLeading;

    m_vertRes = pDC->GetDeviceCaps(VERTRES);
    m_linesPerPage = m_vertRes / m_printerCharHeight;
    int numPages = m_numLines / m_linesPerPage + 1;

    pInfo->SetMinPage(1);
    pInfo->SetMaxPage(numPages);
}
```

After setting the value of m_printerCharHeight (which you add as a member variable to the view class), you can use the value in the OnDraw() function to properly space the text. How can you determine whether MFC calls OnDraw() on behalf of the screen or the printer? The CDC object passed to the function defines a member function called IsPrinting() that returns TRUE if MFC is calling the function to render data for the printer. Listing 11-4 shows one way to write the OnDraw() function so that it displays text correctly on both the screen and the printer. Figure 11-10 shows the print preview window when the application uses Listing 11-4's OnDraw().

Listing 11-4: An OnDraw() function that uses different character sizes for the screen and printer

```
void CPrintAppView::OnDraw(CDC* pDC)
{
    CPrintAppDoc* pDoc = GetDocument();
    ASSERT_VALID(pDoc);

    // TODO: add draw code for native data here

    int charHeight;

    if (pDC->IsPrinting())
        charHeight = m_printerCharHeight;
    else
        charHeight = m_charHeight;

    for(int x=0; x<m_numLines; ++x)
    {
        char str[81];
        wsprintf(str, "This is text line #%d of \
the PrintApp test document.", x+1);
        pDC->TextOut(20, x*charHeight, str);
    }
}
```

This version of OnDraw() calls IsPrinting() to determine whether the output is going to the screen or the printer. If IsPrinting() returns TRUE, the data is about to be rendered on the printer, so OnDraw() sets charHeight to m_printerCharHeight, which got its value in OnBeginPrinting(). If IsPrinting() returns FALSE, the data is about to be rendered on the screen, so OnDraw() sets charHeight to m_charHeight, which holds the character height for the screen.

Where does m_charHeight come from? It's a member variable that you add to the view class. You then override the class's OnCreate() function, which responds to the Windows WM_CREATE message. MFC calls OnCreate() after the application's window has been created, but right before it displays the window on the screen. To initialize m_charHeight to the screen character size, you create a DC for the client window and call its GetTextMetrics() member function. Listing 11-5 shows the entire process.

![Untitled - PrintApp print preview window]

```
This is text line #1 of the PrintApp test document.
This is text line #2 of the PrintApp test document.
This is text line #3 of the PrintApp test document.
This is text line #4 of the PrintApp test document.
This is text line #5 of the PrintApp test document.
This is text line #6 of the PrintApp test document.
This is text line #7 of the PrintApp test document.
This is text line #8 of the PrintApp test document.
This is text line #9 of the PrintApp test document.
This is text line #10 of the PrintApp test document.
This is text line #11 of the PrintApp test document.
This is text line #12 of the PrintApp test document.
This is text line #13 of the PrintApp test document.
This is text line #14 of the PrintApp test document.
This is text line #15 of the PrintApp test document.
This is text line #16 of the PrintApp test document.
This is text line #17 of the PrintApp test document.
This is text line #18 of the PrintApp test document.
This is text line #19 of the PrintApp test document.
This is text line #20 of the PrintApp test document.
```

Figure 11-10: The print preview window now shows that the text spacing is correct for the printer.

Listing 11-5: An `OnCreate()` **function that determines the screen character height**

```
int CPrintAppView::OnCreate(LPCREATESTRUCT lpCreateStruct)
{
    if (CView::OnCreate(lpCreateStruct) == -1)
        return -1;

    // TODO: Add your specialized creation code here

    TEXTMETRIC textMetric;
    CClientDC clientDC(this);
    clientDC.GetTextMetrics(&textMetric);
    m_charHeight = textMetric.tmHeight +
        textMetric.tmExternalLeading;

    return 0;
}
```

Note

If you use `OnBeginPrinting()` to create GDI objects for a print job, don't select the new GDI objects into the printer DC right away. Instead, select them in the `OnPrint()` member function that gets called for each page. This rule applies because the DC is reinitialized for each page of the document. MFC calls `OnBeginPrinting()` only once for the entire document, but calls `OnPrint()` for each page. That is, you can access information about the printer in `OnBeginPrinting()`, but you shouldn't modify the DC until `OnPrint()`.

The OnPrepareDC() function

This brings you to the third function in the list, OnPrepareDC(). After MFC calls OnBeginPrinting(), it calls OnPrepareDC() for each page in the document, right before the page gets printed. When you're using OnDraw() to render data for both the screen and the printer, it's in OnPrepareDC() that your program can control exactly what portion of the document MFC will output to the printer. So, you might override this function when the application must print multiple-page documents. You can also use OnPrepareDC() to set mapping modes and other attributes of the printer device context for each page of the document.

For example, in the previous section, you learned how to determine the character size for printer output. Using this character size when sending data to the printer ensures that the text lines get spaced properly. However, if the document length exceeds one page, it still won't print correctly. You'll get all the pages, but each page will start with the first text line and run off the bottom of the page. This phenomenon occurs because for each page of the document, OnDraw() draws the entire document. To paginate properly, you need some way to tell OnDraw() to start printing further into the document, as appropriate for each page. You do this by calling the printer DC's SetViewportOrg() function, as shown in Listing 11-6.

Listing 11-6: An OnPrepareDC() function that sets the viewport origin

```
void CPrintAppView::OnPrepareDC(CDC* pDC,
    CPrintInfo* pInfo)
{
    // TODO: Add your specialized code here
    //    and/or call the base class

    if (pDC->IsPrinting())
    {
        int start = (pInfo->m_nCurPage - 1) * m_vertRes;
        pDC->SetViewportOrg(0, -start);
    }

    CView::OnPrepareDC(pDC, pInfo);
}
```

You'll learn more about SetViewportOrg() in Chapter 13, "Advanced GDI." For now, just know that SetViewportOrg() tells Windows that the document starts at a different point. The function's two arguments are the X and Y coordinates of the new origin (where the document starts). MFC calls OnPrepareDC() once for each page in the document.

The first time MFC calls OnPrepareDC(), for the first page, the function sets the document's origin to 0,0, which is the real beginning of the document. The program sends the entire document to the page, starting at coordinate 0,0. The part of the document that doesn't fit on the page just runs off the bottom of the page and doesn't appear.

The second time MFC calls `OnPrepareDC()`, for the second page, the function sets the origin to the coordinate that marks the start of the second page. Again, the program sends the entire document to the page, but now the program thinks the document starts at the new origin. If the document is still too long for the second page, the remaining data runs off the bottom of the second page and doesn't appear.

This process continues for each page in the document, with `OnPrepareDC()` moving the document's origin forward a page at a time.

Note

Notice that `OnPrepareDC()` calls the DC's `IsPrinting()` member function before doing anything. This function call is important because MFC calls `OnPrepareDC()` when displaying data on the screen, as well as on the printer. When displaying data on the screen, you may not want to fiddle with the origin.

You may think you've got this printing thing licked, now that you've been able to space and paginate the output. And for some printing tasks, you've probably done enough. But there's still a problem. For many printers, the number of lines that fit on the printed page will not be a whole number. For example, a printer with a vertical page resolution of 3,175 and a character height of 50 can display 63.5 lines per page. And when you print the document, that's exactly what you'll get. For example, Figure 11-11 shows the print preview for the bottom of a document's first page, whereas Figure 11-12 shows the print preview for the top of a document's second page. As you can see, the printer has split line 64 between the two pages.

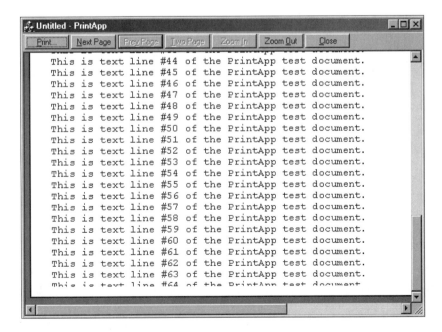

Figure 11-11: The print preview shows the bottom line running off the document's first page.

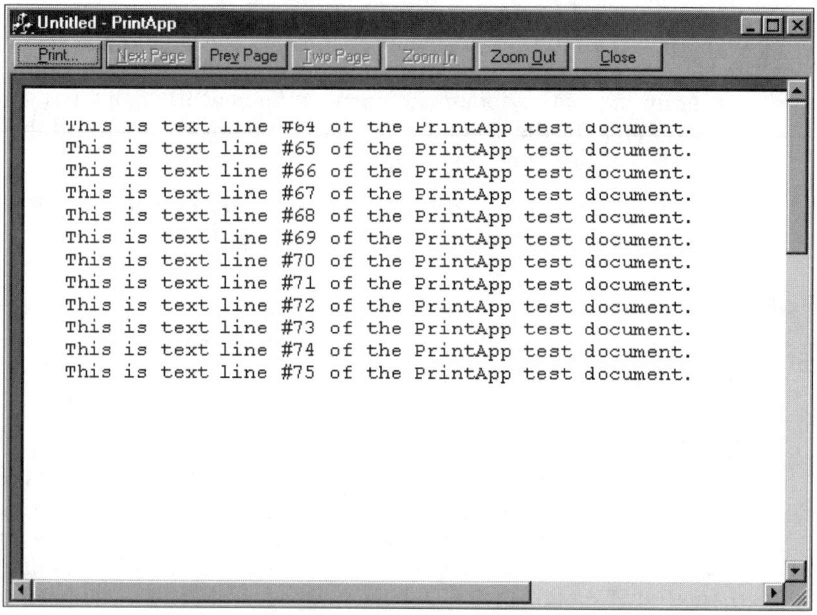

Figure 11-12: The second page then shows the rest of the line.

The application has gotten to the point where it no longer makes sense to let OnDraw() render the document both on the screen and the printer. To rectify this problem, you'll now need to move the printing tasks to the OnPrint() function, which you do in the next section.

When you create your application with AppWizard, AppWizard doesn't automatically override OnPrepareDC() in your view window's class. You must override OnPrepareDC() using ClassWizard (or add it by hand).

The OnPrint() function

After calling OnPrepareDC(), MFC calls OnPrint() for each page. Not only can you set the viewport origin (which controls what portion of the document is output for the page) in OnPrepareDC(), you can also set it in OnPrint(). Usually, though, you'll override OnPrint() when you want to output the document's data differently for the printer than for the screen. You can also use OnPrint() to output headers and footers before the document itself is rendered by the OnDraw() function.

When you create your application with AppWizard, AppWizard doesn't automatically override OnPrint() in your view window's class. You must override OnPrint() using ClassWizard. When you do, make sure that you comment out the call to CView::OnPrint() because that's where MFC calls the OnDraw() function, which your application should not do when it's doing all its printing in OnPrint().

In the previous examples of text output, each document's page had its last line cut in half. To get pagination to work properly in this case, the easiest thing to do is completely separate the code that draws the screen display from the code that draws to the printer. Then, the program can handle the entire printing task in one place, rather than having to keep calling IsPrinting() and performing different tasks based on the result. Listing 11-7 shows how OnPrint() might look for this section's text example. The listing also shows the functions that need to be changed to accommodate the OnPrint() function. For example, OnPrepareDC() no longer sets the viewport origin for each page. OnDraw(), on the other hand, contains only the code needed to draw the document in the application's window.

Listing 11-7: The OnPrint() **and** OnPrepareDC() **functions**

```
void CPrintAppView::OnPrint(CDC* pDC, CPrintInfo* pInfo)
{
    // TODO: Add your specialized code here
    //    and/or call the base class

    int startLine = (pInfo->m_nCurPage - 1) *
        m_linesPerPage + 1;
    int endLine = startLine + m_linesPerPage - 1;
    if (endLine > m_numLines)
        endLine = m_numLines;

    int curLine = 0;
    for(int x=startLine; x<=endLine; ++x)
    {
        char str[81];
        wsprintf(str, "This is text line #%d of \
the PrintApp test document.", x);
        pDC->TextOut(20, curLine*m_printerCharHeight,
            str);
        ++ curLine;
    }
    //CView::OnPrint(pDC, pInfo);
}

void CPrintAppView::OnPrepareDC(CDC* pDC,
    CPrintInfo* pInfo)
{
    // TODO: Add your specialized code here
    //     and/or call the base class

    CView::OnPrepareDC(pDC, pInfo);
}
void CPrintAppView::OnDraw(CDC* pDC)
{
    CPrintAppDoc* pDoc = GetDocument();
    ASSERT_VALID(pDoc);

    // TODO: add draw code for native data here

    for(int x=0; x<m_numLines; ++x)
    {
```

```
        char str[81];
        wsprintf(str, "This is text line #%d of \
the PrintApp test document.", x+1);
        pDC->TextOut(20, x*m_charHeight, str);
    }
}
```

This version of `OnPrint()` works by determining exactly which lines of the document need to be drawn on the current page, and drawing only those lines. MFC passes the current page to `OnPrint()` in the `CPrintInfo` object member `m_nCurPage`. Here's a quick rundown on what the `OnPrint()` function does in Listing 11-7:

- Calculates the number of the first line to print
- Calculates the number of the last line to print
- Uses the first and last line numbers as the control values in a `for` loop
- Prints a line of text in each iteration of the loop

Figures 11-13 and 11-14 show how the application's pagination now works. In Figure 11-13 you can see that the program no longer prints partial lines on the first page. In Figure 11-14, you can see that the document's second page starts with the next full line of text.

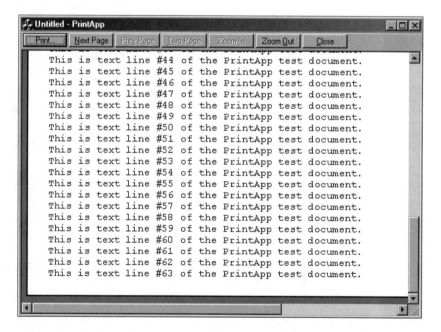

Figure 11-13: Print preview now shows the first page ending with a complete line.

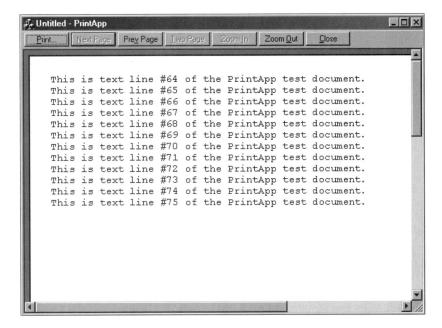

Figure 11-14: The second page shows the rest of the document, starting with the next full line.

The `OnEndPrinting()` function

The last function to explore is `OnEndPrinting()`, which is the counterpart for the `OnBeginPrinting()` function. MFC calls `OnEndPrinting()` when the print job has been completed, giving your application a chance to release resources allocated in `OnBeginPrinting()`. AppWizard overrides `OnEndPrinting()` in your application as shown here:

```
void CCircleAppView::OnEndPrinting(CDC* /*pDC*/,
    CPrintInfo* /*pInfo*/)
{
    // TODO: add cleanup after printing
}
```

Notice that the `CDC` and `CPrintInfo` objects passed to the function are commented out. You'll need to remove the comments if you want to access these objects in the body of the function.

Now that you've had some experience with printing text documents, it's time to move on to graphics printing. In most cases, graphical screens don't need to deal with text sizes and line spacing. Instead, scaling is accomplished using a physical measurement, such as inches or millimeters. In the following sections, you'll learn how this scaling works.

Printing Graphics in an MFC Application

When you print a text document, you need to be aware of text sizes in order to space the lines of the document correctly. When you print a document that contains graphics, you need to scale all the elements that comprise the document, so that the output looks reasonably similar to that on the screen. How you want to perform this scaling depends on the application's needs, and is a choice you need to make as you design your application's user interface. For example, will you want to print the output so that it's the same size as that on the screen, or will you enable the user to scale the screen image and printer images separately?

The PrintCircleApp sample application

On CD-ROM

In the Chapter11\PrintCircleApp directory of this book's CD-ROM, you can find the PrintCircleApp application, which demonstrate the concepts you learned in this section. PrintCircleApp is based on the CircleApp application you created in Chapter 3, "Programming with Visual C++." This version, however, prints circle documents scaled properly on both the screen and printer.

When you run the application, you can draw circles in the window just as you did with the Chapter 3 version, by clicking in the window. Also like the previous version, you can change the size or color of the circles by clicking buttons on the toolbar. This version, however, features a ruler at the top of the screen, which indicates the size of the screen's logical inches, as shown in Figure 11-15. Figure 11-16 shows how the circle document appears in print preview. As you can see, the printer output is now properly scaled.

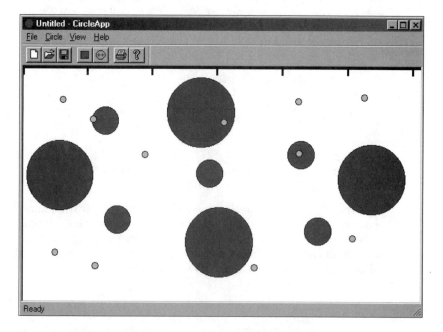

Figure 11-15: The PrintCircleApp screen displaying a set of circles

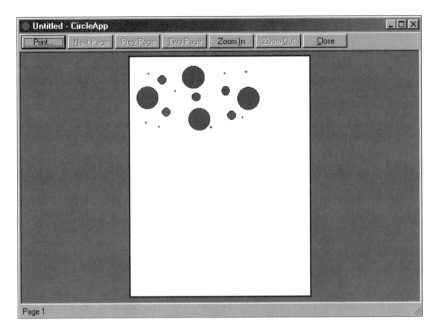

Figure 11-16: PrintCircleApp's print preview showing the document just created

Scaling between the screen and printer

As you now know, the screen's display and the printer usually have different resolutions. That is, the horizontal and vertical dots per inch on the screen may be 96, while the printer's horizontal and vertical dots per inch may be 300 or more. (The horizontal and vertical values aren't necessarily the same.) Because the screen has larger dots, when you print an image on both the screen and the printer, the printer's image looks small.

Note

If you have a hard time understanding how the dots-per-inch measurement of a device affects the size of printed output, imagine that you have a box of BBs and a box of marbles. Lay 100 BBs in a row, and then lay 100 marbles in a row. Which line is longer? Obviously, because marbles are larger than BBs, the 100-marble line will be longer than the 100-BB line. A device's dots-per-inch measurements are no more mysterious that BBs and marbles. If you tell Windows to draw a line 100 units long on a 96 DPI device and on a 300 DPI device, the 300 DPI device's line will be shorter, because the device's dots are smaller.

You can solve this problem in a number of ways. You can use a different mapping mode (instead of the default MM_TEXT) for drawing and printing your graphics. (You'll learn about mapping modes in Chapter 13, "Advanced GDI.") You can have the user choose a final size for the printed output and scale the output based on that choice. Or, one of the simplest solutions, if it suits your application, is to draw the images so that a logical inch on the screen comes out as an inch on the printer.

To do this, you call upon the services of your old friend, `GetDeviceCaps()` (see Chapter 5, "Graphics Device Interface Basics"). When you call `GetDeviceCaps()` with the constant `LOGPIXELSX` as its single argument, the function returns the number of dots per logical horizontal inch on the screen. Similarly, when you call `GetDeviceCaps()` with the argument `LOGPIXELSY`, you get the number of dots per logical vertical inch on the screen . The keyword here is "logical." Because monitors come in different sizes, but display the same resolutions, a logical inch on one screen may truly be an inch, whereas on a larger or smaller screen, a logical inch will be larger or smaller than an inch.

To perform printer output scaling, the first step is to get the logical dots per inch for the screen. Following is an example of how this could be done:

```
CClientDC clientDC(this);
screenHDotsPerInch =
    clientDC.GetDeviceCaps(LOGPIXELSX);
screenVDotsPerInch =
    clientDC.GetDeviceCaps(LOGPIXELSY);
```

Here, the program first gets a DC for the application's client window. It then calls the DC's `GetDeviceCaps()` member function to get the screen's logical inch. You can place the previous lines anywhere in the program after the system has created the application's window. In an MFC program, a good place is in the `OnCreate()` function, which responds to the Windows `WM_CREATE` message.

After getting the screen's logical inch, you need to get the printer's logical inch. To do that, you would use code similar to the following snippet:

```
int printerHDotsPerInch =
    pDC->GetDeviceCaps(LOGPIXELSX);
int printerVDotsPerInch =
    pDC->GetDeviceCaps(LOGPIXELSY);
```

Notice that the `GetDeviceCaps()` function is called through a pointer called `pDC`. The `pDC` pointer is the address of a printer DC, so in order to call `GetDeviceCaps()` for the printer, you must already have a printer DC. If you're using `OnDraw()` to send data to the printer, you can place the previous lines there, checking the DC's `IsPrinting()` flag to be sure that the DC is a printer DC and not the screen DC, as shown in Listing 11-8.

Listing 11-8: Checking for a printer DC and calculating scaling values for the printer

```
float hScale = 1.0;
float vScale = 1.0;

if (pDC->IsPrinting())
{
    int printerHDotsPerInch =
        pDC->GetDeviceCaps(LOGPIXELSX);
    int printerVDotsPerInch =
        pDC->GetDeviceCaps(LOGPIXELSY);
```

```
hScale = (float)printerHDotsPerInch /
    (float)screenHDotsPerInch;
vScale = (float)printerVDotsPerInch /
    (float)screenVDotsPerInch;
}
```

In this code example, the program not only gets the printer's logical inch, but also creates horizontal and vertical scaling values by dividing the printer's logical inch by the screen's logical inch. You can then use these scaling factors with output coordinates in order to create a display that's appropriate for both the screen and the printer. For example, suppose the variables x1, y1, x2, and y2 contain the screen coordinates for a shape. You might scale the coordinates as follows:

```
x1 = (int)(x1 * hScale);
y1 = (int)(y1 * vScale);
x2 = (int)(x2 * hScale);
y2 = (int)(y2 * vScale);
```

Referring back to Listing 11-8, if the DC passed to OnDraw() is a screen DC, hScale and vScale end up set to 1.0. The coordinates, when multiplied by hScale and vScale, stay the same, with the scaling values replaced by the actual values:

```
x1 = (int)(x1 * 1.0);
y1 = (int)(y1 * 1.0);
x2 = (int)(x2 * 1.0);
y2 = (int)(y2 * 1.0);
```

If the DC is a printer DC, however, hScale and vScale get set to the results of dividing printer logical inches by screen logical inches. Suppose, for example, that the screen logical inch is 96 pixels, both horizontally and vertically, and the printer's logical inch is 300, both horizontally and vertically. Substituting actual values for the printerHDotsPerInch and screenHDotsPerInch variables, you get the following calculation:

```
hScale = 300 / 96;
vScale = 300 / 96;
```

This calculation yields the following results:

```
hScale = 3.125;
vScale = 3.125;
```

These scaling values indicate that the screen's logical inch contains a little over three times as many dots as the printer's logical inch. When printing, all screen coordinates must be multiplied by the scaling values, so that a logical inch on the screen equals an inch on the printer:

```
x1 = (int)(x1 * 3.125);
y1 = (int)(y1 * 3.125);
x2 = (int)(x2 * 3.125);
y2 = (int)(y2 * 3.125);
```

The `OnCreate()` function

Now that you've experimented with the program a bit, it's time to see how it performs its printing magic. In order to perform the scaling, the program gets the screen's logical inch in the `OnCreate()` function, which was added to the application using ClassWizard (see Figure 11-17). Listing 11-9 shows the program's `OnCreate()` function.

Listing 11-9: Calculating scaling values for the printer

```
int CCircleAppView::OnCreate(LPCREATESTRUCT
    lpCreateStruct)
{
    if (CView::OnCreate(lpCreateStruct) == -1)
        return -1;

    // TODO: Add your specialized creation code here

    CClientDC clientDC(this);
    m_winHDotsPerInch =
        clientDC.GetDeviceCaps(LOGPIXELSX);
    m_winVDotsPerInch =
        clientDC.GetDeviceCaps(LOGPIXELSY);

    return 0;
}
```

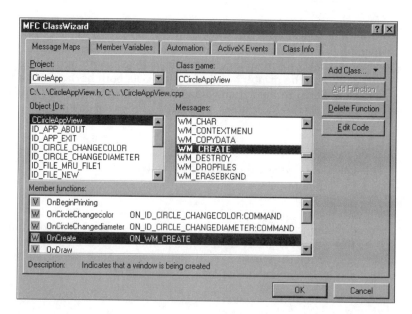

Figure 11-17: Use ClassWizard to add `OnCreate()` to the view window class.

The `OnDraw()` **function**

PrintCircleApp uses `OnDraw()` for drawing on both the screen and the printer.
Listing 11-10 shows the `OnDraw()` function, which performs the following
tasks:

- Initializes the horizontal and vertical scaling variables to 1.0

- If the DC is for the printer, gets the printer's logical inch and divides it
  by the window's logical inch, resetting the horizontal and vertical scaling
  variables

- Processes the application's circle document, scaling the output as
  appropriate

- If the DC is not for the printer, draws a ruler on the screen

Listing 11-10: PrintCircleApp's `OnDraw()` **function**

```
void CCircleAppView::OnDraw(CDC* pDC)
{
    CCircleAppDoc* pDoc = GetDocument();
    ASSERT_VALID(pDoc);

    // TODO: add draw code for native data here
    float hScale = 1.0;
    float vScale = 1.0;

    if (pDC->IsPrinting())
    {
        int printHDotsPerInch =
            pDC->GetDeviceCaps(LOGPIXELSX);
        int printVDotsPerInch =
            pDC->GetDeviceCaps(LOGPIXELSY);
        hScale = (float)printHDotsPerInch /
            (float)m_winHDotsPerInch;
        vScale = (float)printVDotsPerInch /
            (float)m_winVDotsPerInch;
    }

    int size = pDoc->m_circleArray.GetSize();

    for (int x=0; x<size; ++x)
    {
        CircleStruct* circle =
            (CircleStruct*)pDoc->m_circleArray.GetAt(x);
        int radius = circle->diameter/2;
        int x1 = circle->point.x-radius;
        int y1 = circle->point.y-radius;
        int x2 = circle->point.x+radius;
        int y2 = circle->point.y+radius;
        COLORREF color = circle->color;
        CBrush brush(color);
        CBrush* oldBrush = pDC->SelectObject(&brush);
```

```
                    x1 = (int)(x1 * hScale);
                    y1 = (int)(y1 * vScale);
                    x2 = (int)(x2 * hScale);
                    y2 = (int)(y2 * vScale);

                    pDC->Ellipse(x1, y1, x2, y2);
                    pDC->SelectObject(oldBrush);
                }

            if (!pDC->IsPrinting())
            {
                CPen newPen(PS_SOLID, 3, RGB(0,0,0));
                CPen* pOldPen = pDC->SelectObject(&newPen);
                pDC->MoveTo(0, 1);
                pDC->LineTo(800, 1);

                for (int i=0; i<10; ++i)
                {
                    pDC->MoveTo(i*m_winHDotsPerInch, 1);
                    pDC->LineTo(i*m_winHDotsPerInch, 10);
                }
                pDC->SelectObject(pOldPen);
            }
        }
```

The OnPreparePrinting() function

Unlike the text-printing application you learned about earlier in this chapter,
PrintCircleApp doesn't take advantage of the OnPreparePrinting(),
OnBeginPrinting(), and OnEndPrinting() functions, except to set the
maximum page count to 1, as shown here:

```
BOOL CCircleAppView::OnPreparePrinting(CPrintInfo* pInfo)
{
    // default preparation

    pInfo->SetMaxPage(1);

    return DoPreparePrinting(pInfo);
}
```

 PROBLEMS & SOLUTIONS

Using Physical Measurements as Scaling Factors

PROBLEM: *In the program I'm writing, I don't want to use proportional values as
scaling factors; I just want to use inches. That is, when I draw a scaled line, I want
to use inches as line coordinates instead of pixel or dot coordinates. Is this possible?*

Continued

SOLUTION: Sort of. Although you can't directly tell Windows to draw a line six inches long, you can set up your scaling so that you use inch values as scaling factors (as the numbers you multiply coordinate values by). The trick is to avoid hard-coded screen coordinates completely. Instead, express all coordinates in terms of the scale you want to use. For example, if you want to draw a rectangle that's six-inch inches long and three-and-a-half inches high, use 6 and 3.5 in the `Rectangle()` function's arguments, but multiply those inch values by the device's logical inch.

To accomplish this, call `GetDeviceCaps()` in your `OnCreate()` function, as shown in Listing 11-11, in order to obtain the screen device's logical inch.

Listing 11-11: The `OnCreate()` function

```
int CInchAppView::OnCreate(LPCREATESTRUCT lpCreateStruct)
{
    if (CView::OnCreate(lpCreateStruct) == -1)
        return -1;

    // TODO: Add your specialized creation code here

    CClientDC clientDC(this);
    m_screenHInch =
        clientDC.GetDeviceCaps(LOGPIXELSX);
    m_screenVInch =
        clientDC.GetDeviceCaps(LOGPIXELSY);

    return 0;
}
```

Then, override the view window class's `OnBeginPrinting()` function. In that function, call `GetDeviceCaps()` to get the printer's logical inch:

```
void CInchAppView::OnBeginPrinting(CDC* pDC,
    CPrintInfo* /*pInfo*/)
{
    // TODO: add extra initialization before printing

    m_printerHInch = pDC->GetDeviceCaps(LOGPIXELSX);
    m_printerVInch = pDC->GetDeviceCaps(LOGPIXELSY);
}
```

Now that you have the size of a logical inch for each of the devices, you can use inches as coordinates, as long as you multiply those inch coordinates by the appropriate device logical inch. For example, Listing 11-12 shows the code needed to draw a 6 x 3.5-inch rectangle on the screen one inch from the left and top of the window. Listing 11-13, on the other hand, shows the code for the `OnPrint()` function, which handles sending the rectangle to the printer.

Continued

Listing 11-12: The `OnDraw()` **function**

```
void CInchAppView::OnDraw(CDC* pDC)
{
    CInchAppDoc* pDoc = GetDocument();
    ASSERT_VALID(pDoc);

    // TODO: add draw code for native data here
    int x1 = (int)(1.0 * m_screenHInch);
    int y1 = (int)(1.0 * m_screenVInch);
    int x2 = (int)(7.0 * m_screenHInch);
    int y2 = (int)(4.5 * m_screenVInch);

    pDC->Rectangle(x1, y1, x2, y2);
}
```

Listing 11-13: The `OnPrint()` **function**

```
void CInchAppView::OnPrint(CDC* pDC, CPrintInfo* pInfo)
{
    // TODO: Add your specialized code here
    //    and/or call the base class

    int x1 = (int)(1.0 * m_printerHInch);
    int y1 = (int)(1.0 * m_printerVInch);
    int x2 = (int)(7.0 * m_printerHInch);
    int y2 = (int)(4.5 * m_printerVInch);

    pDC->Rectangle(x1, y1, x2, y2);
}
```

On CD-ROM

To see how all this inch-scaling stuff works, you'll now use MFC AppWizard and ClassWizard to put together an application, called *InchApp*. This application displays and prints a six-inch rectangle on the screen and on whatever printer is connected to your system, demonstrating the concepts you covered in this section. For those of you who are not yet comfortable with building Visual C++ applications, the following steps make clear what you need to do to add simple printing capabilities to your own applications. If you would like to examine InchApp before you get started, take a look at the Chapter11\InchApp file on this book's CD-ROM.

1. Select the File menu's New command and create a new AppWizard project called InchApp, as shown in Figure 11-18.

2. Select Single Document in the Step 1 dialog box, as shown in Figure 11-19.

3. Click the Next button three times, accepting the default settings in the Step 2 of 6 and Step 3 of 6 dialog boxes.

Continued

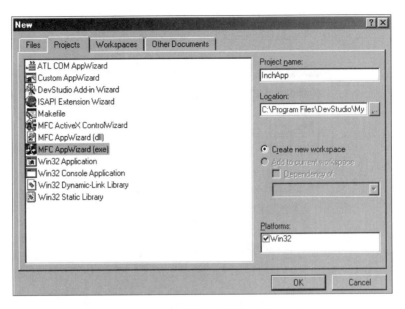

Figure 11-18: The new application will be called *InchApp*.

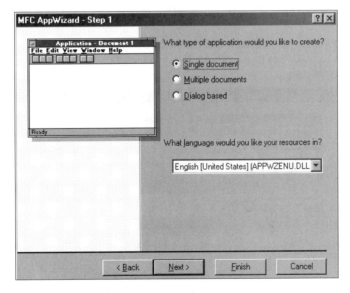

Figure 11-19: The new application will use the single document interface.

Continued

4. Turn off the Docking Toolbar and Initial Status Bar options in the Step 4 of 6 dialog box, as shown in Figure 11-20.

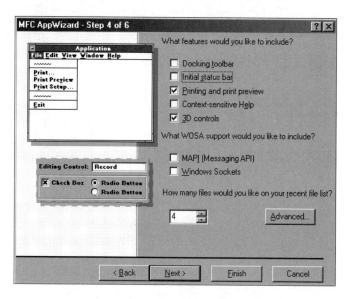

Figure 11-20: The new application will have no toolbar or status bar.

5. Click the Next button and select the As a Statically Linked Library option in the Step 5 of 6 dialog box (see Figure 11-21).

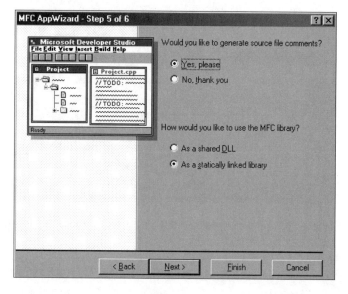

Figure 11-21: The new application will link statically to the MFC libraries.

Continued

6. Click the Finish button. Your New Project Information dialog box appears and should look like the one shown in Figure 11-22.

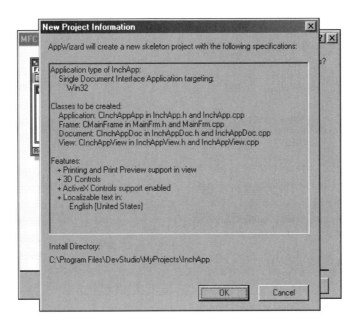

Figure 11-22: The New Project Information dialog box shows the final options for the InchApp application.

7. Use ClassWizard to add the `OnCreate()` function to the application's `CInchAppView` class (see Figure 11-23).

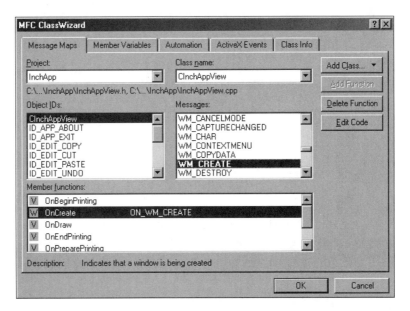

Figure 11-23: You use ClassWizard to add the `OnCreate()` function.

Continued

8. Click the **Edit Code** button and add the following lines to `OnCreate()`, right after the `TODO: Add your specialized creation code here` comment:

```
CClientDC clientDC(this);
m_screenHInch =
    clientDC.GetDeviceCaps(LOGPIXELSX);
m_screenVInch =
    clientDC.GetDeviceCaps(LOGPIXELSY);
```

9. Use ClassWizard to override view class's `OnPrint()` function, as shown in Figure 11-24.

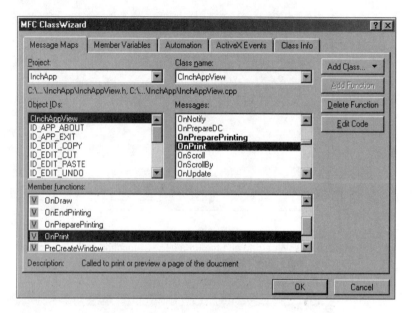

Figure 11-24: You use ClassWizard to override the `OnPrint()` function.

10. Click the **Edit Code** button and add the following lines to `OnPrint()`, right after the `TODO: Add your specialized code here and/or call the base class` comment:

```
int x1 = (int)(1.0 * m_printerHInch);
int y1 = (int)(1.0 * m_printerVInch);
int x2 = (int)(7.0 * m_printerHInch);
int y2 = (int)(4.5 * m_printerVInch);

pDC->Rectangle(x1, y1, x2, y2);
```

11. At the end of the `OnPrint()` function, comment out or remove the call to the base class's `OnPrint()` function.

12. Add the following lines to the `CInchAppView` class's `OnDraw()` function, right after the `TODO: add draw code for native data here` comment:

```
int x1 = (int)(1.0 * m_screenHInch);
int y1 = (int)(1.0 * m_screenVInch);
```

```
int x2 = (int)(7.0 * m_screenHInch);
int y2 = (int)(4.5 * m_screenVInch);

pDC->Rectangle(x1, y1, x2, y2);
```

13. Add the following line to the `CInchAppView` class's `OnPreparePrinting()` function, right after the `default preparation` comment:

    ```
    pInfo->SetMaxPage(1);
    ```

14. Add the following lines to the `CInchAppView` class's `OnBeginPrinting()` function, right after the `TODO: add extra initialization before printing` comment:

    ```
    m_printerHInch = pDC->GetDeviceCaps(LOGPIXELSX);
    m_printerVInch = pDC->GetDeviceCaps(LOGPIXELSY);
    ```

15. Also in `OnBeginPrinting()`, remove the comments from the `pDC` DC object's name in the function's parameter list.

16. Load the `CInchAppView` class's header file, and add the following lines to the class's Implementation section, right after the `protected` keyword:

    ```
    int m_printerVInch;
    int m_printerHInch;
    int m_screenVInch;
    int m_screenHInch;
    ```

You've now completed the InchApp application. Press Ctrl+F5 on your keyboard to compile and run the application. When you do, you see the window shown in Figure 11-25. The window displays a rectangle six inches long and 3.5 inches high. Moreover, it displays the rectangle one inch from the left and top of the window. Remember, however, that the window uses logical inches. The actual size of the rectangle will depend on the size of your monitor.

Figure 11-25: The InchApp application displays a six-inch rectangle.

Continued

To see that the scaling works as advertised, select the File menu's Print command. Your printer should then print the rectangle. Go ahead and measure it with a ruler. If you don't want to print the page, you can see the printed result in the print preview window, shown in Figure 11-26. Because the print preview display is scaled for the screen, you'll have to estimate the size of the rectangle compared to the rest of the page.

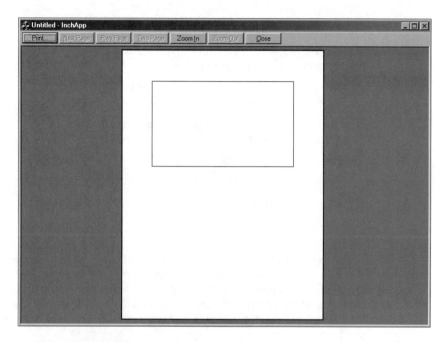

Figure 11-26: InchApp's print preview shows the scaled rectangle.

Summary

Many of the applications you write for Windows 98 will require the capability to print documents. Although printing under Windows can become a complex task, MFC takes over some of the burden by providing not only a printer context for the print job, but also handling the Print dialog box and providing functions that enable you to access the printing process at various points.

Also discussed in this chapter:

▶ Printing in a traditional Windows program requires six main steps: getting the printer DC, starting the document, starting pages, rendering the document, ending pages, and ending the document.

▶ The easiest way to add printing capabilities to an MFC program is to select the Printing and Print Preview option when creating the application with AppWizard.

▶ In an MFC program, the view window's OnDraw() function can render simple documents on both the screen and the printer.

▶ MFC calls the OnPreparePrinting() function when a print or print preview job begins.

▶ The OnBeginPrinting() function is the first place the class has access to the printer DC.

▶ The OnPrepareDC() function is the last chance an MFC application has to manipulate the printer DC before the document is sent to the printer.

▶ You can override the OnPrint() function when you want to output the document's data differently for the printer than for the screen.

▶ MFC calls the OnEndPrinting() when the print job is complete.

▶ When printing graphics, you're usually more concerned with scaling than you are with text sizes, line spacing, pagination, and displaying headers and footers.

▶ Because screen pixels are usually much larger than a printer's dots, an application must scale text and images when printing.

Chapter 12

Bitmaps

Windows applications can create attractive displays using only the GDI drawing functions. However, sometimes you want to display detailed images—maybe even photographs—in an application's window. That's when you call upon the power of a bitmap. Bitmaps are the most common type of image file used in Windows, and can be as simple as a button icon or as complex as a photographic-quality image. But no matter how you use them, bitmaps will make your application look more professional. You got a brief introduction to bitmaps in Chapter 5, "Graphics Device Interface Basics," when you created a bitmapped brush. In this chapter, you'll learn even more ways to use bitmaps.

Introducing DDBs and DIBs

A bitmap is nothing fancier than an image that can be displayed on the screen. You might, for example, use a bitmap to display a photo on the screen or to provide an icon for a button. The only way a bitmap differs from other types of images, such as GIF or JPEG pictures, is in the file format. That is, bitmaps are stored differently than other types of image files. In fact, one type of bitmap, the device-dependent bitmap, is rarely found on disk at all, being created in memory instead. Bitmaps come in two varieties: *device-dependent bitmaps (DDBs)* and *device-independent bitmaps (DIBs)*.

DDBs are rarely, if ever, stored on a disk. Instead, applications create and manipulate DDBs in memory. A DDB is device-dependent because it doesn't contain a color palette; its colors depend on the device on which it's displayed (usually the screen). Nor does a DDB contain other informational structures that a device-independent bitmap contains to indicate how the bitmap should be displayed. Usually, applications use DDBs to transfer image information between memory and the screen. For example, a common use for a DDB is to store a copy of a window's contents so that the window can be redrawn quickly from memory.

A DIB, on the other hand, is stored on disk. Any application that can read bitmap files—which usually have the BMP file name extension—can read and display the image. Even applications running on different platforms (such as the Macintosh) can read and display bitmap files. Unlike DDBs, DIBs include color information. This color information may be in the form of a palette (such as in a 256-color image) or stored in the data for each pixel (such as in a 24-bit image). In any case, all the information an application needs to display the bitmap is in a DIB's file, including even the bitmap's size and other attributes. One example of a DIB might be a scanned image that's been saved in the BMP format.

The rest of this chapter explores how you can use both DDBs and DIBs in your Windows applications.

Programming with Device-Dependent Bitmaps

As stated previously, applications usually use DDBs to transfer image information between memory and the screen. Sometimes, different applications running concurrently in Windows 98 can share image data by passing the information as a DDB in the Clipboard, from which it can be pasted into another application's window. No matter how an application uses a DDB, however, there are several steps that the application must perform to create a bitmap object, associate it with the device, and display it. These steps, as performed by an MFC application, are as follows:

1. Create a `CBitmap` object.
2. Initialize the `CBitmap` object with a bitmap that's compatible with the current device context.
3. Create a memory device context that's compatible with the current device context.
4. Select the bitmap into the memory DC.
5. Draw on the bitmap through the memory DC.
6. Copy the bitmap to the display device.

What the application does with the bitmap after creating it depends on the application. In many cases, the application will copy the bitmap from memory to the screen. An application can also copy image data from the screen to the bitmap in order to store a copy of the screen in memory or to transfer all or part of the screen image to another application, such as a screen-capture program might do. The following sections describe each of the previous steps.

Creating and initializing a bitmap object

The MFC libraries feature a class for creating and manipulating device-dependent bitmaps, also called *GDI bitmaps*. This class, named CBitmap, features several ways to create and initialize bitmaps, as well as member functions for changing or obtaining bitmap information. These functions include the following:

FromHandle()	Gets a pointer to a CBitmap object
GetBitmap()	Obtains information about a bitmap and places it into a BITMAP structure
GetBitmapBits()	Copies a bitmap's data into a buffer
GetBitmapDimension()	Gets a bitmap's width and height
SetBitmapBits()	Changes the bitmap's data to the given values
SetBitmapDimension()	Changes a bitmap's width and height

Creating a CBitmap object in your program is easy:

```
CBitmap bitmap;
```

The tricky part is associating the CBitmap object with the actual bitmap that the object will manipulate. You must do this by calling one of the following seven initialization functions:

LoadBitmap()	Associates a bitmap from the application's resources with the CBitmap object. In this case, you will have already created the bitmap image using Visual C++'s bitmap editor and added the bitmap to the project's resources.
LoadOEMBitmap()	Associates a standard Windows bitmap with the CBitmap object. The standard bitmaps represent images such as checks and arrows that are part of the Windows system.
LoadMappedBitmap()	Associates a bitmap from the application's resources with the CBitmap object, mapping the bitmap's colors to the system colors. As with the LoadBitmap() function, you will have already created the bitmap image using Visual C++'s bitmap editor. This bitmap may represent something like a button that you want to appear on the screen using system colors the user has set.

(continued)

Continued	
CreateBitmap()	Creates a new, blank bitmap and associates it with the CBitmap object. Because of all the information you must provide to this function, you probably won't use it much with MFC. You can usually get the same results by calling CreateCompatibleBitmap(). The exception would be when you need to create a bitmap that's not compatible with any current DC.
CreateBitmapIndirect()	Creates a new bitmap from a BITMAP structure and associates it with the CBitmap object. This function is similar to CreateBitmap(), except you store the bitmap information into a BITMAP structure, rather than passing the information as individual arguments.
CreateCompatibleBitmap()	Creates a bitmap that's compatible with the given DC and associates it with the CBitmap object. This function is the easiest way to create a bitmap that'll be used to transfer information between the screen and memory. Rather than your having to specify all the bitmap's attributes, as you do with CreateBitmap(), you simply specify a DC and the function extracts the attributes it needs from the DC.
CreateDiscardableBitmap()	Creates a discardable bitmap that's compatible with the given DC and associates it with the CBitmap object. This function is similar to CreateCompatibleBitmap(), except that Windows can discard the resultant bitmap whenever the bitmap is not selected into a DC.

An example for using one of the above functions would be if you wanted to create a new bitmap that you could display on the screen. You'd then call CreateCompatibleBitmap() to create the bitmap. However, because CreateCompatibleBitmap() requires a pointer to a DC as one of its arguments, you would have to first create the DC object. The entire process looks like this:

```
CBitmap bitmap;
CClientDC windowDC(this);
bitmap.CreateCompatibleBitmap(&windowDC, 200, 100);
```

These lines create and initialize a 200x100 bitmap that's compatible with (can be displayed in) the current client window.

Creating the memory DC

Now that you have the bitmap created, you'll want to draw something on it. After all, a blank bitmap doesn't do you much good. In order to draw on the bitmap, you must select it into a memory DC. This process is similar to selecting a new pen or brush into a window DC. You can think of the bitmap as just another GDI object like a pen or brush. But what the heck is a memory DC? A memory DC is very similar to a window DC, the big difference being that a memory DC sits invisibly in memory and is never directly displayed on the screen. In a way, you could say that a memory DC is a buffer that has GDI objects such as pens, brushes, and fonts (not to mention bitmaps) associated with it.

You create a memory DC by creating an object of MFC's `CDC` class, which is the class from which MFC derives the other DC classes:

```
CDC memoryDC;
```

Notice that, unlike when you create a window DC, when you create a memory DC, you don't pass the window's `this` pointer as an argument. That's because `CDC` is a general class for any kind of DC, and not every DC has to be compatible with a client window.

Once you've created the `CDC` object you'll be using as a memory DC, you must associate the `CDC` object with an actual DC. The `CDC` class provides a couple of ways to do this, but the most useful for this example is to call the DC object's `CreateCompatibleDC()` function:

```
memoryDC.CreateCompatibleDC(&windowDC);
```

This function takes as its single parameter a pointer to the DC object with which the memory DC should be compatible. Because you want to display the bitmap on the screen, and because the bitmap is compatible with the window's DC, `CreateCompatibleDC()`'s argument is the address of the window DC.

Selecting the bitmap into the memory DC

So far, you have a client window with a DC, a bitmap that's compatible with the window DC, and a memory DC that's compatible with the window DC. Although these three distinct objects are fully compatible, somehow you've got to get them to work together. The first step toward accomplishing that goal is to select the bitmap into the memory DC:

```
CBitmap* pOldBitmap =
    memoryDC.SelectObject(&bitmap);
```

As you can see, you select the bitmap into the DC exactly as you would any other GDI object, by calling the DC's `SelectObject()` function. `SelectObject()`'s single argument is the address of the `CBitmap` object. The call to `SelectObject()` returns a pointer to the DC's previous bitmap. You'll want to hold onto this pointer in order to reselect the original bitmap back into the DC. However, don't get any ideas about making use of this default bitmap. It's a single, monochrome pixel.

Note

A bitmap can be selected only into a memory DC. Don't try to select a bitmap into a window or printer DC.

Drawing on the bitmap

When you select a bitmap into a memory DC, you've given that DC a useful drawing surface. In the case of a memory DC, this drawing surface is not unlike the drawing surface of a window. You just can't see it. You can, however, direct the same sorts of drawing commands to the memory DC that you would direct to a window or printer DC.

To prepare your bitmap, you'll first want to fill it with a background color. This is because the bitmap contains whatever random values happened to be in memory at the location the bitmap was created. Figure 12-1 shows what happens if you forget to clear the bitmap with a background color—a cool effect, but probably not what you're looking for!

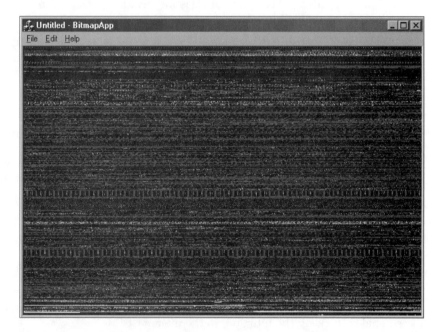

Figure 12-1: A window displaying a bitmap that wasn't cleared

To clear the bitmap, call the DC object's FillRect() function:

```
CBrush* pWhiteBrush = new CBrush(RGB(255,255,255));
CRect rect(0, 0, 199, 99);
memoryDC.FillRect(rect, pWhiteBrush);
```

These lines create a white brush and a CRect object representing the bitmap's coordinates, and then call FillRect() with the newly created objects. The result is a bitmap filled with white. You can, of course, clear the bitmap to any color you like. Black is another common choice.

With the bitmap cleared, you can draw whatever you like on it by calling the memory DC's drawing functions. For example the lines in Listing 12-1 draw a line of text and a rectangle on the bitmap. The program draws the rectangle using a thick pen and red brush that are created and selected into the memory DC. Figure 12-2 shows the resulting bitmap displayed in a window.

Listing 12-1: Drawing text and a rectangle on the bitmap

```
CBrush* pRedBrush = new CBrush(RGB(255,0,0));
CPen* pThickPen =
    new CPen(PS_SOLID, 3, RGB(0,0,0));
CBrush* pOldBrush =
    memoryDC.SelectObject(pRedBrush);
CPen* pOldPen =
    memoryDC.SelectObject(pThickPen);
memoryDC.TextOut(10, 10,
    "This text is going to the bitmap");
memoryDC.Rectangle(50, 50, 150, 75);
memoryDC.SelectObject(pOldBrush);
memoryDC.SelectObject(pOldPen);
memoryDC.SelectObject(pOldBitmap);
delete pRedBrush;
delete pThickPen;
```

Notice how, in Listing 12-1, the program selects objects in and out of the DC just as it would for a normal window DC.

Figure 12-2: A window displaying the bitmap drawn in Listing 12-1

Copying the bitmap to the display

Now you've got your bitmap drawn and ready to go. The only problem is that you can't see it. To display the bitmap, you must copy it from the memory DC to the window's DC. There are a couple of ways to do this, depending on whether you want the bitmap displayed at exactly the same size or if you need to display it larger or smaller. The most common functions you'll use for copying bitmaps are BitBlt() and StretchBlt().

Copying a bitmap without changing its size

To copy a bitmap to a window without changing the bitmap's size, use BitBlt(), which is prototyped as follows. The function's argument descriptions are listed in Table 12-1.

```
BOOL BitBlt(
    int x,
    int y,
    int nWidth,
    int nHeight,
    CDC* pSrcDC,
    int xSrc,
    int ySrc,
    DWORD dwRop);
```

Table 12-1 The BitBlt() function's arguments

Argument	Description
x	The X coordinate of the destination rectangle's upper-left corner
y	The Y coordinate of the destination rectangle's upper-left corner
nWidth	The destination rectangle's and the bitmap's width
nHeight	The destination rectangle's and the bitmap's height
pSrcDC	A pointer to the DC that contains the bitmap
xSrc	The X coordinate of the bitmap's upper-left corner
ySrc	The Y coordinate of the bitmap's upper-left corner
dwRop	The specification for the raster operation. For copying a bitmap, use SRCCOPY.

Whew! Got all that? The BitBlt() function is not as difficult to use as it looks, although it may take you a few tries to get the coordinates just right in some cases. With BitBlt()'s arguments, all you're doing is telling Windows where to copy the bitmap and where the bitmap should be copied from. Just think of each DC as a piece of paper with a drawing on it. Now imagine that you're telling someone what part of the first paper should display what part of the second paper.

To copy an entire bitmap, you'd use a BitBlt() call that looks something like this:

```
windowDC.BitBlt(0, 0, 200, 100,
    &memoryDC, 0, 0, SRCCOPY);
```

The DC through which you're calling BitBlt() (in this case, windowDC) is the destination DC. The first two BitBlt() arguments tell Windows that the bitmap should be copied to the point 0,0 in windowDC. The coordinates 0,0 represent the extreme upper-left corner of the window's display area. The second two arguments tell Windows that the bitmap being copied is 200x100 pixels. The third argument tells windows that memoryDC holds the bitmap to be copied, whereas the next two arguments tell Windows the upper-left coordinates of the bitmap at which to start copying. These coordinates don't have to be 0,0. You can also copy only a portion of the bitmap if you like. Finally, the last argument tells Windows how to combine the source and destination pixels, an advanced topic you'll learn more about in Chapter 13, "Advanced GDI." For now, stick with SRCCOPY for this argument.

Copying a bitmap and changing its size

The other function you might use to copy the bitmap is StretchBlt(), which enables you to stretch or compress the bitmap on the destination DC. Using StretchBlt(), you can make any bitmap fit into any size rectangle, although the image may suffer a little from the scaling operation. StretchBlt()'s signature follows. Table 12-2 lists the function's argument descriptions.

```
BOOL StretchBlt(
    int x,
    int y,
    int nWidth,
    int nHeight,
    CDC* pSrcDC,
    int xSrc,
    int ySrc,
    int nSrcWidth,
    int nSrcHeight,
    DWORD dwRop);
```

Table 12-2 The StretchBlt() function's arguments

Argument	Description
x	The X coordinate of the destination rectangle's upper-left corner
y	The Y coordinate of the destination rectangle's upper-left corner
nWidth	The destination rectangle's width
nHeight	The destination rectangle's height
pSrcDC	A pointer to the DC that contains the bitmap
xSrc	The X coordinate of the bitmap's upper-left corner
ySrc	The Y coordinate of the bitmap's upper-left corner
nSrcWidth	The source rectangle's width
nSrcHeight	The source rectangle's height
dwRop	The specification for the raster operation. For copying a bitmap, use SRCCOPY.

As you can see from the argument list, `StretchBlt()` differs from `BitBlt()` in that `StretchBlt()` specifies the size of both the destination and source rectangles. `StretchBlt()` stretches or reduces the source bitmap so that it fits inside the destination rectangle. For example, if you had a 200x100 pixel bitmap that you wanted to display four times its normal size, you might use a `StretchBlt()` call like the following:

```
windowDC.StretchBlt(0, 0, 800, 400,
    &memoryDC, 0, 0, 200, 100, SRCCOPY);
```

Notice that the specified destination rectangle is four times larger than the specified source rectangle. These values cause Windows to display the bitmap at four times its normal size, as shown in Figure 12-3, which quadruples the size of the bitmap in Figure 12-2.

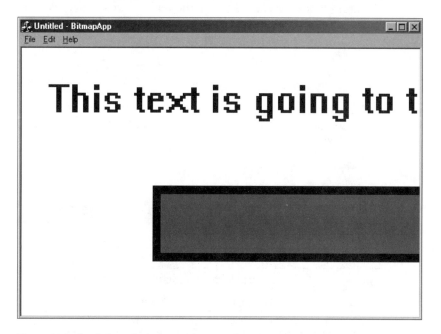

Figure 12-3: A window displaying a bitmap at four times its normal size

Creating the BitmapApp application

On CD-ROM

Now that you know something about creating and displaying device-dependent bitmaps, you can put what you've learned to some practical use. To demonstrate topics already discussed in this chapter, this section builds the BitmapApp application, which allows applications to reproduce their displays more quickly. You can find a complete copy of this application and its source code in the Chapter11\BitmapApp directory of this book's CD-ROM.

There may be times when an application you're writing takes a noticeable amount of time to reproduce its display when the window must be repainted. This problem often arises when the window must repaint many objects in its display.

In a case like this, you can supercharge that sluggish display by holding a duplicate of the window's client area in a bitmap in memory. When the application draws to the screen, it should also draw to the bitmap, keeping the bitmap up-to-date. Then, when the window needs to repaint, the application just copies the bitmap to the screen, rather than reproducing the display by replaying all the drawing commands.

To get some practice in building bitmap applications, as well as to see bitmap programming techniques in action, start up Visual C++ and perform the following steps to build your own version of the BitmapApp application.

1. Select the File menu's New command, and start a new MFC AppWizard project called *BitmapApp* in the Projects window, as shown in Figure 12-4.

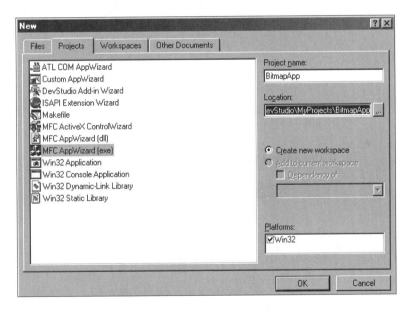

Figure 12-4: The new MFC AppWizard project is called *BitmapApp*.

2. In the MFC AppWizard - Step 1 dialog box, select the Single Document option, as shown in Figure 12-5.

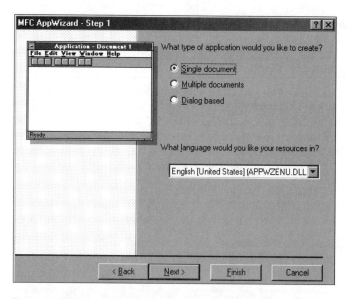

Figure 12-5: The new application will use the single document interface.

3. Click the Next button three times, accepting the default settings in the Step 2 and Step 3 dialog boxes.

4. In the Step 4 dialog box, turn off the Docking Toolbar, Initial Status Bar, and Printing and Print Preview options (see Figure 12-6).

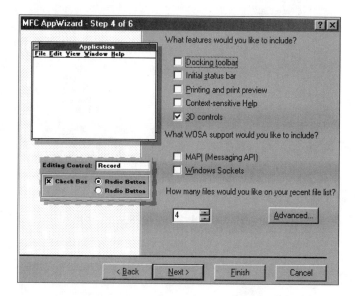

Figure 12-6: The new application will have no toolbar, status bar, or print commands.

5. Click the Next button. Accept the "Yes, please" default option to generate source file comments, and then select the As a Statically Linked Library option in the Step 5 dialog box, as shown in Figure 12-7.

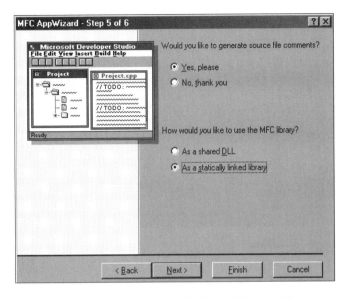

Figure 12-7: The new application will link to MFC's static library.

6. Click the Finish button. The New Project Information dialog box appears and should look like the one shown in Figure 12-8.

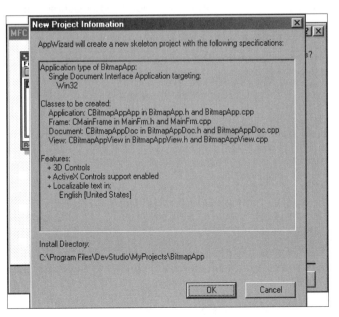

Figure 12-8: The New Project Information dialog box shows a summary of your AppWizard selections.

7. Click the OK button and AppWizard generates the new project.

8. Press Ctrl+W to display ClassWizard, and add the `OnCreate()` function to the `CBitmapAppView` class as shown in Figure 12-9. Make sure you have `CBitmapAppView` selected in the Class Name box.

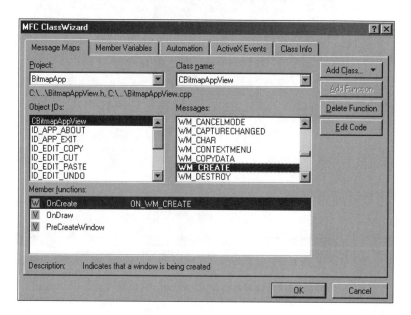

Figure 12-9: ClassWizard adds the `OnCreate()` function to the program.

9. Click the Edit Code button and add the lines shown in Listing 12-2 to `OnCreate()`, right after the `TODO: Add your specialized creation code here` comment:

Listing 12-2: Lines for the `OnCreate()` function

```
CClientDC windowDC(this);
m_bitmap.CreateCompatibleBitmap(&windowDC, 800, 600);
CDC memoryDC;
memoryDC.CreateCompatibleDC(&windowDC);
CBitmap* pOldBitmap =
    memoryDC.SelectObject(&m_bitmap);
CBrush* pWhiteBrush = new CBrush(RGB(255,255,255));
CRect rect(0, 0, 799, 599);
memoryDC.FillRect(rect, pWhiteBrush);
memoryDC.TextOut(10, 10, "BITMAP");
memoryDC.SelectObject(pOldBitmap);
delete pWhiteBrush;
```

10. In the Project Workspace window, right-click the `CBitmapAppView` class and select Add Member Variable from the menu that appears (see Figure 12-10).

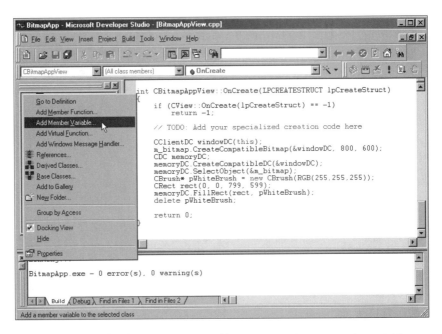

Figure 12-10: The class's pop-up menu enables you to create new member variables.

11. In the Add Member Variable dialog box, create a member variable with the variable type CBitmap and the variable declaration m_bitmap. Select Protected access, as shown in Figure 12-11. Click OK to dismiss the dialog box.

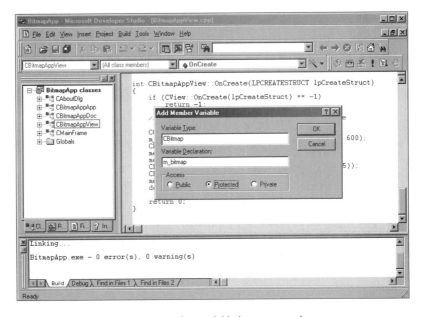

Figure 12-11: The m_bitmap member variable has protected access.

12. Press Ctrl+W to display ClassWizard, and add the `OnLButtonDown()` function to the `CBitmapAppView` class.

13. Click the Edit Code button and add the lines shown in Listing 12-3 to `OnLButtonDown()`, **right after the** `TODO: Add your message handler code here and/or call default` **comment.**

Listing 12-3: Lines for the `OnLButtonDown()` function

```
CClientDC windowDC(this);

CDC memoryDC;
memoryDC.CreateCompatibleDC(&windowDC);
CBitmap* pOldBitmap =
    memoryDC.SelectObject(&m_bitmap);

CBrush* pRedBrush = new CBrush(RGB(255,0,0));
CPen* pThickPen =
    new CPen(PS_SOLID, 3, RGB(0,0,0));

CBrush* pOldMemoryDCBrush =
    memoryDC.SelectObject(pRedBrush);
CBrush* pOldWindowDCBrush =
    windowDC.SelectObject(pRedBrush);
CPen* pOldMemoryDCPen =
    memoryDC.SelectObject(pThickPen);
CPen* pOldWindowDCPen =
    windowDC.SelectObject(pThickPen);

for (int x=0; x<100; ++x)
{
    int x1, y1;

    do
    {
        x1 = rand() % 769;
        y1 = rand() % 569;
    }
    while (y1 < 30);

    CPoint* pNewPoint = new CPoint(x1, y1);
    m_pointArray.Add(pNewPoint);

    memoryDC.Rectangle(x1, y1, x1+30, y1+30);
    windowDC.Rectangle(x1, y1, x1+30, y1+30);
}

memoryDC.SelectObject(pOldMemoryDCBrush);
memoryDC.SelectObject(pOldMemoryDCPen);
memoryDC.SelectObject(pOldBitmap);
windowDC.SelectObject(pOldWindowDCBrush);
windowDC.SelectObject(pOldWindowDCPen);

delete pRedBrush;
delete pThickPen;
```

14. Create a member variable with the variable type `CPtrArray` and the variable declaration `m_pointArray`. Select Protected access. Click OK to dismiss the dialog box.

15. Press Ctrl+W to display ClassWizard, and add the `OnRButtonDown()` function to the `CBitmapAppView` class.

16. Click the Edit Code button, and add the following lines to `OnRButtonDown()`, right after the `TODO: Add your message handler code here and/or call default` comment:

```
m_draw = !m_draw;
Invalidate();
```

17. Create a member variable with the variable type `BOOL` and the variable declaration `m_draw`. Select Protected access. Click OK to dismiss the dialog box.

18. Add the following lines to the `CBitmapAppView` class's constructor, after the `TODO: add construction code here` comment:

```
m_draw = FALSE;
srand((unsigned)time(NULL));
```

19. Add the following lines to the `CBitmapAppView` class's destructor:

```
int size = m_pointArray.GetSize();

for (int x=0; x<size; ++x)
{
    CPoint* point =
        (CPoint*)m_pointArray.GetAt(x);
    delete point;
}

m_pointArray.RemoveAll();
```

20. Add the lines shown in Listing 12-4 to the `CBitmapAppView` class's `OnDraw()` function, after the `TODO: add draw code for native data here` comment:

Listing 12-4: Lines for the `OnDraw()` function

```
if (m_draw)
{
    CBrush* pRedBrush = new CBrush(RGB(255,0,0));
    CPen* pThickPen =
        new CPen(PS_SOLID, 3, RGB(0,0,0));
    CBrush* pOldBrush =
        pDC->SelectObject(pRedBrush);
    CPen* pOldPen = pDC->SelectObject(pThickPen);

    int size = m_pointArray.GetSize();

    for (int x=0; x<size; ++x)
    {
```

```
                    CPoint* point =
                        (CPoint*)m_pointArray.GetAt(x);
                    int x1 = point->x;
                    int y1 = point->y;
                    pDC->Rectangle(x1, y1, x1+30, y1+30);
                }

                pDC->TextOut(10, 10, "NO BITMAP");

                pDC->SelectObject(pOldBrush);
                pDC->SelectObject(pOldPen);
                delete pRedBrush;
                delete pThickPen;
            }
            else
            {
                CDC memoryDC;
                memoryDC.CreateCompatibleDC(pDC);
                CBitmap* pOldBitmap =
                    memoryDC.SelectObject(&m_bitmap);
                pDC->BitBlt(0, 0, 800, 600,
                    &memoryDC, 0, 0, SRCCOPY);
                memoryDC.SelectObject(pOldBitmap);
            }
```

You've now completed BitmapApp. Press Ctrl+F5 to compile and run the application.

Running the BitmapApp application

When you run BitmapApp, the main window appears, displaying the word BITMAP in the upper-left corner. The word BITMAP means that the window is currently displaying a bitmap that the application created in memory. Click the right mouse button to switch the display from the bitmap to the display that the application draws from scratch. When you do, the words NO BITMAP appear in the window, showing that the application is not displaying the bitmap but is redrawing the window from scratch. You'll soon discover that switching between the BITMAP and NO BITMAP displays enables you to see the difference a bitmap can make when it comes time to repaint a window.

Don't see much of a difference yet? That's because the window is only displaying a line of text. To give the application something challenging to display, left-click in the window, which causes 100 randomly placed rectangles to appear on the screen. Keep clicking to fill the window with rectangles, as shown in Figure 12-12. Now when you switch between the BITMAP and NO BITMAP displays, you should see a difference in the redraw rate. Keep adding rectangles. The more you add, the longer it takes the NO BITMAP display to refresh itself, whereas the BITMAP display always pops up instantly.

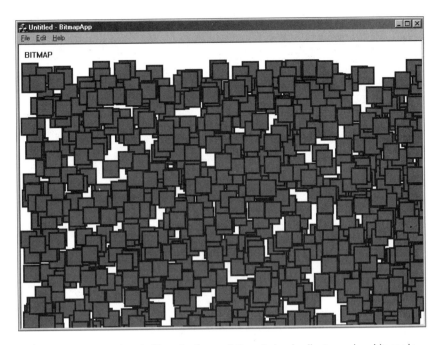

Figure 12-12: BitmapApp holds a duplicate of the window's client area in a bitmap in memory, enabling the application to draw to the screen from the bitmap. This speeds up the recovery process.

Programming with Device-Independent Bitmaps

DIBs are probably the type of bitmaps with which you're most familiar from a user point of view. DIBs are all those files you see with the BMP file name extension in your Windows folder. You've probably even used DIBs as wallpaper on your Windows desktop. DIBs are image files not unlike other types of image files, such as GIF, PCX, TIFF, and JPEG. Unlike many of the other image file types, however, DIBs are rarely compressed, which means that their files tend to be much larger than the files of other types of images.

Because DIBs live in disk files, you need to know their file format before you can load them into your application. A DIB file contains four major parts, each of which contains a structure defined by Windows:

File header	BITMAPFILEHEADER
Bitmap header	BITMAPINFOHEADER
Bitmap color table	RGBQUAD
Bitmap image data	[No formal structure exists for this element as data represents the actual image]

The `BITMAPINFOHEADER` and an array of `RGBQUAD` structures are themselves contained in a `BITMAPINFO` structure. Figure 12-13 illustrates the structure of a DIB file.

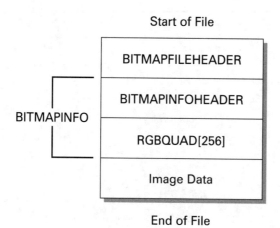

Start of File

| BITMAPFILEHEADER |
| BITMAPINFOHEADER |
| RGBQUAD[256] |
| Image Data |

BITMAPINFO

End of File

Figure 12-13: A DIB file comprises several types of data structures.

Note

Not all DIBs contain a color table. A 24-bit color DIB, for example, has no color table because the color of each pixel in the image is contained in the data for the pixel.

Loading a DIB file

Loading a bitmap file requires not only reading the file from disk, but also using the various structures to calculate important information about the bitmap. Before you can even load the file, however, you must first open the DIB's file. There are several ways to do this, but using MFC's `CFile` class is among the easiest methods of handling file I/O. (You'll learn more about the `CFile` class in Chapter 17, "File Handling.") Following is one method of opening the DIB file:

```
CFile dibFile(fileName, CFile::modeRead);
```

Here, `fileName` is the DIB's file name (including the path) and `modeRead` is the mode in which the file should be opened—in this case, read-only mode.

Loading the file header

At the start of the DIB file is the `BITMAPFILEHEADER` structure, which is defined by Windows as follows. The structure member descriptions follow the declaration:

```
typedef struct tagBITMAPFILEHEADER {
    WORD bfType;
    DWORD bfSize;
    WORD bfReserved1;
```

```
    WORD bfReserved2;
    DWORD bfOffBits;
} BITMAPFILEHEADER;
```

bfType	The ASCII values of the letters BM
bfSize	The bitmap file's size
bfReserved1	Always 0
bfReserved2	Always 0
bfOffBits	The number of bytes from the start of the file to the bitmap's data

After opening the DIB file, you want to load the file's BITMAPFILEHEADER structure, because this structure contains the information you need to load the bitmap. You might handle that task like this:

```
BITMAPFILEHEADER bitmapFileHeader;
dibFile.Read((void*)&bitmapFileHeader,
    sizeof(BITMAPFILEHEADER));
```

Here, you first declare a BITMAPFILEHEADER structure into which you can read the structure's data, and then you call the CFile object's Read() method to read the data from the file into the structure. Read()'s two arguments are the address where to store the data and the number of bytes to read.

Before you process the remainder of the file, you want to make sure that the file is indeed a DIB. You can do this by checking the bfType structure member for the ASCII values of "BM," which, of course, stands for bitmap. You might check for the bitmap ID in an if statement like this:

```
if (bitmapFileHeader.bfType == 0x4d42)
{
    // Process bitmap here
}
```

If the file checks out as a bitmap, you're ready to read the rest of the bitmap file. To do this, you must know the size of the rest of the file. You can calculate this value by getting the size of the entire file and subtracting the size of the BITMAPFILEHEADER structure, which you've already read into memory. The calculation looks something like this:

```
DWORD fileLength = dibFile.GetLength();
DWORD size = fileLength -
    sizeof(BITMAPFILEHEADER);
```

Of course, before you can read in the rest of the bitmap file, you have to have a place to put it. You can solve this problem by allocating a chunk of memory:

```
BYTE* pDib = (BYTE*)GlobalAllocPtr(GMEM_MOVEABLE, size);
```

You'll learn more about memory allocation in Chapter 14, "Memory Management." For now, just know that a call to GlobalAllocPtr() returns a pointer to a block of memory. The function's second argument specifies the size of this block. So, after the above function call, pDib contains the address of a memory block that's just the right size for the remainder of the DIB's file. You might read the remainder of the file like this:

```
dibFile.Read((void*)pDib, size);
dibFile.Close();
```

Loading the bitmap header and color table

You now have the complete DIB in memory. You may recall that the BITMAPINFO structure (which contains the BITMAPINFOHEADER and RGBQUAD structures) follows the BITMAPFILEHEADER structure in the DIB file. Windows defines the BITMAPINFO structure like this:

```
typedef struct tagBITMAPINFO {
    BITMAPINFOHEADER bmiHeader;
    RGBQUAD bmiColors[1];
} BITMAPINFO;
```

Because the buffer to which pDib points contains all the data following the BITMAPFILEHEADER structure, pDib also points to the BITMAPINFO structure. You'll want to save that address like this:

```
BITMAPINFO* pBitmapInfo = (BITMAPINFO*) pDib;
```

Moreover, because the BITMAPINFOHEADER structure is the first member of the BITMAPINFO structure, pDib also contains its address, which you can save like this:

```
BITMAPINFOHEADER* pBitmapInfoHeader =
    (BITMAPINFOHEADER*) pDib;
```

The BITMAPINFOHEADER structure is defined by Windows in the following structure declaration. Table 12-3 lists the structure's members.

```
typedef struct tagBITMAPINFOHEADER{
    DWORD   biSize;
    LONG    biWidth;
    LONG    biHeight;
    WORD    biPlanes;
    WORD    biBitCount;
    DWORD   biCompression;
    DWORD   biSizeImage;
    LONG    biXPelsPerMeter;
    LONG    biYPelsPerMeter;
    DWORD   biClrUsed;
    DWORD   biClrImportant;
} BITMAPINFOHEADER;
```

Table 12-3 BITMAPINFOHEADER's members

Member	Description
biSize	The size of the structure
biWidth	The bitmap's width
biHeight	The bitmap's height
biPlanes	Number of bit planes; always 1
biBitCount	The number of bits per pixel
biCompression	The image's compression type, usually set at 0 for none
biSizeImage	The size of the image in bytes
biXPelsPerMeter	The target device's horizontal resolution in pixels per meter
biYPelsPerMeter	The target device's vertical resolution in pixels
biClrUsed	The number of colors actually used by the bitmap; 0 = all colors used
biClrImportant	The number of important colors; 0 = all colors important

Because the DIB's color table follows the BITMAPINFOHEADER structure, you can calculate its address by adding the size of the BITMAPINFOHEADER to the address stored in pDib:

```
RGBQUAD* pRGB = (RGBQUAD*)(pDib +
    pBitmapInfoHeader->biSize);
```

Windows then defines the RGBQUAD structure as follows:

```
typedef struct tagRGBQUAD {
    BYTE        rgbBlue;
    BYTE        rgbGreen;
    BYTE        rgbRed;
    BYTE        rgbReserved;
} RGBQUAD;
```

The first three members of this structure hold the red, green, and blue color values, respectively, for the color being defined. The fourth member is always 0. The DIB's color table contains one RGBQUAD structure for every color in the bitmap: A color table for a 256-color bitmap is a 256-element array of RGBQUAD structures.

At this point, you have pointers to the BITMAPFILEHEADER, BITMAPINFO, and BITMAPINFOHEADER structures, as well as a pointer to the bitmap's color table. You now need the address of the bitmap's image data. To get this address you need to know the size of the DIB's color table, a value that's not directly included in any of the DIB structures. You do know, however, that each color is represented by an RGBQUAD structure. If you can get the number of colors, you can get the size of the color table by multiplying the number of colors by the size of the RGBQUAD structure. You'll learn more about the RGBQUAD structure later in this chapter, when you study color palettes.

Although the biClrUsed structure specifies the number of colors in the DIB, a value of 0 means all the colors are used. So, biClrUsed may or may not be useful in determining the number of colors. If biClrUsed contains a value other than 0, you're home free. However, if biClrUsed is 0, you're going to have to use the biBitCount member to determine the number of colors.

The biBitCount member tells you the number of bits used to represent each pixel of the image. In images of 256 colors or less, these pixel values represent an index into the color table. (If a DIB contains more than 256 colors, it doesn't have a color table.) That is, if a pixel's value is 25, Windows will find the pixel's color in the twenty-fifth entry in the DIB's color table. So, for example, if a pixel uses eight bits, the pixel can be one of 256 colors. (An 8-bit value must be in the range of 0 to 255).

You can see now how you can get the number of colors from the bit count. If the bit count is 1, the image uses only two colors; if the bit count is 4, the image uses 16 colors; and if the bit count is 8, the image uses 256 colors. Anything over 256 colors is not relevant to loading the bitmap, because in that case you don't have to deal with a color table at all. So, to determine the number of colors in a DIB, you might use code like that shown in Listing 12-5.

Listing 12-5: Calculating the number of colors in a DIB

```
int numberOfColors;

if ((pBitmapInfoHeader->biClrUsed == 0) &&
    (pBitmapInfoHeader->biBitCount < 9))
{
    switch (pBitmapInfoHeader->biBitCount)
    {
        case 1: numberOfColors = 2; break;
        case 4: numberOfColors = 16; break;
        case 8: numberOfColors = 256;
    }
}
else
    numberOfColors =
        (int) pBitmapInfoHeader->biClrUsed;

if (pBitmapInfoHeader->biClrUsed == 0)
    pBitmapInfoHeader->biClrUsed = numberOfColors;
```

Now you're getting somewhere! With the number of colors in hand, you can figure out the size of the color table and so calculate where the bitmap image data starts. You do this by adding the size of the color table to the pDib pointer:

```
DWORD clrTableSize = numberOfColors * sizeof(RGBQUAD);
BYTE* pData = pDib + pBitmapInfoHeader->biSize
    + clrTableSize;
```

Often, folks who create bitmap files leave the BITMAPINFOHEADER structure's biSizeImage member set to 0. You can fill in that value by calculating the image size in your program, which you can do by multiplying the image's width and height. For example:

```
if (pBitmapInfoHeader->biSizeImage == 0)
{
    DWORD height = pBitmapInfoHeader->biHeight;
    DWORD width = pBitmapInfoHeader->biHeight;
    pBitmapInfoHeader->biSizeImage = height * width;
}
```

And that's all there is to it. Now that you know all the details of loading a bitmap into memory, you'll use that knowledge to design a class that manages this sticky task for you.

The custom CDib class

Sure, the process of loading a bitmap is complicated. The good news is that you can write the code for managing a bitmap and then use it again and again as needed for any bitmap. In fact, you can place the code into a class and load a bitmap simply by creating an instance of the class. The really good news is that your humble author has already written just such a class, which you can see in Listings 12-6 and 12-7. Listing 12-6 is the class's header file, whereas as Listing 12-7 is the class's implementation file.

Listing 12-6: The CDib class's header file

```
#ifndef __CDIB_H
#define __CDIB_H

class CDib : public CObject
{
protected:
    char m_fileName[256];
    RGBQUAD* m_pRGB;
    BYTE* m_pData;
    UINT m_numberOfColors;
    BOOL m_valid;
    BITMAPFILEHEADER* m_pBitmapFileHeader;
    BITMAPINFOHEADER* m_pBitmapInfoHeader;
    BITMAPINFO* m_pBitmapInfo;

public:
    CDib(const char* dibFileName);
    ~CDib();

    char* GetFileName();
    BOOL IsValid();
    DWORD GetSize();
    UINT GetWidth();
    UINT GetHeight();
    UINT GetNumberOfColors();
    RGBQUAD* GetRGB();
    BYTE* GetData();
```

```
    BITMAPINFO* GetInfo();

protected:
    void LoadFile();

};

#endif
```

Listing 12-7: The CDib class's implementation file

```
#include "stdafx.h"
#include "cdib.h"
#include "windowsx.h"

CDib::CDib(const char* dibFileName)
{
    strcpy(m_fileName, dibFileName);
    LoadFile();
}

CDib::~CDib()
{
    GlobalFreePtr(m_pBitmapInfo);
}

void CDib::LoadFile()
{
    CFile dibFile(m_fileName, CFile::modeRead);

    BITMAPFILEHEADER bitmapFileHeader;
    dibFile.Read((void*)&bitmapFileHeader,
        sizeof(BITMAPFILEHEADER));

    if (bitmapFileHeader.bfType == 0x4d42)
    {
        DWORD fileLength = dibFile.GetLength();
        DWORD size = fileLength -
            sizeof(BITMAPFILEHEADER);
        BYTE* pDib =
            (BYTE*)GlobalAllocPtr(GMEM_MOVEABLE, size);
        dibFile.Read((void*)pDib, size);
        dibFile.Close();

        m_pBitmapInfo = (BITMAPINFO*) pDib;
        m_pBitmapInfoHeader = (BITMAPINFOHEADER*) pDib;
        m_pRGB = (RGBQUAD*)(pDib +
            m_pBitmapInfoHeader->biSize);
        int m_numberOfColors = GetNumberOfColors();
        if (m_pBitmapInfoHeader->biClrUsed == 0)
            m_pBitmapInfoHeader->biClrUsed =
                m_numberOfColors;
        DWORD colorTableSize = m_numberOfColors *
            sizeof(RGBQUAD);
        m_pData = pDib + m_pBitmapInfoHeader->biSize
            + colorTableSize;
        m_pBitmapInfoHeader->biSizeImage = GetSize();
```

```
        m_valid = TRUE;
    }
    else
    {
        m_valid = FALSE;
        AfxMessageBox("This isn't a bitmap file!");
    }
}

BOOL CDib::IsValid()
{
    return m_valid;
}

char* CDib::GetFileName()
{
    return m_fileName;
}

UINT CDib::GetWidth()
{
    return (UINT) m_pBitmapInfoHeader->biWidth;
}

UINT CDib::GetHeight()
{
    return (UINT) m_pBitmapInfoHeader->biHeight;
}

DWORD CDib::GetSize()
{
    if (m_pBitmapInfoHeader->biSizeImage != 0)
        return m_pBitmapInfoHeader->biSizeImage;
    else
    {
        DWORD height = (DWORD) GetHeight();
        DWORD width = (DWORD) GetWidth();
        return height * width;
    }
}

UINT CDib::GetNumberOfColors()
{
    int numberOfColors;

    if ((m_pBitmapInfoHeader->biClrUsed == 0) &&
        (m_pBitmapInfoHeader->biBitCount < 9))
    {
        switch (m_pBitmapInfoHeader->biBitCount)
        {
            case 1: numberOfColors = 2; break;
            case 4: numberOfColors = 16; break;
            case 8: numberOfColors = 256;
        }
    }
    else
        numberOfColors =
```

```
            (int) m_pBitmapInfoHeader->biClrUsed;

    return numberOfColors;
}

BYTE* CDib::GetData()
{
    return m_pData;
}

RGBQUAD* CDib::GetRGB()
{
    return m_pRGB;
}

BITMAPINFO* CDib::GetInfo()
{
    return m_pBitmapInfo;
}
```

Using the CDib class couldn't be easier. First you create an object of the class:

```
CDib* pBitmap = new CDib("c:\Images\MyBitmap.bmp");
```

The constructor's single argument is a string containing the bitmap's path and file name. That single line is all you need to not only create the CDib object, but also to load the DIB file and set all the appropriate pointers. And you thought loading a bitmap was hard.

To ensure that the bitmap file is valid, call the class's IsValid() member function:

```
BOOL dibOkay = pBitmap->IsValid();
```

The remaining CDib member functions give you access to the information you need to display a DIB. Table 12-4 describes each of the functions.

Table 12-4 The remaining CDib member functions

Function	Description
GetData()	Gets a pointer to the DIB's image data
GetFileName()	Gets the bitmap's file name
GetHeight()	Gets the image's height
GetInfo()	Gets a pointer to the DIB's BITMAPINFO structure
GetNumberOfColors()	Gets the number of colors used in the image
GetRGB()	Gets a pointer to the DIB's color table, or NULL if there is no color table
GetSize()	Gets the image's size in bytes
GetWidth()	Gets the image's width
IsValid()	Returns TRUE if the CDib object is valid

Displaying a DIB

Once you have your bitmap initialized and loaded, you'll want to copy it to the screen. Copying a DIB to the screen is different from copying a DDB to the screen. One big difference is that you don't need to select the DIB into a memory device context. You can copy the image's data directly to the screen. Another big difference is the function you use to copy a DIB. Rather than use `BitBlt()`, as you do with a DDB, you use `StretchDIBits()` to display a DIB. That function's signature is provided below, followed by its arguments in Table 12-5.

```
int StretchDIBits(
    HDC hdc,
    int XDest,
    int YDest,
    int nDestWidth,
    int nDestHeight,
    int XSrc,
    int YSrc,
    int nSrcWidth,
    int nSrcHeight,
    CONST VOID *lpBits,
    CONST BITMAPINFO *lpBitsInfo,
    UINT iUsage,
    DWORD dwRop
);
```

Table 12-5 `StretchDIBits()`**'s arguments**

Argument	Description
hdc	Handle of the destination DC
XDest	X coordinate of the destination rectangle's upper-left corner
Ydest	Y coordinate of the destination rectangle's upper-left corner
nDestWidth	Width of the destination rectangle
nDestHeight	Height of the destination rectangle
XSrc	X coordinate of the source rectangle's upper-left corner
YSrc	Y coordinate of the source rectangle's upper-left corner
nSrcWidth	Width of the source rectangle
nSrcHeight	Height of the source rectangle
lpBits	Pointer to the bitmap's image data
lpBitsInfo	Pointer to the bitmap's BITMAPINFO structure
iUsage	Color table usage, usually DIB_RGB_COLORS
dwRop	Raster operation; determines how source and destination pixels are combined

As you can see, StretchDIBits() is similar to BitBlt(), but the source bitmap doesn't need to supply a memory context handle. Instead, the source bitmap supplies the address of its image data, as well as the address of its BITMAPINFO structure. To load and display a bitmap as a CDib object, you might use code like that shown in Listing 12-8.

Listing 12-8: Loading and displaying a bitmap

```
CDib* pBitmap = new CDib("mybitmap.bmp");

if (!pBitmap->IsValid())
    MessageBox("Couldn't find mybitmap.bmp.",
        "Error", MB_OK | MB_ICONEXCLAMATION);
else
{
    BYTE* pBitmapData = pBitmap->GetData();
    LPBITMAPINFO pBitmapInfo = pBitmap->GetInfo();

    CClientDC windowDC(this);
    StretchDIBits(windowDC.m_hDC, 0, 0, 500, 300,
        0, 0, 500, 300, pBitmapData, pBitmapInfo,
        DIB_RGB_COLORS, SRCCOPY);
}
```

In Listing 12-8, the program first creates a CDib object from the mybitmap.bmp file. The program then calls the bitmap object's IsValid() member function to make sure that the bitmap object is OK to use, displaying an error message box if IsValid() returns FALSE. If the bitmap object was created successfully, a call to the object's GetData() function gets a pointer to the bitmap's image data, and a call to GetInfo() gets a pointer to the bitmap's BITMAPINFO structure. Both of these pointers are used as arguments in the call to StretchDIBits(), which displays the bitmap.

Managing palettes

Although the previous section discusses a general procedure for loading and displaying a bitmap, one important detail was left out: palettes. Any DIB with 256 or less colors carries with it a color palette. In order to display the DIB correctly, you must give the DIB's color palette to Windows. Because Windows can run many applications concurrently, dealing with palettes is trickier than you might expect. This is because any of the running applications may need to display images using a color palette at the same time. Since no two color palettes are likely to be exactly alike (unless they were created alike by design), how can Windows show two or more applications using two or more different palettes? In this section, you get the answer to that question.

Logical palettes

Windows can display only so many colors at a time. For example, if you're running your system in 256-color mode, Windows can display only 256 colors. These 256 colors can be any 256 colors you like (well, except for the twenty colors Windows reserves for its own use), but 256 colors is the limit that the screen can display in this mode. Windows has a *system palette*, which holds the 256 colors that the system can currently display. In most cases, applications need only twenty of these colors to display their windows and data in color. However, when you start displaying more complex graphics like bitmaps, twenty colors doesn't cut it.

Any application that displays complex images must create a *logical palette*, which is similar to the system palette except that the logical palette belongs only to one application. Every running application can create and store its own logical palette. When the application is the topmost window, it gives its logical palette to Windows, which loads the application's colors into the system palette. Then, the application can display its graphics correctly. When the user switches windows, the new topmost application gives Windows its logical palette, which Windows loads into the system palette.

There is one minor complication. When an application with a palette loses its focus (call this the background application) and a new application (call this the foreground application) gives Windows its logical palette, Windows still needs to display the image in the background application as best as it can. Windows does this by matching the background application's colors as closely as possible to the foreground application's colors. Then, although the background application's display may not be perfect, it'll usually at least be close. However, if the foreground application's logical palette is significantly different from the background application's logical palette, the background application's display will suffer a great deal.

An application creates a logical palette by loading color values into a `LOGPALETTE` structure and calling the `CreatePalette()` function. A program might define its `LOGPALETTE` structure like this:

```
struct
{
    WORD Version;
    WORD NumberOfEntries;
    PALETTEENTRY aEntries[256];
} palette = { 0x300, 256 };
```

The structure's three members are a version number (usually `0x300`), the number of colors in the palette, and an array of `PALETTEENTRY` structures. There is one element for each color. Windows defines the `PALETTEENTRY` structure like this:

```
typedef struct tagPALETTEENTRY {
    BYTE peRed;
    BYTE peGreen;
    BYTE peBlue;
    BYTE peFlags;
} PALETTEENTRY
```

The structure's first three members are the values for the color's red, green, and blue components. The last member contains a flag that specifies how Windows should handle the color being defined. Usually, you'll just put a 0 in this member and leave the color management to Windows.

To initialize a palette from a `CDib` object that has loaded a DIB file, you might use code like that shown in Listing 12-9.

Listing 12-9: Loading palette colors from a `CDib` object

```
LPRGBQUAD pRGBTable = pBitmap->GetRGB();
UINT numberOfColors = pBitmap->GetNumberOfColors();

for(UINT x=0; x<numberOfColors; ++x)
{
    palette.aEntries[x].peRed =
        pRGBTable[x].rgbRed;
    palette.aEntries[x].peGreen =
        pRGBTable[x].rgbGreen;
    palette.aEntries[x].peBlue =
        pRGBTable[x].rgbBlue;
    palette.aEntries[x].peFlags = 0;
}
```

In the above listing, `pBitmap` is a pointer to a valid `CDib` object. The program copies the color values from the DIB's color table (pointed to by `pRGBTable`) to the members of each `PALETTEENTRY` structure.

After initializing the `LOGPALETTE` structure, you create the palette by calling the aptly named `CreatePalette()` Windows API function, which returns a handle to the newly created palette (or `NULL` if the function call fails):

```
HPALETTE hPalette =
    ::CreatePalette((LPLOGPALETTE)&palette);
```

Finally, you can give the new palette to Windows. Windows programmers call this process *realizing the palette*. To realize the bitmap's palette, you first select the new palette into the DC, and then you call the `RealizePalette()` function. The entire process looks like this:

```
HPALETTE hOldPalette =
    SelectPalette(pDC->m_hDC, hPalette, FALSE);
RealizePalette(pDC->m_hDC);

// Display bitmap here.

SelectPalette(pDC->m_hDC, hOldPalette, FALSE);
DeleteObject(hPalette);
```

Notice that when the program is through with the palette, it selects the old palette back into the DC and calls `DeleteObject()` to get rid of the now unneeded palette.

Managing palette changes

When an application realizes its palette, Windows sends messages to other currently running applications, giving them a chance to realize their own palettes as well. It's when a background application realizes its palette that Windows maps the application's palette to the new system palette. Your application must handle two messages—`WM_PALETTECHANGED` and `WM_QUERYNEWPALETTE`—if it is to work properly under Windows 98.

Windows sends the WM_PALETTECHANGED message whenever an application changes the system palette. This message signals all applications to realize their palettes and so be remapped to the new palette. If an application fails to respond to the WM_PALETTECHANGED message, the palette change may corrupt the application's display beyond what is reasonable.

Windows sends the WM_QUERYNEWPALETTE message to an application when the application becomes the topmost window. This message signals the application that it should realize its palette in order to take over the system palette. The application that receives and responds to WM_QUERYNEWPALETTE will have the best display, because all of its colors will be available in the system palette.

In an MFC program, you respond to these important palette messages in the main window's class, which is usually called CMainFrame. Use ClassWizard to add the OnPaletteChanged() and OnQueryNewPalette() functions to the class. In each function, you must realize the application's current logical palette. How you do this depends on how your application is set up. If you normally realize the palette in the application's OnDraw() function, you can just call the view window's Invalidate() function, which causes MFC to call OnDraw().

However, in the case of OnPaletteChanged(), you must make sure your application can differentiate between itself and another application changing the palette, as you don't want it to respond to its own message. If it does, the application will end up in an infinite loop as it changes its palette, generating another WM_PALETTECHANGED message. To determine whether it was the application's own view window that changed the palette, have your application check the pFocusWnd pointer that's passed to the function against a pointer to the view window. If they are the same, write your program so it doesn't realize the application's palette. Listing 12-10 shows the source code for typical OnPaletteChanged() and OnQueryNewPalette() functions.

Listing 12-10: Managing palette changes in an MFC program

```
void CMainFrame::OnPaletteChanged(CWnd* pFocusWnd)
{
    CFrameWnd::OnPaletteChanged(pFocusWnd);

    // TODO: Add your message handler code here

    CView* pView = GetActiveView();
    if (pFocusWnd != pView)
        pView->Invalidate();
}

BOOL CMainFrame::OnQueryNewPalette()
{
    // TODO: Add your message handler code here
    //    and/or call default

    CView* pView = GetActiveView();
    pView->Invalidate();
```

```
        return CFrameWnd::OnQueryNewPalette();
}
```

In the `OnPaletteChanged()` function in Listing 12-10, the program first gets a pointer to the application's view window. It then compares this pointer to the pointer that represents the window that generated the palette change. Only if they aren't the same window does the program invalidate the window, which causes it to realize its palette. In the `OnQueryNewPalette()` function, the program simply gets a pointer to the view window, and calls the window's `Invalidate()` function to force the window to redraw its display and realize its palette.

Creating the BitmapApp2 application

On CD-ROM

Now that you've learned a little about device-independent bitmap programming, you can apply that knowledge to building a simple bitmap viewer. Perform the following steps to create your copy of the BitmapApp2 application. These steps will not only give you additional experience with Visual C++'s tools, but also show you, step-by-step, how to manage DIBs in a full-fledged application. If, however, you'd rather not build the application, you can find a complete copy in the Chapter12\BitmapApp2 directory of this book's CD-ROM.

1. Select the File menu's New command and start a new MFC AppWizard project called *BitmapApp2* in the Projects window.

2. In the MFC AppWizard - Step 1 dialog box, select the Single Document option.

3. Click the Next button three times, accepting the default settings in the Step 2 and Step 3 dialog boxes.

4. In the Step 4 dialog box, turn off the Docking Toolbar, Initial Status Bar, and Printing and Print Preview options.

5. Click the Next button and then select the As a Statically Linked Library option in the Step 5 dialog box.

6. Click the Finish button. The New Project Information dialog box appears.

7. Click the OK button and AppWizard generates the new project.

8. Copy the CDib.h and CDib.cpp files from the Chapter12\BitmapApp2 folder of this book's CD-ROM to your BitmapApp2 project's folder.

9. Select the Project menu's Add to Project command, and then select Files from the submenu that appears, as shown in Figure 12-14. You use the File command to add new files to your project.

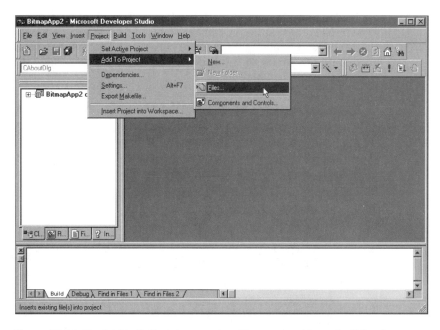

Figure 12-14: The Add to Project command enables you to add non-AppWizard-generated files to your project.

10. Select the cdib.cpp file in the Insert Files Into Project dialog box (see Figure 12-15), and click the OK button. Visual C++ adds the file to the project.

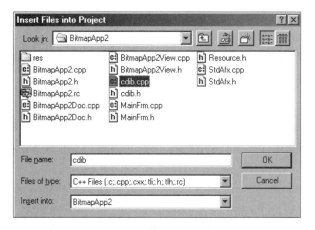

Figure 12-15: Adding the cdib.cpp file to the project gives the program access to the `CDib` class.

You've now completed the basic BitmapApp2 project. You can, if you like, compile and run the project by pressing Ctrl+F5 on your keyboard. However, the program doesn't do much at this point. You still have to modify the default resources and add the source code needed to give the application bitmap-loading capabilities.

Customizing the application's resources

Now that you have the basic project set up, you can work on the application's resources. In this section, you'll add menu commands and a dialog box, as well as modify a few of the default resources. Just perform the steps below to complete this portion of the BitmapApp2 application.

1. Select the ResourceView tab in the project workspace window, and then bring up the application's accelerators in the resource editor, as shown in Figure 12-16.

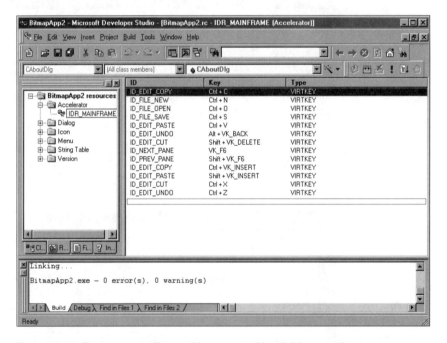

Figure 12-16: The resource editor enables you to add and delete accelerators.

2. Delete all the accelerators except ID_FILE_OPEN (see Figure 12-17).

3. Load the application's About dialog box into the editor, and change the copyright string to read Copyright © 1998 by IDG Books Worldwide, as shown in Figure 12-18.

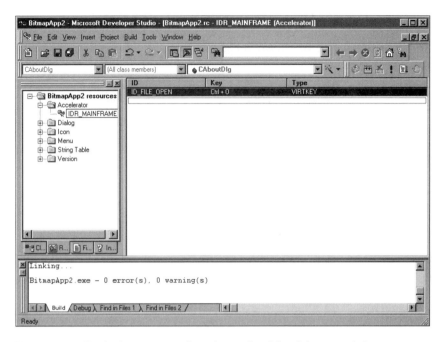

Figure 12-17: Here's the resource editor after you've deleted the unneeded accelerators.

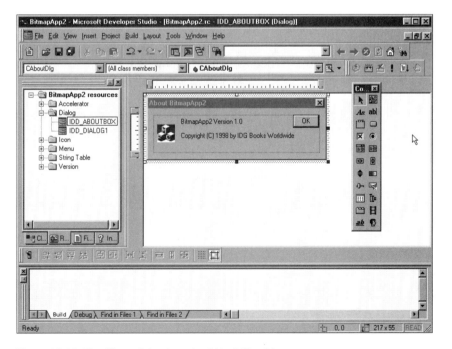

Figure 12-18: The About dialog box should look like this.

4. Load the application's menu bar into the editor and delete the Edit menu. Also, delete all commands from the File menu except Open and Exit, as shown in Figure 12-19.

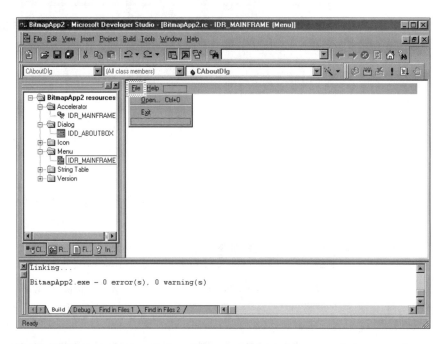

Figure 12-19: The menu bar displayed after you've deleted the unneeded commands

5. Create a Scale menu in the Menu Item Properties dialog box and give it one item called Set Scaling... with an ID of ID_SCALE_SETSCALING, as shown in Figure 12-20.

6. Select the Insert menu's Resource command and add a new dialog box to the resources.

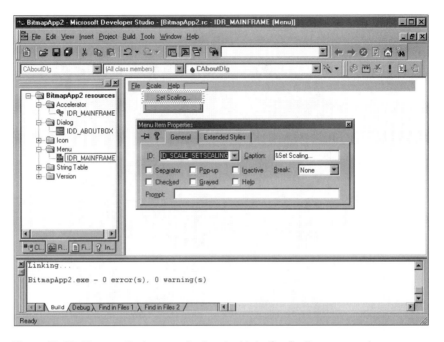

Figure 12-20: The new Scale menu displayed with its Set Scaling command

7. Modify the Set Scaling dialog box so that it looks like the one shown in Figure 12-21. Keep the default ID of IDC_EDIT1 for the edit control.

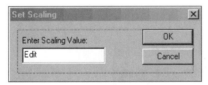

Figure 12-21: Here's the new Set Scaling dialog box.

8. Double-click the new dialog box. Select the Create a New Class option in the Adding a Class dialog box (see Figure 12-22), and click OK.

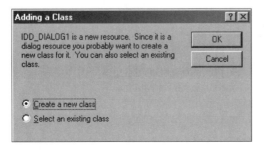

Figure 12-22: This dialog box is the first step of creating a new dialog class.

9. In the New Class dialog box, type `CScaleDlg` into the Name box (see Figure 12-23), and click OK.

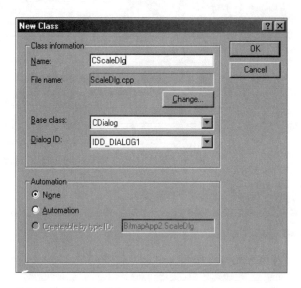

Figure 12-23: This dialog box enables you to specify information about the new class, including its class name, file name, and base class.

10. In the MFC ClassWizard property sheet, select the Member Variables tab. Double-click the `IDC_EDIT1` control ID, and associate the `m_scale` variable with the control. The `m_scale` variable should have the variable type float, as shown in Figure 12-24.

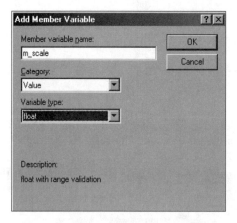

Figure 12-24: The Add Member Variable dialog box allows you to associate variables with the dialog box's controls.

11. Click OK, and then enter 1 into the Minimum Value box and 5 into the Maximum Value box (see Figure 12-25). Click OK to dismiss ClassWizard.

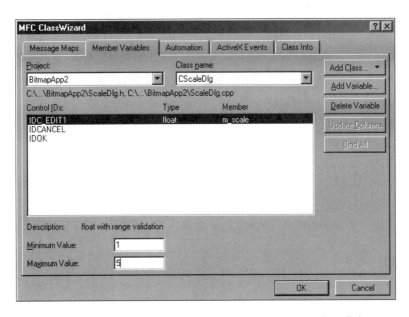

Figure 12-25: The user must enter a value between 1 and 5 into the edit boxes.

The application's resources are now complete. You should save your work at this point, by selecting the File menu's Save All command. If you like, you can compile and run the program by pressing Ctrl+F5. If you run the program, you'll see the new menu bar, as well as be able to select the Help menu's About BitmapApp2 command to call up the application's modified About dialog box.

Adding source code

The last thing you must do to finish the BitmapApp2 application is to add the functions and source code required to give the application bitmap-loading and -displaying capabilities. Follow the next set of steps to accomplish that task.

1. Click the ClassView tab of the project workspace window, and then right-click the CBitmapApp2Doc class. A menu will appear.

2. Select Add Member Variable from the menu, and then define the variable `m_pBitmap` in the Add Member Variable dialog box as shown in Figure 12-26. The variable's type should be `CDib*` and the access should be Public. Click OK to dismiss the dialog box, and Visual C++ adds the new member variable to the class.

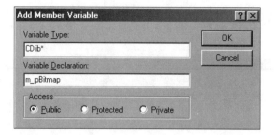

Figure 12-26: BitmapApp2's document class has a single member variable that holds a pointer to the CDib object.

3. Load the BitmapApp2Doc.h header file and add the following line near the top of the file, right after the line `#endif // _MSC_VER >= 1000` that's already there. This line enables the document class to access the CDib class.

```
#include "CDib.h"
```

4. Load the BitmapApp2Doc.cpp file and add the following line to the CBitmapApp2Doc class's constructor, right after the `TODO: add one-time construction code here` comment. This line ensures that the bitmap object's pointer starts off NULL.

```
m_pBitmap = NULL;
```

5. Press Ctrl+W to display ClassWizard, and add the `OnFileOpen()` function to the class, as shown in Figure 12-27. (Make sure you have CBitmapApp2Doc selected in the Class Name box.) When the user selects the Open command on the File menu, the program receives a `ID_FILE_OPEN` message, which causes MFC to call the `OnFileOpen()` function.

6. Click the Edit Code button and add the lines shown in Listing 12-11 to the new `OnFileOpen()` function, right after the `TODO: Add your command handler code here` comment.

Listing 12-11: Lines for the `OnFileOpen()` function

```
CFileDialog dlg(TRUE, "bmp", "*.bmp");
int result = dlg.DoModal();

if (result == IDOK)
{
    CString path = dlg.GetPathName();
    m_pBitmap = new CDib(path);
    if (m_pBitmap->IsValid())
        SetTitle(path);
    else
        DeleteContents();
}

UpdateAllViews(0);
```

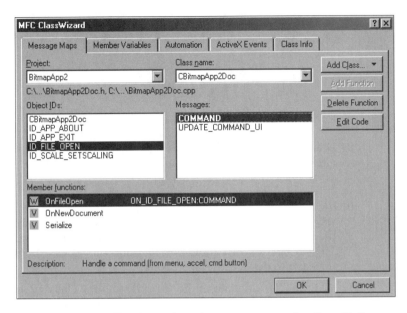

Figure 12-27: ClassWizard associates the `OnFileOpen()` function with the `ID_FILE_OPEN` menu command.

7. Use ClassWizard to override the `DeleteContents()` function in the `CBitmapApp2Doc` class, as shown in Figure 12-28.

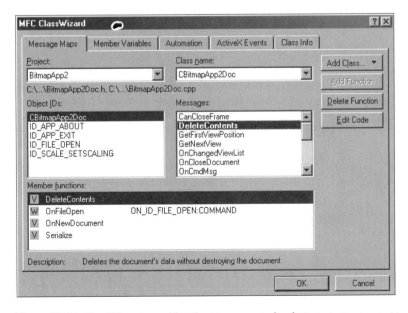

Figure 12-28: ClassWizard overrides the `CDocument` class's `DeleteContents()` function in the `CBitmapApp2Doc` class.

8. Click the Edit Code button and add the following lines to the `DeleteContents()` function, right after the `TODO: Add your specialized code here and/or call the base class` comment:

```
if (m_pBitmap)
{
    delete m_pBitmap;
    m_pBitmap = NULL;
}
```

9. Load the BitmapApp2View file and add the following line near the top, after the line #include "BitmapApp2View.h" that's already there:

```
#include "ScaleDlg.h"
```

10. Right-click the CBitmapApp2View class in the project workspace window, select Add Member Variable from the menu that appears, and then define the variable `m_scale` in the Add Member Variable dialog box. The variable's type should be `float` and the access should be Protected. Click OK to dismiss the dialog box.

11. Add the following line to the `CBitmapApp2View` class's constructor, right after the `TODO: add construction code here` comment:

```
m_scale = 1.0;
```

12. Add the lines shown in Listing 12-12 to the `CBitmapApp2View` class's `OnDraw()` function, right after the `TODO: add draw code for native data here` comment:

Listing 12-12: Lines for the `OnDraw()` function

```
CDib* pBitmap = pDoc->m_pBitmap;

if (pBitmap)
{
    BYTE* pBitmapData = pBitmap->GetData();
    LPBITMAPINFO pBitmapInfo = pBitmap->GetInfo();
    int bitmapHeight = pBitmap->GetHeight();
    int bitmapWidth = pBitmap->GetWidth();
    int scaledWidth = (int)(bitmapWidth * m_scale);
    int scaledHeight = (int)(bitmapHeight * m_scale);

    if (pBitmap->GetRGB()) // Has a color table
    {
        HPALETTE hPalette =
            CreateBitmapPalette(pBitmap);
        HPALETTE hOldPalette =
            ::SelectPalette(pDC->m_hDC, hPalette, FALSE);
        ::RealizePalette(pDC->m_hDC);

        StretchDIBits(pDC->m_hDC,
            10, 10, scaledWidth, scaledHeight,
            0, 0, bitmapWidth, bitmapHeight,
            pBitmapData, pBitmapInfo,
            DIB_RGB_COLORS, SRCCOPY);
```

```
            ::SelectPalette(pDC->m_hDC, hOldPalette, FALSE);
            ::DeleteObject(hPalette);
    }
    else
        StretchDIBits(pDC->m_hDC,
            10, 10, scaledWidth, scaledHeight,
            0, 0, bitmapWidth, bitmapHeight,
            pBitmapData, pBitmapInfo,
            DIB_RGB_COLORS, SRCCOPY);


}
```

13. Right-click the CBitmapApp2View class in the project workspace
    window, select Add Member Function from the menu that appears,
    and then define the variable `CreateBitmapPalette()` function in the
    Add Member Function dialog box as shown in Figure 12-29. The
    function's type should be `HPALETTE`, its signature should be
    `CreateBitmapPalette(CDib* pBitmap)`, and the access should be
    Protected. Click OK to dismiss the dialog box.

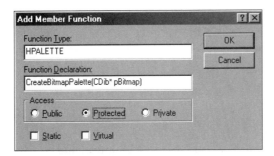

Figure 12-29: BitmapApp2's view class gets a new function called
`CreateBitmapPalette()`.

14. Add the lines shown in Listing 12-13 to the `CreateBitmapPalette()`
    function.

Listing 12-13: Lines for the `CreateBitmapPalette()` **function**

```
struct
{
    WORD Version;
    WORD NumberOfEntries;
    PALETTEENTRY aEntries[256];
} palette = { 0x300, 256 };

LPRGBQUAD pRGBTable = pBitmap->GetRGB();
UINT numberOfColors = pBitmap->GetNumberOfColors();

for(UINT x=0; x<numberOfColors; ++x)
{
    palette.aEntries[x].peRed =
        pRGBTable[x].rgbRed;
    palette.aEntries[x].peGreen =
```

```
                pRGBTable[x].rgbGreen;
        palette.aEntries[x].peBlue =
                pRGBTable[x].rgbBlue;
        palette.aEntries[x].peFlags = 0;
    }

    HPALETTE hPalette =
        ::CreatePalette((LPLOGPALETTE)&palette);

    return hPalette;
```

15. Use ClassWizard to add the `OnScaleSetscaling()` function to the `CBitmapApp2View` class.

16. Click the Edit Code button and add the lines shown in Listing 12-14 to the `OnScaleSetscaling()` function, right after the `TODO: Add your command handler code here` comment.

Listing 12-14: Lines for the `OnScaleSetscaling()` function

```
CScaleDlg dlg(this);
dlg.m_scale = m_scale;

int result = dlg.DoModal();

if (result == IDOK)
{
    m_scale = dlg.m_scale;
    Invalidate();
}
```

17. Use ClassWizard to add the `OnPaletteChanged()` function (which responds to the `WM_PALETTECHANGED` Windows message) to the `CMainFrame` class. Make sure that you select CMainFrame in ClassWizard's Class Name box.

18. Click the Edit Code button and add the following lines to the `OnPaletteChanged()` function, right after the `TODO: Add your command handler code here` comment:

```
CView* pView = GetActiveView();
if (pFocusWnd != pView)
    pView->Invalidate();
```

19. Use ClassWizard to add the `OnQueryNewPalette()` function (which responds to the `WM_QUERYNEWPALETTE` Windows message) to the `CMainFrame` class.

20. Click the Edit Code button, and add the following lines to the `OnQueryNewPalette()` function, right after the `TODO: Add your command handler code here and/or call default` comment:

```
CView* pView = GetActiveView();
pView->Invalidate();
```

You've now completed BitmapApp2. To compile and run the application, press Ctrl+F5 on your keyboard.

Running the BitmapApp2 application

When you run BitmapApp2, the application's window appears. Select the File menu's Open command and use the Open dialog box to select and load a bitmap file. There are four bitmaps included with the program: 1-bit.bmp, 4-bit.bmp, 8-bit.bmp, and 24-bit.bmp. These files contain 2-color, 16-color, 256-color, and True-Color images, respectively. You can also use the application to load and display any valid bitmap file. Figure 12-30 shows the application displaying the 24-bit.bmp file.

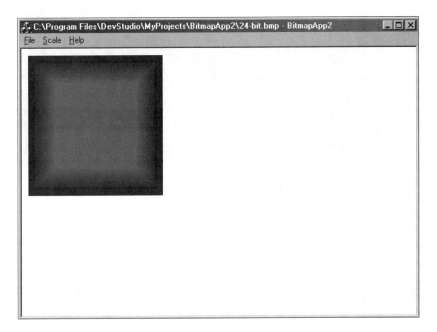

Figure 12-30: Here's BitmapApp2 displaying a 24-bit bitmap.

You can use the Scale menu to enlarge the image of a loaded bitmap. First select the Scale menu's Set Scaling command. Then type a value between 1 and 5 into the dialog box that appears. When you click the dialog box's OK button, the displayed bitmap—and any other bitmap you load—gets scaled to the value you chose (see Figure 12-31). You don't have to choose whole numbers for the scaling, you could enter something like 2.75 if you like.

Figure 12-31: The bitmap is now scaled by a factor of five.

When the user selects the File menu's Open command, the `CBitmapApp2Doc` document class's `OnFileOpen()` function (see Listing 12-15) takes over. In `OnFileOpen()`, the program creates and displays a File dialog box that'll list files with a BMP extension. If the user exits the dialog box via the OK button, the program gets the selected file's path name and calls the `CDib` class's constructor to create and load the bitmap. If the bitmap loads successfully, `OnFileOpen()` calls `SetTitle()` to set the document's title to the file's path name. This title will appear in the application's title bar. If the bitmap ends up not valid, the program calls `DeleteContents()` to delete the `CDib` object.

Listing 12-15: BitmapApp2's `OnFileOpen()` **function**

```
void CBitmapApp2Doc::OnFileOpen()
{
    // TODO: Add your command handler code here

    CFileDialog dlg(TRUE, "bmp", "*.bmp");
    int result = dlg.DoModal();

    if (result == IDOK)
    {
        CString path = dlg.GetPathName();
        m_pBitmap = new CDib(path);
        if (m_pBitmap->IsValid())
            SetTitle(path);
        else
            DeleteContents();
```

```
    }

    UpdateAllViews(0);
}
```

MFC calls the document class's `DeleteContents()` function (see Listing 12-16) when the application first runs and whenever you load a new bitmap. `DeleteContents()` makes sure that the application's document (which consists of only the currently selected bitmap) starts fresh each time the user loads a bitmap.

Listing 12-16: BitmapApp2's `DeleteContents()` function

```
void CBitmapApp2Doc::DeleteContents()
{
    // TODO: Add your specialized code here
    //    and/or call the base class

    if (m_pBitmap)
    {
        delete m_pBitmap;
        m_pBitmap = NULL;
    }

    CDocument::DeleteContents();
}
```

The `OnDraw()` function is where most of the bitmap handling occurs. First `OnDraw()` gets a pointer to the bitmap from the application's document class:

```
CDib* pBitmap = pDoc->m_pBitmap;
```

Then the program calls various `CDib` member functions to get pointers to the DIB's image data and `BITMAPINFO` structure, as well as to get the bitmap's dimensions:

```
BYTE* pBitmapData = pBitmap->GetData();
LPBITMAPINFO pBitmapInfo = pBitmap->GetInfo();
int bitmapHeight = pBitmap->GetHeight();
int bitmapWidth = pBitmap->GetWidth();
```

The program then scales the bitmap's dimensions with the scaling value set by the user:

```
int scaledWidth = (int)(bitmapWidth * m_scale);
int scaledHeight = (int)(bitmapHeight * m_scale);
```

If the bitmap has 256 or less colors, it has a color table. In this case, `OnDraw()` creates and realizes a logical palette for the DIB:

```
HPALETTE hPalette =
    CreateBitmapPalette(pBitmap);
HPALETTE hOldPalette =
    ::SelectPalette(pDC->m_hDC, hPalette, FALSE);
::RealizePalette(pDC->m_hDC);
```

`CreateBitmapPalette()` is a function you added to the view class. This function creates a logical palette exactly as described in the previous section on palette handling.

With the palette created and realized, the program displays the currently loaded bitmap:

```
StretchDIBits(pDC->m_hDC,
    10, 10, scaledWidth, scaledHeight,
    0, 0, bitmapWidth, bitmapHeight,
    pBitmapData, pBitmapInfo,
    DIB_RGB_COLORS, SRCCOPY);
```

Finally, the program restores the old palette to the DC and deletes the now unneeded DIB palette:

```
::SelectPalette(pDC->m_hDC, hOldPalette, FALSE);
::DeleteObject(hPalette);
```

DIBs without color tables don't require all the palette processing. A simple call to `StretchDIBits()` is all it takes to display the bitmap's image in the window.

Note

The double colons (::) in front of function calls indicate Windows API functions and not member functions of an MFC class.

PROBLEMS & SOLUTIONS

Managing Multi-Image Device-Independent Bitmaps

PROBLEM: *I want to put all of my application's images into a single bitmap file and then extract the individual images as I need them. Is there some way to do this with Visual C++ under Windows 98?*

SOLUTION: Placing multiple images into a single bitmap file is a time-honored technique for reducing the number of files that must accompany an application. This technique also enables an application to run faster, because all its images get loaded into memory at one time, rather than the application having to constantly access the user's disk. In fact, Visual C++ uses the multi-image bitmap technique to organize the images it uses for the toolbar's buttons. Figure 12-32 shows a toolbar bitmap loaded into Microsoft Paint.

Continued

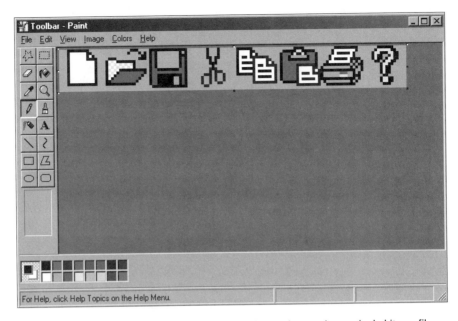

Figure 12-32: Visual C++ places all the toolbar's button images into a single bitmap file.

The first step, of course, is to create your bitmap. There are a number of ways you can organize images in your bitmap. The only rule is that you must know the coordinates and size of each image in the bitmap. If the images you're using are all the same size, you might end up with a grid of images, like that shown in Figure 12-33. However, there's nothing to stop you from putting images of many different sizes in the same bitmap, as long as you know their coordinates.

Figure 12-33: This bitmap contains six images, all the same size.

Continued

Notice that the bottom row of images in Figure 12-33 is labeled 1 through 3, whereas the top row is labeled 4 through 6. The images were created this way because Windows bitmaps (except in special cases) are stored as *bottom-up images*. Bottom-up images are stored upside-down in memory, which places the images labeled 1 through 3 at the top of the bitmap. Figure 12-34 shows the same grid as Figure 12-33, but this time as it appears in memory.

The `StretchDIBits()` function knows how to reverse a bottom-up image so that it appears right-side-up on the screen. If it didn't, the images would appear upside down. This is still a problem if you have to write your own library of video and image functions (not an easy task). Give a silent thank-you to the Windows programmers for making `StretchDIBits()` as smart as it is.

When you're ready to display one of the images in the bitmap, you call `StretchDIBits()`, providing the source coordinates for the image. For example, if you wanted to display block 2 in Figure 12-33's bitmap, you'd call `StretchDIBits()` like this:

```
BYTE* pBitmapData = pBitmap->GetData();
LPBITMAPINFO pBitmapInfo = pBitmap->GetInfo();

StretchDIBits(pDC->m_hDC, 20, 20, 128, 128,
    128, 0, 128, 128, pBitmapData,
    pBitmapInfo, DIB_RGB_COLORS, SRCCOPY);
```

The result of the above call to `StretchDIBits()` would look something like Figure 12-30, shown in the previous section. The destination coordinates (20, 20) could be just about anything that fits in the window, as long as the width and height values (128, 128) are correct. The source coordinates (128, 0) are where you have to be careful. They specify where in the bitmap the specific image you want is located (see Figure 12-34).

Coordinate 128,0

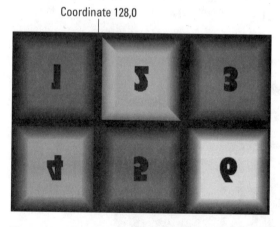

Figure 12-34: DIBs are usually stored upside-down in memory. The source coordinates for this DIB's chosen image is the upper-left corner at coordinates 128,0.

`StretchDIBits()` then gets that portion of the bitmap (see Figure 12-35), flips it right-side-up (see Figure 12-36), and displays it on the screen at the destination coordinates (see Figure 12-37).

Figure 12-35: Here's the selected portion of the bitmap.

Figure 12-36: The `StretchDIBits()` function flips the image before displaying it.

Figure 12-37: This application displays the single chosen image from the multi-image bitmap.

On CD-ROM

In the Chapter12\ColorRecApp directory of this book's CD-ROM, you can find the ColorRecApp application from which the previous code examples and figures were drawn. When you run the application, you see the window shown in Figure 12-38. Click any box and the boxes reorder themselves with the selected box first.

Continued

Figure 12-38: This application displays the multi-image bitmap as a single image.

How does the application work? First, the application loads the main bitmap in the OnCreate() function, which MFC calls in response to Windows' WM_CREATE message. Listing 12-17 shows the OnCreate() function.

Listing 12-17: The OnCreate() **function**

```
int CColorRecAppView::OnCreate
    (LPCREATESTRUCT lpCreateStruct)
{
    if (CView::OnCreate(lpCreateStruct) == -1)
        return -1;

    // TODO: Add your specialized creation code here

    pBitmap = new CDib("colorrec.bmp");
    if (!pBitmap->IsValid())
        MessageBox("Couldn't find colorrec.bmp.",
            "ColorRecApp Error",
            MB_OK | MB_ICONEXCLAMATION);

    return 0;
}
```

Because the application creates a bitmap object on the heap (that is, by using the new operator), the program should delete the bitmap at the end. ColorRecApp performs this task in its OnDestroy() function, which MFC calls in response to Windows' WM_DESTROY message. OnDestroy(), below, is OnCreate()'s counterpart. Usually, anything you allocate in OnCreate() can be deleted in OnDestroy().

Continued

```
void CColorRecAppView::OnDestroy()
{
    CView::OnDestroy();

    // TODO: Add your message handler code here

    if (pBitmap)
        delete pBitmap;
}
```

The program incorporates a simple, six-element array to keep track of the order in which each numbered `block` should be displayed. Each number in the array, from 0 through 5, represents a block. At the start of the program, the blocks should be displayed in order, so the program initializes the array in the view class's constructor, as shown here:

```
CColorRecAppView::CColorRecAppView()
{
    // TODO: add construction code here

    for (int x=0; x<6; ++x)
        m_colors[x] = x;
}
```

It's the `OnDraw()` function's task to display the blocks. The `OnDraw()` function first fills the window's background with black, and then it gets pointers to the bitmap's image data and `BITMAPINFO` structure. Next, `OnDraw()` sets up a `for` loop that iterates six times, once for each block image. In the `for` loop, `OnDraw()` calculates the destination and source coordinates for the current block. A call to `StretchDIBits()` then displays the block on the screen in its correct location. Listing 12-18 shows the `OnDraw()` function.

Listing 12-18: The `OnDraw()` function

```
void CColorRecAppView::OnDraw(CDC* pDC)
{
    CColorRecAppDoc* pDoc = GetDocument();
    ASSERT_VALID(pDoc);

    // TODO: add draw code for native data here

    if (!pBitmap)
        return;

    CBrush blackBrush(RGB(0,0,0));
    pDC->FillRect(CRect(0,0,435,345), &blackBrush);

    BYTE* pBitmapData = pBitmap->GetData();
    LPBITMAPINFO pBitmapInfo = pBitmap->GetInfo();

    for (int x=0; x<6; ++x)
    {
        int destX = x * 128 + 20;
        if (x > 2)
            destX = (x-3) * 128 + 20;
```

Continued

```
    int destY = 20;
    if (x > 2)
        destY = 148;

    int srcX = m_colors[x] * 128;
    if (m_colors[x] > 2)
        srcX = (m_colors[x] - 3) * 128;

    int srcY = 0;
    if (m_colors[x] > 2)
        srcY = 128;

    StretchDIBits(pDC->m_hDC, destX, destY, 128, 128,
        srcX, srcY, 128, 128, pBitmapData,
        pBitmapInfo, DIB_RGB_COLORS, SRCCOPY);
    }
}
```

When the user clicks in the window, the program must determine whether the user clicked a block and, if so, rearrange the block array as appropriate to the user's selection. All this happens in the OnLButtonDown() function, which MFC calls in response to the WM_LBUTTONDOWN Windows message. In OnLButtonDown(), the program first checks the coordinates at which the user clicked to see whether the coordinates are on the area of the window that contains blocks. If so, the program uses the coordinates to calculate the block on which the user clicked. A for loop then reorders the block array into a temporary array, which is then copied back into the original array. The call to Invalidate() forces a call to OnDraw(), which draws the blocks using the new order in the block array. Listing 12-19 shows the OnLButtonDown() function.

Listing 12-19: The OnLButtonDown() function

```
void CColorRecAppView::OnLButtonDown
    (UINT nFlags, CPoint point)
{
    // TODO: Add your message handler code here
    //    and/or call default

    if ((point.x > 20) && (point.x < 404) &&
        (point.y > 20) && (point.y < 276))
    {
        UINT col = ((point.x-20)/128)*128+20;
        UINT row = ((point.y-20)/128)*128+20;
        UINT index = (col/128) + (row/128) * 3;

        UINT temp[6];
        int x;

        for (x=0; x<6; ++x)
        {
            temp[x] = m_colors[index];
            ++index;
            if (index > 5)
                index = 0;
        }
```

```
    for (x=0; x<6; ++x)
        m_colors[x] = temp[x];

    Invalidate(FALSE);
    }

    CView::OnLButtonDown(nFlags, point);
}
```

 PROBLEMS & SOLUTIONS

Displaying Nonrectangular Bitmaps

PROBLEM: *The program I'm working on must display images of various shapes, not just rectangles. Unfortunately,* StretchDIBits() *only displays rectangular images. How can I get around this limitation?*

SOLUTION: First the bad news: Windows can display only rectangular images. The good news is that you can trick Windows into displaying a rectangular image so that it looks nonrectangular. The trick involves knowing a little about image masks and raster operations.

A mask is an image that's used to prepare a window's client area to receive a "nonrectangular" image. In a way, the mask—when displayed properly—cuts a hole in the window's background image. This hole is the exact shape and size of the nonrectangular image you want to display. To get the mask and image to display properly, you have to use a couple of special raster operations.

What's a raster operation? A raster operation determines the way in which a source pixel (such as from a bitmap) is combined with a destination pixel (such as in a window). These operations calculate the final value for the pixel by ANDing, ORing, or XORing the values in various ways. Windows defines fifteen standard raster operations: BLACKNESS, DSTINVERT, MERGECOPY, MERGEPAINT, NOTSRCCOPY, NOTSRCERASE, PATCOPY, PATINVERT, PATPAINT, SRCAND, SRCCOPY, SRCERASE, SRCINVERT, SRCPAINT, and WHITENESS.

You'll learn more about raster operations in Chapter 13, "Advanced GDI." For now, keep the SRCCOPY, SRCAND, and SRCPAINT raster operations in mind. You specify one of these operations when you call StretchDIBits() to display a bitmap. For example, you're already used to seeing SRCCOPY as StretchDIBits()'s last argument:

```
StretchDIBits(pDC->m_hDC, 0, 0, 500, 300,
    0, 0, 500, 300, pBitmapData, pBitmapInfo,
    DIB_RGB_COLORS, SRCCOPY);
```

Continued

All the DIBs you've displayed so far have been displayed with the SRCCOPY raster operation, which tells Windows to replace the destination pixels with the source pixels. You'll use the SRCAND raster operation to display a mask, and the SRCPAINT raster operation to display the final image.

To prepare your nonrectangular image for display, you must first create a mask. Suppose that you want to display the cone-like image shown in Figure 12-39. Notice that the cone image is surrounded with black. The black area is the part of the bitmap that you don't want to appear on the screen. You need to create a second bitmap, exactly the same size as the first, that has the black area filled with white and the rest of the image area filled with black, as shown in Figure 12-40. This second image is the mask.

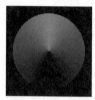

Figure 12-39: Although the bitmap is rectangular, the application needs to display only the cone image.

Figure 12-40: This is the image's mask.

After creating your two images, you're ready to display them in your application. First, you display the mask using the SRCAND raster operation, which gives you the result shown in Figure 12-41. Notice how the mask cuts a hole in the window's background that's just right for the final image. The StretchDIBits() call that displays the mask looks like this:

```
StretchDIBits(windowDC.m_hDC, 20, 20, 128, 128,
    0, 0, 128, 128, pBitmapData, pBitmapInfo,
    DIB_RGB_COLORS, SRCAND);
```

Continued

Figure 12-41: This is the image mask displayed with the SRCAND raster operation.

Now, to display the nonrectangular image, you copy the image to the exact same coordinates to which you copied the mask. This time, though, you use the SRCPAINT raster operation, which combines the source and destination pixels in such a way that only the portion of the image that fits into the mask "cutout" appears on the screen, as shown in Figure 12-42.

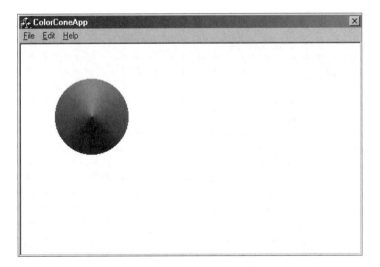

Figure 12-42: This is the image displayed on top of the mask using the SRCPAINT raster operation.

Continued

On CD-ROM

In the Chapter12\ColorConeApp directory of this book's CD-ROM, you can find the ColorConeApp application, which demonstrates the techniques discussed here. When you run the application, click anywhere in the window to display the nonrectangular bitmap over the window's background colors. Figure 12-43 shows the application after the user has clicked several places in the window.

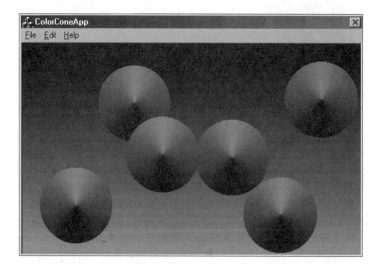

Figure 12-43: The ColorConeApp application demonstrates a display of nonrectangular images.

The program creates and loads its bitmaps in the view window class's OnCreate() function, as shown in Listing 12-20. There are three bitmaps: the background image, the image mask, and the cone image.

Listing 12-20: The OnCreate() **function**

```
int CColorConeAppView::OnCreate
    (LPCREATESTRUCT lpCreateStruct)
{
    if (CView::OnCreate(lpCreateStruct) == -1)
        return -1;

    // TODO: Add your specialized creation code here

    m_pBackBitmap = new CDib("backgrnd.bmp");
    if (!m_pBackBitmap->IsValid())
        MessageBox("Couldn't find backgrnd.bmp.",
            "ColorConeApp Error",
            MB_OK | MB_ICONEXCLAMATION);

    m_pConeBitmap = new CDib("cone.bmp");
    if (!m_pConeBitmap->IsValid())
        MessageBox("Couldn't find cone.bmp.",
```

Continued

```
                    "ColorConeApp Error",
                    MB_OK | MB_ICONEXCLAMATION);

    m_pMaskBitmap = new CDib("conemask.bmp");
    if (!m_pMaskBitmap->IsValid())
        MessageBox("Couldn't find conemask.bmp.",
            "ColorConeApp Error",
            MB_OK | MB_ICONEXCLAMATION);

    return 0;
}
```

Because the program creates the bitmaps on the heap, using the `new` operator, the bitmap objects should be deleted when the program ends. The program handles this task in the `OnDestroy()` function, as shown in Listing 12-21.

Listing 12-21: The `OnDestroy()` function

```
void CColorConeAppView::OnDestroy()
{
    CView::OnDestroy();

    // TODO: Add your message handler code here

    if (m_pBackBitmap)
        delete m_pBackBitmap;
    if (m_pConeBitmap)
        delete m_pConeBitmap;
    if (m_pMaskBitmap)
        delete m_pMaskBitmap;
}
```

The ColorConeApp application doesn't store the coordinates of the images that are displayed on the screen, so `OnDraw()` cannot reproduce the entire display when the window needs repainting. However, `OnDraw()` does display the background image, as shown in Listing 12-22.

Listing 12-22: The `OnDraw()` function

```
void CColorConeAppView::OnDraw(CDC* pDC)
{
    CColorConeAppDoc* pDoc = GetDocument();
    ASSERT_VALID(pDoc);

    // TODO: add draw code for native data here

    if (!m_pBackBitmap)
        return;

    BYTE* pBitmapData = m_pBackBitmap->GetData();
    LPBITMAPINFO pBitmapInfo = m_pBackBitmap->GetInfo();

    StretchDIBits(pDC->m_hDC, 0, 0, 500, 300,
        0, 0, 500, 300, pBitmapData, pBitmapInfo,
        DIB_RGB_COLORS, SRCCOPY);
}
```

Continued

The last function of interest in ColorConeApp is `OnLButtonDown()`, which displays a cone image wherever the user clicks in the application's window. It's here that the program uses the `SRCAND` and `SRCPAINT` raster operations to display the image mask and the image, as shown in Listing 12-23.

Listing 12-23: The `OnLButtonDown()` function

```
void CColorConeAppView::OnLButtonDown
    (UINT nFlags, CPoint point)
{
    // TODO: Add your message handler code here
    //    and/or call default

    CClientDC windowDC(this);

    int destX = point.x - 64;
    int destY = point.y - 64;

    BYTE* pBitmapData = m_pMaskBitmap->GetData();
    LPBITMAPINFO pBitmapInfo = m_pMaskBitmap->GetInfo();

    StretchDIBits(windowDC.m_hDC, destX, destY, 128, 128,
        0, 0, 128, 128, pBitmapData, pBitmapInfo,
        DIB_RGB_COLORS, SRCAND);

    pBitmapData = m_pConeBitmap->GetData();
    pBitmapInfo = m_pConeBitmap->GetInfo();

    StretchDIBits(windowDC.m_hDC, destX, destY, 128, 128,
        0, 0, 128, 128, pBitmapData, pBitmapInfo,
        DIB_RGB_COLORS, SRCPAINT);

    CView::OnLButtonDown(nFlags, point);
}
```

Summary

Bitmaps are a versatile form of image that are used in virtually every Windows application. However, if you want to do more with bitmaps than use them as button icons, you have to know how to load and display them. This process can be as simple as accessing a bitmap in the application's resources or as complex as loading a device-independent bitmap from a file, creating a palette, and drawing the image on the screen.

Also discussed in this chapter:

▶ Device-dependent bitmaps (DDBs) are used mostly to transfer image data between the screen and memory.

▶ Device-independent bitmaps (DIBs) hold images that include color tables and other display information.

▶ To draw on a DDB, you must select it into a memory DC.

▶ To display a DDB, you copy the image from the memory DC to a window DC.

▶ To display a DIB, you copy the image data buffer to a window DC.

▶ DIBs contain several types of data structures that an application must be able to read and interpret.

▶ DIBs reside in their own memory buffers and don't need to be selected into a memory device context.

▶ An application must create a palette for any DIB containing 256 or less colors.

▶ DIBs with more than 256 colors don't use color tables.

▶ Applications with palettes must respond to Windows' palette messages.

▶ You can trick Windows into displaying a rectangular image so that it looks nonrectangular.

▶ Placing multiple images into a single bitmap enables you to reduce the number of files that must accompany an application.

Chapter 13

Advanced GDI

Whenever you display data in a window, even something as simple as text, Windows has to go through a complex mapping process, which converts logical coordinates into physical coordinates. This mapping process depends on a number of device context attributes, including the mapping mode, the window, and the viewport. If all this sounds like Greek to you, don't despair. In this chapter, you get the skinny on mapping modes and everything that goes with them. You also learn about drawing modes, specifically raster operations, which help determine what you see on the screen, as well as regions, paths, and two ways to specify areas and lines on the screen. All this coordinate, mode, raster operation, region, and path stuff is managed by Windows' Graphics Device Interface (GDI), which, as you learned in Chapter 5, comprises Windows' graphics system.

Physical and Logical Coordinates

As you already know, your monitor's screen displays data by lighting dots in various combinations and colors. These dots, called *pixels,* are the smallest thing the monitor can display. To keep everything orderly, pixels are arranged in horizontal rows. How many dots there are in each row, as well as how many rows make up the entire screen, depends on your system's current resolution setting. For example, if you have your monitor set to 640x480, the screen has 480 rows of 640 dots each, whereas if you have your monitor set to 800x600, the screen has 600 rows of 800 pixels each.

Moreover, Windows manages these rows of dots in several ways, using the following:

Screen coordinates	Origin (the position 0,0) in the screen's upper-left corner
Window coordinates	Origin in the upper-left corner of the full window
Client-window coordinates	Origin in the upper-left corner of the client window

Figure 13-1 illustrates this concept. No matter which coordinate system you're working with, these are the *physical coordinates* of the display device. Simply stated, physical coordinates are actual coordinates on the screen. They're called physical coordinates because they have an actual physical presence in the pixels on the screen.

Figure 13-1: Three coordinate systems determine where objects appear on the screen.

Logical coordinates are the coordinates you give to GDI functions that display data on the screen. They have no meaning except in relationship to the physical coordinates. For example, when a call to TextOut() tells Windows to display a line of text at the coordinates 20, 50, Windows must determine where on the physical device the coordinates 20, 50 happen to be.

Depending on the mapping mode, which determines how Windows interprets the coordinates, the text could end up anywhere on the screen. You can't, in fact, even calculate where the text will appear unless you know the mapping mode, as well as the window and viewport settings. Any set of logical coordinates may or may not end up equal to the physical coordinates. This will all become clearer as you learn more about mapping modes.

Note

You probably won't have a lot of use for screen or window coordinates in your applications. For that reason, as well as to simplify the following discussions, this chapter uses the client-window system for all physical coordinates.

Mapping Modes

All this talk of physical and logical coordinates may be confusing. After all, up until now, when you told Windows to display a line of text at coordinates 20, 50 in a window, that line of text showed up at coordinates 20, 50, right? You didn't need to monkey around with physical and logical coordinates. This bit of good fortune, however, was due only to the fact that Windows' default mapping mode, MM_TEXT, defines a one-to-one relationship between physical and logical coordinates. That is, the logical coordinates you specified mapped exactly to the same physical coordinates.

For the most part, the default MM_TEXT mapping mode is all you need for most programs. Using the MM_TEXT mapping mode and a little arithmetic, you can even perform scaling and other graphics techniques. However, the title of this chapter contains the word "Advanced," which means you're not going to get off the hook so easily. The truth is that Windows defines eight mapping modes that determine the way Windows maps logical coordinates to physical coordinates. Those modes are listed and described in Table 13-1.

Experimenting with window and viewport origins

On CD-ROM

Before you take a look at each mode, it would be helpful for you to first experiment with window and viewport origins. Take a look in the Chapter13\MapModeApp folder for the MapModeApp application. When you run the application, you see the window shown in Figure 13-2. As you can see, the window displays a set of lines drawn at the window's origin, as well as text that shows the current viewport and window origins.

Table 13-1	Windows mapping modes
Mode	**Description**
MM_ANISOTROPIC	The GDI converts logical units to arbitrary units with arbitrarily scaled axes.
MM_HIENGLISH	The GDI converts a logical unit to 0.001 inches, with values of X increasing to the right and values of Y increasing upwards.
MM_HIMETRIC	The GDI converts a logical unit to 0.01 millimeters, with values of X increasing to the right and values of Y increasing upwards.
MM_ISOTROPIC	The GDI converts logical units to arbitrary units with equally scaled axes.
MM_LOENGLISH	The GDI converts a logical unit to 0.01 inches, with values of X increasing to the right and values of Y increasing upwards.
MM_LOMETRIC	The GDI converts a logical unit to 0.1 millimeters, with values of X increasing to the right and values of Y increasing upwards.
MM_TEXT	The GDI converts a logical unit to one pixel, with values of X increasing to the right and values of Y increasing down.
MM_TWIPS	The GDI converts a logical unit to one twip (1/1440 inches), with values of X increasing to the right and values of Y increasing upwards.

Select the Origins menu's Set Viewport Origin or Set Window Origin commands to change an origin. When you do, a dialog box appears, into which you can type the new origin values. Figure 13-3, for example, shows the results when you change the viewport origin to 150,75. Try setting the viewport and window origins to the same value. You'll discover that they cancel each other out.

The MapModeApp application draws its display in the view class's OnDraw() function (see Listing 13-1). The application starts the viewport and window origins—represented by the m_vprtOrgX, m_vprtOrgY, m_winOrgX, and m_winOrgY member variables—at all zeroes. When the user changes an origin, the application redraws the window with the new origins.

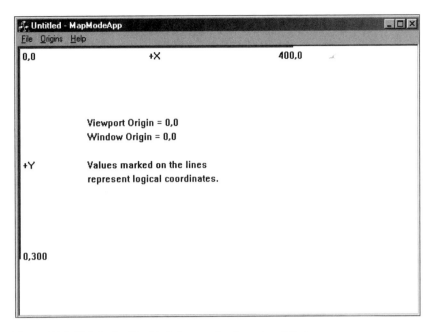

Figure 13-2: This is the MapModeApp application when it first appears.

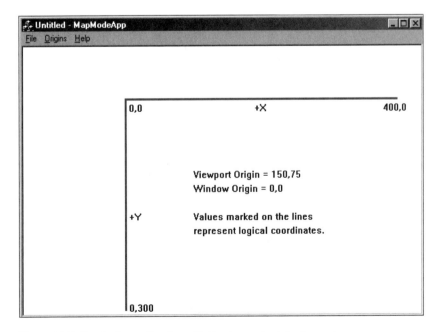

Figure 13-3: Here's the application with its viewport origin changed.

Listing 13-1: MapModeApp's OnDraw( ) function

```
void CMapModeAppView::OnDraw(CDC* pDC)
{
    CMapModeAppDoc* pDoc = GetDocument();
    ASSERT_VALID(pDoc);

    // TODO: add draw code for native data here

    CPen newPen(PS_SOLID, 3, RGB(255,0,0));
    CPen* oldPen = pDC->SelectObject(&newPen);

    pDC->SetViewportOrg(m_vprtOrgX, m_vprtOrgY);
    pDC->SetWindowOrg(m_winOrgX, m_winOrgY);

    pDC->MoveTo(0, 0);
    pDC->LineTo(400, 0);
    pDC->MoveTo(0, 0);
    pDC->LineTo(0, 300);

    pDC->TextOut(5, 5, "0,0");
    pDC->TextOut(190, 5, "+X");
    pDC->TextOut(5, 160, "+Y");
    pDC->TextOut(380, 5, "400,0");
    pDC->TextOut(5, 290, "0,300");

    char s[81];
    wsprintf(s, "Viewport Origin = %d,%d",
        m_vprtOrgX, m_vprtOrgY);
    pDC->TextOut(100, 100, s);
    wsprintf(s, "Window Origin = %d,%d",
        m_winOrgX, m_winOrgY);
    pDC->TextOut(100, 120, s);
    pDC->TextOut(100, 160, "Values marked on the lines");
    pDC->TextOut(100,180,"represent logical coordinates.");

    pDC->SelectObject(oldPen);
}
```

When the user selects the Set Viewport Origin or Set Window Origin command, the application displays a dialog box. This occurs in the view class's OnOriginsSetviewportorigin() or OnOriginsSetwindoworigin() function, as appropriate for the selected command. The program creates and displays the dialog box, after which, if the user clicked the OK button, the program resets the appropriate member variables with the values extracted from the dialog box. Listing 13-2 shows the OnOriginsSetviewportorigin() and OnOriginsSetwindoworigin() functions.

Listing 13-2: MapModeApp's `OnOriginsSetviewportorigin()` **and** **OnOriginsSetviewportorigin() functions**

```
void CMapModeAppView::OnOriginsSetviewportorigin()
{
    // TODO: Add your command handler code here

    CVprtDialog dlg;
    dlg.m_x = m_vprtOrgX;
    dlg.m_y = m_vprtOrgY;

    int result = dlg.DoModal();
    if (result == IDOK)
    {
        m_vprtOrgX = dlg.m_x;
        m_vprtOrgY = dlg.m_y;
        Invalidate();
    }
}

void CMapModeAppView::OnOriginsSetwindoworigin()
{
    // TODO: Add your command handler code here

    CWinDialog dlg;
    dlg.m_x = m_winOrgX;
    dlg.m_y = m_winOrgY;

    int result = dlg.DoModal();
    if (result == IDOK)
    {
        m_winOrgX = dlg.m_x;
        m_winOrgY = dlg.m_y;
        Invalidate();
    }
}
```

The MM_TEXT mode

You're now ready to examine the mapping modes in more detail. The first one you'll examine is MM_TEXT, Windows' default mapping mode. If you don't set the mapping mode explicitly in your program, MM_TEXT is what you'll get. If you've programmed other computers, MM_TEXT is the closest mapping mode to what you're probably used to using. In this mode, the coordinate system's origin is in the upper-left corner of the client window, with X values increasing to the right and Y values increasing as you go down. Figure 13-4 shows the MM_TEXT mapping mode illustrated in a window. Listing 13-3 shows the C++ lines that created the display.

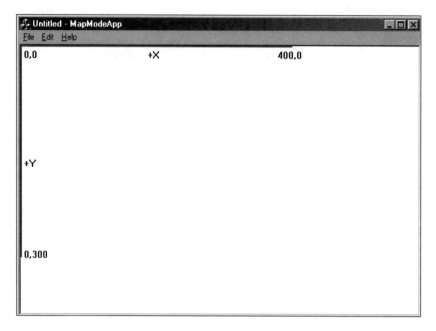

Figure 13-4: This window shows MM_TEXT's X and Y coordinates.

Listing 13-3: Drawing the MM_TEXT **display**

```
pDC->MoveTo(0, 0);
pDC->LineTo(400, 0);
pDC->MoveTo(0, 0);
pDC->LineTo(0, 300);

pDC->TextOut(5, 5, "0,0");
pDC->TextOut(190, 5, "+X");
pDC->TextOut(5, 160, "+Y");
pDC->TextOut(380, 5, "400,0");
pDC->TextOut(5, 290, "0,300");
```

One thing you should notice about Figure 13-4 and Listing 13-3 is that the logical coordinates in the calls to the GDI functions MoveTo(), LineTo(), and TextOut() map to exactly equivalent physical coordinates. That is, the call to MoveTo(0,0) moves the drawing cursor to the physical coordinates 0,0. When you leave the MM_TEXT mode in its default state, this will always be true. In the figure, the text labeling the onscreen coordinates represent both logical and physical coordinates.

However, to illustrate how physical and logical coordinates can differ, you can mess with the device context's window and viewport origins. The *window origin* represents the origin related to the logical coordinates, whereas the *viewport origin* represents the origin related to the physical, client-window coordinates. In this use of the word, you can think of the "window" as the entire data view, all or part of which will appear on the screen. The viewport represents that portion of the window that actually appears onscreen.

Note

When used in the context of windows and viewports, The word "window" should not be confused with the window object you see on the screen. They have nothing to do with each other, except that the window coordinates (logical coordinates) get mapped to the on-screen window object's client area.

To change the viewport origin, call the DC object's `SetViewportOrg()` function, whose signature looks like this:

```
BOOL SetViewportOrg(int X, int Y);
```

This function takes two arguments. The first, X, is the device X coordinate of the new origin; and the second, Y, is the device Y coordinate of the new origin.

When you move the viewport origin, you're telling Windows to display the logical 0,0 origin at the new viewport origin. As an example, suppose the program that created the display in Figure 13-4 calls `SetViewportOrg()` as follows before drawing the display:

```
clientDC.SetViewportOrg(50, 50);
```

This line tells Windows to display the logical coordinate 0,0 at the physical coordinate 50,50. The display then ends up looking like Figure 13-5. Notice how the entire display has shifted 50 pixels to the right and 50 pixels down. Now, the coordinates marked on the lines in the figure represent only the logical coordinates.

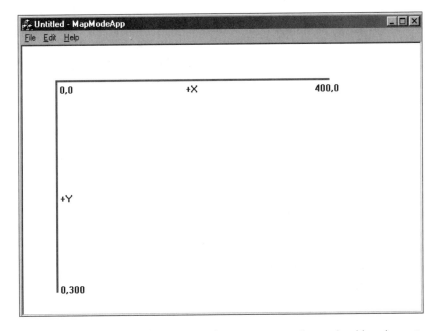

Figure 13-5: This window demonstrates the MM_TEXT mapping mode with a viewport origin of 50,50.

You can also change the window origin, which, as you may guess, has the opposite effect of setting the viewport origin. To set the window origin, call the DC object's `SetWindowOrg()` function, whose signature follows:

```
BOOL SetWindowOrg(int X, int Y);
```

When you move the window origin, you're telling Windows to display the new logical origin at the viewport's 0,0 physical coordinate. As an example, suppose the program that created the display in Figure 13-4 calls `SetWindowOrg()` as follows before drawing the display:

```
clientDC.SetWindowOrg(-50, -50);
```

This line tells Windows to display the logical coordinate -50,-50 at the physical coordinate 0,0. The display again ends up looking like Figure 13-5. If the call to `SetWindowOrg()` had not specified negative coordinates, the display would have shifted up and to the left, taking it out of view.

Mapping with a physical unit of measurement

The `MM_TEXT` mode is great for most general-purpose programs. Best of all, using the `MM_TEXT` mode is easy, thanks to the fact that there's a one-to-one relationship between the coordinates you provide for functions and the pixels of the display device. Sooner or later, though, you're going write a program for which it makes sense to scale graphical output using real-word measurements such as inches or millimeters. A drafting program, for example, would require using these types of measurements. For these situations, Windows offers the mapping modes you'll study in this section.

The `MM_LOENGLISH` and `MM_HIENGLISH` modes

Although the `MM_TEXT` mapping mode is the one you'll use the most, you have many other options, two of which are the `MM_LOENGLISH` and `MM_HIENGLISH` modes, which are similar in that they both work with measurements in inches. In the `MM_LOENGLISH` mapping mode, the logical unit is 0.01 inches, rather than one pixel, as it is in `MM_TEXT`. In `MM_HIENGLISH`, the logical unit is 0.001 inches, giving you an even higher degree of precision.

But the logical units are just one way these mapping modes differ from `MM_TEXT`. In the `MM_LOENGLISH` and `MM_HIENGLISH` modes, the Y coordinates decrease as you move down the display, rather than increase as they do with the `MM_TEXT` mapping mode. (The X coordinates still increase from left to right.) This means that, with the default window and viewport origins of 0,0, you have to use negative values for Y in order to see anything on the screen. Figure 13-6 illustrates how the `MM_LOENGLISH` mode looks. Listing 13-4 shows the C++ lines that created the display.

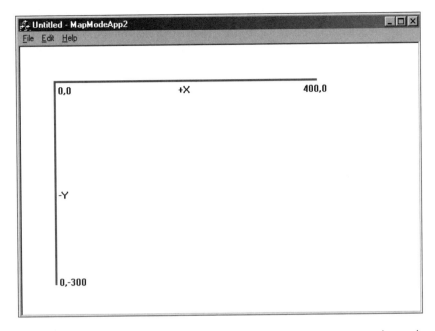

Figure 13-6: This application shows a display drawn in MM_LOENGLISH mapping mode. Notice that the X and Y coordinates use numbers in the hundreds.

Listing 13-4: Drawing a display in MM_LOENGLISH mapping mode

```
pDC->SetMapMode(MM_LOENGLISH);
pDC->SetViewportOrg(50, 50);

pDC->MoveTo(0, 0);
pDC->LineTo(400, 0);
pDC->MoveTo(0, 0);
pDC->LineTo(0, -300);

pDC->TextOut(5, -5, "0,0");
pDC->TextOut(190, -5, "+X");
pDC->TextOut(5, -160, "-Y");
pDC->TextOut(380, -5, "400,0");
pDC->TextOut(5, -290, "0,-300");
```

You should notice a few things about Listing 13-4. First, the program sets the mapping mode by calling the device context object's SetMapMode() member function, supplying the new mode as the function's single argument. Second, the program sets the viewport origin (in physical coordinates) to 50, 50 so that you can more easily see the lines that are drawn starting with the logical origin (the point marked 0,0 in Figure 13-6). Third, you should notice that all Y coordinates in the MoveTo(), LineTo(), and TextOut() functions are negative. Remember: Y coordinates in these mapping modes increase upwards, which means to move down the screen, you must use negative Y values, assuming your origin is in the upper-left corner of the screen. Finally, because the logical unit in MM_LOENGLISH mapping mode is 0.01 inches, the horizontal line in the display represents four logical inches (400 × 0.01), and the vertical line represents three logical inches (300 × 0.01).

The MM_HIENGLISH mapping mode uses units ten times as small as those used with MM_LOENGLISH. This means that, to create the same display shown in Figure 13-6, you'd have to multiply all the MM_LOENGLISH coordinates by 10. Listing 13-5 shows the code that results, and Figure 13-7 shows the resultant display.

Listing 13-5: Drawing a display in MM_HIENGLISH mapping mode

```
pDC->SetMapMode(MM_LOENGLISH);
::SetViewportOrgEx(pDC->m_hDC, 50, 50, NULL);

pDC->MoveTo(0, 0);
pDC->LineTo(400, 0);
pDC->MoveTo(0, 0);
pDC->LineTo(0, -300);

pDC->TextOut(5, -5, "0,0");
pDC->TextOut(190, -5, "+X");
pDC->TextOut(5, -160, "-Y");
pDC->TextOut(380, -5, "400,0");
pDC->TextOut(5, -290, "0,-300");
```

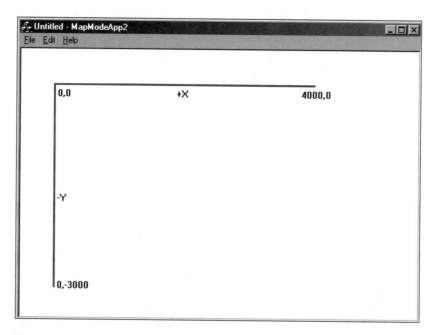

Figure 13-7: This application shows a display drawn in MM_LOENGLISH mapping mode. Notice that the X and Y coordinates use numbers in the thousands.

The MM_LOMETRIC and MM_HIMETRIC modes

The MM_LOMETRIC and MM_HIMETRIC mapping modes are very similar to MM_LOENGLISH and MM_HIENGLISH in that they enable you to scale output to a real-world measurement. The difference is that they use millimeters as logical units, rather than inches. More specifically, in the MM_LOMETRIC mode, the logical unit is 0.1 millimeters, whereas in MM_HIMETRIC, the logical unit is 0.01 millimeters. So, when you want to scale to millimeters, these modes are just the ticket. In both modes, the X coordinates still increase from left to right, and the Y coordinates still decrease from top to bottom. For example, the following code lines would draw two lines 100 millimeters long, one line running left to right and the other running top to bottom:

```
pDC->SetMapMode(MM_LOMETRIC);
pDC->MoveTo(0, 0);
pDC->LineTo(1000, 0);
pDC->LineTo(1000, -1000);
```

The MM_TWIPS mode

The MM_TWIPS mode uses a form of measurement called *twips* to calculate X and Y coordinates. If you've ever programmed with Visual Basic, you've heard the word "twip" before. If not, a twip is a tiny unit of measurement; there are 1,440 twips in an inch. Outside of the different logical unit, the MM_TWIPS mapping mode works exactly like the MM_LOENGLISH, MM_HIENGLISH, MM_LOMETRIC, and MM_HIMETRIC modes, with X values increasing to the right and Y values decreasing down. Because a twip is equal to 1/20th of a point, this mapping mode might be useful for working with some types of text displays, although this author never recalls seeing it used. For example, the following code lines would draw two lines four inches (5,760 twips) long, one line running left to right and the other running top to bottom:

```
pDC->SetMapMode(MM_TWIPS);
pDC->MoveTo(0, 0);
pDC->LineTo(5760, 0);
pDC->LineTo(5760, -5760);
```

Note

Don't bother to look up the word "twip" in your dictionary; you won't find it. Twip is a word Microsoft made up.

Scaling logical units to arbitrary coordinates

When none of the other mapping modes will do, you have to roll you own, so to speak. Two of the mapping modes—MM_ISOTROPIC and MM_ANISOTROPIC— enable you to decide how your coordinates are mapped to physical units. These mapping modes are handy for when you're scaling to a display that changes size (such as a window that can be resized), as well as for other special uses. In this section, you'll see how these mapping modes work.

The MM_ISOTROPIC and MM_ANISOTROPIC modes

Now the fun really starts. All the previous mapping modes represent some specific unit of measure, whether in inches, millimeters, or twips. What if you don't want to use any of these logical units? What if you've got something else in mind? Then you can resort to the MM_ISOTROPIC and MM_ANISOTROPIC mapping modes, which enable you to decide how logical units should be scaled to physical coordinates. The only difference between MM_ISOTROPIC and MM_ANISOTROPIC is that the former forces X units of measure to exactly equal Y units of measure, whereas the latter enables you to change even that small restriction. But before you can experiment with the MM_ISOTROPIC and MM_ANISOTROPIC mapping modes, you have to know about window and viewport extents. As you'll see, these weird mapping modes have a close relationship with the extents.

When you decide to use the MM_ISOTROPIC or MM_ANISOTROPIC mapping mode, you must deal with something called window and viewport extents. The window extents are like the logical coordinates, and the viewport extents are like the physical coordinates to which Windows must map the logical coordinates. The extents really have no meaning by themselves; they are meaningful only when taken as a pair. That is, the ratio between the window and viewport extents is what's important, not the extents' specific values.

Because Windows needs the window extents to set up its mapping properly, you should set the window extents before the viewport extents. You do this by calling the DC object's SetWindowExt() function, whose signature looks like this:

```
BOOL SetWindowExt(int nXExtent, int nYExtent);
```

The function's two arguments are the horizontal window extent and the vertical window extent.

After setting the window extents, you can set the viewport extents. Windows can then determine how logical coordinates will be mapped to physical coordinates. To set the viewport extents, you call the SetViewportExt() function, whose signature looks like this:

```
BOOL SetViewportExt(int nXExtent, int nYExtent);
```

The function's two arguments are the horizontal viewport extent and the vertical viewport extent.

If you're confused about how the window and viewport extents work together, consider this example: suppose that you want to use logical coordinates from 0 to 1000, and you want those logical coordinates mapped to a viewport that's 100 units square. First, you set the mapping mode to MM_ISOTROPIC:

```
CClientDC clientDC(this);
clientDC.SetMapMode(MM_ISOTROPIC);
```

Next, you set the window extents:

```
clientDC.SetWindowExt(1000, 1000);
```

Finally, you set the viewport extents:

```
clientDC.SetViewportExt(100, 100);
```

With the extents set up this way, Windows will map a logical X or Y coordinate of 0 to a viewport coordinate of 0, and will map a logical X or Y coordinate of 1000 to a viewport coordinate of 100, with all other logical coordinates falling somewhere in-between. Here's a one-question pop quiz: Given the extents set in this example, where will Windows map a logical X or Y coordinate of 500? If you said, "To a viewport coordinate of 50," you get an A for the day.

Note

In the previous example, the window extents were set to 1000,1000. The two extents are the same because the mapping mode is MM_ISOTROPIC, which requires equal horizontal and vertical extents. If you were to try to set the extents to unequal values, Windows would reset them to be equal.

Note

You can get the current mapping mode and extents by calling the GetMapMode(), GetWindowExtEx(), and GetViewportExtEx() functions.

PROBLEMS & SOLUTIONS

Mapping Modes and the Cartesian System

PROBLEM: *I'm writing a graphing program that needs to plot values into a Cartesian coordinate system. How can I do this with mapping modes?*

SOLUTION: It's important to note that, in most mapping modes, you can use negative or positive logical coordinates, just as you would when plotting values in a Cartesian coordinate system. For example, although positive Y values and negative X values don't appear on the screen when the window and viewport origins are set to their default 0,0 values, you can still use positive Y values and negative X values. If you want these coordinates to appear on the screen, just change the window or viewport origin.

On CD-ROM

Figure 13-8, for example, shows an application called CartesianApp that displays a Cartesian coordinate system in the MM_LOMETRIC mapping mode. You can find this application in the Chapter13\CartesianApp folder of this book's CD-ROM. When you run the application, select the Graph menu's Graph Line command. A dialog box appears into which you can type the end points for a line. When you exit the dialog box, the program graphs the line on the display.

Continued

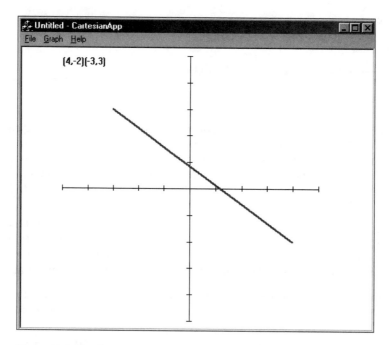

Figure 13-8: The CartesianApp application graphs lines.

CartesianApp holds the coordinates for the current line in four member variables of the view class. These member variables—called m_x1, m_y1, m_x2, and m_y2—start off at all zeroes, so all you see on the screen is a dot at the graph's origin. When you enter new values for the line's coordinates, the view class's OnDraw() function redraws the display, as shown in Listing 13-6.

Listing 13-6: CartesianApp's OnDraw() function

```
void CCartesianAppView::OnDraw(CDC* pDC)
{
    CCartesianAppDoc* pDoc = GetDocument();
    ASSERT_VALID(pDoc);

    // TODO: add draw code for native data here

    pDC->SetMapMode(MM_LOMETRIC);
    pDC->SetViewportOrg(250, 200);

    // Draw the X and Y axes.
    pDC->MoveTo(-500, 0);
    pDC->LineTo(500, 0);
    pDC->MoveTo(0, 500);
    pDC->LineTo(0, -500);
```

Continued

```
// Draw the X axis tick marks.
for (int x=0; x<11; ++x)
{
    pDC->MoveTo(-500+(x*100), 10);
    pDC->LineTo(-500+(x*100), -10);
}

// Draw the Y axis tick marks.
for (int y=0; y<11; ++y)
{
    pDC->MoveTo(-10, 500-(y*100));
    pDC->LineTo(10, 500-(y*100));
}

// Graph the line.
CPen newPen(PS_SOLID, 5, RGB(255,0,0));
CPen* oldPen = pDC->SelectObject(&newPen);

pDC->MoveTo(m_x1*100, m_y1*100);
pDC->LineTo(m_x2*100, m_y2*100);
char s[81];
wsprintf(s, "(%d,%d)(%d,%d)",
    m_x1, m_y1, m_x2, m_y2);
pDC->TextOut(-500, 500, s);

    pDC->SelectObject(oldPen);
}
```

When it comes to graphing programs, CartesianApp is pretty limited. However, if you're a math whiz, you might want to try adding other types of graphing to the program. How about graphing various types of equations? Good luck!

 PROBLEMS & SOLUTIONS

Mapping Modes and Aspect Ratio

PROBLEM: *In the application I'm working on, I want to be sure that square images always look square and round images always look round. Also, I want the current image to always be displayed at its largest possible size. Is there a way to solve this problem with mapping modes?*

Continued

SOLUTION: Sure is. What you're talking about is retaining aspect ratio, the perfect task for the MM_ISOTROPIC mapping mode, which always has equal horizontal and vertical extents. For example, when drawing in MM_ISOTROPIC mode, a 100-unit horizontal line will always be the same length as a 100-unit vertical line. By setting the window extents to whatever values are appropriate for your application, you're assured of retaining the aspect ratio of shapes.

To solve your second problem, you need only set the viewport extents to the current width and height of the client window. The only complication here is that, whenever the user resizes the window, you have to reset the viewport extents. You can do this by using ClassWizard to add the OnSize() function to your application, as shown in Figure 13-9. OnSize() responds to the WM_SIZE Windows message that Windows sends to the application whenever the user resizes the window.

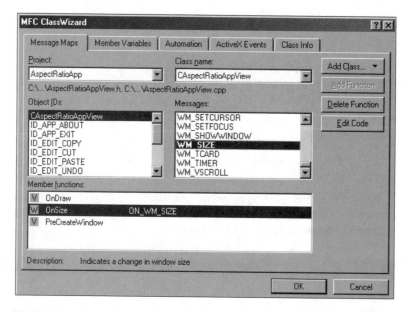

Figure 13-9: Adding the OnSize() message-response function to your application enables you to reset the viewport extents.

On CD-ROM

In the Chapter13\AspectRatioApp folder of this book's CD-ROM, you can find the AspectRatioApp application. When you run the application, you see the window shown in Figure 13-10. The program is set to the MM_ISOTROPIC mapping mode, so that the square will always look square.

Continued

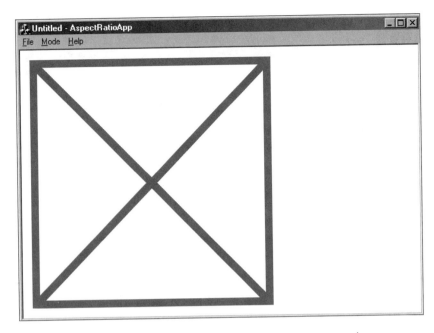

Figure 13-10: AspectRatioApp displays a square in `MM_ISOTROPIC` mode.

Thanks to the viewport extents, the shape will always display as large as possible, no matter how you resize the window (see Figure 13-11).

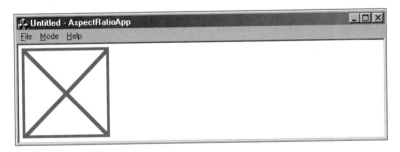

Figure 13-11: The shape stays square no matter the window size.

In the Mode menu, you can change the mapping mode from `MM_ISOTROPIC` to `MM_ANISOTROPIC`, after which the shape's aspect ratio changes to fit the window (see Figure 13-12).

Continued

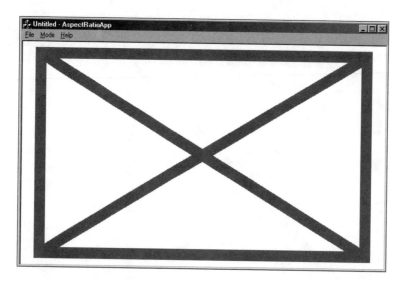

Figure 13-12: In MM_ANISOTROPIC mode, the shape stretches both horizontally and vertically to fit the window.

AspectRatioApp holds the currently selected mapping mode in the m_mapMode member variable of the view-window class and holds the client window's width and height in the m_clientWidth and m_clientHeight variables. The OnDraw() function sets the mapping mode with the m_mapMode variable, and sets the viewport extents with the m_clientWidth and m_clientHeight variables, before drawing its display. Listing 13-7 shows the OnDraw() function.

Listing 13-7: AspectRatioApp's OnDraw() function

```
void CAspectRatioAppView::OnDraw(CDC* pDC)
{
    CAspectRatioAppDoc* pDoc = GetDocument();
    ASSERT_VALID(pDoc);

    // TODO: add draw code for native data here

    CPen newPen(PS_SOLID, 30, RGB(255,0,0));
    CPen* oldPen = pDC->SelectObject(&newPen);

    pDC->SetMapMode(m_mapMode);
    pDC->SetWindowExt(1000, 1000);
    pDC->SetViewportExt(m_clientWidth,
        m_clientHeight);

    pDC->Rectangle(50, 50, 950, 950);
    pDC->MoveTo(55, 55);
```

Continued

```
    pDC->LineTo(945, 945);
    pDC->MoveTo(945, 55);
    pDC->LineTo(55, 945);

    pDC->SelectObject(oldPen);
}
```

Whenever the window gets resized—including when the window first appears—the program must set the values of the `m_clientWidth` and `m_clientHeight` variables. This happens in the view class's `OnSize()` function, shown in Listing 13-8. `OnSize()`'s two parameters are the new width and height of the client window. The program copies these values into the `m_clientWidth` and `m_clientHeight` variables.

Listing 13-8: AspectRatioApp's `OnSize()` function

```
void CAspectRatioAppView::OnSize
    (UINT nType, int cx, int cy)
{
    CView::OnSize(nType, cx, cy);

    // TODO: Add your message handler code here

    m_clientWidth = cx;
    m_clientHeight = cy;
}
```

Raster Operations

You may recall from Chapter 12, "Bitmaps," how you used the raster operations SRCAND and SRCPAINT to draw nonrectangular images on the screen. These raster operations are an example of the many ways in which you can display any type of data on the screen. The raster operations determine the way that Windows combines a source and destination pixel using logical operations such as AND, OR, and XOR. Many of these raster operations have only esoteric uses that you'll probably never run into. However, a few have special uses that can make the difference between an amateur application and a professional one. You'll examine two sets of raster operations in this chapter:

Bitmap raster operations   Used to draw images on the screen

Line raster operations   Used to draw lines on the screen

Bitmap raster operations

Bitmap raster operations are the operations you use with functions like `StretchDIBits()` or `BitBlt()`. As you learned in Chapter 12, these operations can be used to display bitmaps and bitmap masks in various ways. These raster operations actually do more than combine source and destination rectangles; some also combine the current brush with the final image. The fifteen operation codes are listed in Table 13-2

Table 13-2   Raster Operations for bitmaps

Operation	Description
BLACKNESS	Fills the destination rectangle with black
DSTINVERT	Inverts the colors of the destination rectangle
MERGECOPY	ANDs the source rectangle's colors with the brush
MERGEPAINT	Inverts the source rectangle and ORs the result with the destination rectangle
NOTSRCCOPY	Inverts the source rectangle and copies it to the destination rectangle
NOTSRCERASE	ORs the source and destination rectangles and then inverts the result
PATCOPY	Replaces the destination rectangle with the brush
PATINVERT	XORs the destination rectangle with the brush
PATPAINT	Inverts the source rectangle and ORs the brush with the result, which is then ORed with the destination rectangle
SRCAND	ANDs the source and destination rectangles
SRCCOPY	Replaces the destination rectangle with the source rectangle
SRCERASE	Inverts the destination rectangle and ANDs the result with the source rectangle
SRCINVERT	XORs the source and destination rectangles
SRCPAINT	ORs the source and destination rectangles
WHITENESS	Fills the destination rectangle with white

To display any type of bitmap with one of these raster operations, use the operation code as the last argument in the `StretchDIBits()` or `BitBlt()` functions. For example, the following line transfers a bitmap from a memory DC to the screen using the `SRCAND` raster operation:

```
pDC->BitBlt(370, 100, 80, 80,
    &memoryDC, 0, 0, SRCAND);
```

On CD-ROM

The best way to explore these different raster operations is to see them in action. In the Chapter13\RasterOpApp folder of this book's CD-ROM, you'll find the RasterOpApp application. When you run the application, you see the window shown in Figure 13-13. In the window, the program displays a bitmap fifteen times, using each of the raster operations in the order in which they were listed above.

Figure 13-13: RasterOpApp demonstrates the 15 bitmap raster operations.

If you looked over the list of raster operations, you may recall that several of them not only combine the source and destination rectangles, but also throw in the current brush as well. A DC's default brush is solid white and has no effect on the appearance of any of the raster operations. However, if you were to select a different brush into the DC, you'd see the effect immediately. To see this happen, click in the application's window. The application selects a patterned, black brush into the DC so you can see how the raster operations combine the brush with the source and destination rectangles (see Figure 13-14).

Finally, although the solid background color does affect the raster operations, the results aren't very obvious. To get a better look at how the window background affects the process, right-click in the window. The application then draws lines on the background, so you can better see how the raster operations combine the source and destination rectangles (see Figure 13-15).

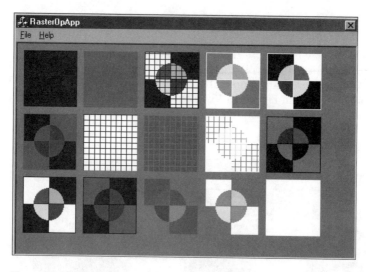

Figure 13-14: RasterOpApp adds a patterned brush to the mix.

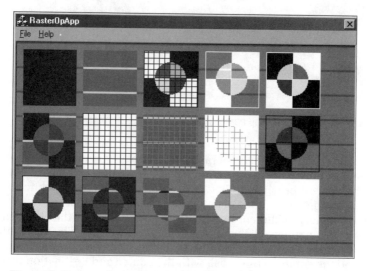

Figure 13-15: RasterOpApp adds lines to the background.

Virtually all of the interesting source code for this program is found in the view class's OnDraw() function (see Listing 13-9), which draws the window's background and then draws the fifteen bitmaps over the background. Notice especially how the different calls to BitBlt() display exactly the same bitmap, but do so using a different raster operation.

Listing 13-9: RasterOpApp's `OnDraw()` **function**

```
void CRasterOpAppView::OnDraw(CDC* pDC)
{
    CRasterOpAppDoc* pDoc = GetDocument();
    ASSERT_VALID(pDoc);

    // TODO: add draw code for native data here

    pDC->FillRect(CRect(0,0, 500, 350),
        new CBrush(RGB(176,150,33)));

    if (m_drawLines)
    {
        CPen* pNewPen =
            new CPen(PS_SOLID, 3, RGB(255,0,0));
        CPen* pOldPen = pDC->SelectObject(pNewPen);

        for (int x=0; x<10; ++x)
        {
            pDC->MoveTo(0, x*35);
            pDC->LineTo(500, x*35);
        }

        pDC->SelectObject(pOldPen);
        delete pNewPen;
    }

    CDC memoryDC;
    memoryDC.CreateCompatibleDC(pDC);
    CBitmap bitmap;
    bitmap.LoadBitmap(IDB_BITMAP1);
    CBitmap* pOldBitmap =
        memoryDC.SelectObject(&bitmap);

    CBrush* pNewBrush = new CBrush(HS_CROSS, RGB(0,0,0));
    CBrush* pOldBrush;

    if (m_showBrush)
        pOldBrush = pDC->SelectObject(pNewBrush);

    pDC->BitBlt(10, 10, 80, 80,
        &memoryDC, 0, 0, BLACKNESS);
    pDC->BitBlt(100, 10, 80, 80,
        &memoryDC, 0, 0, DSTINVERT);
    pDC->BitBlt(190, 10, 80, 80,
        &memoryDC, 0, 0, MERGECOPY);
    pDC->BitBlt(280, 10, 80, 80,
        &memoryDC, 0, 0, MERGEPAINT);
    pDC->BitBlt(370, 10, 80, 80,
        &memoryDC, 0, 0, NOTSRCCOPY);

    pDC->BitBlt(10, 100, 80, 80,
            &memoryDC, 0, 0, NOTSRCERASE);
    pDC->BitBlt(100, 100, 80, 80,
        &memoryDC, 0, 0, PATCOPY);
```

```
pDC->BitBlt(190, 100, 80, 80,
    &memoryDC, 0, 0, PATINVERT);
pDC->BitBlt(280, 100, 80, 80,
    &memoryDC, 0, 0, PATPAINT);
pDC->BitBlt(370, 100, 80, 80,
    &memoryDC, 0, 0, SRCAND);

pDC->BitBlt(10, 190, 80, 80,
    &memoryDC, 0, 0, SRCCOPY);
pDC->BitBlt(100, 190, 80, 80,
    &memoryDC, 0, 0, SRCERASE);
pDC->BitBlt(190, 190, 80, 80,
    &memoryDC, 0, 0, SRCINVERT);
pDC->BitBlt(280, 190, 80, 80,
    &memoryDC, 0, 0, SRCPAINT);
pDC->BitBlt(370, 190, 80, 80,
    &memoryDC, 0, 0, WHITENESS);

if (m_showBrush)
{
    pDC->SelectObject(pOldBrush);
    delete pNewBrush;
}

memoryDC.SelectObject(pOldBitmap);
}
```

The `OnDraw()` function in Listing 13-9 performs the following tasks:

- Fills the window with the background color

- Draws background lines on the display if the user has selected this option

- Creates and loads a bitmap

- Creates a patterned brush and selects the brush if the user has selected the patterned brush option

- Copies the bitmap to the screen once for each of the defined raster operations

- Restores the DC

Line drawing modes

Displaying bitmaps is only one way Windows uses raster operations. Windows also uses raster operations when it draws lines on the screen. When you draw lines on a display, whether you're drawing a rectangle, an ellipse, a straight line, or some other shape, Windows replaces the source pixels with the color of the current pen. This is similar to using the SRCCOPY operation with bitmaps. However, you're not stuck with this one type of raster operation. Windows defines sixteen raster operations that you can use when drawing lines. These raster operations are listed in Table 13-3.

Table 13-3	Raster Operations for drawing lines
Operation	*Description*
R2_BLACK	Draws a black line
R2_WHITE	Draws a white line
R2_NOP	Draws no line
R2_NOT	Draws a line that's the inverse of the screen color
R2_COPYPEN	Draws a line in the pen color
R2_NOTCOPYPEN	Draws a line that's the inverse of the pen color
R2_MERGEPENNOT	Draws a line that ORs the pen color and the inverse of the screen color
R2_MASKPENNOT	Draws a line that ANDs the pen and the inverse of the screen
R2_MERGENOTPEN	Draws a line that ORs the screen color and the inverse of the pen color
R2_MASKNOTPEN	Draws a line that ANDs the screen color and the inverse of the pen
R2_MERGEPEN	Draws a line that ORs the pen color and the screen color
R2_NOTMERGEPEN	Draws a line that is the inverse of the pen ORed with the screen color
R2_MASKPEN	Draws a line that ANDs the pen and the screen color
R2_NOTMASKPEN	Draws a line that's the inverse of the pen ANDed with the screen color
R2_XORPEN	Draws a line that XORs the pen with the screen color
R2_NOTXORPEN	Draws a line that is the inverse of the pen XORed with the screen color

For normal drawing, you don't need to be concerned with the drawing mode at all. But when you need them, the different raster operations are one function call away. To set the drawing mode for the current DC, call the DC object's SetROP2() member function:

```
pDC->SetROP2(R2_NOT);
```

The function's single argument is one of the previously listed raster operation codes.

On CD-ROM

As with the bitmap raster operations, the best way to understand line drawing modes is to see them in action. In the Chapter13\LineModeApp folder of this book's CD-ROM, you'll find the LineModeApp application. When you run the application, you see the window shown in Figure 13-16. In the window, the program draws sixteen lines, using each of the raster operations in the order in which they were listed in Table 13-3.

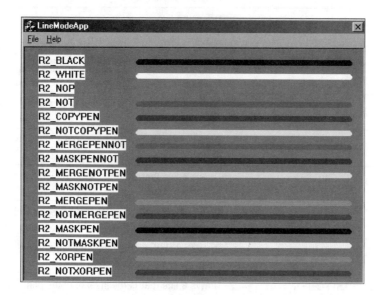

Figure 13-16: LineModeApp draws lines using all 16 raster operations.

Although the solid background color does affect the raster operations, the results aren't obvious. To get a better look at how the window background affects the process, click in the window. The application then draws lines on the background, so you can better see how the raster operations combine the pen and screen colors (see Figure 13-17).

The view class's OnDraw() function—which draws the window's background and then draws the sixteen lines and their labels over the background—contains all of the pertinent source code for LineModeApp, as shown in Listing 13-10. At this point, you should be able to read through the listing and understand what's going on. Notice especially how the different calls to BitBlt() display exactly the same line, but do so using a different raster operation. And, yes, the OnDraw() function could be shortened by drawing the lines in a loop, but that would also make the program a little more difficult to follow.

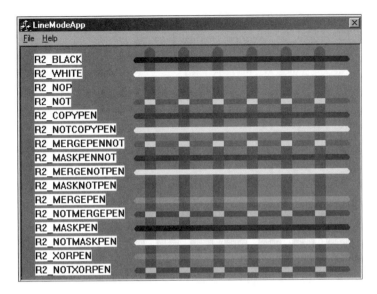

Figure 13-17: LineModeApp adds lines to the background.

Listing 13-10: LineModeApp's `OnDraw()` **function**

```
void CLineModeAppView::OnDraw(CDC* pDC)
{
    CLineModeAppDoc* pDoc = GetDocument();
    ASSERT_VALID(pDoc);

    // TODO: add draw code for native data here

    pDC->FillRect(CRect(0,0, 500, 380),
        new CBrush(RGB(176,150,33)));

    CPen* pOldPen;

    if (m_drawLines)
    {
        CPen redPen(PS_SOLID, 16, RGB(255,0,0));
        pOldPen = pDC->SelectObject(&redPen);

        for (int x=0; x<6; ++x)
        {
            pDC->MoveTo(190+x*50, 10);
            pDC->LineTo(190+x*50, 380);
        }

        pDC->SelectObject(pOldPen);
    }

    CPen newPen(PS_SOLID, 8, RGB(0,0,255));
    pOldPen = pDC->SelectObject(&newPen);

    pDC->TextOut(20, 10, "R2_BLACK");
```

```
pDC->SetROP2(R2_BLACK);
pDC->MoveTo(170, 20);
pDC->LineTo(480, 20);
pDC->TextOut(20, 30, "R2_WHITE");
pDC->SetROP2(R2_WHITE);
pDC->MoveTo(170, 40);
pDC->LineTo(480, 40);
pDC->TextOut(20, 50, "R2_NOP");
pDC->SetROP2(R2_NOP);
pDC->MoveTo(170, 60);
pDC->LineTo(480, 60);
pDC->TextOut(20, 70, "R2_NOT");
pDC->SetROP2(R2_NOT);
pDC->MoveTo(170, 80);
pDC->LineTo(480, 80);
pDC->TextOut(20, 90, "R2_COPYPEN");
pDC->SetROP2(R2_COPYPEN);
pDC->MoveTo(170, 100);
pDC->LineTo(480, 100);
pDC->TextOut(20, 110, "R2_NOTCOPYPEN");
pDC->SetROP2(R2_NOTCOPYPEN);
pDC->MoveTo(170, 120);
pDC->LineTo(480, 120);
pDC->TextOut(20, 130, "R2_MERGEPENNOT");
pDC->SetROP2(R2_MERGEPENNOT);
pDC->MoveTo(170, 140);
pDC->LineTo(480, 140);
pDC->TextOut(20, 150, "R2_MASKPENNOT");
pDC->SetROP2(R2_MASKPENNOT);
pDC->MoveTo(170, 160);
pDC->LineTo(480, 160);
pDC->TextOut(20, 170, "R2_MERGENOTPEN");
pDC->SetROP2(R2_MERGENOTPEN);
pDC->MoveTo(170, 180);
pDC->LineTo(480, 180);
pDC->TextOut(20, 190, "R2_MASKNOTPEN");
pDC->SetROP2(R2_MASKNOTPEN);
pDC->MoveTo(170, 200);
pDC->LineTo(480, 200);
pDC->TextOut(20, 210, "R2_MERGEPEN");
pDC->SetROP2(R2_MERGEPEN);
pDC->MoveTo(170, 220);
pDC->LineTo(480, 220);
pDC->TextOut(20, 230, "R2_NOTMERGEPEN");
pDC->SetROP2(R2_NOTMERGEPEN);
pDC->MoveTo(170, 240);
pDC->LineTo(480, 240);
pDC->TextOut(20, 250, "R2_MASKPEN");
pDC->SetROP2(R2_MASKPEN);
pDC->MoveTo(170, 260);
pDC->LineTo(480, 260);
pDC->TextOut(20, 270, "R2_NOTMASKPEN");
pDC->SetROP2(R2_NOTMASKPEN);
pDC->MoveTo(170, 280);
pDC->LineTo(480, 280);
pDC->TextOut(20, 290, "R2_XORPEN");
```

```
pDC->SetROP2(R2_XORPEN);
pDC->MoveTo(170, 300);
pDC->LineTo(480, 300);
pDC->TextOut(20, 310, "R2_NOTXORPEN");
pDC->SetROP2(R2_NOTXORPEN);
pDC->MoveTo(170, 320);
pDC->LineTo(480, 320);

pDC->SelectObject(pOldPen);
}
```

The OnDraw() function in Listing 13-10 performs the following tasks:

- Fills the window with the background color

- Draws background lines on the display if the user has selected this option

- Creates and selects a blue pen

- Draws one line in each of the defined line-drawing raster operations

- Restores the DC

PROBLEMS & SOLUTIONS

The Magic of R2_XORPEN

PROBLEM: *I heard somewhere about a drawing mode that can draw and erase lines without changing the background image. Is there really a way to do this seemingly magical feat?*

SOLUTION: Yep. What you heard about is the R2_XORPEN drawing mode. Using this drawing mode, you can draw a line over any background image and then restore the image by redrawing the same line a second time, still using the R2_XORPEN drawing mode. Many Windows applications use this drawing technique to implement things like rubber-band lines, boxes, and ellipses.

On CD-ROM

In the Chapter13\MagicRectApp folder of this book's CD-ROM, you'll find the MagicRectApp application, which demonstrates the R2_XORPEN drawing technique. When you run the application, you see the window shown in Figure 13-18. Click in the window to draw a series of rectangles in R2_XORPEN mode (see Figure 13-19). When you click a second time, the rectangles vanish, without disturbing the background image.

Continued

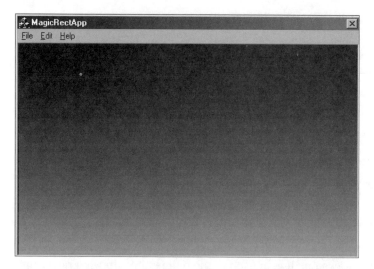

Figure 13-18: MagicRectApp displays a bitmapped background.

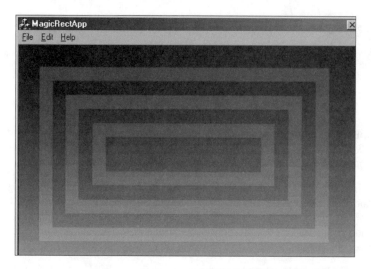

Figure 13-19: The program draws rectangles in R2_XORPEN mode.

The program displays its bitmap in the OnDraw() function. This ensures that the window's background will always be drawn properly when the window needs repainting. Listing 13-11 shows the OnDraw() function. If you don't understand how the bitmap gets displayed, you might want to review Chapter 12, "Bitmaps."

Continued

Listing 13-11: MagicRectApp's `OnDraw()` **function**

```
void CMagicRectAppView ::OnDraw(CDC* pDC)
{
    CMagicRectAppDoc* pDoc = GetDocument();
    ASSERT_VALID(pDoc);

    // TODO: add draw code for native data here

    if (!m_pBackBitmap)
        return;

    BYTE* pBitmapData = m_pBackBitmap->GetData();
    LPBITMAPINFO pBitmapInfo = m_pBackBitmap->GetInfo();

    StretchDIBits(pDC->m_hDC, 0, 0, 500, 300,
        0, 0, 500, 300, pBitmapData, pBitmapInfo,
        DIB_RGB_COLORS, SRCCOPY);
}
```

When the user clicks in the application's window, Windows sends the application a `WM_LBUTTONDOWN` message, which causes MFC to call the `CMagicRectAppView` class's `OnLButtonDown()` message-response function. In that function, shown in Listing 13-12, the program creates a window DC, selects a wide blue pen, selects the stock `NULL_BRUSH`, sets the drawing mode to `R2_XORPEN`, and then draws several nested rectangles. The next time the user clicks in the window, `OnLButtonDown()` again draws the rectangles in `R2_XORPEN` mode, but this time the rectangles are drawn on top of the previous rectangles, which restores the background image.

Listing 13-12: MagicRectApp's `OnLButtonDown()` **function**

```
void CMagicRectAppView::OnLButtonDown
    (UINT nFlags, CPoint point)
{
    // TODO: Add your message handler code here
    //    and/or call default

    CClientDC windowDC(this);

    CPen bluePen(PS_SOLID, 20, RGB(0,0,255));
    CPen* pOldPen = windowDC.SelectObject(&bluePen);
    windowDC.SelectStockObject(NULL_BRUSH);

    windowDC.SetROP2(R2_XORPEN);
    windowDC.Rectangle(40, 40, 450, 270);
    windowDC.Rectangle(80, 80, 410, 230);
    windowDC.Rectangle(120, 120, 370, 190);

    windowDC.SelectObject(pOldPen);

    CView::OnLButtonDown(nFlags, point);
}
```

Continued

Note The SelectStockObject() function enables you to select GDI objects that Windows has already created. Selecting the NULL_BRUSH object effectively tells Windows not to fill shapes such as rectangles with a color. Other stock objects include BLACK_BRUSH, DKGRAY_BRUSH, GRAY_BRUSH, HOLLOW_BRUSH, LTGRAY_BRUSH, WHITE_BRUSH, BLACK_PEN, NULL_PEN, and WHITE_PEN.

Now, the next time you drag a rubber-band line in a drawing program or drag a rectangle around a group of icons, you'll remember raster operations and be pleased with yourself because you know how this little bit of graphics magic works.

Using Regions

In many programs shown so far in this book, you've used rectangles not only as shapes on the screen, but also to determine what portion of the screen or a bitmap you want to work with. Rectangles are everywhere in Windows programming, so much so that MFC even has a class, CRect, for managing them. However, rectangles aren't the only way you can specify a portion of the screen; you can also use a *region*. A region can be as simple as a rectangle or as complex as a set of rectangles, ellipses, and polygons. In a nutshell, a region is an area of the screen that isn't restricted to a rectangular shape.

Creating and drawing a region

In MFC, the CRgn class represents Windows regions. Thanks to the class's member functions, you can use a CRgn object to manage more easily a nonrectangular area. But before you can call upon those member functions, you must create a CRgn object, which you do like this:

```
CRgn region;
```

After creating the region, you must tell MFC what the region looks like. There are several types of regions from which to choose, each with its own creation function. Those functions, all of which are members of the CRgn class, are as follows:

You can paint a region in several ways, using the FillRgn(), FrameRgn(), InvertRgn(), and PaintRgn() member functions of the DC object. For example, the code in Listing 13-13 paints regions with the FillRgn() function, as seen in Figure 13-20.

CreateEllipticRgn()	**Creates an elliptical region**
CreateEllipticRgnIndirect()	**Creates an elliptical region from a** RECT **structure**
CreatePolygonRgn()	**Creates a polygonal region**
CreatePolyPolygonRgn()	**Creates a region containing multiple polygons**
CreateRectRgn()	**Creates a rectangular region**
CreateRectRgnIndirect()	**Creates a rectangular region from a** RECT **structure**
CreateRoundRectRgn()	**Creates a rectangular region with rounded corners**

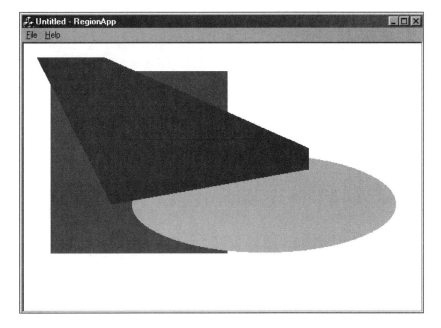

Figure 13-20: This window displays regions created with the FillRgn() function.

Listing 13-13: Displaying three simple regions

```
CClientDC* pDC = new CClientDC(this);

CRgn region1;
CRgn region2;
CRgn region3;

region1.CreateRectRgn(40, 40, 300, 300);
```

```
region2.CreateEllipticRgn(160, 160, 550, 300);
POINT points[5] = {
    120, 20, 420, 150, 420, 180, 130, 230, 20, 20};
region3.CreatePolygonRgn(points, 5, WINDING);

pDC->FillRgn(&region1, new CBrush(RGB(255,0,0)));
pDC->FillRgn(&region2, new CBrush(RGB(0,255,0)));
pDC->FillRgn(&region3, new CBrush(RGB(0,0,255)));

delete pDC;
```

As you can see in Listing 13-13, CreateRectRgn() and CreateEllipticRgn() both take the coordinates of a rectangle as their arguments. The CreatePolygonRgn() function, however, takes as arguments an array of POINT structures, the number of points in the array, and a filling mode, which can be ALTERNATE or WINDING.

Combining regions

On CD-ROM

One thing that makes regions so powerful is that you can combine several regions into one. You do this by calling a region object's CombineRgn() member function. This function takes three arguments: the address of the first region to combine, the address of the second region to combine, and the combine mode (RGN_AND, RGN_COPY, RGN_DIFF, RGN_OR, or RGN_XOR). The RegionApp sample application in the Chapter13\RegionApp folder of this book's CD-ROM shows how to combine regions using different modes. When you run the application, you see the window shown in Figure 13-21, which displays the three combined regions using the RGN_XOR mode. This is the result you'd get from Listing 13-14.

Listing 13-14: Combining three regions

```
CClientDC* pDC = new CClientDC(this);

CRgn region1;
CRgn region2;
CRgn region3;

region1.CreateRectRgn(40, 40, 300, 300);
region2.CreateEllipticRgn(160, 160, 550, 300);
POINT points[5] = {
    120, 20, 420, 150, 420, 180, 130, 230, 20, 20};
region3.CreatePolygonRgn(points, 5, WINDING);

region1.CombineRgn(&region1, &region2, RGN_XOR);
region1.CombineRgn(&region1, &region3, RGN_XOR);
pDC->FillRgn(&region1, new CBrush(RGB(255,0,0)));

delete pDC;
```

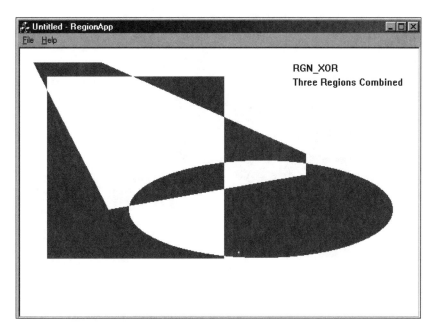

Figure 13-21: RegionApp displaying three regions in RGN_XOR mode

When two regions are combined with the RGN_XOR mode, only areas that are unique to one area or the other appear in the combined region. That is, no overlapping areas are included.

Figure 13-21 may appear to show overlapping areas because the display is the result of two calls to CombineRgn() rather than just one. That is, three regions are being combined. If you want to get a clearer picture of the combination process, right-click in the window. The application then removes the third region from the combined region, showing that the RGN_XOR mode really does remove overlapped areas (see Figure 13-22). Right-click in the window again to put the third region back, and you'll see that what appeared to be an overlapped area really fell over an area that was removed by the first combination.

Figure 13-23 shows the three regions combined in RGN_AND mode. In this mode, only areas the regions have in common appear in the combination. Whereas RGN_XOR showed only non-overlapped areas, RGN_AND shows only overlapped areas. Again, if you want to simplify the display, right-click to remove the third region from the combined regions.

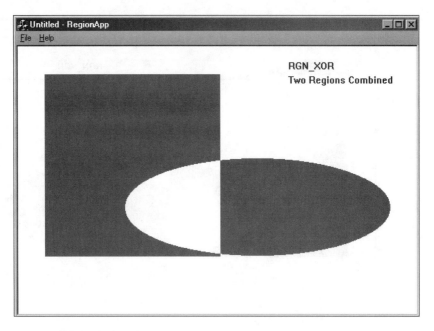

Figure 13-22: RegionApp displaying two regions in RGN_XOR mode

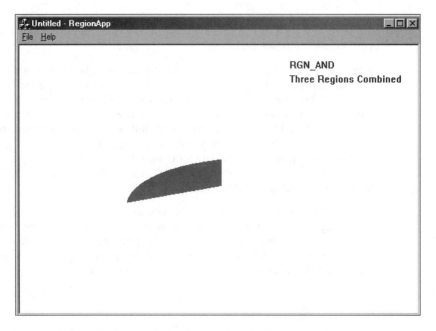

Figure 13-23: RegionApp displaying three regions in RGN_AND mode

Figure 13-24 shows the three regions combined in RGN_COPY mode. In this mode, the region given in CombineRgn( )'s first argument is copied to the new region. In this case, the display looks the same whether you're viewing two or three regions combined into one. The first region is the only one that makes it through the process.

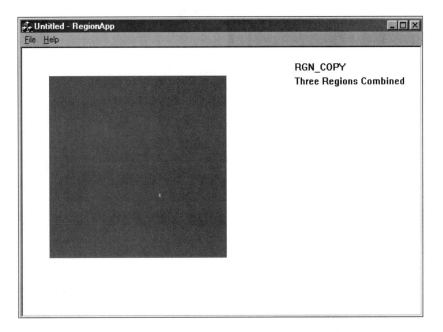

Figure 13-24: RegionApp displaying three regions in RGN_COPY mode

Figure 13-25 shows the three regions combined in RGN_DIFF mode. Now, the areas of the second and third regions are removed from the first region, leaving only a portion of the original rectangle.

Finally, Figure 13-26 shows the three regions combined in RGN_OR mode. This is probably the easiest mode to understand. All the areas of all the regions become part of the combined region, including overlapped and non-overlapped areas. When you think of combining regions, this is probably the result that first springs to mind, because the combined region includes all of the source regions.

As is typical for this chapter's programs, in RegionApp, all the fun shows up in the view class's OnDraw( ) function, which is shown in Listing 13-15. There's nothing too tricky going on in OnDraw( ). The previous discussion should amply prepare you to understand the code.

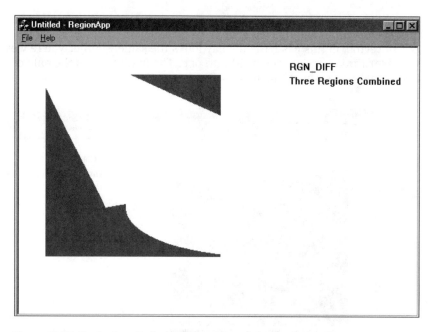

Figure 13-25: RegionApp displaying three regions in RGN_DIFF mode

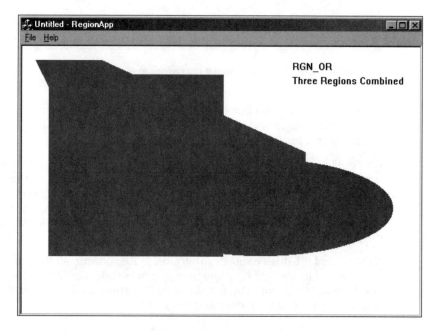

Figure 13-26: RegionApp displaying three regions in RGN_OR mode

Listing 13-15: RegionApp's OnDraw() function

```
void CRegionAppView::OnDraw(CDC* pDC)
{
    CRegionAppDoc* pDoc = GetDocument();
    ASSERT_VALID(pDoc);

    // TODO: add draw code for native data here

    switch (m_combineMode)
    {
    case RGN_AND:
        pDC->TextOut(400,20, "RGN_AND"); break;
    case RGN_COPY:
        pDC->TextOut(400,20, "RGN_COPY"); break;
    case RGN_DIFF:
        pDC->TextOut(400,20, "RGN_DIFF"); break;
    case RGN_OR:
        pDC->TextOut(400,20, "RGN_OR"); break;
    case RGN_XOR:
        pDC->TextOut(400,20, "RGN_XOR"); break;
    }

    if (m_showOnlyTwo)
        pDC->TextOut(400, 40, "Two Regions Combined");
    else
        pDC->TextOut(400, 40, "Three Regions Combined");

    CRgn region1;
    CRgn region2;
    CRgn region3;

    region1.CreateRectRgn(40, 40, 300, 300);
    region2.CreateEllipticRgn(160, 160, 550, 300);
    POINT points[5] = {
        120, 20, 420, 150, 420, 180, 130, 230, 20, 20};
    region3.CreatePolygonRgn(points, 5, WINDING);

    region1.CombineRgn(&region1, &region2,
        m_combineMode);
    if (!m_showOnlyTwo)
        region1.CombineRgn(&region1, &region3,
            m_combineMode);

    pDC->FillRgn(&region1, new CBrush(RGB(255,0,0)));
}
```

The OnDraw() function in Listing 13-15 performs the following tasks:

- Prints a text label for the selected region mode
- Prints a text label specifying whether the display combines two or three shapes
- Creates and initializes three region objects

- Combines the regions according to the currently selected options
- Draws the combined region in the window

The CRgn class has several other member functions you might find useful. Take some time to look the class up in your online Visual C++ documentation and see what the class has to offer.

Using Paths

Paths are similar to regions, except that paths contain lines and curves, rather than shapes like rectangles and ellipses. Like regions, however, paths must be created before they can be displayed. Once the path is created, the program can render it on the screen in various ways. In this section, you learn how to create and display paths.

Creating a path

You start a path by calling the DC object's BeginPath() member function. The system then stores any lines you draw, rather than displaying the lines on the screen. When you're through creating the path, you call the DC object's EndPath() member function. The following example creates a path that represents a four-sided polygon:

```
pDC->BeginPath();

pDC->MoveTo(20, 20);
pDC->LineTo(400, 100);
pDC->LineTo(500, 300);
pDC->LineTo(100, 200);
pDC->LineTo(20, 20);

pDC->EndPath();
```

Here, the program starts a path and then draws four lines, all of which are stored in the path, rather than rendered on the screen. The call to EndPath() ends the path.

Rendering a path

Now that you have all those lines stored, you might wonder what to do with them. As you may have guessed, Windows 98 supplies functions for displaying paths. Those functions, which are encapsulated in MFC's DC classes, are as follows:

StrokePath()	Draws the path using the current pen
FillPath()	Fills the path with the current brush
StrokeAndFillPath()	Draws and fills the path

So, to draw the path used in the previous example, you might use the following line:

```
pDC->StrokePath();
```

Because there can be only one path defined at a time, you don't need to supply any kind of path ID, handle, or object to `StrokePath()`, `FillPath()`, or `StrokeAndFillPath()`. However, rendering the path also destroys it.

Defining subpaths

A path can contain any number of subpaths, which are nothing more than paths within a path. When you call a function in a path that changes the drawing position, such as `MoveTo()`, you start a new subpath at the new position. When you render the path, such as by calling `StrokePath()`, the system renders all subpaths of the path. In this way, a path can define a set of shapes on the screen. For example, the lines in Listing 13-16 create three distinct figures when rendered. Notice the call to the `CloseFigure()` function.

Listing 13-16: Creating subpaths within a path

```
pDC->BeginPath();

pDC->MoveTo(20, 20);
pDC->LineTo(400, 100);
pDC->LineTo(500, 300);
pDC->LineTo(100, 200);
pDC->CloseFigure();

pDC->MoveTo(450, 50);
pDC->LineTo(550, 50);
pDC->LineTo(550, 150);
pDC->LineTo(450, 150);
pDC->CloseFigure();

pDC->MoveTo(50, 250);
pDC->LineTo(100, 250);
pDC->LineTo(100, 300);
pDC->LineTo(50, 300);
pDC->CloseFigure();

pDC->EndPath();
```

Here, the call to `BeginPath()` starts the path. The first call to `MoveTo()` then starts the first subpath, which comprises three lines. The call to `CloseFigure()` causes the system to finish the first figure by drawing a line between the starting and ending points. After creating the first subpath, the second call to `MoveTo()` starts another subpath, also consisting of three lines. Finally, the program creates a third subpath before calling `EndPath()` to end the path.

The PathApp sample program

On CD-ROM

In the Chapter13\PathApp folder of this book's CD-ROM, you can find the PathApp application, which demonstrates rendering paths. When you run the application, you see the window shown in Figure 13-27, which displays a path rendered with the StrokePath() function. To see the other types of path rendering, click in the window. With the first click, the program renders the path with FillPath() (see Figure 13-28); and with the second click, the program renders the path with StrokeAndFillPath() (see Figure 13-29).

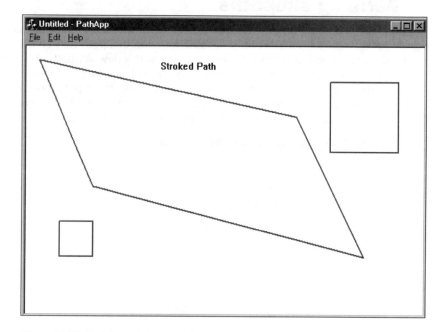

Figure 13-27: PathApp rendering with StrokePath()

Listing 13-17 shows the PathApp application's OnDraw() function, in which the program creates and renders the path according to the currently selected rendering style. The function first creates a path containing three subpaths, after which it creates a thick, red pen and a patterned brush, and then selects these new GDI objects into the DC. The m_renderStyle member variable determines whether the program renders the path with StrokePath(), FillPath(), or StrokeAndFillPath(). The value of this variable changes each time the user clicks in the window.

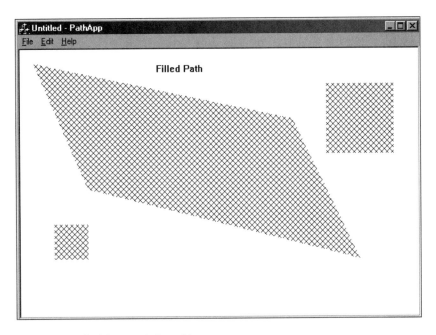

Figure 13-28: PathApp rendering with `FillPath()`

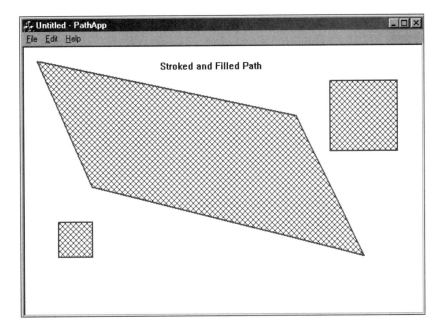

Figure 13-29: PathApp rendering with `StrokeAndFillPath()`

Listing 13-17: PathApp's `OnDraw()` function

```
void CPathAppView::OnDraw(CDC* pDC)
{
    CPathAppDoc* pDoc = GetDocument();
    ASSERT_VALID(pDoc);

    // TODO: add draw code for native data here

    pDC->BeginPath();

    pDC->MoveTo(20, 20);
    pDC->LineTo(400, 100);
    pDC->LineTo(500, 300);
    pDC->LineTo(100, 200);
    pDC->CloseFigure();

    pDC->MoveTo(450, 50);
    pDC->LineTo(550, 50);
    pDC->LineTo(550, 150);
    pDC->LineTo(450, 150);
    pDC->CloseFigure();

    pDC->MoveTo(50, 250);
    pDC->LineTo(100, 250);
    pDC->LineTo(100, 300);
    pDC->LineTo(50, 300);
    pDC->CloseFigure();

    pDC->EndPath();

    CPen redPen(PS_SOLID, 2, RGB(255,0,0));
    CPen* pOldPen = pDC->SelectObject(&redPen);
    CBrush patBrush(HS_DIAGCROSS, RGB(0,0,255));
    CBrush* pOldBrush = pDC->SelectObject(&patBrush);

    if (m_renderStyle == 0)
    {
        pDC->StrokePath();
        pDC->TextOut(200, 20, "Stroked Path");
    }
    else if (m_renderStyle == 1)
    {
        pDC->FillPath();
        pDC->TextOut(200, 20, "Filled Path");
    }
    else
    {
        pDC->StrokeAndFillPath();
        pDC->TextOut(200, 20, "Stroked and Filled Path");
    }

    pDC->SelectObject(pOldPen);
    pDC->SelectObject(pOldBrush);
}
```

Tip

Paths are a powerful tool for creating complex regions because any path can be converted to a region by calling the region object's `CreateFromPath()` member function. `CreateFromPath()` takes as a single argument the address of the DC containing the path.

Summary

By manipulating window and viewport origins and extents, you can control how Windows maps logical coordinates to the screen. This gives you the power to create displays that represent any type of coordinate system you need. Drawing modes enable you to pull off some seemingly magical stunts when displaying bitmaps or drawing lines. You can even make graphics appear and disappear without damaging a background image, regardless of how complex the background is. Finally, regions and paths provide techniques for specifying nonrectangular areas of the screen.

Also discussed in this chapter:

▶ Physical coordinates represent the pixels on the screen, whereas logical coordinates are the coordinates you supply to GDI drawing functions.

▶ Windows automatically maps logical coordinates to physical coordinates.

▶ By changing the window or viewport origin, an application can control where on the display it draws data, without changing the logical coordinates supplied to drawing functions.

▶ Mapping modes determine how Windows orients the X and Y axes and specifies the unit of measure applied to logical coordinates.

▶ When using the `MM_ISOTROPIC` and `MM_ANISOTROPIC` mapping modes, you can specify the window and viewport extents, which control how Windows maps logical coordinates to physical coordinates.

▶ Bitmap drawing modes, such as `SRCAND` and `SRCPAINT`, enable you to combine source pixels, screen pixels, and the current brush in various ways.

▶ Line drawing modes, such as `R2_COPYPEN` and `R2_XORPEN`, determine how the current pen is combined with the screen color.

▶ Regions are areas of the screen defined by rectangles, polygons, and ellipses.

▶ Paths comprise a set of lines or subpaths that can be rendered on the screen is various ways or that can be converted to a complex region.

Part III

OS Core

Chapter 14

Memory Management

In This Chapter

▶ Introducing memory management

▶ Applying standard C library functions for memory allocation

▶ Using the Windows 98 API for memory allocation

▶ Allocating movable memory

▶ Allocating discardable memory

Today's computers boast large amounts of memory, much more than anyone could have imagined having in a computer a decade ago. In 1982, my first Radio Shack computer had 4K, while 32 megabytes of RAM is now common for new computers. The best part is that, as a Windows programmer, most of this memory now is at your beck and call. You can use it to store text, pictures, database records, spreadsheet cells, and any other kind of data you can think of. However, although C++ allocates memory for the data objects you create in a program, sooner or later you're going to need to allocate and manipulate memory directly. In this chapter, you'll learn the techniques Windows programmers rely upon to handle these cases.

The Development of Memory Management

Memory management has come a long way since the early days. If it's been a while since you programmed an IBM-compatible computer, you may be used to dealing with memory under DOS, which requires manipulating segmented addresses. A *segmented address* is a 20-bit value that contains a 4-bit segment address and a 16-bit offset. Because a 20-bit value can be one of 1,048,576 values, a segmented address can access a megabyte of memory.

Handling segmented addresses was a bit sticky. You couldn't just increment the 20-bit value to get the next address. You had to watch for the 16-bit offset to reach its maximum value, at which point you had to change the segment in order to access the next address. If you failed to deal with the segment address when your offset wrapped around, you ended up with an address 64K too small, usually not what you wanted. Back in those days, C compilers required that you choose from the small, medium, large, and huge memory models, depending upon how much code and data space your program needed.

Thankfully, those days are gone forever. Starting with Windows 95, the Windows operating system uses a 32-bit flat addressing scheme. This means that each 32-bit address directly represents an address in memory, without having to consider segments and offsets. A 32-bit address can access up to four gigabytes of memory, much more than any desktop computer has available. (Still, I hesitate to say that 4GB is a lot of memory. Remember when we thought 64K was more memory than we'd ever need? That naïve assumption is what lead us to complications like segmented addresses.)

Although desktop computers don't have 4GB of memory, Windows 98 uses all that memory anyway. How? By creating virtual memory. *Virtual memory* enables Windows to present your application with a 4GB memory space, even though you have nowhere near that much memory installed in your computer. Windows simulates this extra memory by swapping memory to and from the hard disk. The memory addresses your application sees are not the actual physical addresses the system uses. Windows internally translates the virtual memory address to the actual physical address. This translation is all handled in the background. As far as your application is concerned, it has 4GB.

Note

Although Windows 98 gives your application 4GB of virtual memory space, your application can access only about half of that for its own private use. Windows uses the rest of the virtual memory for system purposes.

PROBLEMS & SOLUTIONS

Determining Available Memory

PROBLEM: *How can I determine how much physical and virtual memory is available to my application?*

SOLUTION: The Windows 98 API provides the `GlobalMemoryStatus()` function for this purpose. Following is that function's signature:

```
GlobalMemoryStatus(LPMEMORYSTATUS memoryStatus);
```

The `GlobalMemoryStatus()` function's single argument is a pointer to a `MEMORYSTATUS` structure, which the function uses to return information about the system's memory. Windows declares the `MEMORYSTATUS` structure like this:

```
typedef struct _MEMORYSTATUS { // mst
    DWORD dwLength; // sizeof(MEMORYSTATUS)
    DWORD dwMemoryLoad; // percent of memory in use
    DWORD dwTotalPhys; // bytes of physical memory
    DWORD dwAvailPhys; // free physical memory bytes
    DWORD dwTotalPageFile; // bytes of paging file
    DWORD dwAvailPageFile; // free bytes of paging file
    DWORD dwTotalVirtual; // user bytes of address space
```

Continued

```
    DWORD dwAvailVirtual; // free user bytes
} MEMORYSTATUS, *LPMEMORYSTATUS;
```

The comments in the structure definition tell you what each data member returns. Before calling `GlobalMemoryStatus()`, you should set the `dwLength` data member. The following lines demonstrate how to call `GlobalMemoryStatus()`:

```
MEMORYSTATUS memoryStatus;
memoryStatus.dwLength = sizeof(MEMORYSTATUS);
GlobalMemoryStatus(&memoryStatus);
```

Memory Allocation with C Library Functions

When performing memory allocation under Windows 98, you can use the old tried-and-true C library functions, or opt for Windows 98 API functions. You have four standard functions at your beck and call when using C memory management:

`malloc()`	Allocates a block of memory of the given size
`calloc()`	Allocates a block of memory based on the number of data elements the memory block must hold
`realloc`	Changes the size of a previously allocated memory block
`free()`	Releases a block of memory

malloc()

The `malloc()` function's signature looks like this:

```
void* malloc(UINT size);
```

The `malloc()` function takes as a single parameter the number of bytes to allocate. A typical call to `malloc()` follows:

```
int* p = (int*) malloc(2048);
```

The above line allocates 2,048 bytes of memory. The `malloc()` function returns a pointer to `void`, so you must usually cast the pointer to the data type you need. In the above case, the pointer returned from `malloc()` is cast to `int`. Because the Windows 98 integer is four bytes, the shown call to `malloc()` allocates enough memory for 512 integers. If the call to `malloc()` fails, the function returns `NULL`.

calloc()

When you want to allocate memory for a specific number of data elements, it might make for clearer code to use calloc() instead of malloc(). Following is the calloc() function's signature:

```
void* calloc(UINT num, UINT dataSize);
```

The calloc() function has two parameters:

num	The number of data elements for which you want to allocate memory
dwBytes	The size of a single data element

The total amount of memory allocated is equal to the first parameter multiplied by the second. Like malloc(), calloc() returns a void pointer that you'll usually want to cast to another data type. If the call to calloc() fails, the function returns a NULL pointer.

To reserve the same amount of memory as in the malloc() example, you might make the following function call:

```
int* p = (int*) calloc(512, sizeof(int));
```

realloc()

There may be times when you've allocated a block of memory and then later in the program need to resize the block. You can do this by calling the realloc() function. The realloc() function's signature looks like this:

```
void* realloc(void* memPointer, UINT size);
```

The realloc() function's two parameters are *memPointer*, designating a pointer to the existing memory block; and *size*, designating the memory block's new size.

A typical call to realloc() looks like this:

```
p = (int*) realloc(p, 4096);
```

The new size may be larger or smaller than the original block. The realloc() function returns a pointer to void, so you'll probably need to cast it to a specific data type. If the memory reallocation fails, realloc() returns a NULL pointer.

free()

When you're through with a block of allocated memory, the rules of good programming dictate that the block should be released. You do this with the free() function:

```
void free(p);
```

Here, the function's single argument is a pointer to the block of memory to release.

Note

Under Windows 98, every application gets its own 4GB virtual memory space. When the application ends, this memory space is released, including any unreleased memory blocks you may have allocated. For this reason, failing to release a block of memory, while a bad programming practice, has no effect on other applications running in the system. Contrast this with versions of Windows previous to Windows 95, in which objects and memory blocks that weren't released stayed around until Windows itself shut down.

Memory Allocation with Windows 98 Functions

Windows 98 defines its own large set of memory management functions. In most cases, the C library functions work just fine. There may be times, however, when you want your allocated memory blocks to be managed by the Windows 98 system. This enables you to allocate movable or discardable memory. Moreover, Windows 98 provides utility functions that enable you to initialize, move, and copy memory blocks. Windows 98's memory management functions are listed in Table 14-1:

Table 14-1 Memory Management Functions

Function	Description
Copy Memory()	Copies a block of memory from one location to another
FillMemory()	Fills a block of memory with a given value
GlobalAlloc()	Allocates a block of memory of the given size
GlobalDiscard()	Discards an allocated memory block
GlobalFlags()	Returns the flags associated with a memory block
GlobalFree()	Releases an allocated memory block
GlobalHandle()	Gets the handle of an allocated memory block
GlobalLock()	Locks an allocated memory block
GlobalMemoryStatus()	Returns the amount of physical and virtual memory available to the application
GlobalReAlloc()	Changes the size of a previously allocated memory block
GlobalSize()	Gets the size of an allocated memory block
GlobalUnlock()	Unlocks an allocated memory block
LocalAlloc()	Same as GlobalAlloc()
LocalDiscard()	Same as GlobalDiscard()

(continued)

Table 14-1 *(Continued)*	
LocalFlags()	Same as GlobalFlags()
LocalFree()	Same as GlobalFree()
LocalHandle()	Same as GlobalHandle()
LocalLock()	Same as GlobalLock()
LocalReAlloc()	Same as GlobalReAlloc()
LocalSize()	Same as GlobalSize()
LocalUnlock()	Same as GlobalUnlock()
MoveMemory()	Moves a block of memory from one location to another
VirtualAlloc()	Allocates virtual memory
VirtualFree()	Releases virtual memory
ZeroMemory()	Fills a block of memory with zeroes

Note

You may have noticed in Table 14-1 that many of the functions starting with the word "Global" also have an equivalent function that starts with the word "Local." The local functions are included in Windows 98 only for backward compatibility with 16-bit Windows; they work exactly like the global functions. In fact, you can pretty much ignore the local functions altogether. They're included in the list because you may see them used in older source code, and you should know what they do.

For most of your Windows 98 memory management needs, you'll only need GlobalAlloc(), GlobalFree(), and GlobalReAlloc(). You can use these three functions in much the same way you use the C library memory management functions. For example, you use GlobalAlloc() to allocate a block of memory. GlobalAlloc()'s signature looks like this:

```
HGLOBAL GlobalAlloc(UINT uFlags, DWORD dwBytes);
```

The function's two arguments are as follows:

uFlags	A set of flags that describe the memory allocation attributes
dwBytes	The size, in bytes, of the memory block to allocate

Windows defines a set of constants that represent the values you can use for the uFlags argument. Following are the most useful of the flags:

GMEM_FIXED	Allocates a fixed memory block
GMEM_ZEROINIT	Initializes the memory block to all zeroes
GMEM_MOVEABLE	Allocates a movable memory block
GPTR	Combines GMEM_FIXED and GMEM_ZEROINIT
GHND	Combines GMEM_MOVEABLE and GMEM_ZEROINIT
GMEM_DISCARDABLE	Allocates discardable memory

Suppose you want to allocate a fixed 2,048-byte block of memory. The call to GlobalAlloc() might look like this:

```
int* p = (int*) GlobalAlloc(GMEM_FIXED | GMEM_ZEROINIT, 2048);
```

or

```
int* p = (int*) GlobalAlloc(GPTR, 2048);
```

When used with the GMEM_FIXED or GPTR flag, GlobalAlloc() returns a pointer to void that you can cast to whatever data type is appropriate for your program.

Note

Windows defines constants other than those listed here for the uFlags argument. However, the other constants are too esoteric to bother with in this chapter. You can find the additional flags by looking up GlobalAlloc() in your Visual C++ online documentation.

When you want to change the size of an allocated memory block, you call GlobalReAlloc(), whose signature looks like this:

```
HGLOBAL GlobalReAlloc(HGLOBAL hMem, DWORD dwBytes,
    UINT uFlags);
```

The function's arguments are as follows:

hMem	The memory block's handle
dwBytes	The size, in bytes, of the memory block to reallocate
uFlags	A set of flags that describe the memory allocation attributes

In the case of a fixed memory block, hMem can be the pointer to the memory block, rather than a handle. So, a call to GlobalReAlloc() might look something like this:

```
p = (int*) GlobalReAlloc(p, 4096, GMEM_ZEROINIT);
```

Finally, when it comes time to release allocated memory, call GlobalFree():

```
GlobalFree(p);
```

PROBLEMS & SOLUTIONS

Validating Pointers and Memory

PROBLEM: *How can I determine whether a pointer points to a valid location, and also whether the entire memory block is valid?*

SOLUTION: Windows 98 features six functions you can use to validate pointers and the memory to which those pointers point. The following list shows each of these functions' signatures, as well as describes the function. Each of the functions returns a BOOL value indicating the validity of the pointer and the memory block. For additional information, look the functions up in your Visual C++ online documentation.

`BOOL IsBadCodePtr(FARPROC lpfunction)`	Checks the validity of a pointer for read access
`BOOL IsBadHugeReadPtr` `(CONST void* lpMemory, UINT uSize)`	Checks the validity of a pointer and a memory range for read access
`BOOL IsBadHugeWritePtr` `(LPVOID lpMemory, UINT uSize)`	Checks the validity of a pointer and a memory range for write access
`BOOL IsBadReadPtr` `(CONST VOID lpMemory, UINT uSize)`	Checks the validity of a pointer and a memory range for read access
`BOOL IsBadStringPtr` `(LPCTSTR lpString, UINT uSize)`	Checks the validity of a string pointer
`BOOL IsBadWritePtr` `(LPVOID lp, UINT uSize)`	Checks the validity of a pointer and a memory range for write access

Allocating Movable Memory

If your program does a lot of memory allocation and memory releasing, it's possible that the application's virtual memory space could become fragmented, which could start to slow the system down. One way to avoid this is to let Windows manage the memory as it sees fit. That is, rather than allocate fixed memory, allocate movable memory.

Before you do this, however, you might want to know exactly how fixed memory and movable memory differ.

Fixed memory   Although these allocations always remain fixed at
                      their virtual addresses, Windows can move their
                      blocks around in physical memory. This is
                      because your application only accesses the
                      memory block through its virtual address. Even
                      though Windows may have moved the memory
                      block in physical memory, your application
                      doesn't notice the change.

Movable memory   Windows doesn't have to keep the allocated
                      memory block at the same virtual address, and it
                      can do anything it wants to with the memory
                      block. This makes it easier for Windows to keep
                      your application's virtual memory from becoming
                      too fragmented.

How then, you ask, can your application know where the memory block is
located when the program needs it? That's where handles come in. When
you allocate a movable block of memory, your application doesn't receive a
pointer to the memory. Instead, the program receives a handle. This handle
acts as an ID for the memory block. You give Windows the handle, and
Windows then looks to see where it has placed the block in memory.

You allocate movable memory by calling `GlobalAlloc()` with the
`GMEM_MOVEABLE` or `GHND` flags:

```
GLOBALHANDLE hMemHandle = GlobalAlloc(GMEM_MOVEABLE | GMEM_ZEROINIT,
2048);
```

or

```
GLOBALHANDLE hMemHandle = GlobalAlloc(GHND, 2048);
```

In this case, `GlobalAlloc()` returns a handle to the memory block, rather than
a pointer. In order to get a pointer to the block, you must first lock the block
in memory, which temporarily makes the block fixed, rather than movable.
The function that gets this done is `GlobalLock()`, whose signature follows:

```
LPVOID GlobalLock(GLOBALHANDLE hMem);
```

The function's single argument is a handle to the memory block to lock. A
call to `GlobalLock()` might look like this:

```
int* p = (int*) GlobalLock(hMemHandle);
```

Now that you have a pointer to a fixed block of memory, you can manipulate
the memory block as needed. When you're finished accessing the block, you
must unlock it, which tells Windows that it can go back to moving the block
around. You do this by calling `GlobalUnlock()`:

```
BOOL GlobalUnlock(hMemHandle);
```

Finally, and as a good programmer should, when you're completely finished
with the allocated memory block, you must release it. Windows 98 offers the
`GlobalFree()` function in order to handle this task:

```
GlobalFree(hMemHandle);
```

As you can see, this function's single argument is a handle to the memory block.

Allocating Discardable Memory

Windows likes to have complete control over your allocated memory blocks. In the previous section, you saw one way to give Windows some extra control by allocating memory as a movable block. Another way is to make the memory block discardable, which enables Windows to throw the block away whenever it wants to reuse the physical memory where the block is stored.

If Windows does discard the block, it's up to you to recreate it, which can be a bit of a hassle. Of course, just because Windows wants control over your memory blocks, it doesn't mean you have to give up that control. But if for some reason you like the idea of discardable memory blocks, just allocate the block using the GMEM_DISCARDABLE flag along with GMEM_MOVEABLE. (A discardable memory block must also be movable.) You might create a discardable memory block like this:

```
GLOBALHANDLE hMemHandle =
    GlobalAlloc(GMEM_MOVEABLE | GMEM_DISCARDABLE | GMEM_ZEROINIT,
2048);
```

or

```
GLOBALHANDLE hMemHandle = GlobalAlloc(GHND | GMEM_DISCARDABLE, 2048);
```

Tip

How do you know when Windows has discarded your memory block? When you call GlobalLock(), the function returns NULL. That NULL means that you must recreate the memory block.

Summary

You have many options for managing memory under Windows 98. You can use either the standard C library functions, or Windows 98's large set of memory management functions. Windows' memory management functions are more complicated to use than the C functions, but offer greater flexibility, such as the ability to create movable and discardable memory blocks.

Also discussed in this chapter:

▶ Windows 98 uses a flat memory model with 32-bit addresses.

▶ A running Windows application gets 4GB of virtual memory, but can access only about half of that memory space for its private use.

▶ If you stick with the standard C library functions, memory management under Windows isn't much different from memory management under DOS.

▶ When you allocate memory using `GlobalAlloc()`, you must supply flags that represent the memory allocation attributes. These attributes enable you to specify fixed, movable, or discardable memory, as well as to initialize memory to all zeroes.

▶ Windows can move fixed memory in physical memory, but the memory's virtual address stays the same. Because your application knows about only the virtual address, the changing physical address has no effect on the application.

▶ Windows can move movable memory blocks both in physical and virtual memory, which guards against virtual memory becoming fragmented.

▶ To access movable memory, you must first lock the memory block, which gives you a pointer to the block. When you're finished with the block, you must unlock it so that Windows can move the block if it needs to.

▶ Windows can throw away discardable memory blocks any time it wants access to more physical memory. If Windows discards your memory block, you must recreate the block from scratch.

Chapter 15

Process Control

Windows 98 is a complex operating system that does an impressive job juggling multiple processes so they seem to execute concurrently. From the user's point of view, Windows 98's multitasking enables Windows to run multiple applications at the same time. Windows 98 programmers, however, know that there's a lot more going on under the hood, where each application may contain several threads. Each of these, in turn, acts as a kind of mini-process.

Programming multiple threads can be a sticky process. You can't just throw a bunch of code into a thread and expect everything to run smoothly. You must be concerned with how the threads work together, and especially how the threads use shared resources. In this chapter, you examine thread programming and learn a few tricks that might keep you out of trouble.

Processes, Threads, and Priorities

Under Windows 98, a *process* is more or less equivalent to a running application. For example, when you run your Web browser, you're creating a Windows process. But a process doesn't necessarily have to have a window or even appear on the screen at all. Any program running on your computer is a process. A *thread*, on the other hand, is a distinct path of execution within a process. All processes have at least one thread, which is called the *primary thread*. A process may also start any number of secondary threads, which can perform concurrent tasks on behalf of the process.

Each process and thread has a priority setting that determines when it runs and how much CPU time it gets. Specifically, Windows 98's scheduler assigns CPU time to each process and thread based on the process's and thread's priority. These priorities change constantly as Windows attempts to keep every thread running smoothly. Normally, a high-priority thread gets the first crack at CPU time. The high-priority thread then runs until it no longer has messages to process, at which point Windows schedules another thread.

Because most threads — including high-priority threads — spend a lot of time waiting for messages, low-priority threads usually get all the CPU time they need. However, Windows raises the priority level of threads that haven't run for a while in order to ensure that every thread gets its fair share of CPU time. Windows may also raise a thread's priority if that thread is holding a resource needed by a higher-priority thread. This is because the higher-priority thread is effectively blocked until the low-priority thread releases the shared resource. Finally, Windows slightly raises the priority of threads whose containing process is the foreground application. Conversely, Windows slightly lowers the priority of threads whose containing process is in the background.

Both processes and threads receive their own priority settings. Processes are assigned one of four priority levels. Normally, a process should be assigned the `NORMAL_PRIORITY_CLASS` priority level. The other priority classes are for special circumstances. The `HIGH_PRIORITY_CLASS` and `REALTIME_PRIORITY_CLASS`, in particular, should be used with caution, as they are capable of slowing other processes to a crawl. Following are the process priority classes defined by Windows 98:

`HIGH_PRIORITY_CLASS`	Process is scheduled over `IDLE_PRIORITY_CLASS` and `NORMAL_PRIORITY_CLASS` processes.
`IDLE_PRIORITY_CLASS`	Process is scheduled only when all other processes are blocked (i.e., have no messages to process).
`NORMAL_PRIORITY_CLASS`	Process is scheduled as normal.
`REALTIME_PRIORITY_CLASS`	Process is scheduled over all other priority classes.

Threads get a relative priority setting that's calculated from both the priority that the programmer requests for the thread and the priority of the thread's containing process. This final thread priority, which can be a value from 0 to 31, is called the *base priority level*. Windows 98 defines thread priority classes to enable you to set the appropriate priority level for a thread's task. For example, a thread that receives data from a modem requires a higher priority than a thread that reads data from a disk file because the modem thread cannot afford to miss even a single byte of incoming data, whereas the file thread's data is available whenever the thread needs it. Table 15-1 lists the thread priority classes and their descriptions:

Table 15-1   Thread Priority Classes

Thread Priority Classes	Descriptions
THREAD_PRIORITY_IDLE	Thread's base priority level is 1 when the thread is contained in a HIGH_PRIORITY_CLASS or lower process. Thread's base priority level is 16 when the thread is contained in a REALTIME_PRIORITY_CLASS process.
THREAD_PRIORITY_LOWEST	Thread's base priority level is two less than the containing process's priority level.
THREAD_PRIORITY_BELOW_NORMAL	Thread's base priority level is one less than the containing process's priority level.
THREAD_PRIORITY_NORMAL	Thread's base priority level is the same as the containing process's priority level.
THREAD_PRIORITY_ABOVE_NORMAL	Thread's base priority level is one higher than the containing process's priority level.
THREAD_PRIORITY_HIGHEST	Thread's base priority level is two higher than the containing process's priority level.
THREAD_PRIORITY_CRITICAL	Thread's base priority level is 15 when the thread is contained in a HIGH_PRIORITY_CLASS or lower process. Thread's base priority level is 31 when the thread is contained in a REALTIME_PRIORITY_CLASS process.

Note

Always remember that the CPU is a shared resource and that other applications running on the user's system are vying for their fair share of CPU time. Never set a process's or thread's priority level higher than it needs to be. In most cases the NORMAL_PRIORITY_CLASS and THREAD_PRIORITY_NORMAL settings work just fine.

Note

You can temporarily set a thread's priority to a higher level in order to ensure better performance for the user. (This is what Windows does when a process moves from the background to the foreground.) However, when the thread's need for a higher priority expires, remember to return the priority to its previous lower setting.

MFC provides a special class for threads, called CWinThread. You can derive your own thread classes from CWinThread and then use the class's member functions to manipulate the thread. You can do this in two ways, depending upon whether you're creating a user interface thread or a worker thread.

User Interface Threads and Worker Threads

Windows applications programmed with MFC feature two types of threads:
user interface (UI) threads and worker threads. A *UI thread* processes
Windows messages, and so can create and manage user-interface elements
such as windows and controls. A *worker thread* does not process Windows
messages and is used to perform background tasks, such as controlling an
animation sequence or calculating the contents of a spreadsheet.

Creating a worker thread

Obviously, because a worker thread handles no Windows messages, it's often
much easier to program than a UI thread. In fact, in your MFC programs, you
can get a worker thread going with a single function call:

```
CWinThread* thread = AfxBeginThread(ThreadProc, pParam);
```

This function call creates and runs a thread with normal priority. `ThreadProc`
is the address of the function that represents the thread, and `pParam` is a 32-
bit value that gets passed to the thread function. In other words, when the
above call executes, MFC calls `ThreadProc()`, running the function as a
secondary thread. `ThreadProc()` receives the `pParam` value as its single
parameter, as you can see in the following `ThreadProc()` signature:

```
UINT ThreadProc(LPVOID pParam);
```

Of course, you can call your thread's function anything you like; you don't
have to stick with `ThreadProc()`. For example, the following is a thread
function that displays a message box on the screen and then exits, ending
the thread:

```
UINT MessageThread(LPVOID pParam)
{
    char* pMessage = (char*) pParam;
    CWnd* pMainWnd = AfxGetMainWnd();
    ::MessageBox(pMainWnd->m_hWnd,
        pMessage, "Thread Message", MB_OK);
    return 0;
}
```

The `MessageThread()` function performs the following tasks:

- Casts the `pParam` parameter to a `char` pointer
- Gets a pointer to the application's main window
- Displays a message box, using the main window's handle and the
  message passed to the function

Note

For more information on window handles, please refer to Chapter 6,
"Windows and Dialogs."

The line that starts the thread might look like this:

```
AfxBeginThread (MessageThread,
    "Greetings from your thread!");
```

Tip

Notice the way that `MessageThread()` uses the `pParam` parameter in order to pass the address of the string to display in the message box. You can use this parameter to pass any 32-bit value, including something simple like a window handle or something more snazzy like a pointer to a structure containing information needed by the thread.

On CD-ROM

In the ThreadApp1 directory of this book's CD-ROM, you'll find a simple program that implements the `MessageThread()` function in the application's view class. Although `MessageThread()` is defined in the view class's implementation file, it is not a member function of the class. Defining `MessageThread()` in the view class's implementation file is just a convenience, because the view class's `OnLButtonDown()` function starts the thread. Figure 15-1 shows ThreadApp1 in action, sending you a message from a running thread. When you run the application, click inside the window to start the thread.

How does the thread end? When the `MessageThread()` function ends, so does the thread it represents. As ThreadApp1's user, to end the thread in ThreadApp1, you dismiss the message box. `MessageThread()` then executes its return statement and ends, taking the thread with it.

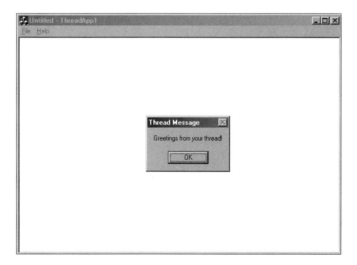

Figure 15-1: The ThreadApp1 application's thread displays its message box, informing you that the thread is running.

The call to `AfxBeginThread()` isn't quite as simple as it looks. There are actually many more parameters than those shown in the previous sample code segment. However, most of the parameters have default values. The complete `AfxBeginThread()` signature looks like this:

```
CWinThread* AfxBeginThread(
    AFX_THREADPROC pfnThreadProc,
    LPVOID pParam,
    int nPriority = THREAD_PRIORITY_NORMAL,
    UINT nStackSize = 0,
    DWORD dwCreateFlags = 0,
    LPSECURITY_ATTRIBUTES lpSecurityAttrs = NULL);
```

As you can see, the full `AfxBeginThread()` takes six parameters:

`pfnThreadProc`	The address of the function that implements the thread
`pParam`	A 32-bit value that is passed to the thread function
`nPriority`	The thread's initial priority level
`nStackSize`	The maximum stack size
`dwCreateFlags`	A flag specifying how the thread should be started. A value of 0 executes the thread immediately upon creation; a value of `CREATE_SUSPENDED` suspends the thread after it's created.
`lpSecurityAttrs`	A pointer to a `SECURITY_ATTRIBUTES` structure

In most cases, the default values for `AfxBeginThread()`'s parameters work fine. If you want to dig further into the innards of threads, you can find more information on these parameters in your Visual C++ online documentation.

Creating a UI thread

Because UI threads must contain a message loop, they are more complicated to deal with than worker threads. Instead of just writing a thread function and calling `AfxBeginThread()` to start it, you must derive a custom thread class from MFC's `CWinThread` class. This thread class must override the class's `InitInstance()` function, where the thread can perform any initialization tasks. MFC calls `InitInstance()` when it first creates the thread. It's also a good idea to override `ExitInstance()`, which is `InitInstance()`'s counterpart. MFC calls `ExitInstance()` before it destroys the thread object, so that the thread can clean up after itself.

When you create your main application with AppWizard, you can use ClassWizard to create your thread class:

1. Press Ctrl+W to display ClassWizard.

2. Click the Add Class button, and select New from its menu, as shown in Figure 15-2.

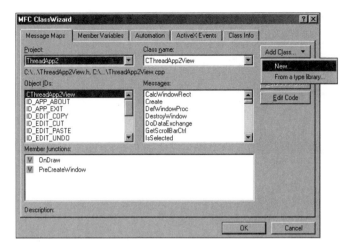

Figure 15-2: The MFC ClassWizard dialog box displayed while creating a new class

3. After the New Class dialog box appears, type the name of the new class in the Name box; then, select CWinThread in the Base Class box, as shown in Figure 15-3.

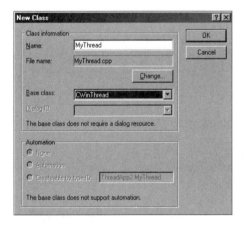

Figure 15-3: The New Class dialog box displayed with the name and base class of the new class

4. Click OK to create the thread class. ClassWizard reappears with the thread class selected, as shown in Figure 15-4. Notice how ClassWizard has already overridden the `InitInstance()` and `ExitInstance()` member functions for you, listing their names in the Member Functions box.

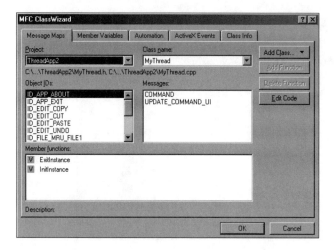

Figure 15-4: ClassWizard displaying the new thread class

Listings 15-1 and 15-2 show the thread class that ClassWizard creates for you. (Some of the ClassWizard stuff has been edited from the files.) Whether or not you take advantage of ClassWizard to create your thread class, you can use the source code in the listings as the skeleton for other UI thread classes you might want to create.

Listing 15-1: The MyThread **class's header file,** MyThread.h

```
class MyThread : public CWinThread
{
    DECLARE_DYNCREATE(MyThread)
protected:
    MyThread();

// Attributes
public:

// Operations
public:

// Overrides
    // ClassWizard generated virtual function overrides
    //{{AFX_VIRTUAL(MyThread)
    public:
    virtual BOOL InitInstance();
    virtual int ExitInstance();
    //}}AFX_VIRTUAL

// Implementation
protected:
    virtual ~MyThread();
```

```
    // Generated message map functions
    //{{AFX_MSG(MyThread)
        // NOTE - the ClassWizard will add and remove member
functions here.
    //}}AFX_MSG

    DECLARE_MESSAGE_MAP()
};
```

Listing 15-2: The MyThread **class's implementation file,** MyThread.cpp

```
#include "stdafx.h"
#include "ThreadApp2.h"
#include "MyThread.h"

#ifdef _DEBUG
#define new DEBUG_NEW
#undef THIS_FILE
static char THIS_FILE[] = __FILE__;
#endif

///////////////////////////////////////////////////////
// MyThread

IMPLEMENT_DYNCREATE(MyThread, CWinThread)

MyThread::MyThread()
{
}

MyThread::~MyThread()
{
}

BOOL MyThread::InitInstance()
{
    // TODO:  perform and per-thread initialization here
    return TRUE;
}

int MyThread::ExitInstance()
{
    // TODO:  perform any per-thread cleanup here
    return CWinThread::ExitInstance();
}

BEGIN_MESSAGE_MAP(MyThread, CWinThread)
    //{{AFX_MSG_MAP(MyThread)
        // NOTE - the ClassWizard will add and\
remove mapping macros here.
    //}}AFX_MSG_MAP
END_MESSAGE_MAP()
```

In order to give this thread something to do, you might have it create a window in its `InitInstance()` function. That source code might look something like this:

```
BOOL MyThread::InitInstance()
{
    CFrameWnd* pFrameWnd = new CFrameWnd();
    pFrameWnd->Create(NULL, "Thread Window");
    pFrameWnd->ShowWindow(SW_SHOW);
    pFrameWnd->UpdateWindow();
    return TRUE;
}
```

Finally, the main program needs to start the UI thread. This is done much like starting a worker thread, by calling a version of `AfxBeginThread()`:

```
AfxBeginThread(RUNTIME_CLASS(MyThread));
```

Here, the function's single parameter is a pointer to the `CRuntimeClass` structure representing the thread class. The `RUNTIME_CLASS` MFC macro very nicely generates the structure for you. All you have to do is give the macro the class's name. Although it doesn't require the 32-bit `pParam` parameter, this version of `AfxBeginThread()` has exactly the same default parameters as the version you used to create a worker thread.

You probably won't have much call for creating UI threads in your programs. Most secondary threads, after all, are worker threads. For that reason, the remainder of this chapter concentrates on worker threads.

 PROBLEMS & SOLUTIONS

Process-to-Thread Communication

PROBLEM: *How can my program communicate with a thread?*

SOLUTION: Often when you program threads, you need a way for the thread and its containing process to communicate. There are actually several ways to do this. The easiest method is to define a global variable that both the thread and the process can access. You could, for example, set up an integer variable as a flag to signal when a thread should end.

To implement this technique, first define a global variable that the program and thread can use as a communication channel:

```
int threadFlag;
```

Continued

Then, set the global variable to an appropriate starting value and start the thread:

```
threadFlag = 1;
HWND hWnd = GetSafeHwnd();
AfxBeginThread(FlagThread, hWnd);
```

The thread function then gets to work, doing whatever processing it needs to do while constantly checking the value of the global variable:

```
UINT FlagThread(LPVOID pParam)
{
    while(threadFlag == 1)
    {
        // The thread does its work here.
    }
    return 0;
}
```

To stop the thread, the program only needs to change the value of the global variable:

```
threadFlag = 0;
```

When the thread's `while` loop checks `threadFlag`, the loop ends, which, in this case, also ends the thread.

Using global variables to communicate between a process and a thread is a simple method, but not always the best. A more elegant way to perform similar communication is with an **event object**. To learn more about event objects, read "Using event objects," later in this chapter.

Thread Synchronization

You might think at this point that using threads is downright easy. This is a perfect example of how a little knowledge can be dangerous. When you start programming threads, you can quickly run into serious trouble if you don't consider something called *thread synchronization*. Using thread synchronization techniques ensures that multiple threads don't simultaneously access critical shared resources.

Suppose your program defines a data structure that holds information the application requires to generate its display. This data might be, for example, the contents of a spreadsheet. The application has a thread that reads the spreadsheet data in order to display values in each cell on the screen. Meanwhile, another thread enables the user to edit the contents of the spreadsheet.

Without thread synchronization, this situation is a disaster waiting to happen. Why? You can't allow the calculation thread to access the data at the same time the edit thread does. If the threads access the data simultaneously, the calculation thread may read a data element that is in the process of being edited, getting a value of, say, 30, instead of 3,000. Obviously, such bad data reads would make the spreadsheet useless.

In order to avoid such problems, Visual C++ defines four MFC synchronization objects you can use in your multithreaded programs:

Events	Used as flags to pass signals between threads
Critical Sections	Used within a process as keys to gain access to shared resources
Mutexes	Work like critical sections, except they can synchronize threads in multiple processes, rather than in just a single process
Semaphores	Enables multiple threads, up to a given limit, to access shared resources

For a more in-depth explanation of each object, please refer to their extended definitions in Chapter 1, "A Windows 98 Overview."

Using event objects

Event objects are really little more than sophisticated flags—that is, an event object can be on or off. When an event object is on, it is said to be in its signaled state. Conversely, when the event object is off, it is in its nonsignaled state. Threads can watch for changes in an event object's signal state in order to determine whether it's safe to run. With MFC, you can create automatic or manual event objects.

Automatic event objects

In Visual C++, the MFC class CEvent represents event objects. To create an event object, you usually create a global CEvent object:

```
CEvent eventObj;
```

Although they're not shown in this line, CEvent's constructor actually has four parameters. All of these have default values, as you can see in the following function signature:

```
CEvent(
    BOOL bInitiallyOwn = FALSE,
    BOOL bManualReset = FALSE,
    LPCTSTR lpszName = NULL,
    LPSECURITY_ATTRIBUTES lpsaAttribute = NULL );
```

The four parameters are as follows:

bInitiallyOwn	Determines the starting signal state (TRUE = signaled; FALSE = nonsignaled)
bManualReset	Determines whether this is a manual (TRUE) or automatic (FALSE) event. An automatic event automatically sets itself back to the nonsignaled state.
lpszName	Assigns a name to the event object
lpsaAttribute	Acts as a pointer to a SECURITY_ATTRIBUTES structure

Note

In order to use the CEvent class (and other thread synchronization classes) in your program, you must add the line #include "afxmt.h" to the file that references the CEvent class.

After creating the event object, you start the secondary thread that you'll synchronize using the event object. For example, you might start the thread like this:

```
AfxBeginThread(EventThread, hWnd);
```

EventThread is the thread that must wait for the event object to be signaled; however, when you call AfxBeginThread(), the thread starts to execute immediately. Inside the thread function, therefore, you need to add code that forces the thread to wait for the signaled event. You do this by calling the event object's Lock() member function.

For example, Listing 15-3 shows an event function that displays a message box when it first starts. The function performs the following tasks:

- Displays a message box telling the user that the thread has started

- Calls the event object's Lock() member function, which blocks the thread from continuing until the event object is placed in its signaled state

- Displays a second message box when the event object is signaled

Listing 15-3: A thread function that uses an event object for synchronization

```
UINT EventThread(LPVOID pParam)
{
    HWND hWnd = (HWND) pParam;
    ::MessageBox(hWnd, "Thread started",
        "Thread Message", MB_ICONEXCLAMATION | MB_OK);

    eventObj.Lock();
```

```
    ::MessageBox(hWnd, "Thread unblocked",
        "Thread Message", MB_ICONEXCLAMATION | MB_OK);

    return 0;
}
```

How, you might ask, does a program set an event object to its signaled state? You signal an event object by calling its SetEvent() member function:

```
eventObj.SetEvent();
```

On CD-ROM

To see all this event object stuff in action, check out the ThreadApp2 directory on this book's CD-ROM. There you'll find a sample application that demonstrates the use of CEvent objects to control a thread. When you run the application, its frame window appears, after which you can click in the window's client area to start a secondary thread. When the thread starts, it displays the message box shown in Figure 15-5.

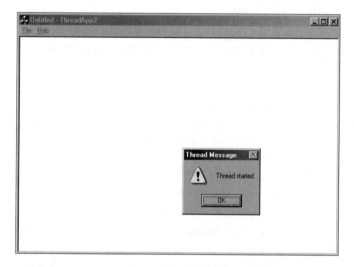

Figure 15-5: The Thread Message message box displays when the secondary thread begins.

Listing 15-3 is the thread function from ThreadApp2. If you examine the listing, you can see that, after displaying the message box, the thread blocks itself by locking the event object. At this point, the thread is suspended, waiting for the event object to become signaled. In a full application, the program's primary thread might be, at this time, preparing a data structure that the second thread must process. In that case, the second thread mustn't start processing the data structure until the first thread has finished with it.

To unblock ThreadApp2's secondary thread, right-click in the window's client area. You then see the message box shown in Figure 15-6. At this point in a full application, the thread would begin whatever task it was designed to do, after which the thread would end or go back into a blocked state, waiting for more data to process. In ThreadApp2, you can stop the thread by dismissing the second message box.

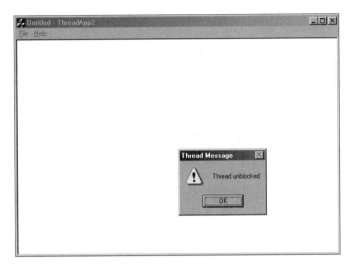

Figure 15-6: After right-clicking in your window's client area, this message box appears, enabling you to unblock the secondary thread.

To see automatic events in action, start more than one instance of the thread by clicking several times in the window. (You have to close a thread's message box before you can click again, of course.) Each time you click, an instance of the `EventThread()` thread begins and then suspends in order to wait for the event object to be signaled.

The next step is to signal the event object, which you do by right-clicking in the window. When you right-click in the window the first time, the program sets the event object to its signaled state and the first thread wakes up. Because the event object is automatic, it immediately goes back to its nonsignaled state, which means other threads you have started stay suspended. Another right click signals the event object and wakes up the next running thread, and so on for all threads you started.

PROBLEMS & SOLUTIONS

Thread Communication with Event Objects

PROBLEM: *How can I use event objects to communicate between a program and a secondary thread?*

On CD-ROM

SOLUTION: Earlier in this chapter, you learned the secret of using a global variable to communicate between a program and a thread. You can also establish this type of communication using event objects in place of global variables. This technique is more elegant and a bit safer. On this book's CD-ROM, you can find the EventThread application, which demonstrates using event objects to communicate between the program and the thread.

To implement the event object communication technique, the program first includes the afxmt.h header file in the view class's implementation file:#include "afxmt.h".

Then, the program defines global event objects that the program and thread can use as communication channels. In this example, the event objects control the starting and stopping of the thread:

```
CEvent comEventStart;
CEvent comEventEnd;
```

The program starts the thread in response to the WM_CREATE message, which occurs when the program is first started. In an MFC program, you can respond to WM_CREATE by using ClassWizard to create the OnCreate() message-response function, as shown in Listing 15-4:

Listing 15-4: The OnCreate() function

```
int CEventThreadView::OnCreate
    (LPCREATESTRUCT lpCreateStruct)
{
    if (CView::OnCreate(lpCreateStruct) == -1)
        return -1;

    // TODO: Add your specialized creation code here

    HWND hWnd = GetSafeHwnd();
    AfxBeginThread(EventThread, hWnd);

    return 0;
}
```

As you can see, OnCreate() starts the thread. However, because the thread is designed so that it doesn't start processing until the comEventStart event object becomes signaled, the thread immediately suspends. Listing 15-5 shows the thread function:

Continued

Listing 15-5: A thread function that uses an event object to control processing

```
UINT EventThread(LPVOID pParam)
{
    BOOL runThread = TRUE;

    HWND hWnd = (HWND) pParam;
    ::MessageBox(hWnd, "Thread started.",
        "Thread Message",
        MB_ICONEXCLAMATION | MB_OK);

    comEventStart.Lock();

    ::MessageBox(hWnd, "Thread processing.",
        "Thread Message",
        MB_ICONEXCLAMATION | MB_OK);

    while(runThread)
    {
        // Perform the thread's task here.
        int retCode = ::WaitForSingleObject(
            comEventEnd.m_hObject, 0);
        if (retCode == WAIT_OBJECT_0)
            runThread = FALSE;
    }

    ::MessageBox(hWnd, "Thread ending.",
        "Thread Message",
        MB_ICONEXCLAMATION | MB_OK);

    return 0;
}
```

When you click in the application's window, MFC calls the `OnLButtonDown()` function. This then calls the `comEventStart` event object's `SetEvent()` member function to set the event to its signaled state:

```
void CEventThreadView::OnLButtonDown(UINT nFlags,
    CPoint point)
{
    // TODO: Add your message handler code here
    // and/or call default

    comEventStart.SetEvent();

    CView::OnLButtonDown(nFlags, point);
}
```

Continued

The thread unblocks and enters its `while` loop, where it begins whatever processing it was designed to do. Inside the `while` loop the thread constantly calls the Windows API function `WaitForSingleObject()` in order to monitor the state of the `comEventEnd` event object. The advantage of calling `WaitForSingleObject()`, rather than the usual `Lock()` member function, is that `WaitForSingleObject()` returns a value. This means that the thread can poll the event object without actually blocking.

`WaitForSingleObject()` takes two arguments, which are the handle of the event object and length of time (in milliseconds) to wait. A value of 0 for the wait time causes `WaitForSingleObject()` to return a value immediately. When `WaitForSingleObject()` returns `WAIT_OBJECT_0`, the event object has entered its signaled state, meaning, in this case, that the thread should end.

To end the thread, right-click in the application's window. MFC calls the program's `OnRButtonDown()` function, which calls the `comEventEnd` event object's `SetEvent()` function and the thread ends:

```
void CEventThreadView::OnRButtonDown(UINT nFlags,
    CPoint point)
{
    // TODO: Add your message handler code here
    // and/or call default

    comEventEnd.SetEvent();

    CView::OnRButtonDown(nFlags, point);
}
```

Tip

In Listing 15-5, you may have noticed the double colon (::) in front of the call to `WaitForSingleObject()`. Use this symbol to indicate that a function call is a Windows API function, rather than an MFC function. The double colon makes it possible to call Windows API functions that are also defined in MFC with the same name. For example, if you call `MessageBox()` within an MFC class, MFC assumes you want to call the MFC version of `MessageBox()`. If, for some reason, you actually wanted to call the Windows API version, you'd preface the function call with the double colon:

```
::MessageBox();
```

However, you can use the double colon any time you call a Windows API function, even if the function doesn't have an MFC counterpart. By doing this, you make it easy to see when you're calling MFC functions and when you're calling Windows API functions.

Manual event objects

In the previous section, you saw how automatic event objects wake a single thread instance and then go back into their nonsignaled state. If you want to wake up all instances of a thread simultaneously, you need to create a manual event object, which you might do like this:

```
CEvent eventObj(FALSE, TRUE);
```

If you remember the arguments for the CEvent constructor, you know that the first FALSE parameter above specifies that the event object will start in its nonsignaled state; the second argument of TRUE specifies that the event object is manual, rather than automatic.

On CD-ROM

When the manual event object becomes signaled, it stays signaled until the program explicitly calls the object's ResetEvent() member function. This means that all threads waiting for the event object can unblock, as you can discover with the ThreadApp3 program, found in the ThreadApp3 directory of this book's CD-ROM.

When you run ThreadApp3, you see a window much like ThreadApp2's window. Now, however, the program assigns numbers to the threads you start. You can start as many instances of the program's secondary thread as you like, with each getting a unique number. Figure 15-7 shows the program creating a third thread.

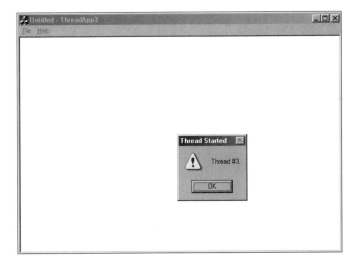

Figure 15-7: ThreadApp3 creating a third thread instance

After creating the number of threads you want, each thread is blocked, waiting for the event object to become signaled. To signal the event object, right-click in the window. When you do, all threads become unblocked, as shown in Figure 15-8.

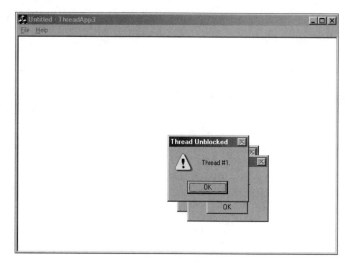

Figure 15-8: ThreadApp3's secondary threads unblock simultaneously.

ThreadApp3's `OnLButtonDown()` and `OnRButtonDown()` functions look exactly like ThreadApp2's. The thread function, `EventThread()`, however, has some new wrinkles, as shown in Listing 15-6. Now `EventThread()` uses a static variable, `threadNum`, to hold the thread number. Each time the user starts a thread, the program increments `threadNum` and uses its new value to construct a text string for the message box.

Listing 15-6: A new `EventThread()` function

```
UINT EventThread(LPVOID pParam)
{
    static int threadNum = 0;
    char str[81];

    ++threadNum;
    wsprintf(str, "Thread #%d.", threadNum);
    HWND hWnd = (HWND) pParam;
    ::MessageBox(hWnd, str, "Thread Started",
        MB_ICONEXCLAMATION | MB_OK);

    eventObj.Lock();

    ::MessageBox(hWnd, str, "Thread Unblocked",
        MB_ICONEXCLAMATION | MB_OK);

    return 0;
}
```

Note

When you use a thread function to create multiple instances of a thread, you must be sure that the function causes no reentrancy problems. That is, the function must be very careful how it deals with data objects, because each thread instance may access the same objects. This isn't a problem for local variables, because each thread instance gets its own stack. However, global and static variables are potential land mines. For instance, the `threadNum` variable in Listing 15-6 could cause trouble if two thread instances tried to access it at the same time, although that shouldn't happen in ThreadApp3.

Using critical sections

You can think of a critical section object as a kind of key that unlocks access to a shared resource. When one thread owns the critical section object, other threads that want to access the locked resource must suspend their execution until the first thread hands over the key.

Visual C++ supports critical sections through its MFC `CCriticalSection` class. Creating a critical section object is even easier than creating an event object. This is because the class's constructor takes no arguments:

```
CCriticalSection criticalSection;
```

When a thread wants to access a shared resource, the thread calls the critical section object's `Lock()` member function, which effectively hands the resource key to the calling thread (assuming no other thread already owns the critical object):

```
criticalSection.Lock();
```

If some other thread has already locked the critical section, the thread calling `Lock()` is blocked until the critical section is again freed. Otherwise, the thread becomes the critical section's owner and can access the shared resource. When the thread has completed whatever task it must perform on the shared resource, it releases the critical section object, by calling the `Unlock()` member function:

```
criticalSection.Unlock();
```

On CD-ROM

In the ThreadApp4 directory of this book's CD-ROM, you can find an application that demonstrates critical sections. When you run the program, click in the window's client area. When you do, the program starts two separate threads. The first thread grabs the critical section object and displays a message box, telling you that the thread has started. The second thread also starts and attempts to gain ownership of the critical section object. Because the first thread already owns the critical section, however, the second thread blocks.

When you dismiss the message box, the first thread unlocks the critical section and displays a message box informing you of that fact. This action wakes up the second thread, which grabs the critical section object and displays its own message box. At this point, you have two message boxes on the screen, as shown in Figure 15-9. Finally, when you dismiss the second thread's start-up message box, the thread releases the critical section object and displays its final message box.

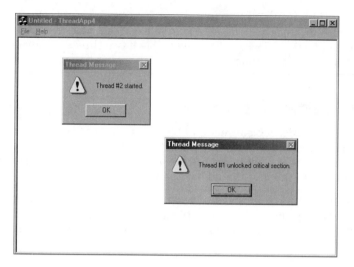

Figure 15-9: ThreadApp4's first thread releases the critical section object.

Was all that hard to follow? Take a look at Listing 15-7, which shows the OnLButtonDown() function defined in ThreadApp4's view class. When the user clicks in the application's window, MFC calls OnLButtonDown(), where CriticalThread1 and CriticalThread2 are started together. This results in the CriticalThread1() and CriticalThread2() functions executing one after the other.

Listing 15-7: ThreadApp4's OnLButtonDown() function

```
void CThreadApp4View::OnLButtonDown(UINT nFlags, CPoint point)
{
    // TODO: Add your message handler code here and/or call default

    HWND hWnd = GetSafeHwnd();
    AfxBeginThread(CriticalThread1, hWnd);
    AfxBeginThread(CriticalThread2, hWnd);

    CView::OnLButtonDown(nFlags, point);
}
```

Now look at Listing 15-8, which is the source code for the first thread function, CriticalThread1(). As you can see, this thread function immediately locks the critical section, which prevents the second thread from doing so. After locking the critical section, the function displays the message box, which halts the thread until you dismiss the message box from the screen. The instant you do, the function unlocks the critical section, giving the second thread a chance to lock it and commence executing. The source code for CriticalThread2() looks almost exactly like that for CriticalThread1(). The only difference is the name of the thread and the strings that identify the thread.

Listing 15-8: ThreadApp4's `CriticalThread1()` **function**

```
UINT CriticalThread1(LPVOID pParam)
{
    criticalSection.Lock();

    HWND hWnd = (HWND) pParam;
    ::MessageBox(hWnd, "Thread #1 started.",
        "Thread Message", MB_ICONEXCLAMATION | MB_OK);

    criticalSection.Unlock();

    ::MessageBox(hWnd,
        "Thread #1 unlocked critical section.",
        "Thread Message", MB_ICONEXCLAMATION | MB_OK);

    return 0;
}
```

 PROBLEMS & SOLUTIONS

Suspended and Sleeping Threads

PROBLEM: *How can I suspend a thread for a set period of time?*

SOLUTION: There may be times when your thread must have a built-in timer. For example, you may want to use a thread to control an animation sequence. To do this, the thread must time the interval between one frame of the animation and the next. Although you can call `SuspendThread()` to suspend a thread, you can't specify a time limit. Moreover, the thread cannot reawaken itself. To awaken the suspended thread, some other process or thread must call `ResumeThread()`.

Luckily, there is a thread function that works well for timing purposes, `Sleep()`, which you call like this:

`Sleep(1000);`

The function's single parameter is the number of milliseconds the thread should sleep. So, the previous line puts the thread to sleep for approximately 1,000 ms, or one second.

Using mutexes

You use a mutex (which is short for "mutually exclusive") almost exactly as you use a critical section. The big difference is that, whereas critical sections can only communicate from within a single process, mutexes can communicate across process boundaries. This means that you can use a mutex to synchronize resources between different running applications, something that's way beyond a critical section's abilities.

Visual C++ supports mutexes with the MFC CMutex class. You create a mutex in the application as a global object:

```
CMutex mutex(FALSE, "mutex1");
```

Here, the CMutex constructor takes two arguments. However, the CMutex constructor actually has three parameters, all of which have default values. The full signature looks like this:

```
CMutex(
    BOOL bInitiallyOwn = FALSE,
    LPCTSTR lpszName = NULL,
    LPSECURITY_ATTRIBUTES lpsaAttribute = NULL );
```

The parameters, which are very similar to those used for automatic event objects, are used as follows:

bInitiallyOwn	Specifies whether the mutex starts off locked (TRUE) or unlocked (FALSE).
lpszName	Assigns a name to the mutex. The name is how different processes identify the mutex in the system.
lpsaAttribute	Acts as a pointer to a SECURITY_ATTRIBUTES structure.

Once you have the mutex created, you use it exactly like a critical section object, calling the object's Lock() member function when the program is about to access a shared resource:

```
mutex.Lock();
```

When the program is finished with the resource, it calls the mutex's Unlock() member function:

```
mutex.Unlock();
```

On CD-ROM

If you'd like to experiment with mutexes, take a look at the ThreadApp5 program that you can find in the ThreadApp5 directory of this book's CD-ROM. Listing 15-9 shows the application's thread function, which performs the following tasks:

- Displays a message box telling the user that the thread has started

- Locks the mutex

- Displays a message box telling the user that the mutex is locked

- Unlocks the mutex

- Displays a message box telling the user that the mutex is unlocked

Listing 15-9: ThreadApp5's MutexThread() **function**

```
UINT MutexThread(LPVOID pParam)
{
    HWND hWnd = (HWND) pParam;
    ::MessageBox(hWnd, "Thread started.",
        "Thread Message", MB_ICONEXCLAMATION | MB_OK);

    mutex.Lock();

    ::MessageBox(hWnd, "Mutex locked.",
        "Thread Message", MB_ICONEXCLAMATION | MB_OK);

    mutex.Unlock();

    ::MessageBox(hWnd, "Mutex unlocked.",
        "Thread Message", MB_ICONEXCLAMATION | MB_OK);

    return 0;
}
```

To see the mutex in action, follow these steps:

1. Run two instances of the application, and resize the windows so that they fit next to each other on the screen.

2. Click in each of the windows to start the secondary threads. When you do, a message box appears for each application, telling you that the threads have started, as shown in Figure 15-10.

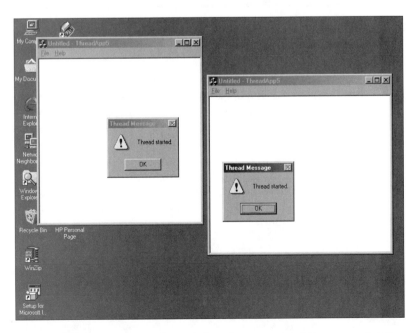

Figure 15-10: After clicking in each window, these message boxes appear to tell you the secondary threads have started.

3. Dismiss one of the message boxes. The associated application instance locks the mutex and displays a message box telling you that the mutex is locked, as shown in Figure 15-11.

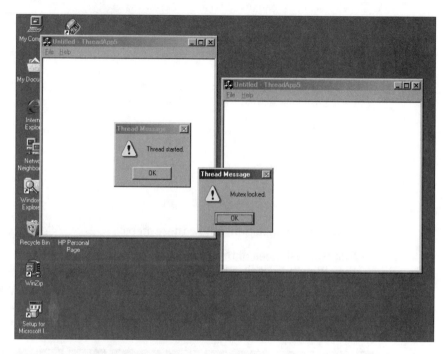

Figure 15-11: After the associated application instance locks the mutex, it displays this message box.

4. Without dismissing the "Mutex locked" message box (which will cause the application to unlock the mutex), dismiss the second instance's "Thread started" message box. Nothing happens. You don't see a "Mutex locked" message box for the second instance because the first instance still has the mutex locked (see Figure 15-12).

5. Click the first application instance's "Mutex locked" message box in order to unlock the mutex. Immediately, the first thread releases the mutex and the second one grabs it, shown by the message boxes that appear in Figure 15-13. As you can see, mutexes really do work across process boundaries.

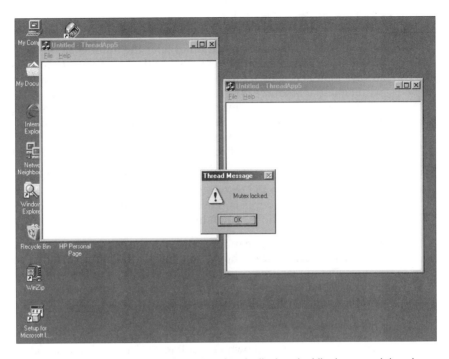

Figure 15-12: The "Mutex locked" message box is displayed while the second thread waits for the mutex to be unlocked.

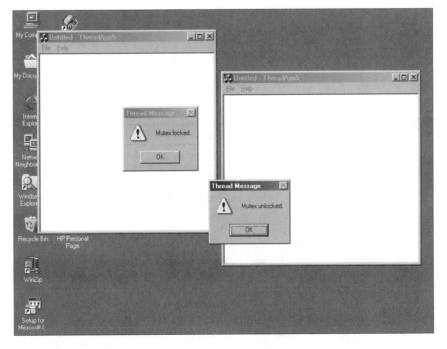

Figure 15-13: The first thread unlocks the mutex, and the second thread locks it.

Using semaphores

Semaphores enable an application to limit the number of threads that access a resource. This is very different from critical sections or mutexes, which always limit accessibility to a single thread at a time. A semaphore starts with an initial resource count, which represents the current status of the semaphore; and a maximum resource count, which represents the greatest number of threads that can access the resource simultaneously. Like a mutex, a semaphore can be used to synchronize threads within a single process, as well as to synchronize threads between multiple processes.

When a thread locks a semaphore, the semaphore reduces its resource count by one. When the resource count reaches zero, any other thread that tries to lock the resource is blocked; it can't resume until another thread releases the semaphore, which increments the resource count.

Visual C++ supports semaphores through the MFC CSemaphore class. When you create a semaphore object, you specify the initial resource count and the maximum resource count. If you're going to use the semaphore across process boundaries, you also need to specify a semaphore name. You might create a semaphore object like this:

```
CSemaphore semaphore(3, 3, "semaphore1");
```

Although they're not shown in this line, CSemaphore's constructor actually has four parameters, all of which have default values, as you can see in the following function signature:

```
CSemaphore(
    LONG lInitialCount = 1,
    LONG lMaxCount = 1,
    LPCTSTR pstrName = NULL,
    LPSECURITY_ATTRIBUTES lpsaAttributes = NULL);
```

The four parameters are as follows:

lInitialCount	Specifies the semaphore's initial resource count
lMaxCount	Specifies the semaphore's maximum resource count
pstrName	Assigns a name to the semaphore object
lpsaAttributes	Acts as a pointer to a SECURITY_ATTRIBUTES structure

Just as with other synchronization objects, such as critical sections and mutexes, when a thread is about to access the shared resource, it calls the semaphore's Lock() member function. This causes the semaphore to decrement its resource count. When the thread is finished with the shared resource, it calls the semaphore object's Unlock() member function, which increments the semaphore's resource count.

On CD-ROM

In the ThreadApp6 directory of this book's CD-ROM, you can find the ThreadApp6 application, which demonstrates using semaphores to control a resource between several running applications. In the application's view class, the program creates a semaphore as described previously:

```
CSemaphore semaphore(3, 3, "semaphore1");
```

To start a thread, the user clicks in ThreadApp6's window. This causes MFC to call the view class's OnLButtonDown() member function, shown in Listing 15-10. As you can see, OnLButtonDown() calls AfxBeginThread() to start the SemaphoreThread secondary thread, represented by the SemaphoreThread() function.

Listing 15-10: ThreadApp6's OnLButtonDown() function

```
void CThreadApp6View::OnLButtonDown(UINT nFlags,
    CPoint point)
{
    // TODO: Add your message handler code here
    // and/or call default

    HWND hWnd = GetSafeHwnd();
    AfxBeginThread(SemaphoreThread, hWnd);

    CView::OnLButtonDown(nFlags, point);
}
```

Listing 15-11 shows the SemaphoreThread() function. Notice how much it looks like MutexThread() from the ThreadApp5 application. The only real difference is that SemaphoreThread() locks and unlocks a semaphore, rather than a mutex.

Listing 15-11: ThreadApp6's SemaphoreThread() function

```
UINT SemaphoreThread(LPVOID pParam)
{
    HWND hWnd = (HWND) pParam;
    ::MessageBox(hWnd, "Thread started.",
        "Thread Message", MB_ICONEXCLAMATION | MB_OK);

    semaphore.Lock();

    ::MessageBox(hWnd, "Semaphore locked.",
        "Thread Message", MB_ICONEXCLAMATION | MB_OK);

    semaphore.Unlock();

    ::MessageBox(hWnd, "Semaphore unlocked.",
        "Thread Message", MB_ICONEXCLAMATION | MB_OK);

    return 0;
}
```

The `SemaphoreThread()` function performs the following tasks:

- Displays a message box telling the user that the thread has started

- Locks the semaphore, which decrements the semaphore's resource count

- Displays a message box telling the user that the semaphore is locked

- Unlocks the semaphore, which increments the semaphore's resource count

- Displays a message box telling the user that the semaphore is unlocked

When you run a single instance of ThreadApp6, nothing interesting happens. The application simply displays message boxes that show what the program is up to, when threads start, and when semaphores lock and unlock. Things get interesting when you run more instances of the application than the semaphore's maximum resource count allows. To see what I mean, follow the steps below:

1. Run four instances of ThreadApp6.

2. Resize and position the windows so that they all fit on the screen.

3. Click in each of the windows in order to start each application's secondary thread. Four message boxes appear, informing you that the threads have started (see Figure 15-14).

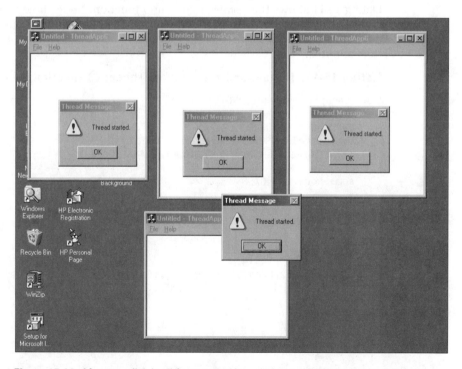

Figure 15-14: After you click in all four application windows, these message boxes appear to inform you that the secondary threads have started.

4. Click the OK button on three of the message boxes. Three new message boxes appear, informing you that the three associated threads have locked the semaphore, as shown in Figure 15-15. (You may have to move the message boxes around in order to see them all.)

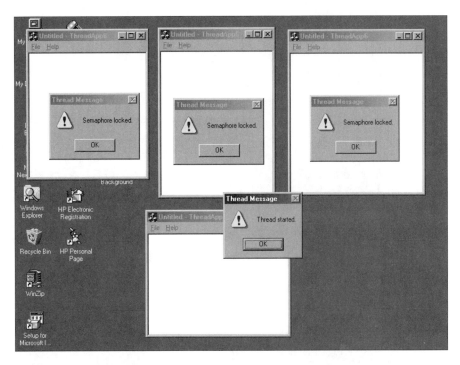

Figure 15-15: To inform you that you've exceeded the semaphore's maximum resource count, message boxes appear, showing that their threads have locked the semaphore.

5. Click the OK button on the remaining "Thread started" message box. The message box goes away, but no new message box tells you that the thread has locked the semaphore (see Figure 15-16). This is because the semaphore has a maximum resource count of three, and three threads have already locked the semaphore.

6. Dismiss one of the "Semaphore locked" message boxes. The associated thread displays its "Semaphore unlocked" message box. At the same time, the fourth, waiting thread immediately grabs the semaphore and locks it, as indicated by its "Semaphore locked" message box (see Figure 15-17).

7. Close all message boxes. Each thread unlocks the semaphore and ends.

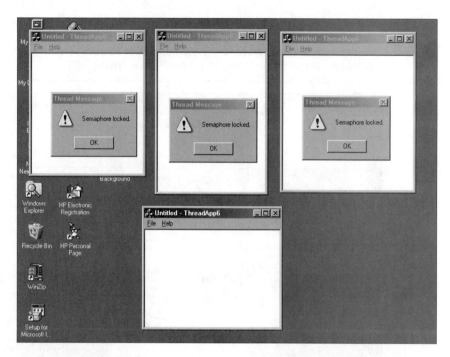

Figure 15-16: The fourth instance cannot yet lock the semaphore, as it has a maximum resource count of three.

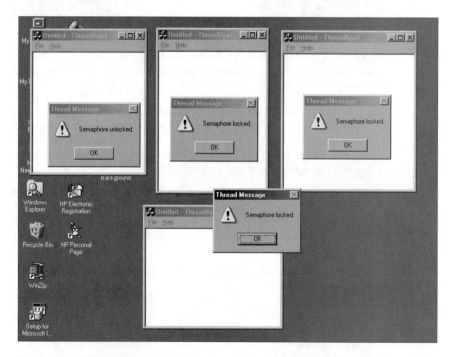

Figure 15-17: While one thread unlocks the semaphore, another locks it.

Summary

Using threads, you can assign time-consuming tasks to functions that run concurrently with the main program. In this way, you take better advantage of the Windows operating system to provide your application's user with a more responsive interface. However, multithreaded applications can become very complex and lead to unexpected and sometimes disastrous problems. You should use multithreading only when there is a clear advantage to doing so and not just because you want your application to incorporate the latest technology.

Also discussed in this chapter:

▶ Processes are more or less equivalent to running applications.

▶ Threads are distinct paths of execution within a process.

▶ Processes and threads both have priority settings that determine how much CPU time they get.

▶ A worker thread does not process Windows messages and so has no user interface.

▶ A UI thread does process Windows messages and so can display windows and other UI elements.

▶ Thread synchronization enables you to protect shared resources from concurrent access by multiple threads.

▶ Event objects pass signals between threads.

▶ Critical section objects act as keys that enable access to protected resources.

▶ Mutexes are like critical sections that work across process boundaries.

▶ Semaphores enable a maximum number of threads to access shared resources.

Chapter 16

Input Devices: The Mouse and the Keyboard

In This Chapter

▶ Understanding input events

▶ Responding to mouse messages

▶ Responding to keyboard messages

A computer can have any number of input devices, but the mouse and the keyboard are the most common. Because the mouse and keyboard are everywhere, this chapter describes how Windows 98 handles their input. Once you know the basics, it's simple to add input routines to your MFC programs. In fact, basic mouse and keyboard handling is as easy to implement as adding a message-response function or two to your MFC program, something that Visual C++'s ClassWizard can help you do.

Input Events and Messages

As you already know, virtually everything that happens in a Windows application happens in response to events. Input devices like the mouse and the keyboard are no different. Whenever the user moves the mouse or types on the keyboard, the system captures the input events and sends a flood of messages to the application. The application then must decide which messages to handle and which to pass back to Windows for default processing.

Because many of the user interface objects used in a Windows program, such as menus and dialog boxes, handle mouse and keyboard input automatically, a Windows application responds to input messages only for special, application-specific purposes. For example, a paint program may respond to mouse events so that the user can draw a line in the application's window, whereas a word-processing application may respond to keyboard events so that the user can type a document.

Both the mouse and the keyboard generate their own types of messages. For example, the mouse generates Windows messages such as WM_MOUSEMOVE, WM_LBUTTONDOWN, and WM_RBUTTONDBLCLK. The keyboard, on the other hand, generates messages such as WM_KEYDOWN and WM_KEYUP. When you want your application to respond to a specific mouse or keyboard event, you simply create a message-response function for the message. MFC then automatically routes the message to the message-response function, where you can handle it as you see fit.

Handling the Mouse

Now that you have a general idea of how the mouse and the keyboard communicate with a Windows application, you can explore the details and learn exactly how to add mouse and keyboard support to your Windows applications. In this section, you will concentrate on the mouse, which most users rely upon at least as much as a keyboard—if not more.

Client-area mouse messages

Previously, you learned that the mouse communicates with an application using mouse event messages such as WM_MOUSEMOVE. More specifically, Windows sends *client-area mouse messages* to your application whenever the mouse pointer is over the client area of a window owned by your application. Client-area mouse messages are the type of messages that you normally handle in a Windows application. For example, when the user moves the mouse over the application window's client area (the area of the window in which the application can draw), the application receives a stream of WM_MOUSEMOVE messages, which tell the application not only that the mouse is moving, but also the location of the mouse at the time Windows generated the message.

When the mouse moves outside of the application window's client area, the application stops receiving client-area mouse messages. Instead, Windows sends the mouse messages to whatever window (including the desktop) the mouse happens to be over. When the mouse moves back over the window's client area, Windows redirects the mouse messages to the application. (An exception to this rule is when the application has *captured* the mouse, which means that Windows directs all mouse messages to the application even when the mouse is outside of the application's window. You learn about capturing the mouse a little later in this chapter.)

There are ten client-area mouse messages that your application may receive. Table 16-1 lists these messages and their descriptions.

Table 16-1   Client-area mouse messages

Message	Description
WM_LBUTTONDBLCLK	Left mouse button was double-clicked
WM_LBUTTONDOWN	Left mouse button was pressed
WM_LBUTTONUP	Left mouse button was released
WM_MBUTTONDBLCLK	Middle mouse button was double-clicked
WM_MBUTTONDOWN	Middle mouse button was pressed
WM_MBUTTONUP	Middle mouse button was released
WM_MOUSEMOVE	Mouse has moved over the client area
WM_RBUTTONDBLCLK	Right mouse button was double-clicked
WM_RBUTTONDOWN	Right mouse button was pressed
WM_RBUTTONUP	Right mouse button was released

Nonclient-area mouse messages

Windows also sends *nonclient-area mouse messages* to your application. These types of mouse messages occur when the mouse is over any area of the application's window except the client area. For example, the application receives nonclient-area mouse messages when the mouse is over the window's title bar or control buttons. Most applications ignore nonclient-area mouse messages, because they are best handled by Windows itself. When the user double-clicks a window's title bar, for example, Windows restores the window's size to its previous setting.

You don't usually want to interfere with Windows' default handling of nonclient-area mouse messages because, if you do, the application's window may stop responding to the user as the user expects it to. However, there are times when responding to nonclient-area mouse messages enables an application to implement extra features. An application might, for example, intercept nonclient messages in order to enhance the way a window's title bar responds to the mouse.

Normally, an application ignores nonclient-area mouse messages. In case you want to get into trouble, however, there are ten nonclient-area mouse messages that your application may receive. These are similar to their client-area counterparts, as you can see in Table 16-2, which lists the nonclient-area mouse messages and their descriptions.

Table 16-2   Nonclient-area mouse messages

Message	Description
WM_NCLBUTTONDBLCLK	Left mouse button was double-clicked
WM_NCLBUTTONDOWN	Left mouse button was pressed
WM_NCLBUTTONUP	Left mouse button was released
WM_NCMBUTTONDBLCLK	Middle mouse button was double-clicked
WM_NCMBUTTONDOWN	Middle mouse button was pressed
WM_NCMBUTTONUP	Middle mouse button was released
WM_NCMOUSEMOVE	Mouse has moved over the client area
WM_NCRBUTTONDBLCLK	Right mouse button was double-clicked
WM_NCRBUTTONDOWN	Right mouse button was pressed
WM_NCRBUTTONUP	Right mouse button was released

 PROBLEMS & SOLUTIONS

Responding to Nonclient-Area Mouse Messages

PROBLEM: *How can I respond to nonclient-area mouse messages in an MFC program? ClassWizard doesn't allow me to add nonclient messages to a class's message map.*

SOLUTION: Although ClassWizard tries to dissuade you from capturing nonclient-area messages (with good reason), MFC does define message-map macros and message-response functions for all the nonclient messages. To handle these messages in an application, you must add the macros and functions to your program by hand, without the help of ClassWizard. For example, the following message map associates the WM_NCMOUSEMOVE message with the OnNcMouseMove() message-response function:

```
BEGIN_MESSAGE_MAP(CMainFrame, CFrameWnd)
    //{{AFX_MSG_MAP(CMainFrame)
        // NOTE - the ClassWizard will add and remove mapping macros
here.
        //     DO NOT EDIT what you see in these blocks of generated
code !
    //}}AFX_MSG_MAP
    ON_WM_NCMOUSEMOVE()
END_MESSAGE_MAP()
```

Continued

Notice that the message map is from the `CMainFrame` class, which represents the main frame window in an MFC application. It is the frame window that owns the nonclient areas, so it is the frame window that gets the nonclient-area messages.

You must also provide the `OnNcMouseMove()` function, because ClassWizard won't do it for you. In your frame window's declaration, you declare the message-response function like this:

```
afx_msg void OnNcMouseMove(UINT nHitTest, CPoint point);
```

The `OnNcMouseMove()` function itself looks something like this:

```
void CMainFrame::OnNcMouseMove(UINT nHitTest, CPoint point)
{
    // Do stuff here...

    CFrameWnd::OnNcMouseMove(nHitTest, point);
}
```

On CD-ROM

Don't forget to pass the message on to the base class's `OnNcMouseMove()` function. You want to be sure that nonclient messages get their normal, default processing. You can find a sample program called NCMouse on this book's CD-ROM. NCMouse tracks `WM_NCMOUSEMOVE` messages, displaying the mouse coordinates in the application's window. To generate the messages, move the mouse pointer over the nonclient areas of the window, as shown in Figure 16-1.

Nonclient mouse coordinates   Mouse over nonclient area

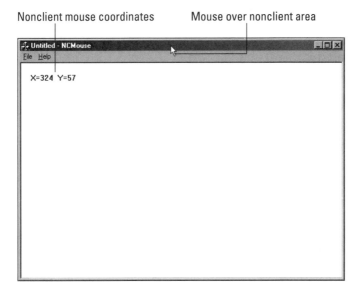

Figure 16-1: The NCMouse application displays mouse coordinates when the mouse is over the window's nonclient area.

The Mouse Sample Application

Now that you have mouse-handling concepts tucked under your belt, you can put those concepts to work. In this section, you'll examine, and experiment with, an application that demonstrates the mouse programming techniques discussed in this chapter. You'll see how to respond to mouse messages, as well as how to capture the mouse in an application.

Responding to mouse messages

On CD-ROM

The Mouse sample program on this book's CD-ROM illustrates how to intercept and respond to mouse messages. When you run the program, its main window appears. At first this window is blank, but the instant you move the mouse over the window, WM_MOUSEMOVE messages appear in the window, showing the mouse's coordinates at the time of the message. Click the left mouse button when the mouse is over the window, and not only do the WM_LBUTTONDOWN and WM_LBUTTONUP messages appear in the window, but the coordinates where the event took place also appear. Ditto for right mouse button clicks. Figure 16-2 shows the Mouse application in action, with the various events it handles displayed in the window.

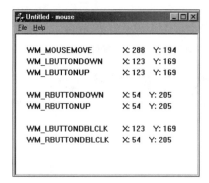

Figure 16-2: The Mouse application displayed with the events it's currently handling

The Mouse application also demonstrates mouse capture techniques. There may be times when your application needs to receive mouse messages even when the mouse isn't over the application's client area. For example, in a paint program, the user may hold down the left mouse button as she draws a line in the window. If the user accidentally drags the mouse pointer outside of the paint application's window, the application must continue to receive mouse messages. Otherwise, if the user releases the mouse button outside of the widow, the application will have no way of knowing the user isn't still drawing.

Capturing mouse messages

To see mouse capture working, place the mouse pointer over the Mouse application's client area. Then, hold down the right mouse button as you move the mouse around the screen. Even when the mouse leaves the application's window, the window continues to receive mouse messages. When you move the mouse without holding down the right mouse button, the application stops receiving mouse messages the instant the mouse pointer leaves the application's client area.

For a more detailed look at message flow with and without mouse capture, run a second instance of the Mouse application. When the mouse pointer is over the first instance, Windows sends all mouse messages to that instance. Figure 16-3 shows two instances of the Mouse application. Notice that the mouse pointer is over the first instance, so Windows directs mouse messages to that window.

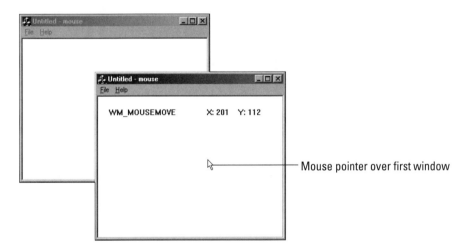

Figure 16-3: The first instance of the Mouse application displayed while receiving mouse messages

In Figure 16-4, the user has moved the mouse pointer over the second instance of the Mouse application. Now, Windows sends all mouse messages to the second instance's window, as you can tell by the appearance of the WM_MOUSEMOVE message in the window's client area.

Mouse pointer over second window

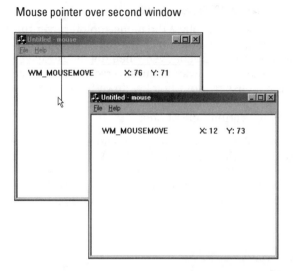

Figure 16-4: The second instance of the Mouse application displays while receiving mouse messages

Finally, Figure 16-5 shows the results of the user holding the right mouse button when moving the mouse from the first instance of Mouse to the second instance. The first instance captures the mouse, so Windows sends all mouse messages to the first instance even when the mouse pointer is over the second (or over any other window). Notice that the WM_MOUSEMOVE coordinates are now negative. This is because WM_MOUSEMOVE coordinates are always relative to the upper-left corner of the window that has captured the mouse.

Mouse pointer over second window

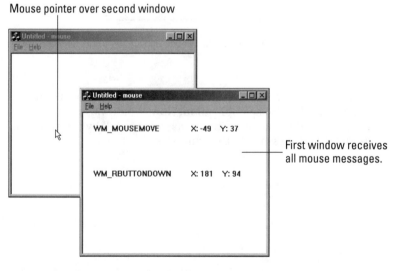

First window receives all mouse messages.

Figure 16-5: After the first instance of the Mouse application captures the mouse, mouse coordinates appear in the first instance's window.

Examining the Mouse application

On CD-ROM

As you've surely guessed, the Mouse application responds to mouse messages thanks to the message-response functions defined in the view window's class, CMouseView. This class is contained in the mouseView.cpp file that you can find in the Chapter 016 folder of this book's CD-ROM. As is the rule in an MFC program, CMouseView uses a message map to associate messages with the appropriate message-response functions. Listing 16-1 shows how the CMouseView class defines its message map.

Listing 16-1: The CMouseView **class's message map**

```
BEGIN_MESSAGE_MAP(CMouseView, CView)
    //{{AFX_MSG_MAP(CMouseView)
    ON_WM_MOUSEMOVE()
    ON_WM_LBUTTONDOWN()
    ON_WM_LBUTTONUP()
    ON_WM_RBUTTONDOWN()
    ON_WM_RBUTTONUP()
    ON_WM_LBUTTONDBLCLK()
    ON_WM_RBUTTONDBLCLK()
    //}}AFX_MSG_MAP
END_MESSAGE_MAP()
```

Each of the macros that comprise the body of the message map associates a mouse message with its appropriate message handler. For example, the ON_WM_MOUSEMOVE macro tells MFC to call the OnMouseMove() function when the window receives a WM_MOUSEMOVE message. Similarly, the message map tells MFC to call OnLButtonDown() when the window receives a WM_LBUTTONDOWN message.

The text that appears in the Mouse application's window is displayed from the view class's message-response functions. For example, Listing 16-2 shows the OnMouseMove() function. The Mouse application receives a stream of these messages as the mouse pointer moves over the application's window. The CPoint object that's passed as the function's second parameter contains the location of the mouse pointer at the time of the event. OnMouseMove() creates a display string from the CPoint object and displays the string in the application's window.

Listing 16-2: The OnMouseMove() **message-response function**

```
void CMouseView::OnMouseMove(UINT nFlags, CPoint point)
{
    // TODO: Add your message handler code here and/or call default
    char str[50];
    CClientDC dc(this);
    dc.TextOut(20, 20, "WM_MOUSEMOVE");
    wsprintf(str, "X: %d    Y: %d    ", point.x, point.y);
    dc.TextOut(200, 20, str);

    CView::OnMouseMove(nFlags, point);
}
```

The OnLButtonDown(), OnLButtonUp(), OnLButtonDblClk(), and OnRButtonDblClk() functions all work similarly, translating the CPoint object into a display string that's drawn in the application's window. The OnRButtonDown() and OnRButtonUp() functions, however, have a little extra work to do, because it's in those functions that the application captures and releases the mouse.

 PROBLEMS & SOLUTIONS

Handling Mouse and Keyboard Events

PROBLEM: *How can I tell if the user has clicked a mouse button with either the Shift or Ctrl key pressed?*

SOLUTION: You may have noticed that the MFC message-response functions for mouse messages receive two parameters: nFlags and point. You already know that point is a CPoint object containing the mouse's coordinates at the time of the message. The secret to discovering whether the user has performed a Shift-click or a Ctrl-click is to examine the nFlags parameter. In fact, you can determine the state of both the Ctrl and Shift keys, as well as all the mouse buttons, from the bits contained in nFlags. You can even tell whether the user has pressed more than one mouse button simultaneously.

Visual C++ defines a number of constants that you can use as bit masks to discover the contents of the bit flags in nFlags. The constants are MK_CONTROL (the Ctrl key flag); MK_LBUTTON (the left mouse button flag); MK_MBUTTON (the middle mouse button flag); MK_RBUTTON (the right mouse button flag); and MK_SHIFT (the Shift key flag). To determine the state of a key or mouse button, perform a bitwise AND against nFlags. For example, to determine whether the Shift key was pressed at the time of a mouse click, perform the following calculation:

```
BOOL shift = nFlags & MK_SHIFT;
```

Listing 16-3 shows the OnRButtonDown() function, which not only displays information about the mouse message, but also calls SetCapture() to capture the mouse. After the call to SetCapture(), Windows directs all mouse messages to the Mouse application, régardless of where the mouse pointer happens to be.

Listing 16-3: The OnRButtonDown() message-response function

```
void CMouseView::OnRButtonDown(UINT nFlags, CPoint point)
{
    // TODO: Add your message handler code here and/or call default

    SetCapture();
```

```
        char str[50];
        CClientDC dc(this);
        dc.TextOut(20, 100, "WM_RBUTTONDOWN");
        wsprintf(str, "X: %d    Y: %d    ", point.x, point.y);
        dc.TextOut(200, 100, str);

        CView::OnRButtonDown(nFlags, point);
}
```

When the user releases the right mouse button, the Mouse application
releases the mouse capture. This event happens in the OnRButtonUp()
function. As shown in Listing 16-4, OnRButtonUp() calls the ReleaseCapture()
function, which is the counterpart to SetCapture(). After the call to
ReleaseCapture(), Windows goes back to sending mouse messages to the
window over which the mouse is positioned. That is, the Mouse application
goes back to receiving mouse messages only when the mouse pointer is over
the application's client area.

Listing 16-4: The OnRButtonUp() message-response function

```
void CMouseView::OnRButtonUp(UINT nFlags, CPoint point)
{
    // TODO: Add your message handler code here and/or call default
ReleaseCapture();

    char str[50];
    CClientDC dc(this);
    dc.TextOut(20, 120, "WM_RBUTTONUP");
    wsprintf(str, "X: %d    Y: %d    ", point.x, point.y);
    dc.TextOut(200, 120, str);

    CView::OnRButtonUp(nFlags, point);
}
```

Note

Windows 3.x allowed an application to capture the mouse for an indefinite
amount of time. If the application that captured the mouse failed to release
the mouse, no other application could ever receive mouse messages.
Windows 98 (and Windows 95) solve this problem by allowing the mouse
capture to continue for only as long as a mouse button remains pressed.
That is, the Mouse application would run fine under Windows 95 and
Windows 98 if the call to ReleaseCapture() were left out of the
OnRButtonUp() function. However, in the spirit of good programming, you
should always release the mouse after capturing it.

Handling the Keyboard

Just as Windows sends messages to an application when the user moves or
clicks the mouse, so too does Windows send messages to an application
when the user types on the keyboard. The big difference between mouse
messages and keyboard messages is that mouse messages get sent to the
window where the mouse is positioned, and keyboard messages always get
sent to the window with the input focus, which is usually the topmost
window on the screen.

There are several ways your application can capture and respond to keyboard events. Which keyboard message you respond to depends on how you plan to use the keystrokes in your program. For example, one type of keyboard message sends only printable characters to your application, while others enable you to respond to the many special keys on the keyboard, such as the F keys, the arrow keys, the Delete key, and so on.

Keyboard messages

Your application can respond to three main keyboard messages: WM_CHAR, WM_KEYDOWN, and WM_KEYUP. There are also two special messages—WM_SYSKEYDOWN and WM_SYSKEYUP—for system keystrokes. These system keys are Alt and F10, for which Windows reserves special functions. Just as with nonclient-area mouse messages, you must be careful how you handle system keys. If you cripple their default behaviors, Windows will stop working the way the user expects it to work.

When the user presses and releases a key, Windows actually sends all three main keyboard messages. When the key goes down, Windows sends the WM_KEYDOWN and WM_CHAR messages. When the user releases the key, Windows sends the WM_KEYUP message. By responding to the appropriate message, you can create just about any kind of keyboard handler you need.

One exception to the above series of events is when the user presses a system key. For example, if the user presses the Alt key, Windows sends the application a WM_SYSKEYDOWN message. If the user presses another key along with the Alt key, Windows still sends WM_SYSKEYDOWN, instead of WM_KEYDOWN. Of course, when the user releases the Alt key, Windows sends the WM_SYSKEYUP message.

Another exception is when the user presses a key that doesn't represent a printable character. Such keys are the F1 through F12 function keys, the Delete key, the arrow keys, and so on. Pressing and releasing one of these keys results in WM_KEYDOWN and WM_KEYUP messages, but no WM_CHAR messages. This is because WM_CHAR messages are sent only for keys that represent printable characters.

Each of the keyboard messages includes additional information about the keystroke. This additional information is packaged in the wParam and lParam parameters that the application receives as part of the message. If you're programming with MFC, the appropriate message-response functions "crack" these parameters into their individual components. For example, the signature for MFC's OnChar() function, which responds to the WM_CHAR message, looks like this:

```
void OnChar(UINT nChar, UINT nRepCnt, UINT nFlags)
```

Here, the cracked parameters are `nChar`, `nRepCnt`, and `nFlags`. The `nChar` parameter holds the keystroke's character, `nRepCnt` holds the number of times the key repeated, and `nFlags` holds more detailed information stored in its bits, as described in Table 16-3. The MFC `OnKeyDown()` and `OnKeyUp()` message-response functions, which respond to the `WM_KEYDOWN` and `WM_KEYUP` messages, receive the same parameters as `OnChar()`.

Table 16-3	`nFlag` data fields
Bits	***Description***
0-7	The key's scan code
8	Extended key flag (0=not extended key; 1=extended key, such as a function key or a numeric keypad key)
9-12	Currently unused
13	Alt key flag (0=Alt not pressed; 1=Alt pressed)
14	Previous key state flag (0=single stroke; 1=repeating stroke)
15	Press or release flag (0=key pressed; 1=key released)

The Keys sample application

On CD-ROM

The Keys sample program on this book's CD-ROM illustrates how to intercept and respond to `WM_CHAR` messages. When you run the program, its main window appears. At first this window is blank, but when you press a key on your keyboard, the key's character appears in the window. As long as you press a key that represents a printable character, the appropriate character appears in the window. However, because the Keys application responds only to `WM_CHAR` messages, special keys such as F2, Ctrl, Insert, and End have no effect on the application's display. Figure 16-6 shows the Keys application in action, with a keystroke displayed in its window.

Figure 16-6: The Keys application with the "W" keystroke displayed in its window

Examining the Keys application

Thanks to MFC's powerful message mapping, there's not a heck of a lot to know about the Keys application. As with any MFC window that responds to Windows messages, Keys' view window, represented by the `CKeysView` class, defines a message map that associates the `WM_CHAR` message with the `OnChar()` function, as shown here:

```
BEGIN_MESSAGE_MAP(CKeysView, CView)
    //{{AFX_MSG_MAP(CKeysView)
    ON_WM_CHAR()
    //}}AFX_MSG_MAP
END_MESSAGE_MAP()
```

The character that appears in the Keys application's window is stored in a `CString` member variable called `m_displayString`. The string is initialized with a new character every time a `WM_CHAR` message is processed by the `OnChar()` function, as shown here:

```
void CKeysView::OnChar(UINT nChar, UINT nRepCnt, UINT nFlags)
{
    // TODO: Add your message handler code here and/or call default

    m_displayString = nChar;
    Invalidate();

    CView::OnChar(nChar, nRepCnt, nFlags);
}
```

After assigning the new character to `m_displayString`, `OnChar()` calls `Invalidate()`, which forces the window to redraw itself. The view class's `OnDraw()` function displays the character, after creating a suitably large font. Listing 16-5 shows the Keys application's `OnDraw()` function. If you don't understand how to create fonts, you can find the gory details in Chapter 7, "Text."

Listing 16-5: The Keys application's `OnDraw()` function

```
void CKeysView::OnDraw(CDC* pDC)
{
    CKeysDoc* pDoc = GetDocument();
    ASSERT_VALID(pDoc);

    // TODO: add draw code for native data here

    CFont font;
    font.CreateFont(200, 0, 0, 0, FW_BOLD, 0, 0, 0, DEFAULT_CHARSET,
        OUT_CHARACTER_PRECIS, CLIP_CHARACTER_PRECIS, DEFAULT_QUALITY,
        DEFAULT_PITCH | FF_DONTCARE, NULL);
    pDC->SelectObject(&font);
    pDC->TextOut(60, 40, m_displayString);
}
```

The KeyDown sample application

When programming Windows and MFC, there's always more than one way to skin the proverbial cat. While responding to the WM_CHAR message may be all you need for some applications, the other mouse messages pass more keystrokes to your application, giving you better control over the keyboard.

On CD-ROM

The KeyDown sample program on this book's CD-ROM illustrates how to intercept and respond to WM_KEYDOWN and WM_KEYUP messages. When you run the program, you see a blank window. Start typing, and WM_KEYDOWN and WM_KEYUP messages appear in the window. Each WM_KEYDOWN message displayed in the window also provides useful information about the keystroke. Moreover, the KeyDown application responds to almost every key on the keyboard, rather than just the keys associated with printable characters.

Figure 16-7 shows KeyDown's display after the user has held down the F2 key for a second or two. Notice how the key repeated 12 times, but the Repeat value is always 1. This indicates that the system was able to keep up with the incoming keystrokes. Had the system been bogged down, it might have lumped several WM_KEYDOWN messages into a single one and then set nRepCnt to the number of keystrokes represented by the single message.

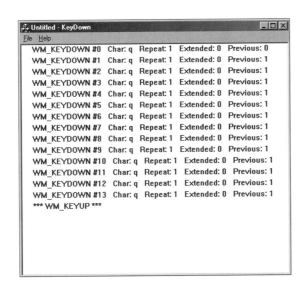

Figure 16-7: KeyDown displayed after the F2 key is held down for one to two seconds

Another thing to notice in Figure 16-7 is how the character associated with the F2 keystroke is reported as "q." This anomaly is caused by the fact that the nChar value for the F2 key, as well as for other special keys, represents a virtual key code, which you learn about in the following "Problems & Solutions" section.

Also, notice how the first `WM_KEYDOWN` message has a Previous value of 0. This is how you can tell that this `WM_KEYDOWN` message represents the first keystroke for the key. The remaining F2 keystrokes all have Previous values of 1, indicating that they resulted from the user's holding down the key, rather than pressing the key repeatedly.

Finally, the Extended value for all of the F2 keystrokes is 0, indicating that F2 is not an extended key. The extended keys include Insert, Home, PgUp, PgDn, Delete, and End. The arrow keys and the keypad's Enter and forward-slash keys are also extended keys. For example, Figure 16-8 shows the KeyDown application after the user has pressed several of the arrow keys. As you can see, the Extended value indicates that the keystrokes were made on extended keys.

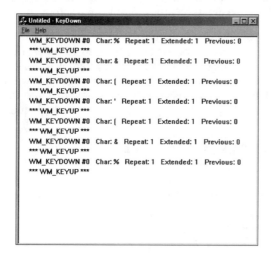

Figure 16-8: The KeyDown application showing extended keys

PROBLEMS & SOLUTIONS

Using Virtual Key Codes

PROBLEM: *How can I respond to special keys like F2 or the arrow keys when receiving keyboard messages?*

SOLUTION: Previously, I mentioned that the `nChar` parameter that MFC keyboard message-response functions receive can contain the actual character pressed or, in this case of special keys, a virtual key code. Visual C++ defines constants that represent all the virtual key codes you'll ever need, as you can see in Table 16-4. Just compare the `nChar` value with the appropriate constant in order to determine the key that was pressed. For example, to determine whether the user pressed the F2 key, you might write something like this:

Continued

```
if (nChar == VK_F2)
{
    // Handle F2 key here
}
```

Remember that if you want to respond to special keys, your application must watch for the WM_KEYDOWN and WM_KEYUP messages. The WM_CHAR message reports only keystrokes that result in printable characters.

Table 16-4 Virtual key codes

Code	Key
VK_ADD	+ on keypad
VK_BACK	Backspace
VK_CANCEL	Ctrl-Break
VK_CAPITAL	Caps Lock
VK_CLEAR	5 on keypad, Num Lock off
VK_CONTROL	Ctrl
VK_DECIMAL	. on keypad
VK_DELETE	Delete
VK_DIVIDE	/ on keypad
VK_DOWN	Down arrow
VK_END	End
VK_ESCAPE	Esc
VK_F1	F1
VK_F10	F10
VK_F11	F11
VK_F12	F12
VK_F2	F2
VK_F3	F3
VK_F4	F4
VK_F5	F5
VK_F6	F6
VK_F7	F7
VK_F8	F8
VK_F9	F9
VK_HOME	Home

Continued

Table 16-4 *(Continued)*

Code	Key
VK_INSERT	Insert
VK_LEFT	Left arrow
VK_MENU	Alt
VK_MULTIPLY	* on keypad
VK_NEXT	PgDn
VK_NUMLOCK	Num Lock
VK_NUMPAD0	0 on keypad
VK_NUMPAD1	1 on keypad
VK_NUMPAD2	2 on keypad
VK_NUMPAD3	3 on keypad
VK_NUMPAD4	4 on keypad
VK_NUMPAD5	5 on keypad
VK_NUMPAD6	6 on keypad
VK_NUMPAD7	7 on keypad
VK_NUMPAD8	8 on keypad
VK_NUMPAD9	9 on keypad
VK_PAUSE	Pause
VK_PRIOR	PgUp
VK_RETURN	Enter
VK_RIGHT	Right arrow
VK_SCROLL	Scroll Lock
VK_SHIFT	Shift
VK_SNAPSHOT	Print Screen
VK_SPACE	Spacebar
VK_SUBTRACT	- on keypad
VK_TAB	Tab
VK_UP	Up arrow

Examining the KeyDown application

As you've come to expect, KeyDown sets up a message map in its view class, CKeyDownView, that associates the messages it wants to handle with the message-response functions that handle them. In this case, the application must respond to WM_KEYDOWN and WM_KEYUP messages, so the message map looks like this:

```
BEGIN_MESSAGE_MAP(CKeyDownView, CView)
    //{{AFX_MSG_MAP(CKeyDownView)
    ON_WM_KEYDOWN()
    ON_WM_KEYUP()
    //}}AFX_MSG_MAP
END_MESSAGE_MAP()
```

The application stores the incoming messages into a CStringArray object. The view class's OnDraw() function is then charged with the task of displaying the contents of the array, as shown in Listing 16-6.

Listing 16-6: The KeyDown application's OnDraw() function

```
void CKeyDownView::OnDraw(CDC* pDC)
{
    CKeyDownDoc* pDoc = GetDocument();
    ASSERT_VALID(pDoc);

    // TODO: add draw code for native data here

    for (int x=0; x<20; ++x)
    {
        CString s = m_stringArray.GetAt(x);
        pDC->TextOut(20, x*20, s);
    }
}
```

Using the string array enables the program to create a pseudoscrolling display without getting stuck with all the code required to set up a real scrolling window. The array is updated in the OnKeyDown() and OnKeyUp() functions. These functions manipulate the contents of the array such that it appears in the window as a scrolling list. Listing 16-7 shows OnKeyDown(), which has the more complicated task of not only reporting the message, but also of deciphering the extra information that the KeyDown application displays with the WM_KEYDOWN message. Listing 16-8 shows OnKeyUp().

Listing 16-7: The OnKeyDown() function

```
void CKeyDownView::OnKeyDown(UINT nChar, UINT nRepCnt,
    UINT nFlags)
{
    // TODO: Add your message handler code here
    //    and/or call default

    char c[80];
```

```
        wsprintf(c, "WM_KEYDOWN #%d    Char: %c    \
Repeat: %d    Extended: %d    Previous: %d",
        m_keyDownCount++, nChar, nRepCnt,
        (nFlags > 8) & 0x01, (nFlags > 14) & 0x01);

    CString str(c);

    if (m_stringCount < 20)
        m_stringArray.SetAt(m_stringCount++, str);
    else
    {
        for (int x=0; x<19; ++x)
        {
            CString s = m_stringArray.GetAt(x+1);
            m_stringArray.SetAt(x, s);
        }
        m_stringArray.SetAt(19, str);
    }

    Invalidate();

    CView::OnKeyDown(nChar, nRepCnt, nFlags);
}
```

Listing 16-8: The OnKeyUp( ) function

```
void CKeyDownView::OnKeyUp(UINT nChar, UINT nRepCnt,
    UINT nFlags)
{
    // TODO: Add your message handler code here
    //    and/or call default

    m_keyDownCount = 0;

    if (m_stringCount < 20)
        m_stringArray.SetAt(m_stringCount++,
            "*** WM_KEYUP ***");
    else
    {
        for (int x=0; x<19; ++x)
        {
            CString s = m_stringArray.GetAt(x+1);
            m_stringArray.SetAt(x, s);
        }
        m_stringArray.SetAt(19, "*** WM_KEYUP ***");
    }

    Invalidate();

    CView::OnKeyUp(nChar, nRepCnt, nFlags);
}
```

PROBLEMS & SOLUTIONS

Tracking the Shift, Ctrl, and Alt Keys

PROBLEM: *How can I determine whether the user has pressed the Shift, Ctrl, or Alt key along with a keystroke?*

SOLUTION: The keyboard messages don't include information on the Shift and Ctrl keys, but they do give you the state of the Alt key in bit 13 of the `nFlags` parameter. To discover the state of the Alt key, you might write a code line like this:

```
BOOL altDown = (nFlags > 13) & 0x01;
```

Normally, though, you don't need to check explicitly for the Alt key, because if the Alt key is pressed, you get `WM_SYSKEYDOWN` and `WM_SYSKEYUP` messages instead of `WM_KEYDOWN` and `WM_KEYUP`.

What about Shift and Ctrl? Although information about these keys is not included with the keyboard messages' other baggage, you can still get this state information easily enough, by calling the Windows API function `GetKeyState()`. This handy function takes a single argument, which is a value representing the key you want to check. Visual C++ defines constants—`VK_SHIFT`, `VK_CONTROL`, and `VK_MENU`—for these values (see Table 16-4). For example, to check the state of the Shift key, you'd write something like this:

```
int shiftDown = ::GetKeyState(VK_SHIFT);
```

`GetKeyState()` returns a negative value if the key is pressed, and a nonnegative value if the key is not pressed.

Summary

Virtually every program you write will require some sort of mouse and keyboard handling. These two devices are, after all, the main way that users enter information into a computer. This chapter has shown you the basic techniques for responding to the mouse and the keyboard in an MFC application. Along the way, you learned a few extra tricks, such as capturing the mouse and determining when the user is holding down the Shift, Ctrl, or Alt keys.

Also discussed in this chapter:

▶ Windows sends messages to an application when the user manipulates the mouse or types on the keyboard.

▶ When the mouse pointer is over a window's client area, the window receives client-area mouse messages.

▶ When the mouse pointer is over the window's nonclient area (title bar, border, controls), the window receives nonclient-area mouse messages.

▶ A window can capture the mouse in order to force Windows to send all mouse messages to the window, even when the mouse pointer is outside the window's boundaries.

▶ Windows sends various types of character codes with the WM_CHAR message, including ASCII values and key codes for extended keys.

▶ A Windows application can capture key-down and key-up messages or just receive character messages.

▶ Windows defines a set of virtual key-code constants that represent the keys of the keyboard.

Chapter 17

File Handling

In This Chapter

▶ Implementing document/view architecture

▶ Understanding persistent objects

▶ Handling files with the `CFile` class

When you're programming with Visual C++, you have several methods
of file handling available. These include taking advantage of MFC's
document/view architecture, using archive objects to create persistent
classes, and using MFC's `CFile` class to manipulate files more directly. If you
create your application using MFC's document/view architecture, file
handling comes almost for free, with the document class's `Serialize()`
member function doing most of the work for you. When you use the `File`
class, you can manipulate files more like you used to in DOS programs, by
opening a file, writing data to the file, and then closing the file. In this
chapter, you examine the various ways you can save and load data to and
from a disk file.

The Document/View Architecture

Back in Chapter 3, "Programming with Visual C++," you got a quick look at
MFC's document/view architecture, which enables your application to
separate the way data is stored from how it's viewed. Specifically, the
application's document class is responsible for holding the data for the
currently open document, as well as for *serializing* the data to and from a
disk file. The view class, on the other hand, displays the data and enables
the user to edit the data in whatever way is appropriate for the application.

Although many things about the document/view architecture relate only
indirectly to file I/O, the document and view classes work together so tightly
that it's difficult to separate one element of the architecture from another.
So, in this section, you see not only how to save and load documents using
the document and view classes, but also how to construct an application
that employs the document/view architecture.

The easiest way to implement the document/view architecture in an application is to create the application with AppWizard. The source code that AppWizard generates contains all the nuts and bolts required to implement functioning document and view classes. You only need to add the source code to handle the specific type of data for your application. To implement the document/view architecture, you must complete the following steps:

1. Use AppWizard to create a skeleton application.

2. Declare the data objects needed to hold the document's data in the document class.

3. Complete the document class's `OnNewDocument()` function in order to initialize a new document.

4. Override the `DeleteContents()` function in the document class in order to delete data from the previous document.

5. Complete the document class's `Serialize()` function in order to save and load document data.

6. Complete the view class's `OnDraw()` function in order to display the contents of the current document.

7. In the view class, add the code needed to enable the user to edit the document's data.

On CD-ROM

On this book's CD-ROM, you can find the source code and executable file for the String application, a program that uses the document/view architecture to enable the user to save, load, and edit an array of strings. In the following sections, you examine each of the seven previous steps as they apply to the building of the String application.

Step 1: Create a skeleton application

Back in Chapter 3, "Programming with Visual C++," you learned how to create an application with AppWizard. If you need a refresher course, please refer back to that chapter. To create the String application, start a new project workspace called **string**. Then, use the following settings in AppWizard's six wizard pages to finish the skeleton application:

Step 1 page—Select the single document interface.

Step 2 page—Accept all default settings.

Step 3 page—Accept all default settings.

Step 4 page—Shut off all features except 3D controls.

Step 5 page—Select the statically linked library.

Step 6 page—Accept all default settings.

When you click the Finish button on the Step 6 wizard page, you should see the New Project Information dialog box shown in Figure 17-1.

Figure 17-1: After choosing settings in the six wizard pages for the String application, AppWizard displays the New Project Information dialog box.

Step 2: Declare the document's data objects

The next step is to declare member variables where the application can store its data. Because the String application's data consists of an array of strings, the MFC CStringArray class is the perfect data type. Add a data member called m_strArray to the CStringDoc document class. This data member should be an object of the CStringArray class and have public access, as shown in Figure 17-2.

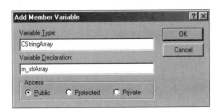

Figure 17-2: Here's the document class's new data member after adding m_strArray to the CStringDoc document class

Step 3: Complete the OnNewDocument() function

Whenever the user creates a new document, MFC calls the document class's OnNewDocument() function, which gives the application a chance to initialize the new document. In the case of the String application, OnNewDocument() adds a header string to the string array. Every String document has this editable header string, which the application displays at the top of the window. Listing 17-1 shows the completed OnNewDocument() function.

Listing 17-1: The OnNewDocument() **function**

```
BOOL CStringDoc::OnNewDocument()
{
    if (!CDocument::OnNewDocument())
        return FALSE;

    // TODO: add reinitialization code here
    // (SDI documents will reuse this document)

    m_strArray.Add("DEFAULT HEADER STRING");

    return TRUE;
}
```

Step 4: Override the DeleteContents() function

When the user creates a new application document (either explicitly or just by starting the application), MFC calls DeleteContents() so the application can delete any data objects that remain from the previous document. This gives the new document a fresh start. Because MFC calls DeleteContents() when the application first runs, you must be sure to check for empty documents in order to avoid crashing the program when there is no previous document. You don't want to try and access objects before they've been created. You can override DeleteContents() using ClassWizard, as shown in Figure 17-3. Listing 17-2 shows String's completed DeleteContents() function. The call to m_strArray.RemoveAll() is safe even if the array is empty.

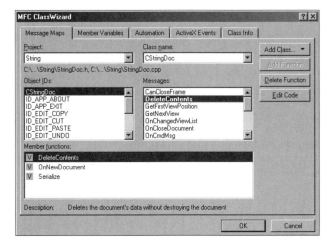

Figure 17-3: Override `DeleteContents()` with ClassWizard.

Listing 17-2: The `DeleteContents()` **function**

```
void CStringDoc::DeleteContents()
{
    // TODO: Add your specialized code here and/or call the base
class

    m_strArray.RemoveAll();

    CDocument::DeleteContents();
}
```

Step 5: Complete the `Serialize()` function

The document class's `Serialize()` function is where the document's data is loaded from or saved to disk. `Serialize()`'s single parameter is a `CArchive` object that can serialize many types of data, including classes like `CString`. To serialize data to the archive, use the `<<` operator. To serialize data from the archive, use the `>` operator. MFC defines both of these operators in the `CArchive` class so that you can easily save and load many types of data.

Unfortunately, a `CStringArray` object is not one of the data types supported by the `CArchive` class. So, in order to save or load the strings contained in the `m_strArray` data member, the program extracts the strings from the array before serializing them. Listing 17-3 shows the completed `Serialize()` function.

Note

In the `Serialize()` function, notice the call to `UpdateAllViews()` after loading a document. This call ensures that the document's view is updated with the newly loaded data.

Listing 17-3: The `Serialize()` **function**

```
void CStringDoc::Serialize(CArchive& ar)
{
    int size;

    if (ar.IsStoring())
    {
        // TODO: add storing code here

        size = m_strArray.GetSize();
        ar << size;
        for (int x=0; x<size; ++x)
        {
            CString str = m_strArray.GetAt(x);
            ar << str;
        }
    }
    else
    {
        // TODO: add loading code here

        ar > size;
        for (int x=0; x<size; ++x)
        {
            CString str;
            ar > str;
            m_strArray.Add(str);
        }
        UpdateAllViews(NULL);
    }
}
```

One great thing about many MFC classes is that they are *persistent*, which means that they are fully capable of serializing their contents without your having to extract the data manually. You learn more about persistent classes later in this chapter. For now, take a look at Listing 17-4, which shows an alternative way to write the `Serialize()` function, taking advantage of the `CStringArray` class's persistence. In this version of the function, the program merely calls `m_strArray`'s `Serialize()` function to handle the saving and loading tasks. The only other thing `Serialize()` must do is call `UpdateAllViews()` to update the application's view window.

Listing 17-4: The alternative `DeleteContents()` **function**

```
void CStringDoc::Serialize(CArchive& ar)
{
    m_strArray.Serialize(ar);

    if (ar.IsStoring())
    {
        // TODO: add storing code here

    }
    else
    {
```

```
    // TODO: add loading code here

    UpdateAllViews(NULL);
    }
}
```

Step 6: Complete the OnDraw() function

In your application's view class, the OnDraw() function is charged with displaying the current document in the application's window. How you display this data in your own applications is, of course, completely dependent upon the data and how you think it's best displayed. In the case of the String application, the display is just a list of the string array's contents, as shown in Figure 17-4. Listing 17-5 shows the CStringView class's completed OnDraw() function.

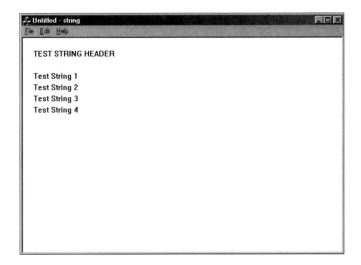

Figure 17-4: The String application displaying its document

Listing 17-5: The OnDraw() function

```
void CStringView::OnDraw(CDC* pDC)
{
    CStringDoc* pDoc = GetDocument();
    ASSERT_VALID(pDoc);

    // TODO: add draw code for native data here

    int row = 20;
    int size = pDoc->m_strArray.GetSize();
    for (int x=0; x<size; ++x)
    {
        CString str = pDoc->m_strArray.GetAt(x);
        pDC->TextOut(20, row, str);
```

```
            if (x=0)
                row += 40;
            else
                row += 20;
    }
}
```

Step 7: Add editing code

On CD-ROM

The final task in implementing an application with the document/view architecture is enabling the user to edit the document. In the String application, the user can add strings to the array, as well as change the header string, by selecting the Add String or Change Header commands, respectively. These commands display a dialog box in which the user types the new information. Listing 17-6 shows the functions that display the dialog boxes and add the new data to the document. Figure 17-5 shows the dialog box that adds a string to the document. The dialog box that changes the header looks about the same. You can find the complete String project on this book's CD-ROM if you want to explore the project's resources.

Figure 17-5: The String application provides a dialog box for adding a string.

Listing 17-6: The editing functions

```
void CStringView::OnEditAddstring()
{
    // TODO: Add your command handler code here

    CStringDoc* pDoc = GetDocument();
    CAddStringDlg dialog;
    int result = dialog.DoModal();

    if (result == IDOK)
    {
        CString str = dialog.m_string;
        pDoc->m_strArray.Add(str);
        Invalidate();
    }
}

void CStringView::OnEditChangeheader()
{
    // TODO: Add your command handler code here

    CStringDoc* pDoc = GetDocument();
```

```
        CChangeHeaderDlg dialog;
        int result = dialog.DoModal();

        if (result == IDOK)
        {
            CString str = dialog.m_header;
            pDoc->m_strArray.SetAt(0, str);
            Invalidate();
        }
}
```

Persistent Objects

A persistent object can serialize its state and contents. A good example of a persistent object is the CStringArray object you used in the previous section to store document data. To save or load the object's contents to and from a file, you only needed to call the object's Serialize() function with a reference to a CArchive object. MFC classes, however, aren't the only classes that can be serialized. Any class that you create can be made persistent, simply by following a few easy steps:

1. Derive your new class from MFC's CObject class.

2. Include the DECLARE_SERIAL macro in the class's declaration.

3. Provide a default constructor for the class.

4. Provide a Serialize() function in the class.

5. Include the IMPLEMENT_SERIAL macro in the class's definition.

On CD-ROM

In the Chapter17\PersistCircleApp directory of this book's CD-ROM is a new version of CircleApp. You originally developed CircleApp in Chapter 3. The new version uses a persistent class to store the document's circles. From the user's point of view, this new version works just like the old one; the differences are all internal. For example, Listing 17-7 shows the header file for the class that the program uses to store its document data.

Listing 17-7: The header file for the CCircles **class**

```
///////////////////////////////////////////////////
// CCircles.h
///////////////////////////////////////////////////

struct CircleStruct
{
    CPoint point;
    COLORREF color;
    int diameter;
};

class CCircles : public CObject
{
    DECLARE_SERIAL(CCircles)

    CCircles();
```

```
protected:
    CPtrArray m_circleArray;

public:
    void AddCircle(CPoint point, COLORREF color,
        int diameter);
    int GetCircleCount();
    void GetCircle(int circleNum, CircleStruct* circle);
    void DeleteAllCircles();
    void Serialize(CArchive& ar);
};
```

As you can see, CCircles is derived from CObject. The class declaration also includes the DECLARE_SERIAL macro. (The macro's single argument is the name of the class you're declaring as serializable.) The new class also provides a default constructor. The constructor is defined in the class's implementation file.

The CCircles class has a single data member, which is an object of the CPtrArray class. You used the CPtrArray class in the original version of the CircleApp application to store the circles that make up a CircleApp document (see Chapter 3). The CCircles class uses the CPtrArray object, m_circleArray, in exactly the same way. Now, however, the details of handling m_circleArray are hidden from the main program, which accesses the array only through the public member functions provided by CCircles. The public member functions, along with their descriptions, are listed below:

AddCircle()	Adds a circle to the circle array
DeleteAllCircles()	Deletes all circles from the circle array
GetCircle()	Gets the data for a given circle
GetCircleCount()	Returns the current number of circles in the circle array
Serialize()	Performs object serialization for the class

The header file declares the class's Serialize() function. The class also has to define the Serialize() function, which it does in its implementation file, shown in Listing 17-8. The first thing to notice here is the IMPLEMENT_SERIAL macro. The macro's three arguments are the name of the class you're declaring as serializable, the name of the immediate base class, and a schema, or version, number.

Listing 17-8: The implementation file for the CCircles class

```
///////////////////////////////////////////////
// CCircles.cpp
///////////////////////////////////////////////

#include "stdafx.h"
#include "CCircles.h"
```

```
IMPLEMENT_SERIAL(CCircles, CObject, 1)

CCircles::CCircles()
{
}

void CCircles::AddCircle(CPoint point,
    COLORREF color, int diameter)
{
    CircleStruct* circle = new CircleStruct;
    circle->point = point;
    circle->color = color;
    circle->diameter = diameter;
    m_circleArray.Add(circle);
}

int CCircles::GetCircleCount()
{
    return m_circleArray.GetSize();
}

void CCircles::GetCircle(int circleNum,
    CircleStruct* circle)
{
    CircleStruct* circleStruct =
        (CircleStruct*)m_circleArray.GetAt(circleNum);
    circle->point = circleStruct->point;
    circle->color = circleStruct->color;
    circle->diameter = circleStruct->diameter;
}

void CCircles::DeleteAllCircles()
{
    int size = GetCircleCount();
    for (int x=0; x<size; ++x)
    {
        CircleStruct* circle =
            (CircleStruct*)m_circleArray.GetAt(x);
        delete circle;
    }
    m_circleArray.RemoveAll();
}

void CCircles::Serialize(CArchive& ar)
{
    CObject::Serialize(ar);

    if (ar.IsStoring())
    {
        CircleStruct circle;
        int size = GetCircleCount();
        ar << size;

        for (int x=0; x<size; ++x)
        {
            GetCircle(x, &circle);
```

```
            ar << circle.point;
            ar << circle.color;
            ar << circle.diameter;
        }
    }
    else
    {
        int size;
        ar > size;

        for (int x=0; x<size; ++x)
        {
            CPoint point;
            COLORREF color;
            int diameter;
            ar > point;
            ar > color;
            ar > diameter;
            AddCircle(point, color, diameter);
        }

    }
}
```

The most important part of this class (at least from the point of view of file handling) is the `Serialize()` function, which is what makes `CCircles` persistent. The `Serialize()` function, which transfers the object's data (or state) to and from a file, looks quite a bit like the `Serialize()` function you wrote for the document class in the original version of CircleApp. Listing 17-9 shows the original document class's `Serialize()` function. Compare it with the `Serialize()` function in Listing 17-8. The main difference is that `CCircles`'s `Serialize()` function calls the class's own member functions where appropriate, rather than always calling `CPtrArray` member functions.

Listing 17-9: The original document class's `Serialize()` function

```
void CCircleAppDoc::Serialize(CArchive& ar)
{
    if (ar.IsStoring())
    {
        // TODO: add storing code here
        int size = m_circleArray.GetSize();
        ar << size;

        for (int x=0; x<size; ++x)
        {
            CircleStruct* circle =
                (CircleStruct*)m_circleArray.GetAt(x);
            ar << circle->point;
            ar << circle->color;
            ar << circle->diameter;
        }
    }
    else
    {
        // TODO: add loading code here
```

```
        int size;
        ar > size;
        m_circleArray.SetSize(size);

        for (int x=0; x<size; ++x)
        {
            CPoint point;
            COLORREF color;
            int diameter;
            ar > point;
            ar > color;
            ar > diameter;
            CircleStruct* circle = new CircleStruct;
            circle->point = point;
            circle->color = color;
            circle->diameter = diameter;
            m_circleArray.SetAt(x, circle);
        }

        UpdateAllViews(NULL);
    }
}
```

Now that CCircles handles most of the serialization, how does the document
class save a CircleApp document? Listing 17-10 shows the document class's
new Serialize() function. As you can see, all it does is call
m_circles.Serialize() (m_circles is a CCircles object). The m_circles
object then handles the serialization, whether the application is loading or
saving the object. In the case of loading a document,
CCircleAppDoc::Serialize() must also call UpdateAllViews() to ensure that
the view window gets updated with the newly loaded document.

Listing 17-10: The document class's new Serialize() function

```
void CCircleAppDoc::Serialize(CArchive& ar)
{
    m_circles.Serialize(ar);

    if (ar.IsStoring())
    {
        // TODO: add storing code here
    }
    else
    {
        // TODO: add loading code here

        UpdateAllViews(NULL);
    }
}
```

Other functions in the original CircleApp application have also changed in
this new version. For example, Listing 17-11 shows how the new view class's
OnLButtonDown() adds a circle to the document, by calling a CCircles
member function, rather than a CPtrArray member function. Ditto for
OnDraw(), which displays the circles in the view window. Listing 17-12 shows
the new OnDraw() function. There are a few other changes to CircleApp's

On CD-ROM

document and view classes in order to accommodate the change from the CPtrArray data storage to the persistent CCircles object. If you want to examine those changes, you can find the complete source code in the PersistCircleApp directory of this book's CD-ROM.

Listing 17-11: The new OnLButtonDown() function

```
void CCircleAppView::OnLButtonDown(UINT nFlags,
    CPoint point)
{
    // TODO: Add your message handler code here
    //    and/or call default

    // Draw the new circle.
    CClientDC clientDC(this);
    CBrush brush(m_currentColor);
    CBrush* oldBrush = clientDC.SelectObject(&brush);
    int radius = m_currentDiameter / 2;
    clientDC.Ellipse(point.x-radius, point.y-radius,
        point.x+radius, point.y+radius);
    clientDC.SelectObject(oldBrush);

    // Store the new circle in the document.
    CCircleAppDoc* pDoc = GetDocument();
    pDoc->m_circles.AddCircle(point,
        m_currentColor, m_currentDiameter);

    CView::OnLButtonDown(nFlags, point);
}
```

Listing 17-12: The new OnDraw() function

```
void CCircleAppView::OnDraw(CDC* pDC)
{
    CCircleAppDoc* pDoc = GetDocument();
    ASSERT_VALID(pDoc);

    // TODO: add draw code for native data here
    int size = pDoc->m_circles.GetCircleCount();

    for (int x=0; x<size; ++x)
    {
        CircleStruct circle;
        pDoc->m_circles.GetCircle(x, &circle);
        int radius = circle.diameter/2;
        int x1 = circle.point.x-radius;
        int y1 = circle.point.y-radius;
        int x2 = circle.point.x+radius;
        int y2 = circle.point.y+radius;
        COLORREF color = circle.color;
        CBrush brush(color);
        CBrush* oldBrush = pDC->SelectObject(&brush);
        pDC->Ellipse(x1, y1, x2, y2);
        pDC->SelectObject(oldBrush);
    }
}
```

PROBLEMS & SOLUTIONS

Saving Persistent and Nonpersistent Objects with Document/View Architecture

PROBLEM: *How do I save and load both persistent objects and nonpersistent objects in a program using the document/view architecture?*

SOLUTION: In order to avoid a lot of confusing source code, the program examples in this book tend to be overly simplified compared to real-world applications. For example, a real paint application would have much more complex data to serialize than does the trivial circle sample program you created in Chapter 3 and modified in this chapter. Some of this complex data may be stored in persistent classes, whereas other document data may be stored in nonpersistent data objects.

The good news is that a document's Serialize() function doesn't force you into an either/or situation. If you need to save both persistent objects and nonpersistent objects, write a Serialize() function like that shown in Listing 17-13. In this listing, the function first serializes persistent objects and then, in the if statement, saves or loads nonpersistent objects.

Note

If you try this combined approach to serialization, be sure that you save the data objects in the same order that you load them. This is true, of course, for any type of file handling. There's nothing magical about serialization.

Listing 17-13: A Serialize() **function that serializes both persistent and nonpersistent data objects**

```
void CCircleAppDoc::Serialize(CArchive& ar)
{
    m_circles.Serialize(ar);

    if (ar.IsStoring())
    {
        // TODO: add storing code here

        ar << msg;
    }
    else
    {
        // TODO: add loading code here

        ar > msg;

        UpdateAllViews(NULL);
    }
}
```

Continued

On CD-ROM

In the PersistCircleApp2 directory of this book's CD-ROM, you'll find yet another version of the CircleApp program. This version displays a message string in the window along with the circles, as shown in Figure 17-6. You can edit the message string by selecting the Circle menu's Change Message command. The program's document class serializes the circle data and the message string as shown in Listing 17-13.

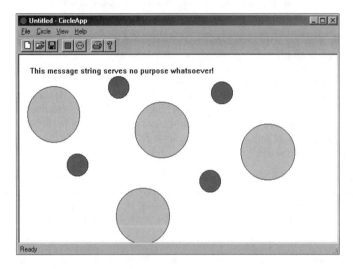

Figure 17-6: CircleApp displayed with its message string and the file's circles; this version serializes both persistent and nonpersistent data objects.

 PROBLEMS & SOLUTIONS

Reminding Users to Save Modified Files

PROBLEM: *How can I remind a user to save a modified file before closing it?*

SOLUTION: This handy feature is actually built into the MFC document classes. To take advantage of the feature, call the `SetModifiedFlag()` member function whenever the user changes the document. Then, when the user goes to close the document, MFC warns that the file needs saving. When the user saves the file, the document class clears the modified flag.

Continued

Listing 17-14 shows the OnCircleChangemessage() function from the PersistCircleApp2 version of the CircleApp application. This is the function that enables the user to change the message string displayed in the window. Notice the call to pDoc⊞SetModifiedFlag() in the if statement. That call is all it takes to tell the document class that the document needs to be saved. There's another call to SetModifiedFlag() in the view class's OnLButtonDown() function, where the view class adds circles to the display in response to the user's button clicks. Figure 17-7 shows CircleApp when the user tries to exit the application before saving a modified file.

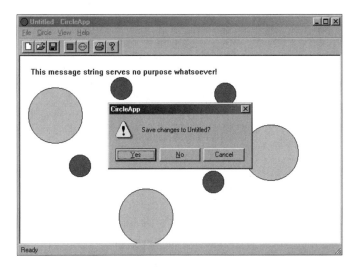

Figure 17-7: CircleApp displayed with a dialog asking whether the user wants to save the file; this dialog box appears when the user attempts to exit CircleApp before saving a modified file.

Listing 17-14: Calling the document class's SetModifiedFlag() **function**

```
void CCircleAppView::OnCircleChangemessage()
{
    // TODO: Add your command handler code here

    CCircleAppDoc* pDoc = GetDocument();
    CMessageDlg dialog;
    dialog.m_message = pDoc->msg;
    int result = dialog.DoModal();
    if (result == IDOK)
    {
        pDoc->msg = dialog.m_message;
        pDoc->SetModifiedFlag();
        Invalidate();
    }
}
```

File Handling with the `CFile` Class

Taking advantage of the document/view architecture and creating persistent objects are both great ways to manipulate files in your Visual C++ programs. However, sometimes you just want to handle the file yourself—opening, closing, reading, and writing a file directly. When you're in this state of mind, you might want to look into MFC's `CFile` class, which enables you to manipulate files more directly. Table 17-1 lists the member functions of the `CFile` class.

Table 17-1   `CFile` Member functions

Function	*Description*
`Abort()`	Closes a file regardless of errors
`Close()`	Closes a file
`Duplicate()`	Creates a duplicate file object
`Flush()`	Flushes data not yet written
`GetFileName()`	Retrieves the file's name
`GetFilePath()`	Retrieves the file's complete path
`GetFileTitle()`	Retrieves the file's title
`GetLength()`	Returns the file's length
`GetPosition()`	Returns the file pointer
`GetStatus()`	Retrieves the file's status
`LockRange()`	Locks a portion of the file
`Open()`	Opens a file
`Read()`	Reads data from a file
`Remove()`	Deletes a file
`Rename()`	Renames a file
`Seek()`	Positions the file pointer
`SeekToBegin()`	Positions the file pointer at the beginning of the file
`SeekToEnd()`	Positions the file pointer at the end of the file
`SetFilePath()`	Sets the file's path
`SetLength()`	Changes the file's length
`SetStatus()`	Sets the file's status
`UnlockRange()`	Unlocks a portion of the file
`Write()`	Writes data to a file

To create a file, you simply create a `CFile` object by calling the `CFile` class's constructor with a file name and the appropriate access flags:

```
CFile file("testfile.txt",
    CFile::modeCreate | CFile::modeWrite);
```

Writing to the file is as easy as calling the file object's `Write()` member function:

```
file.Write("This is a test", 14);
```

`Write()`'s two arguments are the address of the data to write and the length of the data.

Finally, you close the file by calling...you guessed it...the `Close()` member function:

```
file.Close();
```

The `CFile` class defines a number of access flags that you can use when you open or create a file. Table 17-2 lists these flags along with their descriptions.

Table 17-2   `CFile` file mode flags

Flag	Description
CFile::modeCreate	Creates a new file. If the file exists, its length is truncated to 0 length.
CFile::modeNoInherit	Disallows file inheritance by child processes
CFile::modeNoTruncate	Disallows the file to be truncated if the file exists
CFile::modeRead	Opens the file as read-only
CFile::modeReadWrite	Opens the file for read and write access
CFile::modeWrite	Opens the file as write-only
CFile::shareDenyNone	Opens the file, but doesn't deny read or write access to other processes
CFile::shareDenyRead	Opens the file and denies read access to other processes
CFile::shareDenyWrite	Opens the file and denies write access to other processes
CFile::shareExclusive	Opens the file and denies read and write access to other processes
CFile::typeBinary	Sets the binary mode in derived classes
CFile::typeText	Sets the text mode in derived classes

Reading from a file is just as easy as writing to one, as the following source code lines show:

```
CFile file("testfile.txt", CFile::modeRead);
char s[81];
int numBytes = file.Read(s, 80);
s[numBytes] = 0;
file.Close();
```

These lines perform the following actions:

- Open the file for reading
- Read up to 80 bytes into a character array
- Append a zero to the character array in order to form a C string
- Close the file

As you can see, the Read() function returns the number of bytes read from the file. The other CFile member functions are just as easy to use, especially if you're already familiar with C file handling.

 PROBLEMS & SOLUTIONS

Detecting Errors When Handling Files with the CFile Class

PROBLEM: *When I'm handling files with the* CFile *class, how do I know whether the operations went OK or whether an error occurred?*

SOLUTION: Many of the CFile member functions throw CFileException exceptions when file operations fail. To handle errors, you should enclose your file-handling code in try/catch program blocks and then watch for the specific errors your program may generate. Listing 17-15 shows how you might add error handling to your CFile file operations. You place the code that may generate errors in the try program block, and then place the error-handling code in the catch block.

Listing 17-15: CFile **error handling**

```
try
{
    CFile file("testfile.txt", CFile::modeRead);
    char s[81];
    int numBytes = file.Read(s, 80);
    s[numBytes] = 0;
    file.Close();
}
catch (CFileException* fe)
{
    switch (fe->m_cause)
    {
        case CFileException::fileNotFound:
```

Continued

```
        MessageBox("File not found",
            fe->m_strFileName);
    break;
case CFileException::generic:
    MessageBox("Generic file error",
        fe->m_strFileName);
    break;
case CFileException::badPath:
    MessageBox("Bad path",
        fe->m_strFileName);
    break;
case CFileException::tooManyOpenFiles:
    MessageBox("Too many open files",
        fe->m_strFileName);
    break;
case CFileException::accessDenied:
    MessageBox("Access denied",
        fe->m_strFileName);
    break;
case CFileException::invalidFile:
    MessageBox("Invalid file",
        fe->m_strFileName);
    break;
case CFileException::removeCurrentDir:
    MessageBox("Can't remove directory",
        fe->m_strFileName);
    break;
case CFileException::directoryFull:
    MessageBox("Directory full",
        fe->m_strFileName);
    break;
case CFileException::badSeek:
    MessageBox("Bad seek",
        fe->m_strFileName);
    break;
case CFileException::hardIO:
    MessageBox("Hardware error",
        fe->m_strFileName);
    break;
case CFileException::sharingViolation:
    MessageBox("Sharing violation",
        fe->m_strFileName);
    break;
case CFileException::lockViolation:
    MessageBox("Lock violation",
        fe->m_strFileName);
    break;
case CFileException::diskFull:
    MessageBox("Disk full",
        fe->m_strFileName);
    break;
case CFileException::endOfFile:
    MessageBox("End of file",
        fe->m_strFileName);
    break;
```

Continued

                    }
               }

A CFileException object contains the error that occurred in its m_cause member variable and the name of the file that caused the error in its m_strFileName member variable. As you can see in Listing 17-15, CFile objects can generate many different errors. Of course, in the sample listing, not all the errors could be generated by the calls to the CFile constructor and the Read() and Close() functions. The other error types are included in the listing for the sake of completeness.

Summary

No matter what type of application you're programming, Visual C++ features a file-handling method perfect for the task. Whether you want to deal with files directly or whether you want to incorporate persistent objects into your project, MFC's document/view architecture provides a framework that makes it easy to provide professional-level document saving and loading features.

Also discussed in this chapter:

▶ MFC's document/view architecture separates the data that makes up a document from the way the user views and edits the document.

▶ Using AppWizard, you can create a skeleton program that supports the document/view architecture with a few mouse clicks.

▶ The document class's Serialize() member function is where data loading and saving occurs.

▶ You can create your own persistent objects (objects that can serialize their contents and states) easily by using the DECLARE_SERIAL and IMPLEMENT_SERIAL macros and by writing a Serialize() function for the class.

▶ MFC's CFile class provides object-oriented advantages, while at the same time enabling you to manage files directly.

Chapter 18

The Clipboard

In This Chapter

▶ Understanding the Clipboard's standard data formats

▶ Using registered and private Clipboard formats

▶ Providing multiple types of Clipboard data

One of the big advantages of an operating system like Windows 98 is its ability to share data between applications. Under Windows, you can share data in several ways, including using ActiveX to link or embed data objects. You learn about ActiveX in Part 4 of this book. For now, the easiest way to get data from one application to another is through the Clipboard.

When using the Clipboard, you can specify your application's document data type in various ways. Other applications that understand the data type can use their cut and paste functions to transfer the data to and from the Clipboard, as well as render the data in their windows. It's up to you, as the programmer, to decide how your application's data should be represented in the Clipboard. Windows gives you several choices:

Standard formats	Windows defines a number of standard formats, such as text and bitmap, that applications can use to transfer data to and from the Clipboard.
Private "display" formats	Windows also defines formats that the Windows Clipboard viewer can display in a standard format, but that are interpreted differently by an application that knows how to extract additional information from the data.
Registered formats	Applications can create their own Clipboard formats and register the format with Windows. Then, any application that understands the custom format can copy and paste data to and from the Clipboard, as well as render the data in its window.

In the following sections, you explore these methods of managing data with the Clipboard.

Standard Formats

Often when you think about the Clipboard, you think in terms of copying text from one application and pasting it into another. Although this is the Clipboard's most common use, it can handle other types of data as well. In fact, Windows defines a set of constants that programs use to identify the current contents of the Clipboard. These constants and their meanings are listed in Table 18-1.

Table 18-1   Constants used to identify Clipboard contents

Constant	Description
CF_BITMAP	A device-dependent bitmap
CF_DIB	A device-independent bitmap (DIB)
CF_DIF	Data Interchange Format (DIF) data
CF_ENHMETAFILE	An enhanced metafile handle
CF_METAFILEPICT	A special type of metafile that includes data stored in a METAFILEPICT structure
CF_OEMTEXT	Text that uses the OEM character set
CF_PALETTE	A palette handle
CF_SYLK	Microsoft Symbolic Link (SYLK) data
CF_TEXT	Plain text that's terminated with a NULL character. The text has carriage return and linefeed characters at the end of each line.
CF_TIFF	Tagged Image File Format (TIFF) picture data

As you can see, many of these Clipboard formats have specific uses that you don't run into too often. The most commonly used formats are CF_TEXT and CF_BITMAP, for transferring text and image data between applications.

A Clipboard example application

As an example of transferring data in a standard format to the Clipboard, you will examine a new version of the CircleApp application that you created in Chapter 3. This new version has been modified to include a Copy command that creates a bitmap from the current document data and transfers the bitmap to the Clipboard. Any application that can display bitmaps—such as Microsoft Paint—can then display a CircleApp document.

Note

The type of data created by an application's Copy command is completely dependent on the application; Windows really has nothing to do with it. But when working with images, a Copy command usually creates bitmaps because there is no standard Clipboard format. If the application wanted to copy data in another format to the Clipboard, such as PCX, the application would have to register a custom Clipboard format.

On CD-ROM

You can find this new version of CircleApp in the Chapter18\CBCircleApp folder of this book's CD-ROM. When you run the program, you will immediately see that this version of the program has an Edit menu containing Copy and Paste commands. The Copy command copies the entire current document as a bitmap to the Clipboard. You can then display the bitmap in an application such as Microsoft Paint, Microsoft Word, or any other application that can display bitmaps, by selecting the appropriate command, usually Paste.

To see the Copy command in action, follow these steps:

1. Run the new version of CircleApp.

2. When the application's main window appears, paint a few circles, as shown in Figure 18-1.

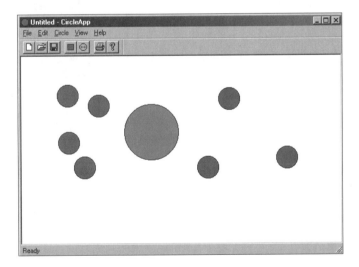

Figure 18-1: CircleApp, with circles drawn in its display area

3. Select CircleApp's Copy command, as shown in Figure 18-2.

4. Run Microsoft Paint.

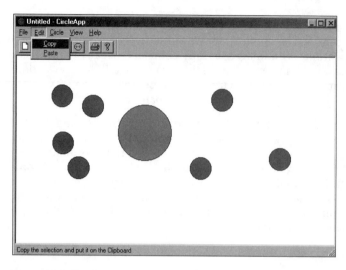

Figure 18-2: The Copy command copies the CircleApp document to the Clipboard as a bitmap.

5. Select Microsoft Paint's Paste command from the Edit menu. The CircleApp document appears in Paint's window, as shown in Figure 18-3.

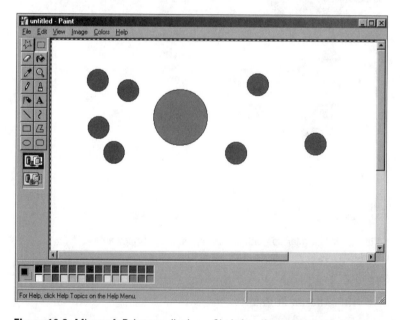

Figure 18-3: Microsoft Paint can display a CircleApp document that's been copied as a bitmap.

Copying a bitmap to the Clipboard

Now that you've seen the Clipboard in action, it's time to look behind the scenes and see how an application copies an image to the Clipboard. Copying a bitmap to the Clipboard is an easy process if you already have the bitmap created and ready to go. First, you call `OpenClipboard()` to open the Clipboard:

```
BOOL open = OpenClipboard();
```

This function, which is a member function of the MFC `CWnd` class, returns `TRUE` if the Clipboard opens successfully, and `FALSE` otherwise.

If the Clipboard opens, you call `EmptyClipboard()`:

```
::EmptyClipboard();
```

This Windows function call not only removes all previous data from the Clipboard, but also makes your application the Clipboard owner. As long as your application owns the Clipboard, other applications cannot access it.

With the Clipboard open and empty, you can then call Windows' `SetClipboardData()` function to copy the bitmap to the Clipboard:

```
::SetClipboardData(CF_BITMAP, hBitmap);
```

`SetClipboardData()`'s two arguments are the data format (in this case, `CF_BITMAP`) and a handle to the data object. At this point, the Clipboard owns the data, and your application should no longer access the data directly.

Note

Most applications pass a copy of the data object to the Clipboard, so that the application can continue to access the original data.

The final step is to close the Clipboard:

```
::CloseClipboard();
```

When you close the Clipboard, you release your application's hold on it, so that other applications can access the Clipboard if they need to.

Note

Because the Clipboard is a shared system resource, an application should retain control of the Clipboard only for a short period of time. The application should close the Clipboard the instant it's finished with it.

The CBCircleApp version of CircleApp does its Clipboard copying in the view class's `OnEditCopy()` function, which is the function that responds to the Edit menu's Copy command (see Listing 18-1).

Listing 18-1: Source code for the `OnEditCopy()` function

```
void CCircleAppView::OnEditCopy()
{
    // TODO: Add your command handler code here

    BOOL open = OpenClipboard();
```

```
    if (open)
    {
        ::EmptyClipboard();

        CClientDC clientDC(this);
        CBitmap* pBitmap = new CBitmap();
        pBitmap->CreateCompatibleBitmap(&clientDC,
            800, 600);

        CDC memoryDC;
        memoryDC.CreateCompatibleDC(&clientDC);
        memoryDC.SelectObject(pBitmap);

        CBrush whiteBrush(RGB(255,255,255));
        memoryDC.FillRect(CRect(0,0,799,599),
            &whiteBrush);

        RenderDisplay(&memoryDC);

        HBITMAP hBitmap = (HBITMAP) *pBitmap;
        ::SetClipboardData(CF_BITMAP, hBitmap);

        ::CloseClipboard();
    }
}
```

If you're not familiar with bitmap handling, `OnEditCopy()` is probably befuddling. To learn more about bitmaps, go back to Chapter 12, "Bitmaps," read up on the subject, and meet the rest of us back here. The following overview of the function provides a general idea of what's going on. The `OnEditCopy()` function performs the following tasks:

- Opens and empties the Clipboard:

```
BOOL open = OpenClipboard();
if (open)
{
    ::EmptyClipboard();
```

- Creates an 800x600 bitmap that's compatible with the current display:

```
CClientDC clientDC(this);
CBitmap* pBitmap = new CBitmap();
pBitmap->CreateCompatibleBitmap(&clientDC,
    800, 600);
```

- Creates a memory device context and selects the bitmap into it:

```
CDC memoryDC;
memoryDC.CreateCompatibleDC(&clientDC);
memoryDC.SelectObject(pBitmap);
```

- Fills the bitmap with white:

```
CBrush whiteBrush(RGB(255,255,255));
memoryDC.FillRect(CRect(0,0,799,599),
    &whiteBrush);
```

■ Calls the member function that draws the circle document onto the bitmap:

```
RenderDisplay(&memoryDC);
```

■ Transfers the bitmap to the Clipboard:

```
HBITMAP hBitmap = (HBITMAP) *pBitmap;
::SetClipboardData(CF_BITMAP, hBitmap);
```

■ Closes the Clipboard:

```
::CloseClipboard();
```

RenderDisplay() is a member function of the view class and does almost exactly what the original CircleApp's OnDraw() function did. In fact, in this version of CircleApp, the OnDraw() function calls RenderDisplay() too. Listing 18-2 shows RenderDisplay(), while Listing 18-3 shows OnDraw() for your comparison.

Listing 18-2: Source code for the RenderDisplay() function

```
void CCircleAppView::RenderDisplay(CDC* pDC)
{
    CCircleAppDoc* pDoc = GetDocument();

    int size = pDoc->m_circleArray.GetSize();

    for (int x=0; x<size; ++x)
    {
        CircleStruct* circle =
            (CircleStruct*)pDoc->m_circleArray.GetAt(x);
        int radius = circle->diameter/2;
        int x1 = circle->point.x-radius;
        int y1 = circle->point.y-radius;
        int x2 = circle->point.x+radius;
        int y2 = circle->point.y+radius;
        COLORREF color = circle->color;
        CBrush brush(color);
        CBrush* oldBrush = pDC->SelectObject(&brush);
        pDC->Ellipse(x1, y1, x2, y2);
        pDC->SelectObject(oldBrush);
    }
}
```

Listing 18-3: Source code for the original OnDraw() function

```
void CCircleAppView::OnDraw(CDC* pDC)
{
    CCircleAppDoc* pDoc = GetDocument();
    ASSERT_VALID(pDoc);

    // TODO: add draw code for native data here
    int size = pDoc->m_circleArray.GetSize();

    for (int x=0; x<size; ++x)
    {
        CircleStruct* circle =
```

```
            (CircleStruct*)pDoc->m_circleArray.GetAt(x);
        int radius = circle->diameter/2;
        int x1 = circle->point.x-radius;
        int y1 = circle->point.y-radius;
        int x2 = circle->point.x+radius;
        int y2 = circle->point.y+radius;
        COLORREF color = circle->color;
        CBrush brush(color);
        CBrush* oldBrush = pDC->SelectObject(&brush);
        pDC->Ellipse(x1, y1, x2, y2);
        pDC->SelectObject(oldBrush);
    }
}
```

As I mentioned before, when you pass the bitmap (or any other data) to the Clipboard, you should no longer access the bitmap in your application. The data belongs to the Clipboard. If you need to access the data, you can extract it from the Clipboard just as any other application would have to, or you can make a private copy of the data before passing it to the Clipboard.

Once the Clipboard is closed, it owns the data it contains. You should not attempt to access the data except through the Clipboard. For this reason, if your application needs continuous access to the data, it must make a copy of that data.

For example, if CircleApp needed to keep the bitmap's image on its display, it would have to redraw the bitmap when the window gets redrawn. This requires having continual access to the bitmap retrieved from the Clipboard, which requires that the application copy the bitmap before closing the Clipboard. You might copy the bitmap in the OnEditPaste() function as follows.

1. Create a new MFC bitmap object from the data returned into the BITMAP structure:

```
CBitmap myBitmap;
myBitmap.CreateBitmapIndirect(&bitmapStruct);
```

2. Create a second memory DC into which the application can copy the bitmap:

```
CDC dstMemDC;
dstMemDC.CreateCompatibleDC(&clientDC);
```

3. Select the new bitmap object into the new memory DC:

```
dstMemDC.SelectObject(myBitmap);
```

4. Copy the Clipboard's bitmap (which is selected into the srcMemDC memory DC) into the new memory DC:

```
dstMemDC.BitBlt(0, 0, bitmapStruct.bmWidth,
    bitmapStruct.bmHeight, &srcMemDC,
    0, 0, SRCCOPY);
```

Pasting a bitmap from the Clipboard

Once you have copied a bitmap to the Clipboard, you'll probably want to do something with it. Luckily, the new version of CircleApp can not only copy bitmaps to the Clipboard, it can also paste a bitmap from the Clipboard into its display. However, because the program doesn't retain a copy of the bitmap, the bitmap display is only temporary. That is, when the window redraws itself, it draws only the current CircleApp document, without any pasted bitmaps. Nor can CircleApp print the pasted bitmap image.

To see the Paste command in action, follow these steps:

1. Run the CBCircleApp version of CircleApp.

2. Run Microsoft Paint.

3. Draw something in Paint's display, as shown in Figure 18-4.

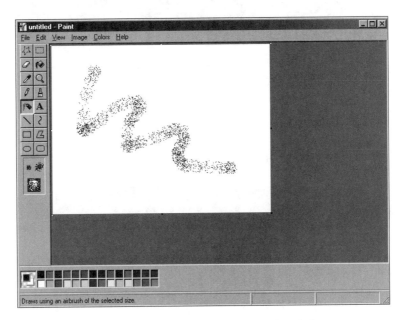

Figure 18-4: Use Microsoft Paint's tools to scribble in the window.

4. Use Paint's selection tool to select and copy a piece of the display area (see Figure 18-5).

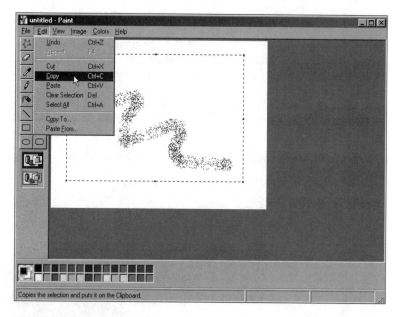

Figure 18-5: You can select a rectangular area and copy it to the Clipboard as a bitmap.

5. Switch to CBCircleApp and select the Paste command. The Paint bitmap appears in the application's window, as shown in Figure 18-6.

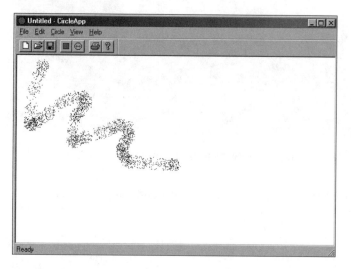

Figure 18-6: CBCircleApp can grab a bitmap from the Clipboard and display it in its window.

Accessing and displaying data stored in the Clipboard is a fairly simple process. First you call IsClipboardFormatAvailable() to see whether the Clipboard holds the type of data the application's looking for:

```
BOOL bitmapAvailable =
    IsClipboardFormatAvailable(CF_BITMAP);
```

The function's single argument is the format of the data for which you're checking. IsClipboardFormatAvailable() returns TRUE if the requested format is available, and FALSE otherwise.

If the format the application needs is available in the Clipboard, you open the Clipboard and call GetClipboardData() to obtain a handle to the data in the Clipboard:

```
OpenClipboard();
HBITMAP hBitmap =
    (HBITMAP)::GetClipboardData(CF_BITMAP);
```

The GetClipboardData() function's single argument is the format of the data. If the call is successful, the function returns a handle to the data object. Otherwise, the return value is NULL.

As always, when you're through with the Clipboard, you close it:

```
CloseClipboard();
```

The CBCircleApp version of CircleApp does its Clipboard pasting in the view class's OnEditPaste() function, which responds to the Edit menu's Paste command (see Listing 18-4).

Listing 18-4: Source code for the OnEditPaste() function

```
void CCircleAppView::OnEditPaste()
{
    // TODO: Add your command handler code here

    BOOL bitmapAvailable =
        IsClipboardFormatAvailable(CF_BITMAP);
    if (bitmapAvailable)
    {
        OpenClipboard();
        HBITMAP hBitmap =
            (HBITMAP)::GetClipboardData(CF_BITMAP);

        CBitmap* bitmap = CBitmap::FromHandle(hBitmap);
        BITMAP bitmapStruct;
        bitmap->GetBitmap(&bitmapStruct);

        CClientDC clientDC(this);

        CDC srcMemDC;
        srcMemDC.CreateCompatibleDC(&clientDC);
        srcMemDC.SelectObject(bitmap);

        clientDC.BitBlt(0, 0, bitmapStruct.bmWidth,
            bitmapStruct.bmHeight, &srcMemDC,
            0, 0, SRCCOPY);
```

```
            CloseClipboard();
        }
    }
```

Listing 18-4 retrieves the bitmap from the Clipboard exactly as previously described. However, before closing the Clipboard, the function displays the bitmap in the window's client area. To do this, the program first creates an MFC bitmap object from the bitmap handle returned from the Clipboard:

```
CBitmap* bitmap = CBitmap::FromHandle(hBitmap);
```

It then gets information about the bitmap, storing the information in a BITMAP structure:

```
BITMAP bitmapStruct;
bitmap->GetBitmap(&bitmapStruct);
```

Next, the program creates a device context for the window's client area:

```
CClientDC clientDC(this);
```

With a client DC in hand, the program can create a memory DC that's compatible with the client DC:

```
CDC srcMemDC;
srcMemDC.CreateCompatibleDC(&clientDC);
```

The memory DC will hold the bitmap just retrieved from the Clipboard. To get the bitmap into the DC, the program calls SelectObject():

```
srcMemDC.SelectObject(bitmap);
```

Finally, the program displays the bitmap by copying it from the memory DC to the client DC, which represents the window's client area:

```
clientDC.BitBlt(0, 0, bitmapStruct.bmWidth,
    bitmapStruct.bmHeight, &srcMemDC,
    0, 0, SRCCOPY);
```

Again, for a more detailed description of bitmaps and MFC's CBitmap class, please consult Chapter 12, "Bitmaps." You may also want to look over Chapter 5, "Graphics Device Interface Basics," for information on using device contexts and GDI objects.

Registered and Private Clipboard Formats

Although the standard Clipboard formats defined by Windows include many common types of data, you may create an application containing data that doesn't fall into one of these types. For example, think about the CircleApp application you created in Chapter 3, "Programming with Visual C++." If that application supported Clipboard copy and paste functions, what data format would you use to copy the file? You could transfer data as a bitmap, but using the bitmap format would cause the document to lose the data that defines the size, location, and color of each circle. This would leave you with nothing more than a picture of the document at the time it was copied into the Clipboard, instead of a complete CircleApp document.

To overcome this type of problem, applications can define their own types of Clipboard data. One way to do this is to transfer data using the standard Clipboard types, but interpret the data differently in the application. For example, the CircleApp application could use the plain text format to transfer the size, location, and color of each circle in a document as a series of text lines:

```
APP=CIRCLEAPP
COUNT=3
DIAMETER=40
X=116
Y=59
RED=255
GREEN=0
BLUE=0
DIAMETER=40
X=140
Y=206
RED=255
GREEN=0
BLUE=0
DIAMETER=100
X=266
Y=145
RED=128
GREEN=128
BLUE=255
```

The previous lines fully describe three circles in a CircleApp document. But, whereas a text application would paste these text lines as they are into the document window, the CircleApp application (or an application that understands the CircleApp data format) would know that it needs to parse the individual values from the text in order to recreate the `CircleStruct` structures that these lines represent.

When this data was pasted into the Clipboard, it might not use the `CF_TEXT` format. Instead, it might use the `CF_DSPTEXT` format, which tells an application that the data is in text form, but should be interpreted in some other way. An application that knows how to render data from the CircleApp application watches for data in the `CF_DSPTEXT` format.

When the Clipboard contains `CF_DSPTEXT` data, the application checks the first line of the text to see whether the CircleApp application created the data (after all, any application can use `CF_DSPTEXT` in its own way for its own document data). If the text checks out as a CircleApp document, the application then parses the text lines, recreating the original CircleApp document.

Following are the constants you can use when copying or pasting Clipboard data in special formats:

CF_DSPTEXT	Data of the CF_TEXT type not necessarily interpreted as text
CF_DSPBITMAP	Data of the CF_BITMAP type not necessarily interpreted as image data
CF_DSPMETAFILEPICT	Data of the CF_METAFILEPICT type not necessarily interpreted as a metafile picture
CF_DSPENHMETAFILE	Data of the CF_ENHMETAFILE type not necessarily interpreted as a metafile handle

Note

The "DSP" in the previous constant names stands for "display," meaning that Windows's Clipboard viewer can display these data types in their normal format (i.e., as text, bitmaps, and so on), but applications that understand the special data format can display the data as it was designed to be displayed.

Another way to manage custom data types with the Clipboard is to register a private Clipboard data format. To do this, you devise your own format name, such as CF_CIRCLES, and register it with Windows. Your application, and other applications that understand the private data type, can then transfer data to and from the Clipboard using the private format.

To register the private format in your program, call

RegisterClipboardFormat():

int formatID = ::RegisterClipboardFormat("CF_CIRCLES");

The function returns an ID that identifies the format, and the function's single argument is the string that identifies the format.

PROBLEMS & SOLUTIONS

Delayed Rendering

PROBLEM: *If my application needs to copy a large data object, such as a full-screen bitmap, to the Clipboard, doesn't the object continue to consume a lot of memory as long as it's in the Clipboard? Is there some way to make better use of memory in this case?*

SOLUTION: It's true that any data object in the Clipboard continues to take up memory until the object is removed. If that data object happens to be very large, a lot of memory can be wasted. If you're concerned about the wasted memory, there's a more memory-efficient way of handling the Clipboard. This method involves something called *delayed rendering*.

Continued

When you use delayed rendering, you give the Clipboard the data type (for example, CF_BITMAP) of a data object, but you don't provide the data object itself until an application tries to paste the data into a document. At that point, you create the data object and pass it to the Clipboard.

Setting up the Clipboard for delayed rendering is easy — just pass NULL as SetClipboardData()'s second argument, rather than passing the handle to the data object. For example, if you wanted to use delayed rendering with a bitmap, you might write the following lines:

```
BOOL open = OpenClipboard();
if (open)
{
    ::EmptyClipboard();
    ::SetClipboardData(CF_BITMAP, NULL);
    ::CloseClipboard();
}
```

That's all there is to it. However, you still need to supply the bitmap (or whatever data format you're using) when an application tries to paste from the Clipboard. Windows uses three messages to manage delayed rendering:

WM_RENDERFORMAT	Windows sends this message when an application calls GetClipboardData() in order to obtain the contents of the Clipboard. This is your application's signal to supply the data object.
WM_RENDERALLFORMATS	Windows sends this message if your application tries to terminate while it is still the owner of a Clipboard containing NULL data objects. In response, you must supply handles for all data objects originally given to the Clipboard as NULL.
WM_DESTROYCLIPBOARD	Windows sends this message when another application becomes the Clipboard owner. In this case, the NULL data objects no longer exist, so your application is no longer responsible for providing handles to them.

When your application receives WM_RENDERFORMAT, you must pass the data object to the Clipboard. You do this by calling SetClipboardData(), this time supplying a handle to the object, rather than supplying NULL. Note that you *should not* call OpenClipboard() or CloseClipboard() in response to the WM_RENDERFORMAT message.

When your application receives WM_RENDERALLFORMATS, you must open and empty the Clipboard, after which you must supply data objects to the Clipboard for every NULL data object the application placed on the Clipboard. The difference between WM_RENDERFORMAT and WM_RENDERALLFORMATS is that, with the latter, you supply all data formats the application passed to the Clipboard, rather than just a requested format. Also, you must call OpenClipboard(), EmptyClipboard(), and CloseClipboard() when handing WM_RENDERALLFORMATS.

Continued

When your application receives `WM_DESTROYCLIPBOARD` you don't have to do anything except release any resources you were holding in order to be able to handle `WM_RENDERFORMAT` or `WM_RENDERALLFORMATS` messages.

On CD-ROM

In the Chapter18\DelayedRender folder of this book's CD-ROM, you can find an application that demonstrates delayed rendering under MFC. To see delayed rendering work, run both the DelayedRender application and Notepad, sizing and positioning the windows so that they are both fully visible. Select DelayedRender's Copy command, and a message box tells you that the application is setting up delayed rendering (see Figure 18-7).

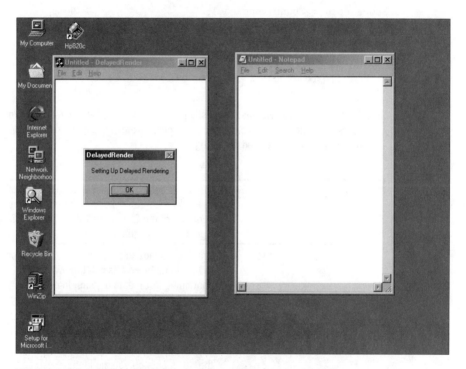

Figure 18-7: DelayedRender displays a message box when it's setting up the Clipboard for delayed rendering.

Now, dismiss the message box, switch to Notepad, and select its Paste command. The text "A Test of Delayed Rendering" appears in the window (see Figure 18-8). This text line wasn't passed to the Clipboard until Notepad asked for it, an example of delayed rendering.

Next, highlight some text in Notepad's window and select Notepad's Copy command. Notepad takes over ownership of the Clipboard, so Windows sends a `WM_DESTROYCLIPBOARD` message to DelayedRender, which you can verify by the message box that appears over DelayedRender's window (see Figure 18-9).

Continued

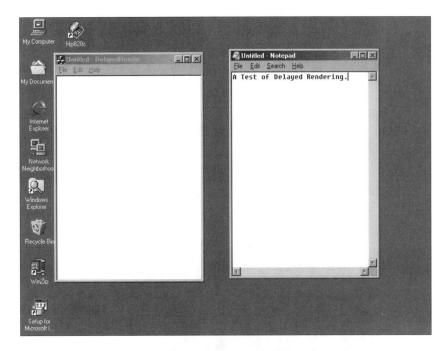

Figure 18-8: After being rendered, the text appears in Notepad's window.

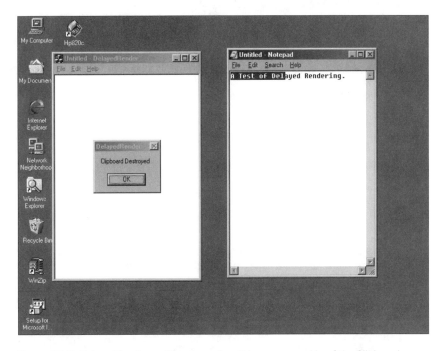

Figure 18-9: DelayedRender notifies you when it loses ownership of the Clipboard.

Continued

As a last experiment, switch back to DelayedRender, dismiss the message box, and select the Copy command. A message box tells you that the application is again setting up for delayed rendering. Dismiss the message box and close DelayedRender. A message box appears, telling you that the application is rendering all formats (in this case, there's only one), as shown in Figure 18-10.

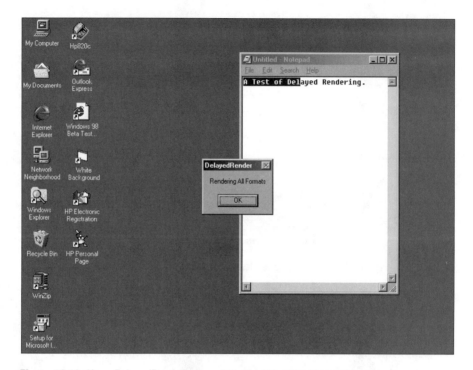

Figure 18-10: Here, DelayedRender responds to the `WM_RENDERALLFORMATS` message.

The source code that accomplishes this Clipboard magic is fairly simple. When the user selects the Copy command, the view class's `OnEditCopy()` function creates a global memory block containing a line of text:

```
m_hText = ::GlobalAlloc(GHND, 29);
m_pText = (char*) ::GlobalLock(m_hText);
strcpy(m_pText, "A Test of Delayed Rendering.");
::GlobalUnlock(m_hText);
```

This line of text represents the object that'll utilize delayed rendering, simulating the user's selecting and copying a large block of text from a document.

After storing the text in its memory block, `OnEditCopy()` passes the data type to the Clipboard, but passes `NULL` as the data object handle:

Continued

```
BOOL open = OpenClipboard();
if (open)
{
    ::EmptyClipboard();
    ::SetClipboardData(CF_TEXT, NULL);
    ::CloseClipboard();
}
```

When the user tries to paste from the Clipboard, MFC calls the view class's `OnRenderFormat()` function:

```
void CDelayedRenderView::OnRenderFormat(UINT nFormat)
{
    if (nFormat == CF_TEXT)
        ::SetClipboardData(CF_TEXT, m_hText);
}
```

As you can see, `OnRenderFormat()` checks for the Clipboard data type and, if the type is `CF_TEXT`, calls `SetClipboardData()` to give the text to the Clipboard.

When DelayedRender terminates while owning the Clipboard, MFC calls `OnRenderAllFormats()`. The `OnRenderAllFormats()` function, which handles the `WM_RENDERALLFORMATS` message, is similar to `OnRenderFormat()`, except it must open and close the Clipboard, as well as render the text object:

```
void CDelayedRenderView::OnRenderAllFormats()
{
    MessageBox("Rendering All Formats");

    OpenClipboard();
    ::EmptyClipboard();
    ::SetClipboardData(CF_TEXT, m_hText);
    ::CloseClipboard();
}
```

Finally, `OnDestroyClipboard()`, which handles the `WM_DESTROYCLIPBOARD` message, simply deletes the text block, because the Clipboard no longer needs it:

```
void CDelayedRenderView::OnDestroyClipboard()
{
    MessageBox("Clipboard Destroyed");

    if (m_pText != NULL)
        delete m_pText;
}
```

Multiple Clipboard Data Formats

In the spirit of sharing, applications that copy data to the Clipboard should enable as many target applications as possible to display the data. This often means supplying data to the Clipboard in more than one format. For example, the CircleApp application could supply both a private Clipboard data format and a normal bitmap image of the current display. Then, although bitmap-compatible applications wouldn't be able to edit a CircleApp document, they could at least display an image of the document that was created by the CircleApp application.

Supplying multiple data formats to the Clipboard is as easy as creating the various types of data and passing them to the Clipboard one after the other. Other applications can then check for a specific type (for example, CF_BITMAP) and if the data exists in that format, extract it from the Clipboard and display it. The more formats your application can provide to the Clipboard, the better the chance that other applications can display the document.

Multiple formats in action

On CD-ROM

In the Chapter18\CBCircleApp2 folder of this book's CD-ROM, you can find a version of CircleApp that copies its document to the Clipboard in two forms: as a bitmap and as a text file. The text file is a list of each circle's attributes as described in the previous section. The data this version of CircleApp copies to the Clipboard makes it possible for three types of applications to display data from CircleApp:

Any CircleApp-compatible application	Currently, only CircleApp itself fits this bill, but you could design your own applications that understand the text data format that CircleApp copies to the Clipboard. These types of applications can recreate the actual CircleApp document and even enable the user to edit the document.
Most paint programs	Any program that can display a bitmap can display the bitmap CircleApp copies to the Clipboard. Such an application can display the CircleApp document exactly as it originally appeared. However, the display is only an image and not a real CircleApp document. (Many full-fledged word processors and other types of applications can also display bitmaps.)
Any text application	Most text-editing applications can display the text form of a CircleApp document. Unfortunately, such an application cannot recreate the actual document or even necessarily display the graphical image of the original document.

As you can see, although several types of applications can read CircleApp data from the Clipboard, applications other than CircleApp-compatible applications lose something in the translation. A bitmap-compatible application loses all the data that describes the individual circles in the document, whereas a plain-text application loses all visual aspects of a CircleApp document, although it retains a complete description of each circle.

To see how CircleApp's multiple Clipboard formats work, perform the following steps:

1. Start Microsoft Paint, Notepad, and the DBCircleApp2 version of CircleApp.

2. Draw a few circles in CircleApp's display, as shown in Figure 18-11.

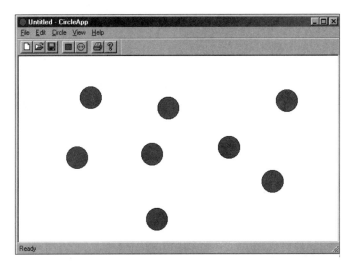

Figure 18-11: Start by drawing a few circles in CircleApp's display.

3. Select the Copy command on CircleApp's Edit menu. CircleApp copies the current document to the Clipboard, both as a bitmap and as a text description.

4. Switch to Microsoft Paint and select its Paste command. The CircleApp bitmap appears in Paint's display (see Figure 18-12).

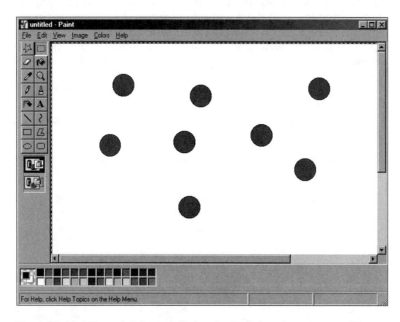

Figure 18-12: Microsoft Paint can display the CircleApp document as a bitmap.

5. Switch to Notepad and select its Paste command. The text version of the CircleApp document appears in Notepad's window, as shown in Figure 18-13.

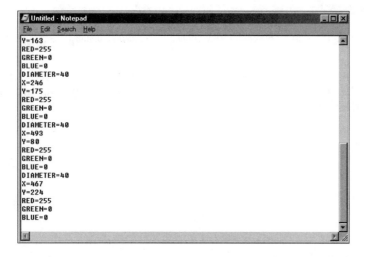

Figure 18-13: Notepad can display the CircleApp text from the Clipboard.

6. Switch back to CircleApp and select the New command, either from the File menu or from the toolbar. CircleApp clears its window.

7. Create a few new circles in CircleApp's window, as shown in Figure 18-14.

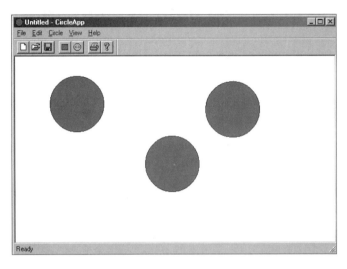

Figure 18-14: Draw a few larger circles in a new circle document to demonstrate how CircleApp's Paste command works.

8. Select CircleApp's Paste command. CircleApp reads the text version of the old CircleApp document from the Clipboard and recreates the original document from the information, pasting the old circle document in with the new one, as shown in Figure 18-15.

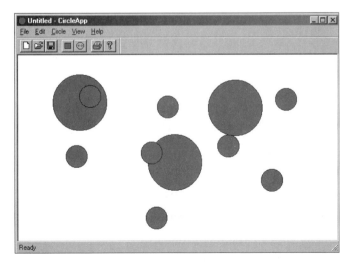

Figure 18-15: Here, CircleApp has pasted the circles from the Clipboard in with the new circles.

The document you created by merging the Clipboard data with the current document is a full CircleApp document. You can save it, add circles to it, and reload it. You can even copy it to the Clipboard.

Copying CircleApp data in multiple formats

Listing 18-5 shows the OnEditCopy() function, which MFC calls when the user selects the Edit menu's Copy command. This function creates two versions of the CircleApp document and makes both versions available to the Clipboard. This enables several types of applications to display the document in one form or another. The function performs the following tasks:

- Opens and empties the Clipboard

- Creates a bitmap version of the document

- Gives the bitmap to the Clipboard

- Creates a text version of the document

- Gives the text version to the Clipboard

- Closes the Clipboard

Listing 18-5: Source code for the new OnEditCopy() **function**

```
void CCircleAppView::OnEditCopy()
{
    // TODO: Add your command handler code here

    BOOL open = OpenClipboard();
    if (open)
    {
        ::EmptyClipboard();
        CBitmap* pBitmap = RenderAsBitmap();
        HBITMAP hBitmap = (HBITMAP) *pBitmap;
        ::SetClipboardData(CF_BITMAP, hBitmap);
        HGLOBAL hText = RenderAsText();
        ::SetClipboardData(CF_TEXT, hText);
        ::CloseClipboard();
    }
}
```

As you can see in Listing 18-5, all of the details of rendering the document in its different formats are contained in the RenderAsBitmap() and RenderAsText() functions. The RenderAsBitmap() function is not unlike the OnEditCopy() function in the previous version of CircleApp, as seen in Listing 18-6. The function performs the following tasks:

- Creates a bitmap that's compatible with the current display

- Creates a memory device context

- Selects the bitmap into the memory DC

- Clears the bitmap with white

- Draws the current CircleApp document onto the bitmap

- Returns from the function a pointer to the bitmap

Listing 18-6: Source code for the new `RenderAsBitmap()` **function**

```
CBitmap* CCircleAppView::RenderAsBitmap()
{
    CClientDC clientDC(this);
    CBitmap* pBitmap = new CBitmap();
    pBitmap->CreateCompatibleBitmap(&clientDC,
        800, 600);

    CDC memoryDC;
    memoryDC.CreateCompatibleDC(&clientDC);
    memoryDC.SelectObject(pBitmap);

    CBrush whiteBrush(RGB(255,255,255));
    memoryDC.FillRect(CRect(0,0,799,599),
        &whiteBrush);

    RenderDisplay(&memoryDC);

    return pBitmap;
}
```

The `RenderDisplay()` function called from `RenderAsBitmap()` is exactly the same as the `RenderDisplay()` function in the previous CBCircleApp version of CircleApp. And, as in that previous version, `RenderDisplay()` not only draws the document when a bitmap is needed for the Clipboard, but also draws the document in CircleApp's window.

The `RenderAsText()` function is fairly complicated, because it must take the data that represents each circle in the document and convert it into an ASCII representation. Listing 18-7 shows the function, which performs the following tasks:

- Gets a pointer to the document object, which holds the document's data

- Allocates a block of memory for the text

- Creates the text header elements that identify the text and specify the number of circles defined in the text

- Iterates through the circle array, converting each data member to a text description

- Returns from the function a handle to the memory block containing the text

Listing 18-7: Source code for the `RenderAsText()` **function**

```
HGLOBAL CCircleAppView::RenderAsText()
{
    CCircleAppDoc* pDoc = GetDocument();

    HGLOBAL hMemBlock = ::GlobalAlloc(GHND, 64000);
    char* pMemBlock = (char*) ::GlobalLock(hMemBlock);
```

```
strcpy(pMemBlock, "APP=CIRCLEAPP");
int index = 13;
pMemBlock[index++]='\r';
pMemBlock[index++]='\n';
int size = pDoc->m_circleArray.GetSize();
ValueToText("COUNT", size, index, pMemBlock);

for (int x=0; x<size; ++x)
{
    CircleStruct* circle =
        (CircleStruct*)pDoc->m_circleArray.GetAt(x);
    int diameter = circle->diameter;
    int x1 = circle->point.x;
    int y1 = circle->point.y;
    COLORREF color = circle->color;

    ValueToText("DIAMETER", diameter,
        index, pMemBlock);
    ValueToText("X", x1, index, pMemBlock);
    ValueToText("Y", y1, index, pMemBlock);
    int red = GetRValue(color);
    ValueToText("RED", red, index, pMemBlock);
    int green = GetGValue(color);
    ValueToText("GREEN", green, index, pMemBlock);
    int blue = GetBValue(color);
    ValueToText("BLUE", blue, index, pMemBlock);
}

pMemBlock[index] = 0;
::GlobalUnlock(hMemBlock);

return hMemBlock;
}
```

As you can see in Listing 18-7, the ValueToText() function actually creates a line of text and copies it into the text buffer. Listing 18-8 shows the function. ValueToText() takes four parameters: the text label for the line, the integer that's associated with the label, the current index into the text buffer, and a pointer to the text buffer. The function turns these values into a text line that looks something like this:

DIAMETER=40

Of course, the function also creates lines for the X, Y, RED, GREEN, and BLUE labels associated with a circle's data.

Listing 18-8: Source code for the ValueToText() function

```
void CCircleAppView::ValueToText(char* label,
    int value, int& index, char* pMemBlock)
{
    char s[80];
    wsprintf(s, "%s=%d\r\n", label, value);
    int len = strlen(s);
    for (int i=0; i<len; ++i)
        pMemBlock[index++] = s[i];
}
```

Pasting CircleApp data in multiple formats

When the user selects the Paste command from CircleApp's Edit menu, the program must determine whether the Clipboard contains CircleApp data. If it does, the program can copy the data from the Clipboard and then extract the information needed to recreate the document. OnEditPaste(), shown in Listing 18-9, is the function that handles the Paste command.

Listing 18-9: Source code for the OnEditPaste() function

```
void CCircleAppView::OnEditPaste()
{
    // TODO: Add your command handler code here

    BOOL textAvailable =
        ::IsClipboardFormatAvailable(CF_TEXT);
    if (!textAvailable)
        return;

    OpenClipboard();
    HANDLE hCircleText = ::GetClipboardData(CF_TEXT);
    char* pClipboardText =
        (char*)GlobalLock(hCircleText);
    int textSize = ::GlobalSize(hCircleText);
    char* pCircleText = (char*)malloc(textSize);
    strcpy(pCircleText, pClipboardText);
    ::CloseClipboard();

    char s[80];
    int index = 0;
    do
        s[index] = pCircleText[index];
    while (pCircleText[index++] != '\n');

    int result = strcmp(s, "APP=CIRCLEAPP\r\n");

    if (result != 0)
        return;

    int count = ParseCircleText(index, pCircleText);
    for (int x=0; x<count; ++x)
    {
        CircleStruct* circle = new CircleStruct;
        circle->diameter =
            ParseCircleText(index, pCircleText);
        circle->point.x =
            ParseCircleText(index, pCircleText);
        circle->point.y =
            ParseCircleText(index, pCircleText);
        int red = ParseCircleText(index, pCircleText);
        int green = ParseCircleText(index, pCircleText);
        int blue = ParseCircleText(index, pCircleText);
        COLORREF color = RGB(red,green,blue);
        circle->color = color;

        CCircleAppDoc* pDoc = GetDocument();
```

```
        pDoc->m_circleArray.Add(circle);
    }

    Invalidate();
}
```

Because the `OnEditPaste()` function is so important to understanding the way CircleApp handles the Paste command, the following paragraphs describe the function a piece at a time.

`OnEditPaste()` first checks whether the Clipboard holds data in the `CF_TEXT` format:

```
BOOL textAvailable =
    ::IsClipboardFormatAvailable(CF_TEXT);
if (!textAvailable)
    return;
```

If the Clipboard contains no data in the `CF_TEXT` format, the function immediately returns because this version of CircleApp cannot process any Clipboard data except its own private type of text data.

If `CF_TEXT` data is available, the program opens the Clipboard and gets a handle to the text contained in the Clipboard:

```
OpenClipboard();
HANDLE hCircleText = ::GetClipboardData(CF_TEXT);
```

Next, `OnEditPaste()` gets a pointer to the Clipboard text, gets the size of the text, and creates a memory block where it can copy the text:

```
char* pClipboardText =
    (char*)GlobalLock(hCircleText);
int textSize = ::GlobalSize(hCircleText);
char* pCircleText = (char*)malloc(textSize);
```

With the new text buffer in hand, the program copies the Clipboard text to the new buffer and then closes the Clipboard:

```
strcpy(pCircleText, pClipboardText);
::CloseClipboard();
```

The next task is to determine whether the text in the Clipboard was created by CircleApp. To do this, the program gets the first text line:

```
    char s[80];
    int index = 0;
    do
        s[index] = pCircleText[index];
    while (pCircleText[index++] != '\n');
```

In CircleApp text data, the first line should be `APP=CIRCLEAPP`, followed by a carriage return and linefeed. The program checks for this signature and returns if it doesn't find it:

```
int result = strcmp(s, "APP=CIRCLEAPP\r\n");
if (result != 0)
    return;
```

At this point in `OnEditPaste()`, the program has confirmed that the text in the Clipboard is CircleApp data. The next step is to extract from the text the values that define each circle in the document. The local member function `ParseCircleText()` handles this task, with `OnEditPaste()` first getting the circle count:

```
int count = ParseCircleText(index, pCircleText);
```

The `ParseCircleText()` function returns the next integer in the text data. The function's two arguments are the current index into the data and a pointer to the data. Because the index is passed by reference, `ParseCircleText()` changes the index value to point to the next line of text in the data.

The program uses the circle count in a `for` statement that extracts the data needed to recreate each circle in the document. In the loop, the program first creates a new `CircleStruct` object for the current circle:

```
CircleStruct* circle = new CircleStruct;
```

The program then calls `ParseCircleText()` several times in order to extract the diameter and location values for the circle:

```
circle->diameter =
    ParseCircleText(index, pCircleText);
circle->point.x =
    ParseCircleText(index, pCircleText);
circle->point.y =
    ParseCircleText(index, pCircleText);
```

The program also extracts the red, green, and blue color components and uses them to create a `COLORREF` value for the circle:

```
int red = ParseCircleText(index, pCircleText);
int green = ParseCircleText(index, pCircleText);
int blue = ParseCircleText(index, pCircleText);
COLORREF color = RGB(red,green,blue);
circle->color = color;
```

Finally, the loop gets a pointer to the document and adds the newly recreated circle object to the document class's circle array:

```
CCircleAppDoc* pDoc = GetDocument();
pDoc->m_circleArray.Add(circle);
```

The loop repeats this process until it has recreated each of the circle objects represented in the text data. The loop then ends and `OnEditPaste()` calls `Invalidate()` to force the application to redisplay the current document, which now has new circle objects pasted from the Clipboard.

Listing 18-10 shows the `ParseCircleText()` function, which is responsible for extracting the integer values that represent the circles in the text data. The function is straight C++, with no Windows code complicating things, so you should have little difficulty seeing how it works.

Listing 18-10: Source code for the `ParseCircleText()` function

```
int CCircleAppView::ParseCircleText(int& index,
    char * pCircleText)
{
    while (pCircleText[index++] != '=');

    char s[80];
    int i = 0;
    while (pCircleText[index] != '\r')
        s[i++] = pCircleText[index++];

    s[i] = 0;
    index += 3;
    int value = atoi(s);

    return value;
}
```

Summary

Applications can share data in several ways, but the Clipboard is the easiest method to implement. Using the Clipboard you can transfer many types of data—including text and bitmaps—from one application to another.

Also discussed in this chapter:

▶ You can transfer Clipboard data using standard formats, standard private formats, or registered private formats.

▶ Opening and emptying the Clipboard transfers Clipboard ownership to the program that opened and emptied the Clipboard.

▶ Closing the Clipboard releases the application's ownership of the Clipboard.

▶ When trying to paste data from the Clipboard, you must determine what type of data is stored in the Clipboard.

▶ Because the Clipboard owns data it contains, you must make a copy of the data before manipulating it.

▶ When copying large data objects to the Clipboard, a program can implement delayed rendering, and so use memory more efficiently.

▶ By copying data in multiple formats to the Clipboard, many different applications can better share the data.

Part IV

ActiveX

Chapter 19

Introduction to ActiveX

In This Chapter

- Looking back at OLE 1.0
- Advancing the technology with OLE 2.0
- Introducing ActiveX and COM
- Understanding ActiveX applications and components

If you've ever cracked open an ActiveX programming manual and started to read, you most likely had a humbling experience. ActiveX, and the COM system upon which it's built, is a complex beast—downright mind-boggling. Expert programmers take a year or more to wade through all the documentation and figure out how to put the concepts to work. Although your chances of mastering this new technology without a year of full-time work on ActiveX is slim, you shouldn't give up hope.

MFC encapsulates much of ActiveX into the classes that make up the MFC application frameworks. Moreover, AppWizard can create skeleton applications that support ActiveX, leaving you to only fine-tune the result. This makes ActiveX manageable even for the weekend programmer. In this chapter, you get an introduction to ActiveX. The remaining chapters in Part 4 provide hands-on projects to get you started with ActiveX.

OLE 1.0

Microsoft has long been pursuing the idea that documents, rather than applications, should be the focus of an operating system. In other words, the user should never be concerned with what application does what job. She should need to know only the type of document she wants to create, letting the operating system find and load the appropriate application. Moreover, when the user wants to create a document containing different types of data elements—for example, both text and graphics—she shouldn't have to leave the editing environment in order to create the new data. Instead, the appropriate editing tools should merge with the current application, providing a seamless document creation and editing experience. This whole idea of a "document-centric" operating system started with a technology Microsoft dubbed *OLE*. Figure 19-1 illustrates this concept.

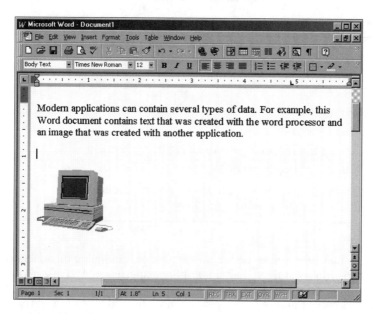

Figure 19-1: With OLE, applications can contain more than one type of data.

OLE stands for Object Linking and Embedding, and is a system that enables applications to more easily share data in two ways: data linking and data embedding. The application that holds the linked or embedded data is called a *container application*, whereas the application that supplies editing services for the linked or embedded data is called the *server application*. (And there's nothing to stop an application from being both a container and a server.) When a data set is linked into a document (see Figure 19-2), the document maintains a connection to the data set as part of the document. However, the linked data stays in its own file as a discrete object. Because the document maintains only a link to the data set, the document stays up-to-date as the data set changes.

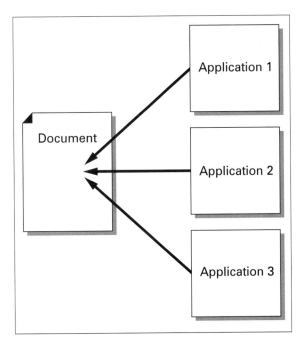

Figure 19-2: Linked data remains in its own file.

When a data set is embedded into a document, the document no longer maintains a connection with the data set's file. Instead, the data set is actually copied into the document. Because there is no longer a connection between the containing document and the original data set, when the data set changes, the document doesn't reflect the changes, as seen in Figure 19-3. To update the embedded data, the user has to load the document and change the data manually.

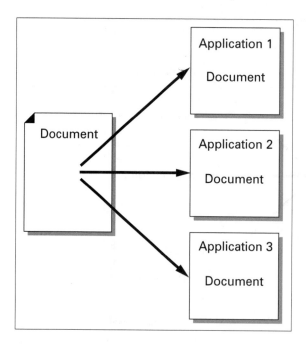

Figure 19-3: Embedded data is copied into the containing document.

Whether a document links or embeds a data set, the data can be edited easily by the application that created the data. Usually, the user double-clicks the linked or embedded item, which causes the editing application to appear in its own window, or, if it supports in-place editing, the editor can actually merge its toolbars and menus with the application that contains the linked or embedded data.

OLE 2.0

OLE was a step in the right direction, but lacked many features that would enable applications to take a second seat to documents. OLE 2.0 extends OLE's abilities to include not only data sharing between applications, but also functionality sharing between applications. By creating an application as a set of *programmable objects* (also called *OLE components*), applications can call upon each other for the capabilities they need, further generalizing the concept of an application.

For example, if a text-editing application needs to spell-check a document, it doesn't necessarily need to have its own spell-checker. Instead, it can call upon a spell-checker object that some other application has already registered with the system. Figure 19-4 illustrates this idea. Notice how the word processor in the figure supplies three programmable objects that can be accessed by other applications. The text editor is currently calling upon the services of the spell-checking component.

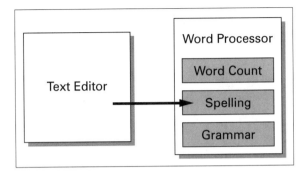

Figure 19-4: Applications can supply programmable objects
that can be accessed by other applications.

In Figure 19-4, the word processor is the *OLE server* (because it's providing a
service), and the text editor is an *OLE client* (because it's using a service).
The process of controlling another application's programmable objects is
called *OLE automation*. So, you could also call the word processor an
automation server and the text editor an *automation client*. Whatever
terminology you want to use, programmable objects blur the boundaries
between one application and another, making all the applications in the
system seem to work together.

As you can see, OLE automation provides advantages to both application
users and developers. Users can take full advantage of the capabilities
represented by all applications installed in the system, without having to
know where those capabilities originate. The user can concentrate on the
document and let the applications take care of themselves.

Developers, on the other hand, must face a double-edged sword. Although
they no longer need to reinvent software that's been developed and installed
on the user's system, they must now support OLE, which adds another layer
of complexity to the development process—one that's perceived as
insurmountable by many programmers. Luckily, as you'll see in the following
chapters, Visual C++ developers can let MFC handle most of the intricacies
of developing OLE applications.

OLE 2.0 also introduced the concept of *OLE controls*, programmable objects
that can be embedded into an application and so become an integral part of
the application in much the same way an embedded document becomes a
part of a containing document. Originally, OLE controls were conceived as a
way to create buttons, sliders, progress indicators, and other types of
custom controls. (They are called OLE *controls*, after all.) However, the idea
soon grew to include mini-applications that offer complex services to host
applications. For example, Figure 19-5 shows an application containing a
Microsoft calendar control. As you can see, this control goes way beyond a
custom button or slider, being more akin to a complete application than a
lowly button.

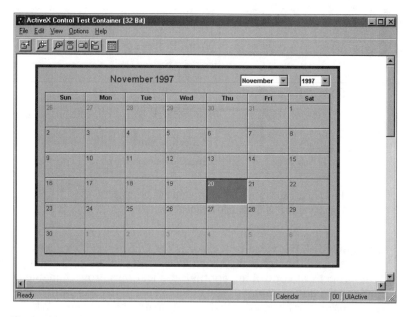

Figure 19-5: Microsoft's calendar control demonstrates how OLE controls can be complex, mini-applications.

COM

COM stands for Component Object Model and is the technology that provides the underpinnings of OLE. Put simply, COM is a specification for creating binary objects. These binary objects can communicate with one another, controlling functions and setting properties. In a nutshell, a binary object is like a program that loads into the system, but is not necessarily visible on the screen. DLLs are a similar type of object, in that they contain functions that other modules in the system can call.

The COM specification is a set of rules that dictate how binary objects are created. These rules define a method through which applications can query a binary object to discover the types of interfaces the object supports. Some of these interfaces are standard, whereas others are proprietary. In any case, by adhering to the specifications, objects can be accessed and manipulated by any OLE-capable application.

Luckily, if you're programming with Visual C++ and MFC, you don't have to know much about COM, although it's always a good idea to have a little background on the technology you're using. As you'll soon discover, Visual C++'s amazing AppWizard can provide your application with most of the basic OLE functionality your program needs. All you have to do is refine the generated source code for your specific purposes.

ActiveX

A couple of years ago, COM and OLE were the big programming buzzwords. Now, the word "ActiveX" is thrown around by programmers like celebrity names at a Hollywood party. When Microsoft recently turned its attention to the Internet, it occurred to the powers that be at the big "M" that there was no reason the Internet should not be treated as just another peripheral like a disk drive or CD-ROM drive. Why not make the Internet so accessible from the user's computer that it seemed to become part of the operating system? With this idea came the necessity of extending OLE 2.0 so that it encompassed not just the user's local system, but also any network to which the local system was connected. ActiveX was born.

ActiveX could have been called OLE 3.0, but the capabilities of OLE had gone so far beyond object linking and embedding that the original moniker was more confusing than descriptive. So Microsoft named this newly expanded technology ActiveX. Now, virtually everywhere the word OLE would have been used, the word ActiveX is substituted. For example, OLE components are now ActiveX components, OLE controls are now ActiveX controls, and OLE documents are now ActiveX documents.

All of these objects that share the word ActiveX in their names are more powerful than their old OLE counterparts, however. They are now objects that expand the original OLE concepts to the Web. ActiveX controls, for example, can be placed in Web pages and transmitted automatically to the browser that's viewing the Web page. ActiveX documents, too, are much more powerful than OLE documents. Not only can these objects be transmitted over the Web, ActiveX documents also tell the receiving browser how the document should be displayed. You can think of an ActiveX document as being a storage object for information that can be interpreted, displayed, and manipulated by a receiving application.

ActiveX Applications and Components

In the following chapters, you'll learn to program several types of ActiveX projects using AppWizard and MFC. As you work through these chapters, keep in mind that ActiveX is an immense technology that's worthy of a complete book (or books) of its own. In fact, Microsoft's own ActiveX manuals run to thousands of pages. Although Part 4 of this book provides only an introduction to ActiveX, the following chapters cover the major types of ActiveX projects: containers, servers, automation, and ActiveX controls. The following sections in this chapter introduce you to these concepts. If, however, you'd like still more information, take a look at *Discover ActiveX* by Richard Mansfield, published by IDG Books Worldwide (1997). Advanced programmers may want to check out *Inside OLE* by Kraig Brockschmidt, published by Microsoft Press (1995).

ActiveX container applications

An ActiveX container is an application that contains linked or embedded data. Such an application must not only be able to display the linked or embedded data, but also enable the user to select, move, delete, and edit the data. Figure 19-6, for example, shows Microsoft Word displaying a document that contains an embedded graphic.

Embedded graphic

Sizing Handles

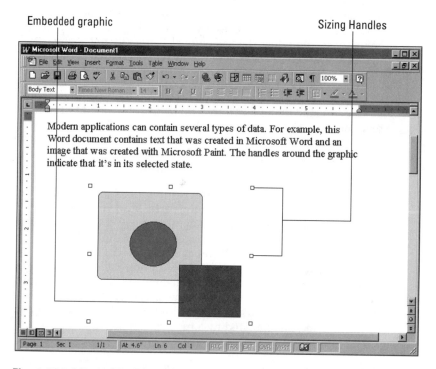

Figure 19-6: Microsoft Word can act as a container application.

In the figure, you can see that the graphic object displays sizing handles that the user can use to resize the image. The user can also move the image to any position in the document, as well as delete the image by selecting the Edit menu's Clear command, or by pressing the Delete key on the keyboard.

When Microsoft Word contains linked or embedded data, it's acting as an ActiveX container. Many Windows applications support ActiveX in this way. In Chapter 20, "Containers," you'll discover how to program your own ActiveX container applications.

ActiveX server applications

In the previous section, you saw Microsoft Word acting as a container application. The graphic (a real masterpiece, eh?) embedded in the Word document was created with Microsoft Paint, which makes Paint the server application. If the user wants to edit the embedded graphic, he can double-click the item. The server then should respond in one of two ways: by opening the graphic in a separate editing window or by merging its user interface with Word's.

Which way the server responds depends on how the client and server were programmed. If the applications support in-place editing (recommended), ActiveX merges the server's toolbars and menus with the container application's. This enables the user to edit the item without ever switching windows or applications. Figure 19-7 shows Microsoft Word after the user has double-clicked the Paint graphic. In the figure, Paint has merged its toolbars and menus with Word's.

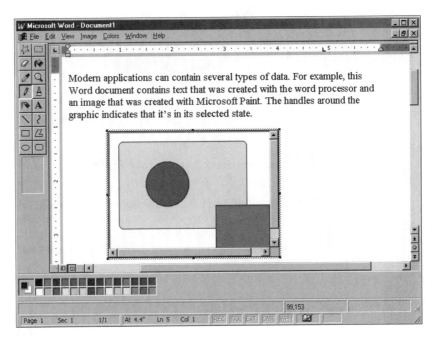

Figure 19-7: Paint's toolbars and menu bars are now merged with Word's.

The user can now edit the graphic just as if the graphic were loaded into Paint. In Figure 19-8, for example, the user has used Paint's ellipse tool to add two filled ellipses to the image. Because ActiveX makes all of Paint's tools available in the toolbar, adding the ellipses takes only seconds.

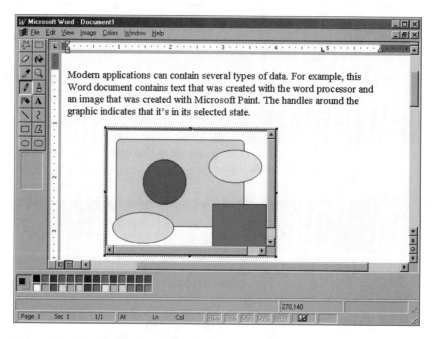

Figure 19-8: Here the user has edited the image using Paint's tools.

When he's finished editing, the user clicks somewhere outside of the graphic, and Word's window returns to normal, restoring its own toolbars and menus. The newly edited graphic appears in the document, as shown in Figure 19-9. In Chapter 21, "Servers," you'll learn to create server applications that support in-place editing.

ActiveX automation applications

Just as you have containers and servers with object linking and embedding, so you have automation clients and automation servers with ActiveX automation. An automation-client application reaches out in the system to control a component of another application, called the *automation server*. Of course, the process isn't quite that simple. Both applications must be specially programmed to take advantage of ActiveX automation.

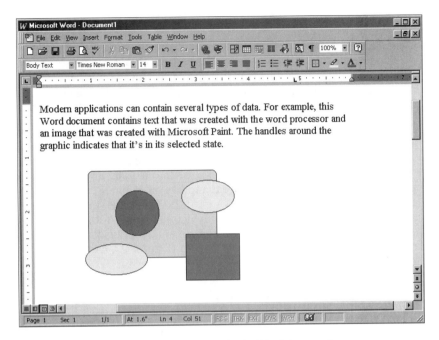

Figure 19-9: The edited image now appears in the Word document.

For example, an application that hasn't been programmed to be an automation client cannot access programmable objects made available by an automation server. Conversely, an application that hasn't been programmed as an automation server cannot share its functionality with other applications in the system, even if the other applications support ActiveX automation.

Creating automation servers means defining interfaces that provide access to properties and methods of the programmable objects supplied by the server. On the client side, when an application wants to access a programmable object, it must know how to obtain a reference to the object's interface, as well as how to manage the object's properties and call the object's methods. For example, reusing the spell-checker example, an application that wanted to take advantage of another application's spell-checker (assuming that the spell-checker is a programmable object) would acquire a reference to the spell-checker's interface and call the spell-checker's functions through that interface. You learn to create automation applications, both clients and servers, in Chapter 22, "Automation."

ActiveX controls

The last type of ActiveX project you'll learn about in Part 4 is ActiveX controls. As mentioned previously in this chapter, ActiveX controls are like mini-applications that you can embed into other applications. They take the idea of programmable components and separate those components from the server. That is, ActiveX components are complete entities unto themselves, and do not need to be managed by a server application.

One of the biggest advantages of ActiveX controls is their capability to provide computing power to Web pages on the Internet. In this way, ActiveX controls can act much like Java applets. Virtually any type of program you can conceive of can be programmed as an ActiveX control and included in a Web page. When the user logs onto the Web page, the system checks whether the ActiveX control is available locally. If it isn't, the system automatically downloads the control and displays it in the Web page. You learn to program ActiveX controls in Chapter 23, "ActiveX Controls."

ActiveX documents

Once the Web took over nearly everyone's computers, Microsoft decided it needed to expand its new document-oriented philosophy to the Internet. ActiveX documents are Microsoft's answer to enabling Web browsers and other ActiveX client applications to interpret and display documents in much the same way OLE documents enabled data sharing on a local computer system. ActiveX documents are, to put it simply, super-powered OLE documents.

One way ActiveX documents are super-powered compared with OLE documents is their capability to be transmitted over the Internet to a remote ActiveX client application, usually a Web browser. In much the same way your local computer system can link or embed a Microsoft Paint document into a Microsoft Word document, so too can a Web browser embed an ActiveX document in its window. However, this ActiveX document may or may not be located on the local computer. It may have been received from the other side of the world.

ActiveX documents are also super-powered in the way they take the concept of a document to a whole new level. In fact, many ActiveX documents don't look like documents at all, but rather like complete applications running inside a client application's window. For example, an ActiveX document that represents a 3D scene would contain not only the data that defines the scene (the traditional idea of a document), but also all the information needed for a client application to display and manipulate the 3D scene. An ActiveX document is a complete document package that includes not only the document's data, but also the tools needed to manage the document. You could say that an ActiveX document knows how to manage itself, making it easy for a client application to display the document.

Summary

Now that you have a general idea of what ActiveX is and what it does, you're ready to get your hands dirty with some actual ActiveX programming. In the following chapter, you create your first ActiveX container application. In the remaining ActiveX chapters, you discover even more about this complex but exciting technology.

Also discussed in this chapter:

▶ OLE 1.0 enables applications to link and embed data.

▶ Linked data maintains a connection to its data set and therefore changes automatically when the original data is updated.

▶ Embedded data is copied into a document and so doesn't update itself when the original data changes.

▶ OLE 2.0 extended OLE to include OLE controls.

▶ ActiveX is the most recent version of OLE, which has been extended to support a networked environment.

▶ ActiveX controls, which are like mini-applications, can be embedded in other applications and in Web pages.

▶ An ActiveX document is a complete document package that includes not only the document's data, but also the tools needed to manage the document.

▶ An ActiveX container application can link or embed data created by another application.

▶ An ActiveX client application uses services supplied by an ActiveX server application.

▶ Automation enables applications to manipulate another application's programmable components.

Chapter 20

Containers

In This Chapter

▶ Creating a skeleton container application

▶ Modifying an ActiveX item's class

▶ Using the mouse to select items

▶ Deleting embedded items

To be a fully compliant Windows 98 application, a program must support ActiveX. One way a program can support ActiveX is to be an ActiveX container, which is an application that can link or embed files created by other applications. You got an introduction to container applications in Chapter 19, "Introduction to ActiveX." In this chapter, you build your own ActiveX container application using AppWizard and other Visual C++ tools. This application, called *ContainerApp,* shows you how to link or embed objects in an application's document, as well as how to enable users to edit, move, and delete objects. You can find the complete ContainerApp application in the Chapter20\ContainerApp folder of this book's CD-ROM.

Note

Programming container applications is a complex task that cannot be fully explained in a single chapter. This chapter is only an introduction to the programming techniques required to create a basic container application. After you master the topics in this chapter, if you want to learn more about ActiveX, you should pick up a book that concentrates on ActiveX programming, such as *Inside OLE* by Kraig Brockschmidt and published by Microsoft Press (1995).

Creating a Skeleton Container Application

Just as with all AppWizard applications, your container application begins as an AppWizard project for which Visual C++ generates the basic source code for the program's classes. In a container application, these classes include not only the usual application, frame window, document (now derived from the COleDocument class instead of CDocument), and view window classes, but also an additional class derived from MFC's COleClientItem class. In this application, AppWizard will call the derived class CContainerAppCntrItem.

This class represents any linked or embedded item in the application's window. To create the skeleton for ContainerAPP, perform the following steps.

1. Start a new AppWizard project called *ContainerApp,* as shown in Figure 20-1.

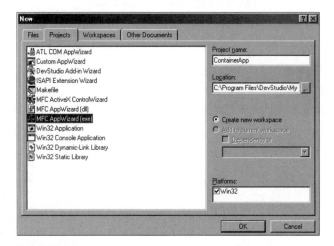

Figure 20-1: The new container application project is called *ContainerApp.*

2. In the MFC AppWizard - Step 1 dialog box, select the Single Document option (see Figure 20-2).

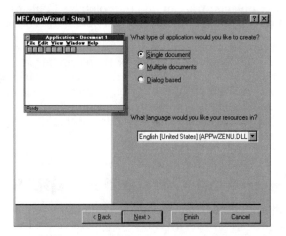

Figure 20-2: The new container application will have an SDI window.

3. Click the Next button twice, accepting the default options in the Step 2 dialog box.

4. In the Step 3 of 6 dialog box, select the Container option, as shown in Figure 20-3, and click the Next button.

Selecting the Container feature tells AppWizard to generate the ActiveX source code needed to create a skeleton container application. The skeleton application will be able to link and embed data created by other applications.

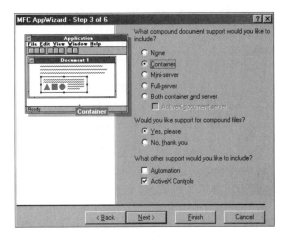

Figure 20-3: AppWizard can generate the code needed to create a container application.

5. In the Step 4 of 6 dialog box, turn off all features except 3D Controls, as shown in Figure 20-4, and then click the Next button.

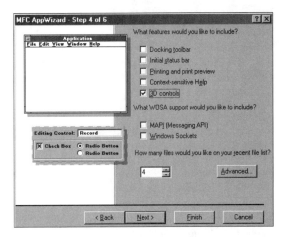

Figure 20-4: The new container application won't have a toolbar, status bar, or printing and print preview support.

6. In Step 5 of 6 dialog box, select the As a Statically Linked Library option. Accept the default "Yes, please" to generate source file comments (see Figure 20-5).

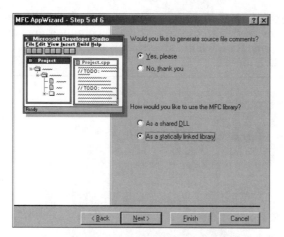

Figure 20-5: The new container application will link to the static MFC library.

7. Click the Finish button. Your New Project Information dialog box should then look like the one in Figure 20-6, except your install directory may be different depending on the directory you chose when you created the project in Step 1.

Figure 20-6: The New Project Information dialog box displays the container application's final options.

8. Click the OK button and AppWizard generates the source code files for the skeleton application.

You've now completed the ContainerApp skeleton application. Save your work by selecting the Save All command on Visual C++'s File menu.

If you compile and run the application, you can test it by linking or embedding an item into the application's current document. To do this, select the Edit menu's Insert New Object command. The Insert Object dialog box appears, as shown in Figure 20-7. You can choose to create a new item of the type selected in the Object Type box, or you can choose a file to link or embed into the document.

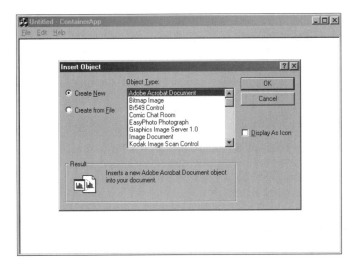

Figure 20-7: The skeleton application already supports linking and embedding.

Double-click the Bitmap Image object type. The application creates a new bitmap image and embeds it into the document. At the same time, Microsoft Paint's toolbars and menus merge with ContainerApp's, as shown in Figure 20-8. You haven't added even one line of code on your own, yet the application already has ActiveX functionality, thanks to AppWizard's Container option.

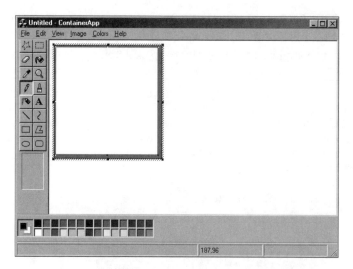

Figure 20-8: Here, an empty bitmap object is embedded into the application's document.

Use Paint's tools to draw a few shapes on the bitmap, as shown in Figure 20-9. Because the container application now sports all of Paint's tools and menus, you can do almost anything with the bitmap that you could do if you were actually running Paint.

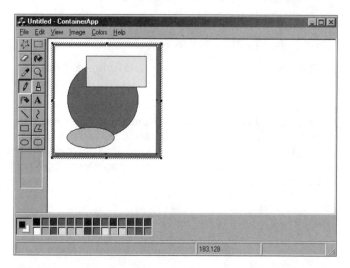

Figure 20-9: You can draw on the bitmap just as if you had started Paint as a stand-alone application.

Unfortunately, the skeleton application supports no item-selection functions, so you can't deselect the bitmap and get back to the regular application. You can, however, save the current document (including its embedded item) and then reload it, which has the same effect of deselecting the embedded item. To do this, select the File menu's Save command. After saving the file, select the File menu's New command to clear the window and start a new document. Now, use the Open command to reopen the saved document. You can also select the document from the File menu's document list.

When you reload the document, you see a window something like that in Figure 20-10. (What you see depends on the figure you drew, of course.) If you want to bring back Paint's tools in order to edit the bitmap, you can find the bitmap item represented on the Edit menu. If you select Edit from Bitmap Image Object's submenu (see Figure 20-11), ActiveX again merges Paint's tools and menus into ContainerApp. If you select the Open command from the submenu, Paint itself runs as a stand-alone application.

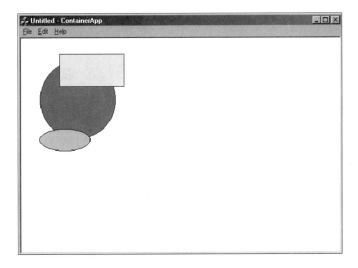

Figure 20-10: The reloaded document displays the embedded item in its deselected state.

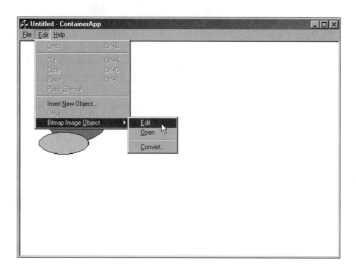

Figure 20-11: Embedded objects have their own submenus.

Managing Embedded Object Size and Position

The first step toward completing ContainerApp is to add code to the `CContainerAppCntrItem` class so that embedded items can manage their own sizes and positions. When AppWizard generated the `CContainerAppCntrItem` class, it created hard-coded coordinates for objects of the class. You don't want to use hard-coded sizes and coordinates because the user will want to size and position embedded items as is appropriate for his current document. Perform the following steps to complete the `CContainerAppCntrItem` class:

1. In the Project Workspace window, select the ClassView tab, and then right-click `CContainerAppCntrItem` and select the Add Member Variable command from the menu that appears.

2. In the Add Member Variable dialog box, type `CRect` in the Variable Type box, type `m_objectRect` in the Variable Declaration box, and select Public access, as shown in Figure 20-12.

   Here, you're adding the `m_objectRect` member variable to the class that represents items embedded in the application's document. This member variable will hold the object's size and position.

Figure 20-12: The `m_objectRect` member variable will hold the object's size and position.

3. In the Project Workspace window, double-click the
CContainerAppCntrItem class's OnChangeItemPosition() function (see
Figure 20-13). The function appears in Visual C++'s edit window.

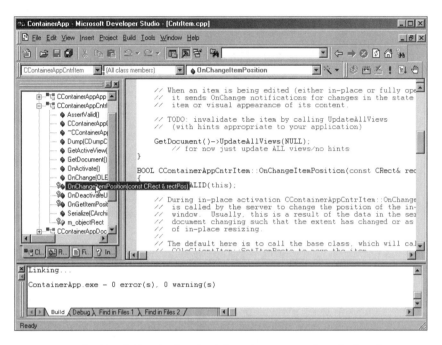

Figure 20-13: Double-clicking the function brings the source code up in the edit
window.

4. Add the following lines to the function, right after the TODO comment:

```
m_objectRect = rectPos;
CContainerAppDoc* pDoc = GetDocument();
pDoc->SetModifiedFlag();
pDoc->UpdateAllViews(NULL);
```

When the user changes the position of an embedded item, MFC calls the
OnChangeItemPosition() function. The lines you added to the function
save the item's new position and update all views of the document to
reflect the new position.

5. Add the following line to the OnGetItemPosition() function, after
deleting the call to SetRect() that's already there:

```
rPosition = m_objectRect;
```

When the frameworks needs the location of an embedded item, it calls the `OnGetItemPosition()` function. The line you added sets the position to the coordinates saved in the `m_objectRect` object.

6. Add the following line to the `CContainerAppCntrItem` class's constructor:

```
m_objectRect.SetRect(20, 20, 150, 150);
```

This line initializes the item's starting position. That is, when the user creates a new item, the item will first appear in the size and position contained in `m_objectRect`.

7. Add the following line to the `CContainerAppCntrItem` class's `Serialize()` function, right after the `TODO: add storing code here` comment:

```
ar << m_objectRect;
```

This line saves the item's size and position when the rest of the document gets saved.

8. Add the following line to the `CContainerAppCntrItem` class's `Serialize()` function, right after the `TODO: add loading code here` comment:

```
ar > m_objectRect;
```

This line loads the item's size and position when the rest of the document gets loaded.

You now have completed the `CContainerAppCntrItem` class. You should save your work before continuing. You can also compile and run the application, although at this point the application won't run any differently than the previous version, except that new objects start off smaller when first added to the document, as shown in Figure 20-14.

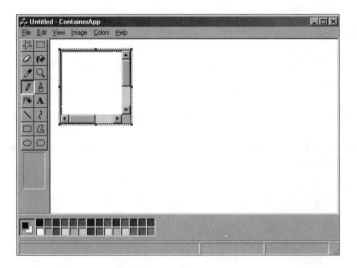

Figure 20-14: Now new objects are smaller when they first appear.

Using the Mouse to Select Items

The next step toward completing ContainerApp is to enable the user to select and deselect embedded items. This includes not only clicking on the object for selection, but also starting the editing process by double-clicking the object. The following steps show how to add item selection to ContainerApp:

1. In the CContainerAppView class's OnDraw() function, remove or comment out all the lines following the TODO: remove this code when final draw code is complete comment.

   The lines you removed displayed an embedded object in the default location in the container application's window. You've removed these lines so that the application can display multiple items at the locations contained in their m_objectRect member variables.

2. Add the lines shown in Listing 20-1 to the OnDraw() function, in place of the lines you removed in Step 1.

   These lines step through all the items embedded in the current document, drawing the items in their proper positions. The CRectTracker object draws the appropriate outline around the object, depending on the item's state. (CRectTracker objects also display the appropriate mouse cursor for an object.) SetupTracker(), which initializes a tracker object, is a function you'll add to the program yourself later in these steps.

Listing 20-1: Lines for the OnDraw() function

```
POSITION pos = pDoc->GetStartPosition();

while(pos != NULL)
{
    CContainerAppCntrItem* pObject =
        (CContainerAppCntrItem*) pDoc->GetNextItem(pos);
    pObject->Draw(pDC, pObject->m_objectRect);
    CRectTracker tracker;
    SetupTracker(&tracker, pObject);
    tracker.Draw(pDC);
}
```

3. Press Ctrl+W on your keyboard to display ClassWizard. Then add the OnSetCursor() function (which MFC calls in response to a WM_SETCURSOR Windows message) to the CContainerAppView class, as shown in Figure 20-15. Make sure you have CContainerAppView selected in ClassWizard's Class Name box.

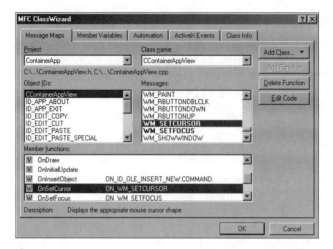

Figure 20-15: ClassWizard adding the `OnSetCursor()` function to the program

4. Add the lines shown in Listing 20-2 to the `OnSetCursor()` function, right after the `TODO` comment.

   The lines in Listing 20-2 check whether the cursor is over a selected embedded item. If it is, the program creates a `CRectTracker` object to set the cursor to the appropriate shape for the selected item. The `pWnd` variable is a pointer to the window that received the `WM_SETCURSOR` message, and `m_pSelection`, which is a member variable of the view class, is a pointer to any selected item.

Listing 20-2: Lines for the `OnSetCursor()` function

```
if ((m_pSelection != NULL) && (pWnd == this))
{
    CRectTracker tracker;
    SetupTracker(&tracker, m_pSelection);
    BOOL cursorSetByTracker =
        tracker.SetCursor(this, nHitTest);
    if (cursorSetByTracker)
        return TRUE;
}
```

5. Press Ctrl+W on your keyboard to display ClassWizard. Then add the `OnLButtonDown()` function to the `CContainerAppView` class, as shown in Figure 20-16.

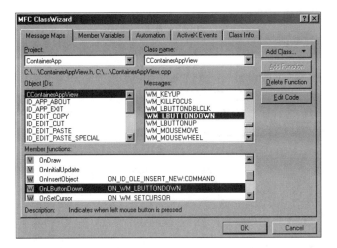

Figure 20-16: ClassWizard adding the `OnLButtonDown()` function to the program

6. Add the lines shown in Listing 20-3 to the `OnLButtonDown()` function, right after the `TODO` comment.

The lines in Listing 20-3 first determine whether the button click is to select or deselect an item. If the click is to select the item, a `CRectTracker` object draws the appropriate border around the item. Calling the tracker's `Track()` member function enables the user to manipulate the item, after which the window is updated and the document marked as dirty (needing to be saved). The `GetHitItem()` function determines whether the mouse was clicked over an embedded item. You'll add `GetHitItem()` to the program later in these steps.

Listing 20-3: Lines for the `OnLButtonDown()` function

```
CContainerAppCntrItem* pHitItem = GetHitItem(point);
SetObjectAsSelected(pHitItem);

if (pHitItem == NULL)
    return;

CRectTracker tracker;
SetupTracker(&tracker, pHitItem);
UpdateWindow();

if (!tracker.Track(this, point))
    return;

Invalidate();

pHitItem->m_objectRect = tracker.m_rect;
CContainerAppDoc* pDoc = GetDocument();
pDoc->SetModifiedFlag();
```

7. Press Ctrl+W on your keyboard to display ClassWizard. Then add the `OnLButtonDblClk()` function to the `CContainerAppView` class, as shown in Figure 20-17.

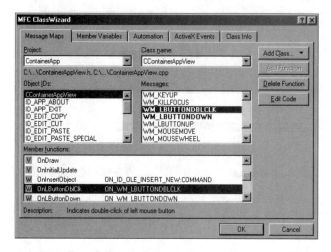

Figure 20-17: ClassWizard adding the `OnLButtonDblClk()` function to the program

8. Add the lines shown in Listing 20-4 to the `OnLButtonDblClk()` function, right after the `TODO` comment.

The lines in Listing 20-4 first call `OnLButtonDown()` to tackle the item-selection task. Then, if the user has selected an item (rather than deselected an item), the program gets the state of the keyboard's Ctrl key. Holding down the Ctrl key when double-clicking an item signals that the item should be opened. If the Ctrl key isn't pressed, the double-click should trigger the item's primary verb, which is often edit. As you can see, Visual C++ defines constants for these standard OLE verbs. (An OLE verb is an action that can be performed on an ActiveX object.)

Listing 20-4: Lines for the `OnLButtonDblClk()` function

```
OnLButtonDown(nFlags, point);

if (m_pSelection == NULL)
    return;

SHORT keyState = GetKeyState(VK_CONTROL);
LONG oleVerb;

if (keyState < 0)
    oleVerb = OLEIVERB_OPEN;

else
    oleVerb = OLEIVERB_PRIMARY;

m_pSelection->DoVerb(oleVerb, this);
```

9. Right-click the `CContainerAppView` class in the Project Workspace window, select Add Member Function from the menu, and add the `SetupTracker()` function to the class. To do this, the Function Type should be `void`, the Function Declaration should be `SetupTracker(CRectTracker* pTracker, CContainerAppCntrItem* pObject)`, and the Access should be Protected, as shown in Figure 20-18.

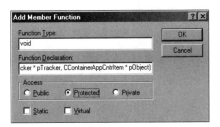

Figure 20-18: Adding the `SetupTracker()` function to the program

10. Add the lines shown in Listing 20-5 to the `SetupTracker()` function.

The `SetupTracker()` function is where you can really see the tracker object at work. In the function, the program gets the size of the selected item and then, through the tracker object, draws resize handles on the item. Then the program determines whether the item is linked or embedded, and draws the appropriate outline for the item's OLE state. Finally, if the item is being edited, the program draws a crosshatch pattern on the item in the document, indicating that it's not currently available.

Listing 20-5: Lines for the `SetupTracker()` function

```
pTracker->m_rect = pObject->m_objectRect;

if (pObject == m_pSelection)
    pTracker->m_nStyle |= CRectTracker::resizeInside;

OLE_OBJTYPE objType = pObject->GetType();

if (objType == OT_EMBEDDED)
    pTracker->m_nStyle |= CRectTracker::solidLine;
else if (objType == OT_LINK)
    pTracker->m_nStyle |= CRectTracker::dottedLine;

UINT objectState = pObject->GetItemState();

if ((objectState == COleClientItem::activeUIState) ||
    (objectState == COleClientItem::openState))
    pTracker->m_nStyle |= CRectTracker::hatchInside;
```

11. Right-click the `CContainerAppView` class in the Project Workspace window, select Add Member Function from the menu, and add the `GetHitItem()` function to the class. To do this, the Function Type should

be `CContainerAppCntrItem*`, the Function Declaration should be `GetHitItem(CPoint point)`, and the Access should be Protected, as shown in Figure 20-19.

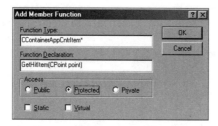

Figure 20-19: Adding the `GetHitItem()` function to the program

12. Add the lines shown in Listing 20-6 to the `GetHitItem()` function.

In the `GetHitItem()` function, the program loops through all the items, comparing their positions with the point passed into the function as its single parameter. If the given point falls inside an item, that item is considered "hit" and passed back from the function.

Listing 20-6: Lines for the `GetHitItem()` function

```
CContainerAppCntrItem* pObjectHit = NULL;
CContainerAppDoc* pDoc = GetDocument();
BOOL objectHit;

POSITION pos = pDoc->GetStartPosition();

while (pos != NULL)
{
    CContainerAppCntrItem* pObject =
        (CContainerAppCntrItem*)pDoc->GetNextItem(pos);
    objectHit = pObject->m_objectRect.PtInRect(point);

    if (objectHit)
        pObjectHit = pObject;
}

return pObjectHit;
```

13. Right-click the `CContainerAppView` class in the Project Workspace window, select Add Member Function from the menu, and add the `SetObjectAsSelected()` function to the class. To do this, the Function Type should be `void`, the Function Declaration should be `SetObjectAsSelected(CContainerAppCntrItem* pObject)`, and the Access should be Protected, as shown in Figure 20-20.

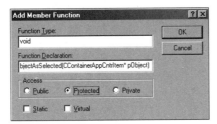

Figure 20-20: Adding the `SetObjectAsSelected()`
function to the program

14. Add the lines shown in Listing 20-7 to the `SetObjectAsSelected()`
    function.

    In the `SetObjectAsSelected()` function, the program determines whether
    the user clicked on an empty portion of the window or on an item. If an
    item is being selected, and there's already another item selected, the
    function closes the previously selected item. The `m_pSelection` member
    variable gets the pointer to the selected item, and the call to
    `Invalidate()` updates the window.

Listing 20-7: Lines for the `SetObjectAsSelected()` function

```
CContainerAppDoc* pDoc = GetDocument();

if ((m_pSelection != pObject) || (pObject == NULL))
{
    COleClientItem* pActiveObject =
        pDoc->GetInPlaceActiveItem(this);

    if ((pActiveObject != pObject) &&
            (pActiveObject != NULL))
        pActiveObject->Close();
}

m_pSelection = pObject;
Invalidate();
```

You now have completed the `ContainerApp` application. You should save
your work and then compile and run the application. When you do, the main
window appears. You can embed an object in the current document just as
you did with earlier versions of the program. Now, however, when you click
in the window outside of the embedded object, the program reverts to its
own menus, as shown in Figure 20-21.

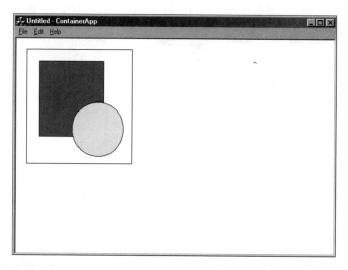

Figure 20-21: The application can now discard a server application's toolbars and menus.

If you click the object to select it, sizing handles appear on the object's border and the mouse pointer changes into a cross cursor, which indicates that the object can be dragged to a new location (see Figure 20-22). By dragging the object's sizing handles with the mouse pointer, you can make the object any size you like (see Figure 20-23). The image in the object automatically resizes as well.

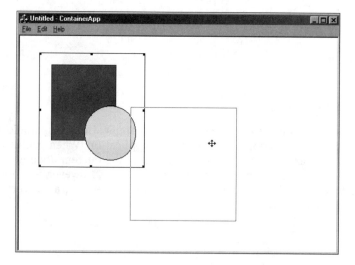

Figure 20-22: The user can now move embedded objects in ContainerApp.

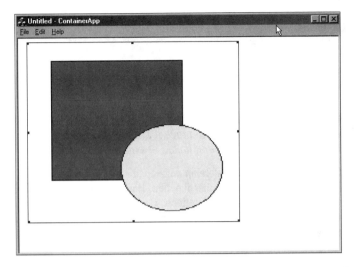

Figure 20-23: The user can now resize embedded objects in ContainerApp.

One problem with the earlier versions of ContainerApp was that its documents could hold only a single embedded object. This new version can hold multiple embedded and linked items. Figure 20-24, for example, shows the application with both a bitmap and a WordPad object embedded in the window.

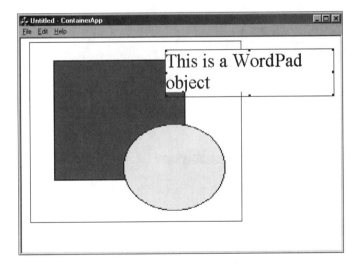

Figure 20-24: ContainerApp can manage multiple embedded objects.

PROBLEMS & SOLUTIONS

Deleting Embedded Items

PROBLEM: *OK, the ContainerApp application works. But once I embed an item in the application's window, although I can move it around and resize it, I can't get rid of it. There must be some way of deleting linked or embedded objects, right?*

SOLUTION: Enabling the user to delete an embedded item isn't difficult. You just have to call the selected item's `Delete()` member function. However, you do need to add the delete command to the application's user interface. Commonly, you'll add some sort of delete command to the application's Edit menu, as well as respond to the keyboard's Delete key. You should already be familiar with creating and responding to menu commands. Here, you'll see how to respond to the Delete key in order to delete an embedded item.

To add a delete command to the ContainerApp application, load the project, and then press Ctrl+W to display ClassWizard. Add the `OnKeyDown()` function to the program, as shown in Figure 20-25. In `OnKeyDown()`, you need to check whether the user pressed the Delete key and whether an item is selected. If both of these conditions are true, you call the selected items `Delete()` function and then call `UpdateAllViews()` to redraw all the view windows that may be displaying the document. Listing 20-8 shows the final `OnKeyDown()` function.

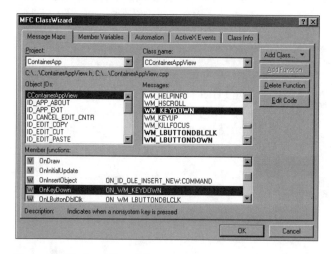

Figure 20-25: ClassWizard adds the `OnKeyDown()` function to the program.

Listing 20-8: Lines for the `OnKeyDown()` **function**

```
void CContainerAppView::OnKeyDown
    (UINT nChar, UINT nRepCnt, UINT nFlags)
{
    // TODO: Add your message handler code here
    //    and/or call default
```

```
    if ((m_pSelection == NULL) || (nChar != VK_DELETE))
        return;

    m_pSelection->Delete();
    m_pSelection = NULL;
    CContainerAppDoc* pDoc = GetDocument();
    pDoc->UpdateAllViews(NULL);

    CView::OnKeyDown(nChar, nRepCnt, nFlags);
}
```

Summary

AppWizard does an amazing job of generating the code an application needs to be an ActiveX container. Still, the basic functionality supplied by AppWizard is rarely adequate for a complete application. AppWizard leaves many details of implementing a container to the programmer. In this chapter, you learned how to give the skeleton container application extra capabilities, such as enabling the user to select, move, and delete embedded items. In the next chapter, you'll learn how to create a server application, which is an application that supplies the editing capabilities to embedded or linked data.

Also discussed in this chapter:

▶ AppWizard provides options for generating several types of ActiveX applications.

▶ In an MFC program, embedded items are represented by an object of the `COleClientItem` class.

▶ MFC calls a `COleClientItem`-derived object's `OnChangeItemPosition()` member function when the user moves an embedded item.

▶ MFC calls a `COleClientItem`-derived object's `OnGetItemPosition()` member function when the program needs the item's current position.

▶ Embedded objects can store their sizes and positions in data members of the class, as well as save and load their sizes and positions in their `Serialize()` function.

▶ `CRectTracker` objects draw the appropriate borders around embedded items, as well as set mouse cursors.

▶ By overloading the view class's `OnSetCursor()` function, a container application can change the mouse cursor when the cursor passes over embedded items.

▶ When the user double-clicks an embedded item, the program should perform the appropriate OLE verb on the item.

▶ To delete an embedded item, call the item's `Delete()` member function.

Chapter 21

Servers

In This Chapter

▶ Creating a skeleton server application

▶ Modifying the application's resources

▶ Completing the document class

▶ Completing the server item class

▶ Customizing the view class

▶ Running a server application

As you learned in the previous chapter, to be fully compliant with Windows 98 application guidelines, a program must support ActiveX. You previously learned that a program can support ActiveX by being an ActiveX container, which is an application that can link or embed files created by other applications. Another way an application can support ActiveX is by being an ActiveX server, which is an application that can link or embed its documents into a container application's window, although it can also run as a stand-alone application if needed. As you'll learn, creating a basic server application with Visual C++ is even easier (compared to writing one from scratch, that is) than creating a container application.

On CD-ROM

In this chapter, you put together the ServerApp application, which supports ActiveX server features such as OLE menus, ActiveX document classes, ActiveX frame-window classes, and server item classes. You'll also see how to program a server to draw its items when those items are embedded in another application's window. You can find the complete application in the Chapter21\ServerApp folder of this book's CD-ROM.

Note

Programming server applications is a complex task that cannot be fully explained in a single chapter. This chapter is only an introduction to the programming techniques required to create a basic server application. After you master the topics in this chapter, if you want to learn more about ActiveX, you should pick up a book that concentrates on ActiveX programming, such as *Inside OLE* by Kraig Brockschmidt, published by Microsoft Press.

Creating a Skeleton Server Application

Just as with all AppWizard applications, your server application begins as an AppWizard project for which Visual C++ generates the basic source code for the program's classes. In a server application, these classes include not only the usual application, frame window, document (now derived from the `COleServerDoc` class instead of `CDocument`), and view window classes, but also an additional class derived from MFC's `COleServerItem` class. In ServerApp, AppWizard names the derived class `CServerAppSrvrItem`. This class represents the server side of any of the application's items, linked or embedded, in a container application's window. To create the skeleton server application, perform the following steps:

Note

You should read through all the application-building steps in this chapter, whether or not you actually build the server application yourself, because the steps include explanations of the programming techniques needed to build a server application.

1. Start a new AppWizard project called *ServerApp,* as shown in Figure 21-1.

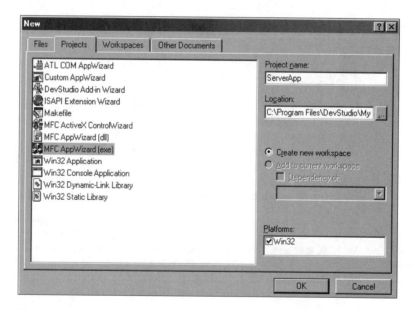

Figure 21-1: The new server application project is called *ServerApp.*

2. In the MFC AppWizard - Step 1 dialog box, select the Single Document option (see Figure 21-2).

3. Click the Next button twice, accepting the default options in the Step 2 dialog box.

4. In the Step 3 of 6 dialog box, select the Full-server option, as shown in Figure 21-3, and click the Next button.

Selecting the Full-server feature tells AppWizard to generate the source code needed to create a skeleton ActiveX server application. The skeleton application will be able to link and embed its documents into applications that act as ActiveX containers. (A mini-server application, another option you can select, cannot run as a stand-alone application, and supports only embedded objects.)

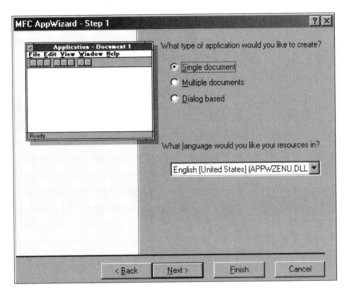

Figure 21-2: The new server application will have an SDI window.

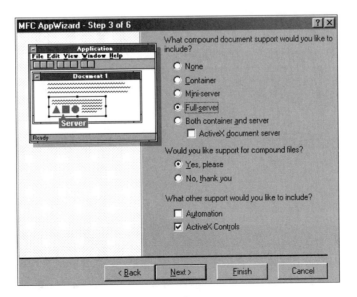

Figure 21-3: AppWizard can generate the code needed to create a server application.

5. In the Step 4 of 6 dialog box, turn off all features except 3D Controls, as shown in Figure 21-4, and then click the Next button.

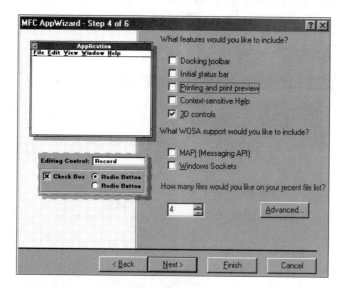

Figure 21-4: The new server application will have no toolbar, status bar, or printing and print preview support.

6. In the Step 5 of 6 dialog box, select the As a Statically Linked Library option. Accept the "Yes, please" default option to generate source file comments (see Figure 21-5).

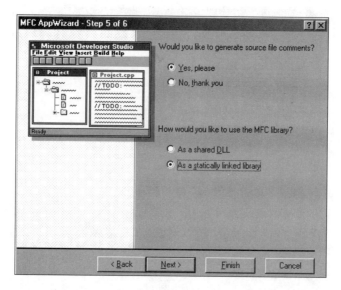

Figure 21-5: The new server application will link to the static MFC library.

7. Click the Finish button. Your New Project Information dialog box should then look like the one in Figure 21-6, except your install directory may be different depending on the directory you chose when you created the project in Step 1.

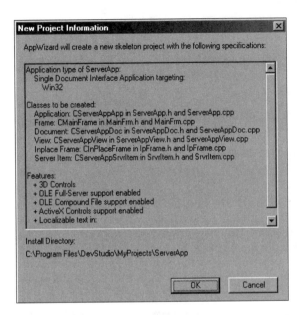

Figure 21-6: The New Project Information dialog box displays the server application's final options.

8. Click the OK button, and AppWizard generates the source code files for the skeleton application.

You've now completed the ServerApp skeleton application. Save your work by selecting the Save All command on Visual C++'s File menu.

If you compile and run the application, you can test it by linking or embedding its document into the ContainerApp application you created in Chapter 20, "Containers." To do this, start ContainerApp and select the Edit menu's Insert New Object command. The Insert Object dialog box appears. In the Object Type box, find Server Document, as shown in Figure 21-7.

Note

Make sure you have compiled and run ServerApp before running Container App. If you fail to run ServerApp, Visual C++ won't register the application's document type in your system Registry, and you won't find the Server Document document type in the Insert Object dialog box.

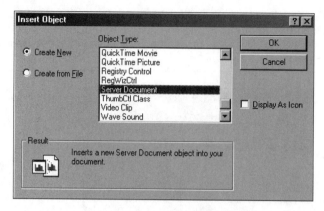

Figure 21-7: The ServerApp application has already registered
its document type with the Windows system Registry.

Server Document is the default document type provided by ServerApp. If
you select this document type from the Insert New Object dialog box,
Windows embeds a document from ServerApp into the currently open
ContainerApp document, as shown in Figure 21-8. Something interesting has
happened as well. As long as the Server Document object is selected for
editing, ServerApp's menus take the place of ContainerApp's.

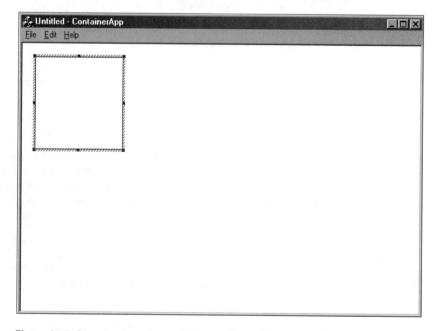

Figure 21-8: ContainerApp shows off its new Server Document object along with
ServerApp's menu bar.

To see that this ActiveX feature is working, click the ContainerApp window to deselect the Server Document object. Then, look at the Help menu. You'll see the command About ContainerApp. Now double-click the Server Document object to select it for editing. Again, look at the Help menu. The About ContainerApp command has been replaced with About ServerApp, proving that ServerApp's menus have appeared in ContainerApp's window. If you had created a toolbar for the ServerApp application, it would have appeared in ContainerApp's window as well.

Customizing the Application's Resources

Now that you have the basic application built, you can customize the resources in order to add a dialog box and complete the application's menus. Perform the following steps to complete the ServerApp application's resources:

1. Select the Resource command from Visual C++'s Insert menu. When the Insert Resource box appears, select the Dialog resource (see Figure 21-9), and click the New button.

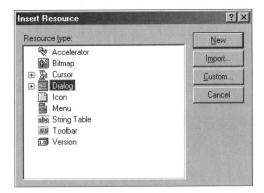

Figure 21-9: Adding a dialog box to the ServerApp application

2. Use the dialog-box editor to create the dialog box shown in Figure 21-10, using the default IDs for all controls.

The server application will display a single rectangle as the contents of its document. The dialog box will enable the user to specify the size of the rectangle.

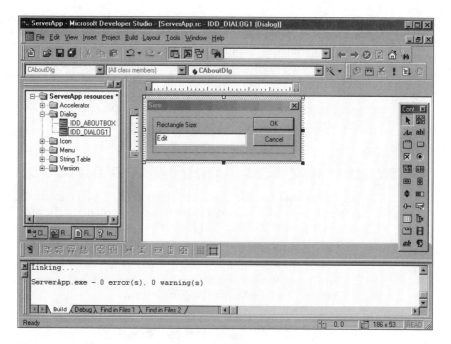

Figure 21-10: The finished dialog box looks like this.

3. Double-click the dialog box you just created to bring up the Adding a Class dialog box, as shown in Figure 21-11. Select the Create a New Class option and click OK.

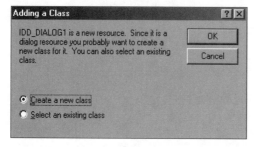

Figure 21-11: You must create a new class for the dialog box.

4. Name the new class CSizeDlg in the New Class dialog box (see Figure 21-12), and click the OK button.

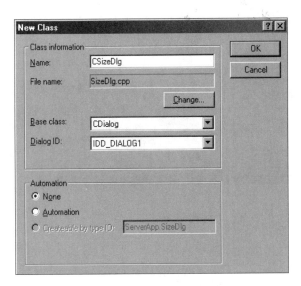

Figure 21-12: The new dialog class will be called `CSizeDlg`.

5. In the MFC Class Wizard property sheet, click the Member Variables tab to display the Member Variables page. Double-click `IDC_EDIT1` and create a variable for the control, as shown in Figure 21-13.

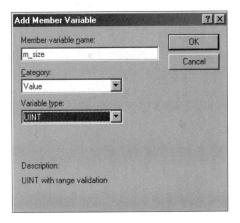

Figure 21-13: The `m_size` member variable will hold the value the user enters into the edit box.

6. Back in ClassWizard, enter 10 and 100 as `m_size`'s minimum and
   maximum allowable values (see Figure 21-14). Then, click OK to close
   the ClassWizard property sheet.

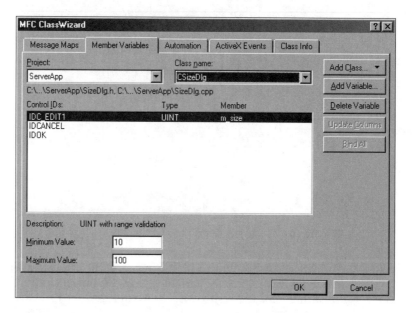

Figure 21-14: The minimum and maximum acceptable values for `m_size` are 10
and 100, respectively.

7. In the ResourceView page of the Project Workspace window, double-click
   the `IDR_MAINFRAME` menu ID to display the menu in the menu editor.

8. Add the Rectangle menu shown in Figure 21-15 with the Size submenu,
   giving the Size command the ID `ID_RECTANGLE_SIZE`.

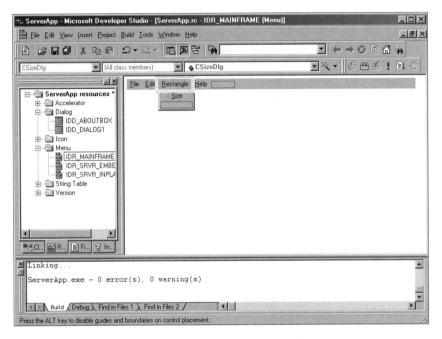

Figure 21-15: The user will be able to call up the Size dialog box using the Rectangle menu's Size command.

9. Add the Rectangle menu to the IDR_SRVR_EMBEDDED (see Figure 21-16) and IDR_SRVR_INPLACE (see Figure 21-17) menus. Use the ID_RECTANGLE_SIZE ID for the Size command on each menu.

As you can tell from the menu IDs, Windows will use these additional menus to display menu bars in a container application that's editing a ServerApp document. The double bars in the IDR_SRVR_INPLACE menu specify where additional menus can be merged into the menu bar.

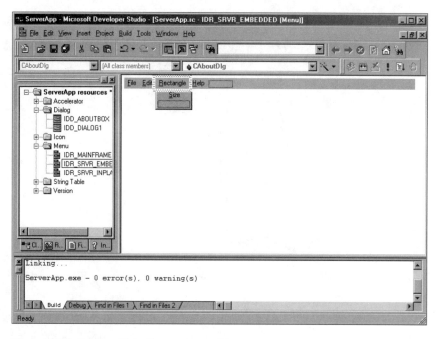

Figure 21-16: You should duplicate server editing commands in the IDR_SRVR_ EMBEDDED menu.

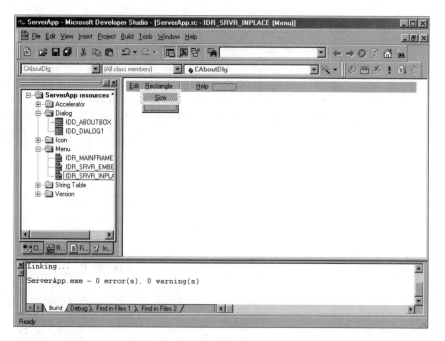

Figure 21-17: You should also duplicate server editing commands in the IDR_SRVR_INPLACE menu.

You've now completed the application's resources. To save your work, select the Save All command from Visual C++'s File menu.

Completing the Application's Document Class

As in any MFC program, ServerApp's document class holds the data that represents the application's currently open document. An ActiveX server application's document class is much like any other application's document class, providing not only member variables to hold the document's data, but also providing the code needed to initialize a new document, as well as to save and load a document. Perform the following steps to complete ServerApp's document class, CServerAppDoc:

1. Right-click CServerAppDoc in the ClassView page of the Project Workspace window, and select Add Member Variable from the menu that appears.

2. When the Add Member Variable dialog appears, type UINT in the Variable Type box, type m_size in the Variable Declaration box, and select the Public access option, as shown in Figure 21-18.

   The m_size variable will hold the size of the rectangle that appears in the ServerApp document. This variable is the only value that determines how a ServerApp document looks on the screen.

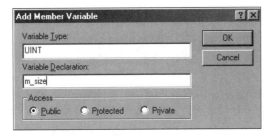

Figure 21-18: A ServerApp document consists of only the value of a single variable.

3. Add the following line to the document class's Serialize() function. Place the line after the add storing code here comment.

   ```
   ar << m_size;
   ```

4. Add the following line to the document class's Serialize() function. Place the line after the add loading code here comment.

   ```
   ar > m_size;
   ```

5. Press Ctrl+W to display ClassWizard, and add the `OnEditCopy()` function to the document class, as shown in Figure 21-19.

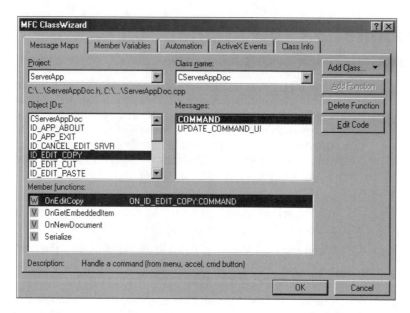

Figure 21-19: You use ClassWizard to add the `OnEditCopy()` function to the document class.

6. Click the Edit Code button and then add the following lines to the new `OnEditCopy()` function:

```
CServerAppSrvrItem* pItem = GetEmbeddedItem();
pItem->CopyToClipboard(TRUE);
```

Now, when the user selects a Paste Link command, the `OnEditCopy()` function copies the Server Document item to the Clipboard.

7. Add the following line to the `CServerAppDoc` class's `OnNewDocument()` member function, right after the `TODO` comment:

```
m_size = 50;
```

This line initializes the rectangle size to its default value.

You have now completed the ServerApp application's document class. Select the File menu's Save All command to save your work.

Completing the Server Item's Class

In the previous chapter, you learned that AppWizard creates a class derived from `COleClientItem` that represents the ActiveX object currently embedded in the container's document. The server, too, has a similar class, but the server version of the class represents an ActiveX item for which the server is supplying editing functions. You could say that this server item class, derived from COleServerItem, is the other side of the ActiveX item coin.

On the container side, the ActiveX object (represented by an object of the COleClientItem class) has to know its own size and where it's positioned. On the server side of things, the same object (now represented by the COleServerItem class) has to know how to draw itself. That is, although the container application positions the ActiveX item in the window, it is the server application that displays the item.

To complete ServerApp's server item class, you need to provide the code that draws the item. Similar to an application's view class, a server item class contains an OnDraw() function, which determines how the item looks when drawn in a container application's window. To complete ServerApp's CServerAppSrvrItem class, add the following lines to the class's OnDraw() function:

```
pDC->SetMapMode(MM_TEXT);
int x = pDoc->m_size + 10;
int y = pDoc->m_size + 10;
pDC->Rectangle(10, 10, x, y);
```

The OnDraw() function displays the inactive embedded object in a container application's window. The mapping mode should be set to the same mode used in the view class's OnDraw() function, which draws the document in the server's window when the server is being run as a stand-alone application.

Completing the View Class

In an ActiveX server application, the view class is responsible for displaying a document when the application is running as a stand-alone application. The view class also supplies editing functions for the application. These editing functions are usually callable from a container application through the server menus that Windows merges with the container's menus (when the user selects an embedded item for editing). In the following steps, you complete the view class's OnDraw() function, as well as enable the user to display the Size dialog box. Using the Size dialog box, the user can edit a ServerApp document, by changing the size of the rectangle that represents the document.

1. Add the following lines to the CServerAppView class's OnDraw() function:

```
pDC->SetMapMode(MM_TEXT);
int x = pDoc->m_size + 10;
int y = pDoc->m_size + 10;
pDC->Rectangle(10, 10, x, y);
```

These lines draw the document when it's being displayed in the server application's own window. Notice that these lines are identical to the lines you added to the item's OnDraw() function.

2. Press Ctrl+W to display ClassWizard, and then add the OnRectangleSize() message-response function, as shown in Figure 21-20.

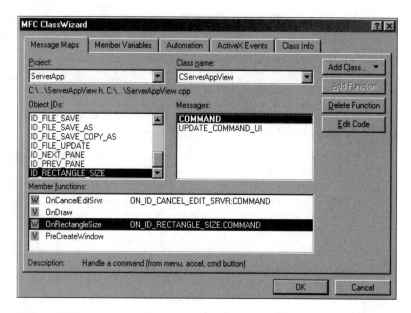

Figure 21-20: Use ClassWizard to add the `OnRectangleSize()` function to the document class.

3. Add the lines in Listing 21-1 to the `OnRectangleSize()` function:

Listing 21-1: Lines for the `OnRectangleSize()` function

```
CSizeDlg dlg;

CServerAppDoc* pDoc = GetDocument();
dlg.m_size = pDoc->m_size;

int result = dlg.DoModal();
if (result == IDOK)
{
    pDoc->m_size = dlg.m_size;
    pDoc->SetModifiedFlag();
    pDoc->NotifyChanged();
    Invalidate();
}
```

The `OnRectangleSize()` function sets up the Size dialog box and displays it to the user. If the user dismisses the dialog with the OK button, `OnRectangleSize()` sets the document's `m_size` member variable to the new value entered by the user, and then updates both the locally displayed document and the embedded (if any) item. Calling the document class's `NotifyChanged()` function is all it takes to notify any items embedded in containers that their displays need to be repainted.

4. Add the following line to the top of the view class's implementation file (ServerAppView.cpp), after the line `#include "ServerAppView.h"` that's already there:

```
#include "SizeDlg.h"
```

You've now completed the ServerApp sample ActiveX server application. Select the Build ServerApp.exe command from Visual C++'s Build menu to compile and link your changes.

Running the Server Application

There are actually several ways to run a server application. First, you can run the server just like any other application, as a stand-alone program that enables the user to create and edit documents. Second, you can run a server application as an in-place editing tool in a container application by selecting for editing an embedded item in a container application's window. Finally, you can run the server application by selecting for editing a linked item in a container application. In this case, the server runs in its own window, editing the file to which the linked item is associated.

Running ServerApp as a stand-alone application

To run ServerApp on its own, double-click the program's executable file or run the application from Visual C++ by selecting the execute command. When you do, you see the window shown in Figure 21-21. The rectangle in the window's upper-left corner represents the application's default document, which consists of a rectangle with a size of 50.

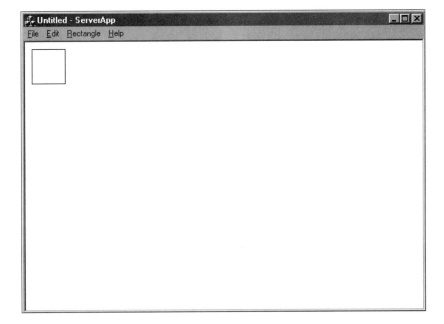

Figure 21-21: This is ServerApp running as a stand-alone application.

The only way you can edit the document in this simple example is to change the size of the rectangle. You do this by selecting the Rectangle menu's Size command, which displays the Size dialog box (see Figure 21-22). In this dialog box, you can specify a size from 10 to 100 for the rectangle. Figure 21-23 shows the application after the user has given the rectangle a new size of 100.

Figure 21-22: You edit the document by changing the rectangle's size.

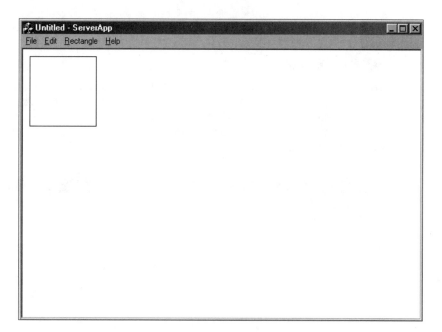

Figure 21-23: Here, the rectangle has been reset to size 100.

Before closing the ServerApp application, save the document under the name test.srv. Later in this chapter, you'll use this file to link an item into a container application's window.

Running ServerApp as an in-place editor

To run ServerApp in-place, you must first start a container application. Luckily, you created just such an application in the previous chapter. So, run ContainerApp and select its Insert New Object command from the Edit menu. Select Server Document in the Object Type box of the Insert Object dialog (refer back to Figure 21-7 for a refresher of what this looks like). Click OK to embed the item into the container application's window (see Figure 21-24).

Notice in Figure 21-24 that not only did the application embed a ServerApp document object, but it also ran ServerApp in-place, so that you can edit the embedded object. You can see that ServerApp is running in-place because its menus have replaced ContainerApp's menus. Go ahead and select the Size command from the Rectangle menu. The Size dialog box appears just as if you were running ServerApp rather than Container App (which, in a way, you are). Change the rectangle size to 10 and then click outside of the object to deselect it. Windows restores ContainerApp's menus, as shown in Figure 21-25. The solid line around the ServerApp item means that the item is embedded in the container window.

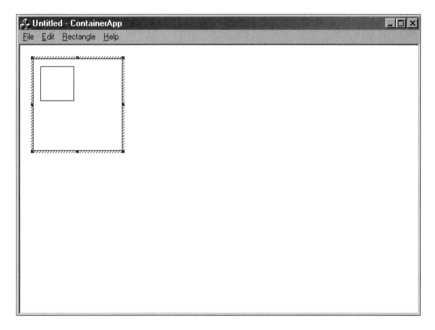

Figure 21-24: Here's ContainerApp with its embedded Server Document item.

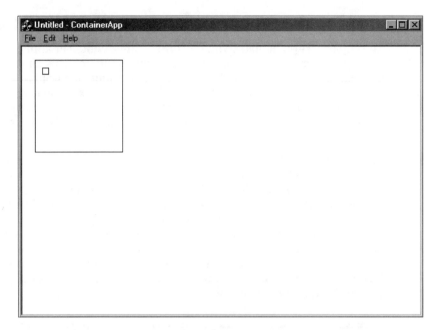

Figure 21-25: The rectangle has been reset to size 10.

Running ServerApp as an editor for a linked item

In the previous section, you embedded a ServerApp item into ContainerApp's window. Because the item is embedded, the item's data (the rectangle) exists only as a part of the container application's document. That is, the item used in ContainerApp doesn't have a file of its own. When you link a ServerApp item, on the other hand, you select a ServerApp file. In this case, when the file is edited, the linked item in the container window changes automatically to the new version of the document.

To try this out, again select the Insert New Object command from ContainerApp's Edit menu. When the Insert Object dialog box appears, select the Create From File option. The Object Type box changes to a File box with a Browser button, as shown in Figure 21-26. Use the Browse button to locate and select the test.srv file you saved when running ServerApp as a stand-alone application. Then, select the Link option in the Insert Object dialog box. Click OK to link the file into ContainerApp's window.

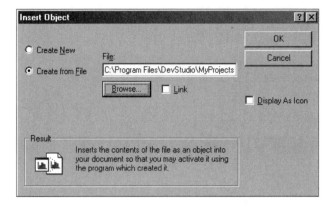

Figure 21-26: You can use the Insert Object dialog to link, as well as embed, items.

When the newly linked ServerApp item first appears, it covers the previously embedded item. Use your mouse to drag the linked item to a new location in the window, as shown in Figure 21-27. Notice that the new item sports a dashed border, which indicates that the item is linked.

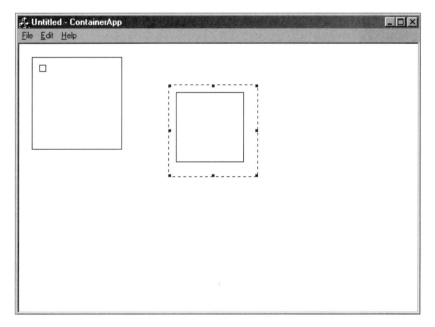

Figure 21-27: Now there are embedded and linked ServerApp items in ContainerApp's window.

To edit the linked item, double-click it. Windows starts ServerApp in a separate window and loads the linked file into the window (see Figure 21-28).

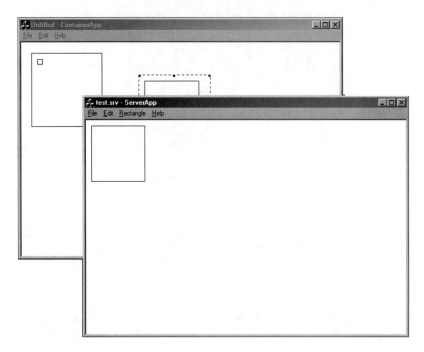

Figure 21-28: When editing a linked item, both ContainerApp and ServerApp are on the screen.

You can now edit the item by bringing up the Size dialog box (select the Rectangle menu's Size command) and changing the rectangle's size. When you close the ServerApp application and save the changed file, the linked item in ContainerApp changes too, as shown in Figure 21-29.

That's all there is to building and running a basic server application. Of course, your own server applications will feature more complex document types and will require more sophisticated programming. Still, this chapter's sample program ought to get you started with creating your own ActiveX server applications.

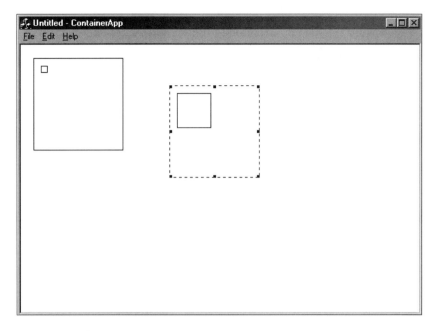

Figure 21-29: Once a linked item has been edited, it changes in the container application to reflect the changes made to the source file.

Summary

A basic server application is easier to build than a container application. Still, there's a lot to learn in order to master the programming of ActiveX server applications. This chapter presented an introduction to server programming. If you want to know more, you should pick up an ActiveX programming book that covers writing container and server applications with Visual C++ and MFC.

Also discussed in this chapter:

▶ When you select AppWizard's Full-server option, AppWizard can generate a complete server skeleton application.

▶ In an MFC program, server items are represented by an object of the `COleServerItem` class.

▶ AppWizard-generated server applications have three menu resources that enable the application's menus to appear in the stand-alone application, as well as in in-place and linked-item versions of the application.

▶ A server application's document class holds the document's data, as well as supplies the programming needed to save and load the document.

▶ MFC calls a `COleClientItem`-derived object's `OnDraw()` member function to render the item in a container application's window.

▶ A server application creates an object derived from the `COleServerItem` class for each item linked or embedded in a container application's window.

▶ A server application's view class contains the `OnDraw()` function that displays the application's data when the application runs in its own window (rather than in-place).

Chapter 22

Automation

In This Chapter

- ▶ Building an automation server application
- ▶ Building an automation client application
- ▶ Controlling an automation server from the client application

Automation enables you to create applications that can control each other. Using automation, you can design features in one program and then be able to use those features in any other program you write — reusability at its best. You might, for example, have an application that can, among other things, count the number of words in a document. If you make this application into an automation server, other applications can call the function that counts words, and not need to implement that function themselves. In this chapter, you'll learn how to create both automation server and automation client applications.

On CD-ROM

In this chapter, you'll put together the *AutoServerApp* application, which supports automation features such as properties and methods that can be accessed by a client application. Along the way, you'll learn to define an interface through which client applications can control an automation server. Because a server application is only half the picture, you'll also create a client application called *AutoClientApp*. You can find these applications in the Chapter22\AutoServerApp and Chapter22\AutoClientApp folders of this book's CD-ROM.

Note

Programming automation applications is a complex task that cannot be fully explained in a single chapter. This chapter is only an introduction to the programming techniques required to create basic automation server and client applications. After you master the topics in this chapter, if you want to learn more about ActiveX, you should pick up a book that concentrates on ActiveX programming, such as *Inside OLE* by Kraig Brockschmidt, published by Microsoft Press.

The Automation Server Application

On CD-ROM

In the first part of this chapter, you'll learn to program a simple automation server. As you already know, an automation server provides some sort of service that can be accessed and controlled by a client application. For example, an automation server might provide a spell-checker that other applications can use to spell-check their documents. In this chapter, you won't create a server that sophisticated, but you will get a quick look at how this handy technology works. You can find this section's sample application, AutoServerApp, in the Chapter22\AutoServerApp folder of this book's CD-ROM.

Creating a skeleton automation server

AppWizard can get your automation server started, leaving you to fill in the details appropriate for your specific application. Creating an automation server using AppWizard is not unlike creating any other type of application. You just specify slightly different AppWizard options. Perform the following steps to create the AutoServerApp skeleton application:

Note

You should read through all the application-building steps in this chapter, whether or not you actually build the automation server application yourself, because the steps include explanations of the programming techniques needed to build an automation server application.

1. Start a new AppWizard project called *AutoServerApp,* as shown in Figure 22-1.

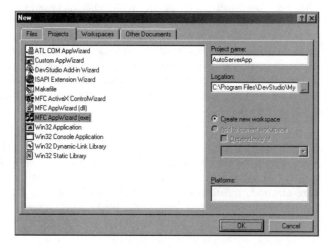

Figure 22-1: The new automation server application is called *AutoServerApp*.

2. In the MFC AppWizard - Step 1 dialog box, select the Single Document option (see Figure 22-2).

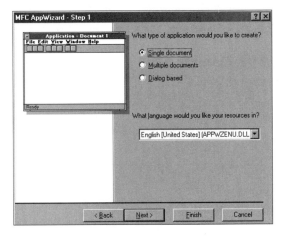

Figure 22-2: The new automation server will have an SDI window.

3. Click the Next button twice, accepting the default options in the Step 2 dialog box.

4. In the Step 3 of 6 dialog box, select the Automation and ActiveX Controls options, as shown in Figure 22-3. Click the Next button.

   Selecting the Automation feature tells AppWizard to generate the source code needed to create a skeleton automation server application. The skeleton application will be able to define properties and methods that can be accessed by other applications.

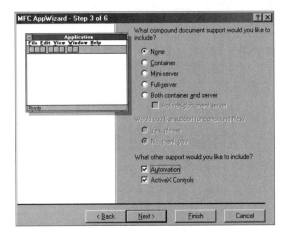

Figure 22-3: AppWizard can generate the code needed to create an automation application.

5. In the Step 4 of 6 dialog box, turn off all features except 3D Controls, as shown in Figure 22-4, and then click the Next button.

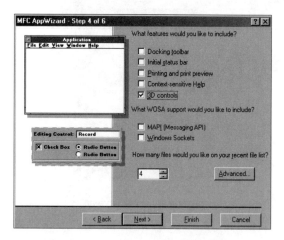

Figure 22-4: The new automation application will have no toolbar, status bar, or printing and print preview support.

6. In the Step 5 of 6 dialog box, select the As a Statically Linked Library option (see Figure 22-5).

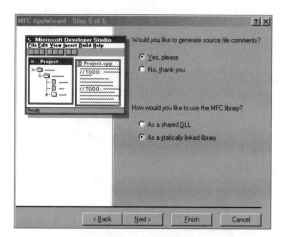

Figure 22-5: The new automation server will link to the static MFC library.

7. Click the Finish button. Your New Project Information dialog box should then look like the one in Figure 22-6, except your install directory may be different depending on the directory you chose when you created the project in Step 1.

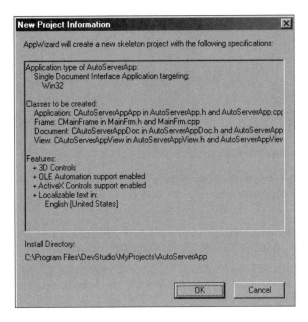

Figure 22-6: The New Project Information dialog box displays the automation server's final options.

8. Click the OK button, and AppWizard generates the source code files for the skeleton application.

You've now completed the AutoServerApp skeleton application. Save your work by selecting the Save All command on Visual C++'s File menu. At this point, the application does nothing useful, so you don't need to compile the source files. Instead, continue on to the next set of steps, where you complete the automation server's resources.

Customizing the automation server's resources

Now that you have the basic application built, you can customize the resources in order to add a dialog box and complete the application's menus. Perform the following steps to complete the AutoServerApp application's resources:

1. Select the Resource command from Visual C++'s Insert menu. When the Insert Resource dialog box appears, select the Dialog resource (see Figure 22-7), and click the New button.

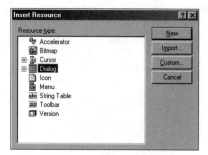

Figure 22-7: Add a dialog box to the
AutoServerApp application.

2. Create the dialog box shown in Figure 22-8, using the IDs `IDC_XPOS`,
   `IDC_YPOS`, and `IDC_DIAMETER` for the edit controls.

   The automation server will display a single circle as the contents of its
   document. The dialog box will enable the user to specify the position
   and size of the circle.

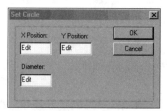

Figure 22-8: The finished dialog
box looks like this.

3. Double-click the dialog you just created to bring up the Adding a Class
   dialog box, as shown in Figure 22-9. Select the Create a New Class option
   and click OK.

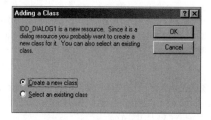

Figure 22-9: You must create a new class
for the dialog box.

4. Name the new class `CCircleDlg` in the New Class dialog box (see Figure 22-10), and click the OK button.

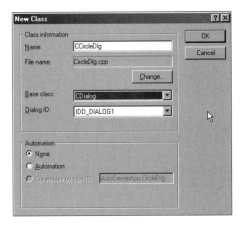

Figure 22-10: The new dialog class will be called `CCircleDlg`.

5. In the MFC Class Wizard property sheet, click the Member Variables tab to display the Member Variables page. Double-click `IDC_DIAMETER` to display the Add Member Variable dialog box and create a `UINT` variable called `m_diameter` for the control, as shown in Figure 22-11. This member variable will hold the document's circle-diameter value.

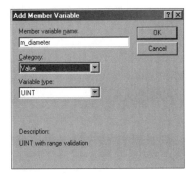

Figure 22-11: The `m_diameter` member variable will hold the value the user enters into the Diameter edit box.

6. Create `UINT` member variables called `m_xpos` and `m_ypos` for the `IDC_XPOS` and `IDC_YPOS` edit controls. The Member Variables page should then look like the one in Figure 22-12. Click ClassWizard's OK button to finalize the dialog box's class.

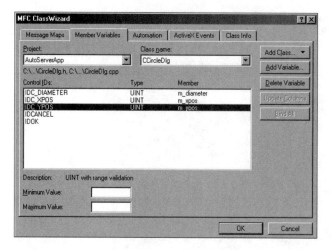

Figure 22-12: The final variables should look as shown here.

7. In the ResourceView page of the Project Workspace window, double-click the IDR_MAINFRAME menu ID to display the menu in the menu editor.

8. Add the Circle menu shown in Figure 22-13, giving the submenu's Set Circle command the ID ID_CIRCLE_SETCIRCLE.

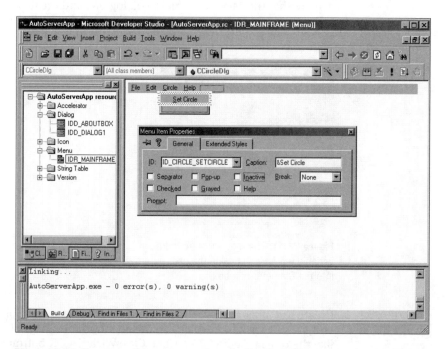

Figure 22-13: The user will be able to call up the Set Circle dialog box using the Circle menu's Set Circle command.

You've now completed the application's resources. To save your work, select the Save All command from Visual C++'s File menu.

Completing the automation server's document class

As in any MFC program, AutoServerApp's document class holds the data that represents the application's currently open document. An automation server application's document class is much like any other application's document class, providing not only member variables to hold the document's data, but also providing the code needed to initialize a new document, as well as to save and load a document. Perform the following steps to complete AutoServerApp's document class, CAutoServerAppDoc:

1. Right-click CAutoServerAppDoc in the ClassView page of the Project Workspace window, and select Add Member Variable from the menu that appears.

2. When the Add Member Variable dialog appears, type UINT in the Variable Type box, type m_diameter in the Variable Declaration box, and select the Public access option, as shown in Figure 22-14.

   The m_diameter variable will hold the diameter of the circle that appears in the AutoServerApp document.

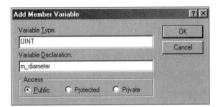

Figure 22-14: An AutoServerApp document consists of values that determine the position and size of a circle.

3. Create two more public UINT member variables called m_xpos and m_ypos.

   These variables will hold the position of the circle that appears in the AutoServerApp document.

4. Add the following lines to the document class's Serialize() function. Place the lines after the add storing code here comment:

```
ar << m_diameter;
ar << m_xpos;
ar << m_ypos;
```

5. Add the following line to the document class's `Serialize()` function. Place the line after the `add loading code here` comment:

    ```
    ar > m_diameter;
    ar > m_xpos;
    ar > m_ypos;
    ```

6. Add the following lines to the `CAutoServerAppDoc` class's `OnNewDocument()` member function, right after the `TODO` comment:

    ```
    m_diameter = 100;
    m_xpos = 30;
    m_ypos = 30;
    ```

    These lines initialize the circle's size and position to the default values.

    You have now completed the AutoServerApp application's document class. Select the File menu's Save All command to save your work.

Completing the automation server's view class

In the following steps, you complete the view class's `OnDraw()` function, as well as enable the user to display the Set Circle dialog box. Using the Set Circle dialog box, the user can edit an AutoServerApp document by changing the size and position of the circle that represents the document.

1. Add the following lines to the `CAutoServerAppView` class's `OnDraw()` function:

    ```
    pDC->Ellipse(pDoc->m_xpos, pDoc->m_ypos,
        pDoc->m_diameter + pDoc->m_xpos,
        pDoc->m_diameter + pDoc->m_ypos);
    ```

    These lines draw the circle that's displayed as the application's document.

2. Press Ctrl+W to display ClassWizard, and then add the `OnCircleSet circle()` message-response function, as shown in Figure 22-15.

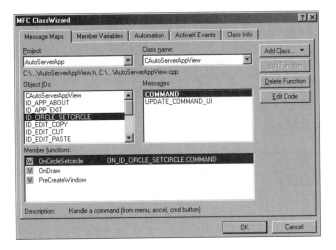

Figure 22-15: Use ClassWizard to add the `OnCircleSetcircle()` function to the view class.

3. Add the lines in Listing 22-1 to the `OnCircleSetcircle()` function:

Listing 22-1: Lines for the `OnCircleSetcircle()` function

```
CCircleDlg dlg;
CAutoServerAppDoc* pDoc = GetDocument();
dlg.m_diameter = pDoc->m_diameter;
dlg.m_xpos = pDoc->m_xpos;
dlg.m_ypos = pDoc->m_ypos;

int result = dlg.DoModal();

if (result == IDOK)
{
    pDoc->m_diameter = dlg.m_diameter;
    pDoc->m_xpos = dlg.m_xpos;
    pDoc->m_ypos = dlg.m_ypos;
    pDoc->SetModifiedFlag();
    Invalidate();
}
```

The `OnCircleSetcircle()` function sets up the Set Circle dialog box and displays it to the user. If the user dismisses the dialog with the OK button, `OnCircleSetcircle()` sets the document's member variables to the new values entered by the user, and then updates the displayed document.

4. Add the following line to the top of the view class's implementation file (AutoServerAppView.cpp), after the line `#include "AutoServerAppView.h"` that's already there:

```
#include "CircleDlg.h"
```

You've now completed AutoServerApp's view class. Select the File menu's Save All command to save your work. At this point, you can compile and run the application. If you do, you'll discover that it runs just like any other AppWizard application, with no obvious automation features. You can select the Circle menu's Set Circle command to change the circle's size and location (see Figure 22-16), but that's about it. To create the automation server, you must define properties and methods, which you do in the next section.

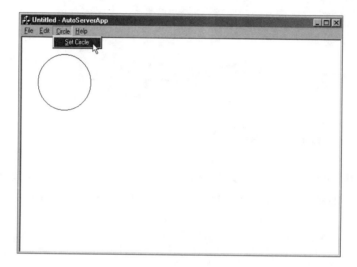

Figure 22-16: At this point, AutoServerApp runs with no obvious automation features.

Defining the server's properties and methods

To enable an automation client application to control the automation server, the server must define an interface consisting of properties and methods. Properties are similar to member variables, and methods are similar to member functions, the difference being that properties and methods are part of the automation server's interface, rather than part of a class. To add properties and methods to AutoServerApp, perform the following steps:

1. Press Ctrl+W to display ClassWizard, and then select the Automation page, as shown in Figure 22-17.

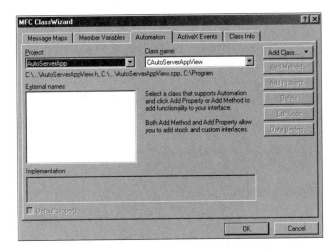

Figure 22-17: You use ClassWizard's Automation page to add properties and methods.

2. Select `CAutoServerAppView` in the Class Name box, and click the Add Property button.

3. In the Add Property dialog, enter `Diameter` in the External Name box, select `short` in the Type box, and select the Get/Set methods option (see Figure 22-18).

   `Diameter` will be the name of the property that client applications will use to control the size of the circle object. To retrieve this value from the automation server, a client application calls the `GetDiameter()` method. Similarly, to change the Diameter property, a client application calls the `SetDiameter()` method.

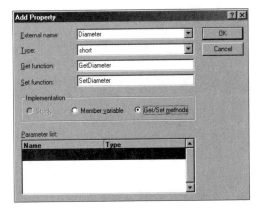

Figure 22-18: The Diameter property controls the circle's size.

4. Add two more properties, called xPosition and yPosition, to the interface, following the same procedure given in Step 3. ClassWizard's Automation page should look like the one shown in Figure 22-19 when you're finished.

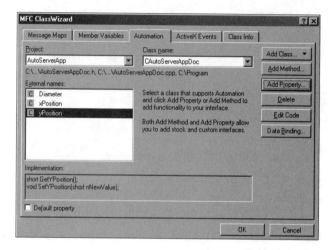

Figure 22-19: ClassWizard displays the three new properties.

5. In ClassWizard, click the Add Method button. In the Add Method dialog, type DisplayServerWindow in the External Name box (the Internal Name box will mirror your typing), select void in the Return Type box, as shown in Figure 22-20. Click OK to dismiss the Add Method dialog.

The DisplayServerWindow() method enables client applications to display the server application's window.

Figure 22-20: ClassWizard can also define methods for the automation interface.

6. With `DisplayServerWindow` highlighted in ClassWizard's External Name box, click the Edit Code button. Add the following lines to the `DisplayServerWindow()` method:

```
CFrameWnd* pWnd = (CFrameWnd*)AfxGetMainWnd();
pWnd->ActivateFrame(SW_SHOW);
```

Now, when a client application calls `DisplayServerWindow()`, the server gets a pointer to the main window and displays the window by calling its `ActivateFrame()` function.

7. In the `GetDiameter()` method, replace the return statement with the following line:

```
return (short)m_diameter;
```

When a client application calls `GetDiameter()`, the method returns the value of `m_diameter`, which is the circle's current size.

8. Add the following lines to the `SetDiameter()` method:

```
m_diameter = nNewValue;
UpdateAllViews(NULL);
SetModifiedFlag();
```

When a client application calls `SetDiameter()`, the method receives the new value in the `nNewValue` parameter. The method saves the new value in `m_diameter` and then redraws all views so that the new diameter has an immediate effect on the display.

9. In the `GetXPosition()` method, replace the return statement with the following line:

```
return (short)m_xpos;
```

When a client application calls `GetXPosition()`, the method returns the value of `m_xpos`, which is the circle's horizontal position.

10. Add the following lines to the `SetXPosition()` method:

```
m_xpos = nNewValue;
UpdateAllViews(NULL);
SetModifiedFlag();
```

When a client application calls `SetXPosition()`, the method receives the new value in the `nNewValue` parameter. The method saves the new value in `m_xpos` and then redraws all views so that the new horizontal position has an immediate effect on the display.

11. In the `GetYPosition()` method, replace the return statement with the following line:

```
return (short)m_ypos;
```

When a client application calls `GetYPosition()`, the method returns the value of `m_ypos`, which is the circle's vertical position.

12. Add the following lines to the SetYPosition() method:

```
m_ypos = nNewValue;
UpdateAllViews(NULL);
SetModifiedFlag();
```

When a client application calls SetYPosition(), the method receives the new value in the nNewValue parameter. The method saves the new value in m_ypos and then redraws all views so that the new vertical position has an immediate effect on the display.

You've now completed the AutoServerApp sample application. Select the Build AutoServerApp.exe command from Visual C++'s Build menu to compile and link your changes. Although AutoServerApp now supports ActiveX automation through its new interface, you still need a client application that knows how to control the server. You'll build the client application in the next section.

The Automation Client Application

On CD-ROM

Automation is a two-sided process. Once you have a server application that supplies automation services, you need a client application to take advantage of those services. In this section, you'll construct a client application that knows how to access AutoServerApp's automation interface. After completing the client application, you'll discover how the server and client work together. You can find this section's sample application, AutoClientApp, in the Chapter22\AutoClientApp folder of this book's CD-ROM.

Creating the automation client skeleton

AppWizard can get your client server started just as easily as it got your server application started. Then you can fill in the details that are appropriate for your specific client application. As you'll soon see, creating an automation client application using AppWizard is not unlike creating any other type of application. Perform the following steps to create the AutoServerApp skeleton application.

1. Start a new AppWizard project called *AutoClientApp*, as shown in Figure 22-21.

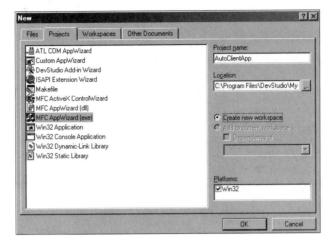

Figure 22-21: The new automation client application project is called *AutoClientApp*.

2. In the MFC AppWizard - Step 1 dialog box, select the Single Document option (see Figure 22-22).

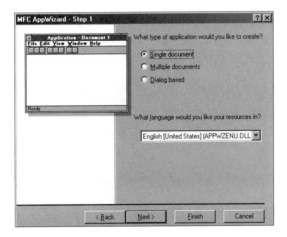

Figure 22-22: The new automation client will have an SDI window.

3. Click the Next button three times, accepting the default options in the Step 2 and Step 3 dialog boxes.

4. In the Step 4 of 6 dialog box, turn off all features except 3D Controls, as shown in Figure 22-23, and then click the Next button.

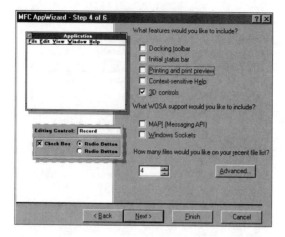

Figure 22-23: The new automation client will have no toolbar, status bar, or printing and print preview support.

5. In the Step 5 of 6 dialog box, select the As a Statically Linked Library option. Accept the "Yes, please" default option to generate source file comments (see Figure 22-24).

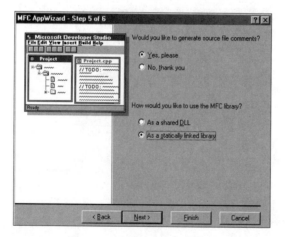

Figure 22-24: The new automation client will link to the static MFC library.

6. Click the Finish button. Your New Project Information dialog box should then look like the one in Figure 22-25, except your install directory may be different depending on the directory you chose when you created the project in Step 1.

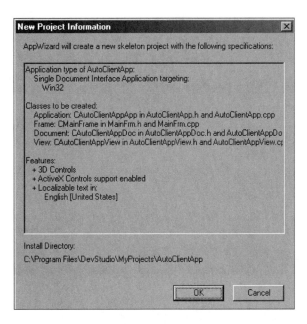

Figure 22-25: The New Project Information dialog box displays the automation client's final options.

7. Click the OK button, and AppWizard generates the source code files for the skeleton application.

Customizing the client application's resources

Now that you have the basic client application built, you can customize the resources in order to complete the application's menus. In the ResourceView page of the Project Workspace window, double-click the IDR_MAINFRAME menu ID to display the menu in the menu editor. Then, add the Automation menu shown in Figure 22-26, giving the Set Diameter, Set X Position, Set Y Position, and Display Window commands the IDs ID_AUTOMATION_SETDIAMETER, ID_AUTOMATION_SETXPOSITION, ID_AUTOMATION_SETYPOSITION, and ID_AUTOMATION_DISPLAYWINDOW, respectively.

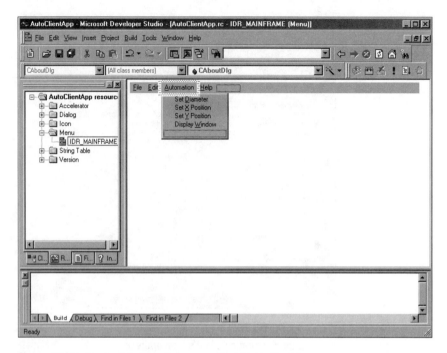

Figure 22-26: The final Automation menu should look like this.

You've now completed the application's resources. To save your work, select the Save All command from Visual C++'s File menu.

Completing the client application's view class

The client application's view class is charged with responding to menu messages. Because some of those menu messages must manipulate the server application, the view class must have access to the server application's properties and methods. This access is provided by an interface that you can create from the server application's type library. To create that interface and the menu commands' message-response functions, follow these steps:

1. Press Ctrl+W to display ClassWizard, and then select the Message Maps page. Click the Add Class button, and select the From a Type Library option, as shown in Figure 22-27. The Import From Type Library dialog box appears.

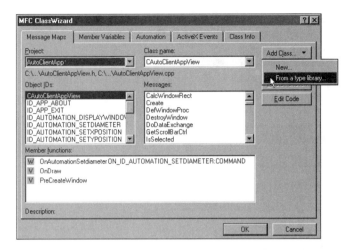

Figure 22-27: ClassWizard can create classes from type libraries.

2. In the Import from Type Library dialog, navigate to the AutoServerApp.tlb file in your server application's Release or Debug directory, as shown in Figure 22-28. Double-click the AutoServerApp.tlb file to select it.

Figure 22-28: The required type library is part of your AutoServerApp project.

3. In the Confirm Classes dialog (see Figure 22-29), click OK to accept the suggested names for the new class and the class's source code files. Click OK to dismiss ClassWizard.

   The type library contains information about the server's properties and methods. ClassWizard can read the type library and create a class that represents the interface represented by the class library. This new class makes it easy for your application to access the server's properties and call the server's methods.

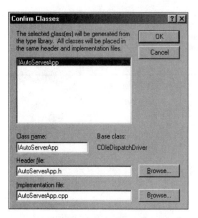

Figure 22-29: ClassWizard converts the server's interface into a class.

4. In the ClassView page of the Project Workspace window, right-click the `CAutoClientAppView` class, and select Add Member Variable from the menu that appears.

5. In the Add Member Variable dialog, type `IAutoServerApp` into the Variable Type box, type `m_server` into the Variable Declaration box, and select the Protected access option, as shown in Figure 22-30. Click OK to add the member variable to the view class.

   `IAutoServerApp` is the class you created from the server application's type library. The `m_server` object, which the program creates from `IAutoServerApp`, will represent the server's interface in the client application. That is, the client application will be able to access the server through the `m_server` object.

Figure 22-30: Creating an object of the interface class enables the automation client to access the automation server.

6. If it's not already there, add the following line to the top of the AutoClientAppView.h file, right after the `#endif` directive that's already there:

```
#include "AutoServerApp.h"
```

7. Press Ctrl+W to display ClassWizard, and add the `OnAutomation Setdiameter()` message-response function. (Make sure you select `CAutoClientAppView` in the Class Name box.)

8. Add the following lines to the new `OnAutomationSetdiameter()` function:

```
int diameter = m_server.GetDiameter();
diameter += 25;
if (diameter > 300)
    diameter = 100;
m_server.SetDiameter(diameter);
```

These lines get the current circle diameter from the server, calculate a new diameter, and call the server to set the new diameter.

9. Press Ctrl+W to display ClassWizard, and add the `OnAutomation Setxposition()` message-response function.

10. Add the following lines to the new `OnAutomationSetxposition()` function:

```
int xpos = m_server.GetXPosition();
xpos += 50;
if (xpos > 320)
    xpos = 30;
m_server.SetXPosition(xpos);
```

These lines get the current circle's horizontal position from the server, calculate a new position, and call the server to set the new position.

11. Press Ctrl+W to display ClassWizard, and add the `OnAutomationSetyposition()` message-response function.

12. Add the following lines to the new `OnAutomationSetyposition()` function:

```
int ypos = m_server.GetYPosition();
ypos += 50;
if (ypos > 320)
    ypos = 30;
m_server.SetYPosition(ypos);
```

These lines get the current circle's vertical position from the server, calculate a new position, and call the server to set the new position.

13. Press Ctrl+W to display ClassWizard, and add the `OnAutomationDisplaywindow()` message-response function.

14. Add the following line to the new `OnAutomationDisplaywindow()` function:

```
m_server.DisplayServerWindow();
```

This line calls the server's `DisplayServerWindow()` method to display the server's main window, which remains hidden unless the client calls this method.

15. Press Ctrl+W to display ClassWizard, and add the `OnCreate()` message-response function, as shown in Figure 22-31.

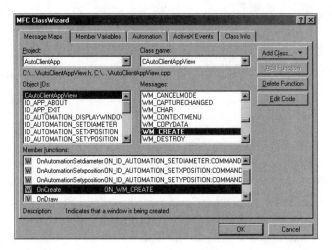

Figure 22-31: Use ClassWizard to add the `OnCreate()` function.

16. Add the following lines to the new `OnCreate()` function, right after the
    `TODO: Add your specialized creation code here` comment:

    ```
    BOOL loaded =
        m_server.CreateDispatch("AutoServerApp.Document");

    if (!loaded)
        return -1;
    ```

    These lines load the automation server. If the server fails to load, the
    return value of -1 tells MFC that the window cannot be created properly
    and the application should terminate.

You've now completed the client application's view class. Next you'll add the
code needed to initialize ActiveX, after which you'll experiment with the server
and client applications to get a firsthand look at how they work together.

Initializing ActiveX in the client application

You'll be pleased to know that the AutoClientApp application is almost
complete. The final step is to enable ActiveX by calling the MFC
`AfxOleInit()` function. If you fail to do this, your client application will be
unable to access the server. The best place to call `AfxOleInit()` is in the
application class's `InitInstance()` function. Load the `CAutoClientAppApp`
class's implementation file, and add the following lines to the very beginning
of the `InitInstance()` function, right after the function's opening brace:

```
BOOL OleEnabled = AfxOleInit();
    if (!OleEnabled)
        return FALSE;
```

You've now completed the automation client application. In the following
section, you'll finally get to run both the server and the client and see the
power of automation.

Controlling the Server from the Client

Now that you've created both an automation server application and a client application, you're ready to see ActiveX automation in action. First, be sure that you've run the server application at least once. When you run the server the first time, it registers itself with Windows as an automation server. Until the server has been registered with Windows, the client application cannot control it.

Now, if the server application is still running, close it. You don't need to have the server running in order to control it from the client; the client application loads the server automatically. Run the AutoClientApp application, and you'll see the window shown in Figure 22-32.

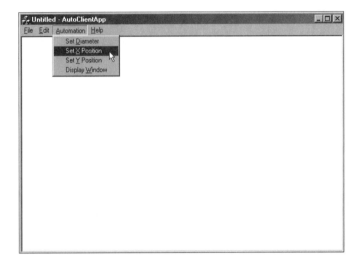

Figure 22-32: This is AutoClientApp when you first run it.

When you start AutoClientApp, although you can't see the server application, it's already loaded into memory. To prove this, select the Set Diameter command from the AutoClientApp's Automation menu. What happened? Nothing? Select the Set Diameter command a few more times. Still nothing? Actually, a lot is going on behind the scenes. Every time you select the Set Diameter command, AutoClientApp calls the automation server and changes the circle's diameter. The problem is that the server's window isn't visible, so you can't see the changes.

To remedy this problem, select the Display Window command from AutoClientApp's Automation menu. Up pops the server's window, and there you can see that your Set Diameter selections really did have an effect, because the circle is much larger that its default size, as shown in Figure 22-33. Arrange both windows (you can make the client application window smaller to save on room) so that you can see them both.

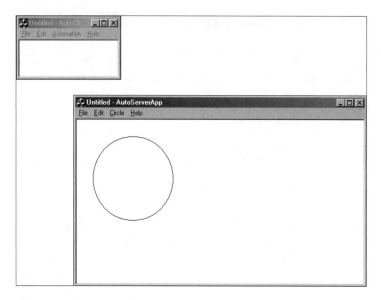

Figure 22-33: To make both windows visible on the screen, you can make the client window fairly small.

Now, select the Set Diameter, Set X Position, or Set Y Position commands in the client application's Automation menu. As you select these commands, you can watch the server application responding just as if you were selecting the commands from its own menu. Changing the X and Y positions results in moving the circle, as shown in Figure 22-34.

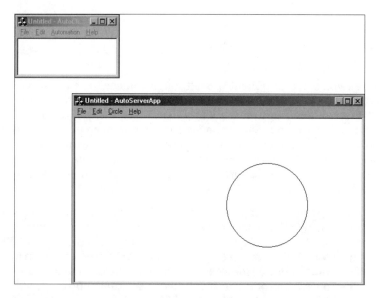

Figure 22-34: You can use the client application to move around the circle shown in the server application's window.

PROBLEMS & SOLUTIONS

Accessing Properties Directly

PROBLEM: *I want to be able to provide access to an automation server's properties without bothering with Get and Set methods. Is there some way I can give the properties public access, but still keep the application aware of when a property changes?*

SOLUTION: For most automation servers, indirect access to property values (using Get and Set methods) is the best way to go, in the same way that you usually give a class's member variables protected or private access attributes. However, rules are made to be broken, and there may be times when it makes sense to enable direct access of properties. In these cases, you can create a notification method for each property, which will be called whenever the property changes. Other applications, however, will be able to access the property's storage variable directly.

When you use ClassWizard to create your automation server's interface, select the Member Variable option in the Add Property dialog box instead of Get/Set Methods. For example, in Figure 22-35, the programmer is creating AutoServerApp's Diameter property using the Member Variable option. Notice in the figure how ClassWizard defines a notification method for the property. In the figure, the notification method is called `OnDiameterChanged()`. This is the function that gets called whenever an application changes the associated property directly.

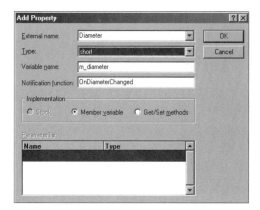

Figure 22-35: ClassWizard can also create notification functions for properties.

Summary

Using automation servers, you can provide program functionality to any application that can access the server. In this way, you can develop features once and reuse those features in future projects. In fact, any application that can create an interface class from the server's type library can access an object's properties and methods. A server can even provide multiple interfaces, and so offer a set of features to other programs.

Also discussed in this chapter:

► AppWizard provides options for generating ActiveX automation applications.

► An automation server provides programmable objects comprised of properties and methods to other applications.

► An automation client uses the features of an automation server.

► Automation servers expose their programmable objects to clients through an interface that ClassWizard can convert to a class.

► Normally, a client application indirectly accesses an object's properties through Get and Set methods.

► An interface can also include public properties that are associated with notification methods.

Chapter 23

ActiveX Controls

In This Chapter

▶ Creating a skeleton ActiveX control

▶ Creating an ActiveX control's user interface

▶ Creating a control's properties and methods

▶ Responding to the control button

▶ Testing an ActiveX control

ActiveX controls are like mini-applications that you can embed in other applications' windows. ActiveX controls are popping up all over the Word Wide Web, used in much the same way that some people use Java applets. Because ActiveX controls can do just about anything a small application can do, they enable Web developers to create Web pages that actually do something inside the user's browser, rather than just present information. On Web sites, you can find ActiveX controls that do everything from play tic-tac-toe to calculate the payment schedule on a loan. In this chapter, you get an introduction to creating ActiveX controls. Along the way, you'll create a working ActiveX control called *Scramble*. You can find the sample control in the Chapter23\Scramble folder of this book's CD-ROM.

Note

Programming ActiveX controls is a complex task that cannot be fully explained in a single chapter. This chapter is only an introduction to the programming techniques required to create a basic ActiveX control. After you master the topics in this chapter, if you want to learn more about ActiveX controls, you should pick up a book that concentrates on ActiveX control programming, such as *ActiveX Controls with Visual Basic 5.0* by Jose Mojica, published by IDG Books Worldwide.

Creating a Skeleton ActiveX Control

Just as you used AppWizard in previous projects to create skeleton programs, so too can you use Visual C++'s ActiveX ControlWizard to create a skeleton control. The resultant skeleton control is fully functional without your having to enter even one line of code. Of course, if you want to create a useful control, you'll have to do a little programming. In this section, you use ActiveX ControlWizard to create the basic control. In later sections, you'll change this skeleton control into a simple word-scramble game. Perform the following steps to create the skeleton control.

Note

You should read through all the application-building steps in this chapter, whether or not you actually build the ActiveX control yourself, because the steps include explanations of the programming techniques needed to build an ActiveX control.

1. Start a new MFC ActiveX ControlWizard project called *Scramble,* as shown in Figure 23-1.

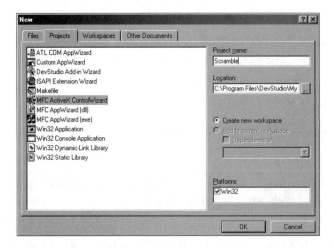

Figure 23-1: The new control project is called ***Scramble***.

2. In the MFC ActiveX ControlWizard - Step 1 of 2 dialog box, accept all default options and click the Finish button (see Figure 23-2).

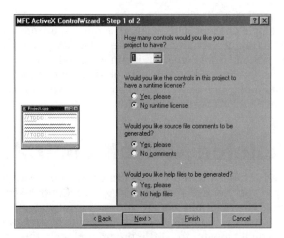

Figure 23-2: The default options will work fine for the sample ActiveX control.

3. Your New Project Information dialog box should look like the one in Figure 23-3, except your install directory may be different depending on the directory you chose when you created the project in Step 1.

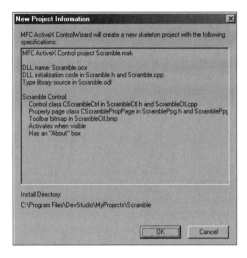

Figure 23-3: The New Project Information dialog box displays the ActiveX control's final options.

4. Click the OK button and ControlWizard generates the source code files for the skeleton application.

You've now completed the Scramble skeleton ActiveX control. Save your work by selecting the Save All command on Visual C++'s File menu. At this point, the application does nothing useful, so you don't need to compile the source files. Instead, continue on to the next set of steps, where you complete the control's user interface.

Creating the ActiveX Control's User Interface

Not all ActiveX controls are interactive in nature. For example, an ActiveX control might do nothing more than display a line of scrolling text. However, Scramble, being a simple game, requires a user interface through which the user can communicate with the control. In this section, you create that interface by completing the following steps:

1. Right-click `CScrambleCtrl` in the ClassView page of the Project Workspace window, and select the Add Member Variable command in the menu that appears.

2. In the Add Member Variable dialog box, type `CEdit` in the Variable Type box, type `m_edit` in the Variable Declaration box, and select the

Protected access option, as shown in Figure 23-4. The edit box you're adding to the class allows the user to enter information into the control.

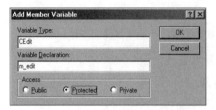

Figure 23-4: The edit control will enable the user to enter information into the control.

3. Bring up the Add Member Variable dialog box again and type `CButton` in the Variable Type box, type `m_button` in the Variable Declaration box, and select the Protected access option (see Figure 23-5). This button will be another interactive element of the ActiveX control, enabling the user to tell the control to process text entered into the edit box.

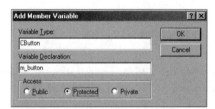

Figure 23-5: The button control will enable the user to finalize entries in the edit control.

4. Press Ctrl+W to display ClassWizard, and add the `OnCreate()` function, as shown in Figure 23-6.

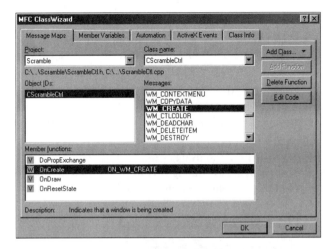

Figure 23-6: ClassWizard adding the OnCreate() function

5. Add the following lines to the OnCreate() function:

```
m_edit.Create(WS_CHILD | WS_BORDER | WS_VISIBLE |
    ES_AUTOHSCROLL, CRect(20, 70, 120, 100),
    this, IDC_EDIT);
m_button.Create("Submit", WS_CHILD | WS_BORDER |
    WS_VISIBLE | BS_PUSHBUTTON,
    CRect(130, 70, 230, 100), this, IDC_BUTTON);
```

6. Replace the pdc->Ellipse(rcBounds) line in the OnDraw() function with the lines in Listing 23-1.

Listing 23-1: Lines for the OnDraw() function

```
pdc->TextOut(20, 50, "Enter Answer:");

LOGFONT logFont;
logFont.lfHeight = 32;
logFont.lfWidth = 0;
logFont.lfEscapement = 0;
logFont.lfOrientation = 0;
logFont.lfWeight = FW_BOLD;
logFont.lfItalic = 0;
logFont.lfUnderline = 0;
logFont.lfStrikeOut = 0;
logFont.lfCharSet = ANSI_CHARSET;
logFont.lfOutPrecision = OUT_DEFAULT_PRECIS;
logFont.lfClipPrecision = CLIP_DEFAULT_PRECIS;
logFont.lfQuality = PROOF_QUALITY;
logFont.lfPitchAndFamily = VARIABLE_PITCH | FF_ROMAN;
strcpy(logFont.lfFaceName, "Times New Roman");
```

```
CFont font;
font.CreateFontIndirect(&logFont);
CFont* pOldFont = pdc->SelectObject(&font);
pdc->TextOut(20, 10, "ERSBCMLA");
pdc->SelectObject(pOldFont);
```

7. The OnDraw() function draws the control in the same way the OnDraw() function in a regular MFC application draws an application's window. In this case, OnDraw() displays two strings in the control, one of them with a large font.

   Select the Resource Symbols command from Visual C++'s View menu. The Resource Symbols dialog box appears, displaying the resource IDs defined in the program (see Figure 23-7).

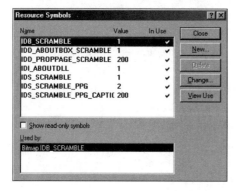

Figure 23-7: The Resource Symbols dialog box enables you to see defined IDs and how the IDs are used.

8. Click the New button, and type IDC_EDIT in the New Symbol dialog's Name box, as shown in Figure 23-8. (Visual C++ automatically provides a value.) Click OK to add the new resource symbol to the project. You'll use this ID to identify the ActiveX control's edit box.

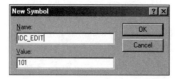

Figure 23-8: You can add resource symbols for the controls you added.

9. Click the New button again, and type IDC_BUTTON in the New Symbol dialog's Name box. Click OK to add the new symbol to the project. You'll use this ID to identify the ActiveX control's button.

You've now completed the control's basic user interface. At this point, you can see what the control looks like when its embedded in a program. First, select the Build Scramble.ocx command from Visual C++'s Build menu. Visual C++ compiles and links the control. Just as important, Visual C++ registers the new control with the system, so that you can include it in other applications or in Web pages.

To get a look at the new control, select the ActiveX Control Test Container command from Visual C++'s Tools menu. The test container application appears. In the text container's Edit menu, select the Insert OLE Control command (see Figure 23-9). In the Insert OLE Control dialog, find the Scramble Control in the Object Type box (see Figure 23-10), and double-click it. The control appears in the test container's window.

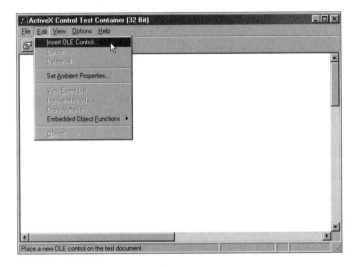

Figure 23-9: Selecting the Insert OLE Control command enables you to display your new control.

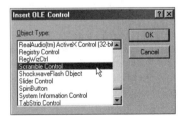

Figure 23-10: The Insert OLE Control dialog box lists the controls that are registered on your machine.

When the control first appears, use your mouse to resize and move it. Figure 23-11 shows the control after it's been resized and moved. That strange word at the top of the control is a scrambled version of "Scramble," the control's default puzzle. When the control is fully functioning, the user will be able to enter the answer to the puzzle in the edit box and click the Submit button to submit the answer to the control.

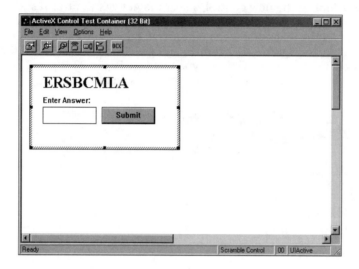

Figure 23-11: Here's the Scramble control displayed in a container window.

Creating Properties and Methods

As you know, an ActiveX control is a mini-application that can be placed in other applications' windows or in Web pages. By creating properties and methods for the control, you enable the control's user (user in this case means the person adding the control to a window) to customize the way the control looks and acts. For example, currently the Scramble control presents only a single word to unscramble. Once a player has solved that puzzle, there needs to be a way to replace the old puzzle with a new one. You can do this by making the scrambled word a property.

Methods are another feature of a control that determines how the control looks and acts. Methods are functions in a control that can be called from the control's container. The Scramble control already has one method generated by AppWizard, the function that displays its About dialog box. This method is called `AboutBox()` and looks like the following:

```
void CScrambleCtrl::AboutBox()
{
    CDialog dlgAbout(IDD_ABOUTBOX_SCRAMBLE);
    dlgAbout.DoModal();
}
```

You can add other methods to your controls as well. The scramble control, for example, will have methods for setting and getting properties. You create control properties in much the same way you create properties for automation applications. Perform the following steps to add properties and methods to the Scramble control:

1. Press Ctrl+W to display ClassWizard, and then click the Automation tab to display the Automation page.

2. Click the Add Property button. When the Add Property dialog appears, select the Get/Set Methods option, type ScrambleString in the External Name box (ClassWizard automatically fills in the Get and Set function names as you type), and select BSTR in the Type box, as shown in Figure 23-12. Click OK to create the property.

   The ScrambleString property of the Scramble control will hold the scrambled string. The BSTR is a data type used with strings in automation functions.

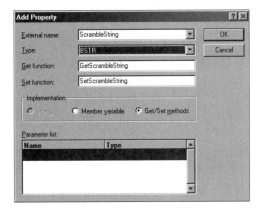

Figure 23-12: You use the Add Property dialog box to create your control's properties.

3. Click the Add Property button again. When the Add Property dialog appears, select the Get/Set Methods option, type AnswerString in the External Name box, and select BSTR in the Type box. Click OK to create the property.

   The AnswerString property of the Scramble control will hold the unscrambled string.

4. Right-click CScrambleCtrl in the ClassView page of the Project Workspace window and select Add Member Variable from the menu that appears.

5. In the Add Member Variable dialog, type CString in the Variable Type box, type m_scrambleStr in the Variable Declaration box, and select the Protected access option, as shown in Figure 23-13.

The m_scrambleStr member variable will hold the string assigned to the ScrambleString property.

Figure 23-13: Controls, like other classes, can define member variables.

6. Display the Add Member Variable dialog again; type CString in the Variable Type box, type m_answerStr in the Variable Declaration box, and select the Protected access option.

   The m_answerStr member variable will hold the string assigned to the AnswerString property.

7. Add the following line to the GetScrambleString() method, after the TODO comment:

   ```
   strResult = m_scrambleStr;
   ```

   This line sets the string to be returned by the function to the string stored in the m_scrambleStr member variable.

8. Add the following lines to the SetScrambleString() method, after the TODO comment:

   ```
   m_scrambleStr = lpszNewValue;
   InvalidateControl();
   ```

   These lines set the m_scrambleStr member variable to the new string value and then redraw the control.

9. Add the following line to the GetAnswerString() method, after the TODO comment:

   ```
   strResult = m_answerStr;
   ```

   This line sets the string to be returned by the function to the string stored in the m_answerStr member variable.

10. Add the following lines to the SetAnswerString() method, after the TODO comment:

    ```
    m_answerStr = lpszNewValue;
    InvalidateControl();
    ```

    These lines set the m_answerStr member variable to the new string value and then redraw the control.

11. In the OnDraw() function, change the "ERSBCMLA" in the call to TextOut() to m_scrambleStr.

The `OnDraw()` function will now display the current value of the `ScrambleString` property instead of a hard-coded value.

12. Add the following lines to the end of the `CScrambleCtrl()` constructor:

```
m_scrambleStr = "ERSBCMLA";
m_answerStr = "SCRAMBLE";
```

These lines give the `ScrambleString` and `AnswerString` properties their default values.

You've now created your ActiveX control's properties and methods. In the next section, you'll write the code that makes the control's button act as it should.

Responding to the Control's Button

You're almost there now. All you have to do is make the control's button respond to the user's clicks. You can do this using Windows messages, as you'll see when you complete the following steps:

1. Right-click `CScrambleCtrl` in the ClassView page of the Project Workspace window, and select Add Member Function from the menu that appears.

2. In the Add Member Function dialog, type `afx_msg void` in the Function Type box, type `OnButtonClicked()` in the Variable Declaration box, and select the Protected access option, as shown in Figure 23-14.

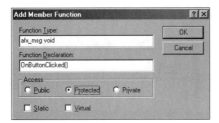

Figure 23-14: Controls can also define member functions.

3. Add the following line to the `CScrambleCtrl` class's message map (found near the top of the ScrambleCtrl.cpp file), right after the `ON_OLEVERB()` macro that's already there:

```
ON_BN_CLICKED(IDC_BUTTON, OnButtonClicked)
```

4. Add the lines in Listing 23-2 to the `OnButtonClicked()` function:

Listing 23-2: Lines for the `OnButtonClicked( )` **function**

```
CString str;
m_edit.GetWindowText(str);
str.MakeUpper( );

if (str == m_answerStr)
    m_edit.SetWindowText("Correct!");
else
    m_edit.SetWindowText("Incorrect");
```

Now, when the user clicks the Submit button, the control's `OnButtonClicked( )` function gets called, which extracts the contents of the edit box and compares the contents with the string that holds the scramble puzzle's answer. The function changes the edit box's contents to "Correct!" or "Incorrect," depending on the result of the comparison. You'll see this in action in just a moment.

You've now completed the Scramble control. Select the Build menu's Build Scramble.ocx command to compile, link, and register the control.

Testing the ActiveX Control

Now that you're done building the control, you can see Scramble do its stuff. Run ActiveX Control Text Container from Visual C++'s Tools menu. When the application appears, select the Insert OLE Control command from the container's Edit menu. Double-click Scramble Control in the Insert OLE Control dialog box, and then resize and position the control as shown in Figure 23-15.

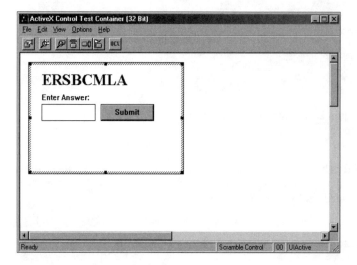

Figure 23-15: Here's the container application with the Scramble control.

Type the word "Scramble" into the edit box and click the Submit button. The word "Correct!" should appear in the edit box, because you've typed the answer to the default scramble, as shown in Figure 23-16.

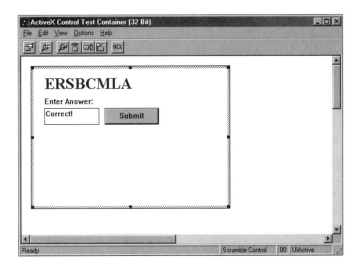

Figure 23-16: Here's the Scramble control after the user solves the puzzle.

The control wouldn't be much good if it were only capable of supplying one scramble puzzle. Fortunately, Scramble enables you to change its properties and create your own scramble puzzles. To try this, select the Properties command from the container application's View menu. The Properties dialog box appears. Select AnswerString in the Property list box, type **CONTROL** (all uppercase) into the Value box (see Figure 23-17), and click the Apply button.

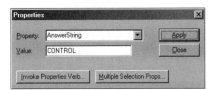

Figure 23-17: You can change Scramble's properties using the Properties dialog box.

Now, using the same procedure you used to set the AnswerString property, set the ScrambleString property to **LORTNOC**. When you click the Apply button, the control's displayed scramble string changes to the new one. If you type **CONTROL** into the text box and click the Submit button, the control tells you that you've entered the correct answer.

PROBLEMS & SOLUTIONS

Placing an ActiveX Control on a Web Page

PROBLEM: *I've got an ActiveX control that was created for my Web site, but I can't figure out how to include it in an HTML document. Help!*

SOLUTION: Including an ActiveX control in your Web page isn't much harder than including a Java applet. The biggest difference is that ActiveX controls are identified by a GUID (globally unique ID), and before you can add a control to a Web page, you have to know what that GUID is. An easy way to find the GUID is to look up the control in your Registry.

First, click your Windows 98 Start menu and select the Run command. When the Run dialog appears, type **regedit** into the Open box, and click the OK button. The Registry Editor appears on your screen and displays the main folders in your systems Registry (see Figure 23-18).

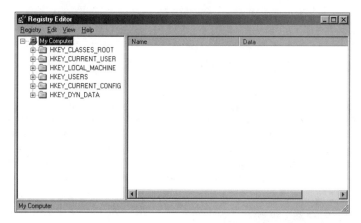

Figure 23-18: Windows 98's Registry Editor is a handy application for exploring your system's Registry.

Select the Edit menu's Find command. In the Find dialog box, type **Scramble Control** and click the Find Next button. The Registry Editor searches for the Scramble control in the registry. Press F3 to search again, until you find the SCRAMBLE.ScrambleCtrl.1 entry in the left-hand pane. You'll see that this entry has a subfolder called CLSID pane (see Figure 23-19). Click CLSID to display the control's GUID (also known as a class ID, or CLSID).

Continued

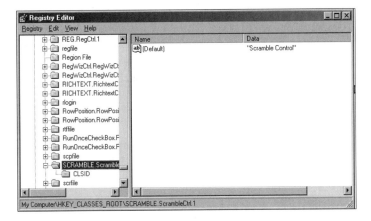

Figure 23-19: This is the Registry entry you're looking for.

Double-click the word "default" in the right-hand pane to bring up the ID in Value Data box of the Edit String dialog box (see Figure 23-20). Then, press Ctrl+C to copy the ID to the Clipboard. You'll need the ID to add the control to your HTML document, and it's a heck of a lot easier to copy it this way than to try to type it manually. Close the Registry Editor.

Figure 23-20: It's easy to copy the GUID from the Edit String dialog box.

The next step is to add the control to your HTML file, which you do with the <OBJECT> tag. Listing 23-3 is an example HTML document for the Scramble control.

Listing 23-3: Loading Scramble in an HTML document

```
<HTML>

<HEAD>
  <TITLE>ActiveX Control Example</TITLE>
</HEAD>

<BODY>
<CENTER>

<OBJECT classid="clsid:3206DCA8-6CA1-11D1-AB9F-50C153C10000"
  id=Scramble height=150 width=300>
</OBJECT>
```

Continued

```
</CENTER>
</BODY>
</HTML>
```

The <OBJECT> tag is similar to many other HTML tags, containing attributes that enable you to control the element's ID and size. The most important thing to notice about the <OBJECT> tag is the way it specifies the control's classid attribute. The value for this attribute is the GUID you found with the Registry Editor.

Summary

ActiveX controls take the idea of automation one step further, by enabling you to embed a programmable object into an application's window or a Web page. Creating an ActiveX control with Visual C++ and MFC is much easier than programming one from scratch, thanks to the MFC ActiveX Control Wizard. Using this handy wizard, you can concentrate on writing the code that makes your control do what it needs to do, rather than having to write the general code common to all ActiveX controls.

Also discussed in this chapter:

▶ Visual C++ provides the ActiveX ControlWizard, which is similar to AppWizard, for creating ActiveX controls.

▶ An MFC ActiveX control paints its display in the OnDraw() function, the same as any other MFC program.

▶ ActiveX controls feature properties that can be changed by applications or by scripts in a Web page.

▶ Container applications can call an ActiveX control's methods.

▶ The ActiveX Control Test Container application enables you to test ActiveX controls without having to write your own container applications or create an HTML document.

▶ You use the <OBJECT> tag to place ActiveX controls in an HTML document.

Part V

Multimedia

Chapter 24

DirectDraw

In This Chapter

▶ Creating a DirectDraw program

▶ Preparing Visual C++ for DirectDraw

▶ Creating a DirectDraw object

▶ Setting the screen access level

▶ Setting the display mode

▶ Creating DirectDraw surfaces

▶ Creating Offscreen surfaces

▶ Creating DirectDraw palettes

▶ Examining a sample DirectDraw application

This is the first chapter in an exploration of Microsoft's DirectX technologies. DirectX enables programmers to create multimedia programs for Windows unlike typical Windows programs. The most substantial feature in new DirectX applications is their ability to attain the graphical speeds needed to create even sophisticated games, something that Windows on its own has historically been poor at doing. In fact, DirectX is almost solely responsible for the explosion of new game titles for the Windows operating system. Previously, most games were written for DOS.

DirectX comprises several libraries, the most important of which are Direct Draw, DirectSound, DirectInput, and Direct3D. This chapter focuses on DirectDraw, whereas succeeding chapters cover the other libraries.

DirectDraw is just one of the several object libraries that make up Microsoft's DirectX applications. That fact notwithstanding, DirectDraw is sophisticated enough to warrant a thousand-page book of its own. Of course, this chapter doesn't have a thousand pages to dedicate to DirectDraw, but there is enough space to give you a taste of DirectDraw programming. You can then decide whether it's a topic that you want to pursue further.

Programming DirectDraw is a complex task that cannot be fully explained in a single chapter. This chapter is only an introduction to the programming techniques required to create a basic DirectDraw application. After you master the topics in this chapter, if you want to learn more about

DirectDraw, you should pick up a book that concentrates on DirectDraw programming, such as *Windows 95 Game SDK Strategy Guide* by Clayton Walnum, published by Que.

In order to run DirectDraw programs, you must have DirectX installed on your system. You can get a copy of the DirectX 5.0 SDK from Microsoft by pointing your Web browser to http://www.microsoft.com/directx/default.asp.

Creating a DirectDraw Program

In this chapter, you'll examine the basic steps you must complete to create most DirectDraw applications and build a sample DirectDraw program. To create a DirectDraw program, you must complete the following main steps:

1. Create a DirectDraw object. The DirectDraw object is the object through which you can access other DirectDraw capabilities.

2. Set the screen access level. Normally, a DirectDraw program requests exclusive control of the screen and palette, which prevents other programs from changing settings behind DirectDraw's back.

3. Set the display mode. The display mode determines the size of the screen and the number of colors that can be displayed.

4. Create a DirectDraw primary surface. A DirectDraw primary surface represents the display you see on the screen. The primary surface is often associated with one or more back buffers, which are used to animate the display.

5. Create offscreen surfaces for bitmaps. Most DirectDraw programs must display bitmaps, probably a lot of bitmaps. Off-screen surfaces are areas of memory where bitmaps reside.

6. Create DirectDraw palettes for surfaces. Just as with a conventional Windows program, the screen colors in a DirectDraw program are determined by a palette. Usually, the program constructs the DirectDraw palette from a bitmap's color table.

After completing these basic steps, your program can use DirectDraw to perform whatever graphics functions are required by your specific application. In many cases, your programs will use back buffers and bitmaps to animate the display. These techniques require additional programming steps. You'll learn how to add back buffers to your program in the "Creating Primary DirectDraw Surfaces" section of this chapter, while you'll take a closer look at bitmaps in the "Creating Offscreen Surfaces" section later in this chapter.

Often, DirectDraw programs are written without the use of application frameworks like MFC. This is because MFC can bring with it a lot of extra baggage that slows down an application—especially a game—that needs to run at its fastest speed. Compared with adding DirectDraw to an MFC program, though, creating a non-MFC DirectDraw program is straightforward.

Getting DirectDraw to run properly in an MFC program is the tricky part. The main part of this chapter focuses on writing an MFC DirectDraw program, while the "Problems & Solutions" section found in this chapter illustrates how to write such a program without MFC.

Adding DirectDraw Files to Your Visual C++ Project

The DirectDrawApp sample program that you'll examine later in this chapter was created by AppWizard as an SDI (single document) application with no extras such as a toolbar or status bar. By now, you should be comfortable with creating this type of skeleton application. There are a couple of extra steps, however, that you need to complete before you can compile and run an MFC DirectDraw program.

Adding the ddraw.h header file to your program

First, you must include in your program the ddraw.h header file, which contains declarations for the various DirectDraw functions, structures, and data types. Because the ddraw.h header file is included with Visual C++'s other header files, you only need to add the following line to modules that access the DirectDraw libraries:

```
#include <ddraw.h>
```

The angle brackets around the file name indicate that the header file is located in one of the default header-file directories, rather than in the project's directory. To see the default directories, select the Options command on Visual C++'s Tools menu. When the Options property sheet appears, select the Directories page and select Include Files in the Show Directories For list box (see Figure 24-1). DirectDrawApp includes the ddraw.h file in its view class's header file, called DirectDrawAppView.h.

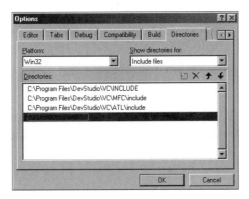

Figure 24-1: You can view and change the default directories in the Options property sheet.

Adding the ddraw.lib file to your program

Now that you've included the ddraw.h header file, you shouldn't have any problems compiling your DirectDraw program. Unfortunately, you'll quickly discover that the program won't link because it can't find the DirectDraw libraries. To correct this problem, you must add the ddraw.lib file to your project as illustrated in the following steps:

1. Select the Add to Project command on Visual C++'s Project menu.

2. Select the Files command from the submenu that appears, as shown in Figure 24-2.

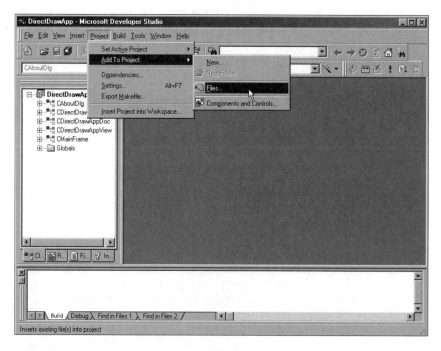

Figure 24-2: Visual C++ enables you to add files to your project.

3. Navigate to your c:\ProgramFiles\DevStudio\Vc\lib directory in the Insert Files Into Project dialog box.

4. Select the ddraw.lib file, as shown in Figure 24-3.

Figure 24-3: DirectDraw programs must link to the ddraw.lib file.

Now Visual C++ is set up to compile and link a DirectDraw program.

Creating a DirectDraw Object

To use DirectDraw in a program, you need to first create a DirectDraw object, through which you'll acquire access to the DirectDraw functions and objects. To create a DirectDraw object, you call `DirectDrawCreate()`, as follows:

```
LPDIRECTDRAW pDDraw;
HRESULT result = DirectDrawCreate(NULL,
    &pDDraw, NULL);
if (result != DD_OK)
{
    // Handle DirectDraw failure.
}
```

`LPDIRECTDRAW` represents a pointer to a DirectDraw object. In this case, the pointer is called `pDDraw`. You pass the address of the pointer as `DirectDrawCreate()`'s second argument (you'll usually use `NULL` for the other two arguments). If the function call succeeds, `DirectDrawCreate()` places the address of the DirectDraw object into the `pDDraw` pointer. To ensure that this pointer is valid, you must check `DirectDrawCreate()`'s return value, which should be `DD_OK` if the call succeeded. If the call fails, you can't use DirectDraw in the program.

Setting the Screen Access Level

With a pointer to a DirectDraw object in hand, your application can take over control of the computer's display. You do this by calling the DirectDraw object's `SetCooperativeLevel()` function:

```
result = pDDraw->SetCooperativeLevel(hFrameWnd,
    DDSCL_EXCLUSIVE | DDSCL_FULLSCREEN);
if (result != DD_OK)
{
    // Handle screen access failure.
}
```

SetCooperativeLevel() takes two arguments: the handle of the application's main window and the screen access flags. Usually, you'll use DDSCL_EXCLUSIVE | DDSCL_FULLSCREEN for the flags, giving your application exclusive access to the entire screen. Such access causes the application to run as a full-screen application, rather than a windowed application. SetCooperativeLevel(), like DirectDrawCreate(), returns DD_OK if the function call succeeds. If the call fails, you probably can't use DirectDraw in the program.

Setting the Display Mode

Your DirectDraw application's next task is to set the screen mode, which determines the size of the screen and the number of colors that can be displayed. You do this by calling the DirectDraw object's SetDisplayMode() function:

```
result = pDDraw->SetDisplayMode(640, 480, 8);
if (result != DD_OK)
{
    // Handle display mode failure.
}
```

SetDisplayMode()'s three arguments are the screen's horizontal resolution, the screen's vertical resolution, and the color depth expressed in color bits. The previous call to SetDisplayMode() creates a 640x480 screen with 256 colors (8-bit color). If the function succeeds, SetDisplayMode() returns DD_OK. If the call fails, you'll probably want to terminate the program, because the display won't be set up properly.

Creating the Primary DirectDraw Surface

Every DirectDraw program must have a primary surface, which is the object that represents the screen display. Often, a DirectDraw program will also have one or more back buffers associated with the primary surface. As mentioned at the beginning of this chapter, a back buffer enables you to add animation functionality to your DirectDraw program. More specifically, when a program creates back buffers, the program can perform page-flipping, a programming technique that makes smooth animation possible. (You'll learn about page-flipping when you examine the DirectDrawApp application later in this chapter.)

To create a primary surface with a back buffer, you call the DirectDraw object's CreateSurface() function, which involves initializing DDSURFACEDESC and DDSCAPS structures, as shown in Listing 24-1.

Listing 24-1: Creating a DirectDraw primary surface with a back buffer

```
LPDIRECTDRAWSURFACE pSurface;
DDSURFACEDESC ddsd;

memset(&ddsd, 0, sizeof(ddsd));
```

```
ddsd.dwSize = sizeof(ddsd);
ddsd.ddsCaps.dwCaps = DDSCAPS_PRIMARYSURFACE |
    DDSCAPS_FLIP | DDSCAPS_COMPLEX;
ddsd.dwBackBufferCount = 1;
ddsd.dwFlags = DDSD_CAPS | DDSD_BACKBUFFERCOUNT;
HRESULT result = pDDraw->CreateSurface(&ddsd,
    &pSurface, NULL);
if (result != DD_OK)
{
    // Handle surface-creation failure.
}
```

The `DDSURFACEDESC` structure, which is defined by DirectDraw, holds the data that describes a DirectDraw surface. There's not enough room in this chapter to fully describe this structure. However, the example in Listing 24-1 creates a primary surface with one back buffer. You can use this code verbatim to accomplish the same task. In Listing 24-1, the program first calls `memset()` to zero out the entire structure. The remaining lines then set the structure to create a flippable (you'll learn about page-flipping soon) primary surface with one back buffer.

The `CreateSurface()` function takes three arguments: the address of the DDSURFACEDESC structure, the address of a LPDIRECTDRAWSURFACE pointer, and NULL.

An `LPDIRECTDRAWSURFACE` pointer is the address of a DirectDraw surface. In the example, the `LPDIRECTDRAWSURFACE` pointer is called `pSurface`. If the call to `CreateSurface()` succeeds, `CreateSurface()` places the address of the new primary surface in `m_pSurface` and returns `DD_OK`. If the call fails, the pointer will be invalid and you won't be able to manipulate the DirectDraw surface.

Once you have the primary surface pointer, you need to get a pointer to the associated back buffer (if you requested a back buffer). You do this by calling the DirectDraw surface object's `GetAttachedSurface()` function. Assuming that the previous example came first in the program, you would call the DirectDraw surface object's `GetAttachedSurface()` function:

```
DDSCAPS ddsCaps;
LPDIRECTDRAWSURFACE pBackBuf;
ddsCaps.dwCaps = DDSCAPS_BACKBUFFER;
result = pSurface->
    GetAttachedSurface(&ddsCaps, &pBackBuf);
if (result != DD_OK)
{
    // Handle function failure.
}
```

The `DDSCAPS_BACKBUFFER` flag in the `DDSCAPS` structure specifies that `GetAttachedSurface()` should get the back-buffer pointer. `GetAttached Surface()` returns `DD_OK` if it succeeds. If the function call fails, the back-buffer pointer will be invalid, and your program will have no way to access the back buffer.

Creating Offscreen Surfaces

Once you have your main DirectDraw surfaces, you'll need additional surfaces for storing images. Most DirectDraw applications create their screens using many bitmaps to animate their displays. These bitmaps (which are usually DIBs) have to be stored in memory, where they'll be easily accessible in the program. DirectDraw uses offscreen surfaces for these bitmap storage areas. Creating an offscreen surface is similar to creating primary and back-buffer surfaces. The difference is the way you initialize the DDSURFACEDESC structure, as shown in Listing 24-2.

Listing 24-2: Creating a DirectDraw offscreen surface

```
LPDIRECTDRAWSURFACE pOffScrnSurf;
DDSURFACEDESC ddsd;
memset(&ddsd, 0, sizeof(ddsd));
ddsd.dwSize = sizeof(ddsd);
ddsd.dwHeight = 200;
ddsd.dwWidth = 200;
ddsd.dwFlags = DDSD_CAPS |
    DDSD_HEIGHT | DDSD_WIDTH;
ddsd.ddsCaps.dwCaps = DDSCAPS_OFFSCREENPLAIN;
HRESULT result = pDDraw->
    CreateSurface(&ddsd, &pOffScrnSurf, NULL);

if (result != DD_OK)
{
    // Handle failure.
}
```

The lines in Listing 24-2 create a 200x200 offscreen surface. As you can see, to create the surface, the program first initializes the DDSURFACEDESC structure and then calls the DirectDraw object's CreateSurface() function. As usual with DirectDraw functions, CreateSurface() returns DD_OK if it succeeds.

Creating DirectDraw Palettes

After creating the offscreen surfaces for your bitmaps, you copy the bitmaps onto the surfaces. You'll see how to tackle that task later in this chapter, when you examine the sample program. Before you can display those bitmaps, however, you have to create another type of DirectDraw object, a DirectDraw palette, which determines the colors you see on the screen. You create a DirectDraw palette by calling the DirectDraw object's CreatePalette() function:

```
PALETTEENTRY paletteEntries[256];
LPDIRECTDRAWPALETTE pDDrawPal;
HRESULT result = pDDraw->CreatePalette(DDPCAPS_8BIT,
    paletteEntries, &pDDrawPal, NULL);
```

```
if (result != DD_OK)
{
    // Handle palette failure.
}
```

`CreatePalette()` **requires four arguments:**

- A flag indicating the type of palette to create (`DDPCAPS_8BIT` for 256 colors)

- The address of a `PALETTEENTRY` structure containing the colors

- The address of a `LPDIRECTDRAWPALETTE` pointer

- `NULL`

If the function call succeeds, `CreatePalette()` returns `DD_OK`. (You already learned about PALETTEENTRY structures in Chapter 12, "Bitmaps." Please refer to that chapter if you need a quick refresher.)

Exploring the DirectDrawApp Sample Application

On CD-ROM

In the Chapter24\DirectDrawApp folder of this book's CD-ROM, you'll find the DirectDrawApp sample application, which is an MFC program that incorporates DirectDraw in order to display a simple animation sequence. When you run the program, your screen turns black, with a pulsing rectangle in the middle, as shown in Figure 24-4. (Before running the program, you may need to change your computer's display settings to any 256-color mode.) To exit the program, press Esc on your keyboard.

Figure 24-4: The DirectDrawApp application showing off its tricks

DirectDrawApp's `OnInitialUpdate()` function

Now that you've seen the program in action, take a look at the source code to see how the application initializes and manipulates DirectDraw. In an MFC program, a good place to initialize DirectDraw is in the view class's `OnInitialUpdate()` function, which you add to the class with ClassWizard, as shown in Figure 24-5. MFC calls `OnInitialUpdate()` once when the view class is first updated. At that point, the application's main window, represented by the `CMainFrame` class, has its window handle, which you need to create DirectDraw surfaces.

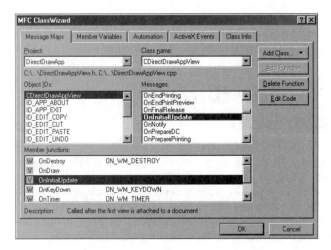

Figure 24-5: ClassWizard overriding the view class's `OnInitialUpdate()` function

Listing 24-3 shows DirectDrawApp's `OnInitialUpdate()` function

Listing 24-3: The `OnInitialUpdate()` function

```
void CDirectDrawAppView::OnInitialUpdate()
{
    CView::OnInitialUpdate();

    // TODO: Add your specialized code here
    //   and/or call the base class

    InitMemberVariables();

    BOOL okay = InitDirectDraw();
    if (!okay)
        return;
```

```
okay = CreateDDrawSurfaces();
if (!okay)
    return;

okay = ClearDDrawSurface(m_pBackBuf);
if (!okay)
    return;

okay = CreateOffScreenSurface();
if (!okay)
    return;

InitImages();

if (m_DDrawOK)
{
    DibToSurface(m_pDib, &CRect(0,0,488,499),
        m_pImages, &CPoint(0,0));
    SetTimer(1, 100, 0);
}
}
```

As you can see, the function calls other member functions—
`InitMemberVariables()`, `InitDirectDraw()`, `CreateDDrawSurfaces()`,
`ClearDDrawSurface()`, `CreateOffScreenSurface()`, `InitImages()`, and
`DibToSurface()`—to get the program set up for its animated display. If any of
these functions fail, `OnInitialUpdate()` immediately returns, discontinuing
any further DirectDraw initialization. This action leaves `m_DDrawOK` (a
member variable of the view class) set to `FALSE`, which indicates to other
functions that they should not call any DirectDraw functions.

DirectDrawApp's `InitMemberVariables()` function

The `InitMemberVariables()` function initializes the view class's member
variables to their default values. The member variables are declared in the
view class's header file like this:

```
UINT m_frame;
CDib* m_pDib;
BOOL m_DDrawOK;
LPDIRECTDRAW m_pDDraw;
LPDIRECTDRAWSURFACE m_pSurface;
LPDIRECTDRAWSURFACE m_pBackBuf;
LPDIRECTDRAWSURFACE m_pImages;
LPDIRECTDRAWPALETTE m_pDDrawPal;
```

Listing 24-4 shows the `InitMemberVariables()` function.

Listing 24-4: The `InitMemberVariables()` function

```
void CDirectDrawAppView::InitMemberVariables()
{
    m_frame = 0;
    m_pDib = NULL;
    m_DDrawOK = FALSE;
    m_pDDraw = NULL;
    m_pSurface = NULL;
    m_pBackBuf = NULL;
    m_pImages = NULL;
    m_pDDrawPal = NULL;
}
```

The program uses the following variables:

`m_frame`	An animation frame counter
`m_pDib`	A pointer to the program's bitmap object
`m_DDrawOK`	A flag indicating whether DirectDraw initialized successfully
`m_pDDraw`	A pointer to the application's DirectDraw object
`m_pSurface`	A pointer to the primary DirectDraw surface
`m_pBackBuf`	A pointer to the DirectDraw back-buffer surface
`m_pImages`	A pointer to the DirectDraw offscreen surface
`m_pDDrawPal`	A pointer to the DirectDraw palette object

DirectDrawApp's `InitDirectDraw()` function

In DirectDrawApp, it's the `InitDirectDraw()` function that creates the DirectDraw object, sets the screen access level, and sets the display mode. Listing 24-5 shows the `InitDirectDraw()` function.

Listing 24-5: The `InitDirectDraw()` function

```
BOOL CDirectDrawAppView::InitDirectDraw()
{
    HRESULT result = DirectDrawCreate(NULL,
        &m_pDDraw, NULL);
    if (result != DD_OK)
        return FALSE;

    CWnd* pFrameWnd = AfxGetMainWnd();
    HWND hFrameWnd = pFrameWnd->m_hWnd;
    result =
        m_pDDraw->SetCooperativeLevel(hFrameWnd,
```

```
                    DDSCL_EXCLUSIVE | DDSCL_FULLSCREEN);
        if (result != DD_OK)
            return FALSE;

        result = m_pDDraw->SetDisplayMode(640, 480, 8);
        if (result != DD_OK)
            return FALSE;

        return TRUE;
}
```

Notice how the function calls `AfxGetMainWnd()` to get a pointer to the frame window and, through the pointer, gets access to the window's handle. If you had tried to place this code in the view class's `OnCreate()` function, you would have discovered that the main window had not yet been created, and so doesn't have a handle. As with other DirectDrawApp initialization functions, if any initialization step fails, the function immediately returns, without trying to perform any further initialization.

DirectDrawApp's `CreateDDrawSurfaces()` function

DirectDrawApp's `CreateDDrawSurfaces()` function creates the DirectDraw primary and back-buffer surfaces. Listing 24-6 shows the `CreateDDrawSurfaces()` function. As with other DirectDrawApp initialization functions, if any step fails, the function immediately returns, without trying to perform further initialization.

Listing 24-6: The `CreateDDrawSurfaces()` function

```
BOOL CDirectDrawAppView::CreateDDrawSurfaces()
{
    DDSURFACEDESC ddsd;
    DDSCAPS ddsCaps;

    memset(&ddsd, 0, sizeof(ddsd));
    ddsd.dwSize = sizeof(ddsd);
    ddsd.ddsCaps.dwCaps = DDSCAPS_PRIMARYSURFACE |
        DDSCAPS_FLIP | DDSCAPS_COMPLEX;
    ddsd.dwBackBufferCount = 1;
    ddsd.dwFlags = DDSD_CAPS | DDSD_BACKBUFFERCOUNT;
    HRESULT result = m_pDDraw->
        CreateSurface(&ddsd, &m_pSurface, NULL);
    if (result != DD_OK)
        return FALSE;

    ddsCaps.dwCaps = DDSCAPS_BACKBUFFER;
    result = m_pSurface->
        GetAttachedSurface(&ddsCaps, &m_pBackBuf);
    if (result != DD_OK)
        return FALSE;

    return TRUE;
}
```

Previously in this chapter, you already saw much of the code in 24-6. If you need a refresher, please refer back to the section "Creating the Primary DirectDraw Surface."

DirectDrawApp's `ClearDDrawSurface()` function

DirectDrawApp's `ClearDDrawSurface()` function (see Listing 24-7) initializes a surface's memory area to all black (always color index 0 in Windows 98). Basically, the function gets a pointer to the memory area and fills the area with zeroes. Little in DirectDraw is that simple, however, including, as you'll soon see, this function.

Listing 24-7: The `ClearDDrawSurface()` function

```
BOOL CDirectDrawAppView::ClearDDrawSurface
    (LPDIRECTDRAWSURFACE pSurface)
{
    BOOL okay = FALSE;
    HRESULT result;
    DDSURFACEDESC ddsd;

    memset(&ddsd, 0, sizeof(ddsd));
    ddsd.dwSize = sizeof(ddsd);

    BOOL endLoop = FALSE;
    do
    {
        result = pSurface->Lock(NULL, &ddsd,
            DDLOCK_SURFACEMEMORYPTR, NULL);

        if (result == DDERR_SURFACELOST)
        {
            m_pSurface->Restore();
            m_pImages->Restore();
        }
        else if (result != DDERR_WASSTILLDRAWING)
            endLoop = TRUE;
    }
    while (!endLoop);

    if (result == DD_OK)
    {
        UINT height = ddsd.dwHeight;
        UINT width = ddsd.lPitch;
        char* buffer = (char*)ddsd.lpSurface;
        memset(buffer, 0, height * width);
        pSurface->Unlock(ddsd.lpSurface);
        okay = TRUE;
    }

    return okay;
}
```

Before manipulating surface memory, the surface must be locked by calling the surface object's Lock() function. When the program tries to lock the surface, it may encounter a couple of problems. First, due to the user's switching to another program or some other similar event, the program may have lost its DirectDraw surfaces. In this case, the program must call every surface's Restore() function. (In a full-featured DirectDraw program, the images in the surfaces may also need to be restored. That is, after restoring the surface objects, your program may have to copy the bitmaps back onto the surfaces.) The Lock() function returns DDERR_SURFACELOST if the surfaces need to be restored. ClearDDrawSurface() handles this error by restoring the surfaces.

Lock()'s function signature looks as shown below. The function's four arguments are described following the signature.

```
HRESULT Lock(
    LPRECT lpDestRect,
    LPDDSURFACEDESC lpDDSurfaceDesc,
    DWORD dwFlags,
    HANDLE hEvent
```

lpDestRect	A pointer to a RECT structure containing the destination rectangle to lock
lpDDSurfaceDesc	A pointer to the DirectDraw surface
dwFlags	Flags indicating the type of lock to perform
hEvent	A handle to an event. Currently not used, so should be NULL.

Another problem the program may encounter is trying to lock a surface while DirectDraw is still drawing the screen. In this case, Lock() returns DDERR_WASSTILLDRAWING, and your program must loop back and try Lock() again. Eventually, Lock() should return DD_OK, and your program can proceed. Lock()'s second argument is the address of a DDSURFACEDESC structure, which, when the function succeeds, will contain the address of the surface memory in its lpSurface member. You'll need this pointer to access the surface memory.

When the function has finished with the surface memory, it unlocks the surface with a call to the surface object's Unlock() function, whose single argument is the address of the surface memory to unlock.

DirectDrawApp's CreateOffScreenSurface() function

DirectDrawApp's CreateOffScreenSurface() function (see Listing 24-8) creates the offscreen surface in which the program stores its single bitmap. The surface gets created exactly as described earlier in this chapter. However, besides creating the offscreen surface, the function also specifies a transparent color for the surface. A transparent color is a color in a bitmap that you don't want to appear on the screen when the bitmap is copied. By defining a transparent color, you can display nonrectangular images on the screen, in much the same way you did in Chapter 12, "Bitmaps," when you displayed bitmaps using masks.

Listing 24-8: The `CreateOffScreenSurface()` **function**

```
BOOL CDirectDrawAppView::CreateOffScreenSurface()
{
    DDSURFACEDESC ddsd;

    memset(&ddsd, 0, sizeof(ddsd));
    ddsd.dwSize = sizeof(ddsd);
    ddsd.dwHeight = 499;
    ddsd.dwWidth = 488;
    ddsd.dwFlags = DDSD_CAPS |
        DDSD_HEIGHT | DDSD_WIDTH;
    ddsd.ddsCaps.dwCaps = DDSCAPS_OFFSCREENPLAIN;
    HRESULT result = m_pDDraw->
        CreateSurface(&ddsd, &m_pImages, NULL);

    if (result != DD_OK)
        return FALSE;

    DDCOLORKEY ddck;
    ddck.dwColorSpaceLowValue = 35;
    ddck.dwColorSpaceHighValue = 35;
    m_pImages->SetColorKey(DDCKEY_SRCBLT, &ddck);

    return TRUE;
}
```

As Listing 24-8 shows, to specify a transparent color for a DirectDraw surface, you first initialize a `DDCOLORKEY` structure with the low and high indexes of the transparent colors. In the case of a single transparent color, the low and high indexes are the same. After setting the index values, you call the surface object's `SetColorKey()` function to set the transparent color. In the `CreateOffScreenSurface()` function, the program selects color index 35 as a transparent color. This selection means that any pixel in the bitmap that has a color index of 35 will not appear when the image is copied.

DirectDrawApp's `InitImages()` **function**

DirectDrawApp's `InitImages()` function (see Listing 24-9) loads the bitmap from disk and calls `CreateDDrawPal()`, which creates a DirectDraw palette from the bitmap's color table.

Listing 24-9: The `InitImages()` **function**

```
void CDirectDrawAppView::InitImages()
{
    m_pDib = new CDib("frames.bmp");
    m_pDDrawPal =
        CreateDDrawPal(m_pDDraw, m_pDib);
    if (m_pDDrawPal != NULL)
```

```
    {
        HRESULT result =
            m_pSurface->SetPalette(m_pDDrawPal);
        if (result == DD_OK)
            m_DDrawOK = TRUE;
    }
}
```

If the program creates the DirectDraw palette object successfully, `InitImages()` calls the surface object's `SetPalette()` function to assign the palette to the surface. `SetPalette()` takes a `LPDIRECTDRAWPALETTE` (which is a pointer to a DirectDraw palette object) value as its single argument, and returns `DD_OK` if the function successfully sets the palette. If you don't remember the `CDib` class, you should review Chapter 12, "Bitmaps."

DirectDrawApp's `CreateDDrawPal()` function

DirectDrawApp's `CreateDDrawPal()` function creates a DirectDraw palette object from a DIB's color table, as shown in Listing 24-10. If you remember creating palettes in Chapter 12, you'll see some familiar stuff here.

Listing 24-10: The `CreateDDrawPal()` function

```
LPDIRECTDRAWPALETTE CDirectDrawAppView::CreateDDrawPal
    (LPDIRECTDRAW pDDraw, CDib * pDib)
{
    PALETTEENTRY paletteEntries[256];
    LPDIRECTDRAWPALETTE pDDrawPal;
    LPRGBQUAD pRGB = pDib->GetRGB();

    for (int x=0; x<256; ++x)
    {
        paletteEntries[x].peRed = pRGB[x].rgbRed;
        paletteEntries[x].peGreen = pRGB[x].rgbGreen;
        paletteEntries[x].peBlue = pRGB[x].rgbBlue;
    }

    HRESULT result = pDDraw->CreatePalette(DDPCAPS_8BIT,
        paletteEntries, &pDDrawPal, NULL);

    if (result != DD_OK)
        pDDrawPal = NULL;

    return pDDrawPal;
}
```

Basically, the function copies the colors from the DIB's color table into a `PALETTEENTRY` structure, and then calls the DirectDraw object's `CreatePalette()` function to create the palette object.

CreatePalette() takes four arguments:

- A flag specifying the palette type (DDPCAPS_8BIT creates a 256-color palette.)
- The address of the PALETTEENTRY structure
- The address of a pointer to a DirectDraw palette object
- NULL

If CreatePalette() returns DD_OK, the function returns a pointer to the palette object. If the call to CreatePalette() succeeds, the function returns DD_OK.

DirectDrawApp's DibToSurface() function

You can use GDI functions to draw on a DirectDraw surface. However, GDI functions are often slow, one of the reasons you're using DirectDraw in the first place. More importantly, there are no GDI functions for displaying DIBs, which are the most common image type used with DirectDraw programs. For these reasons, DirectDraw programmers often write their own graphics display routines. One such routine you've already seen is ClearDDrawSurface(), which fills a DirectDraw surface with black pixels. Now you can take a look at DibToSurface(), a function that copies all or part of a DIB to a DirectDraw surface (see Listing 24-11).

Listing 24-11: The DibToSurface() function

```
void CDirectDrawAppView::DibToSurface(CDib * pDib,
    CRect * srcRect, LPDIRECTDRAWSURFACE pSurface,
    CPoint * destPt)
{
    DDSURFACEDESC ddsd;

    memset(&ddsd, 0, sizeof(ddsd));
    ddsd.dwSize = sizeof(ddsd);

    HRESULT result;
    BOOL endLoop = FALSE;
    do
    {
        result = pSurface->Lock(NULL, &ddsd,
            DDLOCK_SURFACEMEMORYPTR, NULL);

        if (result == DDERR_SURFACELOST)
        {
            m_pImages->Restore();
            m_pSurface->Restore();
        }
        else if (result != DDERR_WASSTILLDRAWING)
            endLoop = TRUE;
    }
    while (!endLoop);
```

```
if (result == DD_OK)
{
    char* pSurfData = (char*)ddsd.lpSurface +
        (destPt->y * ddsd.lPitch) + destPt->x;

    UINT dibH = pDib->GetHeight();
    UINT dibW = pDib->GetWidth();
    UINT srcH = (UINT)srcRect->Height();
    UINT srcW = (UINT)srcRect->Width();

    char* pDibData = (((char*)pDib->GetData()) +
        (dibH-1) * dibW) - srcRect->top *
        dibW + srcRect->left;

    for (UINT x=0; x<srcH; ++x)
    {
        memcpy(pSurfData, pDibData, srcW);

        pSurfData += ddsd.lPitch;
        pDibData -= dibW;
    }

    pSurface->Unlock(NULL);
}
}
```

In Listing 24-11, DibToSurface() gets called in OnInitialUpdate(). There,
DibToSurface() copies the entire frames.bmp image into the m_pImages
offscreen surface. Once DibToSurface() copies the image to the surface,
DirectDraw can do its part to create the program's display. DibToSurface()
requires four arguments:

pDib	A pointer to the CDib object that represents the bitmap to copy
srcRect	A pointer to a CRect object holding the source rectangle
pSurface	A pointer to the destination DirectDraw surface
dstPoint	A pointer to a CPoint object holding the destination coordinates in the surface

Like ClearDDrawSurface(), DibToSurface() must lock the DirectDraw surface
before it can access the surface memory. It must also unlock the surface
when it's finished with it. The part of the function that copies bitmap data to
the surface is straight C++ that calculates the destination address for the
data, calculates the address of a row of bitmap data, and copies that bitmap
data to the surface. There's been no effort to optimize the function. You C++
experts out there should be able to streamline the function quite a bit, if you
feel compelled to do so.

DirectDrawApp's OnTimer() function

DirectDrawApp's OnTimer() function is where the animation actually occurs. The OnInitialUpdate() function gets a Windows timer started, which causes Windows to send WM_TIMER events to the application 10 times a second. In an MFC program, an application can handle these messages in the view class's OnTimer() message-response function, which you add to the class using ClassWizard. Calling the OnTimer function is shown in Listing 24-12.

Listing 24-12: The OnTimer() function

```
void CDirectDrawAppView::OnTimer(UINT nIDEvent)
{
    // TODO: Add your message handler code here
    //    and/or call default

    int x, y;

    m_frame += 1;
    if (m_frame > 7)
        m_frame = 0;

    switch (m_frame)
    {
        case 0: x = 1;    y = 1; break;
        case 1: x = 163; y = 1; break;
        case 2: x = 325; y = 1; break;
        case 3: x = 1;    y = 163; break;
        case 4: x = 163; y = 163; break;
        case 5: x = 325; y = 163; break;
        case 6: x = 1;    y = 325; break;
        case 7: x = 163; y = 325;
    }

    ClearDDrawSurface(m_pBackBuf);

    m_pBackBuf->BltFast(250, 170, m_pImages,
        CRect(x, y, x+160, y+160),
        DDBLTFAST_SRCCOLORKEY | DDBLTFAST_WAIT);

    m_pSurface->Flip(NULL, DDFLIP_WAIT);

    CView::OnTimer(nIDEvent);
}
```

In DirectDrawApp, the OnTimer() function (see Listing 24-12) first increments the animation frame counter in order to determine which image to display next. The function then gets the coordinates in the bitmap for the appropriate image. (The frames.bmp bitmap contains all eight images used in the animation, as seen in Figure 24-6.)

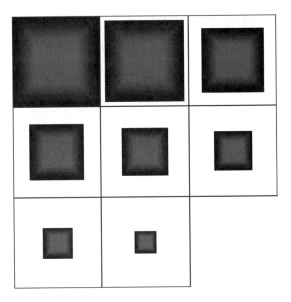

Figure 24-6: The frames that make up the program's animation sequence

The function then clears the back-buffer surface and calls the back-buffer surface's BltFast() function, which copies the appropriate portion of the bitmap to the back buffer. BltFast() takes five arguments:

■ A destination X coordinate

■ A destination Y coordinate

■ A pointer to the offscreen surface containing the image to copy

■ A pointer to a CRect object holding the source rectangle

■ Flags specifying the type of operation

In OnTimer() function, the flags used with BltFast() are DDBLTFAST_, SRCCOLORKEY, and DDBLTFAST_WAIT, with the former specifying that the copy should use the transparent color keys, and the latter specifying that the function should automatically deal with the DDERR_WASSTILLDRAWING error.

Finally, OnTimer() calls the primary surface object's Flip() function, which brings the back buffer into view on the screen and makes the original primary surface memory into the new back buffer. This flipping between the primary and back-buffer surfaces is what produces the animation, similar to those flip books you get in boxes of Cracker Jack.

DirectDrawApp's OnKeyDown() **function**

DirectDrawApp's OnKeyDown() function (see Listing 24-13) enables the user to terminate the program. MFC calls OnKeyDown() whenever the user presses a key on the keyboard, which generates a WM_KEYDOWN message. You add the OnKeyDown() function to your MFC program using ClassWizard.

Listing 24-13: The OnKeyDown() **function**

```
void CDirectDrawAppView::OnKeyDown(UINT nChar,
    UINT nRepCnt, UINT nFlags)
{
    // TODO: Add your message handler code here
    //    and/or call default

    if (nChar == VK_ESCAPE)
    {
        CWnd* pParentWnd = GetParentFrame();
        pParentWnd->PostMessage(WM_CLOSE);
    }

    CView::OnKeyDown(nChar, nRepCnt, nFlags);
}
```

As Listing 24-13 shows, DirectDrawApp's version of OnKeyDown() watches for the Esc key. When that keystroke arrives, the function sends a WM_CLOSE message to the application's frame window, which closes the application.

DirectDrawApp's OnDestroy() **function**

MFC calls the OnDestroy() function just before the window is destroyed, so it's also a good place to release resources that the program may have allocated for the window. In the case of DirectDrawApp, those resources are the various DirectDraw objects and the bitmap object. To release DirectDraw objects, you don't call delete on their pointers. Instead, you call their Release() functions, but you must be sure to release the objects in the right order, as shown in Listing 12-14.

Listing 24-14: The OnDestroy() **function**

```
void CDirectDrawAppView::OnDestroy()
{
    CView::OnDestroy();

    // TODO: Add your message handler code here

    KillTimer(1);

    if (m_pDDrawPal != NULL)
        m_pDDrawPal->Release();

    if (m_pSurface != NULL)
        m_pSurface->Release();
```

```
        if (m_pDDraw != NULL)
            m_pDDraw->Release();

        if (m_pDib != NULL)
            delete m_pDib;
}
```

As Listing 24-14 indicates, you first need to release the palettes, followed by the surfaces, and last of all, the DirectDraw object. You can add the OnDestroy() function to your program using ClassWizard.

Note

DirectDraw creates its objects following the specifications for COM objects. This is why you must call DirectDraw object's Release() functions rather than destroy them via the delete operator. Because COM objects can be used by more than one process, the objects keep internal counters. These counters are incremented when a program creates the object, and decremented when the program calls the object's Release() function. When the object's count is decremented to zero, the system removes the object from memory.

PROBLEMS & SOLUTIONS

Writing a Conventional DirectDraw Windows Application

PROBLEM: *OK, so now I know how to write an MFC DirectDraw program. What if I'd just as soon do without the extra baggage and write my program without MFC? What's the trick?*

SOLUTION: Truth be told, many programmers create their DirectDraw programs without help from MFC. The easiest way to accomplish this task is to write a traditional Windows program, but write it as a C++ program, rather than a C program. The reason for this is that the syntax for calling DirectDraw functions in a C program is fairly clumsy, whereas the C++ syntax is what you're already used to using.

Note

If you've forgotten how to write a traditional Windows application, you might want to take the time now to review Chapter 4, "Application Fundamentals."

To create a DirectDraw application as a conventional Windows program, first write the basic application as you normally would, providing a WinMain() function that defines and registers your window class, as well as contains the application's message loop. You'll also need to provide a Windows procedure that responds to the many messages for which Windows will target your application. In your basic Windows procedure, you'll want to respond at least to the WM_DESTROY message.

Continued

On CD-ROM

Once you have the basic application built, you can add the DirectDraw program code. In your Windows procedure, respond to the WM_CREATE message by initializing your program and setting up DirectDraw. You then might start a Windows timer to control an animation sequence, calling DirectDraw's Flip() method to display the back buffer. As you can see in Listing 24-15, the entire process is actually less complicated than trying to wedge DirectDraw into an MFC program. You can find the program in the Chapter24\DirectDrawApp2 folder of this book's CD-ROM.

Listing 24-15: Source code for the DirectDrawApp2 application

```
#include <windows.h>
#include <ddraw.h>

/* Function prototypes */
LRESULT CALLBACK WndProc(HWND hWnd, UINT message,
    WPARAM wParam, LPARAM lParam);
void InitVariables();
BOOL InitDirectDraw(HWND hWnd);
BOOL CreateDDrawSurfaces();
BOOL ClearDDrawSurface(LPDIRECTDRAWSURFACE pSurface);

/* Global variables */
LPDIRECTDRAW pDDraw;
LPDIRECTDRAWSURFACE pSurface;
LPDIRECTDRAWSURFACE pBackBuf;

int WINAPI WinMain(HINSTANCE hCurrentInst,
    HINSTANCE hPrevInstance, PSTR lpszCmdLine,
    int nCmdShow)
{
    WNDCLASS wndClass;
    HWND hWnd;
    MSG msg;
    UINT width;
    UINT height;

    wndClass.style = CS_HREDRAW | CS_VREDRAW;
    wndClass.lpfnWndProc = WndProc;
    wndClass.cbClsExtra = 0;
    wndClass.cbWndExtra = 0;
    wndClass.hInstance = hCurrentInst;
    wndClass.hIcon = LoadIcon(NULL, IDI_APPLICATION);
    wndClass.hCursor = LoadCursor(NULL, IDC_ARROW);
    wndClass.hbrBackground = GetStockObject(WHITE_BRUSH);
    wndClass.lpszMenuName = NULL;
    wndClass.lpszClassName = "DDrawApp";

    RegisterClass(&wndClass);

    width = GetSystemMetrics(SM_CXSCREEN) / 2;
    height = GetSystemMetrics(SM_CYSCREEN) / 2;
```

Continued

```
        hWnd = CreateWindow(
            "DDrawApp",            /* Window class's name.    */
            "DirectDraw App",      /* Title bar text.         */
            WS_OVERLAPPEDWINDOW,   /* The window's style.     */
            10,                    /* X position.             */
            10,                    /* Y position.             */
            width,                 /* Width.                  */
            height,                /* Height.                 */
            NULL,                  /* Parent window's handle. */
            NULL,                  /* Menu handle.            */
            hCurrentInst,          /* Instance handle.        */
            NULL);                 /* No additional data.     */

        ShowWindow(hWnd, nCmdShow);
        UpdateWindow(hWnd);

        while (GetMessage(&msg, NULL, 0, 0))
        {
            TranslateMessage(&msg);
            DispatchMessage(&msg);
        }

        return msg.wParam;
}

LRESULT CALLBACK WndProc(HWND hWnd, UINT message,
        WPARAM wParam, LPARAM lParam)
{
        switch(message)
        {
            case WM_CREATE:
                InitVariables();
                InitDirectDraw(hWnd);
                CreateDDrawSurfaces();
                ClearDDrawSurface(pBackBuf);
                SetTimer(hWnd, 1, 1000, 0);
                return 0;

            case WM_TIMER:
                pSurface->Flip(NULL, DDFLIP_WAIT);
                return 0;

            case WM_KEYDOWN:
                if (wParam == VK_ESCAPE)
                    PostQuitMessage(0);
                return 0;

            case WM_DESTROY:
                KillTimer(hWnd, 1);

                if (pSurface != NULL)
                    pSurface->Release();
```

Continued

```
                    if (pDDraw != NULL)
                        pDDraw->Release();

                    PostQuitMessage(0);
                    return 0;
        }

    return DefWindowProc(hWnd, message, wParam, lParam);
}

void InitVariables()
{
    pDDraw = NULL;
    pSurface = NULL;
    pBackBuf = NULL;
}

BOOL InitDirectDraw(HWND hWnd)
{
    HRESULT result = DirectDrawCreate(NULL,
        &pDDraw, NULL);
    if (result != DD_OK)
        return FALSE;

    result = pDDraw->SetCooperativeLevel(hWnd,
        DDSCL_EXCLUSIVE | DDSCL_FULLSCREEN);
    if (result != DD_OK)
        return FALSE;

    result = pDDraw->SetDisplayMode(640, 480, 8);
    if (result != DD_OK)
        return FALSE;

    return TRUE;
}

BOOL CreateDDrawSurfaces()
{
    DDSURFACEDESC ddsd;
    DDSCAPS ddsCaps;

    memset(&ddsd, 0, sizeof(ddsd));
    ddsd.dwSize = sizeof(ddsd);
    ddsd.ddsCaps.dwCaps = DDSCAPS_PRIMARYSURFACE |
        DDSCAPS_FLIP | DDSCAPS_COMPLEX;
    ddsd.dwBackBufferCount = 1;
    ddsd.dwFlags = DDSD_CAPS | DDSD_BACKBUFFERCOUNT;
    HRESULT result = pDDraw->
        CreateSurface(&ddsd, &pSurface, NULL);
    if (result != DD_OK)
        return FALSE;
```

Continued

```
            ddsCaps.dwCaps = DDSCAPS_BACKBUFFER;
            result = pSurface->
                GetAttachedSurface(&ddsCaps, &pBackBuf);
            if (result != DD_OK)
                return FALSE;

            return TRUE;
        }

        BOOL ClearDDrawSurface(LPDIRECTDRAWSURFACE pSurface)
        {
            BOOL okay = FALSE;
            HRESULT result;
            DDSURFACEDESC ddsd;

            memset(&ddsd, 0, sizeof(ddsd));
            ddsd.dwSize = sizeof(ddsd);

            BOOL endLoop = FALSE;
            do
            {
                result = pSurface->Lock(NULL, &ddsd,
                    DDLOCK_SURFACEMEMORYPTR, NULL);

                if (result == DDERR_SURFACELOST)
                    pSurface->Restore();
                else if (result != DDERR_WASSTILLDRAWING)
                    endLoop = TRUE;
            }
            while (!endLoop);

            if (result == DD_OK)
            {
                UINT height = ddsd.dwHeight;
                UINT width = ddsd.lPitch;
                char* buffer = (char*)ddsd.lpSurface;
                memset(buffer, 0, height * width);
                pSurface->Unlock(ddsd.lpSurface);
                okay = TRUE;
            }

            return okay;
        }
```

Although Listing 24-15 initializes DirectDraw in much the same way as this chapter's previous program, DirectDrawApp, it doesn't manipulate bitmaps. The bitmap manipulations were left out so that you could better see what it takes to get DirectDraw up and running in a traditional Windows program. The program in Listing 24-15, however, does perform simple animation. When you run the program, it continually flips between the primary and back buffers. To terminate the program, simply press your keyboard's Esc key. All of the DirectDraw code in the program should be familiar to you by now. If you don't understand the program, you need to reread this chapter from the beginning.

Summary

Getting DirectDraw set up and ready to run is actually not as complex a process as you might have thought. You just create a DirectDraw main object, create a few DirectDraw surfaces (primary, back-buffer, and offscreen), create palettes for your bitmaps, and load the bitmaps into their offscreen surfaces. Of course, what you do with DirectDraw after you get it up and running is the real art of DirectDraw programming. This chapter gave you a quick introduction to the technology; it would take hundreds of pages to describe all of DirectDraw's capabilities.

Now that you've had a little experience with DirectDraw, you might want to spend some time on your own, investigating the DirectX libraries. The DirectX SDK includes hundreds of pages of documentation that'll let you pick up where you left off here. In the next chapter, you get a look at DirectSound, the DirectX library that enables Windows applications to better deal with sound cards.

Also discussed in this chapter:

▶ A DirectDraw application must first create a DirectDraw object.

▶ The application can set up the display by calling `SetCooperativeLevel()` and `SetDisplayMode()` through the DirectDraw object.

▶ The primary DirectDraw surface represents the screen display.

▶ Primary DirectDraw surfaces are often associated with back-buffer surfaces that can be used for page-flipping.

▶ Offscreen DirectDraw surfaces provide storage for the images a program needs to create its display.

▶ DirectDraw palettes provide the colors for a display.

Chapter 25

DirectSound

In This Chapter

▶ Creating a DirectSound program

▶ Preparing Visual C++ for DirectSound

▶ Creating a DirectSound object

▶ Setting the sound-hardware access level

▶ Creating DirectSound buffers

▶ Examining a sample DirectSound application

DirectSound is probably the second most important component of the DirectX libraries. What, after all, would a modern game be without sound? Using DirectSound, you can let Windows' drivers worry about the system's sound card. You just create your sound effects, load them into the program, and play them. In this chapter, you'll see how to get started with DirectSound.

Programming DirectSound is a complex task that cannot be fully explained in a single chapter. This chapter is only an introduction to the programming techniques required to create a basic DirectSound application. After you master the topics in this chapter, if you want to learn more about DirectSound, you should pick up a book that concentrates on DirectX programming, such as *Windows 95 Game SDK Strategy Guide* by Clayton Walnum, published by Que.

In order to run DirectSound programs, you must have DirectX installed on your system. You can get a copy of the DirectX 5.0 SDK from Microsoft by pointing your Web browser to http://www.microsoft.com/directx/default.asp.

Creating a DirectSound Program

Because DirectDraw and DirectSound were developed together, you'll see a lot of similarities in the ways you use them in your programs. As with the previous chapter, you will build a sample DirectSound application while examining the basic steps you must complete to create most DirectSound applications.

To create a DirectSound program, you must complete the following main steps:

1. Create a DirectSound object. The DirectSound object is the object through which you can access other DirectSound capabilities.

2. Set the sound-hardware access level. Normally, a DirectSound program requests normal control of the system's sound hardware, which gives the application nonexclusive access to the sound card.

3. Create DirectSound secondary buffers. A DirectSound secondary buffer represents a sound in your program. You'll usually create a secondary sound buffer for each sound you want to play.

After completing these basic steps, your program can use DirectSound to play the sound effects loaded into your application.

Note

Often, DirectSound programs are written without the use of an application frameworks like MFC. This is because MFC can bring with it a lot of extra baggage that slows down an application—especially a game—that needs to run at its fastest speed. Compared with adding DirectSound to an MFC program, though, creating a non-MFC DirectSound program is straightforward. Getting DirectSound to run properly in an MFC program is the tricky part. The main part of this chapter will therefore focus on writing an MFC DirectSound program, while the "Problems & Solutions" section found in this chapter illustrates how to write such a program without MFC.

Adding DirectSound Files to Your Visual C++ Project

The DirectSoundApp sample program that you'll examine later in this chapter was created by AppWizard as an SDI (single document) application with no extras such as a toolbar or status bar. By now, you should be comfortable with creating this type of skeleton application. There are a couple of extra steps, however, that you need to complete before you can compile and run an MFC DirectSound program.

Adding the dsound.h header file

First, you must include in your program the dsound.h header file, which contains declarations for the various DirectSound functions, structures, and data types. Because the dsound.h header file is included with Visual C++'s other header files (in version 5.0), you only need to add the following line to modules that access the DirectSound libraries:

```
#include <dsound.h>
```

The angle brackets around the file name indicate that the header file is located in one of the default header-file directories, rather than in the project's directory.

Now that you've included the dsound.h header file, you should have no trouble compiling your DirectSound program.

Adding the dsound.lib file

As with DirectDraw, you'll quickly discover that the program won't link because it can't find the DirectSound libraries. To correct this problem, you must add the dsound.lib file to your project. To do this, follow these steps:

1. Select the Add to Project command on Visual C++'s Project menu (see Figure 25-1).

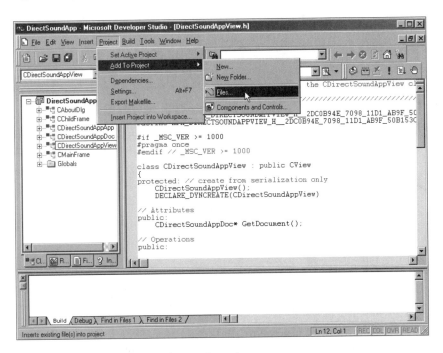

Figure 25-1: You can easily add files to the project.

2. Select the Files command from the submenu that appears.

3. Navigate to your c:\ProgramFiles\DevStudio\Vc\lib directory in the Insert Files Into Project dialog box.

4. Select the dsound.lib file, as shown in Figure 25-2.

Figure 25-2: DirectSound programs must link to the dsound.lib file.

Now, Visual C++ is set up to compile and link a DirectSound program.

Creating a DirectSound Object

To use DirectSound in a program, you must create a DirectSound object, through which you'll acquire access to the DirectSound functions. To create a DirectSound object, call `DirectSoundCreate()`:

```
LPDIRECTSOUND pDS;
HRESULT result =
    DirectSoundCreate(NULL, &pDS, NULL);
if (result != DS_OK)
{
    // Handle DirectSound failure.
}
```

`LPDIRECTSOUND` represents a pointer to a DirectSound object. In this case, the pointer is called `pDS`. You pass the address of the pointer as `DirectSoundCreate()`'s second argument (you'll usually use `NULL` for the other two arguments). If the function call succeeds, `DirectSoundCreate()` places the address of the DirectSound object into the `pDS` pointer. To ensure that this pointer is valid, you must check `DirectSoundCreate()`'s return value, which should be `DS_OK` if the call succeeds.

Note

To see the code applied, examine the DirectSoundApp application.

Setting the Sound-Hardware Access Level

With a pointer to a DirectSound object in hand, your application can get access to the computer's sound card. You do this by calling the DirectSound object's `SetCooperativeLevel()` function:

```
result = pDS ->
    SetCooperativeLevel(hMainWnd, DSSCL_NORMAL);
if (result != DS_OK}
{
```

```
        // Handle sound access failure.
}
```

`SetCooperativeLevel()` **takes two arguments: the handle of the application's**
main window and the sound hardware access flags. Usually, you'll use
`DSSCL_NORMAL` **for the flags, giving your application access to sound**
hardware, but still allowing multitasking to function properly.
`SetCooperativeLevel()`, **like** `DirectSoundCreate()`, **returns** `DS_OK` **if the**
function call succeeds.

Creating the Secondary DirectSound Buffer

Every DirectSound object is associated with a primary sound buffer. You
don't have to create the primary buffer; DirectSound does it for you. You do,
however, have to create secondary buffers for your sound effects. To create
a secondary buffer, you call the DirectSound object's `CreateSoundBuffer()`
function, which involves initializing a `DSBUFFERDESC` structure, as shown in
Listing 25-1.

Listing 25-1: Creating a DirectSound secondary buffer

```
DSBUFFERDESC dsbd;
memset(&dsbd, 0, sizeof(DSBUFFERDESC));
dsbd.dwSize = sizeof(DSBUFFERDESC);
dsbd.dwBufferBytes = bufferSize;
dsbd.lpwfxFormat =
    (LPWAVEFORMATEX) pwfe;
dsbd.dwFlags = DSBCAPS_CTRLDEFAULT;

HRESULT result = pDS->CreateSoundBuffer(&dsbd,
    &pBuffer, NULL);
if (result != DS_OK)
{
    // Handle buffer failure.
}
```

The `DSBUFFERDESC` structure, which is defined by DirectSound, holds the data
that describes a DirectSound surface. The example in Listing 25-1 creates a
secondary buffer for a wave file described in the `pwfe` `WAVEFORMATEX`
structure. (You'll see this structure later in the chapter, when you examine
the DirectSoundApp sample program.) The `bufferSize` variable is the size of
the buffer needed to hold the wave file's data.

The `CreateSoundBuffer()` function takes three arguments: the address of the
`DSBUFFERDESC` structure, the address of a `DIRECTSOUNDBUFFER` pointer, and
`NULL`.

An `LPDIRECTSOUNDBUFFER` pointer is the address of a DirectSound secondary
buffer. In the example, the `LPDIRECTSOUNDBUFFER` pointer is called `pBuffer`. If
the call to `CreateSoundBuffer()` succeeds, `CreateSoundBuffer()` places the
address of the new secondary buffer in `pBuffer` and returns `DD_OK`.

Wave files are the most common form of sound file used with Windows 98. Every time you boot Windows 98, you hear a wave file played (unless you have your system sounds turned off). In fact, during a Windows session, you're likely to hear many wave files. You can spot wave files easily on your disk due to their .wav extensions. Figure 25-3 shows some of the wave files you can find in your Windows\Media folder.

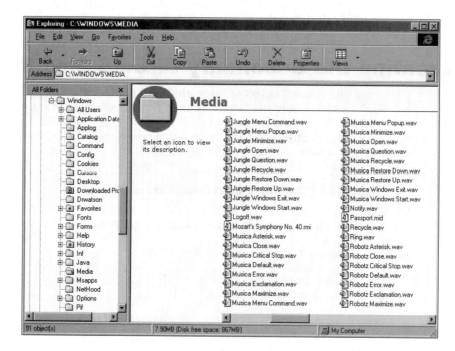

Figure 25-3: Windows 98 comes packed with wave files.

Exploring the DirectSoundApp Application

In the Chapter25\DirectSoundApp folder of this book's CD-ROM, you'll find the DirectSoundApp sample application, which is an MFC program that incorporates DirectSound in order to display a simple sound effect. When you run the program, you see the window shown in Figure 25-4. Click in the window to hear the sound effect played by DirectSound.

In the following sections, you'll examine DirectSoundApp more closely, and see how it implements DirectSound using the techniques described in this chapter.

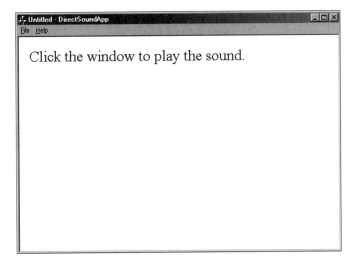

Figure 25-4: The DirectSoundApp application prompts the user to play a DirectSound sound effect.

DirectSoundApp's view-class constructor

Now that you've seen the program in action, take a look at the source code to see how the application initializes and manipulates DirectSound. The view class's constructor (see Listing 25-2) initializes the class's member variables to their default values. The member variables are declared in the view class's header file:

```
DWORD m_bufSize;
LPDIRECTSOUND m_pDS;
BOOL m_DSOK;
CWave* m_pWave;
LPDIRECTSOUNDBUFFER m_pBuffer;
```

The program uses the following variables:

m_bufSize	Size of the wave file's data
m_pDS	Pointer to the application's DirectSound object
m_DSOK	Flag indicating whether DirectSound initialized successfully
m_pWave	Pointer to the CWave object that contains the sound data
m_pBuffer	Pointer to the secondary DirectSound buffer

Listing 25-2: The CDirectSoundAppView **class's constructor**

```
CDirectSoundAppView::CDirectSoundAppView()
{
    // TODO: add construction code here
```

```
        m_pBuffer = NULL;
        m_pWave = NULL;
        m_DSOK = FALSE;
        m_bufSize = 0;
        m_pDS = NULL;
}
```

DirectSoundApp's OnInitialUpdate() function

In an MFC program, a good place to initialize DirectSound is in the view
class's OnInitialUpdate() function, which you add to the class with
ClassWizard, as shown in Figure 25-5. MFC calls OnInitialUpdate() once
when the view class is first updated. At that point, the application's main
window, represented by the CMainFrame class, has its window handle, which
you need to call SetCooperativeLevel(). Listing 25-3 shows
DirectSoundApp's OnInitialUpdate() function.

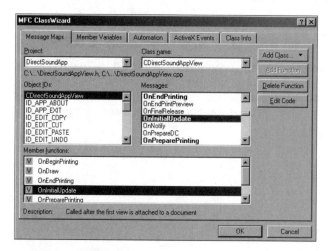

Figure 25-5: ClassWizard overriding the view class's OnInitialUpdate() function

Listing 25-3: The OnInitialUpdate() **function**

```
void CDirectSoundAppView::OnInitialUpdate()
{
        CView::OnInitialUpdate();

        // TODO: Add your specialized code here
        //    and/or call the base class

        BOOL okay = InitDirectSound();
        if (!okay)
                return;
```

```
    okay = CreateSoundBuffer();
    if (!okay)
        return;

    m_DSOK = LoadWaveData();
}
```

As you can see, the function calls other member functions—
InitDirectSound(), CreateSoundBuffer(), and LoadWaveData()—to get the
program set up for playing sound effects. If any of these functions fail,
OnInitialUpdate() immediately returns, discontinuing any further
DirectSound initialization. This action leaves m_DSOK (a member variable of
the view class) set to FALSE, which indicates to other functions that they
should not call DirectSound functions.

DirectSoundApp's InitDirectSound()
function

In DirectSoundApp, it's the InitDirectSound() function that creates the
DirectSound object and sets the sound-hardware access level. Listing 25-4
shows the InitDirectSound() function.

Listing 25-4: The InitDirectSound() function

```
BOOL CDirectSoundAppView::InitDirectSound()
{
    HRESULT result =
        DirectSoundCreate(NULL, &m_pDS, NULL);
    if (result != DS_OK)
        return FALSE;

    CWnd* pMainWnd = AfxGetMainWnd();
    HWND hMainWnd = pMainWnd->m_hWnd;
    result = m_pDS->SetCooperativeLevel(hMainWnd,
        DSSCL_NORMAL);
    if (result != DS_OK)
        return FALSE;

    return TRUE;
}
```

Notice how the function calls AfxGetMainWnd() to get a pointer to the frame
window and, through the pointer, gets access to the window's handle. If you
had tried to place this code in the view class's OnCreate() function, you
would have discovered that the main window had not yet been created, and
so doesn't have a handle. As with other DirectSoundApp initialization
functions, if any step fails, the function immediately returns, without trying
to perform any further initialization.

DirectSoundApp's `CreateSoundBuffer()` function

DirectSoundApp's `CreateSoundBuffer()` function creates the DirectSound secondary buffer, using the techniques described previously in this chapter. Listing 25-5 shows the `CreateSoundBuffer()` function.

Listing 25-5: The `CreateSoundBuffer()` function

```
BOOL CDirectSoundAppView::CreateSoundBuffer()
{
    LPWAVEFORMATEX pwfe;
    DSBUFFERDESC dsbd;

    m_pWave = new CWave("metal.wav");
    if (!m_pWave->IsValid())
        return FALSE;
    pwfe = m_pWave->GetFormat();
    m_bufSize = m_pWave->GetSize();

    memset(&dsbd, 0, sizeof(DSBUFFERDESC));
    dsbd.dwSize = sizeof(DSBUFFERDESC);
    dsbd.dwBufferBytes = m_bufSize;
    dsbd.lpwfxFormat =
        (LPWAVEFORMATEX) pwfe;
    dsbd.dwFlags = DSBCAPS_CTRLDEFAULT;

    HRESULT result = m_pDS->CreateSoundBuffer(&dsbd,
        &m_pBuffer, NULL);
    if (result != DS_OK)
        return FALSE;

    return TRUE;
}
```

Notice that the function defines a pointer to a `WAVEFORMATEX` structure, which holds information about a wave file that's needed in order to create a DirectSound buffer. As with other DirectSoundApp initialization functions, if any step fails, the function immediately returns, without trying to perform further initialization.

The `CWave` class

`CWave` is a custom class, much like the `CBitmap` class you developed in Chapter 12, that loads a wave sound file and provides the information about the file needed by DirectSound. A `CWave` object was created near the beginning of the function in Listing 25-5. Completely describing the programming techniques for loading a wave file is beyond the scope of this chapter. However, if you know something about Windows' multimedia library, you can explore the `CWave` class to see how it works. Listing 25-6 shows the class's header file, and Listing 25-7 shows the implementation file.

Listing 25-6: The CWave class's header file

```
#ifndef __CWAVE_H
#define __CWAVE_H

#include <mmsystem.h>

class CWave : public CObject
{
protected:
    LPCSTR m_filename;
    WAVEFORMATEX m_wfe;
    BYTE* m_pData;
    DWORD m_size;
    BOOL m_valid;

public:
    CWave(LPCSTR filename);
    ~CWave();

    BOOL IsValid();
    DWORD GetSize();
    BYTE* GetData();
    LPCSTR GetFilename();
    LPWAVEFORMATEX GetFormat();

protected:
    BOOL LoadFile(LPCSTR filename);
};

#endif
```

Listing 25-7: The CWave class's implementation file

```
#include <stdafx.h>
#include <afxwin.h>
#include "windowsx.h"
#include "cwave.h"

CWave::CWave(LPCSTR filename)
{
    m_filename = filename;
    m_pData = NULL;
    m_size = 0;
    m_valid = LoadFile(filename);
}

CWave::~CWave()
{
    GlobalFreePtr(m_pData);
}

BOOL CWave::IsValid()
{
    return m_valid;
}
```

```
DWORD CWave::GetSize()
{
    return m_size;
}

LPWAVEFORMATEX CWave::GetFormat()
{
    return &m_wfe;
}

BYTE* CWave::GetData()
{
    return m_pData;
}

LPCSTR CWave::GetFilename()
{
    return m_filename;
}

BOOL CWave::LoadFile(LPCSTR filename)
{
    MMCKINFO mmCkiRiff;
    MMCKINFO mmCkiChunk;

    HMMIO hMMIO = mmioOpen((char*)filename, NULL,
        MMIO_READ | MMIO_ALLOCBUF);
    if (hMMIO == NULL)
        return FALSE;

    mmCkiRiff.fccType = mmioFOURCC('W', 'A', 'V', 'E');
    MMRESULT mmResult = mmioDescend(hMMIO, &mmCkiRiff,
        NULL, MMIO_FINDRIFF);
    if (mmResult != MMSYSERR_NOERROR)
        return FALSE;

    mmCkiChunk.ckid = mmioFOURCC('f', 'm', 't', ' ');
    mmResult = mmioDescend(hMMIO, &mmCkiChunk,
        &mmCkiRiff, MMIO_FINDCHUNK);
    if (mmResult != MMSYSERR_NOERROR)
        return FALSE;

    LONG numBytes = mmioRead(hMMIO, (char*)&m_wfe,
        sizeof(WAVEFORMATEX));
    if (numBytes == -1)
        return FALSE;

    mmResult = mmioAscend(hMMIO, &mmCkiChunk, 0);
    if (mmResult != MMSYSERR_NOERROR)
        return FALSE;

    mmCkiChunk.ckid = mmioFOURCC('d', 'a', 't', 'a');
    mmResult = mmioDescend(hMMIO, &mmCkiChunk,
        &mmCkiRiff, MMIO_FINDCHUNK);
    if (mmResult != MMSYSERR_NOERROR)
        return FALSE;
```

```
    m_size = mmCkiChunk.cksize;
    m_pData = (BYTE*)GlobalAllocPtr(GMEM_MOVEABLE, m_size);
    if (m_pData == NULL)
        return FALSE;

    numBytes = mmioRead(hMMIO, (char*)m_pData, m_size);
    if (numBytes == -1)
        return FALSE;
    mmioClose(hMMIO, 0);

    return TRUE;
}
```

If you're not interested in how to load a wave file, you can just add the class to your programs and call its member functions as needed. To create an object of the class, you call the class's constructor with the file name of the wave file you want to load. The constructor not only creates the CWave object, but it also loads the file and stores information you'll need as you create your DirectSound object and buffers. The CWave class's methods are listed below, along with their descriptions:

CWave()	Constructs a CWave object from the given wave file
IsValid()	Returns TRUE if the CWave object is valid
GetSize()	Returns the size of the sound data as a DWORD
GetData()	Returns a pointer to the sound data
GetFilename()	Returns the wave file's file name
GetFormat()	Returns a pointer to the wave file's WAVEFORMATEX structure

You'll learn more about using the CWave class as you explore the rest of the DirectSoundApp application in the following sections.

DirectSoundApp's LoadWaveData() function

In the LoadWaveData() function, DirectSoundApp transfers the sound data from the CWave object to the secondary DirectSound buffer, as shown in Listing 25-8.

Listing 25-8: The LoadWaveData() function

```
BOOL CDirectSoundAppView::LoadWaveData()
{
    LPVOID pBlock1;
    DWORD bytesBlock1;
    LPVOID pBlock2;
    DWORD bytesBlock2;

    HRESULT result = m_pBuffer->Lock(0, m_bufSize,
        &pBlock1, &bytesBlock1, &pBlock2,
        &bytesBlock2, 0);
```

```
        if (result != DS_OK)
            return FALSE;

        DWORD waveSize = m_pWave->GetSize();
        BYTE* pWaveData = m_pWave->GetData();
        memcpy((void*)pBlock1, pWaveData, waveSize);

        m_pBuffer->Unlock(pBlock1, bytesBlock1,
            pBlock2, bytesBlock2);

        delete m_pWave;

        return TRUE;
}
```

Before transferring data to a buffer, the program must lock the buffer by calling the DIRECTSOUNDBUFFER object's Lock() function. The Lock() function takes seven arguments:

■ The buffer position at which to start locking data (0 = beginning)

■ The number of bytes to lock

■ The address of a pointer that will get the address of the first sound block

■ The address of a DWORD that will hold the number of bytes in the first sound block

■ The address of a pointer that will get the address to the second sound block

■ The address of a DWORD that will hold the number of bytes in the second sound block

■ A locking flag; usually 0

After LoadWaveData() locks the sound buffer, the pBlock1, bytesBlock1, pBlock2, and bytesBlock2 variables will contain the values described above. LoadWaveData() uses the pBlock1 pointer as the destination for the memcpy() command that copies the wave data to the DirectSound buffer. After copying the data, LoadWaveData() calls the buffer object's Unlock() function and deletes the CWave object. Unlock() takes the pBlock1, bytesBlock1, pBlock2, and bytesBlock2 variables as its arguments.

DirectSoundApp's OnLButtonDown() function

Now that the wave file's data has been loaded into the DirectSound secondary buffer, the sound effect is ready to play. When the user clicks in the application's window, DirectSoundApp plays the sound by calling the buffer object's Play() function. This happens in the view class's OnLButtonDown() function (see Listing 25-9), which responds to the WM_LBUTTONDOWN Windows message. (You can add OnLButtonDown() to your AppWizard-generated programs using ClassWizard.)

Listing 25-9: The LoadWaveData( ) **function**

```
void CDirectSoundAppView::OnLButtonDown(UINT nFlags, CPoint point)
{
    // TODO: Add your message handler code here and/or call default

    if (m_DSOK)
    {
        m_pBuffer->SetCurrentPosition(0);
        m_pBuffer->Play(0, 0, 0);
    }

    CView::OnLButtonDown(nFlags, point);
}
```

As you can see in this listing, the program calls the sound buffer object's
SetCurrentPosition( ) to set the starting point to the first byte in the
buffer, and then calls Play( ) to play the sound effect.

DirectSoundApp's OnDestroy( ) function

Finally, when the user closes the application, DirectSoundApp must release
the DirectSound objects it created. Again, as with DirectDraw, you don't call
the delete operator on a DirectSound pointer. Instead, you call the
DirectSound object's Release( ) function. DirectSoundApp takes care of these
final details in the OnDestroy( ) function (see Listing 25-10), which MFC calls
just before the view window is destroyed. OnDestroy( ) releases the
secondary buffer and then releases the main DirectSound object. You can
add OnDestroy( ) to your AppWizard-generated programs using ClassWizard.

Listing 25-10: The OnDestroy( ) **function**

```
void CDirectSoundAppView::OnDestroy()
{
    CView::OnDestroy();

    // TODO: Add your message handler code here

    if (m_pBuffer != NULL)
        m_pBuffer->Release();

    if (m_pDS != NULL)
        m_pDS->Release();
}
```

Note

DirectSound creates its objects following the specifications for COM objects.
This is why you must call DirectSound objects' Release( ) functions, rather
than destroy them via the delete operator. Because COM objects can be
used by more than one process, the objects keep internal counters. These
counters are incremented when a program creates the object, and
decremented when the program calls the object's Release( ) function. When
the object's count is decremented to zero, the system removes the object
from memory.

PROBLEMS & SOLUTIONS

Writing a Conventional DirectSound Windows Application

PROBLEM: *Now I know how to write an MFC DirectSound program. What if I'd just as soon write my program without MFC?*

SOLUTION: Just as with DirectDraw, the easiest way to accomplish this task is to write a traditional Windows program, but write it as a C++ program, rather than a C program. Then you can avoid the clumsy syntax required to call DirectSound functions from a C program.

Note

If you've forgotten how to write a traditional Windows application, you might want to take the time now to review Chapter 4, "Application Fundamentals."

To create a DirectSound application as a conventional Windows program, first write the basic application as you normally would, providing a `WinMain()` function that defines and registers your window class, as well as contains the application's message loop. You'll also need to provide a Windows procedure that responds to the many messages for which Windows will target your application. In your basic Windows procedure, you'll want to respond at least to the `WM_DESTROY` message.

On CD-ROM

Once you have the basic application built, you can add the DirectSound program code. In your Windows procedure, respond to the `WM_CREATE` message by initializing your program and setting up DirectSound. As you can see in Listing 25-11, the entire process is actually less complicated than trying to wedge DirectSound into an MFC program. You can find the program in the Chapter25\DirectSoundApp2 folder of this book's CD-ROM.

Listing 25-11: Source code for the DirectSoundApp2 application

```
#include <windows.h>
#include <windowsx.h>
#include <dsound.h>

/* Function prototypes */
LRESULT CALLBACK WndProc(HWND hWnd, UINT message,
    WPARAM wParam, LPARAM lParam);
void InitVariables();
BOOL InitDirectSound(HWND hWnd);
BOOL LoadWaveFile(char* filename);
BOOL CreateSoundBuffer();

/* Global variables */
LPDIRECTSOUND pDS;
LPDIRECTSOUNDBUFFER pDSBuffer;
WAVEFORMATEX wfe;
BYTE* pSoundData;
DWORD soundSize;

int WINAPI WinMain(HINSTANCE hCurrentInst,
```

Continued

```
        HINSTANCE hPrevInstance, PSTR lpszCmdLine,
        int nCmdShow)
{
        WNDCLASS wndClass;
        HWND hWnd;
        MSG msg;
        UINT width;
        UINT height;

        wndClass.style = CS_HREDRAW | CS_VREDRAW;
        wndClass.lpfnWndProc = WndProc;
        wndClass.cbClsExtra = 0;
        wndClass.cbWndExtra = 0;
        wndClass.hInstance = hCurrentInst;
        wndClass.hIcon = LoadIcon(NULL, IDI_APPLICATION);
        wndClass.hCursor = LoadCursor(NULL, IDC_ARROW);
        wndClass.hbrBackground = GetStockObject(WHITE_BRUSH);
        wndClass.lpszMenuName = NULL;
        wndClass.lpszClassName = "DSoundApp";

        RegisterClass(&wndClass);

        width = GetSystemMetrics(SM_CXSCREEN) / 2;
        height = GetSystemMetrics(SM_CYSCREEN) / 2;

        hWnd = CreateWindow(
                "DSoundApp",            /* Window class's name.    */
                "DirectSound App",      /* Title bar text.         */
                WS_OVERLAPPEDWINDOW,    /* The window's style.     */
                10,                     /* X position.             */
                10,                     /* Y position.             */
                width,                  /* Width.                  */
                height,                 /* Height.                 */
                NULL,                   /* Parent window's handle. */
                NULL,                   /* Menu handle.            */
                hCurrentInst,           /* Instance handle.        */
                NULL);                  /* No additional data.     */

        ShowWindow(hWnd, nCmdShow);
        UpdateWindow(hWnd);

        while (GetMessage(&msg, NULL, 0, 0))
        {
            TranslateMessage(&msg);
            DispatchMessage(&msg);
        }

        return msg.wParam;
}
LRESULT CALLBACK WndProc(HWND hWnd, UINT message,
    WPARAM wParam, LPARAM lParam)
{
    HDC hDC;
    PAINTSTRUCT paintStruct;
```

Continued

```
        switch(message)
        {
            case WM_CREATE:
                InitVariables();
                InitDirectSound(hWnd);
                LoadWaveFile("metal.wav");
                CreateSoundBuffer();
                return 0;

            case WM_PAINT:
                hDC = BeginPaint(hWnd, &paintStruct);
                TextOut(hDC, 10, 10,
                    "Click the window to play the sound.", 35);
                EndPaint(hWnd, &paintStruct);
                return 0;

            case WM_LBUTTONDOWN:
                pDSBuffer->SetCurrentPosition(0);
                pDSBuffer->Play(0, 0, 0);
                return 0;

            case WM_DESTROY:
                if (pDSBuffer != NULL)
                    pDSBuffer->Release();
                if (pDS != NULL)
                    pDS->Release();
                GlobalFreePtr(pSoundData);
                PostQuitMessage(0);
                return 0;
        }

    return DefWindowProc(hWnd, message, wParam, lParam);
}

void InitVariables()
{
    pDSBuffer = NULL;
    pDS = NULL;
}

BOOL InitDirectSound(HWND hWnd)
{
    HRESULT result =
        DirectSoundCreate(NULL, &pDS, NULL);
    if (result != DS_OK)
        return FALSE;

    result = pDS->SetCooperativeLevel(hWnd,
        DSSCL_NORMAL);
    if (result != DS_OK)
        return FALSE;

    return TRUE;
}
```

Continued

```
BOOL LoadWaveFile(char* filename)
{
    MMCKINFO mmCkiRiff;
    MMCKINFO mmCkiChunk;

    HMMIO hMMIO = mmioOpen((char*)filename, NULL,
        MMIO_READ | MMIO_ALLOCBUF);
    if (hMMIO == NULL)
        return FALSE;

    mmCkiRiff.fccType = mmioFOURCC('W', 'A', 'V', 'E');
    MMRESULT mmResult = mmioDescend(hMMIO, &mmCkiRiff,
        NULL, MMIO_FINDRIFF);
    if (mmResult != MMSYSERR_NOERROR)
        return FALSE;

    mmCkiChunk.ckid = mmioFOURCC('f', 'm', 't', ' ');
    mmResult = mmioDescend(hMMIO, &mmCkiChunk,
        &mmCkiRiff, MMIO_FINDCHUNK);
    if (mmResult != MMSYSERR_NOERROR)
        return FALSE;

    LONG numBytes = mmioRead(hMMIO, (char*)&wfe,
        sizeof(WAVEFORMATEX));
    if (numBytes == -1)
        return FALSE;

    mmResult = mmioAscend(hMMIO, &mmCkiChunk, 0);
    if (mmResult != MMSYSERR_NOERROR)
        return FALSE;

    mmCkiChunk.ckid = mmioFOURCC('d', 'a', 't', 'a');
    mmResult = mmioDescend(hMMIO, &mmCkiChunk,
        &mmCkiRiff, MMIO_FINDCHUNK);
    if (mmResult != MMSYSERR_NOERROR)
        return FALSE;

    soundSize = mmCkiChunk.cksize;
    pSoundData =
        (BYTE*)GlobalAllocPtr(GMEM_MOVEABLE, soundSize);
    if (pSoundData == NULL)
        return FALSE;

    numBytes = mmioRead(hMMIO, (char*)pSoundData, soundSize);
    if (numBytes == -1)
        return FALSE;
    mmioClose(hMMIO, 0);
    return TRUE;
}

BOOL CreateSoundBuffer()
{
    DSBUFFERDESC dsbd;
    LPVOID pBlock1;
```

```
DWORD bytesBlock1;
LPVOID pBlock2;
DWORD bytesBlock2;

memset(&dsbd, 0, sizeof(DSBUFFERDESC));
dsbd.dwSize = sizeof(DSBUFFERDESC);
dsbd.dwBufferBytes = soundSize;
dsbd.lpwfxFormat =
    (LPWAVEFORMATEX) &wfe;
dsbd.dwFlags = DSBCAPS_CTRLDEFAULT;

HRESULT result = pDS->CreateSoundBuffer(&dsbd,
    &pDSBuffer, NULL);
if (result != DS_OK)
    return FALSE;

result = pDSBuffer->Lock(0, soundSize,
    &pBlock1, &bytesBlock1, &pBlock2,
    &bytesBlock2, 0);
if (result != DS_OK)
    return FALSE;

memcpy((void*)pBlock1, pSoundData, soundSize);

pDSBuffer->Unlock(pBlock1, bytesBlock1,
    pBlock2, bytesBlock2);

return TRUE;
}
```

Listing 25-11 initializes DirectSound in much the same way as this chapter's previous program, DirectSoundApp. In fact, the program looks and acts very similar. When you run the application, click in the window to hear the sound effect. All of the DirectSound code in the program should be familiar to you by now. If you don't understand the program, you need to reread this chapter from the beginning.

Summary

As you've probably noticed, programming DirectSound is a little easier than programming DirectDraw. All you have to do is create a main DirectSound object, create a buffer for your sound data, load the data into the buffer, and play it. Still, if you decide to explore this DirectX library further, there's a lot more to learn. Once you master DirectDraw and DirectSound, however, you'll be well on your way to creating professional-quality Windows multimedia programs that run properly on any Windows 98 system.

Also discussed in this chapter:

▶ A DirectSound application must create a DirectSound object.

▶ The application can set up the sound hardware by calling
`SetCooperativeLevel()`.

▶ The primary DirectSound buffer, which DirectSound creates automatically, represents the sound being played.

▶ Secondary DirectSound buffers hold the sound data that your program will play.

▶ A DirectSound buffer object's `Play()` function sends sound data to a sound card.

▶ You shut down DirectSound by calling the DirectSound object's and each buffer's `Release()` function.

Chapter 26

DirectInput

In This Chapter

▶ Creating a DirectInput program

▶ Preparing Visual C++ for DirectInput

▶ Creating a DirectInput object

▶ Creating a DirectInput device

▶ Setting the device data format

▶ Setting the device access level

▶ Acquiring a DirectInput device

▶ Examining a sample DirectInput application

All programs need to deal with input devices, which are the link between humans and the computer. Games and other types of multimedia programs are no different. Most games, in fact, enable players to choose between different types of input devices, most notably the mouse, keyboard, and joystick. For computer games the mouse and the keyboard are the most important input devices because, while many computer systems may not have a joystick, virtually all of them have a mouse or keyboard. As with the other DirectX features, DirectInput lets programmers handle these devices in a more efficient manner than is possible with Windows API functions. In this chapter, you'll get a look at how you can add basic DirectInput functionality to your programs.

Note

Programming DirectInput is a complex task that cannot be fully explained in a single chapter. This chapter is only an introduction to the programming techniques required to create a basic DirectInput application. After you master the topics in this chapter, if you want to learn more about DirectInput, you should pick up a book that concentrates on DirectX programming.

In order to run DirectInput programs, you must have DirectX installed on your system. You can get a copy of the DirectX 5.0 SDK from Microsoft by pointing your Web browser to http://www.microsoft.com/directx/default.asp.

Creating a DirectInput Program

DirectInput may not be as famous as its DirectDraw and DirectSound cousins, because it works behind the scenes, rather than on the screen; but it's still an important part of the DirectX libraries. Using DirectInput, applications programmers can gain control over input devices at an almost hardware level. In this chapter, you'll examine the basic steps you must complete to create most DirectInput applications, along with the source code needed to create them.

To create a DirectInput program, you must complete the following main steps. After completing the main steps, other implementation details depend upon the type of DirectInput device you create. The main steps are as follows:

1. **Create a DirectInput object.** The DirectInput object is the object through which you can access other DirectInput capabilities.

2. **Create a DirectInput device.** A DirectInput device is an object that represents a physical input device, such as a mouse, keyboard, joystick, or other type of controller.

3. **Set the device data format.** Setting a device's data format tells DirectInput how the device is to be used and how its data should be arranged.

4. **Set the device access level.** The device access level, also called the *cooperative level,* determines how the device can be shared with other processes.

5. **Acquire the device.** Before an application can receive data from a device, the application must acquire the device. Once the device is acquired, the application begins to receive input data.

After completing these basic steps, your program can use DirectInput to receive input from the DirectInput device.

Note

Often, DirectX programs are written without the use of an application frameworks like MFC. This is because MFC can bring with it a lot of extra baggage that slows down an application—especially a game—that needs to run at its fastest speed. Compared with adding DirectInput to an MFC program, though, creating a non-MFC DirectInput program is straightforward. Getting DirectInput to run properly in an MFC program is the tricky part. The main part of this chapter will therefore focus on writing an MFC DirectInput program, while the "Problems & Solutions" section found in this chapter illustrates how to write such a program without MFC.

Adding DirectInput Files to Your Visual C++ Project

The DirectInputApp sample program that you'll examine later in this chapter was created by AppWizard as an SDI (single document) application with no extras such as a toolbar or status bar. By now, you should be comfortable with creating this type of skeleton application. There are a couple of extra steps, however, that you need to complete before you can compile and run an MFC DirectInput program.

Adding the dinput.h header file

First, you must include in your program the dinput.h header file, which contains declarations for the various DirectInput functions, structures, and data types. Because the dinput.h header file is not, for some reason, included with Visual C++'s other header files, you need to add the c:\dx5sdk\sdk\inc path to your project's header-file directories (assuming you have the SDK installed in its default directory).

To add the DirectX include-file folder to your project's directories, follow these steps:

1. Select the Options command on Visual C++'s Tools menu (Figure 26-1).

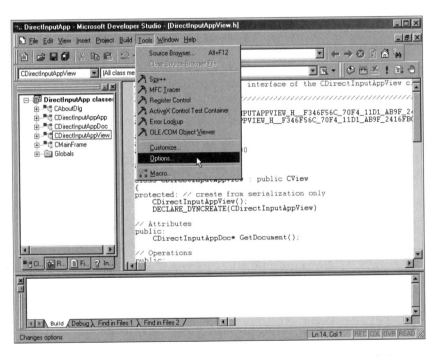

Figure 26-1: To bring up the Options property sheet, select the Tools menu's Options command.

2. Click the Directories tab to get to the Directories page when the Options property sheet appears.

3. Select Include Files in the Show Directories For box.

4. Add the path in the Directories box, as shown in Figure 26-2.

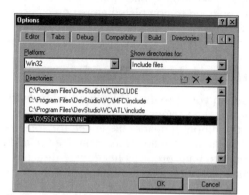

Figure 26-2: Add the include-file directory on the Directories page of the Options property sheet.

Once you add the c:\dx5sdk\sdk\inc path, you need to add the following line to modules that access the DirectInput libraries:

```
#include <dinput.h>
```

The angle brackets around the file name indicate that the header file is located in one of the default header-file directories, rather than in the project's directory.

Adding the dinput.lib and dxguid.lib files

Now that you've included the dinput.h header file, you shouldn't have any difficulty compiling your DirectInput program. Unfortunately, you'll quickly discover that the program won't link because it can't find the DirectInput libraries. To correct this problem, you must add the dinput.lib and dxguid.lib files to your project. To do this, follow these steps:

1. Select the Add to Project command on Visual C++'s Project menu.

2. Select the Files command from the submenu that appears (see Figure 26-3).

3. Navigate to your c:\dx5sdk\sdk\lib directory in the Insert Files Into Project dialog box.

4. Select the dinput.lib and dxguid.lib files, as shown in Figure 26-4.

Now Visual C++ is set up to compile and link a DirectInput program.

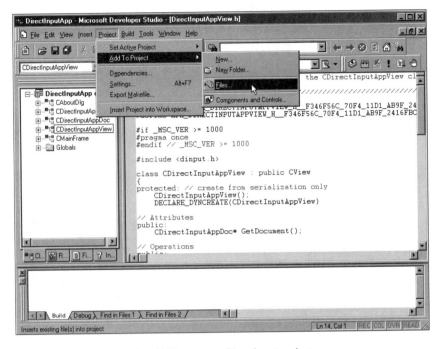

Figure 26-3: You can easily add files to your DirectInput project.

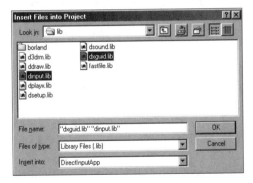

Figure 26-4: DirectInput programs must link to the dinput.lib and dxguid.lib library files.

Creating a DirectInput Object

To use DirectInput in a program, you must create a DirectInput object, through which you'll acquire access to the DirectInput functions. To create a DirectInput object, call `DirectInputCreate()`, as follows:

```
LPDIRECTINPUT pDInput;
HINSTANCE hInstance = AfxGetInstanceHandle();
HRESULT result = DirectInputCreate(hInstance,
```

```
      DIRECTINPUT_VERSION, &pDInput, NULL);
if (FAILED(result))
{
    // Handle DirectInput failure.
}
```

`DirectInputCreate()`'s arguments are as follows:

- The application's instance handle
- The predefined DIRECTINPUT_VERSION constant
- The address of a DIRECTINPUT pointer
- `NULL`

`LPDIRECTINPUT` represents a pointer to a DirectInput main object. In this case, the pointer is called `pDInput`. You pass the address of the pointer as `DirectInputCreate()`'s second argument. If the function call succeeds, `DirectInputCreate()` places the address of the DirectInput main object into the `pDInput` pointer. To ensure that this pointer is valid, you must check `DirectInputCreate()`'s return value. The `FAILED()` macro is a handy tool for discovering whether the DirectInput function call succeeded, when you don't need to handle a specific error return value. There's also a `SUCCEEDED()` macro.

Creating a DirectInput Device

Once you have your main DirectInput object, you can call the function that creates the DirectInput device object, which represents the physical device the application must control. To create the device, call the DirectInput object's `CreateDevice()` function:

```
LPDIRECTINPUTDEVICE pDIMouse;
HRESULT result = pDInput➪CreateDevice(GUID_SysMouse,
    &pDIMouse, NULL);
 if (FAILED(result))
 {
     // Handle device failure.
 }
```

`LPDIRECTINPUTDEVICE` represents a pointer to a DirectInput device. In this case, the pointer is called `pDIMouse`. You pass the address of the pointer as `CreateDevice()`'s second argument. (The first argument is a predefined ID for the device you want to create.) If the function call succeeds, `CreateDevice()` places the address of the DirectInput device into the `pDIMouse` pointer. As with many DirectInput functions, to ensure that the returned pointer is valid, you must check `CreateDevice()`'s return value.

Setting the Data Format

Before you can receive data from a device, DirectInput has to know how to handle that data. You provide this information by calling the device object's `SetDataFormat()` function:

```
HRESULT result = pDIMouse->SetDataFormat(&c_dfDIMouse);
if (FAILED(result))
{
    // Handle the failure.
}
```

The SetDataFormat() function's single argument is a pointer to the structure that describes how the device should return data. DirectInput provides predefined structures for the keyboard, mouse, and joystick. In the above case, the function supplies the c_dfDIMouse structure to specify default mouse handling.

Setting the Device Access Level

With a pointer to a DirectInput device in hand, your application can set the type of device access the application needs. You do this by calling the device object's SetCooperativeLevel() function:

```
CWnd* pMainWnd = AfxGetMainWnd();
HWND hMainWnd = pMainWnd->m_hWnd;
HRESULT result = pDIMouse->SetCooperativeLevel(hMainWnd,
    DISCL_NONEXCLUSIVE | DISCL_FOREGROUND);
if (FAILED(result))
{
    // Handle failure.
}
```

SetCooperativeLevel() takes two arguments: the handle of the application's main window and the device access flags. Usually, you'll use DISCL_NONEXCLUSIVE | DISCL_FOREGROUND for the flags, giving your application nonexclusive access to the device when the application is the foreground process, but still allowing multitasking to function properly.

Acquiring the Device

The last thing your application must do in order to receive data from the device is acquire the device. Acquiring the device associates the device with your application in much the same way capturing the mouse acquires the mouse device in a regular Windows application. When you've acquired a device, all its input goes to your application until another process gets switched to the foreground and acquires the device on its behalf. To acquire a device, you call the device object's Acquire() function:

```
HRESULT result = pDIMouse->Acquire();
if (FAILED(result))
{
    // Handle failure.
}
```

As with most DirectInput functions, Acquire() returns a result value that you can check with the FAILED or SUCCEEDED macro. In this example's case, if the FAILED macro results in a value of TRUE, the body of the if statement will execute.

Exploring the DirectInputApp Application

On CD-ROM

In the Chapter26\DirectInputApp folder of this book's CD-ROM, you'll find the DirectInputApp sample application, which is an MFC program that incorporates DirectInput in order to control the mouse. When you run the program, you see the window shown in Figure 26-5. Move the mouse pointer around the screen and watch how the mouse values change in the window. Also, click the mouse buttons. When you do, the data for the button changes from 0 to 1 on the screen.

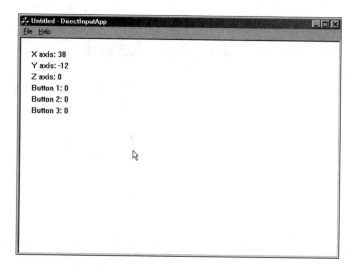

Figure 26-5: The DirectInputApp application tracks relative mouse movement.

When used with DirectInput, a mouse isn't so much a pointing device as it is a replacement for a joystick. That is, the mouse device reports relative mouse movement data, rather than the X and Y coordinates you're used to receiving from a mouse. The relative mouse data indicates the direction the mouse moved and how far the mouse moved since the last time the mouse data was read. Whenever the mouse is at rest, the X, Y, and Z axis data remains zero. The faster the mouse moves from this virtual origin, the higher the reported mouse values become. (Which values change the most depends on the direction you move the mouse.)

In the following sections, you'll examine DirectInputApp more closely, and see how it implements DirectInput using the techniques described previously in this chapter.

DirectInputApp's view-class constructor

Now that you've seen the program in action, take a look at the source code to see how the application initializes and manipulates DirectInput, as shown in Listing 26-1.

Listing 26-1: The `CDirectInputAppView` **class's constructor**

```
CDirectInputAppView::CDirectInputAppView()
{
    // TODO: add construction code here

    m_DIOK = FALSE;
    m_button3 = 0;
    m_button2 = 0;
    m_button1 = 0;
    m_mouseZ = 0;
    m_mouseY = 0;
    m_mouseX = 0;
    m_pDIMouse = NULL;
    m_pDInput = NULL;
}
```

The view class's constructor in Listing 26-1 initializes the class's member variables to their default values. The member variables are declared in the view class's header file like this:

```
BOOL m_DIOK;

int m_button3;
int m_button2;
int m_button1;
int m_mouseZ;
int m_mouseY;
int m_mouseX;
LPDIRECTINPUTDEVICE m_pDIMouse;
LPDIRECTINPUT m_pDInput;
```

The program uses the following variables:

m_DIOK	Flag indicating whether DirectInput initialized successfully
m_button3	Status of mouse button 3
m_button2	Status of mouse button 2
m_button1	Status of mouse button 1
m_mouseZ	Relative mouse movement on the Z axis
m_mouseY	Relative mouse movement on the Y axis
m_mouseX	Relative mouse movement on the X axis
m_pDIMouse	Pointer to the DirectInput mouse device
m_pDInput	Pointer to the application's DirectInput object

DirectInputApp's OnInitialUpdate() function

In an MFC program, a good place to initialize DirectInput is in the view class's OnInitialUpdate() function, which you add to the class with ClassWizard, as shown in Figure 26-6. MFC calls OnInitialUpdate() once when the view class is first updated. At that point, the application's main window, represented by the CMainFrame class, has its window handle, which you need in order to call SetCooperativeLevel().

Listing 26-2 shows DirectInputApp's OnInitialUpdate()function.

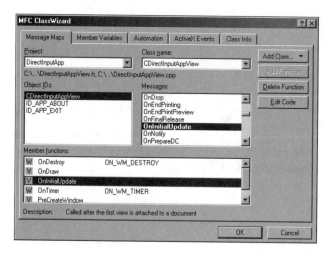

Figure 26-6: ClassWizard overriding the view class's OnInitialUpdate() function

Listing 26-2: The OnInitialUpdate() function

```
void CDirectInputAppView::OnInitialUpdate()
{
CView::OnInitialUpdate();

// TODO: Add your specialized code here
//    and/or call the base class

HINSTANCE hInstance = AfxGetInstanceHandle();
HRESULT result = DirectInputCreate(hInstance,
DIRECTINPUT_VERSION, &m_pDInput, NULL);
if (FAILED(result))
return;

result = m_pDInput->CreateDevice(GUID_SysMouse,
&m_pDIMouse, NULL);
if (FAILED(result))
return;
```

```
result = m_pDIMouse->SetDataFormat(&c_dfDIMouse);
if (FAILED(result))
return;

CWnd* pMainWnd = AfxGetMainWnd();
HWND hMainWnd = pMainWnd->m_hWnd;
result = m_pDIMouse->SetCooperativeLevel(hMainWnd,
DISCL_NONEXCLUSIVE | DISCL_FOREGROUND);
if (FAILED(result))
return;

m_DIOK = TRUE;
SetTimer(1, 100, NULL);
}
```

As you can see, the function initializes DirectInput using the techniques you learned earlier in this chapter. If any of these functions fail, `OnInitialUpdate()` immediately returns, discontinuing any further DirectInput initialization. This action leaves m_DIOK (a member variable of the view class) set to FALSE, which indicates to other functions that they should not call DirectInput functions.

Notice that, near the end of Listing 26-2, the program starts a Windows timer. DirectInputApp uses this timer to simulate a game loop, in which a game program would continually poll its input devices. In this case, the program's `OnTimer()` function, where DirectInputApp reads mouse data, gets called 10 times a second.

DirectInputApp's `OnTimer()` function

DirectInputApp's `OnTimer()` function responds to the WM_TIMER messages that Windows sends to the application when the `OnInitialUpdate()` function starts the Windows timer, as shown in Listing 26-3.

Listing 26-3: The `OnTimer()` function

```
void CDirectInputAppView::OnTimer(UINT nIDEvent)
{
    // TODO: Add your message handler code here
    //    and/or call default

    if (m_DIOK)
    {
        DIMOUSESTATE dims;

        HRESULT result = m_pDIMouse->Acquire();
        if (FAILED(result))
            return;

        result = m_pDIMouse->
            GetDeviceState(sizeof(DIMOUSESTATE), &dims);
        if (FAILED(result))
            return;
```

```
        m_mouseX = dims.lX;
        m_mouseY = dims.lY;
        m_mouseZ = dims.lZ;
        m_button1 = (dims.rgbButtons[0] & 0x80) > 0;
        m_button2 = (dims.rgbButtons[1] & 0x80) > 0;
        m_button3 = (dims.rgbButtons[2] & 0x80) > 0;

        Invalidate();
    }

    CView::OnTimer(nIDEvent);
}
```

In the above listing, the program acquires the mouse and then calls the mouse device's GetDeviceState() function, which returns the state of the mouse in the members of a DIMOUSESTATE structure. After the call to GetDeviceState(), the DIMOUSESTATE structure (called dims) will contain X, Y, and Z axis movement data in its lX, lY, and lZ members, respectively. The structure will also contain mouse button data in its rgbButtons[] byte array, with each element of the array representing a specific button (0 represents button 1, 1 represents button 2, and so on). The button data is tucked into the byte's high-order bit, so to extract the information, you must AND the value with 0x80, which masks out the other bits. OnTimer() not only uses the bit mask to extract the button information, but also uses the result in a Boolean expression that sets the appropriate mouse-button variable to either 0 or 1.

You add OnTimer() to your AppWizard-generated program using ClassWizard.

DirectInputApp's OnDraw() function

After OnTimer() reads the mouse data, it calls Invalidate() to redraw the window with the new information. In an MFC program, this action causes the frameworks to call the view class's OnDraw() function (see Listing 26-4), where the application renders its display.

Listing 26-4: The OnDraw() function

```
void CDirectInputAppView::OnDraw(CDC* pDC)
{
    CDirectInputAppDoc* pDoc = GetDocument();
    ASSERT_VALID(pDoc);

    // TODO: add draw code for native data here

    char s[81];
    wsprintf(s, "X axis: %d", m_mouseX);
    pDC->TextOut(20, 20, s);
    wsprintf(s, "Y axis: %d", m_mouseY);
    pDC->TextOut(20, 40, s);
    wsprintf(s, "Z axis: %d", m_mouseZ);
    pDC->TextOut(20, 60, s);
```

```
    wsprintf(s, "Button 1: %d", m_button1);
    pDC->TextOut(20, 80, s);
    wsprintf(s, "Button 2: %d", m_button2);
    pDC->TextOut(20, 100, s);
    wsprintf(s, "Button 3: %d", m_button3);
    pDC->TextOut(20, 120, s);
}
```

DirectInputApp's `OnDraw()` function displays the most recent mouse data by converting the data to strings and displaying the strings with the `TextOut()` function.

DirectInputApp's `OnDestroy()` function

Finally, when the user closes the application, DirectInputApp must release the DirectInput objects it created. Again, as with DirectDraw and DirectSound, you don't call the `delete` operator on a DirectInput pointer. Instead, you call the `Release()` function. DirectInputApp takes care of these final details in the `OnDestroy()` function, which MFC calls just before the view window is destroyed, as shown in Listing 26-5.

Listing 26-5: The `OnDestroy()` function

```
void CDirectInputAppView::OnDestroy()
{
    CView::OnDestroy();

    // TODO: Add your message handler code here

    KillTimer(1);

    if (m_pDIMouse != NULL)
    {
        m_pDIMouse->Unacquire();
        m_pDIMouse->Release();
    }

    if (m_pDInput != NULL)
        m_pDInput->Release();
}
```

In DirectInputApp, `OnDestroy()` destroys the Windows timer, releases the mouse device, and then releases the main DirectInput object. You can add `OnDestroy()` to your AppWizard-generated programs using ClassWizard.

Note

DirectInput creates its objects following the specifications for COM objects. This is why you must call DirectInput objects' `Release()` functions, rather than destroy them via the `delete` operator. Because COM objects can be used by more than one process, the objects keep internal counters. These counters are incremented when a program creates the object and decremented when the program calls the object's `Release()` function. When the object's count is decremented to zero, the system removes the object from memory.

PROBLEMS & SOLUTIONS

Writing a Conventional DirectInput Windows Application

PROBLEM: *Now I know how to write an MFC DirectInput program. What if I'd just as soon write my program without MFC?*

SOLUTION: Just as with DirectDraw or DirectSound, the easiest way to accomplish this task is to write a traditional Windows program, but write it as a C++ program, rather than a C program. Then you can avoid the clumsy syntax required to call DirectInput functions from a C program.

Note

If you've forgotten how to write a traditional Windows application, you might want to take the time now to review Chapter 4, "Application Fundamentals."

To create a DirectInput application as a conventional Windows program, first write the basic application as you normally would, providing a `WinMain()` function that defines and registers your window class, as well as contains the application's message loop. You'll also need to provide a Windows procedure that responds to the many messages for which Windows will target your application. In your basic Windows procedure, you'll want to respond at least to the `WM_DESTROY` message.

On CD-ROM

Once you have the basic application built, you can add the DirectInput program code. In your Windows procedure, respond to the `WM_CREATE` message by initializing your program and setting up DirectInput. As you can see in Listing 26-6, the entire process is actually less complicated than trying to wedge DirectInput into an MFC program. You can find the program in the Chapter26\DirectInputApp2 folder of this book's CD-ROM.

Listing 26-6: Source code for the DirectInputApp2 application

```
#include <windows.h>
#include <windowsx.h>
#include <dinput.h>

/* Function prototypes */
LRESULT CALLBACK WndProc(HWND hWnd, UINT message,
    WPARAM wParam, LPARAM lParam);
void InitVariables();
BOOL InitDirectInput(HWND hWnd);
/* Global variables */
LPDIRECTINPUT pDInput;
LPDIRECTINPUTDEVICE pDIMouse;
int button3;
int button2;
int button1;
int mouseZ;
int mouseY;
int mouseX;
HINSTANCE hInstance;
```

Continued

```
int WINAPI WinMain(HINSTANCE hCurrentInst,
    HINSTANCE hPrevInstance, PSTR lpszCmdLine,
    int nCmdShow)
{
    WNDCLASS wndClass;
    HWND hWnd;
    MSG msg;
    UINT width;
    UINT height;

    hInstance = hCurrentInst;

    wndClass.style = CS_HREDRAW | CS_VREDRAW;
    wndClass.lpfnWndProc = WndProc;
    wndClass.cbClsExtra = 0;
    wndClass.cbWndExtra = 0;
    wndClass.hInstance = hCurrentInst;
    wndClass.hIcon = LoadIcon(NULL, IDI_APPLICATION);
    wndClass.hCursor = LoadCursor(NULL, IDC_ARROW);
    wndClass.hbrBackground = GetStockObject(WHITE_BRUSH);
    wndClass.lpszMenuName = NULL;
    wndClass.lpszClassName = "DInputApp";

    RegisterClass(&wndClass);

    width = GetSystemMetrics(SM_CXSCREEN) / 2;
    height = GetSystemMetrics(SM_CYSCREEN) / 2;

    hWnd = CreateWindow(
        "DInputApp",          /* Window class's name.   */
        "DirectInput App",    /* Title bar text.        */
        WS_OVERLAPPEDWINDOW,  /* The window's style.    */
        10,                   /* X position.            */
        10,                   /* Y position.            */
        width,                /* Width.                 */
        height,               /* Height.                */
        NULL,                 /* Parent window's handle. */
        NULL,                 /* Menu handle.           */
        hCurrentInst,         /* Instance handle.       */
        NULL);                /* No additional data.    */

    ShowWindow(hWnd, nCmdShow);
    UpdateWindow(hWnd);
    while (GetMessage(&msg, NULL, 0, 0))
    {
        TranslateMessage(&msg);
        DispatchMessage(&msg);
    }

    return msg.wParam;
}

LRESULT CALLBACK WndProc(HWND hWnd, UINT message,
    WPARAM wParam, LPARAM lParam)
```

Continued

```
{
    HDC hDC;
    PAINTSTRUCT paintStruct;
    HRESULT result;

    switch(message)
    {
        case WM_CREATE:
            InitVariables();
            InitDirectInput(hWnd);
            return 0;

        case WM_PAINT:
            hDC = BeginPaint(hWnd, &paintStruct);
            char s[81];
            wsprintf(s, "X axis: %d", mouseX);
            TextOut(hDC, 20, 20, s, strlen(s));
            wsprintf(s, "Y axis: %d", mouseY);
            TextOut(hDC, 20, 40, s, strlen(s));
            wsprintf(s, "Z axis: %d", mouseZ);
            TextOut(hDC, 20, 60, s, strlen(s));

            wsprintf(s, "Button 1: %d", button1);
            TextOut(hDC, 20, 80, s, strlen(s));
            wsprintf(s, "Button 2: %d", button2);
            TextOut(hDC, 20, 100, s, strlen(s));
            wsprintf(s, "Button 3: %d", button3);
            TextOut(hDC, 20, 120, s, strlen(s));
            EndPaint(hWnd, &paintStruct);
            return 0;

        case WM_TIMER:
            DIMOUSESTATE dims;

            result = pDIMouse->Acquire();
            if (FAILED(result))
                return 0;

            result = pDIMouse->
                GetDeviceState(sizeof(DIMOUSESTATE), &dims);
            if (FAILED(result))
                return 0;
            mouseX = dims.lX;
            mouseY = dims.lY;
            mouseZ = dims.lZ;
            button1 = (dims.rgbButtons[0] & 0x80) > 0;
            button2 = (dims.rgbButtons[1] & 0x80) > 0;
            button3 = (dims.rgbButtons[2] & 0x80) > 0;

            InvalidateRect(hWnd, NULL, TRUE);
            return 0;

        case WM_DESTROY:
            KillTimer(hWnd, 1);
```

Continued

```
                    if (pDIMouse != NULL)
                    {
                        pDIMouse->Unacquire();
                        pDIMouse->Release();
                    }

                if (pDInput != NULL)
                    pDInput->Release();

                PostQuitMessage(0);
                return 0;
        }

    return DefWindowProc(hWnd, message, wParam, lParam);
}

void InitVariables()
{
    button3 = 0;
    button2 = 0;
    button1 = 0;
    mouseZ = 0;
    mouseY = 0;
    mouseX = 0;
    pDIMouse = NULL;
    pDInput = NULL;
}

BOOL InitDirectInput(HWND hWnd)
{
    HRESULT result = DirectInputCreate(hInstance,
        DIRECTINPUT_VERSION, &pDInput, NULL);
    if (FAILED(result))
        return FALSE;

    result = pDInput->CreateDevice(GUID_SysMouse,
        &pDIMouse, NULL);
    if (FAILED(result))
        return FALSE;
    result = pDIMouse->SetDataFormat(&c_dfDIMouse);
    if (FAILED(result))
        return FALSE;

    result = pDIMouse->SetCooperativeLevel(hWnd,
        DISCL_NONEXCLUSIVE | DISCL_FOREGROUND);
    if (FAILED(result))
        return FALSE;

    SetTimer(hWnd, 1, 100, NULL);

    return TRUE;
}
```

Continued

Listing 26-6 initializes DirectInput in much the same way as this chapter's previous program, DirectInputApp. In fact, the program looks and acts very similar. When you run the application, move the mouse around and click the mouse's buttons. The application's display continually reports on the mouse actions. All of the DirectInput code in the program should be familiar to you by now. If you don't understand the program, you should reread this chapter from the beginning.

Summary

Besides the mouse, DirectInput also provides support for a keyboard and a joystick. In fact, the word "joystick" really refers to many types of controllers, including not only an actual joystick, but also trackballs, controller pads, and any other input device that doesn't fit into the mouse or keyboard category. As you can see, DirectInput gives your application the tools it needs to support a wide variety of input devices, one or more of which should be perfect for your program.

Also discussed in this chapter:

▶ A DirectInput application must create a DirectInput main object.

▶ A DirectInput application must also create a device object.

▶ The application can set up input-device sharing by calling the device object's `SetCooperativeLevel()` function.

▶ Setting a device's data format tells DirectInput how to present device data to the application.

▶ Before an application can receive data from a DirectInput device, it must acquire the device.

▶ After acquiring a device, the application can obtain data from the device by calling the device object's `GetDeviceState()` function.

Chapter 27

Direct3D

In This Chapter

- Creating a Direct3D program
- Creating a Direct3D main object
- Creating a clipper object
- Creating a Direct3D device
- Creating Direct3D frames
- Creating Direct3D meshes
- Creating a viewport
- Adding lights to a Direct3D scene
- Preparing Visual C++ for Direct3D
- Examining a sample Direct3D application

Now that you've taken a look at most of the DirectX libraries, you should be ready for the real high-tech stuff! Direct3D is without a doubt the most complex of the DirectX libraries (at least from a programmer's point of view). It features a large number of interfaces that you need to learn to program, and requires quite a bit of knowledge of 3D programming basics. Using Direct3D, applications programmers can create fabulous 3D games like Doom or Tomb Raider without having to worry about loading specific drivers for the user's hardware. In this chapter, you'll get a look at how you can add basic Direct3D functionality to your programs.

Note

Programming Direct3D is a complex task that cannot be fully explained in a single chapter. This chapter is only an introduction to the programming techniques required to create a basic Direct3D application. After you master the topics in this chapter, if you want to learn more about Direct3D, you should pick up a book that concentrates on Direct3D programming, such as *Cutting Edge Direct 3D Programming* by Stan Trujillo, published by Coriolis Group Books.

In order to run Direct3D programs, you must have DirectX installed on your system. You can get a copy of the DirectX 5.0 SDK from Microsoft by pointing your Web browser to http://www.microsoft.com/directx/default.asp.

Creating a Direct3D Program

Creating a Direct3D program isn't a process that's easily defined in a list of numbered steps. This is because there are many ways to put together a Direct3D program and many choices you must make along the way. Still, there are certain steps that most Direct3D programs will require. In this section, you'll examine these basic steps and learn how to implement them with source code.

To create a Direct3D program, you usually complete at least the following main steps. After completing the main steps, other implementation details depend upon the type of Direct3D program you're writing. The main steps are as follows:

1. **Create a Direct3D main object.** The Direct3D main object is the object through which you can access other Direct3D capabilities.

2. **Create a DirectDraw clipper object.** Direct3D draws upon DirectDraw for some of its power, the clipper object being a good example. The clipper object enables a Direct3D application's window to update properly without overwriting other windows on the screen.

3. **Create a Direct3D device.** Once you have a clipper object, you can use it to create a Direct3D device that's appropriate for the application's window. It's the device that draws your 3D scenes, as well as interfaces with whatever 3D hardware may be installed on the user's system.

4. **Create a root frame.** Direct3D objects are positioned and oriented using frames. Every Direct3D application has a root frame that acts as the parent (or container, if you like) for other frames.

5. **Create meshes for objects that will be displayed in the scene.** A mesh is a group of polygons that are connected in order to create some sort of 3D shape.

6. **Create frames for the meshes.** Each object in a 3D scene must be associated with a frame, which determines the object's position and orientation in a scene.

7. **Create a viewport for the scene.** Much like a viewfinder in a camera, a viewport determines what part of a 3D scene appears on the screen.

8. **Add lights to the scene.** Like lamps in a dark room, Direct3D lights determine not only how bright a scene can be, but also the color of the scene and the way light reflects from objects in the scene.

After completing these basic steps, your program can use Direct3D to render a 3D scene on the screen. In the following sections, you'll take a closer look at each of these steps, examining the source code required to implement them.

Creating a Direct3D Main Object

To use Direct3D in a program, you must create a Direct3D main object, through which you'll acquire access to the Direct3D interfaces. To create a Direct3D object (in retained mode), call `Direct3DRMCreate()`, as follows:

```
LPDIRECT3DRM pD3D;
HRESULT result = Direct3DRMCreate(&pD3D);
if (result != D3DRM_OK)
{
    // Handle Direct3D failure.
}
```

`LPDIRECT3DRM` represents a pointer to a Direct3D retained-mode main object. In this case, the pointer is called `pD3D`. You pass the address of the pointer as `Direct3DRMCreate()`'s single argument. If the function call succeeds, `Direct3DRMCreate()` places the address of the Direct3D main object into the `pD3D` pointer. To ensure that this pointer is valid, you must check `Direct3DRMCreate()`'s return value, which will be `D3DRM_OK` if the function succeeds.

Direct3D programs can be written in *retained* or *immediate* mode. Retained mode Direct3D programs are easier to write and so are more common. The retained mode is a high-level programming interface that's built on top of the immediate mode. The immediate mode provides programmers with a detailed, low-level programming interface.

Creating a Clipper Object

Although 3D worlds can represent large virtual areas, that image of the world is constrained by the screen, or even the window, through which you must view it. A DirectDraw clipper object that's associated with a window manages the way that the scene can appear on the screen. In a multiwindowed environment, for example, the clipper object ensures that a Direct3D window's display doesn't overwrite other areas of the screen, particularly other applications' windows that may overlap the Direct3D application's window. You create a clipper object by calling `DirectDrawCreateClipper()`:

```
LPDIRECTDRAWCLIPPER pClipper;
HRESULT result =
    DirectDrawCreateClipper(0, &pClipper, 0);
if (result != DD_OK)
{
    // Handle clipper failure.
}
```

`LPDIRECTDRAWCLIPPER` represents a pointer to a `DIRECTDRAWCLIPPER` object. In this case, the pointer is called `pClipper`. You pass the address of the pointer as `DirectDrawCreateClipper()`'s second argument. (The first and third arguments can be zero.) If the function call succeeds, `DirectDrawCreateClipper()` places the address of the clipper object into the `pClipper` pointer. To ensure that this pointer is valid, you must check `DirectDrawCreateClipper()`'s return value, which will be `DD_OK` if the function succeeds.

Once you've created the clipper object, you must associate it with the window it'll manage. You do this by calling the clipper object's `SetHWnd()` function:

```
result = pClipper->SetHWnd(0, hWnd);
if (result != DD_OK)
{
    // Handle clipper failure.
}
```

`SetHWnd()` takes zero as its first argument, and the window's handle as the second argument. The function returns `DD_OK` if it succeeds.

Creating a Direct3D Device

While the clipper object may manage how Direct3D draws its scenes, it's the device that does the actual drawing. Therefore, it should come as no surprise that your program must create a Direct3D device. One way an application can perform this task is by calling the main Direct3D object's `CreateDeviceFromClipper()` function:

```
RECT rect;
::GetClientRect(hWnd, &rect);
LPDIRECT3DRMDEVICE pDevice;
HRESULT result = pD3D->
    CreateDeviceFromClipper(pClipper, NULL,
    rect.right, rect.bottom, &pDevice);
if (result != D3DRM_OK)
{
    // Handle device failure.
}
```

Before calling `CreateDeviceFromClipper()`, the above example calls `GetClientRect()` to obtain the size of the window's client area, which the program needs to create the device. `LPDIRECT3DRMDEVICE` represents a pointer to a `DIRECT3DRMDEVICE` object. In this case, the pointer is called pDevice. You pass the address of the pointer as `CreateDeviceFromClipper()`'s fifth argument. The `CreateDeviceFromClipper()` arguments are as follows:

- A pointer to the clipper object
- A GUID for the device (`NULL` for the ramp color model)
- The width of the window for which the device will be created
- The height of the window for which the device will be created
- The address of the `LPDIRECT3DRMDEVICE` pointer

If the function call succeeds, `CreateDeviceFromClipper()` places the address of the device object into the pDevice pointer. To ensure that this pointer is valid, you must check `CreateDeviceFromClipper()`'s return value, which will be `D3DRM_OK` if the function succeeds.

After creating the device, you can stick with the default flat shading model, or you can go with the more realistic-looking Gouraud shading. The flat shading model applies lighting effects such that you can see each of the polygons that a shape comprises (see Figure 27-1).

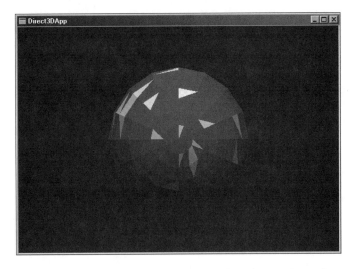

Figure 27-1: With flat shading, you can see the polygons that make up an object.

Gouraud shading, on the other hand, calculates shades using color averages, thus creating more realistic surfaces (see Figure 27-2). To set the shading model, call the device object's SetQuality() function:

```
pDevice->SetQuality(D3DRMRENDER_GOURAUD);
```

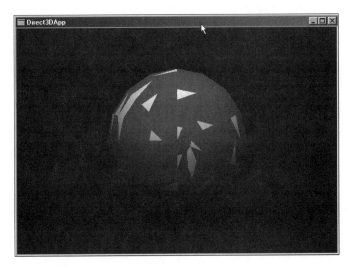

Figure 27-2: With Gouraud shading, surfaces look smoother and more realistic.

Creating the Root Frame

As you've already learned, Direct3D scenes comprise many objects, each of which is positioned inside a frame object. It is the frame object that determines an object's orientation and position in the scene. All the object frames in a scene are children of the root frame. Obviously, before you can create child frames, then, you must have created the root frame, which you do by calling the main Direct3D object's `CreateFrame()` function:

```
LPDIRECT3DRMFRAME pParentFrame;
HRESULT result = pD3D->CreateFrame(0, &pParentFrame);
if (result != D3DRM_OK)
{
    // Handle frame failure.
}
```

`LPDIRECT3DRMFRAME` represents a pointer to a `DIRECT3DRMFRAME` object. In this case, the pointer is called `pParentFrame`. You pass the address of the pointer as `CreateFrame()`'s second argument. The first argument is the address of the parent frame or zero if you're creating a parent frame. If the function call succeeds, `CreateFrame()` places the address of the frame object into the `pParentFrame` pointer. To ensure that this pointer is valid, you must check `CreateFrame()`'s return value, which will be `D3DRM_OK` if the function succeeds.

Creating Meshes for Objects

At this point, you've got Direct3D initialized and raring to go. All you have to do now (as if this were an easy task) is create a 3D scene to display. An object in a Direct3D scene is represented by a mesh, which is a collection of polygons linked together such that they create a 3D object. Direct3D offers several ways to create meshes, but the easiest is to use a mesh builder object, which is represented by the `Direct3DRMMeshBuilder` interface. You create a mesh builder object by calling the main Direct3D object's `CreateMeshBuilder()` function:

```
LPDIRECT3DRMMESHBUILDER pMeshBuilder;
HRESULT result = pD3D->CreateMeshBuilder(&pMeshBuilder);
if (result != D3DRM_OK)
{
    // Handle mesh builder failure.
}
```

`LPDIRECT3DRMMESHBUILDER` represents a pointer to a `DIRECT3DRMMESHBUILDER` object. In this case, the pointer is called `pMeshBuilder`. You pass the address of the pointer as `CreateMeshBuilder()`'s single argument. If the function call succeeds, `CreateMeshBuilder()` places the address of the mesh builder object into the `pMeshBuilder` pointer. To ensure that this pointer is valid, you must check `CreateMeshBuilder()`'s return value, which will be `D3DRM_OK` if the function succeeds.

With the mesh builder created, you can create the actual mesh, by calling the mesh builder object's Load() function:

```
HRESULT result = pMeshBuilder->Load(fileName,
    NULL, D3DRMLOAD_FROMFILE, NULL, NULL );
if (result != D3DRM_OK)
{
    // Handle mesh load failure.
}
```

In this case, thanks to the D3DRMLOAD_FROMFILE flag, Load() is looking for a file whose name is fileName. This file should use Direct3D's X file format (no, Scully and Mulder had nothing to do with it), a type of file that you can create from 3D Studio objects using Direct3D's CONV3DS utility. If the file loads successfully, Load() returns D3DRM_OK.

Creating Frames for Meshes

You may remember that all objects in a Direct3D scene must be associated with frames, which determine the object's orientation and position. A mesh is no different. Once you've created a mesh, you can't add it to your 3D world until you've associated it with a frame. Another call to CreateFrame() takes care of this task:

```
LPDIRECT3DRMFRAME pFrame;
HRESULT result =
    pD3D->CreateFrame(pParentFrame, &pFrame);
if (result != D3DRM_OK)
{
    // Handle frame failure.
}
```

Notice that in this case, CreateFrame() gets the parent frame pointer as its first argument. This is because the new frame will be a child of the parent frame.

Once the child frame exists, a call to the frame's AddVisual() function associates the mesh (represented by the mesh builder object) with the frame:

```
pFrame->AddVisual(pMeshBuilder);
```

The Viewport

Now you've created a 3D scene that contains an object. Unfortunately, there's no way yet to see the object because you haven't told Direct3D the position from which you want to view the scene. You take care of this little detail by creating a viewport, which not only determines your viewing position and angle, but also the clipping planes that determine what portion of the 3D world is available for viewing. Imagine that you're standing in a room facing a window. As you move toward or away from the window, your view of the outside world changes. In this way, a viewport is similar to a window.

Creating the viewport frame

To create a viewport, you first create the frame that'll position and orient the viewport:

```
LPDIRECT3DRMFRAME pEye;
HRESULT result = pD3D->CreateFrame(pParentFrame, &pEye);
if (result != D3DRM_OK)
{
    // Handle frame failure.
}
```

Again, notice that this new frame, whose pointer is called pEye, is being created as a child frame of pParentFrame.

After creating the frame object, you call the SetPosition() function to position the frame inside the parent frame:

```
pEye->SetPosition(pParentFrame, D3DVALUE(0),
    D3DVALUE(0),D3DVALUE(-40.0));
```

As you can see, SetPosition() takes four arguments:

- A pointer to the parent frame
- The new position on the X axis
- The new position on the Y axis
- The new position of the Z axis

Think of the frame as an eye (which is, of course, where the name pEye comes from). Before being positioned, everything added to the 3D scene ends up centered on the 3D world's origin, which is position 0,0,0. So, when you first place the eye in the 3D scene, it'll actually be inside the 3D object (represented by the mesh builder object) that you just placed in the same position. In order to see the object, then, you have to pull the eye back. That's why, in the call to SetPosition(), the Z position is set to -40. Negative numbers pull the eye back from the scene, whereas positive numbers push the eye forward. For example, while the Z value of -40 will enable you to see the object, a positive value in this case will put the eye behind the object, where the object will still be invisible.

Note

The D3DVALUE data type is a floating-point value used in Direct3D. You should cast most numerical values you pass to Direct3D functions to the D3DVALUE type. (Consult the Direct3D documentation for a function's signature to determine the data types of the arguments.) Also, many Direct3D functions return values of the D3DVALUE data type.

Creating the viewport

Once you have the viewport's frame, you can create the viewport, which you do by calling the main Direct3D object's CreateViewport() function:

```
LPDIRECT3DRMVIEWPORT pViewport;
result = pD3D->CreateViewport(pDevice, pEye, 0, 0,
```

```
        pDevice->GetWidth(), pDevice->GetHeight(),
    &pViewport);
if (result != D3DRM_OK)
{
    // Handle viewport failure.
}
```

LPDIRECT3DRMVIEWPORT **represents a pointer to a** DIRECT3DRMVIEWPORT **object.**
In this case, the pointer is called pViewport. You pass the address of the
pointer as one of CreateViewport()'s seven arguments:

- A pointer to the device object
- A pointer to the frame
- The X position of the viewport
- The Y position of the viewport
- The viewport's width
- The viewport's height
- The address of the viewport pointer

If the function call succeeds, CreateViewport() places the address of the
viewport object into the pViewport pointer. To ensure that this pointer is
valid, you must check CreateViewport()'s return value, which will be
D3DRM_OK if the function succeeds.

Adding Lights

You may have placed an eye in the 3D scene, but it's still darn dark in there.
The last thing you must do to prepare your 3D scene is add lighting.
Direct3D supports many types of lighting, including positional, directional,
ambient, and spot lights. In this example, you'll see how to use positional
lighting. As lighting is a complex topic beyond the scope of this chapter, only
positional lighting will be discussed, giving you a taste of what Direct3D is all
about. If you want to learn about the other types of lighting, you can look
them up in the Direct3D documentation or in a Direct3D programming book.

Creating the light object

The first step is to create your light object, by calling the main Direct3D
object's CreateLightRGB() function:

```
LPDIRECT3DRMLIGHT pLight;
HRESULT result = pD3D->
    CreateLightRGB(D3DRMLIGHT_DIRECTIONAL,
    D3DVALUE(1.0), D3DVALUE(1.0),
    D3DVALUE(1.0), &pLight);
if (result != D3DRM_OK)
{
    // Handle light failure.
}
```

LPDIRECT3DRMLIGHT represents a pointer to a DIRECT3DRMLIGHT object. In this case, the pointer is called pLight. You pass the address of the pointer as one of CreateLightRGB()'s five arguments:

- A flag indicating the type of light to create
- The light's red intensity
- The light's green intensity
- The light's blue intensity
- The address of the light's pointer

If the function call succeeds, CreateLightRGB() places the address of the light object into the pLight pointer. To ensure that this pointer is valid, you must check CreateLightRGB()'s return value, which will be D3DRM_OK if the function succeeds. If the function fails, you'll have no lighting for your 3D scene.

Creating the light's child frame

After creating the light, you need to create its child frame, which controls the light's position and orientation in the parent frame:

```
LPDIRECT3DRMFRAME pLightFrame;
result = pD3D->CreateFrame(pParentFrame, &pLightFrame );
if (result != D3DRM_OK)
{
    return FALSE;
}
```

To add the light to the frame, you call the frame's AddLight() function, whose single argument is the light object's pointer:

```
pLightFrame->AddLight(pLight);
```

Finally, you position the light by calling the frame's SetOrientation() function:

```
pLightFrame->SetOrientation(pParentFrame,
    D3DVALUE(0.0), D3DVALUE(-1.0), D3DVALUE(1.0),
    D3DVALUE(0.0), D3DVALUE(1.0), D3DVALUE(0.0));
```

Following are SetOrientation()'s arguments:

- A pointer to the parent frame
- The X coordinate of the forward vector
- The Y coordinate of the forward vector
- The Z coordinate of the forward vector
- The X coordinate of the up vector
- The Y coordinate of the up vector
- The Z coordinate of the up vector

A vector is a line that indicates which way an object is pointing. In the SetOrientation() function, the forward vector is the direction that the light should face, and the up vector is the light's height.

The Direct3DApp Sample Application

The Direct3DApp sample program that you'll examine in this chapter is an MFC program, but it wasn't created by AppWizard. Instead, the program was written "from scratch" in order to avoid having to deal with the document and view classes that AppWizard always adds to the applications it generates. Still, Direct3DApp is an MFC program and takes advantage of the CWinApp and CFrameWnd classes.

Building a new Direct3D application

To run or compile Direct3DApp, you can simply access the project's files on this book's CD-ROM. However, doing so won't help you set up other programs for Direct3D. So, in this section, you'll learn how to build a new project for Direct3DApp, a task that includes getting the project ready for Direct3D.

Assuming that all you have to start with is the application's source code files (Direct3DApp.h, Direct3DApp.cpp, Direct3DWin.h, and Direct3DWin.cpp), you must perform the following steps to get the program compiled and running:

1. Select the New command on Visual C++'s File menu.

2. In the New property sheet, select Win32 Application on the Projects page, type **Direct3DApp** in the Project Name box, and select the project's destination directory in the Location box, as shown in Figure 27-3. Click the OK button to create the project.

   Visual C++ creates an empty project for which you must supply the source code and library files.

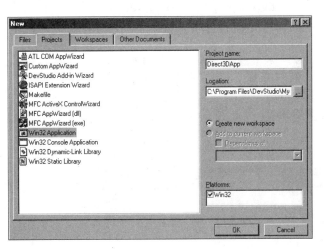

Figure 27-3: Direct3DApp starts off life as a Win32 Application project.

3. Copy the Direct3DApp.h, Direct3DApp.cpp, Direct3DWin.h, and Direct3DWin.cpp files from this book's CD-ROM to your new Direct3DApp project directory.

4. Select the Add to Project command from Visual C++'s Project menu, and then select Files from the submenu that appears (see Figure 27-4).

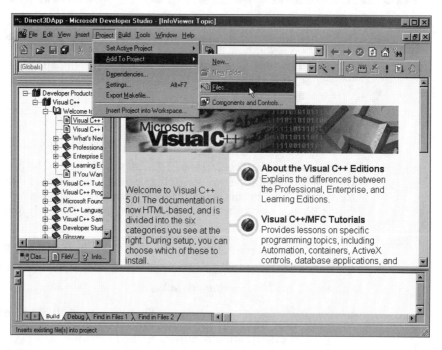

Figure 27-4: You must add files to your new, empty project.

5. In the Insert Files Into Project dialog box, select the Direct3DApp.cpp and Direct3DWin.cpp files (see Figure 27-5), and then click OK.

Visual C++ adds the source code file to the project.

Figure 27-5: Select the project's source code in the dialog box.

6. Again, select the Add to Project command from Visual C++'s Project menu, and then select Files from the submenu that appears.

7. In the Insert Files Into Project dialog box, navigate to your Visual C++ installation's lib folder and select the d3drm.lib and ddraw.lib files (see Figure 27-6), and then click OK.

   Visual C++ adds the DirectDraw and Direct3D library files to the project.

Figure 27-6: Select the library files needed by the project.

8. Select the Set Active Configuration command from Visual C++'s Build menu. In the Set Active Project Configuration dialog box, select Direct3DApp - Win32 Release (see Figure 27-7), and click OK.

   Visual C++ is now set to develop the release version of the program, rather than the debugging version.

Figure 27-7: The release configuration doesn't include debugging information in your files, so the program's executable will be smaller.

9. Select the Settings command from the Project menu. When the Project Settings property page appears, select the Use MFC in Static Library setting in the Microsoft Foundation Classes box, as shown in Figure 27-8.

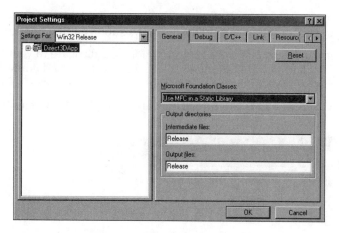

Figure 27-8: When an application uses MFC, it must link to the MFC libraries.

The project is now ready to compile.

Note

Applications that use Direct3D must include the appropriate header files in any modules that access Direct3D interfaces. First, the application must include the #define INITGUID definition. Then, the program must include the d3drm.h header file, and may also require the d3drmwin.h and ddraw.h header files as well.

Running Direct3DApp

On CD-ROM

In the Chapter27\Direct3DApp folder of this book's CD-ROM, you'll find the Direct3DApp program. This program not only shows you how to create a basic Direct3D program, it also shows you how to write MFC programs without the help of AppWizard, which is always handy when you don't want to monkey around with the document and view classes that AppWizard insists on generating.

Before you try to run Direct3DApp, copy it to your hard drive and be sure to copy the Bigship1.x file to the same directory. Rename the file model.x. You can find Bigship1.x in your DirectX 5.0 installation's Media folder, along with other X files you can display with Direct3DApp.

When you run Direct3DApp, you see the window shown in Figure 27-9. (The quality of the 3D model may vary depending on your hardware.) Although you can't tell from the figure, the ship model slowly rotates around its Y axis, giving you a view of the model from all sides. When viewing the program, pay particular attention to the lighting, how the scene's single light causes shadows and reflections on the ship's body. That's a lot of 3D for just a few pages of source code!

Figure 27-9: Direct3DApp showing off its impressive 3D modeling skills

Writing an AppWizardless MFC application

Before you start digging into Direct3DApp's Direct3D code, you might want
to see how to create a non-AppWizard MFC program with only an application
and main-window class. The following sections reveal how you can
accomplish this handy trick, starting with a program's application class.

Creating the application class's header file

If you look at Listing 27-1, you'll see the header file for Direct3DApp's
application class. Two things are important in the listing:

1. The application class is derived from CWinApp.

2. The application class overrides the base class's InitInstance()
   function.

Listing 27-1: The Direct3DApp **class's header file**

```
#ifndef __DIRECT3DAPP_H
#define __DIRECT3DAPP_H

class Direct3DApp : public CWinApp
{
public:
    Direct3DApp();
    ~Direct3DApp();
    virtual BOOL InitInstance();
};

#endif
```

Remember that the application class represents what goes on behind the scenes in a Windows application. For example, the application class handles the message loop that retrieves and dispatches Windows messages. One thing an application object doesn't have is a window—at least, not until you give it one, which you do in `InitInstance()`.

Creating the application class's implementation file

Listing 27-2 shows the application class's implementation file.

Listing 27-2: The `Direct3DApp` class's implementation file

```
#include <AfxExt.h>
#include <d3drm.h>
#include "Direct3DApp.h"
#include "Direct3DWin.h"

Direct3DApp app;

Direct3DApp::Direct3DApp()
{
}

Direct3DApp::~Direct3DApp()
{
}

BOOL Direct3DApp::InitInstance()
{
    Direct3DWin* pMainWnd = new Direct3DWin;
    pMainWnd->ShowWindow(SW_SHOWNORMAL);
    pMainWnd->UpdateWindow();

    m_pMainWnd = pMainWnd;

    return TRUE;
}
```

In the `InitInstance()` function, the program creates an object of the `Direct3DWin` class, which is the application's main-window class and where all the Direct3D stuff lives. After creating the window object, `InitInstance()` calls the `ShowWindow()` and `UpdateWindow()` functions to bring the window up on the screen. Finally, the function assigns the window's pointer to the application class's `m_pMainWnd` member variable, which tells the application that it now owns the window and can begin sending it messages.

And that's all there is to it. The `Direct3DWin` class handles everything else in the program, including not only responding to Windows messages, but also creating, displaying, and animating its 3D scene.

Creating the main window class's header file

Listing 27-3 shows the `Direct3DWin` class's header file. This class represents the application's main window that you see on the screen. It's also the link between the application and Direct3D.

Listing 27-3: The `Direct3DWin` class's header file

```
#ifndef __DIRECT3DWIN_H
#define __DIRECT3DWIN_H

class Direct3DWin : public CFrameWnd
{
public:
    Direct3DWin();
    ~Direct3DWin();

protected:
    LPDIRECT3DRM m_pD3D;
    LPDIRECT3DRMDEVICE m_pDevice;
    LPDIRECT3DRMVIEWPORT m_pViewport;
    LPDIRECT3DRMFRAME m_pParentFrame;
    LPDIRECT3DRMFRAME m_pEye;
    LPDIRECT3DRMMESHBUILDER m_pMeshBuilder;
    LPDIRECTDRAWCLIPPER m_pClipper;
    BOOL m_D3DOK;

    BOOL MakeScene();
    BOOL CreateMesh();
    BOOL CreateViewport();
    BOOL CreateLight();

    afx_msg int OnCreate(LPCREATESTRUCT lpCreateStruct);
    afx_msg void OnPaint();
    afx_msg void OnTimer(UINT nIDEvent);
    afx_msg void OnDestroy();

    DECLARE_MESSAGE_MAP()
};

#endif
```

You should notice a few things about the class declared in the header file:

1. The `Direct3DWin` class is derived from MFC's `CFrameWnd` class.

2. The class declares member variables for all the main Direct3D pointers the program will need.

3. The `MakeScene()`, `CreateMesh()`, `CreateViewport()`, and `CreateLight()` member functions implement the program's Direct3D functionality.

4. The class responds to `WM_CREATE`, `WM_PAINT`, `WM_TIMER`, and `WM_DESTROY` windows messages with functions that are associated with the messages in the class's message map.

Creating the window class's implementation file

Listing 27-4 shows the window class's implementation file. You should take a little time to look over the listing until you understand how it fits in with the application class. You should also understand the general Direct3D programming techniques used in the program. In the sections that follow, you'll examine this application in detail, to see how it creates and displays its Direct3D animated scene.

Listing 27-4: The `Direct3DWin` **class's implementation file**

```
#include <AfxExt.h>
#define INITGUID
#include <d3drm.h>
#include <d3drmwin.h>
#include "Direct3DWin.h"

BEGIN_MESSAGE_MAP(Direct3DWin, CFrameWnd)
    ON_WM_CREATE()
    ON_WM_PAINT()
    ON_WM_TIMER()
    ON_WM_DESTROY()
END_MESSAGE_MAP()

Direct3DWin::Direct3DWin()
{
    m_D3DOK = FALSE;
    m_pD3D = NULL;
    m_pDevice = NULL;
    m_pViewport = NULL;
    m_pParentFrame = NULL;
    m_pEye = NULL;
    m_pMeshBuilder = NULL;
    m_pClipper = NULL;
    Create(NULL, "Direct3DApp");
}

Direct3DWin::~Direct3DWin()
{
}

int Direct3DWin::OnCreate(LPCREATESTRUCT)
{
    HRESULT result = Direct3DRMCreate(&m_pD3D);
    if (result != D3DRM_OK)
        return 0;

    result = DirectDrawCreateClipper(0, &m_pClipper, 0);
    if (result != DD_OK)
        return 0;
    result = m_pClipper->SetHWnd(0, m_hWnd);
    if (result != DD_OK)
        return 0;

    RECT rect;
    ::GetClientRect(m_hWnd, &rect);
```

```
        result = m_pD3D->CreateDeviceFromClipper(m_pClipper,
            NULL, rect.right, rect.bottom, &m_pDevice);
        if (result != D3DRM_OK)
            return 0;
        m_pDevice->SetQuality(D3DRMRENDER_GOURAUD);

        m_pD3D->CreateFrame(0, &m_pParentFrame);
        if (result != D3DRM_OK)
            return 0;

        BOOL succeeded = MakeScene();
        if (!succeeded)
            return 0;

        m_D3DOK = TRUE;

        SetTimer(1, 100, NULL);

        return 0;
    }

BOOL Direct3DWin::MakeScene()
    {
        BOOL succeeded = CreateMesh();
        if (!succeeded)
            return FALSE;

        succeeded = CreateViewport();
        if (!succeeded)
            return FALSE;

        succeeded = CreateLight();
        if (!succeeded)
            return FALSE;

        return TRUE;
    }

BOOL Direct3DWin::CreateMesh()
    {
        HRESULT result =
            m_pD3D->CreateMeshBuilder(&m_pMeshBuilder);
        if (result != D3DRM_OK)
            return FALSE;

        result = m_pMeshBuilder->Load("model.x",
            NULL, D3DRMLOAD_FROMFILE, NULL, NULL );
        if (result != D3DRM_OK)
        {
            MessageBox("MODEL.X file missing. Please place\n\
a Direct3D X file with this name\nin the Direct3DApp folder.");
            return FALSE;
        }

        LPDIRECT3DRMFRAME pFrame;
        result =
```

```
        m_pD3D->CreateFrame(m_pParentFrame, &pFrame);
    if (result != D3DRM_OK)
        return FALSE;
    pFrame->AddVisual(m_pMeshBuilder);
    pFrame->SetRotation(m_pParentFrame, D3DVALUE(0.0),
        D3DVALUE(1.0), D3DVALUE(0.0), D3DVALUE(0.05));
    pFrame->Release();
    pFrame = NULL;

    return TRUE;
}

BOOL Direct3DWin::CreateViewport()
{
    HRESULT result = m_pD3D->
        CreateFrame(m_pParentFrame, &m_pEye);
    if (result != D3DRM_OK)
        return FALSE;
    m_pEye->SetPosition(m_pParentFrame, D3DVALUE(0),
        D3DVALUE(0), D3DVALUE(-40.0));
    result = m_pD3D->CreateViewport(m_pDevice, m_pEye,
        0, 0, m_pDevice->GetWidth(),
        m_pDevice->GetHeight(), &m_pViewport);
    if (result != D3DRM_OK)
        return FALSE;

    return TRUE;
}

BOOL Direct3DWin::CreateLight()
{
    LPDIRECT3DRMLIGHT pLight;
    HRESULT result = m_pD3D->
        CreateLightRGB(D3DRMLIGHT_DIRECTIONAL,
        D3DVALUE(1.0), D3DVALUE(1.0), D3DVALUE(1.0),
        &pLight);
    if (result != D3DRM_OK)
        return FALSE;

    LPDIRECT3DRMFRAME pLightFrame;
    result = m_pD3D->CreateFrame(m_pParentFrame,
        &pLightFrame );
    if (result != D3DRM_OK)
        return FALSE;

    pLightFrame->AddLight(pLight);
    pLightFrame->SetOrientation(m_pParentFrame,
        D3DVALUE(0.0), D3DVALUE(-1.0), D3DVALUE(1.0),
        D3DVALUE(0.0), D3DVALUE(1.0), D3DVALUE(0.0));
    pLight->Release();
    pLight = NULL;
    pLightFrame->Release();
    pLightFrame = NULL;

    return TRUE;
}
```

```
void Direct3DWin::OnPaint()
{
    BOOL repaint = GetUpdateRect(NULL);
    if (!repaint)
        return;

    PAINTSTRUCT pstruct;
    BeginPaint(&pstruct);

    if (m_D3DOK)
    {
        LPDIRECT3DRMWINDEVICE pWndDevice;
        m_pDevice->
            QueryInterface(IID_IDirect3DRMWinDevice,
            (void**)&pWndDevice);
        pWndDevice->HandlePaint(pstruct.hdc);
        pWndDevice->Release();
    }
    else
        ::TextOut(pstruct.hdc, 20, 20,
            "Direct3D failed to start.", 25);

    EndPaint(&pstruct);
}

void Direct3DWin::OnTimer(UINT nIDEvent)
{
    if (m_D3DOK)
        m_pD3D->Tick(D3DVALUE(1));
}

void Direct3DWin::OnDestroy()
{
    if (m_pMeshBuilder)
        m_pMeshBuilder->Release();

    if (m_pEye)
        m_pEye->Release();

    if (m_pViewport)
        m_pViewport->Release();

    if (m_pParentFrame)
        m_pParentFrame->Release();

    if (m_pDevice)
        m_pDevice->Release();

    if (m_pD3D)
        m_pD3D->Release();

    if (m_pClipper)
        m_pClipper->Release();
}
```

In this listing, you can see that the OnCreate() function gets Direct3D up and running. Each step required to build the 3D scene is implemented in its own function. These functions, which you'll soon examine in greater detail, are MakeScene(), CreateMesh(), CreateViewport(), and CreateLight().

The Direct3DWin class's constructor

The window class's constructor has the usual job of initializing member variables:

```
m_D3DOK = FALSE;
m_pD3D = NULL;
m_pDevice = NULL;
m_pViewport = NULL;
m_pParentFrame = NULL;
m_pEye = NULL;
m_pMeshBuilder = NULL;
m_pClipper = NULL;
```

This initialization is especially important for the Direct3D pointers because if the pointers don't start off NULL, the OnDestroy() function may try, even if the objects weren't created successfully, to call their Release() functions when the program terminates. Calling a function through an uninitialized pointer is a good way to give your application's user nasty surprises.

The class's constructor also creates the Window element (the window you see on the screen) that's associated with the class:

```
Create(NULL, "Direct3DApp");
```

Direct3DWin inherits its Create() function from the CMainWnd base class. Its two arguments provide a pointer to the parent window (NULL means no parent) and the window's title.

The OnDestroy() function

As mentioned in the previous section, the OnDestroy() function releases the Direct3D pointers. For example, here's how OnDestroy() releases the mesh builder and viewport frame objects:

```
if (m_pMeshBuilder)
    m_pMeshBuilder->Release();

if (m_pEye)
    m_pEye->Release();
```

OnDestroy() releases the other Direct3D objects the same way. You can see why it's important that the pointers start off NULL. If Direct3D initialization fails, OnDestroy() is going to get those pointers as they were initialized in the class's constructor.

The OnCreate() function

MFC calls the OnCreate() function in response to the WM_CREATE message, which Windows sends just before the window appears. Direct3DApp uses

OnCreate() to set up the basic Direct3D system. First, OnCreate() creates the main Direct3D object:

```
HRESULT result = Direct3DRMCreate(&m_pD3D);
if (result != D3DRM_OK)
    return 0;
```

Notice how if the Direct3D creation process fails, the function returns a zero, which tells the application to go ahead and create the window. In this case, the m_D3DOK flag stays set to FALSE, and the window's OnPaint() function will know to display an error message. Every step of the Direct3D setup uses the same type of error handling, immediately returning from the function if trouble rears its ugly head.

After creating the main Direct3D object, the program creates and initializes its clipper object:

```
result = DirectDrawCreateClipper(0, &m_pClipper, 0);
if (result != DD_OK)
    return 0;
result = m_pClipper->SetHWnd(0, m_hWnd);
if (result != DD_OK)
    return 0;
```

As you learned previously, the SetHWnd() function requires the window's handle. The m_hWnd is a member variable of the Direct3DWin class. The class inherits this member variable from the CWnd class.

The next step is to create the Direct3D device, which OnCreate() does like this:

```
RECT rect;
::GetClientRect(m_hWnd, &rect);
result = m_pD3D->CreateDeviceFromClipper(m_pClipper,
    NULL, rect.right, rect.bottom, &m_pDevice);
if (result != D3DRM_OK)
    return 0;
m_pDevice->SetQuality(D3DRMRENDER_GOURAUD);
```

For the last step of the basic Direct3D setup, OnCreate() creates the application's parent Direct3D frame:

```
m_pD3D->CreateFrame(0, &m_pParentFrame);
if (result != D3DRM_OK)
    return 0;
```

Near the end of its duties, having successfully initialized Direct3D, OnCreate() calls the locally defined MakeScene() function, which, despite its name, doesn't throw a tantrum, but instead creates the application's 3D scene:

```
BOOL succeeded = MakeScene();
if (!succeeded)
    return 0;
```

If MakeScene() executes successfully, OnCreate() sets the m_D3DOK flag to TRUE, so that the rest of the program knows that everything with Direct3D is hunky-dory:

```
m_D3DOK = TRUE;
```

The last thing `OnCreate()` does is set a Windows timer:

```
SetTimer(1, 100, NULL);
```

This Windows timer, which is the engine that drives the program's 3D animation, will cause `WM_TIMER` messages to arrive at the window 10 times a second. As you'll soon see, the `OnTimer()` function handles the `WM_TIMER` messages handily.

The `MakeScene()` function

Direct3DApp's `MakeScene()` function performs the task of putting together a 3D scene for the application to show off. However, rather than perform its tasks directly, it calls other locally defined functions to complete the deed. The first of these functions is `CreateMesh()`, which `MakeScene()` calls like this:

```
BOOL succeeded = CreateMesh();
if (!succeeded)
    return FALSE;
```

`MakeScene()` gets the viewport and light created the same way, by calling `CreateViewport()` (the local version, not the Direct3D version), and `CreateLight()`:

```
succeeded = CreateViewport();
if (!succeeded)
    return FALSE;

succeeded = CreateLight();
if (!succeeded)
    return FALSE;
```

If any of these function calls fail, `MakeScene()` returns a value of `FALSE`, which causes `OnCreate()` to immediately stop and return, leaving `m_D3DOK` with a value of `FALSE`.

The `CreateMesh()` function

`CreateMesh()` is where the real Direct3D scene creation starts. First, the function creates the mesh builder object:

```
HRESULT result =
    m_pD3D->CreateMeshBuilder(&m_pMeshBuilder);
if (result != D3DRM_OK)
    return FALSE;
```

If the mesh builder creation fails, `CreateMesh()` returns `FALSE` to `MakeScene()`, which then returns `FALSE` to `OnCreate()`, which then returns without further Direct3D initialization, which leaves `m_D3DOK` with a value of `FALSE`. (Whew! The webs we weave.)

The next task for `CreateMesh()` is to load the 3D object into the mesh builder:

```
result = m_pMeshBuilder->Load("model.x",
    NULL, D3DRMLOAD_FROMFILE, NULL, NULL );
```

```
if (result != D3DRM_OK)
{
    MessageBox("MODEL.X file missing. Please place\n\
a Direct3D X file with this name\nin the Direct3DApp folder.");
    return FALSE;
}
```

Finally, the new mesh needs an orientation and position in the 3D scene, which means it needs a frame. `CreateMesh()` creates the frame as follows:

```
LPDIRECT3DRMFRAME pFrame;
result =
    m_pD3D->CreateFrame(m_pParentFrame, &pFrame);
if (result != D3DRM_OK)
    return FALSE;
```

Then the program adds the mesh to the frame:

```
pFrame->AddVisual(m_pMeshBuilder);
```

To prepare Direct3D for animation, the program calls the frame object's `SetRotation()` function:

```
pFrame->SetRotation(m_pParentFrame, D3DVALUE(0.0),
    D3DVALUE(1.0), D3DVALUE(0.0), D3DVALUE(0.05));
```

This function call tells Direct3D to rotate the frame around the Y axis. `SetRotation()`'s arguments are described as follows:

- A pointer to the parent frame
- The X coordinate of the vector around which to rotate
- The Y coordinate of the vector around which to rotate
- The Z coordinate of the vector around which to rotate
- The amount of rotation in radians

Finally, because the program doesn't need to access the mesh object's frame, `CreateMesh()` releases the frame object and sets its pointer to `NULL`:

```
pFrame->Release();
pFrame = NULL;
```

The `CreateViewport()` function

Now, with the mesh object created, the program needs to construct a viewport. The first step in completing this task is to create the viewport's frame, which will determine the orientation and position of the view:

```
HRESULT result = m_pD3D->
    CreateFrame(m_pParentFrame, &m_pEye);
if (result != D3DRM_OK)
    return FALSE;
```

Now that the program has its viewport frame, it can position the frame for the required viewing angle and distance:

```
m_pEye->SetPosition(m_pParentFrame, D3DVALUE(0),
    D3DVALUE(0), D3DVALUE(-40.0));
```

The last step is to create the viewport and associate it with its frame:

```
result = m_pD3D->CreateViewport(m_pDevice, m_pEye,
    0, 0, m_pDevice->GetWidth(),
    m_pDevice->GetHeight(), &m_pViewport);
if (result != D3DRM_OK)
    return FALSE;
```

The CreateLight() function

With all the scene objects constructed, and a viewport pointing at the scene, it's time to put some light on the subject. This magic happens in the CreateLight() function, which first creates a single directional light:

```
LPDIRECT3DRMLIGHT pLight;
HRESULT result = m_pD3D->
    CreateLightRGB(D3DRMLIGHT_DIRECTIONAL,
    D3DVALUE(1.0), D3DVALUE(1.0), D3DVALUE(1.0),
    &pLight);
if (result != D3DRM_OK)
    return FALSE;
```

The three color values of 1.0 produce a bright, white light. After its creation, the light needs a frame to orient and position it in the scene:

```
LPDIRECT3DRMFRAME pLightFrame;
result = m_pD3D->CreateFrame(m_pParentFrame,
    &pLightFrame );
if (result != D3DRM_OK)
    return FALSE;
```

With the frame created, the program can add the light to the frame and orient it as needed to light the scene as required by the program:

```
pLightFrame->AddLight(pLight);
pLightFrame->SetOrientation(m_pParentFrame,
    D3DVALUE(0.0), D3DVALUE(-1.0), D3DVALUE(1.0),
    D3DVALUE(0.0), D3DVALUE(1.0), D3DVALUE(0.0));
```

After adding the light to the scene, the program no longer needs to access the light or its frame, so it releases both of these objects and sets their pointers to NULL:

```
pLight->Release();
pLight = NULL;
pLightFrame->Release();
pLightFrame = NULL;
```

The OnPaint() function

In an MFC program that doesn't use a window derived from the CView class, it's the OnPaint() function, rather than OnDraw(), that creates the application's display. In a Direct3D program, creating the display is just a matter of creating a window device and calling its HandlePaint() function. This happens in

Direct3DApp's `OnPaint()` function, which first calls `GetUpdateRect()` to determine whether any portion of the window actually needs to be redrawn:

```
BOOL repaint = GetUpdateRect(NULL);
if (!repaint)
    return;
```

If `GetUpdateRect()` returns `FALSE`, there's really nothing that `OnPaint()` needs to do, so the function returns. If `GetUpdateRect()` returns `TRUE`, however, some portion of the window needs to be redrawn. To handle this eventuality, the program first calls `BeginPaint()`, which, unlike in `OnDraw()`, is required in `OnPaint()`:

```
    PAINTSTRUCT pstruct;
    BeginPaint(&pstruct);
```

Next, `OnPaint()` checks the `m_D3DOK` flag to see whether the program's Direct3D objects are valid. If Direct3D is ready to go, the program creates a window device, calls its `HandlePaint()` function, and finally releases the device:

```
if (m_D3DOK)
{
    LPDIRECT3DRMWINDEVICE pWndDevice;
    m_pDevice->
        QueryInterface(IID_IDirect3DRMWinDevice,
        (void**)&pWndDevice);
    pWndDevice->HandlePaint(pstruct.hdc);
    pWndDevice->Release();
}
```

As you can see, the program gets a pointer to the window device by calling the Direct3D device's `QueryInterface()` function. This function's first argument is the ID for the requested interface, and the second argument is the address of a pointer to the requested interface. If the call to `QueryInterface()` succeeds (which it should, as we already know that the interface exists), the function places the address of the interface into the `pWndDevice` pointer.

If Direct3D didn't initialize properly earlier in the program, `m_D3DOK` will be `FALSE`, and `OnPaint()` will do nothing more than display an error message:

```
    else
        ::TextOut(pstruct.hdc, 20, 20,
            "Direct3D failed to start.", 25);
```

Finally, `OnPaint()` calls `EndPaint()` to tell Windows that the painting is complete:

```
EndPaint(&pstruct);
```

The `OnTimer()` function

The last thing of interest in the Direct3DApp program is the way the Direct3D animation works. Believe it or not, all it takes is a single call to the main Direct3D object's `Tick()` function to advance the animation to the next frame. This happens in the program's `OnTimer()` function, which responds to the `WM_TIMER` messages arriving at the window 10 times a second.

OnTimer() first checks the m_D3DOK flag to be sure that the Direct3D object is valid. Then the function calls Tick() to rotate the 3D model one step:

```
if (m_D3DOK)
    m_pD3D->Tick(D3DVALUE(1));
```

Tick()'s single argument controls the speed of the animation. A value of 1 causes the animation to proceed exactly as was requested when the program called SetRotation() in the locally defined CreateMesh() function. In Direct3DApp, the Tick() argument of 1 causes the model to rotate 0.05 radians. A smaller argument makes the rotation speed proportionately slower, while a larger argument makes the rotation proportionately faster. For example, in Direct3DApp, a Tick() argument of 0.5 causes the model to rotate only 0.025 radians, whereas an argument of 2 causes the model to rotate 0.10 radians.

PROBLEMS & SOLUTIONS

Writing a Conventional Direct3D Windows Application

PROBLEM: *Now I know how to write an MFC Direct3D program. What if I'd just as soon write my program without MFC?*

SOLUTION: Just as with DirectDraw or DirectSound, the easiest way to accomplish this task is to write a traditional Windows program, but write it as a C++ program, rather than a C program. Then you can avoid the clumsy syntax required to call Direct3D functions from a C program.

Note

If you've forgotten how to write a traditional Windows application, you might want to take the time now to review Chapter 4, "Application Fundamentals."

To create a Direct3D application as a conventional Windows program, first write the basic application as you normally would, providing a WinMain() function that defines and registers your window class, as well as contains the application's message loop. You'll also need to provide a Windows procedure that responds to the many messages for which Windows will target your application. In your basic Windows procedure, you'll want to respond at least to the WM_DESTROY message.

On CD-ROM

Once you have the basic application built, you can add the Direct3D program code. In your Windows procedure, respond to the WM_CREATE message by initializing your program and setting up Direct3D. As you can see in Listing 27-5, the entire process is actually less complicated than trying to wedge Direct3D into an MFC program. You can find the program in the Chapter27\Direct3DApp2 folder of this book's CD-ROM.

Continued

Listing 27-5: Source code for the Direct3DApp2 application

```
#define INITGUID
#include <windows.h>
#include <windowsx.h>
#include <d3drm.h>
#include <d3drmwin.h>

/* Function prototypes */
LRESULT CALLBACK WndProc(HWND hWnd, UINT message,
    WPARAM wParam, LPARAM lParam);
void InitVariables();
BOOL InitDirect3D(HWND hWnd);
BOOL MakeScene();
BOOL CreateMesh();
BOOL CreateViewport();
BOOL CreateLight();

/* Global variables */
LPDIRECT3DRM pD3D;
LPDIRECT3DRMDEVICE pDevice;
LPDIRECT3DRMVIEWPORT pViewport;
LPDIRECT3DRMFRAME pParentFrame;
LPDIRECT3DRMFRAME pEye;
LPDIRECT3DRMMESHBUILDER pMeshBuilder;
LPDIRECTDRAWCLIPPER pClipper;

int WINAPI WinMain(HINSTANCE hCurrentInst,
    HINSTANCE hPrevInstance, PSTR lpszCmdLine,
    int nCmdShow)
{
    WNDCLASS wndClass;
    HWND hWnd;
    MSG msg;
    UINT width;
    UINT height;

    wndClass.style = CS_HREDRAW | CS_VREDRAW;
    wndClass.lpfnWndProc = WndProc;
    wndClass.cbClsExtra = 0;
    wndClass.cbWndExtra = 0;
    wndClass.hInstance = hCurrentInst;
    wndClass.hIcon = LoadIcon(NULL, IDI_APPLICATION);
    wndClass.hCursor = LoadCursor(NULL, IDC_ARROW);
    wndClass.hbrBackground = GetStockObject(WHITE_BRUSH);
    wndClass.lpszMenuName = NULL;
    wndClass.lpszClassName = "D3DApp";

    RegisterClass(&wndClass);

    width = GetSystemMetrics(SM_CXSCREEN) / 2;
    height = GetSystemMetrics(SM_CYSCREEN) / 2;
```

Continued

```
        hWnd = CreateWindow(
            "D3DApp",                /* Window class's name.    */
            "Direct3D App",          /* Title bar text.         */
            WS_OVERLAPPEDWINDOW,     /* The window's style.     */
            10,                      /* X position.             */
            10,                      /* Y position.             */
            width,                   /* Width.                  */
            height,                  /* Height.                 */
            NULL,                    /* Parent window's handle. */
            NULL,                    /* Menu handle.            */
            hCurrentInst,            /* Instance handle.        */
            NULL);                   /* No additional data.     */

    ShowWindow(hWnd, nCmdShow);
    UpdateWindow(hWnd);

    while (GetMessage(&msg, NULL, 0, 0))
    {
        TranslateMessage(&msg);
        DispatchMessage(&msg);
    }

    return msg.wParam;
}

LRESULT CALLBACK WndProc(HWND hWnd, UINT message,
    WPARAM wParam, LPARAM lParam)
{
    HDC hDC;
    PAINTSTRUCT paintStruct;
    BOOL repaint;

    switch(message)
    {
        case WM_CREATE:
            InitVariables();
            InitDirect3D(hWnd);
            return 0;

        case WM_PAINT:
            repaint = GetUpdateRect(hWnd, NULL, FALSE);
            if (!repaint)
                return 0;

            hDC = BeginPaint(hWnd, &paintStruct);

            LPDIRECT3DRMWINDEVICE pWndDevice;
            pDevice->QueryInterface(
                IID_IDirect3DRMWinDevice,
                (void**)&pWndDevice);
            pWndDevice->HandlePaint(hDC);
            pWndDevice->Release();

            EndPaint(hWnd, &paintStruct);
```

Continued

```
                    return 0;

            case WM_TIMER:
                pD3D->Tick(D3DVALUE(1));
                return 0;

            case WM_DESTROY:
                if (pMeshBuilder)
                    pMeshBuilder->Release();

                if (pEye)
                    pEye->Release();

                if (pViewport)
                    pViewport->Release();

                if (pParentFrame)
                    pParentFrame->Release();

                if (pDevice)
                    pDevice->Release();

                if (pD3D)
                    pD3D->Release();

                if (pClipper)
                    pClipper->Release();

                PostQuitMessage(0);
                return 0;
        }

    return DefWindowProc(hWnd, message, wParam, lParam);
}

void InitVariables()
{
    pD3D = NULL;
    pDevice = NULL;
    pViewport = NULL;
    pParentFrame = NULL;
    pEye = NULL;
    pMeshBuilder = NULL;
    pClipper = NULL;
}

BOOL InitDirect3D(HWND hWnd)
{
    HRESULT result = Direct3DRMCreate(&pD3D);
    if (result != D3DRM_OK)
        return FALSE;
```

Continued

```
        result = DirectDrawCreateClipper(0, &pClipper, 0);
        if (result != DD_OK)
            return FALSE;
        result = pClipper->SetHWnd(0, hWnd);
        if (result != DD_OK)
            return FALSE;

        RECT rect;
        GetClientRect(hWnd, &rect);
        result = pD3D->CreateDeviceFromClipper(pClipper,
            NULL, rect.right, rect.bottom, &pDevice);
        if (result != D3DRM_OK)
            return FALSE;
        pDevice->SetQuality(D3DRMRENDER_GOURAUD);

        pD3D->CreateFrame(0, &pParentFrame);
        if (result != D3DRM_OK)
            return FALSE;

        BOOL succeeded = MakeScene();
        if (!succeeded)
            return FALSE;

        SetTimer(hWnd, 1, 100, NULL);

        return TRUE;
    }

BOOL MakeScene()
{
        BOOL succeeded = CreateMesh();
        if (!succeeded)
            return FALSE;

        succeeded = CreateViewport();
        if (!succeeded)
            return FALSE;

        succeeded = CreateLight();
        if (!succeeded)
            return FALSE;

        return TRUE;
    }

BOOL CreateMesh()
{
        HRESULT result =
            pD3D->CreateMeshBuilder(&pMeshBuilder);
        if (result != D3DRM_OK)
            return FALSE;
```

Continued

```
        result = pMeshBuilder->Load("model.x",
            NULL, D3DRMLOAD_FROMFILE, NULL, NULL );
        if (result != D3DRM_OK)
        {
            MessageBox(0, "MODEL.X file missing. Please place\n\
a Direct3D X file with this name\nin the Direct3DApp folder.",
                "File Missing", MB_OK | MB_ICONEXCLAMATION);
            return FALSE;
        }

        LPDIRECT3DRMFRAME pFrame;
        result =
            pD3D->CreateFrame(pParentFrame, &pFrame);
        if (result != D3DRM_OK)
            return FALSE;
        pFrame->AddVisual(pMeshBuilder);
        pFrame->SetRotation(pParentFrame, D3DVALUE(0.0),
            D3DVALUE(1.0), D3DVALUE(0.0), D3DVALUE(0.05));
        pFrame->Release();
        pFrame = NULL;

        return TRUE;
}

BOOL CreateViewport()
{
        HRESULT result = pD3D->
            CreateFrame(pParentFrame, &pEye);
        if (result != D3DRM_OK)
            return FALSE;
        pEye->SetPosition(pParentFrame, D3DVALUE(0),
            D3DVALUE(0), D3DVALUE(-40.0));
        result = pD3D->CreateViewport(pDevice, pEye,
            0, 0, pDevice->GetWidth(),
            pDevice->GetHeight(), &pViewport);
        if (result != D3DRM_OK)
            return FALSE;

        return TRUE;
}

BOOL CreateLight()
{
        LPDIRECT3DRMLIGHT pLight;
        HRESULT result = pD3D->
            CreateLightRGB(D3DRMLIGHT_DIRECTIONAL,
            D3DVALUE(1.0), D3DVALUE(1.0), D3DVALUE(1.0),
            &pLight);
        if (result != D3DRM_OK)
            return FALSE;
```

Continued

```
LPDIRECT3DRMFRAME pLightFrame;
result = pD3D->CreateFrame(pParentFrame,
    &pLightFrame );
if (result != D3DRM_OK)
    return FALSE;

pLightFrame->AddLight(pLight);
pLightFrame->SetOrientation(pParentFrame,
    D3DVALUE(0.0), D3DVALUE(-1.0), D3DVALUE(1.0),
    D3DVALUE(0.0), D3DVALUE(1.0), D3DVALUE(0.0));
pLight->Release();
pLight = NULL;
pLightFrame->Release();
pLightFrame = NULL;

return TRUE;
}
```

Listing 27-5 initializes Direct3D in much the same way as this chapter's previous program, Direct3DApp. In fact, the program looks and acts very similar. That is, when you run the application, a rotating 3D model appears in the window. All of the Direct3D code in the program should be familiar to you by now. If you don't understand the program, you should reread this chapter from the beginning.

Summary

This concludes your all-too-brief introduction to the Direct3D programming libraries. As was mentioned before, this introduction is only a starting point. Entire books have been written on Direct3D programming, not to mention on 3D graphics programming in general. If you're new to 3D programming, this chapter may seem more confusing than helpful. If so, get yourself a good 3D graphics programming book and learn the basics. Then, come back to this chapter.

Also discussed in this chapter:

▶ A Direct3D application must create a Direct3D main object.

▶ A DirectDraw clipper object manages a Direct3D window.

▶ A Direct3D application must create a device object.

▶ Direct3D objects are oriented and positioned using frames.

▶ A Direct3D model is created from a mesh, which is a collection of polygons.

▶ A Direct3D viewport determines how a scene can be viewed.

▶ Direct3D lights not only enable you to see objects in a 3D world, but also cause shadows and reflections.

Part VI

Internet

Chapter 28

WinInet

With the Internet slowly but surely dominating our lives, it should come as no surprise that MFC includes classes that enable programmers to create Internet applications more easily than ever before. The WinInet classes make it possible to create HTTP, FTP, and Gopher Internet applications without having to handle (or even know about) all the nitty-gritty details. To introduce you to this topic, this chapter provides an overview of the WinInet classes. Moreover, because HTTP and FTP sessions are the most common type of Internet access, this chapter also features sections on how to use WinInet to create these types of applications. The FTP section, in fact, features an FTP application that enables you to browse FTP servers and download files.

Introducing WinInet

As mentioned previously, WinInet is a collection of MFC classes that simplifies the task of writing Internet applications, including the handling of HTTP, FTP, and Gopher sessions. WinInet includes classes for managing Internet sessions, connections, and files. In fact, using WinInet, you can forget about things like TCP/IP protocol and WinSock, major stumbling blocks for new Internet programmers. Table 28-1 lists the WinInet classes along with their descriptions.

Table 28-1   The WinInet Classes

Class	Description
CFileFind	Enables Internet file searches
CFtpConnection	Manages the connection to an FTP server
CFtpFileFind	Enables Internet file searches on an FTP server
CGopherConnection	Manages a connection to a Gopher server
CGopherFile	Manages files on a Gopher server
CGopherFileFind	Enables Internet file searches on a Gopher server
CGopherLocator	Retrieves a Gopher locator from a gopher server
CHttpConnection	Manages the connection to an HTTP server
CHttpFile	Enables an application to read HTTP files
CInternetConnection	Manages a connection to an Internet server
CInternetException	Represents exceptions that occur during Internet sessions
CInternetFile	Enables high-level Internet file access
CInternetSession	Manages one or more Internet sessions

Virtually all Internet access these days is through HTTP or FTP connections. For that reason, this chapter concentrates on these types of applications, as well as on the WinInet classes that support these types of Internet connections. In the rest of this section, you get a closer look at the following classes, which enable you to create both HTTP and FTP applications: CInternetSession, CInternetConnection, CHttpConnection, CFtpConnection, CInternetFile, CHttpFile, CFileFind, CFtpFileFind, and CInternetException.

The CInternetSession class

No matter what type of Internet program you're writing with WinInet, the first step is to create an Internet session. A CInternetSession object can handle one or more Internet sessions simultaneously and even handle connections to a proxy server. The CInternetSession object can interpret and connect to URLs that you specify using the object's member functions. Moreover, a CInternetSession object can create HTTP, FTP, and Gopher connections on behalf of your application. Table 28-2 lists the class's member functions, along with their descriptions.

Table 28-2   The `CInternetSession` **class's member functions**

Function	Description
`Close()`	Closes the Internet connection
`EnableStatusCallback()`	Enables a status callback function for asynchronous operations
`GetContext()`	Gets the session's context value
`GetFtpConnection()`	Starts an FTP session
`GetGopherConnection()`	Starts a gopher session
`GetHttpConnection()`	Starts an HTTP session
`OnStatusCallback()`	Updates an asynchronous operation's status
`OpenURL()`	Opens a given URL
`QueryOption()`	Provides error handling for operations
`ServiceTypeFromHandle()`	Gets the type of Internet service
`SetOption()`	Sets a session's options

The `CInternetConnection` class

The `CInternetConnection` class is the base class for the other more specific WinInet connection types, such as `CHttpConnection` and `CFtpConnection`. As such, this class defines the basic functionality for an Internet connection. All WinInet programs must establish an Internet session (through `CInternetSession`) and an Internet connection (through a class derived from `CInternetConnection`) to communicate over the Internet. Following is a list of `CInternetConnection`'s member functions, which are all inherited by classes derived from `CInternetSession`.

`GetContext()`	Gets the connection's context ID
`GetSession()`	Gets a pointer to the connection's session object
`GetServerName()`	Gets the name of the connection's server

The `CHttpConnection` class

The `CHttpConnection` class represents a connection to an HTTP server, which is the type of connection that browsers use to display Web pages (see Figure 28-1). Unlike most MFC classes, you don't create a `CHttpConnection` object directly, but rather call the `CInternetSession` `GetHttpConnection()` member function. Or, you can connect to an HTML document from an HTTP connection by calling the `CInternetSession` object's `OpenURL()` function.

Because CHttpConnection has CInternetConnection as a base class, it inherits that class's member functions. It also defines one of its own, OpenRequest(), which opens an HTTP connection.

Figure 28-1: Microsoft Internet Explorer displaying the author's Web page over an HTTP connection

The CFtpConnection **class**

The CFtpConnection class represents a connection to an FTP server, which is used mainly to upload and download files to and from the server (see Figure 28-2). Like CHttpConnection, you don't create a CFtpConnection object directly, but rather call the CInternetSession GetFtpConnection() member function. Because CFtpConnection has CInternetConnection as a base class, it inherits that class's member functions. It also defines many of its own, which are listed and described in Table 28-3.

Table 28-3   The CFtpConnection **class's member functions**

Function	*Description*
Close()	Closes the connection to an FTP server
CreateDirectory()	Creates a directory on an FTP server
GetCurrentDirectory()	Gets the connection's current directory

Function	Description
GetCurrentDirectoryAsURL()	Gets the connection's current directory as an URL
GetFile()	Downloads a file from an FTP server
OpenFile()	Opens a file on an FTP server
PutFile()	Uploads a file to an FTP server
Remove()	Removes a file from an FTP server
RemoveDirectory()	Removes a directory from an FTP server
Rename()	Renames a file on an FTP server
SetCurrentDirectory()	Changes to the given FTP directory

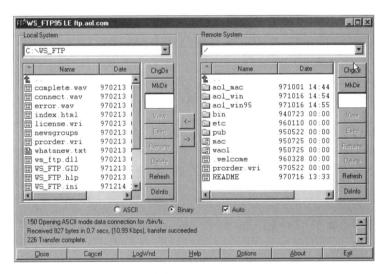

Figure 28-2: A popular FTP application, WS_FTP, connecting to an FTP server

The CInternetFile **class**

The CInternetFile class is the base class for the other more specific WinInet file classes, CHttpFile and CGopherFile. As such, this class defines the basic functionality for an Internet file object, allowing WinInet programs to access files using Internet file transfer protocols. However, you don't create CInternetFile objects in your programs. Instead, you create an object from a class that's derived from CInternetFile. Table 28-4 lists CInternetFile's member functions, which are all inherited by classes derived from CInternetFile.

Table 28-4 The CInternetFile **class's member functions**

Function	Description
Abort()	Closes the file without regard for errors
Close()	Closes a CInternetFile object
Flush()	Flushes the file
Read()	Reads bytes from the file
ReadString()	Reads characters from the file
Seek()	Positions the file's pointer
SetReadBufferSize()	Sets the size of the file's read buffer
SetWriteBufferSize()	Sets the size of the file's write buffer
Write()	Writes bytes to the file
WriteString()	Writes a string to the file

The CHttpFile **class**

The CHttpFile class enables an application to access and read files over an HTTP connection. Because WinInet derives CHttpFile from CInternetFile, the class inherits all of CInternetFile's member functions, as well as defines a set of its own that are specific to handling HTTP files. Table 28-5 lists those functions and their descriptions.

Table 28-5 The CHttpFile **class's member functions**

Function	Description
AddRequestHeaders()	Adds headers to an HTTP server request
Close()	Closes a file
GetFileURL()	Gets a file's URL
GetObject()	Gets a request verb's target object
GetVerb()	Gets a request verb
QueryInfo()	Gets the response or request headers
QueryInfoStatusCode()	Gets an HTTP request's status code
SendRequest()	Sends a request to an HTTP server

The CFileFind **class**

The CFileFind class is the base class for the other more specific WinInet file-find classes, CFtpFileFind and CGopherFileFind. As such, this class defines the basic functionality for a file-find object, allowing WinInet programs to do file searches on the local system, as well as over an Internet connection. Besides finding files, `CFileFind` objects can request information about files, including path, file name, creation time, URL, length, directory, and other file attributes. Table 28-6 lists `CFileFind`'s member functions.

Table 28-6   The `CFileFind` class's member functions

Function	Description
Close()	Terminates a search
FindFile()	Searches for a file
FindNextFile()	Finds the next file in a file search
GetCreationTime()	Gets the file's creation time
GetFileName()	Gets the file's file name
GetFilePath()	Gets the file's path
GetFileTitle()	Gets the file's title, which is the name without the extension
GetFileURL()	Gets the file's URL
GetLastAccessTime()	Gets the file's last access time
GetLastWriteTime()	Gets the files last change time
GetLength()	Gets the file's length
GetRoot()	Gets the file's root directory
IsArchived()	Returns TRUE if the file is archived
IsCompressed()	Returns TRUE if the file is compressed
IsDirectory()	Returns TRUE if the file is a directory
IsDots()	Returns TRUE if the file name is "." or ".."
IsHidden()	Returns TRUE if the file is hidden
IsNormal()	Returns TRUE if the file is normal
IsReadOnly()	Returns TRUE if the file is read-only
IsSystem()	Returns TRUE if the file is a system file
IsTemporary()	Returns TRUE if the file is temporary
MatchesMask()	Specifies attributes of the file for which to search

The `CFtpFileFind` class

The `CFtpFileFind` class, which WinInet derives from `CFileFind`, enables FTP applications to search for files, as well as to obtain information about files. `CFtpFileFind` inherits much of its functionality from `CFileFind`, but also defines three functions of its own that refine certain operations for FTP access. The following list describes these additional member functions:

FindFile()	Finds a file on an FTP server
FindNextFile()	Continues a file search from a previous call to FindFile()
GetFileURL()	Gets the URL, including path, of the found file

The CInternetException class

When an error occurs during a WinInet Internet session, it's an object of the CInternetException class that usually reports it. Many WinInet functions throw CInternetException objects, so your program should supply try and catch program blocks to ensure that the exceptions are handled properly. Because WinInet derives CInternetException from MFC's CException class, you can use the inherited member functions to obtain information about a specific exception.

Writing an HTTP Application

Just about every Internet user on the planet uses an HTTP application to browse the Web, whether they know it or not. It's the HTTP portion of a Web browser that reads HTML code from a Web page and converts it to the page's visual representation. Because HTTP is so important, in this section you'll learn about basic HTTP programming with WinInet.

If you don't consider the task of parsing (reading and interpreting) and rendering an HTTP document (a task that can't be handled with the WinInet classes), creating an HTTP application with WinInet is criminally easy, involving five main steps:

1. Start an Internet session.
2. Open the connection to the HTTP server.
3. Read the HTTP file from the server.
4. Close the HTTP connection.
5. Close the Internet session.

In the following sections, you'll examine these steps in detail, as implemented using the WinInet classes.

Starting an Internet session

No matter what type of Internet program you're writing with WinInet, the first step is to create an Internet session. To set up an Internet session, you create an object of the CInternetSession class:

```
CInternetSession session;
```

On a basic level, that's all there is to creating your Internet session. If you're an advanced Internet programmer, CInternetSession's constructor provides additional control over the session through its many arguments, which all have default values. MFC declares the CInternetSession constructor like this:

```
CInternetSession(
    LPCTSTR pstrAgent = NULL,
    DWORD dwContext = 1,
    DWORD dwAccessType = INTERNET_OPEN_TYPE_PRECONFIG,
    LPCTSTR pstrProxyName = NULL,
    LPCTSTR pstrProxyBypass = NULL,
    DWORD dwFlags = 0);
```

Each of the constructor's arguments are described as follows. If you're interested in supplying any of these arguments to the CInternetSession constructor, please look for additional details in your Visual C++ online documentation.

pstrAgent	A pointer to the name of the application that owns the Internet session
dwContext	The context ID with which the session object will be associated
dwAccessType	The type of Internet access the session will use
pstrProxyName	The CERN proxy name if the access will be through a CERN proxy
pstrProxyBypass	A list of addresses that may be ignored during proxy access
dwFlags	Flags for selecting additional options

Opening the connection to an HTTP server

To establish a connection with an HTTP server, you can call the session object's OpenURL() function to read the HTML document from the given URL. That process looks like this:

```
CHttpFile* httpFile =
    (CHttpFile*)internetSession.OpenURL(url);
```

The OpenURL() function actually has five arguments, all of which except the first have default values. The function's full signature looks like this:

```
CStdioFile* OpenURL(
    LPCTSTR pstrURL,
    DWORD dwContext = 1,
    DWORD dwFlags = INTERNET_FLAG_TRANSFER_ASCII,
    LPCTSTR pstrHeaders = NULL,
    DWORD dwHeadersLength = 0);
```

OpenURL()'s arguments are described below:

pstrURL	The URL from which to read
dwContext	A context value used with callback functions
dwFlags	File-handling flags
pstrHeaders	Headers to be sent to the server
dwHeadersLength	The length of the headers

How you handle the pointer returned by OpenURL() depends on the type of connection. With an FTP connection, the OpenURL() function returns a pointer to a CStdioFile object, which you must cast to an CHttpFile pointer.

After getting the file-object pointer, you can set the file's read-buffer size:

```
httpFile->SetReadBufferSize(4096);
```

Due to a bug in WinInet, before you can use the file object, you must set its buffer size, by calling the file object's SetReadBufferSize() function.

Reading a file from an HTTP server

Once you have your connection established, you can read from the file easily, by calling the file object's ReadString() function:

```
CString string;
httpFile->ReadString(string);
```

The ReadString() function takes a reference to a CString object into which it places the string read from the file. An overloaded version of the function accepts a pointer to a string, as well as a value indicating the maximum number of characters to read, as arguments. Because ReadString() may throw a CInternetException object, you should call this function from within a try program block.

Closing the connection and session

When you've finished with your HTTP session, you must close both the connection and the session:

```
httpFile->Close();
session.Close();
```

Creating an HTTP session

Now that you know all the details, you might like to see those details put together into a block of source code that actually does something. Listing 28-1 shows the source code for creating an HTTP session that connects to an HTTP server and reads 100 lines of the default HTML file. (Of course, the real trick is what you do with those HTML lines once you have them. Rendering an HTML document is an immense task.)

Note

Before you can access WinInet classes in a program, you must include the WinInet header file, afxinet.h. The header file declares the classes, functions, and constants used in WinInet programming.

Listing 28-1: Reading an HTML document from an HTTP server

```
CString htmlLines[100];
CString url = "http://www.microsoft.com";

CInternetSession session;

try
{
    CHttpFile* file =
        (CHttpFile*)session.OpenURL(url);
    file->SetReadBufferSize(2046);

    for (int index=0; index<100; ++index)
        file->ReadString(htmlLines[index]);

    file->Close();
}
catch (CInternetException* pException)
{
    pException->ReportError();
}

session.Close();
```

As an example, if you created an MFC AppWizard program with a OnLButtonDown() function that contained the code shown in Listing 28-1, when you clicked in the application's window, the program would connect to Microsoft's Web site and read 100 lines of HTML code from the default Web page. Of course, you won't see anything happening unless you do something with the HTML code the function reads.

Writing an FTP Application

Writing an FTP application that just connects to an FTP server and reads the root directory isn't much more complicated than connecting to an HTTP server and reading an HTML file. The basic steps are as follows:

1. Start an Internet session.

2. Open the connection to the FTP server.

3. Get the server's current directory.

4. Read file names from the directory.

5. Close the FTP connection.

6. Close the Internet session.

In the following sections, you'll examine these steps in detail, as implemented using the WinInet classes.

Opening an FTP connection

Starting a WinInet Internet session for an FTP application is no different than starting one for an HTTP application. Just create an object of the `CInternetSession` class:

```
CInternetSession session;
```

To open an FTP connection to a server, call the session object's `GetFtpConnection()` function:

```
CFtpConnection* pConnection =
    session.GetFtpConnection(m_site);
```

The `GetFtpConnection()` function actually has five arguments. However, all but the first have default values. In the above code, `m_site` is a string containing the FTP server's address—for example, `ftp.microsoft.com`. The function's full signature looks like this:

```
CFtpConnection* GetFtpConnection(
    LPCTSTR pstrServer,
    LPCTSTR pstrUserName = NULL,
    LPCTSTR pstrPassword = NULL,
    INTERNET_PORT nPort = INTERNET_INVALID_PORT_NUMBER,
    BOOL bPassive = FALSE);
```

The five arguments are described as follows:

pstrServer	A string containing the server's name
pstrUserName	A string containing the user's login name
pstrPassword	A string containing the user's password
nPort	The server's TCP/IP port number
bPassive	A flag that sets active or passive mode

As an example, suppose you want to access a server named `ftp.myserver.com` with a user name of Casper and a password of The Ghost. Your call to `GetFtpConnection()` would look something like this:

```
CFtpConnection* pConnection =
    session.GetFtpConnection("ftp.myserver.com",
    "Casper", "The Ghost");
```

Of course, in a full-featured program, you'd use string variables for the server name, user name, and password, rather than hard-coded values as shown in the example. After all, what good is an FTP program that can connect to only one account on only one sever?

Getting the root directory

Once you've established a connection with the server, you're going to want to at least browse the root directory. The first step in accomplishing that task is to get the name of the root directory, which will probably always be "/". However, getting the directory from the server gives you a chance to use the `CFtpConnection` class's object `GetCurrentDirectory()` function:

```
CString directory;
succeeded = pConnection->
    GetCurrentDirectory(directory);
```

`GetCurrentDirectory()` returns the directory's name in the function's single argument, which is a reference to a `CString` object.

Reading a directory

Now your application is ready to read the contents of the root directory, which is not unlike reading a directory in a regular non-Internet application. First, you create a `CFtpFileFind` object:

```
CFtpFileFind fileFind(pFtpConnection);
```

The class's constructor takes as its single argument a pointer to the `CFtpConnection` object.

Next, you call the `CFtpFileFind` object's `FindFile()` function, which returns a Boolean value indicating whether there was a file to find:

```
BOOL gotAFile = fileFind.FindFile();
```

If `FindFile()` returns `TRUE`, you know that the directory is not empty. (If it returns `FALSE`, there are no files in the directory.) You can then call `FindNextFile()` as many times as needed to read all the directory's file names:

```
gotAFile = fileFind.FindNextFile();
```

`FindNextFile()` returns a Boolean value that indicates whether there is another file to find. To read the entire directory, continually call `FindNextFile()` in a loop until the function returns `FALSE`. The entire process of reading file names from a directory on an FTP server looks like the following code:

```
CString fileName;
CFtpFileFind fileFind(pConnection);
BOOL gotAFile = fileFind.FindFile();
while (gotAFile)
{
    gotAFile = fileFind.FindNextFile();
    fileName = fileFind.GetFileName();
    // Do something with the file name.
}
```

Closing the connection and session

When you've finished with your FTP session, you must close both the connection and the session:

```
pConnection->Close();
session.Close();
```

Running the FTPAccessApp Application

On CD-ROM

Before you write a sample FTP application, it would be helpful for you to take a look at what one can do. In the Chapter28\FTPAccessApp folder of this book's CD-ROM, you'll find the FtpAccessApp application, which really puts the WinInet FTP classes to the test. When you run the application, you see the window shown in Figure 28-3. The main window is divided into three columns that'll display the contents of any FTP directory you log onto.

```
┌─────────────────────────────────────────────────────────────────────────┐
│ Untitled - FTPAccessApp                                          _ □ ×    │
│ File  FTP  Help                                                           │
│                                                                           │
│  FTP SITE:                                                                │
│  DIRECTORY:                                                               │
│  ┌──────────────────────────────┐                                        │
│  └──────────────────────────────┘                                        │
│                                                                           │
│  File Name    File Length    File Name    File Length    File Name    File Length │
│                                                                           │
│                                                                           │
└─────────────────────────────────────────────────────────────────────────┘
```

Figure 28-3: FTPAccessApp's main window will be your view into the Internet.

To get started, select the FTP menu's Connect command in the application. When you do, the Connect dialog box appears (see Figure 28-4), into which you can type the information needed to connect to an FTP server. (Microsoft's FTP server comes up as the default the first time you see the dialog. To connect to Microsoft, just press Enter.) If your connection requires no password, simply enter the name of the FTP server and select OK. You'll then log into the selected FTP server as an anonymous user.

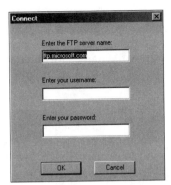

Figure 28-4: You choose an FTP server in the Connect dialog box.

Status messages in the upper-right of the window keep you informed as the program makes its connection and reads file names from the server. After the program completes reading the file names on the server, it displays the results in the window. One limitation of this simple example program is that it can display only 45 files. Any more than that and you're out of luck. (Fixing this limitation sounds like a good project for you folks who like to tinker.) Figure 28-5 shows FtpAccessApp after it logs onto Microsoft's server.

FTP SITE: ftp.microsoft.com
DIRECTORY: /

File Name	File Length	File Name	File Length	File Name	File Length
bussys	0	Services	0		
deskapps	0	Softlib	0		
developr	0	solutions	0		
dirmap.htm	8102				
dirmap.txt	4405				
DISCLAIM.TXT	710				
disclaimer.txt	712				
KBHelp	0				
ls-lR.txt	9503357				
ls-lR.Z	1775951				
LS-LR.ZIP	951200				
MSCorp	0				
peropsys	0				
PRODUCT.TBL	7873				
Products	0				

Figure 28-5: FtpAccessApp explores Microsoft's FTP server.

Now that you're logged onto a server, you can start to browse. To move to another directory, double-click the directory in the window. The entry turns red, the mouse cursor changes into an hourglass, and the program again negotiates with the server. After reading the file names for the new directory, the results appear on the screen. If no file names appear, the directory is empty.

The MOVE TO PREVIOUS DIRECTORY command becomes active when you're no longer on the root directory. You can double-click this command to move back up through the server's directory tree. The directory line near the top of the window keeps you informed of your current location.

As you browse through the server's directory, you may come across a file you want to download. No problem. Just right-click the file's entry. The file's name turns green, and FtpAccessApp asks whether you want to download the file (see Figure 28-6). Click OK to download the file, or click Cancel to terminate the download command. When the download is complete (it could take a while, depending on the size of the file), you'll find the file in FtpAccessApp's directory.

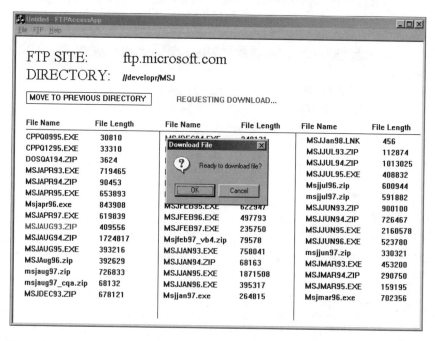

Figure 28-6: You can choose to download a file or abort the download command.

Creating the FTPAccessApp Sample Application

Now that you've seen the application work, in the following sections, you'll examine the source code to see how the application handles the FTP connection.

Examining the member variables

FTPAccessApp is an AppWizard-generated program, and virtually everything that happens in FTPAccessApp happens in the view class. Obviously, then, all the important member variables are declared in the view class's header file. Those declarations look like this:

```
CString m_fileNames[45];
DWORD m_fileLengths[45];
CString m_curDirectory;
CString m_site;
int m_fileCount;
CString m_password;
CString m_username;
```

The following list describes how the program uses each of these variables:

m_fileNames[]	A string array that holds the file names for the current directory
m_fileLengths[]	A DWORD array that holds the lengths of the files in the current directory
m_curDirectory	A string that holds the name of the current directory, complete with path
m_site	A string that holds the name of the currently accessed FTP server
m_fileCount	An integer that holds the number of files in the current directory
m_password	A string that holds the password for the current FTP connection
m_username	A string that holds the user name for the current FTP connection

FTPAccessApp initializes these member variables in the view class's constructor, which looks like Listing 28-2. As you can see in the listing, the constructor initializes all the string variables to empty strings and all the numerical variables to zero.

Listing 28-2: The `CFTPAccessAppView`**'s class's constructor**

```
CFTPAccessAppView::CFTPAccessAppView()
{
    // TODO: add construction code here

    m_fileCount = 0;
    m_site = "";
    m_curDirectory = "";
    m_username = "";
    m_password = "";

    for (int x=0; x<45; ++x)
    {
        m_fileNames[x] = "";
        m_fileLengths[x] = 0;
    }
}
```

Creating the `OnDraw()` function

Many of the variables you examined in the previous section contain information to be displayed on the screen. Because FTPAccessApp is an AppWizard-generated program, it draws its display in the view class's `OnDraw()` function, shown in Listing 28-3.

Listing 28-3: The `CFTPAccessAppView`**'s class's** `OnDraw()` **function**

```
void CFTPAccessAppView::OnDraw(CDC* pDC)
{
    CFTPAccessAppDoc* pDoc = GetDocument();
    ASSERT_VALID(pDoc);

    // TODO: add draw code for native data here

    LOGFONT logFont;
    logFont.lfHeight = 32;
    logFont.lfWidth = 0;
    logFont.lfEscapement = 0;
    logFont.lfOrientation = 0;
    logFont.lfWeight = 400;
    logFont.lfItalic = 0;
    logFont.lfUnderline = 0;
    logFont.lfStrikeOut = 0;
    logFont.lfCharSet = ANSI_CHARSET;
    logFont.lfOutPrecision = OUT_DEFAULT_PRECIS;
    logFont.lfClipPrecision = CLIP_DEFAULT_PRECIS;
    logFont.lfQuality = PROOF_QUALITY;
    logFont.lfPitchAndFamily = VARIABLE_PITCH | FF_ROMAN;
    strcpy(logFont.lfFaceName, "Times New Roman");

    CFont font;
    font.CreateFontIndirect(&logFont);
    CFont* pOldFont = pDC->SelectObject(&font);
```

```
pDC->TextOut(20, 20, "FTP SITE:");
pDC->TextOut(200, 20, m_site);
pDC->TextOut(20, 52, "DIRECTORY:");

pDC->SelectObject(pOldFont);
pDC->TextOut(200, 62, m_curDirectory);

pDC->Rectangle(20, 98, 255, 120);
if (m_curDirectory.GetLength() > 1)
    pDC->TextOut(26, 100,
        "MOVE TO PREVIOUS DIRECTORY");

pDC->TextOut(20, 145, "File Name");
pDC->TextOut(150, 145, "File Length");
pDC->TextOut(280, 145, "File Name");
pDC->TextOut(420, 145, "File Length");
pDC->TextOut(530, 145, "File Name");
pDC->TextOut(660, 145, "File Length");
pDC->MoveTo(20, 165);
pDC->LineTo(750, 165);
pDC->MoveTo(270, 165);
pDC->LineTo(270, 500);
pDC->MoveTo(520, 165);
pDC->LineTo(520, 500);

for (int x=0; x<m_fileCount; ++x)
{
    int col, row;

    if (x < 15)
    {
        col = 20;
        row = 170 + x * 20;
    }
    else if (x < 30)
    {
        col = 280;
        row = 170 + (x - 15) * 20;
    }
    else
    {
        col = 540;
        row = 170 + (x - 30) * 20;
    }

    pDC->TextOut(col, row, m_fileNames[x]);

    if ((m_fileNames[x] != ""))
    {
        char s[80];
        wsprintf(s, "%d", m_fileLengths[x]);
        pDC->TextOut(col+140, row, s);
    }
}
}
```

This function creates a large font for the FTP SITE and DIRECTORY labels near the top of the window. After displaying these labels, OnDraw() returns to the default font, drawing the remaining labels and any file names that may be stored in the file array. OnDraw() draws lines with the Rectangle(), MoveTo(), and LineTo() functions. Near the end of the OnDraw() function, you can see that the program has to go through a few gyrations to get the file names to print properly in the different columns.

Creating the OnFtpConnect() function

Before the application can display data in its OnDraw() function, it must read that data from an FTP site. When the user selects the FTP menu's Connect command, the view class's message map sets the OnFtpConnect() function (see Listing 28-4) into action. This function is charged with the task of bringing up the Connect dialog box, retrieving the user's entries from said dialog box, and turning things over to the locally defined OpenFTPDirectory() function, which takes the user's dialog box entries and turns them into an actual FTP connection.

Note

Notice how the call to OpenFTPDirectory() is sandwiched between calls to BeginWaitCursor() and EndWaitCursor() function calls. This is the magic that displays and removes the hourglass cursor, signaling the user that the system is tied up trying to accomplish something. In this case, that "something" is logging onto an FTP server.

Listing 28-4: The CFTPAccessAppView's **class's** OnFtpConnect() **function**

```
void CFTPAccessAppView::OnFtpConnect()
{
    // TODO: Add your command handler code here

    CFTPDialog dialog(this);
    if (m_site == "")
        m_site = "ftp.microsoft.com";
    dialog.m_ftpEdit = m_site;
    dialog.m_nameEdit = m_username;
    dialog.m_passwordEdit = m_password;

    int result = dialog.DoModal();
    if (result != IDOK)
        return;

    m_site = dialog.m_ftpEdit;
    m_username = dialog.m_nameEdit;
    m_password = dialog.m_passwordEdit;
    BeginWaitCursor();
    OpenFTPDirectory("");
    EndWaitCursor();

    Invalidate();
}
```

Here, the program creates a `CFTPDialog` dialog box, sets the dialog box's edit controls to the current FTP settings, and displays the dialog box with the `DoModal()` function. If the user exits the dialog box by clicking the OK button, the program reads the user's entries from the dialog box, transferring them to the member variables that store the FTP settings for the class. Calling the locally defined `OpenFTPDirectory()` (you'll examine this function in the next section) creates the FTP connection and logs onto the server. The call to `Invalidate()` then causes the program to update its display with any data the program reads from the FTP server.

Creating the `OpenFTPDirectory()` function

The `OpenFTPDirectory()` function overflows with cool FTP stuff, as shown in Listing 28-5.

Listing 28-5: The `CFTPAccessAppView`'s class's `OpenFTPDirectory()` function

```
void CFTPAccessAppView::OpenFTPDirectory(CString directory)
{
    DisplayStatusMessage("ESTABLISHING CONNECTION...");

    try
    {
        CInternetSession session;
        CFtpConnection* pConnection =
            session.GetFtpConnection(m_site,
                m_username, m_password);
        BOOL succeeded;
        if (directory == "")
            succeeded = pConnection->
                GetCurrentDirectory(m_curDirectory);
        else
            succeeded =
             pConnection->SetCurrentDirectory(directory);
        if (succeeded)
        {
            ReadFileNames(pConnection);
            session.Close();
            delete pConnection;
            if (directory != "")
                m_curDirectory = directory;
        }
        else
            MessageBox(
                "Cannot access the\nrequested directory",
                "Open Directory",
                MB_OK | MB_ICONINFORMATION);
    }
    catch (CInternetException* pException)
    {
        pException->ReportError();
    }
}
```

First, it calls the locally defined DisplayStatusMessage() function to tell the user that the program's working to establish a connection. Then it creates a CInternetSession object and establishes an FTP connection by calling the object's GetFtpConnection() member function.

The function then examines the directory variable, the value of which is passed into the function as a parameter. If OpenFTPDirectory() is called with directory equal to an empty string, the calling function wants to open the root directory, rather than move to a new directory. This causes a call to GetCurrentDirectory(), rather than SetCurrentDirectory(), which gets called if directory contains a directory name.

If everything goes okay, the program calls the locally defined ReadFileNames(), which does the actual file-name reading for the directory. When that function returns, OpenFTPDirectory() closes the session and deletes the connection object. If the program wasn't able to open the directory, it displays a message box, notifying the user of the problem. If any CInternetException errors occur, they're handled in the catch program block by calling the exception object's ReportError() function.

Creating the ReadFileNames() function

Whenever FTPAccessApp needs to read file names from a server's directory, it calls ReadFileNames(), which looks like Listing 28-6.

Listing 28-6: The CFTPAccessAppView's class's ReadFileNames() function

```
void CFTPAccessAppView::ReadFileNames(CFtpConnection* pFTP)
{
    DisplayStatusMessage("READING DIRECTORY...");

    int fileCount = 0;
    CFtpFileFind fileFind(pFTP);
    BOOL gotAFile = fileFind.FindFile();
    while (gotAFile && (fileCount < 45))
    {
        gotAFile = fileFind.FindNextFile();
        m_fileNames[fileCount] = fileFind.GetFileName();
        m_fileLengths[fileCount] = fileFind.GetLength();
        ++fileCount;
        if (fileCount == 45)
            MessageBox("Can't Display all files");
    }

    m_fileCount = fileCount;
}
```

This function starts off by displaying a status message in the window, after which it creates a CFtpFileFind object with which the function will examine the current server directory. The program calls the CFtpFileFind object's FindFile() and FindNextFile() functions to read in all the file names in the directory. If there are more than 45 files in the directory, the program presents a message box telling the user that the entire directory could not be read. When ReadFileNames() has done its stuff, the m_fileCount member variable will contain the number of files to display, and the m_fileNames[] and m_fileLengths[] arrays will contain the file information that the program received from the GetFileName() and GetLength() functions.

Creating the OnLButtonDblClk() function

The user can move to a new directory by double-clicking the directory's name in FTPAccessApp's window. That double-click causes MFC to call the OnLButtonDblClk() function (see Listing 28-7), which is associated with the WM_LBUTTONDBLCLK message through the view class's message map.

Listing 28-7: The CFTPAccessAppView's class's OnLButtonDblClk() function

```
void CFTPAccessAppView::OnLButtonDblClk(UINT nFlags, CPoint point)
{
    // TODO: Add your message handler code here
    //    and/or call default

    BeginWaitCursor();

    if ((point.x > 22) && (point.x < 253) &&
        (point.y > 97) && (point.y < 118))
        MoveToPreviousDirectory();

    int index, col, row;
    BOOL selectionOK =
        InitSelection(point, index, col, row);
    if (!selectionOK)
        return;

    CClientDC clientDC(this);
    clientDC.SetTextColor(RGB(255,0,0));
    clientDC.TextOut(col, row, m_fileNames[index]);

    CString targetDir =
        m_curDirectory + '/' + m_fileNames[index];

    OpenFTPDirectory(targetDir);

    EndWaitCursor();
    Invalidate();

    CView::OnLButtonDblClk(nFlags, point);
}
```

This function first displays the hourglass cursor, and then checks the mouse click's coordinates to see whether the user double-clicked the MOVE TO PREVIOUS DIRECTORY button. If so, the MoveToPreviousDirectory() function takes over.

Otherwise, the program calls InitSelection() to check that the mouse click was on a valid entry in the window and to calculate the values needed by the program to manage the selected entry. Those values are stored in the index, col, and row variables, which hold the index of the selected item (its position in the file array), and the column and row, in pixels, at which the item's name appears on the screen.

The program then displays the selected file name in red, adds the selection to the current path, and calls OpenFTPDirectory() to open that new path, after which it turns off the wait cursor and calls Invalidate() to force an update of the screen.

Creating the OnRButtonDown() function

When the user wants to download a file, he right-clicks its name in the application's window. This causes MFC to call the OnRButtonDown() function, which responds to WM_RBUTTONDOWN Windows messages, as shown in Listing 28-8.

Listing 28-8: The CFTPAccessAppView's class's OnRButtonDown() function

```
void CFTPAccessAppView::OnRButtonDown(UINT nFlags, CPoint point)
{
    // TODO: Add your message handler code here
    //    and/or call default

    BeginWaitCursor();

    int index, col, row;
    BOOL selectionOK =
        InitSelection(point, index, col, row);
    if (!selectionOK)
        return;

    CClientDC clientDC(this);
    clientDC.SetTextColor(RGB(0,128,0));
    clientDC.TextOut(col, row, m_fileNames[index]);

    DownloadFile(m_fileNames[index]);
    EndWaitCursor();
    Invalidate();

    CView::OnRButtonDown(nFlags, point);
}
```

In the function, the program first displays the hourglass cursor and then calls InitSelection() to check where the user clicked and to initialize those all-important index, col, and row variables you learned about in the previous section. With the user's click verified, OnRButtonDown() then displays the selected item in green and calls the locally defined DownloadFile() function to do the dirty work, after which the program turns off the wait cursor and updates the screen.

Creating the DownloadFile() function

The DownloadFile() function, called from OnRButtonDown(), transfers a file from the current FTP server to the user's computer, as shown in Listing 28-9.

Listing 28-9: The `CFTPAccessAppView's` **class's** `DownloadFile()` **function**

```cpp
void CFTPAccessAppView::DownloadFile(CString fileName)
{
    DisplayStatusMessage("REQUESTING DOWNLOAD...");

    try
    {
        CInternetSession session;
        CFtpConnection* pConnection =
            session.GetFtpConnection(m_site);
        BOOL succeeded =
            pConnection->
            SetCurrentDirectory(m_curDirectory);
        if (!succeeded)
        {
            MessageBox("Couldn't set directory.",
                "Download File",
                MB_OK | MB_ICONEXCLAMATION);
            delete pConnection;
            session.Close();
            return;
        }

        CFtpFileFind fileFind(pConnection);
        BOOL fileFound = fileFind.FindFile(fileName);
        if (!fileFound)
        {
            MessageBox("Couldn't find file.",
                "Download File",
                MB_OK | MB_ICONEXCLAMATION);
            delete pConnection;
            session.Close();
            return;
        }

        int result =
            MessageBox("Ready to download file?",
                "Download File",
                MB_OKCANCEL | MB_ICONQUESTION);
        if (result == IDOK)
        {
            DisplayStatusMessage(
                "DOWNLOADING FILE.  PLEASE WAIT...");
            pConnection->GetFile(fileName, fileName);
            MessageBox("File retrieved", "Download File",
                MB_OK | MB_ICONEXCLAMATION);
        }

        delete pConnection;
        session.Close();
    }
    catch (CInternetException* pException)
    {
        pException->ReportError();
    }
}
```

As you can see, the function first creates a CInternetSession object and then calls the object's GetFtpConnection() function to create the connection object. If this process fails, the function displays an error message box and returns.

If the program creates the session and connection successfully, it attempts to find the requested file on the server. Because the user can select only files that FTPAccessApp already found on the server, it's unlikely that this process will fail, but if it does, the user gets a message box, and the function returns.

If all goes well up to this point, the program displays a message box that asks the user whether he wants to download the file, giving him a chance to change his mind (maybe the right-click was accidental or on the wrong file). If the user wants to proceed, the program displays a status message and calls the connection object's GetFile() function to retrieve the file from the server. Finally, DownloadFile() displays a "File Retrieved" message box, deletes the connection object, and closes the session.

Creating the MoveToPreviousDirectory() function

If the user clicks the MOVE TO PREVIOUS DIRECTORY command, program execution finds its way to the MoveToPreviousDirectory() function, as shown in Listing 28-10.

Listing 28-10: The CFTPAccessAppView's class's MoveToPreviousDirectory() function

```
void CFTPAccessAppView::MoveToPreviousDirectory()
{
    if (m_curDirectory.GetLength() < 2)
        return;

    BeginWaitCursor();

    CClientDC clientDC(this);
    clientDC.SetTextColor(RGB(255,0,0));
    clientDC.TextOut(26, 100,
        "MOVE TO PREVIOUS DIRECTORY");

    int slash = m_curDirectory.ReverseFind('/');
    CString previousDir = m_curDirectory.Left(slash);
    OpenFTPDirectory(previousDir);

    EndWaitCursor();

    Invalidate();
}
```

Here, the program turns on the hourglass cursor, highlights the MOVE TO PREVIOUS DIRECTORY command in red, modifies the m_curDirectory string so that it contains the path to the previous directory, and calls OpenFTPDirectory() to do the directory change. Finally, the function returns the mouse cursor to normal and updates the window.

Creating the `DisplayStatusMessage()` function

So that the user doesn't get too antsy waiting for FTP commands to finish executing, FTPAccessApp displays status messages in the window. This way, the user knows that the program is at least doing something and hasn't locked up on him. Displaying a status message is as easy as calling the locally defined function `DisplayStatusMessage()`, which supplies the string to display, as shown in Listing 28-11.

Note

Notice that when you call `SelectStockObject()` to replace a DC's drawing object with a system-defined one, you don't have to restore the DC with the original object.

Listing 28-11: The `CFTPAccessAppView`'s class's `DisplayStatusMessage()` function

```
void CFTPAccessAppView::DisplayStatusMessage(CString msg)
{
    CClientDC clientDC(this);
    clientDC.SelectStockObject(NULL_PEN);
    clientDC.Rectangle(300, 100, 800, 120);
    clientDC.SetTextColor(RGB(255,0,0));
    clientDC.TextOut(300, 100, msg);
}
```

The `DisplayStatusMessage()` function creates a device context for the window, erases the old message with a white rectangle, changes the text color to red, and displays the given string. What could be easier?

Creating the `InitSelection()` function

`InitSelection()`, as shown in Listing 28-12, is the last function in FTPAccessApp that you'll explore:

Listing 28-12: The `CFTPAccessAppView`'s class's `InitSelection()` function

```
BOOL CFTPAccessAppView::InitSelection(CPoint point,
    int & index, int & col, int & row)
{
    if ((point.y < 170) || (point.y > 464))
        return FALSE;

    index = (point.y - 170) / 20;
    row = 170 + index * 20;
    col = 20;

    if (point.x > 520)
    {
        index += 30;
        col = 540;
    }
    else if (point.x > 270)
    {
```

```
            index += 15;
            col = 280;
        }

    if (index >= m_fileCount)
        return FALSE;

    return TRUE;
}
```

`InitSelection()`'s task is two-fold. First, the function must verify that the user's mouse click was over a valid file name in the window. Second, the function must determine the selected item's index (its position in the file name array), as well as the item's position on the screen. Because the `index`, `col`, and `row` variables are passed to the function as integer references, the function can directly change their contents on behalf of the calling function.

Summary

As you've learned, WinInet makes creating Internet applications almost as easy as creating applications that access only local files. Whether you want to write an HTTP, FTP, or Gopher Internet program, WinInet can make the process quicker and easier. With the Internet playing such an important role in desktop computing, the WinInet classes are an invaluable part of the MFC libraries.

Also discussed in this chapter:

▶ The `CInternetSession` class represents an Internet session.

▶ The `CHttpConnection`, `CFtpConnection`, and `CGopherConnection` classes represent connections to Internet servers.

▶ The `CHttpFile` class represents HTML files on an HTTP server.

▶ The `CFtpFileFind` class enables programs to locate files on a server, as well as obtain information about the files.

▶ To create an HTTP application with WinInet, you create a `CInternetSession` object, create a `CHttpFile` object with the session object's `OpenURL()` function, and call the file object's `ReadString()` function to read the contents of the HTML file.

▶ To create an FTP application with WinInet, you create a `CInternetSession` object, create a `CFtpConnection` object with the session object's `GetFtpConnection()` function, and access the server's directory with a `CFtpFileFind` object.

▶ Many WinInet functions throw `CInternetException` objects in response to errors.

Chapter 29

Internet Explorer

In This Chapter

▶ The Internet Explorer components

▶ Creating a simple Web browser

▶ Using HTML dialogs

▶ Using Dynamic HTML

▶ Distributing the browser control

▶ Running a sample Web browser

The Internet's growing popularity, especially the popularity of the World Wide Web, has triggered a few changes in software development. One of the major changes has been in the development cycle of programs. New programs are popping up everywhere, and it seems like some programs have new versions released before you finish downloading a copy of the last version. The average time it takes between developing new versions has shortened, and many programs and patches are available for download from the Internet. Another change is that almost every program that appears these days has some connection to the Internet.

Internet Explorer is an example of these changes in software development. Since its first release, Internet Explorer has seen many changes, with new versions and patches appearing almost monthly. Some of these changes represent changes in modern programming. The main change is that Internet Explorer comprises reusable components that are well-documented. This means that you can actually make your own Web browser using these reusable parts that Microsoft is freely distributing to everyone.

Note

Programming Internet Explorer is a complex task that cannot be fully explained in a single chapter. This chapter is only an introduction to the programming techniques required to create a basic Internet Explorer application. After you master the topics in this chapter, if you want to learn more, you should pick up a book that concentrates on Internet Explorer programming.

The Internet Explorer Components

The Internet Explorer components are more than an easy way to create a Web browser. They are a complete set of reusable objects that were specifically created for dealing with HTML files, which means that you can use the Internet Explorer components as all of the following:

- a Web browser
- a rich-content viewer
- an alternative help system
- HTML dialog boxes
- a scripting host
- an HTML parser

The complete documentation with examples for the Internet Explorer components is available in the Internet SDK. This is a free download from `http://www.microsoft.com/msdn/sdk/inetsdk/Asetup`. As the complete SDK is more than 200MB of compressed information, you may want to order the CD. Details on ordering the CD are available at the same site.

Let's first look at the capabilities of the WebBrowser component and how it uses the WebBrowser objects, as shown in Figure 29-1. At the top level is the program—Internet Explorer. Internet Explorer is the framework, or container, required to use the other components. This framework is a relatively small program that provides a user-interface to the Internet components. It uses a toolbar and menus to receive commands from the user, such as a request to return to a previously displayed page, signaled when a user clicks on a Back button. Internet Explorer sends this command to the WebBrowser component for processing.

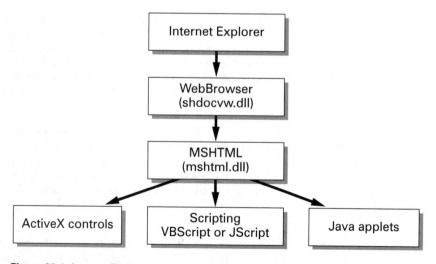

Figure 29-1: Internet Explorer uses components to display HTML pages.

The WebBrowser control—the file shdocvw.dll—makes up the next level of the component hierarchy. This object encapsulates the lower interfaces, providing a higher-level interface and several added features. For example, this control adds the functionality of in-place hyperlinking—the ability to view a link without starting a new instance of the browser object, and the Platform for Internet Content Selection (PICS). This control also maintains a history list, allowing browsers to move backward and forward through previously visited sites.

At the next level, we find MSHTML, or the mshtml.dll. This is the main HTML component, and it does all of the parsing and rendering of HTML files. MSHTML also handles HTML extensions and uses COM hosting to support Java applet hosting, plug-ins, ActiveX controls, and scripting engines, such as VBScript and JScript. When hosted by MSHTML, these COM objects also have the ability to access the Dynamic HTML object model. (The Dynamic HTML object model is described later in this chapter.)

MSHTML is an OLE Document object, or Active Document, that supports the OC96 specification, which basically means that it is a windowless control and doesn't have to be visible. This type of control can gain in performance because it doesn't have to use resources to draw itself or its components. Chapter 19 provides more information about ActiveX Controls.

Java applets and VBScript are examples of components that can be included in your program. Rather than rebuilding your program every time you want to change a feature, you can create parts of the program in Java or a scripting language. These can then be stored on a corporate Web site or another location on the Internet. Then, instead of distributing a new release of the program, you can simply update the linked Java applet or script.

You can use the same object model as MSHTML to create your own programs that access Java VM or the scripting engines in the same manner, without needing the WebBrowser control. The COM object model was introduced in Chapter 19.

Creating a Skeleton Browser Application

The primary use of the WebBrowser object is to create a browser and add Internet browsing to your programs. As mentioned earlier in this chapter, all Internet functionality is built into the WebBrowser control. All that is left up to the programmer is creating the interface and tying the interface to the control. This is quite easy to do with the following steps:

1. Create a new program using App Wizard. This example is created as a dialog box—based program with context-sensitive help, and creatively named *MyBrowser*.

2. Open the dialog box with the ID of IDD_MYBROWSER_DIALOG and enlarge it. After all, a Web page has to fit in the dialog box, and the default size is too small.

3. Rename the default OK and Cancel buttons to Load URL and Exit, respectively. Then, all the buttons can be rearranged at the top of the dialog box to leave more room for the Web Browser control.

4. Next to the buttons, insert an Edit Box for the user to insert URLs, and a label explaining what the Edit box is for. This layout can be seen in the working copy of the program shown in Figure 29-2.

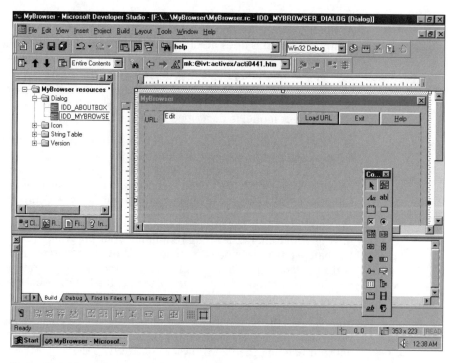

Figure 29-2: The main user interface for a Web Browser is quite simple.

5. From the Project menu, Select Components and Controls in the Add to Project submenu. This opens up the Components and Controls Gallery dialog box, which displays two folders, as shown in Figure 29-3.

6. Double-click the Registered ActiveX Controls folder to find a list of ActiveX controls available on the computer.

7. Double-click the Microsoft Web Browser control to add it to your program. Visual C++ will ask if you really want to add the control. Select OK.

8. The default CWebBrowser2 that is created works fine, so click OK again.

9. After closing the Components and Controls dialog box, select the Web Browser control from the palette and add it to the program. Enlarge the control to fill as much of the remaining space in the dialog box as possible.

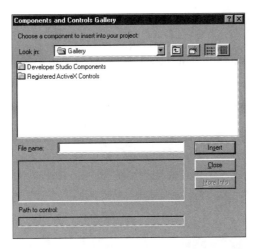

Figure 29-3: The Components and Controls Gallery dialog box lists ActiveX controls on your machine.

10. Click the Save icon to save the work done so far.

After creating the user interface, all that is required for a working browser is a little bit of coding. The following steps go through all of the coding changes needed to make the browser work:

1. Double-click the Load URL button. IDOK and BN_CLICKED should be selected in the dialog box that pops up.

2. Select Add and Edit. Give the new function a name, such as OnLoadURL, and select OK.

3. Add the code in Listing 29-1 to the function.

Listing 29-1: Navigating to a URL

```
// Get a pointer to the browser
CWebBrowser2* pBrowser =
    (CWebBrowser2*)GetDlgItem(IDC_EXPLORER1);
// Get the URL from the text box
CString strURL;
GetDlgItemText(IDC_EDIT1, strURL);
COleVariant* pURL = new COleVariant(strURL);
COleVariant noArgument;
// Have the browser load the URL
pBrowser->Navigate2(pURL, &noArgument, &noArgument,
    &noArgument, &noArgument);
delete pURL;
```

4. Go to the top of the file and add the following code below the list of already included files:

```
#include "MyBrowser2.h"
#include <mshtml.h>
```

Compiling MyBrowser

MyBrowser is now ready to be compiled and run. The browser is a bit
Spartan, but it does the job. Simply add a URL into the text box and click
Load URL for the browser to find its first Web page. Figure 29-4 illustrates
the new MyBrowser displaying pages just as well as Internet Explorer, even
though the window is a bit small.

Figure 29-4: MyBrowser displaying its first Web page

On CD-ROM

In the Chapter29\MyBrowser folder of this book's CD-ROM, you'll find the
MyBrowser application. This program has a few more features than the Web
browser shown in Figure 29-4. The other features of the MyBrowser
application are described in the rest of this chapter.

The sample program included on the CD works fine, but you may want to
modify the source and compile a new modified version. When you go to
compile the CD, there are a few considerations to make. Assuming that you
have Visual C++ installed and the MyBrowser project copied on your
computer, you can compile the program using the following steps:

1. Open the MyBrowser workspace into Visual C++. MyBrowser.dsw should
   be located in the Chapter29/MyBrowser folder.

2. Open the custsit.h file. This file includes some of the MFC source files
   which may or may not be installed on your computer.

3. Change the line that includes the occimpl.h file. The line of code is
   currently set to include this header from the VC++ CD located in the G:
   drive.

4. Insert your VC++ CD into the computer and change the G: drive letter to your CD's drive letter. If you know that the MFC sources were installed, you can modify the statement to find the file in your installation of VC++.

5. Open MyBrowserDlg.cpp and go to line 170. This line of code loads the HTML file used in the About dialog box.

6. Change the location of the about.htm file, or modify the code to load a page from the Web. You could also use a resource, but you would have to include the resource in your project before it can be used.

7. Click on the Build button to compile the program.

After compiling the program, you can use the program as described in the section Running MyBrowser. If there are any problems compiling the program, here are a few hints:

- An error creating the help file may mean that the Help Workshop is not installed. This will not adversely affect the program and can safely be ignored.

- Install the InetSDK. This SDK includes new header files as well as several more examples that you can explore.

- Install the latest Service Pack. While service packs are generally considered bug fixes, they also include newer information which may be needed to create programs. This is especially true when programming for the Internet because of how quickly things change.

One item to note is that it is possible to use Internet Explorer through OLE Automation, rather than using the WebBrowser component. This is important because some of the properties and methods described in this chapter behave differently depending on whether you use the WebBrowser or are using Internet Explorer through OLE—accessing Internet Explorer through OLE adds functionality not available to the WebBrowser control.

Note

If all you want to do is create a simple browser, I would suggest finding a copy of Visual Basic or a Visual Basic programmer. Visual Basic makes creating an interface and adding ActiveX controls such as the WebBrowser so easy that it would take about five minutes to create a functioning browser.

Configuring the WebBrowser control

After adding the WebBrowser control to your program, you will want to configure it to your needs. If you add the component to a dialog box, you can open the Microsoft Web Browser Property box. This allows you to change some of the basic properties listed in Table 29-1. The wrapper class provides methods to access these properties from your program.

Table 29-1	Basic WebBrowser Properties
Value	**Description**
AddressBar	Shows or hides the URL address bar, but is ignored by the WebBrowser component.
Offline	Sets the WebBrowser control to run in offline or online mode. In offline mode, the control will only read HTML pages from the local cache.
RegisterAsBrowser	This is generally set to false, and determines if the WebBrowser should be registered as a top-level browser.
RegisterAsDropTarget	With a default value of false, this property determines if the object can receive objects through Window's drag-and-drop.
Silent	When set to the default value of false, this property allows dialog boxes to be displayed.
TheaterMode	Ignored by the WebBrowser, but allows Internet Explorer to use the full screen for displaying HTML pages.

Navigating with the WebBrowser component

After configuring the WebBrowser component, you will need to provide a way to navigate HTML pages. Generally this is done by adding menus, toolbars, and buttons to your application, which is explained in Part 2: User Interface. The WebBrowser control includes several methods for navigating. When creating a browser, these methods are generally tied to buttons or menu commands (see Table 29-2).

Table 29-2	Important WebBrowser Methods
Value	**Description**
GoBack	Navigates one item backward in the history list
GoForward	Navigates one item forward in the history list
GoHome	Navigates to the default home location. The default search page is set using the Control Panel, or Internet Explorer's Option dialog box.
GoSearch	Navigates to the default search page. The default search page is set using the Control Panel, or Internet Explorer's Option dialog box.
Navigate	Navigates to a target URL or path and file name locations
Navigate2	Extends the Navigate method to support browsing special folders, such as My Computer, along with standard URL or path and file name locations

Each Navigate method comes with its own set of parameters. First, there is the Navigate method:

```
HRESULT CWebBrowser2::Navigate(
    LPCTSTR URL, VARIANT* Flags,
    VARIANT* TargetFrameName, VARIANT* PostData,
    VARIANT* Headers,
);
```

As you can see, the full Navigate() method takes five parameters. Some of the parameters are optional, and you can use a COleVariant variable, as illustrated in Listing 29-1, for those optional parameters you aren't using. A complete description of the parameters follows:

URL	A string expressing the URL, full path, or Universal Naming Convention (UNC) location and name of a resource to display.
Flags	An optional combination of constants (see Table 29-3). Some of the flags are only useful when using Internet Explorer as an OLE object instead of using the WebBrowser.
TargetFrameName	An optional string expression representing a named HTML frame. Four reserved names can be used: _blank, _parent, _self, and _top.
PostData	An optional pointer to data to be sent to the server in a POST transaction. This parameter is ignored if URL is not an HTTP URL.
Headers	An optional value specifying additional HTTP headers to send to the server; ignored if URL is not an HTTP URL.

The value returned by the method will be one of S_OK, E_INVALIDARG, or E_OUTOFMEMORY.

In most cases, you will use the Navigate method. However, there may be times when you want to allow the user to navigate My Computer or the Desktop. These are represented as pointers to an item identifier list (PIDL). In these instances, you need to use the Navigate2 method:

```
HRESULT CWebBrowser2::Navigate2(
    VARIANT* URL, VARIANT FAR* Flags,
    VARIANT* TargetFrameName, VARIANT FAR* PostData,
    VARIANT FAR* Headers);
```

This method uses the same parameters as the Navigate method with the exception of URL. This variation of the URL parameter is a distinction in name only because it is also a string expressing the URL, full path, or Universal Naming Convention (UNC) location and name of a resource to display. Navigate2 also has the same return values as Navigate.

Table 29-3   Navigational Flags

Constant	Value	Description
navOpenInNewWindow	1	Opens the resource in a new window.
navNoHistory	2	Doesn't add the resource to the history list; instead, the new resource replaces the current one in the list.
navNoReadFromCache	4	Not used.
navNoWriteToCache	8	Not used.
navAllowAutoSearch	10	Only for use with IE. If the call to Navigate fails, an autosearch function will attempt to navigate to common root domains, or the URL will be passed to a search engine.
navBrowserBar	20	Only for use with IE, it attempts to have the current Explorer Bar navigate to the resource.

Not all of the navigation methods are appropriate for all applications. For example, the GoHome method opens up the user's default home page. Only add the functionality that is needed for your application. The steps to adding a new button are quite similar to how the Load URL button was created earlier in this chapter. Simply add the button to the dialog box and create a function to respond to the BN_CLICKED message. The sample program included on the CD, MyBrowser, has GoHome and GoForward buttons already added to it.

 PROBLEMS & SOLUTIONS

Implementing Parental Lockout

PROBLEM: *How do I implement a parental lockout for controlling what is seen on my browser?*

SOLUTION: PICS, the Platform for Internet Content Selection, defines a two-part standard used to control access to Web content. Primarily, the standard is concerned with minors accessing adult content, but a little creativity can be used with the standard to create other uses.

PICS only presents a system for creating a rating system. It does not rate, or tell you how to rate, your content. It only provides a standard that allows content developers to tell a browser what rating system is being used and the rating of the content. The particular rating system is up to the developer. For example, the content developer could add the following META tag to an HTML page header:

Continued

```
<HEAD><HEAD>
<TITLE>Corporate Home Page</TITLE>
<META http-equiv="PICS-Label" content='(PICS=1-1
 "http://www.rsac.org/ratingsv01.html"
 l true comment "RSACi North America Server"
 for "http://www.mydomain.com/default.html"
 on "1997.12.01T22:48-0800"
 r (n 0 s 0 v 1 l 0))'>
</HEAD>
```

In this example, the content developer is using RSACi, the rating system developed by the Recreation Software Advisory Council. This rating system comprises four subsystems used to rate nudity, sex, violence, and language. Each one of these has its own value listed in the header.

The RSAC rating system is a good example of a rating system supported by Microsoft and used by the Internet Explorer. You can find out more about this system by visiting www.rsac.org. You can also take a look at the file rsaci.rat, which is used by IE to describe their ratings. PICS does not, however, require that you use this system. You can just as easily create your own system based on the Motion Picture Association of America's rating system. Then, you could give your site a G, PG, PG-13, R, or NC-17 rating.

Because PICS is simply a standard for any type of rating, you could try to devise a system that has nothing to do with adult content. You could, for example, create a system that blocks out content if it is too cute or geeky. Suppose you have a Web site for a shareware program you are distributing. You could rate this content so that owners of the shareware copy are blocked out while owners of the full version have complete access to your site. (Of course, there would also be those hackers who bypassed this simple security measure by using a browser that doesn't use your rating system. But the hacker would have to know where your documentation was located.)

In order to use PICS, you have to use the Internet Ratings API functions listed in Table 29-4 and add content labels. Content labels are easy to add to HTML pages using any of the HTML authoring programs available.

Table 29-4 Internet Ratings API Functions

Function	Description
RatingAccessDeniedDialog	Displays a dialog box when a user has been denied access to a page and may allow the supervisor to override the denial
RatingAccessDeniedDialog2	Displays a dialog box when a user has been denied access to a page and may allow the supervisor to override the denial. If a modal dialog box is already displayed for the same parent, details from this function are added to the existing dialog box.

Continued

Table 29-4 *(Continued)*

Function	Description
RatingCheckUserAccess	Compares a PICS rating with the user-defined settings to determine whether to display the page
RatingEnable	Enables or disables ratings
RatingEnabledQuery	Determines whether ratings are being used
RatingFreeDetails	Frees the pointer of ratings information
RatingObtainCancel	Cancels a call to RatingObtainQuery
RatingObtainQuery	Requests and compares ratings information from various locations
RatingSetupUI	Displays a dialog box allowing a supervisor to set restriction levels

Implementing the API functions in your program is not as simple as adding an HTML tag to a document. The first step to using the Internet Ratings API is to have the supervisor set the ratings level for the browser. Internet Explorer allows the user to set options using the Content Advisor dialog box, as shown in Figure 29-5. A user can change the RSAC settings for the content ratings they want displayed. There is also an option to automatically block content that isn't rated. You may want to provide similar functionality for your program, or hard-code the settings.

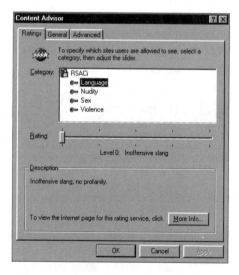

Figure 29-5: Content ratings can be changed using a dialog box.

Continued

After setting the PICS ratings, your program will need to implement the Internet Ratings API functions. The typical sequence for this is listed below:

1. The browser calls `RatingEnabledQuery` to see if content ratings are to be used.

2. If ratings are being used, the browser calls `RatingObtainQuery` with a URL to search for listings of ratings. `RatingCheckUserAccess` is called if a rating is found for the URL.

3. The browser searches the downloading content for a rating to check using `RatingCheckUserAccess`.

4. If a content label isn't found on the page, `RatingCheckUserAccess` is called with a NULL value to see if the user can access unrated content.

5. After both `RatingObtainQuery` and `RatingCheckUserAccess` have been called, the browser should have at least one access-denied or access-allowed report. The browser should defer to the value returned by `RatingObtainQuery`.

6. The `RatingAccessDeniedDialog` function is called, which may allow the user to override the initial denial.

   The browser will display the content if access is allowed.

This list shows one of the benefits of using the WebBrowser control over MSHTML—it already incorporates the Internet Ratings API. For more information on PICS, check out the full documentation at `www.w3.org/PICS/`.

Using HTML Dialog Boxes

HTML can also be used to create dialog boxes. There are two good examples of HTML dialog boxes in Internet Explorer 4. The first example is the About dialog box shown in Figure 29-6. This dialog box uses Dynamic HTML to display the copyright information if the user clicks on the link.

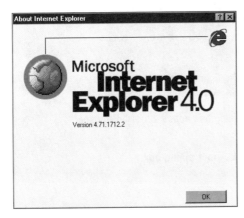

Figure 29-6: Internet Explorer presents information using HTML dialog boxes.

Another example is the Find dialog box shown in Figure 29-7. While this appears as a normal dialog box, Microsoft claims that it is also an HTML dialog box.

Figure 29-7: HTML dialog boxes can also appear as standard dialog boxes.

In order to implement HTML dialog boxes, you will need to access the ShowHTMLDialog function included in MSHTML. After dynamically loading MSHTML with the LoadLibrary function, calling GetProcAddress acquires the address of ShowHTMLDialog. MyBrowser illustrates using this call to show the HTML About dialog box shown in Figure 29-8, instead of the standard MFC dialog box. In order to test out this function, right-click on the title bar. The shortcut menu that pops up includes an option for viewing the About box. Listing 29-2 demonstrates these procedures.

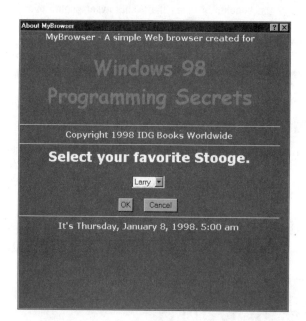

Figure 29-8: An HTML About dialog box appears for MyBrowser.

Listing 29-2: Opening an HTML About dialog box

```
void CMyBrowserDlg::OnSysCommand(UINT nID, LPARAM lParam)
{
    if ((nID & 0xFFF0) == IDM_ABOUTBOX)
    {
```

```
#if 0
       //standard call to a regular About dialog box
       CAboutDlg dlgAbout;
       dlgAbout.DoModal();
#endif
       //use an html dialog box instead
       HINSTANCE hiMSHTML = LoadLibrary(TEXT("MSHTML.DLL"));

       if(hiMSHTML)
       {
           //SHOWHTMLDIALOGFN is defined in mshtmhst.h
           SHOWHTMLDIALOGFN *pfnShowHTMLDialog;

           pfnShowHTMLDialog = (SHOWHTMLDIALOGFN*)
              GetProcAddress( hiMSHTML,
                 TEXT("ShowHTMLDialog"));

           if(pfnShowHTMLDialog)
           {
               // parameter intializiation
               IMoniker *pmk;
               TCHAR    szTemp[MAX_PATH*2];
               OLECHAR  bstr[MAX_PATH*2];

               //for a hardcoded file name
               lstrcpy(szTemp,
TEXT("file:D:/Chapter29/MyBrowser/about.htm"));

               LocalToBSTR(bstr, szTemp, ARRAYSIZE(bstr));

               CreateURLMoniker(NULL, bstr, &pmk);

               if(pmk)
               {
                   HRESULT  hr;
                   VARIANT  varArgs, varReturn;

                   VariantInit(&varReturn);

                   varArgs.vt = VT_BSTR;
                   //send a list of Stooges to the dialog box
                   varArgs.bstrVal
SysAllocString(L"Larry;Moe;Curly;Shem");

                   hr = (*pfnShowHTMLDialog)(NULL, pmk,
                       &varArgs, NULL, &varReturn);
                   VariantClear(&varArgs);
                   pmk->Release();

                   //display the returned information
                   if(SUCCEEDED(hr))
                       {
                       switch(varReturn.vt)
                           {
                           case VT_BSTR:
                               {
```

```
                                   //display the Stooge's name
                                   TCHAR szData[MAX_PATH];
                                   BSTRToLocal(szData,
                                       varReturn.bstrVal,
                                       ARRAYSIZE(szData));

                                   wsprintf(szTemp, TEXT
                                   ("The new stooge is \"%s\"."),
                                    szData);

                                   VariantClear(&varReturn);
                                   }
                                   break;

                               default:
                                   lstrcpy(szTemp, TEXT
                                      ("Cancel was selected."));
                                   break;
                               }
                               MessageBox(szTemp, TEXT
                                   ("HTML Dialog Sample"),
                                    MB_OK | MB_ICONINFORMATION);
                           }
                       else
                           MessageBox(TEXT
                            ("ShowHTMLDialog Failed."),
                            TEXT("HTML Dialog Sample"),
                             MB_OK | MB_ICONERROR);
                   }
               }

           FreeLibrary(hiMSHTML);
       }

   }
   else
   {
       CDialog::OnSysCommand(nID, lParam);
   }
}
```

This same code can easily be added to any program to enable the addition of HTML dialog boxes. All that is required is to initialize the parameters of ShowHTMLDialog:

```
typedef HRESULT STDAPICALLTYPE SHOWHTMLDIALOGFN(
    HWND hwndParent,
    IMoniker *pmk,
    VARIANT *pvarArgIn,
    TCHAR* pchOptions,
    VARIANT *pvarArgOut
);
```

As you can see, the ShowHTMLDialog() function takes five parameters:

hwndParent	A handle for the parent window or NULL for dialog boxes that aren't owned. NULL values are good when you don't want the calling window to be disabled.
pmk	A pointer to an IMoniker interface identifying the HTML source
pvarArgIn	Optionally NULL, pvarArgIn points to a VARIANT filled with parameters being passed to the dialog box.
pchOptions	An optionally NULL pointer to a string containing a combination of values seperated by ';' Table 29-5 lists the various features available as options.
pvarArgOut	An optionally NULL pointer to the data returned from the dialog box

Table 29-5   Optional Features for HTML Dialogs

Syntax	*Description*
center:[yes | no | 1 | 0]	Specifies whether to center the dialog in the desktop. The default is yes.
dialogHeight:number	Sets the dialog's height
dialogLeft:number	Sets the left of the dialog relative to the desktop
dialogTop:number	Sets the top of the dialog relative to the desktop
dialogWidth:number	Sets the dialog's width

Including an HTML resource

In order to access the HTML file that you use in your dialog box, you will probably want to make it a resource. This makes the HTML file easy to find and keeps the user from accidentally modifying the file. Then, the res: protocol, as opposed to http: or file:, is used to access the resource. Of course, only a few functions, such as ShowTMLDialog, support the protocol. You can't Navigate to a resource. Other functions such as FindResource and LocalResource, which are used to work with resources, can use an lptype of RT_HTML to locate an HTML resource.

You can simply include an HTML resource, such as MyProgramHomePage.htm into your application's resource script. The resource will then be listed in your script as something similar to the following:

```
HTML_RESOURCE  23  DISCARDABLE  "MyProgramHomePage.htm"
```

HTML_RESOURCE is the resource identifier. Visual C++ 5.0 uses the value of 23 for an HTML resource type, so you may see HTML in place of 23 for other compilers and future releases of Visual C++. Using the current version of

VC++, opening the file for editing will open an editor window displaying the file's source; you may want to use another program for editing the HTML.

Working in the dialog box

A dialog box that displays only static information has limited usefulness. Eventually you will want to send information or retrieve a value from the user. For example, you may want to fill a list box with values for the user to select. The following code listing is a bit of JScript from the about.htm file used in MyBrowser. It illustrates how to fill a list box, or *select element* as it is called in HTML, named `listOptions` with the values sent to the dialog box:

```
//get the arguments
var arrArgs = new Array();
arrArgs = window.dialogArguments.split(";");

//clear the list
listOptions.options.length = 0;

//add the arguments to the list
var index;
index = 0;
while(index < arrArgs.length)
{
    var tempOption = new Option(arrArgs[index]);
    listOptions.options[listOptions.options.length] =
        tempOption;
    index++;
}

//select the first argument
listOptions.options[0].selected = true;

//set a default return value
window.returnValue = 0;
```

In this example, a default `returnValue` of zero is set. This value will need to be changed when the user selects one of the items in the list. This value is then retrieved from the `pvarArgOut` parameter when the `ShowHTMLDialog` function returns. Figure 29-9 shows a value being returned from the About box of MyBrowser.

Figure 29-9: HTML dialog boxes can return values to MyBrowser.

Using Dynamic HTML

Dynamic HTML (DHTML) is an extension to standard HTML that allows an HTML author to change a document after it has been loaded into the browser. The browser then reformats and displays the content using styles and scripts contained in the HTML page. Because all of this is handled by the browser, nothing is sent back to the server and the whole process is faster than using conventional HTML.

Note

Currently, there isn't an accepted standard to Dynamic HTML. Netscape and Microsoft both have their own Dynamic HTML extensions. As this chapter is devoted to Microsoft's Internet Explorer components, it will also use Microsoft's Dynamic HTML. For more information on this topic, you can take a look at *Dynamic HTML* by Shelley Powers, published by IDG Books Worldwide.

Dynamic HTML uses an object model based on HTML tags. This object model gives the browser and HTML author access to virtually everything on the page. The HTML elements on the page are translated to objects with properties and methods. Other objects, such as ActiveX components, are also included in the model—to be modified and modify other objects. For a complete description of the object model including all of the objects, properties, and models, check out the documentation in the Internet SDK.

Note

Dynamic HTML allows you to turn over some of your application's programming needs to Web page developers.

Introducing the DHTML object model

Applications can access the Dynamic HTML object model using interfaces based on `IDispatch`. `IDispatch` is an interface that allows one application to tell another application what methods are available for use. In other words, the methods available can vary from program to program, but they work in basically the same way. `IHTMLDocument2` is a wrapper class with interface maps to the document object. Basically, this allows you to access all of the different tags that may be on an HTML page. Table 29-6 lists the dynamic HTML objects and their corresponding `IHTMLDocument2` interfaces.

Table 29-6   Dynamic HTML to `IHTMLDocument2` Object Mapping

Object	Interface
A	IHTMLAnchorElement
AREA	IHTMLAreaElement
areas	IHTMLAreasCollection
BASE	IHTMLBaseElement
BASEFONT	IHTMLBaseFontElement

(Continued)

Table 29-6 *(Continued)*

Object	Interface
BGSOUND	IHTMLBGsound
BODY	IHTMLBodyElement
BR	IHTMLBRElement
BUTTON	IHTMLButtonElement
CAPTION	IHTMLTableCaption
COL	IHTMLTableCol
COLGROUP	IHTMLTableCol
COMMENT	IHTMLCommentElement
DD	IHTMLDDElement
DIV	IHTMLDivElement
DL	IHTMLDListElement
document	IHTMLDocument, IHTMLDocument2
DT	IHTMLDTElement
elements	IHTMLElementCollection
EMBED	IHTMLPluginsCollection
event	IHTMLEventObj
FIELDSET	IHTMLFieldSetElement
filters	IHTMLFiltersCollection
FONT	IHTMLFontElement
FORM	IHTMLFormElement
FRAME	IHTMLFrameElement
frames	IHTMLFramesCollection2
FRAMESET	IHTMLFrameSetElement
history	IOmHistory
HR	IHTMLHRElement
IFRAME	IHTMLIFrameElement
INPUT of type file	IHTMLInputFileElement
INPUT of type hidden	IHTMLInputHiddenElement
INPUT of type image	IHTMLInputImage
INPUT of type radio	IHTMLOptionButtonElement
INPUT of type reset or submit	IHTMLInputButtonElement
INPUT of type text	IHTMLInputTextElement

Object	Interface
ISINDEX	IHTMLIsIndexElement
LABEL	IHTMLLabelElement
LEGEND	IHTMLLegendElement
LI	IHTMLLIElement
LINK	IHTMLLinkElement
location	IHTMLLocation
MAP	IHTMLMapElement
MARQUEE	IHTMLMarqueeElement
META	IHTMLMetaElement
navigator	IOmNavigator
NEXTID	IHTMLNextIdElement
OBJECT	IHTMLObjectElement
OL	IHTMLOListElement
OPTION	IHTMLOptionElement
P	IHTMLParaElement
screen	IHTMLScreen
SCRIPT	IHTMLScriptElement
SELECT	IHTMLSelectElement
selection	IHTMLSelectionObject
SPAN	IHTMLSpanFlow
style	IHTMLRuleStyle, IHTMLStyle
STYLE	IHTMLStyleElement
styleSheet	IHTMLStyleSheet, IHTMLStyleSheetRule, IHTMLStyleSheetRulesCollection, IHTMLStyleSheetsCollection
TABLE	IHTMLTable
TBODY	IHTMLTableSection
TD	IHTMLTableCell
TEXTAREA	IHTMLTextAreaElement
TextRange	IHTMLTxtRange
TH	IHTMLTableCell
THEAD	IHTMLTableSection
TFOOT	IHTMLTableSection
TITLE	IHTMLTitleElement
TR	IHTMLTableRow

(Continued)

Table 29-6   *(Continued)*

Object	Interface
UL	IHTMLULlistElement
userProfile	IHTMLOpsProfile
window	IHTMLDialog or IHTMLWindow2

The IHTMLDocument2 class, detailed in Table 29-7, also includes a few additional interfaces to make programming easier, such as the IHTMLElement interface, which is a generic interface for any HTML tags. These interfaces allow you to access a group of related elements rather than just a specific element. An example of using the ITHMLElement is found in MyBrowser.

Table 29-7   All-Purpose IHTMLDocument2 Interfaces

Interface	Applicable Elements
IHTMLElement	All element objects
IHTMLHeaderElement	Any header element (H1 to H6)
IHTMLImgElement	Common properties of IMG and INPUT of type images
IHTMLListElement	OL or UL common properties

Almost everything that can be done to the object model from your application can be done using scripts. This makes it a good idea to prototype and test what you are doing using a script.

Accessing the document interface

In order to access the document model, you must obtain an IHTMLDocument2 interface. This is quite easy to do, but how you do it depends on the type of application host you are using.

Using a WebBrowser control, you can obtain a pointer to the current document in two steps. First call the control's get_Document method to obtain an IDispatch pointer. Then call QueryInterface on the pointer to request IID_IHTMLDocument2. Listing 29-3 illustrates how to access a document's interface to change the background color of an HTML page. Simply click on the Change Background button at the bottom of the page and this function changes the color using the Dynamic HTML model.

Listing 29-3: Accessing an HTML document to change the background color

```
void CMyBrowserDlg::OnChangeBackground()
{
// TODO: Add your control notification handler code here
```

```
CWebBrowser2* pBrowser =
        (CWebBrowser2*)GetDlgItem( IDC_EXPLORER1 );

IDispatch* pDisp = pBrowser->GetDocument();

if (pDisp != NULL )
{
    IHTMLDocument2* pHTMLDocument2;
    HRESULT hr;
    hr = pDisp->QueryInterface(IID_IHTMLDocument2,
                              (void**)&pHTMLDocument2 );

    if (hr == S_OK)
    {
        VARIANT vColor;
        vColor.vt = VT_INT;
        vColor.lVal = 0xFFF8DC;
        hr = pHTMLDocument2->put_bgColor(vColor);

        pHTMLDocument2->Release();
    }
    pDisp->Release();
}

}
```

The process is quite similar when you are using MSHTML. However, you will need to create an object using CoCreateInstance to get an object you can use to call QueryInterface. The CWebBrowser2 class already includes one when using the WebBrowser control.

Using the object model

Once you have a handle on the object model, you can use it to change the content of the current document. This can be done either using a script or from your application. For example, you can change the background color of a document using the following JavaScript code:

```
document.bgColor = "#FFF8DC";
```

You can also use the following code taken from Listing 29-3 to produce the same result:

```
VARIANT vColor;
vColor.vt = VT_INT;
vColor.lVal = 0xFFF8DC;
hr = pHTMLDocument2->put_bgColor(vColor);
```

Extending the DHTML object model

The WebBrowser component allows you to extend the DHTML object model. By extending HTML you can add functionality to scripts that will be run on the browser. Any function or method that you have in your program can be accessed through the object model. This is done using the window object's external object. For example, you may be creating a statistics program and want to show a sample calculation. Because the function you want to use isn't in the VBScript or JScript library, you can add ComplexStatisticalFunction to your program using an IDispatch interface. The script in the HTML page will call ComplexStatisticalFunction using a call similar to Variable = window.external.ComplexStatisticalFunction.

The best way to use the IDispatch interface is to create your own to extend the IDispatch class. Listing 29-4 presents a simple IDispatch class that can be used to extend the Dynamic HTML object model. The CMyIDispatch class in this example creates a simple counter extension to the Dynamic HTML object model used by MyBrowser. Every time the extension, first, is called, an internal counter is incremented and returned.

Listing 29-4: Creating your own IDispatch class

```
#include "stdafx.h"
#include "idisp.h"


// Since there is only one extension, the first
// I will use constants
const    WCHAR pszFirstExtend[10]=L"first";
#define DISPID_FirstExtend 20001


/*
 * Constructors and Destructors
 */

CMyIDispatch::CMyIDispatch( void )
{
    //initialize the counter
    m_ExtensionCounter = 0;
    m_cRef = 0;
}

CMyIDispatch::~CMyIDispatch( void )
{
    ASSERT( m_cRef == 0 );
}


/*
 * Implementation for virtual functions hanging around
 * from IUnKnown.
 */

STDMETHODIMP CMyIDispatch::QueryInterface(
                 REFIID riid, void **ppv )
{
    *ppv = NULL;


    if ( IID_IDispatch == riid )
```

```
    {
        *ppv = this;
    }

    if ( NULL != *ppv )
     {
        ((LPUNKNOWN)*ppv)->AddRef();
        return NOERROR;
     }

    return E_NOINTERFACE;
}


STDMETHODIMP_(ULONG) CMyIDispatch::AddRef(void)
{
    return ++m_cRef;
}

STDMETHODIMP_(ULONG) CMyIDispatch::Release(void)
{
    return —m_cRef;
}


/*
 * Implementation for IDispatch functions
 */
STDMETHODIMP CMyIDispatch::GetTypeInfoCount(UINT*)
{
    return E_NOTIMPL;
}


STDMETHODIMP CMyIDispatch::GetTypeInfo(UINT,
                LCID, ITypeInfo**)
{
    return E_NOTIMPL;
}


/*
 * Implementation required for extending Dynamic HTML
 * the first function goes through the list of IDs
 * to find which ones are valid extensions handled by
 * the application
 */
STDMETHODIMP CMyIDispatch::GetIDsOfNames(
                REFIID riid,
                OLECHAR** rgszNames,
                UINT cNames,
                LCID lcid,
                DISPID* rgDispId)
{
    HRESULT hr;
    UINT    i;

    hr = NOERROR;    // Assume success
```

```
        // check for extension
        for ( i=0; i < cNames; i++)
        {
            if (  2 == CompareString( lcid, NORM_IGNOREWIDTH,
                (char*)pszFirstExtend, 3,
                (char*)rgszNames[i], 3 ) )
            {
                rgDispId[i] = DISPID_FirstExtend;
            }
            else
            {
                // set return code for unknown id's
                hr = ResultFromScode(DISP_E_UNKNOWNNAME);
                rgDispId[i] = DISPID_UNKNOWN;
            }
        }
        return hr;
}


STDMETHODIMP CMyIDispatch::Invoke(
                DISPID dispIdMember,
                REFIID, LCID,
                WORD wFlags,
                DISPPARAMS* pDispParams,
                VARIANT* pVarResult,
                EXCEPINFO*,
                UINT* puArgErr)
{

    // This first extension simply returns the
    // number of times the extension was called
    if ( dispIdMember == DISPID_FirstExtend )
    {
        if ( wFlags & DISPATCH_PROPERTYGET )
        {
            if ( pVarResult != NULL )
            {
                VariantInit(pVarResult);
                pVarResult->vt = VT_UINT;
                pVarResult->lVal = ++m_ExtensionCounter;
            }
        }
    }

    return S_OK;
}
```

In order to use this IDispatch extension, you must include it in your program. MyBrowser adds a new pointer, m_pIDispatch, for the IDispatch which is initialized when the program starts up and calls InitInstance(). In order for the new IDispatch extension to work, idisp.h also has to be included in the MyBrowser source and header files. Another requirement is a class to capture events. A sample class called CCustomOCCManager was included with the InetSDK for just such a use.

```
BOOL MyBrowser::InitInstance()
{
    // Create a custom control manager class so we can overide the
site
    CCustomOccManager *pMgr = new CCustomOccManager;
    //create a pointer to the IDispatch for use by the manager
    m_pIDispatch = new CMyIDispatch;
    //start the manager class up to catch events
    AfxEnableControlContainer(pMgr);    // The rest of you
initialization goes here
}
```

One final step is required before you can see your code in action. You will need to create an HTML file that uses the extension. A sample HTML file is found in Listing 29-5. After loading this file into MyBrowser, every time you click on the button that this file displays, a function is called that uses the first extension. A message box then pops up displaying the number of times you have called the extension, i.e., clicked on the button. Figure 29-10 shows the program with the page loaded and a dialog box on top displaying a number of clicks.

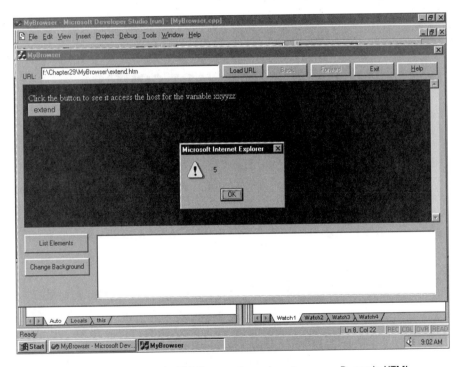

Figure 29-10: A few clicks on the HTML page shows how to access Dynamic HTML extensions.

Listing 29-5: Using HTML to access a Dynamic HTML Extension

```
<HTML>
<HEAD>
<TITLE>My First Dynamic HTML Extension</TITLE>

<script>
function runcounter()
{
  y=window.external.first;
  alert(y);
}
</script>
</HEAD>

Click the button to see how many times you have
used your first Dynamic HTML extension
<BR>
<input type=button
        value="extend"
        onClick="runcounter()">

</BODY>
</HTML>
```

Distributing the browser control

When distributing your application, it is important to note that Internet Explorer must be installed on the target system in order to use the WebBrowser control. This control was first distributed with Internet Explorer version 3.0; it is available for 32-bit Windows, such as Windows 98 and Windows NT, as well as Windows 3.1 and the Apple Macintosh.

Aside from checking to see if IE is installed, you may want to check to see if version 3.0 is already on the computer. You may develop applications that use functionality available starting with version 3.0. There are two ways of checking for a version: You can check the Registry or the version of the components installed.

Determining versions with the Registry

Windows maintains a small database of initialization values and system settings called the Windows Registry. Information is stored hierarchically as strings and integers in multipart keys. For example, Internet Explorer has a registry key of HKEY_LOCAL_MACHINE\Software\Microsoft\Internet Explorer.

This key contains a *version* value, which is a string value containing the Internet Explorer 4.0 version in the following format:

```
"<major version>.<minor version>.<build number>.<sub-build number>".
```

Internet Explorer 3.0x does not install this value, so if this value is retrieved and the major version is "4" and the minor version is "71", then Internet Explorer 4.0 is installed. To check for Internet Explorer 3.0x, use the *Build* value under this same key. For backward compatibility, Internet Explorer 4.0 modifies or adds the *Build* value as well as the *Version* value. Internet Explorer 3.0x's *Build* value is a string that contains a four-character build number. Internet Explorer 4.0's *Build* value is a larger string value in the format of

```
"4<build number>.<sub-build number>".
```

Therefore, if the *Build* value is the character 4 followed by a four-character build number, Internet Explorer 4.0 is installed. Listing 29.6 shows a function used to determine what version of IE is installed. GetIEMajorVersion returns a 4 for IE 4.x; a 3 for IE 3.x; and a zero for anything else.

Listing 29-6: Determining the installed version of Internet Explorer

```
int GetIEMajorVersion()
{
    long retVal;
    char *version[10];    //big enough for sub build
    int IEVersion = 0;
    HKEY hKey;

    //open the key
    retVal = RegOpenKey(HKEY_LOCAL_MACHINE,
        "Software\Microsoft\Internet Explorer", &hKey);
    if (retVal == ERROR_SUCCESS)
    {
        retVal = RegQueryValueEx(hKey, "Build", NULL,
            REG_SZ, version, sizeof(version);
        if (retVal == ERROR_SUCCESS)
        {
            select case version[0] {
            {
                case '4':
                    IEVersion = 4;
                    break;

                case '3':
                    IEVersion = 3;
                    break;
            }
        }
        //close the key
        retVal = RegCloseKey(hKey);
    }
    return (IEVersion);
}
```

Determining versions with shdocvw.dll

The version of the file shdocvw.dll, the WebBrowser dll, can also be used to determine which version of Internet Explorer is installed. If this file is missing completely, you know Internet Explorer needs to be installed. You can use the function in Listing 29-7 to retrieve version information. IE 3.0 is version 4.70, and IE 4.0 is version 4.71.

Listing 29-7: Determining version information from a DLL

```
int GetBrowserVersion()
{
    HINSTANCE    hBrowser;

    int IEVersion = 0;

    //Load the DLL.
    hBrowser = LoadLibrary(TEXT("shdocvw.dll"));

    if(hBrowser)
    {
        HRESULT              hResult;
        DLLGETVERSIONPROC pDllGetVersion;

        pDllGetVersion = (DLLGETVERSIONPROC)GetProcAddress(
            hBrowser, TEXT("DllGetVersion"));
        if(pDllGetVersion)
        {
            DLLVERSIONINFO     versionInfo;

            ZeroMemory(&versionInfo sizeof(versionInfo));
            versionInfo.cbSize = sizeof(versionInfo;

            hResult = (*pDllGetVersion)(&dvi);

            if(SUCCEEDED(hResult))
            {
                if (dvi.dwMajorVersion == 4 &&
                    dvi.dwMinorVersion == 70)
                    IEVersion = 3;

                if (dvi.dwMajorVersion == 4 &&
                    dvi.dwMinorVersion == 71)
                    IEVersion = 4;
            }
        }
        FreeLibrary(hBrowser);
    }

    return IEVersion;
}
```

Using the minimum installation

Internet Explorer is currently designed in such a way that you can't simply install mshtml.dll or shdocvw.dll, the WebBrowser DLL files, with your program and have everything work properly. A number of system files and registry entries are required for the control to work. Simply put, you must have a full installation of the basic IE components in order to use any of them—an all or nothing situation. In order to distribute WebBrowser or any of the other IE technologies with your application, you must obtain a redistribution agreement from Microsoft.

This does not mean that you have to have a full-blown F—that is, every component included—installation of IE 4.0. Microsoft provides an Internet Explorer kit which allows you to customize the installation. The minimum installation includes the IE 4.0 browser, Microsoft's VM for Java, and Direct Show. You can also modify the installation to run with a user interface and prompts, or to be totally automated with the rest of your installation. The Internet Explorer Administration Kit's home page is currently at http://www.microsoft.com/ie/ieak.

This kit provides information on how to create the best installation for your needs. The easiest way to run a minimum installation of IE 4.0 is to use the command-line parameters. For example, to do a minimum installation without user interface, integrated desktop, a reboot prompt, making IE 4.0 the default browser, or adding an icon to the desktop, simply use the following command line:

```
ie4stw95.exe /Q:A /C:"ie4wzd.exe /Q:A /X /I:N /R:N /S:"#e""
```

Note

A new Internet Explorer installation requires the computer to reboot in order to finish installation. You should give the user the option of rebooting or not, but IE 4.0 will not be usable until the computer reboots.

Warning users about uninstalling IE 4.0

Because your application requires Internet Explorer 4.0 services, you will want to add your application to the list of applications that require Internet Explorer 4.0 to be installed. This way, if the user attempts to uninstall Internet Explorer 4.0, a list will be displayed including your program, and the user will be told that your application may not function properly if Internet Explorer 4.0 is uninstalled. The user will still be able to uninstall Internet Explorer 4.0, but they will have been warned.

The Windows Registry stores the list of applications that require IE 4.0 in a string value at the following key: HKEY_LOCAL_MACHINE\Software\Microsoft\IE4\DependentComponents.

The string's value will be something like AWebApp = "Awesome New Web Browser," where AWebApp is a unique identifier in the Registry list for your program and "Awesome New Web Browser" is the value that will be displayed in the list of programs requiring IE 4.0. Of course, your uninstall routine should remove this value when run.

Running MyBrowser

It's now time to look at MyBrowser in action. When you run it, it will look like Figure 29-11.

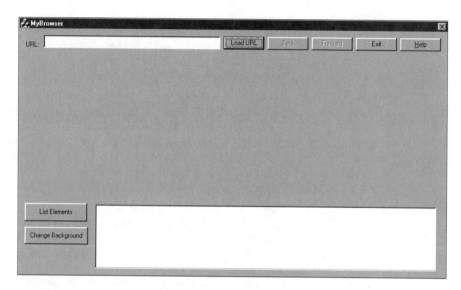

Figure 29-11: MyBrowser, a quick example of a WebBrowser

After starting up MyBrowser, you will need to enter a URL or a file location to load your first file. The program has two sample HTML files included with it, so you can begin by loading one of those files. Open the extend.htm file and you will be able to see most of the functionality of this application, as shown in Figure 29-12.

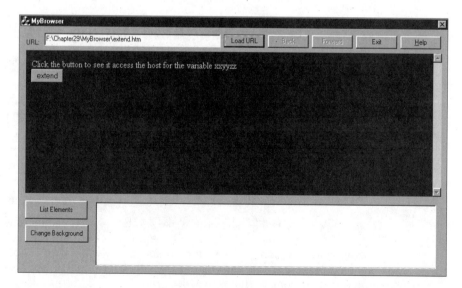

Figure 29-12: MyBrowser displaying an HTML page

At first, the Back and Forward buttons are not enabled, because there isn't a history of loaded pages to traverse. However, a few other buttons can be used. Clicking List Elements will cause a list of all the HTML elements to appear in the list box at the bottom of the program. Clicking Change Background will change the background color of the page, and your program should look like Figure 29-13. You can also click the HTML page's button to increment the program's internal counter.

A few other things that you can try out are loading the About dialog box by right-clicking on the Title bar and selecting About MyBrowser. Currently, the file location for the HTML file is hard-coded, but the source is documented with suggestions on how to change the way the file is loaded, or even use a Web page. The browser is now ready to open any of your favorite HTML pages.

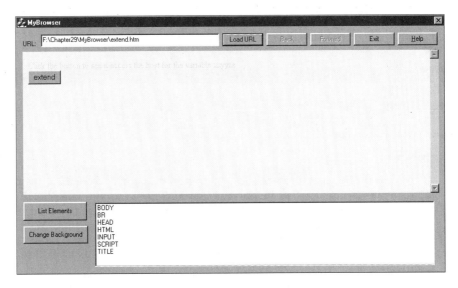

Figure 29-13: Changing the background color isn't always a good idea as it can make your page's text unreadable.

 PROBLEMS & SOLUTIONS

Using Robots

PROBLEM: *How do I retrieve documents using robots?*

SOLUTION: When dealing with the Internet, a *robot* is a program that automatically retrieves documents for you. These documents may be downloaded for later reference or given to another program that will index the files. Robots can also be created to simply make a backup

Continued

copy of a Web site. Unlike a browser, a robot doesn't simply retrieve one document and then display it. The robot is only interested in the information on the page, and does not need to waste the resources required to display the page in any particular format. A robot will look through a document and recursively traverse its hyperlinks. These programs have several uses, including the following:

- Checking for valid links in an HTML page
- Filling hard disk drives with vast amounts of HTML
- Helping to index a Web site
- Creating a mirror of a Web site
- Acting as an example of the uses of MSHTML

The MyBrowser application can quickly be turned into a robot. Simply change the List Elements button so that it only adds a list of links. Then, call a routine that will go through the list and download all of the files in it.

Summary

One of the most important things to remember when looking at using Internet Explorer components in your application is not to limit your thinking to browsing the Web. The Internet has given new life to the client-server model of programming and new solutions to this style of programming. Microsoft and many other companies have spent a lot of time, energy, and money creating new avenues of application development available through the Internet.

A quick overview of the basic functions of Internet Explorer provides an introduction to what you can do with these components. At the most basic level, Internet Explorer retrieves and displays formatted text from the Internet. You no longer have to derive your own format or tools for creating your content. You can use any of the HTML authoring programs on the market to quickly create anything you would normally display on the screen. This includes online documentation, a help system, or dialog boxes. All this and networking, too.

Also discussed in this chapter:

▶ Web browsers are easy to create using Internet Explorer components.

▶ The HTML rendering system can be used to create dialog boxes and help systems.

▶ MSHTML can be used even without a graphical interface for creating robots and other test programs.

▶ Dynamic HTML allows you to change the content of a page that has already been loaded into a browser.

▶ The Dynamic HTML object model can be extended to add functionality to scripts run on HTML pages.

▶ PICS is an advanced feature that can be used with Internet Explorer components to limit access to different HTML pages and Web sites.

Appendixes

Appendix A: Windows 98 Certification

Appendix B: Windows 98 Programming Secrets CD-ROM

Appendix A

Windows 98 Certification

Anybody with a little knowledge can sit down and write a Windows application. However, writing certified applications for Windows 98 is another ball of wax entirely. If you're writing an application that needs the hallowed Windows 98-compatible logo, you'll need to follow a strict set of design rules, as well as present your application for official testing. In this appendix, you'll get an overview of the requirements for Windows 98 certified programs, and learn how you can get your programs tested and certified.

Windows 98 Certification Requirements

Before you get too deep into this topic, you'll probably want to know what you're getting into. Exactly what are the requirements you must fulfill in order to be Windows 98-certified? Generally, the certification process ensures users that the application has been tested and is fully functional under Windows 98; that the application's design provides the user with a familiar and powerful user interface; that the application runs smoothly with the operating system and other applications; and that the application runs properly on both Windows 98 and Windows NT.

If these goals seem a bit nebulous, that's because they are only general descriptions of what a user expects from a Windows 98-certified application. Obviously, if your application is going to be tested, it needs to meet a specific set of testable rules, which don't include vague, undefined statements like "fully functional under Windows 98" and "runs smoothly with the operating system." The following sections will give you a clearer idea of what's involved in fulfilling the expectations of the certification testers. The certification categories covered in this section are listed below, exactly as Microsoft words them in its documentation:

- Provide consistent, up-to-date Windows support
- Be easy to install and remove
- Use the Registry correctly
- Save data to the best locations
- Cooperate with administrators
- Special requirements

Provide consistent, up-to-date Windows support

One of the big advantages of an operating system like Windows 98 is that most applications work similarly, enabling the user to concentrate on the specific details of completing a task with the software, rather than having to figure out how to perform mundane tasks like loading a file, printing a document, or getting access to online help (see Figure A-1). If such a system is to work, developers must design their applications to follow a set of interface rules.

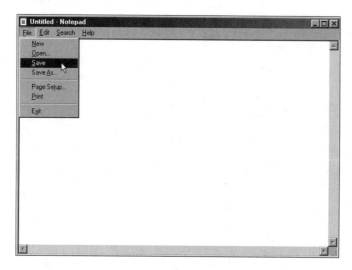

Figure A-1: User's expect to find standard commands in standard places, such as Save, Load, and Print in the File menu.

The rules of interface design for Windows can be found in a book called *The Windows Interface Guidelines for Software Design*, available on the Microsoft Developer Network (MSDN) library CD (see Figure A-2); in the online MSDN on Microsoft's Web site (www.microsoft.com/msdn); or from Microsoft Press in regular book form.

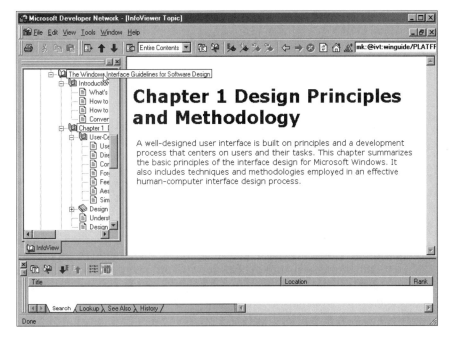

Figure A-2: The Microsoft Developer Network library CD is an excellent resource for application-development guidelines.

Your application needs to follow these interface rules. Also, the application must meet the following specifications. (Please refer to the "Designed for Microsoft Windows Logo, Handbook for Software Applications" document, available on Microsoft's Web site, for detailed implementation advice.)

Your application must:

- Be a 32-bit program that supports multitasking and runs properly on both Windows 98 and Windows NT.

- Have a file system that will support long file names, the Universal Naming Convention for networks, and 2GB for larger hard drives.

- Provide a migration DLL for users who upgrade from one version of Windows to another. This DLL must make the changes needed to ensure that the product works correctly in the new environment.

- Offer keyboard commands for all program features, support the High Contrast option, and provide notification of the location of keyboard focus by moving the system caret or by using Microsoft Active Accessibility.

- Implement OLE as a container or as an object server, and enable a drag-and-drop interface.

- Support the OnNow/Advanced Configuration and Power Interface (ACPI) technologies for handling Sleep/Wake transitions.

- Use Telephony Application Programming Interface (TAPI) if the application manages phone calls on modems and other such equipment.

- Digitally sign any ActiveX controls supplied by the application, and support Authenticode for downloadable code.

Be easy to install and remove

Most users expect software installation programs to require as little input from them as possible. Installation programs should look and act familiar, and provide default answers for every option, if possible. Windows applications must also feature complete uninstallation capabilities, so that a user can remove an application without having to track down the myriad files that the application may have installed in various directories on the hard disk.

Microsoft's certification rules insist that your application employ the new Microsoft Installer Technology, which will become the standard installation method for Windows 98 and Windows NT 5.0. (For more details, please read the document "Introduction to New Microsoft Installer Technology" on the Microsoft Developer Network CD.) By using this technology, you ensure that your application can more easily comply with all the installation and uninstallation requirements. These requirements include providing a graphical setup program, supporting AutoPlay for CD-ROMs, detecting software versions, creating shortcuts, and supplying an automated uninstall program that's registered with the Add/Remove Programs feature of the Control Panel (see Figure A-3).

The application must not, of course, add or remove files that may affect the integrity of the system. Further, the application must register shared components so that the system can track their reference counts. When uninstalling, the uninstall utility must decrement the reference count of any shared components.

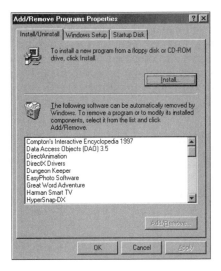

Figure A-3: Your application must uninstall through the Control Panel's Add/Remove Programs feature.

Use the Registry correctly

In the old days, applications used .ini files to store information. Often, such application-specific information was stored in system .ini files, such as Win.ini or System.ini. The addition of the Registry changed all that. Windows 98-certifiable programs cannot add entries to .ini files. Instead, they must take advantage of the Registry to record document types and other information the system or application needs.

Save data to the best locations

If you've ever tried to back up only data files from a hard drive, you probably ran into serious difficulty trying to figure out where everything you needed was stored. That's one reason why Microsoft started pushing its "document-centric" design in Windows 95 and continued with it in Windows 98. Users rarely have to know where applications reside or how they run; they only need to know how to create and edit documents. When a user wants to create a new Word document, for example, he shouldn't have to track down the appropriate application. Instead, he should simply tell Windows to start a new Word document or to load an existing document for editing.

Keeping applications out of the user's face is one reason for Microsoft's Program Files directory. By installing applications only into the Program Files directory, the root directory becomes the exclusive property of the user, without having application installations trespassing and messing things up. Therefore, Microsoft's Windows 98 requirements state that all applications must be installed in the Program Files directory.

Just as important, the application must enable the user to choose default locations for data files, with the information about the storage areas being stored in the Registry for future reference. That is, upon running, the application must access the Registry to discover where the user wants to save data files. Figure A-4, for example, shows how Microsoft Word enables users to specify default directories. These directories are stored in the Registry, as shown in Figure A-5.

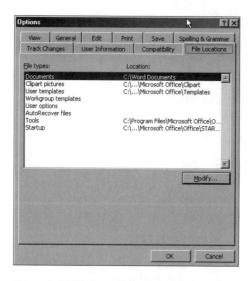

Figure A-4: Windows 98 programs enable the user to specify default data directories.

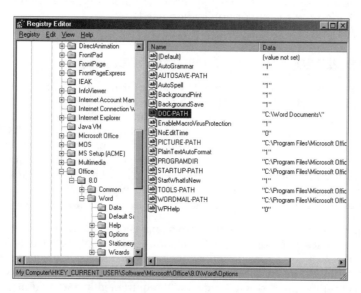

Figure A-5: Default data directories must be stored in the Registry.

Cooperate with administrators

Networks are everywhere, and, as a result, software must enable network administrators to manage the software without difficulty. A Windows 98 application should enable policy settings to uninstall and unadvertise the application. It should also supply administrators with an .adm system policy file and be able to disable Run and Find dialogs. Further, if the application spawns other processes, it must do so with `ShellExecute()`; and if the application extends the Windows 98 shell, it must support the `NoViewContextMenu` key.

Special requirements

Not all Windows 98 applications can be shoehorned into a general category. Some applications, such as development tools and utilities, change the rules due to their nature. Microsoft has, in fact, added a few rules to cover issues that arise when programming development tools, utilities, games, multimedia applications, Java applications, and add-on products.

First, development tools must not only be logo-compliant, they must also generate logo-compliant applications, which themselves must be tested for compliance. As for utilities, Microsoft states "Utilities must provide meaningful functionality on both Windows 95 and on Windows NT." Why anyone would create an application that provided no meaningful functionality is beyond me. Microsoft must mean that the utility must work equally well under both operating systems, eh?

Games and multimedia applications, too, have their own additional requirements, not the least of which is the use of DirectX technologies, including DirectDraw, DirectSound, DirectInput, DirectPlay, and Direct3D. If you see a little conflict of interest here, you're not alone. I guess if you want to create your game with OpenGL instead of Direct3D, Microsoft will punish you by withholding your Windows 98 logo. Convenient, considering that DirectX is Microsoft's own technology. Guess that's one of the advantages of being the guy who makes the rules.

Finally, Java applications must provide and use the 32-Bit Virtual Machine for Java, and add-on products must be used with 32-bit, logo-compliant products.

The Logo Certification Process

When you've completed your application, Microsoft outlines a series of seven steps that you must complete before you can consider yourself "logoed" (to coin a new verb):

1. Make sure your application meets the logo requirements. To avoid wasting time and money trying to certify a product that doesn't fit the bill, do your own complete logo-compliance tests.

2. Test application installation. Use the Installation Analyzer tool from VeriTest to test your product's installation system.

3. Sign agreements. Obtain and sign the legal documents required to begin the logo certification process, including the VeriTest testing agreement and the Windows NT and Windows 98 Logo License Agreement.

4. Send application to VeriTest for testing. Submit your product, pretest results, signed legal documents, and testing fee (currently $950) to VeriTest. For more information about VeriTest, visit their Web site at www.veritest.com.

5. Obtain test results. VeriTest should provide test results within eight business days from receipt of your application. Microsoft also receives a copy of the test results.

6. Get a signed license from Microsoft. If your application passes the certification test, Microsoft signs the license agreement and sends it to you.

7. Use the logo. You can obtain the logo kit from a secure Web server, using the password provided to you.

As you can tell, a lot of work goes into creating logo-compliant applications. Because this appendix is only an overview of the requirements and process, if you plan on going the logo route with your products, please be sure to acquire the full, up-to-date documentation from Microsoft and VeriTest.

Appendix B

Windows 98 Programming Secrets CD-ROM

The CD-ROM that accompanies this book contains all the sample programs described in each chapter. These programs are organized into directories that are named after the chapters. That is, you can find the programs for Chapter 3 in the Chapter03 folder, the programs for Chapter 4 in the Chapter04 folder, and so on. (Note that not every chapter contains a sample program.) At the end of this appendix, you'll find a complete listing of the CD's contents, which will help you find the programs you want to study.

Each program on the CD-ROM includes not only the source code, but also all the project files generated by Visual C++, as well as the ready-to-run executable file. To experiment with any program under Visual C++, copy the appropriate program directory to your hard drive and then double-click the program's .dsw file to load the project into Visual C++. You can then modify the source code, compile the program, or do whatever you like with the project. Feel free to copy code from the CD-ROM into your own programs. Use the code as is or modify it to fit a specific purpose.

Please note that after you copy files from the CD-ROM to your hard drive, you'll need to shut off the read-only attribute on any files you plan to modify. Visual C++ cannot save modified files until you do this. To turn off the read-only attribute on a set of files (after copying them to your hard drive), highlight the files in Windows Explorer and right-click the group. Then, select the Properties command from the context menu, and turn off the Read-Only checkbox in the property sheet that appears. Following is a listing of the CD's contents.

CD-ROM Contents

This list of programs includes the chapter directory names, as well as the names of program directories inside each chapter directory. Each program directory contains the source code, project files, and executable file for the specific program.

File Name	Application
Chapter03	CircleApp
	CircleApp1
	CircleApp2
Chapter04	BasicApp
Chapter05	BasicDCApp
	BitmapBrushApp
	BrushApp
	ClientDCApp
	DeviceCapsApp
	MetafileDCApp
	PatternBrushApp
	PenApp
	PenApp2
Chapter06	BasicApp
	BasicApp2
	CommonDlgApp
	DialogApp
	PropSheet
	WizardApp
Chapter07	CharSpaceApp
	ColorTextApp
	FontApp
	FontApp2
	HorizontalAlignApp
	TabTextApp
	TextMetricsApp
	VerticalAlignApp
Chapter08	MenuApp
Chapter09	ControlApp2
	DialogControlsApp
Chapter10	CommonControlsApp
	CommonControlsApp2
	EditControls
	SliderApp

File Name	Application
Chapter11	BasicPrintApp
	InchApp
	PrintApp
	PrintCircleApp
Chapter12	BitmapApp
	BitmapApp2
	ColorConeApp
	ColorRecApp
Chapter13	AspectRatioApp
	CartesianApp
	LineModeApp
	MagicRectApp
	MapModeApp
	PathApp
	RasterOpApp
	RegionApp
Chapter15	EventThread
	ThreadApp1
	ThreadApp2
	ThreadApp3
	ThreadApp4
	ThreadApp5
	ThreadApp6
Chapter16	KeyDown
	Keys
	Mouse
	NCMouse
Chapter17	PersistCircleApp
	PersistCircleApp2
	String
Chapter18	CBCircleApp
	CBCircleApp2
	DelayedRender

(continued)

File Name	*Application*
Chapter20	ContainerApp
Chapter21	ServerApp
Chapter22	AutoClientApp
	AutoServerApp
Chapter23	Scramble
Chapter24	DirectDrawApp
	DirectDrawApp2
Chapter25	DirectSoundApp
	DirectSoundApp2
Chapter26	DirectInputApp
	DirectInputApp2
Chapter27	Direct3DApp
	Direct3DApp2
Chapter28	FTPAccessApp
Chapter29	MyBrowser

Index

(continued)

(continued)

(continued)

(continued)

(continued)

my2cents.idgbooks.com

Register This Book — And Win!

Visit **http://my2cents.idgbooks.com** to register this book and we'll automatically enter you in our fantastic monthly prize giveaway. It's also your opportunity to give us feedback: let us know what you thought of this book and how you would like to see other topics covered.

Discover IDG Books Online!

The IDG Books Online Web site is your online resource for tackling technology — at home and at the office. Frequently updated, the IDG Books Online Web site features exclusive software, insider information, online books, and live events!

10 Productive & Career-Enhancing Things You Can Do at www.idgbooks.com

- Nab source code for your own programming projects.

- Download software.

- Read Web exclusives: special articles and book excerpts by IDG Books Worldwide authors.

- Take advantage of resources to help you advance your career as a Novell or Microsoft professional.

- Buy IDG Books Worldwide titles or find a convenient bookstore that carries them.

- Register your book and win a prize.

- Chat live online with authors.

- Sign up for regular e-mail updates about our latest books.

- Suggest a book you'd like to read or write.

- Give us your 2¢ about our books and about our Web site.

You say you're not on the Web yet? It's easy to get started with IDG Books' *Discover the Internet,* available at local retailers everywhere.

IDG BOOKS WORLDWIDE, INC.
END-USER LICENSE AGREEMENT

<u>READ THIS</u>. You should carefully read these terms and conditions before opening the software packet(s) included with this book ("Book"). This is a license agreement ("Agreement") between you and IDG Books Worldwide, Inc. ("IDGB"). By opening the accompanying software packet(s), you acknowledge that you have read and accept the following terms and conditions. If you do not agree and do not want to be bound by such terms and conditions, promptly return the Book and the unopened software packet(s) to the place you obtained them for a full refund.

1. <u>License Grant</u>. IDGB grants to you (either an individual or entity) a nonexclusive license to use one copy of the enclosed software program(s) (collectively, the "Software") solely for your own personal or business purposes on a single computer (whether a standard computer or a workstation component of a multiuser network). The Software is in use on a computer when it is loaded into temporary memory (RAM) or installed into permanent memory (hard disk, CD-ROM, or other storage device). IDGB reserves all rights not expressly granted herein.

2. <u>Ownership</u>. IDGB is the owner of all right, title, and interest, including copyright, in and to the compilation of the Software recorded on the disk(s) or CD-ROM ("Software Media"). Copyright to the individual programs recorded on the Software Media is owned by the author or other authorized copyright owner of each program. Ownership of the Software and all proprietary rights relating thereto remain with IDGB and its licensers.

3. <u>Restrictions on Use and Transfer</u>.

   (a) You may only (i) make one copy of the Software for backup or archival purposes, or (ii) transfer the Software to a single hard disk, provided that you keep the original for backup or archival purposes. You may not (i) rent or lease the Software, (ii) copy or reproduce the Software through a LAN or other network system or through any computer subscriber system or bulletin-board system, or (iii) modify, adapt, or create derivative works based on the Software.

   (b) You may not reverse engineer, decompile, or disassemble the Software. You may transfer the Software and user documentation on a permanent basis, provided that the transferee agrees to accept the terms and conditions of this Agreement and you retain no copies. If the Software is an update or has been updated, any transfer must include the most recent update and all prior versions.

4. <u>Restrictions on Use of Individual Programs</u>. You must follow the individual requirements and restrictions detailed for each individual program in Appendix B of this Book. These limitations are also contained in the individual license agreements recorded on the Software

Media. These limitations may include a requirement that after using the program for a specified period of time, the user must pay a registration fee or discontinue use. By opening the Software packet(s), you will be agreeing to abide by the licenses and restrictions for these individual programs that are detailed in Appendix B and on the Software Media. None of the material on this Software Media or listed in this Book may ever be redistributed, in original or modified form, for commercial purposes.

5. **Limited Warranty**.

   (a) IDGB warrants that the Software and Software Media are free from defects in materials and workmanship under normal use for a period of sixty (60) days from the date of purchase of this Book. If IDGB receives notification within the warranty period of defects in materials or workmanship, IDGB will replace the defective Software Media.

   (b) **IDGB AND THE AUTHOR OF THE BOOK DISCLAIM ALL OTHER WARRANTIES, EXPRESS OR IMPLIED, INCLUDING WITHOUT LIMITATION IMPLIED WARRANTIES OF MERCHANTABILITY AND FITNESS FOR A PARTICULAR PURPOSE, WITH RESPECT TO THE SOFTWARE, THE PROGRAMS, THE SOURCE CODE CONTAINED THEREIN, AND/OR THE TECHNIQUES DESCRIBED IN THIS BOOK. IDGB DOES NOT WARRANT THAT THE FUNCTIONS CONTAINED IN THE SOFTWARE WILL MEET YOUR REQUIREMENTS OR THAT THE OPERATION OF THE SOFTWARE WILL BE ERROR FREE.**

   (c) This limited warranty gives you specific legal rights, and you may have other rights that vary from jurisdiction to jurisdiction.

6. **Remedies**.

   (a) IDGB's entire liability and your exclusive remedy for defects in materials and workmanship shall be limited to replacement of the Software Media, which may be returned to IDGB with a copy of your receipt at the following address: Software Media Fulfillment Department, Attn.: *Windows 98 Programming Secrets,* IDG Books Worldwide, Inc., 7260 Shadeland Station, Ste. 100, Indianapolis, IN 46256, or call 1-800-762-2974. Please allow three to four weeks for delivery. This Limited Warranty is void if failure of the Software Media has resulted from accident, abuse, or misapplication. Any replacement Software Media will be warranted for the remainder of the original warranty period or thirty (30) days, whichever is longer.

   (b) In no event shall IDGB or the author be liable for any damages whatsoever (including without limitation damages for loss of business profits, business interruption, loss of business information, or any other pecuniary loss) arising from the use of or inability to use the Book or the Software, even if IDGB has been advised of the possibility of such damages.